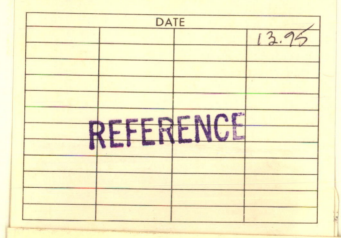

Introduction to Contemporary Music

Second Edition

Introduction to Contemporary Music

Second Edition

Joseph Machlis

Professor of Music
Queens College of the City University of New York

W · W · Norton & Company · New York

Copyright © 1979, 1961 by W. W. Norton & Company, Inc.
Published simultaneously in Canada by George J. McLeod Limited,
Toronto. Printed in the United States of America.
First Edition

Library of Congress Cataloging in Publication Data

Machlis, Joseph, 1906–
    Introduction to contemporary music.

    Bibliography: p.
    Includes index.
    1. Music—History and criticism—20th century.
2. Music—Analysis, appreciation.   I. Title.
ML197.M11   1979   780'.904   78-10327
ISBN 0-393-09026-4

1 2 3 4 5 6 7 8 9 0

For Ernest and Red Heller

Contents

List of Illustrations

Preface

to the Second Edition

THIS BOOK attempts to lead the reader to an understanding and enjoyment of twentieth-century music. It surveys the broad panorama of the contemporary scene and tries to assess the forces that have shaped the musical climate we inhabit.

My primary goal, in preparing a second edition of this book, was to bring it up to date. This entailed adding a full discussion of the tremendous changes that have occurred on the musical scene since 1961, when the first edition was published. Although intended primarily for the interested layman, the book has been widely used as a college text in one-semester courses. Most of the teachers I consulted felt that it would be more suitable for their needs if it were shorter. A number of excellent histories and reference works on twentieth-century music are available for the reader in search of encyclopedic coverage. My aim, rather, is to introduce the student to the contemporary scene in such a way that he will be stimulated to undertake further exploration on his own.

The second edition has therefore been reduced to a size that can be comfortably handled within the framework of a single-semester course. However, like the first edition, it contains considerably more material than can be covered in class. In addition, once the course is finished, the student can use the book to pursue the subject further according to his interests and needs.

I reorganized the material. In the earlier version, composers were grouped according to stylistic labels—Impressionists, Neoclassicists,

Nationalists, Neoromantics, twelve-tone composers, experimentalists. I abandoned this organization for one rooted in chronology: Before World War I, Between the Wars, Since World War II. This not only results in a simpler arrangement of the material; it also enables the reader to relate musical movements and trends to the great social-political events that surround them and to view the composer as a child of his time.

Although it was desirable to compress the book, I had to include a whole body of new material covering the music of the past two decades. I faced a problem. It was manifestly impossible to discuss as many composers as I had done in the first edition; the result would have been a totally unwieldy text. My solution, in the section entitled Since World War II, was to discuss eight representative composers—four Europeans and four Americans—followed by a Dictionary in which well over two hundred composers are succinctly introduced. These entries may be regarded as so many invitations to the reader to continue his investigation of the subject. At the same time, they give him a clear idea of the infinite variety and richness of contemporary music.

I am immeasurably indebted to David Hamilton for his advice and guidance. My editor, Claire Brook, gave unstintingly of her time and patience and came up with invaluable suggestions. I should also like to thank Jeffrey Miller, Hinda Keller Farber, and Donna Seldin for their enthusiastic assistance in bringing this book to completion.

JOSEPH MACHLIS

Acknowledgments

Music and poetry reproduced in this volume have been supplied by the following, whose courtesy is gratefully acknowledged.

Samuel Barber: *Overture for the School for Scandal,* Opus 5 Copyright © 1941 G. Schimer, Inc. Used by permission.

Béla Bartók: *Allegro Barbaro* Copyright 1918 by Universal Edition; renewed 1945. Copyright and renewal assigned to Boosey & Hawkes, Inc. for the U.S.A. Reprinted by permission. *Concerto for Orchestra* Copyright 1946 by Hawkes & Son (London) Ltd.; Renewed 1973. Reprinted by permission of Boosey & Hawkes, Inc. *Fourth String Quartet* Copyright 1929 by Universal Edition; renewed 1956. Copyright and renewal assigned to Boosey & Hawkes, Inc. for the U.S.A. Reprinted by permission. *Mikrokosmos* Copyright 1940 by Hawkes & Son (London) Ltd.; renewed 1967. Reprinted by permission of Boosey & Hawkes, Inc. *Music for Strings, Percussion and Celesta* Copyright 1937 by Universal Edition; renewed 1964. Copyright and renewal assigned to Boosey and Hawkes, Inc. for the U.S.A. Reprinted by permission.

Alban Berg: From *Wozzeck.* Full score copyright 1926 by Universal Edition A. G., Wien. Full score copyright renewed 1954 by Helene Berg. Used by permission of European American Distributors Corporation, sole representative in the U.S.A. and Canada.

Benjamin Britten: *War Requiem* Copyright 1962 by Boosey & Hawkes Music Publishers, Ltd. Reprinted by permission. Text taken from *The Collected Poems of Wilfred Owen,* edited by C. Day Lewis. Used by permission of the Owen Estate and Chatto & Windus Ltd.

Elliot Carter: *Double Concerto* © Copyright 1962, 1964 by Associated Music Publishers, Inc., New York.

Carlos Chávez: *Sinfonia India* Copyright © 1959 by G. Schirmer, Inc. Used by permission.

Aaron Copland: *Billy the Kid* Copyright 1946 by Aaron Copland; renewed 1973. *Statements* Copyright 1947 by Aaron Copland; renewed 1974. Reprinted by permission of Aaron Copland, copyright owner, and Boosey & Hawkes, sole licensees and publishers.

Claude Debussy: *La Cathédrale Engloutie* Copyright 1910 Durand and Cie. *Chansons de Bilitis* Copyright 1971 Société des Editions Jobert. *La Fille Aux Cheveux de Lin* Copyright 1910 Durand and Cie. *General Lavine—Eccentric* Copyright 1913 Durand and Cie. *Ibéria* Copyright 1910 Durand and Cie. *Pelléas and Melisande* Copyright 1907 Durand and Cie. *Soirée Dans Granade* Copyright Durand and Cie. Used by permission of the publisher Theodore Presser Company, sole representative U.S.A.

Frederick Delius: *On Hearing the First Cuckoo in Spring* used by permission of Oxford University Press.

Roy Harris: *Third Symphony in One Movement* Copyright © 1940 by G. Schirmer, Inc. Used by permission.

Paul Hindemith: From *Kleine Kammermusik,* Opus 24/2. Copyright 1922 by B. Schott's Soehne, Mainz, copyright renewed 1949 by Schott & Co., Ltd., London. Used by permission of European American Distributors Corporation, sole representative in the U.S.A. and Mexico. *Ludus Tonalis* used by permission of B. Schott's Soehne, Mainz and European American Distributors Corporation.

John Hollander: *Philomel* © 1968; John Hollander. Reprinted by permission of the author.

Charles Ives: *Concord Sonata* © Copyright 1947 Associated Music Publishers, Inc., New York. Used by permission. *Fourth of July* ©

Russe de Musique. Copyright assigned 1947 to Boosey & Hawkes for all countries of the world. Reprinted by permission. *Symphony of Psalms* Copyright 1931 by Edition Russe de Musique; renewed 1958. Copyright and renewal assigned to Boosey & Hawkes, Inc. Revised version, copyright 1948 by Boosey & Hawkes, Inc. Reprinted by permission.

Edgard Varèse: *Intégrales* Copyright © 1926 by Colfranc Music Publishing Corp., New York. Reprinted by permission.

Ralph Vaughan Williams: *Pastoral Symphony* reprinted by permission of Faber Music Ltd. (for J. Curwen & Sons Ltd.). *Serenade to Music* reprinted by permission of Oxford University Press.

Heitor Villa-Lobos: *Bachianas Brasileiras #5* Copyright © 1947, 1974 by Associated Music Publishers, Inc., New York. Used by permission.

Anton Webern: From *Four Songs,* Op. 13 Copyright 1926 by Universal Edition; copyright renewed 1954 by Anton Webern's Erben. From *Symphonie,* Op. 21 Copyright 1929 by Universal Edition; copyright renewed 1956. Used by permission of European American Music Distributors Corporation, sole representative in the U.S.A. and Canada.

PART ONE

The First Revolution

"Music was chaste and modest so long as it was played on simpler instruments, but since it has come to be played in a variety of manners and confusedly, it has lost the mode of gravity and virtue and fallen almost to baseness."

BOETHIUS (c. 480–524)

"Music was originally discreet, seemly, simple, masculine, and of good morals. Have not the moderns rendered it lascivious beyond measure?"

JACOB OF LIÈGE (c. 1425)

"They are so enamored of themselves as to think it within their power to corrupt, spoil, and ruin the good old rules handed down in former times by so many theorists and most excellent musicians, the very men from whom these moderns have learned to string together a few notes with little grace. For them it is enough to create a tumult of sounds, a confusion of absurdities, an assemblage of imperfections."

G. M. ARTUSI (1600)

"The Overture to Beethoven's opera *Fidelio* was performed recently, and all impartial musicians and music lovers were in complete agreement that never was anything written in music so incoherent, shrill, muddled, and utterly shocking to the ear."

AUGUST VON KOTZEBUE (1806)

"Serious music is a dead art. The vein which for three hundred years offered a seemingly inexhaustible yield of beautiful music has run out. What we know as modern music is the noise made by deluded speculators picking through the slagpile."

HENRY PLEASANTS: *The Agony of Modern Music* (1955)

1 The Old and the New

"The modern and the old have always been."

FERRUCCIO BUSONI

Why Music Changes

One thing in history never changes, and that is the element of change itself. What does change from one age to the next is the pace, the rate of change. Certain periods are comparatively stable; the force of tradition is strong enough to hold back the new modes of thought that are struggling to be born. At other times society is in a state of flux. Changes take place in a single lifetime that, in an earlier age, would have been spread over many generations. As a result, new horizons open up with breathtaking rapidity. Ours is such an era. The rate of change in our time has been enormously accelerated. Life demands from us signal powers of adjustment if we are not to be left behind.

Music has changed constantly through the ages, as every living language must. Each generation of musicians has inherited a tradition, an established body of usages and techniques, which it has

3

When Matisse wrote "Both harmonies and dissonances of color can produce very pleasurable effects," he might well have been speaking for modern composers as well as modern painters. Artists of the early twentieth century sought new expressive solutions to the familiar problems of the past as well as those unique to their time. La Musique, 1939, by Henri Matisse (1869–1954). Albright-Knox Art Gallery, Buffalo, New York, Room of Contemporary Art Fund.

enriched by its own efforts and passed on to the next generation. However, in the early years of the twentieth century, the forces for change became so powerful that the new music seemed—for a time—to have broken completely with the old. Audiences were persuaded that the art as they had known it was coming to an end, and responded accordingly. Perfectly respectable individuals in Paris, Vienna, and elsewhere hissed and hooted, banged chairs, and engaged in fistfights with strangers.

Today, the works that caused these antics are enthroned as classics of the modern repertory. The men who wrote them are acknowledged masters. Their disciples occupy key positions in our conservatories and colleges. The techniques and procedures once regarded as startling have become part of the accepted vocabulary of musical art. Although we like to think that human nature never changes, actually we are more adaptable than we suspect. Music that bewildered and jarred listeners a generation ago is now heard by the public with every evidence of pleasure.

Significantly, the leaders of the modern movement wished only—as composers have done through the ages—to make their music express their own time. They had no desire to lead a revolution. "I hold that it was an error," Igor Stravinsky wrote, "to regard me as a revolutionary. If one only need break habit in order to be labeled a revolutionary, then every artist who has something to say and who in order to say it steps outside the bounds of established convention could be considered revolutionary." And Arnold Schoenberg to the same point: "I personally hate to be called a revolutionary, which I am not. What I did was neither revolution nor anarchy."

These statements attest to what every artist knows: that rules are not broken for the sheer joy of breaking them. The artist accepts the necessity of rules just as all of us do when we play baseball, and for the same reason: to achieve freedom of action within a self-imposed frame. If he discards the inherited rules, it is only because they have ceased to be meaningful—that is, fruitful—for him. He rejects them only so that he may impose other rules upon himself. In short, the rules change, but not the concept of rule, the eternal principle of law and order which is basic to the discipline of art.

When the new music of our century was first heard, people asked why composers could not go on writing like Tchaikovsky or Puccini. The answer is obvious. Art, as an integral part of life, has to change just as life itself changes. The melodies of Tchaikovsky and Puccini were part of the nineteenth-century world. Stravinsky, Schoenberg, Bartók, and their contemporaries no longer inhabited that world. They had perforce to move on, to discover sounds that would express the present as eloquently as those of the masters had expressed the past.

The last eighty years have witnessed a vast expansion of musical resources. New conceptions have enriched the language of music and have had a great impact upon the artistic consciousness of our epoch. Contemporary music, so rich in its diversity of expression, so excitingly attuned to the spirit of the twentieth century, is the latest—consequently the most vivid—chapter in man's age-old attempt to impose his artistic intuitions upon the elusive stuff of sound: that majestic five-thousand-year-old attempt to shape the sonorous material into forms possessing logic and continuity, expressive meaning and nourishing beauty.

2 The Classic-Romantic Tradition

"The pull-away from romanticism was the most important interest of the early twentieth century."

AARON COPLAND

Classic versus Romantic

A work of art exists on two levels. On the one hand it embodies a deeply felt experience, a moment of rapturous awareness projected by a creative temperament. On the other, it embodies a way of shaping the artistic material, whether sounds, colors, blocks of marble, or words, into coherent forms, according to procedures that derive from the nature of that material. In other words, a work of art possesses an expressive aspect and a formal aspect.

Form and content are indivisible parts of the whole. They can no more be separated than can body and mind. However, the emphasis may rest upon the one or the other. We call that attitude classical which seeks above all to safeguard the purity of form. We call that attitude romantic which concerns itself primarily with the expression of emotion.

6

The classicist exalts the values of order, lucidity, restraint. He seeks purity of style and harmonious proportion, striving to bring to perfection what already exists, rather than to originate new forms. Achieving a certain measure of detachment from the artwork, he expresses himself through symbols that have a universal validity. The romanticist, on the other hand, exalts the unique character of his personal reactions and strives always for the most direct expression of his emotions. He rebels against tradition, valuing passionate utterance above perfection of form. He sees the "strangeness and wonder" of life. His is an art of infinite yearning, rich in mood and atmosphere, picturesque detail, and striking color. Music for him is an enchantment of the senses, an outpouring of the heart.

Classic and romantic correspond to two fundamental impulses in man's nature: classicism to his love of traditional standards, his desire that emotion be purged and controlled within a form; romanticism to his longing for the unattainable, his need for ecstasy and intoxication. Both impulses have asserted themselves throughout the history of art. There have been times, however, when one markedly predominated over the other. One such era was the nineteenth century, which has come to be called the Age of Romanticism.

Nineteenth-Century Romanticism

The French Revolution signalized the birth of a new society that glorified the individual as never before. Freedom was its watchword: freedom of religion, freedom of enterprise, political and personal freedom. On the artistic front this need for untrammeled individualism took shape in the Romantic movement. The Romantic spirit pervaded the arts of poetry and painting, as is amply attested by the works of Keats and Shelley, Delacroix, Turner, and their contemporaries. But it was in music that Romanticism found its ideal expression: music, the art of elusive meanings and indefinable moods.

Basic to the Romantic aesthetic was the belief that the prime function of music is to express emotion. Nineteenth-century composers developed a musical language that was associated with specific literary or pictorial images, in which poetic idea, atmosphere, and mood occupied a central place. They viewed their art as much more than a manipulation of melodies and rhythms. For them the sounds were inseparably allied with feelings about life and death, love and romantic yearning, nature, God, man defying his fate. To return to the terminology we established at the beginning of this chapter, the

Romantic art in England was highly personal. For Turner, it consisted of painting masses of color often without obvious representational meaning, but evocative of natural forces. Music at Petworth, c. 1833, by J. M. W. Turner (1775– 1851). The Tate Gallery, London.

Romantic musician valued the expressive content of music more than its purely formal content.

The central figure in the nineteenth-century ferment was Richard Wagner (1813–1883), whose grandiose music-dramas best exemplify the German tendency to attach "deep" meanings to music. In these works he hymned, with unparalleled abandon, German forest and mountain, the Rhine, the ancient Teutonic myths of gods and heroes, the manly man and the womanly woman. In *The Ring of the Nibelung* the proceedings on stage were infused with all manner of political, moral, and philosophical symbolism. Wagner's *Tristan and Isolde* was a landmark that had decisive importance for all the composers who came after. It pointed the way to developments in the harmonic language that were to achieve major significance in the twentieth century.

Increasing reliance on literary and pictorial elements could not but weaken the sense of form and order in music. As the century unfolded, structural values increasingly gave way to an art based on gargantuan orchestral forces and overexpanded forms. One of the first tasks of the new century, consequently, was to shake off the burden of a tradition that hung too heavily upon it. The twentieth century had to assert its independence much as an adolescent has to rebel against his parents. The revolt was twofold. Composers not only had to free themselves from the domination of their immediate predecessors; they had also to fight the romanticism within themselves. The modern movement in art took shape as a violent reaction against everything the nineteenth century had stood for. "The pull-away from romanticism," as Aaron Copland called it, became a crucial issue for the early twentieth century. Out of it came an irresistible swing toward a new classicism. In effect, a revolution in style and taste.

Eighteenth-Century Classicism

The Classical period in music (c. 1775–1825) extended through the half century that preceded the Romantic. It reached its high point with the masters of the Viennese school—Haydn, Mozart, Beethoven, and Schubert.

The Classical era witnessed the American and French Revolutions, as well as the English movement for political reform. These countries passed from absolute monarchy to a system based on political democracy and capitalist technology. The art of the Classical period reflects the unique moment in history when the old order was dying and the new was in process of being born; when the elegance of the aristocratic tradition met the vigor and humanism of a rising middle-class culture. Out of this climate emerged the grand form in both literature and music: the novel and the symphony, both destined to become vehicles of communication with a larger audience than had ever existed before.

The eighteenth-century artist functioned under the system of aristocratic patronage. He was a craftsman in a handicraft society, creating his works for a select audience of connoisseurs who were high above him in social rank, who were interested in his art rather than in him as an individual. To be personal in such circumstances would have been something of an impertinence. As a result, he was impelled to classical objectivity and reserve rather than romantic self-revelation. The Classical composer took for granted the power of

Cézanne's paintings were classically influenced and highly structural. In this work, a sense of substantiality is conveyed by the pictorial elements arranged in a formalistic composition. The Card Players, *1892, by Paul Cézanne (1839–1906). The Metropolitan Museum of Art, Bequest of Stephen C. Clark, 1960.*

music to express emotion; he therefore did not feel it necessary constantly to emphasize this aspect of his art, as did the Romantic. He directed his attention rather to craftsmanship, beauty of design, and purity of style. There resulted an urbane art that continues to appeal, in the words of John Burroughs, to "our sense of the finely carved, the highly wrought, the deftly planned."

The Classical sonata-symphony was a spacious form allowing for the expansion and development of abstract musical ideas. The characters in this instrumental drama were neither Scheherazade nor the Sorcerer's Apprentice. What concerned the listener was the fate not of the lovers but of the themes. The Classical symphony steered clear of specific emotions, literary or pictorial associations. There is profound feeling in the late works of Haydn and Mozart, as in the volcanic symphonism of Beethoven. But this emotion is well contained within the form, lifted from the personal to the universal through the plenary discipline of Classical art. For the Romantic composer melody and rhythm, color and harmony existed as ends in themselves. The Classicist subordinated all of these to the overall unity of the form: form as the principle of law and order in art, born from the ideal mating of reason and emotion. It is this oneness of form and content that impelled Paul Henry Lang to write, in his *Music in Western Civilization:* "When a nation brings its innermost nature to consummate expression in arts and letters, we speak of its classic period."

Nietzsche distinguished the classic from the romantic by two vivid symbols: he opposed Apollo, god of light and harmonious proportion, to Dionysus, god of wine, ecstasy, and intoxication. The shift from the Dionysian principle to the Apollonian, as we shall see, became one of the decisive gestures of the new music of the twentieth century.

3 Melody in Twentieth-Century Music

"The melody is generally what the piece is about."

AARON COPLAND

Of all the elements of music, melody stands first in the affections of the public. "It is the melody," observed Haydn a century and a half ago, "which is the charm of music, and it is that which is most difficult to produce." The statement has retained much of its validity in the twentieth century.

A melody is a succession of tones grasped by the mind as a significant pattern. Some modern theorists tell us that a melody simply is a succession of tones. What they mean is that if we hear any selection of tones often enough, we will impose on it a semblance of pattern. Be that as it may, to understand a melody means to grasp its underlying unity. In order to do this, we must perceive the relationship of the beginning to the middle, of the middle to the end. We must apprehend the tones not singly, but as part of the melodic line, just as we apprehend words in a sentence not separately, but in relation to the thought as a whole. Heard in this way, the melody takes on clarity, direction, meaning.

Melody in the Classic-Romantic Era

Over the course of centuries, certain conventions were evolved in order to help the listener apprehend a melody. These devices, as might be supposed, are particularly prominent in folk music and popular songs. They are also to be found in abundance in the art music of the eighteenth and nineteenth centuries. Melody in the Classic-Romantic era was often based on a structure of four symmetrical phrases, each four measures in length, which were set off by regularly spaced cadences. (The cadence is the point of rest, the "breathing place" in the melodic line.) As soon as the listener heard the first phrase, he knew that the other three would be of equal duration. The balanced phrases and cadences were like so many landmarks that kept him from being lost in the trackless wastes of sound. They set up expectancies that were sure to be fulfilled.

The structure was made even clearer to the ear by the use of repetition. Often, the second phrase was like the first; the third introduced an element of variety; and the fourth established the underlying unity by returning to the material of the first two phrases. (This A-A-B-A structure still prevails in many popular songs.) So too the melody emphasized a central tone that served as a point of departure and return. The fact that there was a keynote to which all the other tones gravitated imparted a clarity of direction to the melody and created an impression of purposeful movement toward a goal. When the listener reached the final cadence he had a sense of tension released, action consummated: the melody had completed its journey. (For an example of symmetrical melody based on four-measure phrases, see Appendix I-a.)

Through symmetrical structure, repetition of phrases, and kindred devices, the masters made themselves understood by a large public. From the time of Haydn and Mozart to that of Tchaikovsky, Brahms, and Dvořák, literally thousands of melodies in Western music were oriented to four-measure phrase patterns. However, although a framework such as this begins by being a support, it ends by becoming a straitjacket. The artist finds it increasingly difficult to achieve significant expression within the conventional pattern. He begins to chafe under the restrictions of a form whose resources, he feels, have been exhausted. He is impelled to seek new modes of expression. At this point the revolt against tradition sets in.

The rebellion against the stereotypes of four-square melody began long before the twentieth century. At the height of the Classical era Haydn and Mozart introduced asymmetries—phrases of three, five, or six measures—which lent their music the charm of the unforeseen. It remained for Wagner to cast off the shackles of symmetrical melody. He aspired to a melodic line that would sensitively reflect the emotions of his characters, and he could not reconcile this aim with slicing up a melody into neatly balanced phrases and cadences. To achieve the necessary intensity, Wagner devised what he called "endless" or "infinite" melody—a melodic line, that is, which avoided stereotyped formations by evolving freely and continuously.

The public, naturally, was much upset at this. Singers maintained that Wagner's music was unsingable; audiences and critics alike insisted that it lacked melody. They meant that it lacked the familiar landmarks on which they had come to rely. When people had had time to become familiar with Wagner's idiom they discovered that it was not lacking in melody at all. In imposing his melodic image upon the nineteenth century, Wagner immeasurably expanded the accepted notion of what a melody could be.

Art music in Europe had employed freely unfolding melody before the Classic-Romantic era, from the sinuous traceries of Gregorian chant to the flowing arabesques of Bach. Western music thus had a rich store of melody that bore little or no trace of four-measure regularity, and Wagner was not inventing anything new when he espoused the cause of "endless" melody. He was merely reclaiming for music some of the freedom it had abdicated under the alluring symmetries of the Classic-Romantic era. Once he had done this, there could be no question of returning to four-measure patterns.

The New Melody

Modern composers do not emulate either the formal beauty of Classical melody or the lyric expansiveness of the Romantics. They range far afield for models, from the free flow of Gregorian chant, the subtle irregularities of medieval and Renaissance music, to the luxuriance of Bach's melodic line. Or, looking beyond the orbit of European music, they aspire to capture for the West the freedom, the improvisational quality of Oriental melody.

The twentieth-century composer is not inclined to shape his melody to standard patterns. He does not eke out a phrase to four or eight measures solely because the preceding phrase was that long. He states a thing once, rather than two or three times. By abandoning symmetry and repetition he hopes to achieve a vibrant, taut melody from which everything superfluous has been excised. His aim is a finely molded, sensitive line packed with thought and feeling, which will function at maximum intensity as it follows the rise and fall of the musical impulse. Such a melody makes greater demands upon us than did the old. It requires alertness of mind and unflagging attention on the part of the listener, for its clipped phrases do not yield their meaning easily.

This condensation of thought is not limited to music. Compare, for example, the rolling sentences of Dickens or Thackeray with the sinewy prose of Hemingway or Steinbeck; or the impassioned rhetoric of Shelley with the terse, wiry utterance of contemporary poets. It must also be remembered that the melodies of Mozart, Schubert, Chopin, and Tchaikovsky were shaped to the curve of the human voice, even when written for instruments. This is why the instrumental themes of these masters can be converted, year after year, into popular song hits. Twentieth-century music, on the other hand, has detached instrumental melody from its vocal origins. The new melody is neither unvocal nor antivocal; it is simply not conceived in terms of what the voice can do. The themes of twentieth-century works contain wide leaps and jagged turns of phrase that are not to be negotiated vocally. Contemporary melody ranges through musical space, striding forward boldly along untrodden paths. Marked by energy and force, its line is apt to be angular rather than curved.

Naturally, many twentieth-century melodies do not depart too radically from tradition. A fine example is the lyric theme from Samuel Barber's *School for Scandal Overture*. The structure is based on two symmetrical four-measure phrases with rhyming cadences, answered by a longer phrase. The leaps are narrow, the melody is singable. After a few hearings of the work, we find ourselves humming along. Here is a twentieth-century tune that finds something fresh to say within the conventional pattern:

The case is different with the second theme in the opening movement of Shostakovich's *First Symphony*. This theme represents the lyrical element of the movement, yet the lyricism is instrumental in character, not vocal. The structure is asymmetrical, with a phrase of five measures answered by one of four:

Painting has often been described in musical terms. Of a spontaneous work like this, the artist said, "The observer must learn to look at the pictures . . . as form and color combinations . . . as a representation of mood and not a representation of objects." Untitled, 1915, by Wassily Kandinsky (1866–1944). Collection, The Museum of Modern Art, New York. Gift of Abby Aldrich Rockefeller.

This angular line, with its wide leaps, will not impress the listener as being very much of a tune. Yet with repeated hearings the difficult skips lose their arbitrary character. Gradually the line takes on profile, engages the listener's fancy, and ultimately reveals itself—for all its wiriness—as a genuinely melodic idea.

When people accuse modern music of having abandoned melody, what they really mean is that it has abandoned the familiar landmarks on which they rely to recognize a melody. Once we have learned to dispense with the punctuation marks of the good old days—just as we do when we read a telegram—we will be ready to respond to the exciting new conceptions of melody that have evolved in our time. We will find that, today as in the past, melody is a prime factor in musical expressiveness. For, as Igor Stravinsky has pointed out, "What survives every change of system is melody."

4 Harmony in Twentieth-Century Music

"The evolution of the harmonic idiom has resulted from the fact that musicians of all generations have sought new means of expression. Harmony is a constant stream of evolution, a constantly changing vocabulary and syntax."

ROGER SESSIONS

The melody, in our music, is heard against a background of harmony. The chords that accompany the melody lend it color, clarify its direction, and enhance its meaning. In effect, they define the musical space in which the melody has its being. Harmony is to music what perspective is to painting: the element of depth, the third dimension.

The Classical System of Harmony

It was the great achievement of the Classical era to perfect a system of harmony in which each chord had its appointed place and function. This was the system of triadic harmony. The triad is the fundamental chord structure in Western music. Hence Paul Hin-

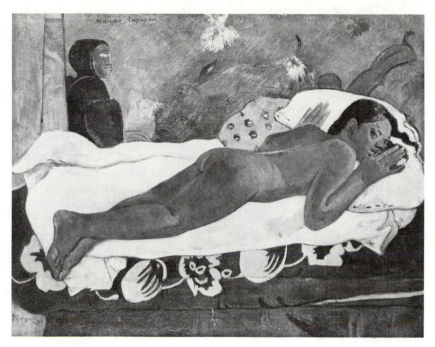

Gauguin created an impression of depth in this painting by his handling of blocks of color which advance and recede. He referred to the "musical aspect" of this work as represented by the undulating lines and strong contrasts. The Spirit of the Dead Watching, *1892, by Paul Gauguin (1848–1903). Albright-Knox Art Gallery, Buffalo, New York. A. Conger Goodyear Collection.*

demith's statement—one with which not all his colleagues might agree—"For as long as it exists, music will always take its point of departure from the triad and return to it." (The structure of the triad is explained in Appendix I-b.)

Melody constitutes the horizontal aspect of music, harmony the vertical. The melody unfolds above the chords that serve as supporting pillars. In the Classical system, the triad on *do* (*do-mi-sol*) is the I chord or tonic, the chord of rest. Around it are ranged the other triads, which are considered, in varying degrees, to be active or incomplete. The active triads seek to be completed or resolved in the rest chord. This seeking for resolution lends direction and purpose to the harmony; it establishes the point of departure and return. The triad on the fifth degree of the scale (*sol-ti-re*) is the dominant or V chord, the chief representative of the active principle. Dominant resolving to tonic (V–I) is a basic formula in our music. We hear it af-

firmed again and again at the end of symphonies or overtures of the
Classic-Romantic period. The IV chord (*fa-la-do*) is the subdominant.
This too is an active chord, although markedly less so than the dominant. The progression IV–I makes a gentler cadence than V–I (the
"Amen" at the end of hymns, for example). Classical harmony related all chords to the three basic functions—tonic, dominant, and
subdominant—allotting to each chord its place in a carefully graded
hierarchy of values. It built these functions into a rational system that
took on meaning for millions of listeners throughout the West. The
ultimate resolution of dominant and subdominant to tonic became
the grand principle of Classical form, a principle that reached its culmination in the symphonies of Haydn, Mozart, and Beethoven.

Romantic Harmony

The Romantic movement sprang from an age of revolution and
social upheaval. Its music reflected the dynamism of this new age.
Spurred on by the desire for passionate utterance, the Romantic composers were increasingly drawn to the possibilities of dissonant harmony. Richard Wagner carried this tendency to its furthest limits. In
his music-dramas Wagner consistently avoided the cadence—that is,
the resolution. Through the imaginative use of dissonance he
achieved extended structures marked by an accumulation of emotional tension greater than any that music had ever known before. In
his work the active, dissonant harmony, seeking resolution in the
chord of rest, came to symbolize one of the most powerful images of
the Romantic movement: the lonely, questing man, whether the
Dutchman or Lohengrin, Siegmund or Tristan, driven to find fulfillment in the all-womanly woman, Senta or Elsa, Sieglinde or Isolde.
Dissonance is the element that supplies dynamic tension, the
forward impulsion that expends itself and comes to rest in consonance. There is a widespread notion that consonance is what is
pleasant to the ear while dissonance is what is disagreeable. This
distinction is much too vague to be useful. What is unpleasant to one
ear may be agreeable to another. We will come closer the mark if we
identify dissonance with the principle of activity and incompleteness, consonance with fulfillment and rest. "It cannot be too
strongly emphasized," Walter Piston has written, "that the essential
quality of dissonance is its sense of movement." And Stravinsky to
the same point: "Dissonance is an element of transition, a complex or
interval of tones which is not complete in itself and which must be

The jarring figures and masks in this pathbreaking painting may be compared to the unfamiliar and disturbing dissonances often associated with modern music. Les Demoiselles d'Avignon, *1907, by Pablo Picasso (1881–1973). Collection, The Museum of Modern Art, New York. Acquired through the Lillie P. Bliss Bequest.*

resolved to the ear's satisfaction into a perfect consonance." Viewed thus, dissonance is seen to be the essential element of dynamism and tension without which music would be intolerably dull and static. The progression of dissonance to consonance mirrors the movement of life itself—its recurrent cycle of hunger and appeasement, desire and fulfillment.

The history of music reflects a steady broadening of the harmonic sense, an ever greater tolerance of the human ear. In the course of this evolution, tone combinations which at first were regarded as dissonant came to be accepted, with time and familiarity, as consonant. The leader in this development has consistently been the composer. Striving to avoid the commonplace, he added a tone that did not properly belong to the chord, or held over a note from the old chord to the new, thereby creating a piquant effect to which, as time went on, people grew accustomed. This dissonance came to be treated with ever greater freedom and gradually became a full-fledged member of the chord in which it had once been a stranger. Ultimately it lost its flavorsome quality, its character of dissonance, whereupon composers cast about for new combinations that would add zest and pungency to their music. "Every tone relationship that has been used too often," wrote Arnold Schoenberg, "must finally be regarded as exhausted. It ceases to have power to convey a thought worthy of it. Therefore every composer is obliged to invent anew."

The history of the development of harmony, Schoenberg pointed out, is a record of dissonance rather than consonance, for dissonance is the dynamic element that leads the composer away from well-trodden paths. By the same token, it is the element which in every age— whether Monteverdi's, Bach's, Wagner's, or our own—has acutely disturbed the adherents of the past. "Dissonances are more difficult to comprehend than consonance," Schoenberg observed. "Therefore the battle about them goes on throughout history."

This battle came to a head in the late nineteenth century. Wagner and his disciples assiduously explored the expressive powers of dissonance and superimposed upon the Classical system of harmony a network of relationships that completely changed the existing harmonic idiom. In so doing they enormously enriched the harmonic resources available to the composer, and set the stage for an exciting break with the past.

Twentieth-Century Harmony

The twentieth century inherited chord structures of three, four, and five tones. Carrying the traditional method of building chords one step further, twentieth-century composers added another "story" to the chord, thus forming highly dissonant combinations of six and seven tones—for instance, chords based on steps 1–3–5–7–9–11 and 1–3–5–7–9–11–13 of the scale. The emergence of these complex "skyscraper" chords imparted a greater degree of tension to music than had ever existed before.

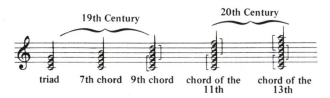

19th Century   20th Century

triad   7th chord   9th chord   chord of the 11th   chord of the 13th

A chord of seven tones, such as the one shown above, hardly possesses the unity of the Classical triad. It includes the notes of no less than three separate triads: the I chord (steps 1–3–5), the V chord (steps 5–7–9), and the II chord (steps 2–4–6 or 9–11–13). In this formation the dominant chord is directly superimposed on the tonic, so that tonic and dominant, the two poles of Classical harmony, are brought together in a kind of montage. What our forebears were in the habit of hearing successively, we today are expected to hear—and grasp—simultaneously. Such a chord, which contains all seven steps of the major scale, not only adds spice to the traditional triad, but also increases the volume of sound, an effect much prized by composers. Here are two effective examples.

A seven-tone "skyscraper" is, in effect, a polychord. It is a block of sound that is heard on two or three planes. A succession of such chords creates several planes of harmony. One of the outstanding achievements of the new age is a kind of polyharmony in which the composer plays two or more streams of harmony against each other, exactly as in former times single strands of melody were combined. The interplay of the several independent streams adds a new dimension to the harmonic space. The following is a famous example of polyharmony from Stravinsky's *Petrushka*. The clash of the two harmonic currents produces a bright, virile sonority that typifies the twentieth-century revolt against the sweet sound of the Romantic era:

No less significant was the appearance of new ways of building chords. Traditionally, these were formed by combining every other tone of the scale; that is to say, they were built in thirds. (See Appendix I-b for an explanation of intervals.) The interval of a third was associated with the music of the eighteenth and nineteenth centuries. To free themselves from the sound of the past, composers cast about for other methods of chord construction; they began to base chords on the interval of the fourth. This turning from tertial to quartal harmony constitutes one of the important differences between nineteenth- and twentieth-century music. Chords based on fourths have a pungency and freshness that are very much of the new age, as the following examples demonstrate.

Scriabin   Stravinsky

Schoenberg, *Chamber Symphony*, Opus 9

Composers also based their harmonies on other intervals. Here is a chord of piled-up fifths from Stravinsky's *Rite of Spring:*

and cluster chords based on seconds from Bartók's *Mikrokosmos:*

Mysterious threads bind artistic expression to the world out of which it stems. Eighteenth-century Classicism was interested above all in the resolution of dissonance to consonance—that is, in the restoration of law and order after momentary disturbance. Our era is interested in the dissonance rather than in the resolution. The greater amount of dissonance in contemporary music reflects the heightened tension and drive of contemporary life. Behind the new harmonic language is the wonderful capacity of the human ear to adapt to new conditions, to receive and assimilate ever more complicated sounds. Availing themselves of this capacity, contemporary composers have created tone combinations of unprecedented complexity capable of expressing the most subtle and elusive meanings.

Twentieth-century harmony, infinitely venturesome in spirit, reveals to us the perspectives of an ever-expanding tonal universe.

5 New Conceptions of Tonality

"Tonality is a natural force, like gravity."

PAUL HINDEMITH

The tones out of which music is fashioned take on coherence and unity if they are apprehended as a family or group; that is to say, if they are heard in relation to a central tone from which musical movement sets out and to which it ultimately returns. This central point is the *do*, the keynote or tonic around which the other tones revolve and to which they gravitate. How basic this gravitation is may be gauged from Stravinsky's dictum, "All music is nothing more than a succession of impulses that converge toward a definite point of repose."

The sense of relatedness to a central tone is known as *tonality*. It has been the fundamental relationship in our music. As Roger Sessions has written, "Tonality should be understood as the principal means which the composers of the seventeenth, eighteenth and nineteenth centuries evolved of organizing musical sounds and giving them coherent shape."

A group of related tones with a common center or tonic is known as a *key*. The tones of the key serve as basic material for a given composition. The key, that is, marks off an area in musical space within which musical growth and development take place.

We have said that dissonance implies movement, consonance represents the desire for rest. But movement and rest in relation to what? Tonality supplies the fixed center, the goal toward which this alternation of movement and rest is directed. By providing a framework for musical events, tonality becomes the first principle of musical architecture, a form-building element which unifies musical space and articulates musical structure. Tonality is no less potent in achieving variety. By moving from one key to another the composer creates a dramatic opposition between two tonal areas. He establishes his piece in the home key, then moves to a contrasting key—that is, he modulates. This modulation to a foreign area increases tension and gives a higher value to the ultimate triumph of the home key. "Modulation is like a change of scenery," said Schoenberg. The movement from home key to contrasting key and back came to be a fundamental pattern of musical structure, and may be described as statement-departure-return. As a result of modulation, a movement of a sonata or symphony did exactly what its name implies—it moved! Out of the dramatic tension between the home key and the foreign emerged the impressive architecture of the Classical symphony. "The development of tonality," Sessions observes, "was a necessary condition of the development of large design in music, since tonality alone carried with it the means of contrast."

The Major-Minor System

In Western music the octave is divided into twelve equal parts. In other words, it contains twelve tones, which comprise what is known as the chromatic scale. A musical work, no matter how complex, is made up of these twelve tones and their duplication in the higher and lower octaves. From any degree of the chromatic scale to its neighbor is a distance of a half tone or semitone. Half tone and whole tone are the units of measurement in our musical system. The music of the Orient, on the other hand, uses smaller intervals, such as third and quarter tones.

The music of the Classic-Romantic era was based on two contrasting scales, the major and the minor. (Information on the major-minor system of scales and keys will be found in Appendix I-c.) The major and minor scales consist of seven tones selected out of the possible twelve. In other words, the Classical system of harmony embodies the "seven-out-of-twelve" way of hearing music that prevailed throughout the eighteenth and nineteenth centuries. When seven tones are chosen to form a key, the other five tones remain foreign to that particular tonality. These extraneous tones are not entirely excluded from a composition in that key. They appear as embellishments of the melody and harmony, and they are used to form the unstable chords which lend spice to the harmony. They are particularly in evidence when the music is moving from the home key to foreign areas, that is, in passages of modulation. If music is to sound firmly rooted in a key, the seven tones that are directly related to the key center must prevail. If the five foreign tones are permitted too conspicuous a role, the magnetic pull to the tonic is weakened, and the tonality becomes ambiguous. The term diatonic refers to movement according to the key—that is, according to the seven tones of the major or minor scale. The term chromatic refers to movement according to the twelve semitones of the octave. Diatonicism connotes the "seven-out-of-twelve" way of hearing music which strengthens the feeling of key. Chromaticism refers to those forces in music which tend to weaken or dissolve the sense of key.

Tonality in the Classic-Romantic Era

The Classical system, with its twelve major and twelve minor keys, may be compared to a house with twenty-four rooms, the modulations being equivalent to corridors leading from one to the next. The Classical composer clearly established the home key, then set out to the next-related area. For him the chief charm of modulation was "the getting there, and not the arrival itself." The home area, the contrasting area, and the corridor between were spaciously designed. Indeed, the forms of the Classic era have a breadth that is the musical counterpart of the ample facades of eighteenth-century architecture and the stately periods of eighteenth-century prose. This amplitude of gesture reached its finest realization in the sonatas and string quartets, symphonies and concertos of Haydn, Mozart, and the younger Beethoven. Basic to the Classical style, of course, was a manner of writing that neatly defined the various key areas: in other words, an emphasis on diatonic harmony.

Under the impetus of nineteenth-century Romanticism, composers sought to whip up emotion and intensify all musical effects; they turned more and more to chromaticism. Besides, by then the system had become familiar, and listeners needed less time to grasp the tonality. Home key and foreign key were established with more concise gestures; the corridors between them steadily shrank. There came into being that restless wandering from key to key which fed the nineteenth-century need for emotional excitement. Modulation was ever more frequent, abrupt, daring. Each modulation led to new excursions. The result was that the distance from the home tonality steadily increased. It was in the music-dramas of Wagner that the chromatic harmony of the Romantic era received its most compelling expression. Wagner's harmonies—ambiguous, volatile, seductive—

represented a new level of musical sensibility. His *Tristan and Isolde*, couched in a language of unprecedented expressivity, carried the chromatic idiom to the limit of its possibilities. The harmonic cadence—the element in music that defines and establishes tonality—was virtually suppressed in this epoch-making score, in favor of a continual scheme of modulation that built up extraordinary tension. Indeed, in the Prelude to the opera one no longer knows exactly what the key is. *Tristan*, the prime symbol of romantic yearning and unfulfillment, made it all too apparent that the Classical system with its neatly defined key areas had begun to disintegrate.

For the better part of three hundred years the major and minor scales had supplied, in Alfredo Casella's phrase, "the tonal loom on which every melody was woven." Nineteenth-century composers began to feel that everything that could possibly be said within this framework had already been said, so that it became more and more difficult for them to achieve fresh expression within the confines of the major-minor system. Just as they turned against the symmetries of the four-measure phrase and the dominant-tonic cadence, so they had perforce to turn against the restrictions of the diatonic scale. In the final years of the nineteenth century the "seven-out-of-twelve" way of hearing music came to its natural end. The twentieth century was ready for a new way: twelve out of twelve.

The Expansion of Tonality in Twentieth-Century Music

In their desire to free music from what Béla Bartók called "the tyrannical rule of the major-minor keys," twentieth-century composers found their way to broader notions of tonality. One of the most fruitful of the new concepts involves the free use of twelve tones around a center. This retains the basic principle of traditional tonality, loyalty to the tonic; but, by considering the five chromatic tones to be as much a part of the key as the seven diatonic ones, it immeasurably expands the borders of tonality.

This expanded conception of tonality has not only done away with the distinction between diatonic and chromatic, but also wiped out the distinction between major and minor that was so potent a source of contrast in the Classic-Romantic era. The composers of the eighteenth and nineteenth centuries presented major-minor in succession; contemporary composers present them simultaneously. A piece today will be, let us say, in F major-minor, using all the twelve tones around the center F, instead of dividing them, as was done in the past, into two separate groups of seven. This serves to create an ambiguous tonality which is highly congenial to the taste of our time.

In general, the key is no longer so clearly defined an area in musical space as it used to be, and the shift from one key center to another is made with a dispatch that puts to shame the most exuberant modulations of the Wagner era. Transitional passages are dispensed with. One tonality is simply displaced by another, in a way that keeps both the music and the listener on the move. An excellent example is the popular theme from *Peter and the Wolf*. Prokofiev is extremely fond of this kind of displacement.

So too, chords utterly foreign to the tonality are included, not even as modulations, but simply as an extension of the key to a new tonal plane. As a result, a passage will sound A major-ish, shall we say, rather than in A major. In their turn away from the major-minor system, composers went back to procedures that had existed long before—to the music of the Middle Ages and Renaissance, and to the medieval scale patterns called the church modes. You can hear some of these medieval scales by playing the white notes on the piano from D to D (Dorian), from E to E (Phrygian), from F to F (Lydian), or from G to G (Mixolydian). The modes served as the basis for European art music for a thousand years—from the Gregorian chants of the sixth century to the masterpieces of Palestrina at the end of the

Twentieth-century tonality may be compared to modern collage, in which discreet, recognizable images from everyday life are combined to create Expressionistic effects. Violin and Pipe, *oil and sand on canvas, 1920–1921, by Georges Braque (1882–1963). Courtesy, Philadelphia Museum of Art: The Louise and Walter Arensberg Collection.*

sixteenth. The adjective modal describes the type of melody and harmony prevailing during this period, as distinguished from tonal, which refers to the major-minor harmony that supplanted the modes.

Based as they are on a white-note scale, the modes stand as far removed as possible from post-Wagnerian chromaticism. Their archaic sound was most attractive to a generation of musicians seeking to escape the overcharged sonorities of an outworn Romanticism. The following passage from Vaughan Williams's *Pastoral Symphony* exemplifies the freshness and charm that modal flavoring brought to twentieth-century music.

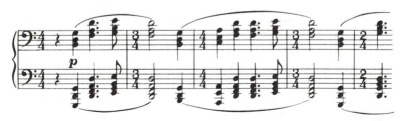

Desirous of exploiting new harmonic resources, composers found inspiration in the exotic scales of China, India, Java, and other Far Eastern countries. They also turned to the ancient scales embodied in European folk music. And they began to experiment with the construction of new scales. Here are two examples—one devised by Béla Bartók, the other by Ferruccio Busoni.

The great developments from the time of Bach and Handel to that of Tchaikovsky and Brahms had unfolded within the frame of the major-minor system. With the disintegration of this three-hundred-year-old structure, music entered upon a new phase. In effect, the twentieth century ushered in far-reaching changes in the basic relationships of the art of music.

Even so, the break with tradition was not as complete as many suppose. Schoenberg himself—who more than any other was instrumental in overthrowing the established order of tonality—declared, "There is still much good music to be written in C major."

6 Rhythm in Twentieth-Century Music

"Rhythm and motion, not the element of feeling, are the foundations of musical art."

IGOR STRAVINSKY

By rhythm we mean the principle of organization that regulates the flow of music in time. Since music is an art that exists only in time, rhythm controls every aspect of a composition, from the minutest detail to the overall unity of its architecture. Hence Roger Sessions's remark that "an adequate definition of rhythm comes close to defining music itself." The decisive role of rhythm in the musical process has always been recognized by composers. Hector Berlioz considered rhythmic pulsation "the very life-blood of the music." Hans von Bülow coined a famous phrase when he remarked, "In the beginning was rhythm." Twentieth-century musicians are no less explicit in acknowledging its importance. Sessions regards rhythm as the "primary fact" of music. Ernst Toch, speaking of rhythmic reiteration and contrast, states, "It is the interplay of these two elementary forces that builds and feeds the skeleton of music." And Aaron Copland calls rhythm "the most primitive element in music."

Metrical Rhythm and Free Rhythm

We distinguish among several types of rhythmic organization in language. One kind of organization is metrical poetry, which utilizes an unmistakable pattern of syllables arranged in units of equal duration, marked by regular recurrence of accent—as in the following lines by Keats:

> Sóuls of Póets déad and góne,
> Whát Elýsium háve ye knówn,
> Háppy fiéld or móssy cávern
> Chóicer thán the Mérmaid Távern?

Free verse, in contrast, is less tightly organized than metrical poetry. Its speech rhythms are more supple, its accents more subtly placed. Still more free in its flow is poetic prose, whose elastic rhythms—as in the prose of the Bible—are capable of a rich and varied music.

Musical rhythm, too, presents varying degrees of organization. At one extreme is the regular beat of a Sousa march or a folk dance, so obvious as to be unmistakable. At the other are the freely flowing arabesques of oriental song, or of Gregorian chant, or of operatic recitative. These are the musical equivalents of free-verse and poetic-prose rhythms. Their rhythmic impulse comes from speech rather than from the symmetries of the dance.

The trend in Western music from 1600 to 1900 was steadily in the direction of tighter organization—that is to say, toward metrical rhythm. There were several reasons for this. To begin with, European music was influenced in ever greater degree by folk dance and folk song, both of which were allied to popular metrical poetry. Then again, as the various literatures of Europe developed highly organized metrical verse forms, these could not but affect the music to which they were set. A similar influence came from the Lutheran chorales, which used simple metrical patterns so that the congregation could keep together. As a result of these and kindred influences, Western music steadily lost the rhythmic freedom it had had during the Middle Ages and the Renaissance.

The movement toward standardized metrical rhythm reached its height in the Classic-Romantic era. Indeed, practically the entire output of the eighteenth and nineteenth centuries—an enormous amount of music—was written in two-four, three-four, four-four, and six-eight time—that is, two, three, four, or six beats to a measure, with a regularly recurring accent on the first beat. Such regular patterns set up expectancies whose fulfillment is a source of pleasure to the listener. People enjoy falling into step with the beat of a march or waltz. Metrical rhythm captures for music an image of the dance, a sense of physical well-being inherent in regular body movement. Besides, by using metrical rhythm, a composer is easily able to organize music in balanced phrases and cadences. Thus the standard meters went hand-in-hand with the four-measure structure of the Classic-Romantic style. (The basic meters are explained in Appendix I-d.)

"The Tyranny of the Barline"

The standardization of musical time into a few basic patterns had great advantages at a time when art music was winning a new mass public. It enabled composers to communicate their intentions more easily. It also helped large groups of performers to sing and play in time, thereby making feasible the huge choruses and orchestras that transformed music into a popular art.

All the same, composers chafed increasingly under "the tyranny of the barline"—the relentless recurrence of the accented ONE. As we have noticed in preceding chapters, what begins by being a support ends as a straitjacket. Musicians found the excessive standardization of meter increasingly hostile to artistic expression, and sought to free themselves from the trip-hammer of the accented beat.

These attempts began long before the twentieth century. Older masters, for instance, made liberal use of syncopation, a technique of shifting the accent to the offbeat, thereby upsetting—and enlivening—the normal pattern of accentuation. Composers also used more complex subsidiary rhythms within the measure. A characteristic subtlety was cross rhythm: shifting the accents within the measure so that a passage written in triple time briefly took on the character of duple time, or the other way around. Much favored too was the simultaneous use of two rhythmic patterns, such as "two against three" or "three against four." These devices figure prominently in the music of Chopin, Schumann, and Brahms.

A great impetus toward the freshening of rhythm came from the nationalist schools of the nineteenth century. Rhythms drawn from

Polish, Hungarian, Bohemian, and Norwegian folk dance enlivened the standard patterns of the older musical cultures. The Russians played a leading role in this development. Musorgsky especially used rugged, uneven rhythms of great expressive power. In the final quarter of the century it became ever clearer that new conceptions of rhythm were in the making.

Twentieth-Century Rhythm

The revolt against the standard meters led twentieth-century composers to explore the possibilities of less symmetrical patterns. At the same time poets were turning from metrical to free verse. Both these developments reflect a general tendency in contemporary art to pull away from conventional symmetry in favor of the unexpected. As one critic expressed it, "We enjoy the irregular more than the regular when we understand it."

The revitalization of Western rhythm was nourished by a number of sources. Composers felt obliged to try to capture the hectic rhythms of the life about them. Nineteenth-century rhythms were derived from peasant dances and bucolic scenes. Twentieth-century rhythms glorify the drive of modern city life, the pulsebeat of factory and machine. It is therefore natural for twentieth-century musicians

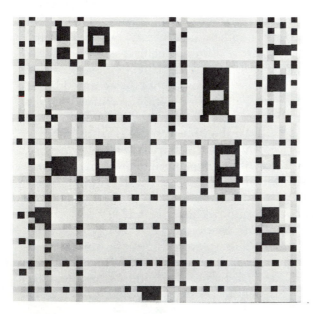

Painters, as well as composers, were fascinated by the excitement of modern city life with its ever-changing patterns of light and rhythm. In Broadway Boogie Woogie, 1942–1943, *Piet Mondrian (1872–1946) captures the spirit of jazz bands and dance halls through the asymmetrical juxtaposition of geometrical shapes. Collection, The Museum of Modern Art, New York.*

to be preoccupied with that element of their art most closely associated with movement and physical activity. Also, the enormous popularity of Russian ballet in the years after the First World War heightened the emphasis on rhythm. Nineteenth-century composers had concentrated on harmony and orchestral color, and had somewhat neglected rhythm. The new music had to correct the imbalance.

In their desire to escape the obvious, composers began to draw inspiration from rhythmic conceptions outside European music. Especially fruitful was the interest in primitive art that arose in the opening years of the century. The pounding, hammering rhythms of Stravinsky and Bartók sent a breath of fresh air through European music. Not unrelated were the syncopations of jazz that became the rage in Europe and exerted a positive influence on modern music. The search for new rhythmic effects led composers far afield in time as well as space. They turned back to the free prose rhythms of Gregorian chant; they studied the supple rhythms of medieval motet and Renaissance madrigal, in which no single strong beat regularized the free interplay of the voices. Nationalism, too, made a vital contribution to the new rhythm. Vaughan Williams in England, Bartók in Hungary, and Charles Ives in the United States prized the rhythms of their cultures precisely for their "offbeat" qualities. From the interaction of all these forces came a new rhythm, tense and resilient, that electrified the world.

New Rhythmic Devices

The twentieth-century composer is apt to avoid four-measure rhythm. He regards it as too predictable, hence unadventurous. He prefers to challenge the ear with nonsymmetrical rhythms that keep the listener on his toes. This rejection of standard patterns has led composers to explore meters based on odd numbers: five beats to the measure $(3 + 2$ or $2 + 3)$; seven $(2 + 2 + 3, 4 + 3,$ or $2 + 3 + 2)$; nine $(5 + 4$ or $4 + 5)$; also rhythms based on groups of eleven or thirteen beats. Within the measure small units of beats are subdivided in a great diversity of rhythmic patterns. In addition, the grouping of the measures into phrases is far more flexible than in earlier music. The result is that today rhythm is freer, more supple than ever before.

Often, in nineteenth-century music, an entire piece or movement is written in a single meter. Twentieth-century composers, striving for the suppleness of free-verse and prose rhythm, began to change from one meter to another with unprecedented rapidity and ease. In a word, they turned to multirhythm. The following passage from Stravinsky's *Rite of Spring* shows changes of meter with every measure. Rhythmic flexibility could hardly be carried any further. Stravinsky had every right to remark, as he did, "It is for the conductor that I make things difficult."

It goes without saying that the barline has lost its former power as the arbiter of the musical flow. As a matter of fact, there are composers who dispense with it altogether. Others retain it, but mainly as a visual aid to the performer. In any case, through the use of multirhythms and other devices that we will explore in later chapters, "the tyranny of the barline" has been broken forever.

Twentieth-century rhythm, like melody and harmony, has abandoned the landmarks on which the mass of music lovers depend. In much modern music (although by no means all!) the listener will miss the reassuring downbeat, the predictable accent that is so pleasant to nod, tap, and sway to, just as he will miss the symmetrical structure based on four-measure phrases. As he accustoms himself to do without those, he will discover a world of fresh and novel rhythms, impregnated with kinetic power and movement, and thoroughly attuned to the modern world. The emancipation of rhythm from the standard metrical patterns of the eighteenth and nineteenth centuries must be accounted one of the major achievements of contemporary music. It has resulted in nothing less than a revitalization of the rhythmic sense of the West.

7　Texture in Twentieth-Century Music

"Counterpoint is just as much subject to constant evolution and flux as are melody and harmony, with which it is indissolubly interwoven."

ERNST TOCH

Three Kinds of Texture

The dictionary defines texture as the arrangement or disposition of the threads of a woven fabric. Musicians have adopted the term, because it applies rather well to their art.

We distinguish three types of texture. First is monophonic or single-voice texture, in which the music is heard as a single strand of melody without harmonic background. All music up to a thousand years ago was monophonic, as is to this day the music of India and the Arab world, China and Japan, Java and Bali. In Western music the great monument of the monophonic period is the fifteen-hundred-year-old liturgical music of the Catholic Church, Gregorian chant, which was conceived as pure melody without reference to harmonic values.

Two or more melodic lines may be combined in a many-voiced or

35

polyphonic texture. Polyphonic music is based on counterpoint, the art of combining several melody lines or "voices" in a unified musical fabric. The essence of contrapuntal style is the contrast between the independent voices, which are set off from each other by contrasts in rhythm and line. These contrasts cause the music to unfold in several planes, creating an impression of depth and unflagging movement that can be attained in no other way.

In the third type of texture a single voice carries the melody line. The accompanying voices surrender their independence and coalesce in blocks of harmony, to become the chords that support and enrich the main part. This is homophonic or chordal texture. Here, as in monophonic music, the listener's attention is directed to a single line, but with a difference: the melody is not conceived as a self-sufficient entity, but is related to the harmonic background. Homophonic texture depends on the vertical tone-mass, the chord, while contrapuntal texture represents a concept of music based on the interplay of horizontal lines.

The three types of texture differ sharply, even graphically.

a. Monophonic—Gregorian Chant

Do-mi-ne De - us   Rex coe - le - stis   De-us   Pa-ter   om - ni-po - tens

b. Polyphonic—Chorus from *Messiah*

etc.

c. Homophonic—Chopin Waltz

p   *cresc.*   *mf*

etc.

Although we draw a clear distinction between the harmonic and contrapuntal elements of music, they really represent two aspects of the same thing. In a contrapuntal work by Bach or Handel, the tones at any given point form a vertical block of sound—in other words, a chord. Conversely, suppose a vocal quartet is harmonizing a tune. We hear a single melody line with chords underneath—that is, homophonic texture. Yet each of the singers as he moves from one chord to the next follows his own horizontal line. Clearly the horizontal and the vertical, the contrapuntal and the harmonic elements, exist side by side in music. The difference is one of emphasis. We regard a texture as polyphonic when the conduct of the voices takes precedence over harmonic considerations. We regard a texture as homophonic when the relationship of the chords takes precedence over the counterpoint. (For information on basic procedures of counterpoint—imitation, canon, fugue—see Appendix I-g.)

Counterpoint exalts the structural and formal values of music. It has a special appeal for the intellectual musician, who sees in its abstraction and refinement of thought the purest, most exalted musical discourse. To fill a contrapuntal structure with feeling and poetry requires consummate mastery of technique and poses problems that cannot fail to challenge the creative imagination.

Texture in the Music of the Past

The late Middle Ages and Renaissance witnessed a magnificent flowering of polyphonic art in sacred and secular choral music, with which composers at that time were primarily concerned. This development continued throughout the Baroque era (1600–1750) and culminated in the music of the two giants of the late Baroque, Johann Sebastian Bach (1685–1750) and George Frideric Handel (1685–1759). Their majestic fugues, both instrumental and choral, crown five centuries of polyphony and superbly reveal the capacities of counterpoint for the manipulation of purely musical means in a purely musical way.

In the period that followed, composers explored the possibilities of a single line of melody heard against a background of chords. They developed a transparent orchestral texture that culminated in the style of Haydn and Mozart. The nineteenth century completed the swing from a horizontal to a vertical conception of music. Texture throughout the Romantic era emphasized harmony and color rather than line. Composers were preoccupied above all with unlocking the magic power of the chord. This striving for luscious harmony impelled them to an ever richer orchestral sound. Texture grew thick and opaque. The mammoth orchestra favored by the disciples of

Wagner—Richard Strauss, Mahler, and the youthful Schoenberg—brought the elaborate textures of the Postromantic era to a point beyond which no further progress was possible.

There is a healthy impulse in art to execute an about-face when an impasse has been reached. Contemporary music found a new direction.

Texture in the Twentieth Century

In pulling away from the emotional exuberance of the Postromantic era, composers turned also against the sumptuous texture that was its ultimate manifestation. They had to lighten the texture, they

In this painting, the impression of movement through space is created by overlapping the same image repeatedly in descending progression. The texture of the work is thereby lightened in order to establish the sense of propulsion. Nude Descending a Staircase, No. 2, 1912, by Marcel Duchamp (1887–1968). The Philadephia Museum of Art: The Louise and Walter Arensberg Collection.

felt, in order to give music once again a sense of unobstructed movement. The twentieth century thus saw a great revival of counterpoint, which represented a return to the aesthetic ideals of the age of
Bach, the last period when the horizontal-linear point of view had
prevailed. Composers broke up the thick chordal fabric of the late
Romantic style; they shifted from opulent tone mass to pure line,
from sensuous harmony and iridescent color to sinewy melody and
transparency of texture. The "return to Bach" extended beyond the
work of that master to the great contrapuntists of the fifteenth and
sixteenth centuries. This new interest in linear thinking served the
desire of the age for condensation of style and purity of expression,
for athletic movement and architectonic unity; above all, for a point
of view that concentrated upon compositional problems rather than
upon the expression of personal feelings.

Consonance unites, dissonance separates. The masters of polyphony in the past used consonant intervals—fifths, fourths, thirds,
and sixths—at the points of contact between the voices, so as to
blend them into a unified texture. Twentieth-century composers, on
the other hand, use dissonant intervals such as seconds and sevenths
to separate the lines and make them stand out against each other.
Dissonant counterpoint has come to denote the modern kind of texture
in which dissonance energizes the movement and propels the texture
forward. Here is an example from Paul Hindemith, one of the masters of dissonant counterpoint:

The reconstitution of contrapuntal values must be regarded as
one of the prime achievements of twentieth-century music. It restored the balance that was upset by nineteenth-century emphasis

upon vertical elements at the expense of horizontal. And it instituted counterpoint not as an accessory technique but as an integral part of the compositional process. As the English critic George Dyson put it, "Ours is an age of texture."

8 New Concepts in Sonority

"We have had enough of this orchestral dappling and these thick sonorities. One is tired of being saturated with timbres and wants no more of all this overfeeding."

IGOR STRAVINSKY

Unquestionably the most exciting instrument of our time is the orchestra. Orchestral sonority is a cardinal fact in our musical experience and is central to the shaping of our musical imagery. A little over two hundred years ago, Bach had at his disposal an orchestra of approximately twenty players. Toward the end of the eighteenth century, when Haydn and Mozart were writing their symphonies, the orchestra consisted of about thirty men. Our great orchestras today number upward of a hundred. To write for such an ensemble is no mean art.

In writing for an orchestra, the composer weaves the multicolored strands of sound into a variegated tapestry, blending and contrasting the different timbres, contracting and expanding the instrumental forces according to his dynamic purpose, and allocating themes to those instruments that will present them most effectively. He sees to it that the melody stands out clearly and vividly from the sonorous background. At the same time he contrives to make the accompanying lines clearly audible in their own right. He distributes the melodic, harmonic, and rhythmic material among the instrumental groups so as to secure the proper balance of tone and consistency of texture. Through the use of color he points up the design, sets off the main ideas from the subordinate, and welds the thousand and one details into a unified whole.

The orchestration, consequently, is associated most closely with his musical conception. As Walter Piston has observed, "The true art of orchestration is inseparable from the creative act of composing music." As a matter of fact, a composer's manner of orchestrating is as personal as is his shaping of the melody, harmony, or rhythm. (For background material on the orchestra and its instruments, see Appendix I-h.)

Orchestration in the Classic-Romantic Era

The orchestra of Haydn and Mozart was capable of subtle nuances by which each timbre was made to stand out luminously. The eighteenth-century masters used their medium with surpassing economy. Color, for them, sprang from the nature of the thing said; it served the idea. Color highlighted form and structure and contributed to achieving architectural unity.

For the Romantic composers, color was an end in itself and a perpetual source of wonder. Richard Strauss well understood this when he remarked that Hector Berlioz "was the first composer consistently to derive his inspiration from the nature of the instruments." In this regard the pioneering Frenchman was a true Romantic. Until his time, as Aaron Copland pointed out, "composers used instruments in order to make them sound like themselves; the mixing of colors so as to produce a new result was his achievement."

It was Richard Wagner who created the sound image of the Romantic orchestra which is most familiar to the world. His habit of blending and mixing colors continually, his technique of reinforcing (doubling) a single melody line with various instruments, and his addiction to sustained tones in the brass produced a rich, massive texture that enchanted the audiences of the late nineteenth century. His was an opulent, multicolored cloud of sound in which the pure timbres of the individual instruments were either veiled or completely swallowed up; hence the frequent remark that Wagner's orchestra plays "with the pedal on." This technique was carried to its farthermost limits in the Postromantic era, culminating in the orchestral virtuosity of Richard Strauss. Orchestration became an art that existed almost independently of composition. The composer displayed his sense of sound with the same mastery that former composers had shown in the field of thematic invention. The Postromantic period saw the emergence of other brilliant orchestrators—Gustav Mahler, Maurice Ravel, Ottorino Respighi. But it happened in more than one work that the magnificence of the orchestral raiment far surpassed the quality of the musical ideas.

Between 1890 and 1910 the orchestra assumed formidable proportions. Strauss, in his score for *Elektra,* called for twelve trumpets, four trombones, eight horns, six to eight kettledrums. In Mahler's *Symphony of a Thousand* several choruses were deployed, in addition to mammoth orchestral forces. The texture of music began to assume a complexity beyond the capacity of the human ear to unravel. Despite the furious interplay of the instrumental lines, what emerged was a swollen, opaque stream of sound that brought to its ultimate development the vertical-harmonic—that is to say, the sheerly Romantic—way of hearing music. The post-Wagnerian orchestra reached a point beyond which further advance was hardly possible.

Such an orchestral style, needless to say, did not appeal to a generation of musicians in revolt against the Romantic aesthetic. Debussy spoke of the "thick polychromatic putty" that Wagner spread over his scores. Stravinsky remarked that Wagner's orchestra "plays the organ." Copland described the German master's orchestration as "an over-all neutral fatness of sound which has lost all differentiation and distinction." This change of taste went hand-in-hand with the simplification of texture described in the last chapter, and brought with it a ligthening of the orchestral sound. Twentieth-century composers forced the Postromantic orchestra to open its window, so to speak: to let in light and air.

The New Orchestration

The turn from harmonic-vertical to contrapuntal thinking determined the new orchestral style. The nineteenth-century musician made his colors swim together; his twentieth-century counterpart aspires above all to make each instrument stand out clearly against the mass. Composers have turned back to classical ideals: clarity of line and transparency of texture. They have thinned out the swollen sound and reinstated the sharply defined colors of the eighteenth-century style. They no longer reinforce or double the melody line with a blend of instruments from various choirs; instead they emphasize individual timbres. As Stravinsky put it, "Doubling is not strengthening."

One may compare this change to a rejection of the rich composite colors of oil painting in favor of the naked lines of etching. The new orchestration reveals the interweaving of the melodic strands, the play of contrapuntal lines rather than the flow of harmonic masses. The result has been a reconstitution of true orchestral polyphony.

There has been a return to the Classical precept that color must function not as a source of enchantment but as a means of clarifying the structural design. The leaders of contemporary musical thought have emphasized again and again the need to free music from the seduction of Romantic sonority. "We must outgrow the sentimental and superficial attachment to sound," wrote Paul Hindemith. Arnold Schoenberg maintained that "Lucidity is the first purpose of color in music. Perhaps the art of orchestration has become too popular, and interesting-sounding pieces are often produced for no better reason than that which dictates the making of typewriters and fountain pens in different colors." Stravinsky also warned against the "fundamental error" of regarding orchestration as "a source of enjoyment independent of the music. The time has surely come to put things in their proper place."

The desire to "decongest" the Romantic sound brought in its wake a strong desire for a reduction of orchestral forces. From the monster ensemble of the 1890s, composers turned back to the smaller orchestra of the early nineteenth century. The lightening of orchestral texture is apparent in the widely spaced lines wherewith contemporary composers "ventilate" their scores. By eliminating all that is

Just as composers were lightening orchestral texture to achieve greater clarity, refinement, and subtlety, painters like Matisse strived for "an art of balance, of purety and serenity. . . ." Joie de vivre, 1905–1906, by Henri Matisse. The Barnes Foundation, Merion, Pennsylvania.

Strauss, *Till Eulenspiegel*

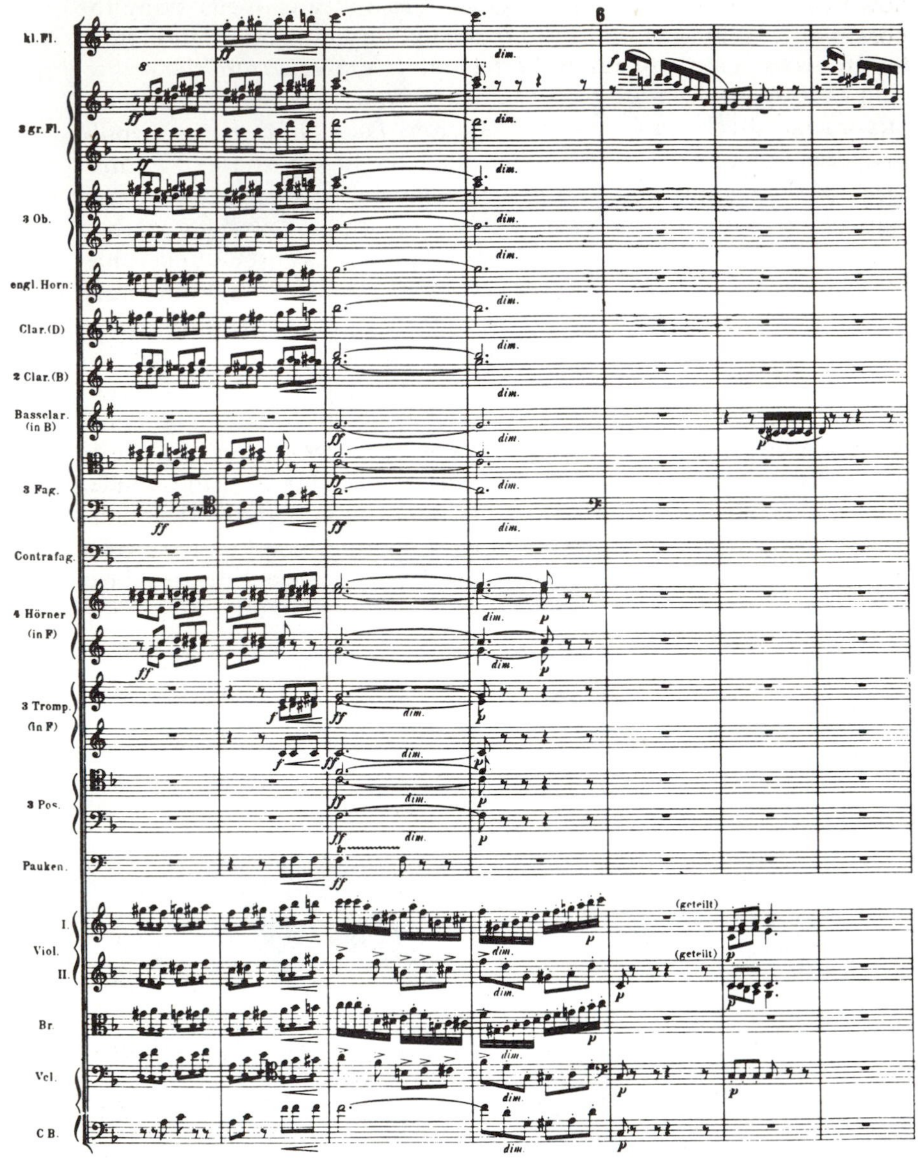

not essential they achieve a new sparseness in their scoring, setting down as few notes (where a Richard Strauss put down as many) as possible. It is instructive, in this regard, to compare a page from Strauss's *Till Eulenspiegel* with one from Stravinsky's *Orpheus.*

In effect, many contemporary composers brought into the orchestra the spirit of chamber music, and by so doing moved closer to what has always been the ideal of the string quartet and similar types of music: limpidity of texture, clarity of thought, refinement of expression, and subtlety of effect. As one writer expressed it, they have "chamberized" the orchestra; their modest linear scoring has taught it to play "without the pedal." Composers today are not afraid to keep part of the orchestra silent if it suits their expressive purpose (unlike nineteenth-century composers, who felt that all the instruments had to play all the time). The pull away from Wagnerian opulence placed a new value upon a sober sound. Lack of brilliance, which the previous age would have regarded as a deficiency, came to be a virtue. "True sobriety," Stravinsky proclaimed, "is a great rarity, and most difficult of attainment." The string choir lost its traditional role as the heart of the orchestra, because its tone was felt to be too personal, too subjective. Composers began to favor the less expressive winds. Because of the distrust of overbrilliant sound, the darker instruments came into prominence; the lyrical violin was re-

Stravinsky, *Orpheus*

placed in favor by the more reserved viola. Among the brass, the caressing horn was supplanted by the more incisive trumpet. All this, during the 1920s, was used as an antidote against the seductions of Romantic sonority.

The exploration of percussive rhythm focused attention on the percussion instruments. These were emancipated from their hitherto subordinate position and brought into soloistic prominence. Indeed, percussion sound pervaded the entire orchestra. Composers were intrigued with the xylophone and glockenspiel, whose metallic, "objective" sonority accorded with the new aesthetic. In addition, they began to model their sound upon instruments that had never been part of the orchestra. A case in point is Stravinsky's fondness for the accordion sound, or Schoenberg's for guitar and mandolin. The piano, which throughout the Romantic era had been a solo instrument, was now included in the ensemble. Composers exploited its capacity for percussive rhythm, often treating it as a kind of xylophone in a mahogany box: a far cry, to say the least, from the instrument of Chopin and Liszt.

At the same time, they continued the nineteenth-century attempt to open up new orchestral resources, using instruments in unusual ways, and exploring the expressive power of extreme registers and novel combinations. They exploited new effects—for example, the trombone glissando that Schoenberg employed so imaginatively. It can safely be said that musicians today are more adept in the art of orchestration than ever before. What with the prevalence of good orchestras, recordings, and radio, they have greater opportunities than did musicians of any earlier generation to hear orchestral music well played. As a result, many a young composer nowadays sets forth on his career with a mastery of orchestral technique it would have taken him half a lifetime to acquire a century ago.

The advances in orchestral technique achieved during the nineteenth century made possible a new orchestral art. In restoring orchestral color to its function in Classical times as the obedient handmaiden of form and idea, twentieth-century composers found a way to make the orchestra serve the aesthetic goals of our time.

9 New Conceptions of Form

"In music there is no form without logic, there is no logic without unity."

ARNOLD SCHOENBERG

We have traced fundamental patterns of organization in melody, harmony, tonality, rhythm and meter, texture and color. Out of the interplay of all these elements there emerges an impression of conscious choice and judicious arrangement, of coherence and continuity of thought: in a word, of artistic form. "Tonal elements," Stravinsky has written, "become music only by being organized." The overall organization of these elements in musical time and space is what we mean by form.

A basic principle of musical form is repetition and contrast, which achieves both unity and variety. The one ministers to man's joy in the familiar and to his need for reassurance. The other satisfies his equally strong craving for the challenge of the unfamiliar. Repetition establishes a relationship between structural elements. Contrast sets off and vitalizes this relationship. The contrasting material brings with it a heightening of tension, which is resolved by the return of the familiar material. Hence Ernst Toch's fine phrase, "Form is the balance between tension and relaxation."

Form is the dwelling place of the idea, its visible shape and embodiment. In the highest art there exists the utmost unity between form and content, the two being as inseparable as are mind and body: *what* is said cannot be conceived as existing apart from *how* it is said. This becomes apparent when we try to retell the content of a poem, a novel, or a play in our own words. We become aware that the content changes when it is removed from its form. The unity of form and content is especially strong in music, where the form is molded to the idea and the idea is shaped by the form. The form helps us grasp the inner content of a musical work. At the same time it can itself be a potent source of aesthetic pleasure. "The principal function of form," declares Schoenberg, "is to advance our understanding. By producing comprehensibility, form produces beauty."

The Classical Forms

The principle of form which operates in all the arts manifests itself in music in a variety of traditional forms. It is important to remember that these are not so many ready-made molds into which the composer pours the stuff of his inspiration, so that it will harden and assume a shape approved by custom. The living forms of the masters grow organically from the material; the nature of the thing said dictates the treatment it receives. We can describe a sonata or fugue in a general way; but the fact remains that no two fugues of Bach, no two sonatas of Mozart are exactly alike. Each is a unique example of the adaptation of form to content. Each solves anew the subtle balancing of tension and relaxation, light and shade, feelingful content and structural logic. "The form," Aaron Copland points out, "is a generalisation which has to be adapted to a particular situation."

In the Baroque and Classical eras, the movement away from and back to the home key came to be the main gesture of musical form. The grand form of the Classical era—the sonata—mobilized to the full the possibilities for unity and contrast, tension and resolution inherent in the major-minor system. Therewith the Classical masters created an architectonic structure whose clarity of design, amplitude of gesture, and diversity of mood continue to command the admiration of the world. The Classical sonata is an ideal tone-drama whose characters are the themes, and whose action is derived from purely musical elements without reference to literary or pictorial association. The first movement is generally a spacious *allegro*. The second, as a rule, is a reflective slow movement. Third is a minuet or scherzo;

and the cycle concludes with a lively finale. First, third, and fourth movements are usually in the home key, while the second is in a related key. The sonata cycle leaves the listener with the sense of a vast action resolved, an eventful journey brought to its conclusion. With its fusion of sensuous, emotional, and intellectual elements, of lyric contemplation and dramatic action, the sonata-symphony may justly claim to be one of the most compelling forms ever devised for the expressing of purely musical ideas in a purely musical way. There is every justification for Aaron Copland's comparing a great symphony to "a man-made Mississippi down which we irresistibly flow from the instant of our leave-taking to a long foreseen destination." (For a detailed analysis of sonata form, see Appendix I-i.)

The four-movement cycle—whether as solo sonata, duo, trio, quartet or quintet, concerto or symphony—satisfied the desire of the Classical masters for an extended work that would derive its character from the nature of the instruments and its materials from the nature of music. Understandably, this cycle had its greatest triumphs in the period when the major-minor system was at its peak: the age of Haydn, Mozart, Beethoven, and Schubert. The composers of the nineteenth century, for their part, adapted the Classical form to Romantic ends. They were concerned with picturesque detail, with mood, atmosphere, and color rather than the triumph of an overall design. They loved expansive lyricism and rhetoric—so they distended the form and dissolved its outlines. Above all, in their preoccupation with chromatic harmony they veiled the boundaries of the key, and therewith undermined the contrast between tonic and dominant that was basic to the form. In their hands the symphony became a grandiose drama concerned with the triumph of faith over doubt, with man's struggle against fate, with the beauty of nature and the glory of one's native land. By the time César Franck, Bruckner, Tchaikovsky, Mahler, and Richard Strauss finished with it, the symphony had traveled a long way from its Classical heritage; but it came to satisfy the expressive needs of the Romantic period as effectively as it had served those of the Classical age.

Form in Twentieth-Century Music

Modern composers have embraced the Classical conception of form as a construction based on purely musical elements. They have restored form to its Classical position as an absolute value in art, the symbol of purity and perfection of style. For the present-day composer the purely musical elements of his art—line, harmony, rhythm, color—have as much appeal has had the literary or descriptive program for his Romantic predecessor. He makes no distinction between the form and the emotion. Indeed, many musicians today affirm that form *is* emotion, and that the form of a piece is its meaning—the only meaning it can have. Even if this is an extreme statement of the formalist position—and one to which, assuredly, not all composers subscribe—it does express a significant current in present-day musical thought.

Considering the great changes that have taken place with respect to melody, harmony, rhythm, color, texture, and tonality, the changes in musical form have been considerably less spectacular. The traditional forms offer such ingenious solutions to the problem of unity and variety in music that they are not easily supplanted. The most important trend has been a moving away from the clear-cut symmetries of the Classic-Romantic era. The phrase is still the unit of musical architecture; but its beginning and end are no longer punched home to the ear. Repetition remains the basic principle of musical structure—but repetition disguised, varied, cropping up at irregular intervals and unexpected places. The whole conception of form based on clearly articulated patterns of two, four, and eight measures has been drastically modified. This veiling of the structural outlines has resulted, naturally, in a certain loss of clarity and simplicity. But it has brought a corresponding gain of subtlety and freshness in expressive resources. "It is the barely perceptible irregularities that infuse life into artistic form," writes Ernst Toch. Twentieth-century music has rediscovered the charm of the irregular.

Dynamic Symmetry

The Classical A-B-A pattern, with its outer sections balancing the middle part, is a clear adaptation to music of an architectural principle. In the Classical view, eight measures of music in the first section had to be balanced by eight in the closing section. Twentieth-century aesthetics has embraced a somewhat different position. When the A section of a three-part structure is repeated, the original statement is already removed from us in time. It has "shrunk" somewhat to our view, exactly as an object does that is removed from us in space. For this reason a shorter version of the A section, when it is repeated, will sound just as long to us as the original statement—especially

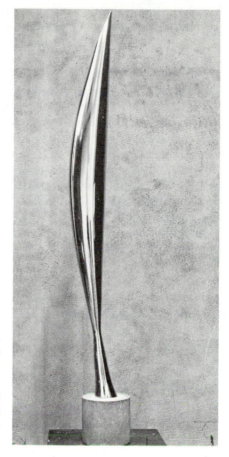

Bird in Space, 1919, by Con-
stantin Brancusi (1876–1958) is
an example of sculpture ex-
pressing a feeling or emotion
through abstract form. Collec-
tion, The Museum of Modern
Art, New York. Given Anony-
mously.

since we already are familiar with the material. Modern composers consequently foreshorten the repetition, achieving the same effect of perspective in time as we are accustomed to in space. They have substituted dynamic symmetry for a symmetry based on exact repetition.

To the contemporary way of thinking, an intensification of style—a rise to more dramatic expression, more striking orchestral color, or more extreme dynamics—will cause six measures in the repetition, or five or four, to equal, psychologically, eight measures in the original version. What counts is not the number of measures, but the importance of the events taking place in them. In accord with this dynamic conception of form, composers today are extremely reluctant to repeat themselves. They abridge the repetition, vary it, or entirely recast it. Their attitude in this regard is summed up by Schoenberg's admonition to students who brought him a piece with a section repeated: "Never do what a copyist can do!"

Our time avoids grandiloquence and verbosity, and rejects the overextended forms of the post-Wagner period. The twentieth-century climate is hospitable to epigrammatic statement, to forms that are forthright and laconic. The emphasis is on nicety of detail, precision of thought, and simplicity of means. Nevertheless, the twentieth-century concept of form derives from the great traditions of the past. Composers have taken from the old forms whatever could be of use to them, and have added new elements, thereby adapting the achievements of the past to the needs of the present. In our time, as formerly, they affirm the primacy of form in the musical tradition of the West: form as the supreme gesture of creative will and imagination; as the subjugation of all that is capricious and arbitrary to the discipline, the logic, the higher unity of art.

PART TWO

Before World War I (1900–1914)

"The secret of the tone must be always pursued anew."

ARNOLD SCHOENBERG

I. *After Romanticism*

"We are all of us children of our time—and can never leap over its shadows."

RICHARD STRAUSS

10 The Postromantic Generation

"Only when I experience intensely do I compose. Only when I compose do I experience intensely."

GUSTAV MAHLER

It was the composers born in the 1860s and '70s who bridged the transition from the Romantic era to the twentieth century. These men came to artistic maturity at the turn of the century—that is to say, in the twilight of Romanticism. Their music constituted both a continuation of the Romantic heritage and a revolt against it. This dualism added an inner strain to their art that on the one hand militated against its achieving perfection and on the other added to its nostalgic charm. Essentially, these men were latecomers, writing under the shadow of a greatness that could no longer be revived. But their music is not merely retrospective: it sets forth new elements in which one can clearly trace the shape of things to come.

A characteristic figure of this generation was Gabriel Fauré (Pamiers, Ariège, 1845–1924, Paris). Fauré is one of those composers who attain an eminence in their native land that they do not duplicate elsewhere. In Fauré's case, this is partly due to the fact that he

55

was basically a lyricist who expressed himself best in the intimate forms of music—songs, piano pieces, chamber music—whereas in our time the big public is reached primarily through symphonies and operas. Moreover, his reticent charm and his unpretentious and fastidious lyricism are traits least likely to impress the multitude.

Fauré's style exemplifies what he called "the eminently French qualities of taste, clarity, and sense of proportion." At a time when his countrymen were seduced by the grandiloquence of Wagner he hoped for a restoration of "our common sense, that is to say, the taste for clear thought, purity of form, and sobriety." Fauré is best known for his *Requiem* (1887). This music has an inner quietude of spirit that displays his characteristic trait of "intimate limpidity." His songs, of which he wrote almost a hundred, rank with the finest that France has produced. The nocturnes, barcarolles, and similar pieces for piano are imbued with personal lyricism. Fauré's chamber works achieve a graceful union of classical form and romantic content. Noteworthy in this category are two quartets for piano and strings (1879, 1886); two piano quintets (1906, 1921); and the string quartet he completed shortly before his death at the age of eighty. As head of the Paris Conservatoire for fifteen years, Fauré was in a position to impress his ideals upon French musical life. Among his pupils were Maurice Ravel and Nadia Boulanger.

In point of time Emmanuel Chabrier (Ambert, Puy de Dôme, 1841–1894, Paris) was contemporary with Tchaikovsky. If he deserves mention in a book on twentieth-century music it is because, while many composers were still exploring the depths of late Romantic subjectivity, this exuberant Frenchman emphasized humor and gaiety in his works, thus pointing to a trend that became increasingly important in the new music and strongly influenced several key figures of the modern French school. Chabrier is best known to the public for his tuneful orchestral rhapsody *España*. He also produced several operas, *Trois Valses romantiques* (1883) for two pianos, choral and piano music, and songs.

A typical figure of this generation was Sir Edward Elgar (Broadheath, near Worcester, 1857–1934, Worcester), the first important British composer in two hundred years—that is, since the death of Purcell. Elgar loved England, her past, her people, her countryside, and he responded to her need for a national artist much as Rudyard Kipling did. Perhaps he responded too eagerly. He became the musician laureate of the late Victorian and Edwardian eras; the mixture of idealism and imperialism prevalent during those years found perfect expression in his music. He was knighted by Edward VII, for whose accession he wrote the *Coronation Ode*. For years the first of his *Pomp and Circumstance* marches was the required accompaniment for newsreel glimpses of Britain's royal family. Elgar was a natural musician of great invention and spontaneity. "It is my idea," he said, "that music is in the air all around us, the world is full of it, and at any given time you simply take as much of it as you require." What he took was not always distinguished. But he shaped it lovingly into something that had enormous gusto and that shone with all the hues of the Postromantic orchestra.

Elgar's music is full of sound and movement. It stems from an eclectic, late nineteenth-century style compounded of Brahms, Strauss, and even a little Verdi; but it bears the imprint of a thoroughly British personality. Having grown up in Worcester, Elgar knew at first hand the cathedral towns whose choir festivals are the backbone of musical life in provincial England. His oratorios met both the religious and musical needs of the time. Elgar's masterpiece in this category is *The Dream of Gerontius* (1900), a setting of the poem by Cardinal Newman. Elgar produced a varied repertoire of religious and secular cantatas, part-songs, and chamber music; two symphonies (1908, 1909); overtures and symphonic poems, among them *Froissart* (1890), *Cockaigne Overture* (In London Town, 1901), and *Falstaff* (1909); and a number of occasional pieces. Of his major works, the *Enigma Variations* (1899) and *Introduction and Allegro* for strings (1905) are the most frequently performed outside his homeland. "He might have been a great composer," his compatriot Cecil Gray said of him, "if he had not been such a perfect gentleman." Nonetheless Elgar served his country well. She will long remember him.

Although Romanticism was not confined to any one country, its stronghold was in those lands that lay under the influence of the Austro-German musical tradition. We may therefore begin our detailed consideration of the late Romantic composers with the two most illustrious representatives of that tradition—Gustav Mahler and Richard Strauss.

11 Gustav Mahler (1860–1911)

"To write a symphony is, for me, to construct a world."

In the last few decades Gustav Mahler has emerged as one of the most widely played composers of our century. A romantic at heart, he created a music that speaks in powerful accents to the sensibility of our time.

His Life

Mahler was born and raised in Bohemia. His father, owner of a small distillery, was not slow in recognizing the boy's talent. Piano lessons began when Gustav was six. He was sent to Vienna and entered the Conservatory at fifteen, the University three years later. Here he came under the influence of Anton Bruckner. Relations between master and disciple were so cordial that when he was eighteen the youth was entrusted with the task of preparing the piano arrangement of Bruckner's *Third Symphony*.

Together with other impecunious young musicians, he

Head of Mahler, *1909, by Auguste Rodin (1840–1917). Fogg Art Museum, Harvard University, Cambridge, Massachusetts. Grenville L. Winthrop Bequest.*

frequented the cafés where were discussed the advanced social and artistic theories of the day. He worshipped Wagner. He was persuaded for a time that mankind would be regenerated by means of a vegetarian diet. He gave piano lessons. He composed. His professional career began modestly enough when, at the age of twenty, he was engaged to conduct operettas at a third-rate summer theater. A dynamic conductor who found his natural habitat in the opera house, Mahler soon achieved a reputation that brought him ever more important posts, until at twenty-eight he became director of the Royal Opera at Budapest. From Budapest Mahler went to Hamburg. Then, at thirty-seven, he was offered the most important musical position in the Austrian Empire—the directorship, with absolute powers, of the Vienna Opera. His ten years there (1897–1907) made history. He brought to his duties a fiery temperament, unwavering devotion to ideals, and the inflexible will of the zealot. When he took over, Massenet was the chief drawing card. By the time his rule ended he had taught a frivolous public to revere Mozart, Beethoven, and Gluck, and made them listen to uncut versions of Wagner's operas.

When it was objected that his innovations flouted tradition, he retorted, "Tradition is laziness! In every performance the work must be born anew." Despite the prodigious outlay of energy entailed by his duties, during his Vienna period he produced five big symphonies—the *Fourth* to the *Eighth*. These were written down in rough draft during the summer months when the Opera was closed—he called himself *der Sommerkomponist*, the summer composer—and orchestrated during the winter, in the morning hours, before he embarked on his duties as director. The conflict between his two careers, each pulling him in a different direction, could not but heighten the tensions within that turbulent temperament.

Shortly before he was appointed to Vienna, Mahler became a convert to Catholicism. This step was motivated in the first instance by the desire to smooth his way in a city where anti-Semitism was rampant. Beyond that, Mahler belonged to a generation of Jewish intellectuals who had lost identification with their religious heritage and who sought roots in the Austro-German culture of which they felt themselves to be a part. His was the inquiring intellect of the perpetual doubter; yet he yearned for the ecstasy of faith and the wholeness of soul that came with certainty. Alma Mahler tells in her *Reminiscences* how, during their courtship, when he played her his *Fifth Symphony,* she admired everything in the work save the triumphal chorale at the end, which she found unconvincing. " 'What about Bruckner!' he protested. 'He yes, but not you,' I said, and tried to make clear to him the radical difference between his nature and Bruckner's. I was touching here on a rift in his being which often brought him into serious conflict with himself." The man's need for roots involved also the artist's vision: hence his inordinate desire to ally his music with the Viennese tradition. "I am thrice homeless," he remarked. "As a Bohemian born in Austria. As an Austrian among Germans. And as a Jew throughout the world."

"Humanly I make every concession, artistically—none!" Such intransigence was bound to create powerful enemies. Mahler's final years in Vienna were embittered by the intrigues against him, which flourished despite the fact that he had transformed the Imperial Opera into the premier lyric theater of Europe. The death of a little daughter left him grief-stricken. A second disaster followed soon after: he was found to have a heart ailment. When he finally was forced to resign his post, the blow was not unexpected. Mahler, now forty-eight (he had only three more years to live), accepted an engagement at the Metropolitan Opera House. He hoped to earn enough to be able to retire at fifty, so that he finally might compose with the peace of mind that had never been granted him. His three years in New York were not free of the storms that his tempestuous personality inevitably provoked. In 1909 he assumed direction of the New York Philharmonic Orchestra. When the ladies of the Board made it plain to Alma that her husband had flouted their wishes, she expostulated, "But in Vienna the Emperor himself did not dare to interfere!"

His summers he spent in the countryside near Vienna. Here he composed his masterpiece, *Das Lied von der Erde* (The Song of the Earth). Although he thought of this as his ninth symphony, he was superstitious enough not to call it by that title, as neither Beethoven nor Schubert, Bruckner nor Dvořák had gone beyond their ninth. His next symphony was therefore named the *Ninth*. Fate, however, was not to be cheated: he did not live to finish his *Tenth*. In the middle of a taxing concert season with the Philharmonic he fell ill with a streptococcus infection. It was decided to bring him to Paris, where a new serum treatment had been developed. Arrived in Paris, he took a turn for the worse. Thus he set forth on his last journey, back to the scene of his greatest triumphs—the enchanting, exasperating Vienna he both loved and detested. On his deathbed he conducted with one finger on the quilt, uttering a single word: "Mozart. . . ."

He was buried, as he had requested, beside his daughter at Grinzing. At last that unquiet heart was at rest.

His Music

"The act of creation in me is so closely bound up with all my experience that when my mind and spirit are at rest I can compose nothing." In this identification of art with personal emotion Mahler was entirely the romantic. Music for him was vision, intoxication, fulfillment: "a mysterious language from beyond." The sounds were symbols of states of mind and soul. "What is best in music," he observed, "is not to be found in the notes." In his notes resound the great themes of an age that was drawing to its close: nature, poetry, and folklore, love of man and faith in God, the sorrow of human destiny and the loneliness of death. Mahler engaged in a gigantic effort to breathe vitality into the Romantic world of thought and feeling that was in process of disintegration. This circumstance imparts to his music its fevered unrest, its nostalgia.

Mahler was the last in the illustrious line of Viennese symphonists that extended from Haydn, Mozart, Beethoven, and Schubert to Bruckner and Brahms. His tone imagery was permeated by the intimately jovial spirit of Austrian popular song and dance, and by the melodious folk tunes of his native Bohemia. He sought to assimilate these humble materials to the grand form of the past and to create a popular (in the best sense of the term) symphonic art for the modern age. In his desire to emulate the Classical masters he sometimes ended by sounding like them. Yet even those who accuse him of being derivative will admit that he set the seal of his own personality upon everything he touched. He has his own sound. It is not to be mistaken for any other's.

Mahler was primarily a lyricist. The spirit of song permeates his art. He followed Schubert and Schumann in cultivating the song cycle, although in keeping with the spirit of his time, Mahler's song cycles are accompanied by orchestra rather than piano. *Lieder eines fahrenden Gesellen* (Songs of a Wayfarer), composed in 1884, is a set of four songs suffused with Schubertian longing. Mahler wrote the texts himself, aroused by an image that appealed strongly to his imagination: the rejected lover wandering alone over the face of the earth. His next cycle was inspired by a famous collection of German folk poetry, *Des Knaben Wunderhorn* (The Youth's Magic Horn, 1892–1896), which had been gathered in the early nineteenth century by the poets Achim von Arnim and Clemens Brentano. The moving *Kindertotenlieder* (Songs on the Death of Children, 1904) is a cycle for voice and orchestra to the grief-laden poems of Friedrich Rückert. Several other Rückert poems were set by Mahler in 1901. The peak of his achievement in this direction is, of course, the cycle of six songs with orchestra that make up *Das Lied von der Erde*.

Song lyricism is the essential ingredient of Mahler's symphonies. These works are monumental frescoes. The melody is long of line, with extravagant leaps which heighten its power to communicate. The harmony is rich and surcharged with emotion. A favorite symbol is the funeral march, now as a solemn cortege, now as a lyrical meditation on life and death. The scherzos speak the Austrian popular dialect, running the gamut from earthy humor and peasant dance to the bizarre and the fantastic. Trumpet and horn calls, an inevitable feature of the language of German Romanticism, supply a sense of mystery and evoke the sound of nature; or, allied with rattling

A scene from the current American Ballet Theater production of Dark Elegies, *choreographed in 1937 by Anthony Tudor to Mahler's* Kindertotenlieder. *The soloist is Terry Orr. Photograph by Martha Swope.*

drums, conjure up the robust din of the town pipers and regimental bands that remain an indelible memory for anyone growing up in Germanic lands. Another important symbol is the chorale, used to create an atmosphere of religious faith. Hardly less important are the motives derived from birdcalls, evoking the out-of-doors. Mahler increased the number of movements in the symphony to five or six, and tried to tighten the structure by bringing back in later movements the thematic material of earlier ones (cyclical structure). His feeling for drama caused him to make the last movement, rather than the first, the most important in the cycle, thereby avoiding any impression of anticlimax.

In his sense of color Mahler ranks with the great masters of the art of orchestration. He contrasts solo instruments in the manner of chamber music, achieving his color effects through clarity of line rather then massed sonorities. His fondness for pure (that is, unmixed) colors gave impetus to an important trend in twentieth-century music. He secures unusual effects by spacing the instrumental lines far apart and writing for the instruments in their extreme range: trumpets and bassoons in high register, flutes in low. His transparent "open-air" sound was not without influence. Composers as diverse as Schoenberg and Prokofiev, Honegger and Alban Berg, Shostakovitch and Britten listened to him with profit.

It was in the matter of texture that Mahler made his most important contribution to contemporary technique. Basing his orchestral style on counterpoint, he caused two or more melodies to unfold simultaneously, each setting off the other. Through this songful polyphony he approached what was to become one of the most important types of new music—the chamber symphony. He was an innovator with respect to key; he would begin a movement—or a symphony!—in one key and end it in another. Characteristic is his dramatic juxtaposition of unrelated keys, as well as a Schubertian wavering between major and minor. Hand-in-hand with his loosening of the key structure went his expansion of symphonic form. He unfolds a large number of thematic groups, which are then subjected to a process of continuous variation, repetition, and development. He did overextend the symphonic form. The first movement of the *Third Symphony* and the finale of the *Sixth* are among the longest movements ever conceived by any composer.

The *First Symphony* (1888, revised in 1893) is related both psychologically and thematically to *Lieder eines fahrenden Gesellen*. Similarly, the next three symphonies utilize material from the *Wunderhorn* songs and call for voices in addition to the instruments. The *Second* (1894) is known as the *Resurrection Symphony*. In it Mahler discourses on a theme that obsessed him—death and the life beyond. The finale is for huge orchestra and double chorus. Amidst the pealing of bells and the fanfares of the brass, the chorus intones Klopstock's *Ode to Immortality*, to which Mahler added his own lines: "Believe, my heart . . . I shall soar upward, I shall die that I may live!" The *Third* (1895) is a hymn to nature and contains two movements for voice—a setting for contralto of lines from Nietzsche's *Thus Spake Zarathustra*, and a song for contralto and women's chorus based on a delightful poem from *Des Knaben Wunderhorn*, *Es sungen drei Engel einem süssen Gesang* (Three Angels Sang a Sweet Song). The *Fourth* (1900), one of the most popular of the Mahler symphonies, ends with another *Wunderhorn* poem, a child's view of heaven that inspired an enchanting song for soprano and orchestra.

The *Fifth* (1902), *Sixth* (1904), and *Seventh* (1905) are purely instrumental works in which he forges his way to a concept of symphonic structure based on contrapuntal procedures. The middle period culminates in the *Eighth* or *Symphony of a Thousand* (1906), so called because of the vast array of performers required: an expanded orchestra with extra brass choir, eight solo voices, double chorus, boys' chorus, and organ. This work crowns the nineteenth century's predilection for the grandiose. The compositions of the final period breathe an inner serenity, a resignation that was new to Mahler. These include *Das Lied von der Erde* and the *Ninth Symphony* (1909). The unfinished *Tenth Symphony* has recently been edited and made available for performance.

Although he never wrote critical articles or formulated his aesthetic creed, Mahler's letters are filled with observations that combine verbal felicity with keen insight. "In art as in life I am at the mercy of spontaneity. . . . Ugliness is an insult to God. . . . My music is, throughout and always, but a sound of nature. . . . Spitting on the floor won't make you Beethoven." After the completion of the *Eighth Symphony* he exulted, "I am the universe when it resounds." Asked to state the essence of his religious belief, he replied: "I am a musician. That tells everything!" In a letter to Bruno Walter: "Strange, when I hear music—even while I conduct—I can hear quite definite answers to all my questions and feel entirely clear and sure." And when his work met with incomprehension: "My time will come!" It did.

Das Lied von der Erde (The Song of the Earth)

Mahler's most sustained song cycle followed the dark period when he was informed by his physician that he had a heart ailment. From initial despair he passed over to a heightened awareness of life. "I see everything in a new light. I thirst for life more than ever before and find the 'habit of existence' more sweet than it ever was." This mood spurred him to a work in which a fierce joy in the beauty of earthly things commingles with resignation.

He found his vehicle in Hans Bethge's translation—more accurately, reconstruction—of old Chinese poems. In their emphasis upon the transience of youth and happiness, these verses are similar in mood to those of FitzGerald's adaptation of the *Rubáiyát* of Omar Khayyám. The lyricist in Mahler responded to these fervid images of joy and despair, while the symphonist expanded the material in the orchestra. The piece was written in the South Tyrol in 1908. Mahler never heard it performed. *Das Lied von der Erde* had its premiere in Munich six months after his death, under the baton of his disciple Bruno Walter.

I. *Das Trinklied vom Jammer der Erde* (The Drinking Song of Earth's

Sorrow). For tenor and orchestra. (The complete text of *Das Lied von der Erde* and an English translation will be found in Appendix II.)

> Now gleams the wine in the golden cup.
> But drink not yet—first will I sing you a song!
> Let the song of sorrow
> Resound with laughter in your soul. . . .

The impassioned opening establishes Mahler's favorite key of A minor. The movement is marked *Allegro pesante.* (For an explanation of tempo terms, see Appendix I-e.) A leaping motive in the horns outlines the interval of a fourth, which is basic to the work.

Almost immediately the violins set forth the germinal theme that serves as the unifying element of the several movements:

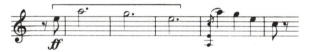

The principal motive (under the bracket), also outlining a fourth, reappears in a number of metamorphoses: in longer note values (augmentation) or shorter (diminution); upside down (inversion) or backward (retrograde). The motive suggests the pentatonic (five-note) scale commonly associated with Chinese music, subtly underlining the exotic flavor of the piece.

The soloistic treatment of winds and strings sets off the lines with exemplary clarity. The music abounds in effects that Mahler loved: arpeggios on the harp; "fluttertonguing" on the flute, suggesting a sinister rattle; muted trumpets. "Dark is life, dark is death. . . ." The poignant refrain, with its fatalistic downward curve, returns thrice, each time a semitone higher, in a kind of intensification. Before the third stanza, which is set to contrasting music, there is a quieter orchestral interlude. The movement reaches its climax with a macabre image dear to the Romantic imagination. "In the moonlight, in the churchyard, there gibbers a wild ghostly shape. . . ." The solo voice descends in an eerie slide over an octave, Mahler demanding from the singer a new kind of agility. In this passage we are well into the twentieth century, especially the Viennese section thereof.

"The time has come, comrades: drain your golden cups. . . ."

The music fluctuates between major and minor, and closes with a last tumultuous outcropping of the germinal motive.

II. *Der Einsame im Herbst* (Autumn Loneliness). For contralto (or baritone) and orchestra.

> Autumn mists drift palely over the sea.
> Touched with frost, the grass stands rigid.
> It is as though an artist's hand had strewn
> Dust of jade on every leaf and blade. . . .

The movement is marked *Etwas schleichend–ermüdet* (somewhat lingering, listless). Oboe, clarinet, and violins trace delicate filaments that intertwine in an attenuated fabric. The opening melody on the oboe features the basic interval of a fourth. Notice the transformations of the germ motive at *a* and *b:*

The listless mood is projected through simple stepwise movement and uneventful rhythms in the voice part. The alternation of major and minor harmonies is typical of Mahler. The turn to subjective feeling in the text is marked by exuberant leaps in the orchestral melody. The movement builds steadily to its emotional peak. There is a gentle subsiding, and a return to the dark D-minor tonality. This music is pale, disembodied, strangely poignant.

III. *Von der Jugend* (Of Youth). For tenor and orchestra. A dainty bit of *chinoiserie* that evokes a teahouse on the river where friends sit, drinking, conversing, or writing verses while their reflections ripple in the water below. The pentatonic patterns exhale a delicate exoticism. The form is a clear-cut A-B-A pattern.

IV. *Von der Schönheit* (Of Beauty). For contralto (or baritone) and orchestra. This movement is more amorous in character. Young maidens pick flowers by the river bank, their graceful movements bathed in sunlight. Suddenly there arrives a company of young gallants, to the sturdy strains of an Austrian regimental band. These gay blades hail from the Tyrol rather than Cathay; but love is stronger than geography, and the final measures, with their tenderly retrospective tones, are inescapably romantic.

V. *Der Trunkene im Frühling* (The Drunkard in Spring). For tenor and orchestra. The poet is awakened from his wine-drugged sleep by a bird in the tree. "I ask him if spring has come, for all is like a dream. He twitters, 'Yes—Spring is here!' " And the poet, contented, refills his cup. . . . The movement is an *Allegro* marked "Boldly, but not too fast." The colloquy between poet and bird is given with all the naïveté of which Mahler was sometimes capable: the enigmatic naïveté of the sophisticate. Notice the vaulting melodic line and the wide leaps, against shifting harmonies that play havoc with a tenor's intonation.

VI. *Der Abschied* (The Farewell). For contralto (or baritone) and orchestra. This movement, which takes about twenty-four minutes, is equivalent in length to a complete Classical symphony. The opening chords establish an atmosphere of brooding. Dark colors are to the fore: oboe, contrabassoon, horn, gong, viola, and double bass, along with two harps.

> The sun sets behind the mountains.
> In every valley the shadows of evening descend. . . .
> I tarry here and await my friend—
> I wait to bid him a last farewell.

The voice enters with a subdued recitative, over a sustained low note in the cello. Eventually, a lyric line of remarkable length unravels against a background of flickering sound set up by clarinets and harps—an effect characteristic of Mahler. "How I long for your presence, O my friend, to share with you the beauty of this evening. . . ." There is an ecstatic apostrophe to beauty: "O world intoxicated with eternal love and life!" A gong tolls, bringing us back to the tragic note—and the C-minor tonality—of the opening measures. A symphonic interlude, based on the themes with which the movement opened, unfolds in the manner of a bizarre march, charged with all the strangeness and wonder that Mahler inherited from the "satanism" of Berlioz and Liszt. The marchlike lamentation—fitting cortege for the dreams of a century—is woven out of a pregnant motive which is an inversion of the first three notes of the germinal theme.

The voice reenters, recapitulating material from the beginning. The major mode breaks through momentarily as Mahler returns to the favorite image of his youth, the lonely wayfarer. "Where do I go? I go wandering in the mountains, seeking rest for my lonely heart!" Eventually, the movement is suspended, poised on the single note E in the strings, which grows and spills into a consolatory C major. And now the shape of things is revealed. For C major is the relative key of A minor, in which the piece began. The vast design, for all its chromatic fluctuation, is seen to rest on a firm foundation of tonality. Celesta, mandolin, and harp impart a radiant lightness to the orchestral tissue as the voice repeats the last word, *ewig* (ever . . . ever . . .) until it is barely audible. The three tones of the germinal motive are reconciled in the final chord.

Mahler knew that in this *Adagio* he had reached the summit of his art. "What do you think?" he wrote Bruno Walter. "Is this to be endured at all? Will not people do away with themselves after hearing it?" The movement is regarded as Mahler's farewell to life. It is, even more, a tender leavetaking of that whole complex of thought and feeling which made up the sulphurous world of Romanticism—that dying world which found in him so visionary a spokesman.

12 Richard Strauss (1864-1949)

"The important thing is not the beginning of the melody but its continuation, its development into a complete melodic form."

His Life

The most publicized composer of the early twentieth century was born in Munich. His father was a virtuoso horn player who belonged to the court orchestra. His mother was the daughter of Georg Pschorr, a successful brewer of Munich beer. In this solid middle-class environment, made familiar to American readers by the novels of Thomas Mann, a high value was placed on music and money. These remained Strauss's twin passions throughout his life.

The boy played the piano when he was four and composed his first pieces at the age of six. His father, a confirmed anti-Wagnerite, saw to it that he was brought up "in a strictly classical way." As a result, his early instrumental works show an allegiance to chamber

A portrait of Richard Strauss in 1918 by Max Lieberman (1847–1935). National Gallery, Berlin.

music, concerto, and symphony. In conservative musical circles the gifted youth was hailed as the future successor to Brahms. But at the age of twenty-one, Strauss, groping for a type of expression that would suit his temperament, found his way into the camp of program music. It became his aim "to develop the poetic, the expressive in music as exemplified in the works of Liszt, Wagner, and Berlioz."

The new orientation is apparent in the symphonic fantasy *Aus Italien* (From Italy, 1886). Strauss now found his metier—the writing of vividly descriptive tone poems. *Macbeth*, the first of the series (1887), was followed by *Don Juan* (1888), an extraordinary achievement for a young man of twenty-four. There followed the works that carried his name throughout the civilized world: *Tod und Verklärung* (Death and Transfiguration, 1889); *Till Eulenspiegels lustige Streiche* (Till Eulenspiegel's Merry Pranks, 1895); *Also sprach Zarathustra* (Thus Spake Zarathustra, 1895); *Don Quixote* (1897); and *Ein Heldenleben* (A Hero's Life, an autobiographical symphonic poem, 1898). These works shocked the conservatives and secured Strauss's position as the *enfant terrible* of modern music—a role he thoroughly enjoyed.

In 1894 he married the singer Pauline de Ahna, daughter of a Bavarian general. A colorful personality, she devoted herself to presenting her husband's songs, often with him as accompanist. By this time he had made a great reputation as a conductor. He appeared all over Europe and in 1896 was summoned to the Berlin Opera. In 1904 Strauss and his wife visited the United States, where he conducted the world premiere of his *Sinfonia domestica;* she performed his songs. Strauss, for the then fabulous fee of a thousand dollars per appearance, conducted two afternoon concerts in the auditorium of John Wanamaker's department store. The incident was seized upon by his detractors to point up his commercialism. His defense made very good sense: "True art ennobles any hall. And earning money in a decent way for wife and child is no disgrace—even for an artist!"

Strauss conquered the operatic stage with *Salome, Elektra,* an *Der Rosenkavalier* (The Knight of the Rose). The international triumph of the last opera, on the eve of the First World War, marked the summit of his career. Strauss was able to extract unprecedented fees for his scores; the publishing rights to *Elektra* brought him twenty-seven thousand dollars. To obtain the New York premiere of this work ahead of the Metropolitan Opera House, Oscar Hammerstein paid him ten thousand dollars and deposited an additional eighteen thousand in advance royalties. Such sums seventy years ago—and in the field of serious music—were something to talk about.

It was Strauss's ambition to become a millionaire, so that he would be free to devote himself to his art. He had achieved his goal by the time he was fifty. His collaboration with Hugo von Hofmannsthal, the librettist of *Elektra* and *Rosenkavalier,* continued until the latter's death in 1929. But the world out of which their art issued had come to an end in 1914. New winds were blowing. The one-time "bad boy of music" was now firmly entrenched as a conservative. Strauss's later operas contain much beautiful music. But they all speak, with various shades of refinement, the musical language of *Rosenkavalier.* To that degree they offer no fresh solution to problems, no real inner growth.

The coming to power of the Nazis in 1933 confronted Strauss with a crucial decision. He was a staunch social-democrat under the Weimar Republic, as he had been a staunch royalist under the Kaiser. The cosmopolitan circles in which he traveled were not susceptible to Hitler's ideology. Hence the challenge to speak out against the Third

Reich, or to leave Germany as Thomas Mann, Hindemith, and scores of artists and intellectuals were doing. On the other hand, the new Germany was courting famous men of art and letters. Strauss saw the road open to supreme power over German music. In 1933, when he was on the threshold of seventy, the former revolutionary artist was elevated to the official hierarchy as president of the *Reichsmusikkammer* (Reich Chamber of Music).

His conscience was uneasy, as was his reign. His opera *Die schweigsame Frau* was withdrawn by the Nazis because the author of the book, Stefan Zweig, like Strauss's earlier librettist, Hofmannsthal, was Jewish. Strauss resigned his post. The war's end found the eighty-one-year-old composer in a somewhat ambiguous position. He was eventually permitted to return to his sumptuous villa at Garmisch, in the Bavarian Alps. To his friends Strauss explained that he had remained in Nazi Germany because someone had to protect culture from Hitler's barbarians. Perhaps he even believed it.

There were speeches at the Bavarian Academy of Fine Arts on the occasion of his eighty-fifth birthday. He died shortly thereafter.

His Music

Strauss inherited the orchestra of Berlioz, Liszt, and Wagner at the moment when it was ready to be transformed into a mammoth virtuoso ensemble. He stood in the forefront of this development. His was a dazzling orchestral style in which all the instruments participated equally. Even those which up to that time had served mainly to support the rest—double bass, trombone, tuba, kettledrums—were thrust into soloistic prominence. For special effects he introduced a quartet of saxophones; machines to simulate wind, thunder, storm; in the *Alpine Symphony*, sixteen horns and cowbells. For the early twentieth century the Straussian orchestra came to represent the last word in musical invention and mastery. To the sober palette of the Germans he added Italian sensuousness and French verve. Strauss, significantly, was one of the first to abandon the traditional concept of writing within the character of the instruments. On the contrary, he forced the instruments beyond their limitations, composing "for the trombone as if it were a piccolo." He loved an intricate orchestral fabric. Page after page is strewn with notes, so that the ear is simply unable to unravel all that is going on. When chided for his complexity he would exclaim, "Hang it all! I cannot express it more simply."

His melodies are tense, nervous, rhythmically alive. When he is at his best, those leaping themes of his have immense vitality and sweep. He spoke the sumptuous language of post-Wagnerian harmony; but he was not averse to daring effects that pointed to the future. The secret of Strauss's art is its furious rhythm. A master of shock and surprise—in other words, of timing—he whipped the sound mass into unheard-of speed and mobility. Characteristic of his works is the tumultuous opening gesture which reveals not only his superabundance of energy but also his constant need to dazzle and overwhelm.

Strauss's operas continue to hold the stage. *Salome* we will discuss. *Elektra* (1908), on Hofmannsthal's version of the Greek tragedy, is a one-acter that moves relentlessly to its climax. In these two lyric tragedies Strauss explored the dark caverns of the soul, dealing respectively with lust and revenge at their psychopathic level. Therewith he gave impetus to the taste for the horrible that was to grow stronger in German lands after the First World War. *Der Rosenkavalier* (1910), on the other hand, harks back nostalgically to the Vienna of Maria Theresa (as the later *Arabella* evokes the Vienna of Emperor Franz Joseph). The score is perfumed eroticism. Its deliberate archaisms offer homage to Mozart and Johann Strauss. The aging Marschallin, the disreputable Baron Ochs, young Octavian and Sophie awakening to the wonder of love—they belong to that memorable company of operatic characters who come truly alive in music.

In *Ariadne auf Naxos* (Ariadne on Naxos, 1911, revised in 1917), Strauss abandoned grand opera for the chamber variety, therewith foreshadowing an important trend. His later stage works include *Die Frau ohne Schatten* (The Woman without a Shadow, 1918); *Intermezzo* (1923); *Die ägyptische Helena* (Helen in Egypt, 1927); *Arabella* (1932); *Die schweigsame Frau* (The Silent Woman, 1935); *Friedenstag* (Day of Peace, 1936, forbidden by the Nazis after the outbreak of war); *Daphne* (1937); *Die Liebe der Danae* (The Loves of Danae, 1940); and *Capriccio* (1941). Several have begun to establish themselves in the international repertory and have been acclaimed by American audiences.

As a writer of songs Strauss stands in the great lineage of the German Romantic lied. The finest among them, such as *Ständchen* (Serenade), *Morgen* (Morning), *Ich schwebe* (I Soar), and *Traum durch die Dämmerung* (Dream through the Twilight), represent a permanent contribution to the literature of this lyric genre. With the *Vier letzte Lieder* (Four Last Songs), written in 1948 when he was eighty-four, the master—in a mood of serene acceptance—bade a tender farewell to his art.

Salome: Final Scene

Salome (1905), a drama in one act after Oscar Wilde's play (1893), displays to the full Strauss's powers as an operatic composer: his capacity for generating excitement, his vivid delineation of character, his sensuous vocal line, his powerful evocation of mood and atmosphere. Oscar Wilde's play makes a stunning libretto. The characters are sharply drawn, the issues clear, the climax overwhelming. The beautiful and perverse Princess of Judaea, inflamed to madness by her passion for the Prophet; her stepfather Herod, cruel and crafty, pursued by fears and hallucinations; her mother Herodias, lascivious and vengeful; the handsome young captain Narraboth, who is hopelessly enamored of her; and Jokanaan the Prophet, unshakable in his faith—all are enveloped in a musical ambience whose spell is not easily forgotten.

The drama unfolds on a terrace in the palace of Herod, Tetrarch of Judaea, who has imprisoned Jokanaan in a cistern deep in the earth because the Prophet spoke out against the abominations of Herodias and the court. Herod has given strict orders that no one is to raise the cover of the well, but Salome appeals to Narraboth to let her speak with the Prophet. The captain is helpless against her blandishments. In profound anguish he commands that Jokanaan be brought from the cistern.

The confrontation is brief and intense. "I am amorous of thy body, Jokanaan!" sings Salome, transported with desire. "Thy body is white, like the lilies of the field that the mower hath never mowed. I will kiss thy mouth, Jokanaan." The Prophet shudders. "Never! daughter of Babylon! Daughter of Sodom—never!" The lovelorn Narraboth can endure his agony no longer. He plunges his sword into his heart and falls between Salome and the Prophet. Jokanaan bids Salome seek Him who is on a boat in the sea of Galilee, to bow at His feet and beg forgiveness for her sins. But Salome is enamored of the Prophet's lips. He curses her and returns to the cistern.

Herod and his evil queen come from the banquet hall, accompanied by the court. The grotesque ruler is obsessed by his fancies. "The moon has a strange look tonight. She is like a mad woman." He orders that the torches be lit, steps in Narraboth's blood, and takes it for an evil omen. Terrified, he commands the soldiers to remove the body.

In the ensuing scene Herod, inflamed with wine, gazes lustfully

A scene from the Strauss opera, showing Salome (Grace Bumbry) with the head of Jokanaan while Herod (Robert Nagy) looks on. From the Metropolitan Opera production. Copyright © Beth Bergman.

at his stepdaughter and asks her to dance for him. Salome, who has been brooding over Jokanaan's rejection of her, at first refuses. When Herod promises to reward her with anything that she will request of him, the thought comes to her for which she has been remembered through the ages. "Whatsoever thou shalt ask of me, even to the half of my kingdom," Herod asserts. "You swear it, Tetrarch?" He swears by his life, his crown, his gods. "You have sworn an oath, Tetrarch! Ominous trills are heard on the clarinets as Salome attires herself in the seven veils and makes ready for the most famous dance in history.

Herod, enchanted by Salome's performance, asks her to name her reward. Salome, "rising, laughing," demands the head of Jokanaan on a silver charger. Herod is horrified, for he regards Jokanaan as a Man of God. He tries to deflect Salome, offering her instead the choicest treasures of his kingdom; but she will not be cheated of her prey. "Give me the head of Jokanaan!" she demands again and again, reminding Herod of his oath. Herodias supports Salome, touched by what she mistakes for a devoted daughter's wish to avenge her mother. Herod, defeated, yields.

The Princess leans over the cistern. There is a terrible stillness as her bidding is done. Herod hides his face in his cloak. Herodias smiles and fans herself. A roll on the kettledrums, and the executioner's arm rises from the cistern, bearing aloft the silver charger.

Thus begins the final scene of the opera, as Salome addresses Jokan-aan's head in as strange and affecting an apostrophe as was ever heard. "Ah, thou woulds't not suffer me to kiss thy mouth, Jokan-aan! Well, I will kiss it now!" (For the complete German-English text, see Appendix II.) What passion Strauss injects into the key word *küssen:*

Notice that Strauss, like Mahler, treats voice and orchestra as two equal protagonists, the latter not only supporting the vocal line but also commenting and enlarging upon it. We are, in effect, in the same realm of symphonic lyricism as in *The Song of the Earth.*

The scene is wreathed in that sense of strangeness and wonder which haunted the art of the nineteenth century, lifted to another dimension through the violent dissonances of the twentieth. The vocal line unfolds in an enormously broad curve, deriving its power from the words and in turn heightening their expressiveness. The orchestral fabric is woven out of themes that have appeared earlier in the opera, treated in the highly chromatic idiom of the post-Wagner epoch. There stands out the eerie little tune on the clarinet that is as-sociated throughout with Salome's capriciousness:

The mood changes as Salome mocks the head. "Wherefore dost thou not look at me? Art thou afraid of me, Jokanaan, that thou wilt not look at me?" Staccato chords and light dotted rhythms in the orchestra echo Salome's mocking. "Thou dist speak evil words against me. Well, I still live, but thou art dead, and thy head belongs to me!" The moment of empty triumph passes as Salome realizes that she can never have the Prophet's love. This psychological change is underlined by a marvelous change of key to C-sharp major:

The principal theme associated with Salome comes to the fore as she remembers his beauty:

From here the music gathers tension to Salome's despairing outburst: "Thou may'st have seen thy God, Jokanaan, but me thou didst never see. If thou hadst looked at me, thou wouldst have loved me. . . ."

Extremely wide leaps in the melody were to become a characteristic of the Expressionist style that we will discuss in connection with Arnold Schoenberg and his disciples. We encounter a foretaste in Strauss's music. Consider his setting of Wilde's line "And the mystery of love is greater than the mystery of death," with a leap of two octaves down to the final word. This kind of sepulchral chest tone linked with the idea of death (on the word *Todes*) had not been heard in the lyric theater since Carmen, in the great card scene, recognized her doom in the Ace of Spades.

Herod is overwhelmed. He turns to the Queen: "She is a monster, your daughter. I tell you, she is a monster!" Overcome with fear, he decides to leave the terrace and orders his attendants to put out the torches. The moon disappears. Salome's voice comes faintly out of the shadows. "Ah, I have kissed thy mouth, Jokanaan. There was a bitter taste on thy red lips. Was it the taste of blood? But perhaps this is the taste of love. . . ." The moon reappears, bathing the Princess in a luminous glow. There is a tremendous upsurge in the orchestra as she repeats in triumph, "I have kissed thy lips, Jokanaan!" Now

Salome's main theme rings out for the last time, wreathed in all the splendor of the Straussian orchestra and colored with a clashing dissonance (x):

And we realize that this is the climactic point, both musically and dramatically, toward which the action has been building from the opening note of the opera. Only a master of lyric drama could have led with such unerring aim and control to the "moment of truth" that now is revealed to us in all its majesty. Herod can bear no more. "Kill that woman!" he commands. The soldiers rush forward and crush Salome under their shields. The curtain quickly falls.

This is theater in the grand style. Salome, Herod, Herodias, Narraboth—each is driven by a magnificent obsession. And since it is in the nature of man to be driven, they rise from the shadows of their phantasmagoric world into the realm of what is humanly comprehensible and moving.

After having dominated the musical firmament for decades, Strauss's star went into a temporary eclipse from which it seems to have emerged almost as brightly as ever. Let there be no mistaking. He was one of the major figures of our century.

13   Other Composers of the Postromantic Era

Jean Sibelius (1865–1957)

"When we see those granite rocks we know why we are able to treat the orchestra as we do."

Jean Sibelius cut an important figure during the twenties and thirties—especially in England and the United States, where his cult was as widespread as in his native Finland. He appeared on the musical scene as a Nationalist and nature poet in the Postromantic tradition. His command of the large forms of orchestral music enabled him to win an international audience.

Sibelius functioned within the frame of the "poematic" symphonism of the late Romantic era. His seven symphonies are impressive tone canvases filled with the imagery of a far northern landscape and with expansive musings—now somber, now jubilantly affirmative—on man, nature, fate. He cultivated every form of music save opera. His huge output includes symphonic poems; orchestral legends and suites; the widely played *Violin Concerto* (1903); works for string orchestra and chamber music; cantatas and choral works; incidental music for plays; and quantities of songs and piano pieces.

In his later symphonies Sibelius moved away from the grandiose manner of the Postromantic era. He strove for sobriety of utterance, sparseness of texture, and condensation of form. It is instructive, in this connection, to compare a movement from his most popular symphony, the *Second* (1901), with a movement from the *Fourth*, which was completed a decade later (1911). The finale of the *Second* presents broad singing melodies decked out in all the lush raiment of late nineteenth-century orchestration. In contrast, the first movement of the *Fourth* is less than half as long. The material is handled with the utmost economy and with a relentless control that verges on the austere. The soloistic writing examplifies the twentieth-century urge to lighten the orchestral texture, to lend it the transparency of chamber music. In this search for stylistic purity we may recognize the beginnings of that return to Classical values (albeit within a Postromantic frame) that was to be one of the main preoccupations of the new era.

Sibelius's music came out of the last period in European culture that was capable of Romantic idealism. It hears the imprint of a dedicated musician who, in the course of a long and fruitful career, won an honorable place for himself in the annals of his art.

Alexander Scriabin (1872–1915)

"For the first time I found light in music; found this rapture, this soaring flight, this suffocation from Joy!"

In the early years of our century Alexander Scriabin represented the progressive trend in Russia. He played an important part in ushering in the new music. It was in the field of harmony that Scriabin made his chief contribution. He was a leader in the attempt to found a new system of harmony on the higher overtones of the Chord of Nature (see Appendix I-j). Guided by a refined sense of hearing and a bold imagination, he created chords that opened up new perspectives. His music in its unbridled chromaticism reached the outermost limits of the traditional key system, and pointed the way to a freer use of the twelve tones. He dispensed with key signatures and helped abolish the traditional distinction between major and minor. Also, he was one of those who led music away from chords based on the interval of a third to those based on the interval of a fourth; in other words, from triadic to quartal harmony. As a result, his music has a distinctly twentieth-century look. (See the Scriabin chord on page 22.)

Chief among Scriabin's large works are three symphonies (1900, 1901, 1905); the *Piano Concerto* (1899); two tone poems in the Wagner-Liszt tradition—*Poem of Ecstasy* (1908) and *Prometheus—The Poem of Fire* (1910); and ten piano sonatas. These last, when played by a master pianist who is sympathetic to Scriabin's style (such as Vladimir Horowitz or Sviatoslav Richter), make an effect of extraordinary intensity and romantic fervor.

A fine example of Scriabin's late manner is *Vers la flamme* (Toward the Flame), written in 1914, a year before the composer's death. At this time he was deep in mystical speculations, according to which flame was the principle of self-consuming yet self-renewing life. Thus this four-minute miniature became a symbol of the progression from total darkness to dazzling light, from nonbeing to passionate self-affirmation.

This concept shapes the course of the piece: In dynamics, from pianissimo to fortissimo. In register, from the somber bass to the brilliant upper range of the piano. In rhythm, from longer note values to shorter. In texture, from simple four-part harmonies to intricate "skyscraper" chords. The final measures, which explode in dissonant trills and dazzling harmonies, illustrate Scriabin's predilection for chords built in fourths:

Scriabin was one of an important group of composers who helped prepare the public for new conceptions. He takes his place in history as one of the picturesque figures in the transition from Romanticism to the nineteenth century.

Ferruccio Busoni (1866–1924)

"Music was born free, and to win freedom is its destiny."

In Ferruccio Busoni we encounter the cerebral composer—a type that, with the intellectualization of art in the twentieth century, has come to be ever more important. He was born in Empoli, in Tuscany, the son of two professional musicians. He came of German-Italian ancestry. To his Latin heritage, he added the intellectuality of the German. He himself, though he made Berlin his home for the greater part of his career, considered himself an Italian. "What refreshes me," he declared, "is the Latin attitude to art, with its cool serenity and its insistence on outer form."

His spiritual development consequently led him to a classical orientation. In this he anticipated the most important development in musical aesthetics during the first quarter of the twentieth century. He moved away from the full, rich scoring of Wagner to an orchestral idiom based on counterpoint. He wrote for the orchestra as though for an assemblage of solo players, therewith reviving the concertante ideal of the age of Bach. He foreshadowed the twentieth-century fondness for small and unusual combinations of instruments, and he cultivated the eighteenth-century forms: rondo, sarabande, gavotte, minuet, gigue; also the fugue and sonatina. He sought clarity of thought, sobriety of feeling, and lucidity of expression. For the grand rhetoric of the Postromantic era he substituted the spirit of comedy and harlequinade, the Latin ideal of brilliancy and grace.

So too he rebelled against the traditional scales which, he was persuaded, had lost their capacity to stimulate and to surprise. "We are tyrannized by Major and Minor—by that bifurcated garment!" He experimented with new scales, and came up with a hundred and thirteen possible ways of arranging whole and half steps within a seven-note series. (See the Busoni scale on page 29.) Taking a leap into the future, he also advocated the use of microtones, that is, intervals smaller than the standard semitone of Western music.

As a composer, Busoni was most successful with works conceived in the antiromantic spirit of Harlequin, such as *Rondo Arlecchinesco* for orchestra (1915); the operas *Arlecchino*, "a theatrical caprice" (1916), and *Turandot*, "a Chinese tale" after Carlo Gozzi (1917), for both of which he wrote the librettos; and the *Concertino* for clarinet and small orchestra (1919). The last years of his life were devoted to his magnum opus, the opera *Doktor Faust*. Left incomplete at his death, it was finished by his pupil Philipp Jarnach. Busoni's artistic beliefs are brilliantly presented in his *Entwurf einer neuen Ästhetik der Tonkunst* (1907), which has been published in English as *Towards a New Esthetic of Music*. "I feel myself to be a beginning. . . ." Busoni correctly estimated his position. His ideas took root because they met the needs of the age. The younger generation of central European composers learned much from his dexterous counterpoint, his light orchestral texture, the originality of certain of his effects. In effect, Busoni's influence has reached well beyond the actual performance of his music.

II. *Impressionism*

"The century of aeroplanes deserves its own music. As there are no precedents, I must create anew."

CLAUDE DEBUSSY

14   The Impressionist Movement

"In comparison with the pure dream, the unanalyzed impression, a definite or positive art is blasphemous."

CHARLES BAUDELAIRE

The art of the nineteenth century aspired to that "embracing of the millions" which Beethoven hymned in the finale of his *Ninth Symphony*. The novels of Dickens, the painting of Delacroix, the operas of Verdi are popular in the best sense. Such art exerts universal appeal and reinforces our common humanity.

In the twilight of an era, however, art tends to lose this directness of speech. The artist seeks greater refinement of style and reticence of feeling; with these, a select public that will respond to his subtleties. In the second half of the nineteenth century artists increasingly cultivated the unusual and the precious. On the one hand, this gesture constituted a revolt against the taste of the bourgeois. On the other, it embodied the desire to rid art of certain modes of expression that had lost their freshness. Paris was the center of the new style, which found its most compelling expression in the movement known as Impressionism.

83

The Impressionist Painters

It was in 1867 that the academic salons rejected a painting entitled *Impression: Sun Rising,* by Claude Monet (1840–1926), which the artist then exhibited under less conventional auspices. Before long *impressionism* was being applied as a term of derision to the painting of Monet and his comrades, such as Camille Pisarro (1830–1903), Edouard Manet (1832–1883), Edgar Degas (1834–1917), and Auguste Renoir (1841–1919). The Impressionist painters were desirous of discarding everything in the Romantic tradition that had hardened into academic formula. They essayed to capture on canvas not the exact representation of things, but the artist's momentary impression of them, and to convey that with all spontaneity and freshness. To this end they took painting out of the studio into the open air. They

This famous modern pastoral created a furious controversy when first exhibited because of its vivid depiction of clothed men and nude women enjoying a picnic in the forest. In this work, Manet manifested the Impressionist preference for painting out of doors in order to capture fleeting effects of light and shadow. Le Déjeuner sur l'herbe, *1863, by Édouard Manet (1832–1883). The Louvre, Paris.*

looked at nature with an "innocent eye." They saw the world in a continual state of flux, its outlines melting in a luminous haze. Nor did they mix their pigments on the palette, as had been the custom hitherto. Instead they juxtaposed bits of pure color on the canvas, leaving it to the eye of the beholder to do the mixing. The result was a fluidity of line and an iridescence of color such as had never been seen before.

The Impressionists were repelled by the heroic themes of the Romantic painters. The hero of their painting was not man, but light. They had an affinity for subject matter that the Romantic painters would have been apt to dismiss as trivial: dancing girls, picnics, boating and café scenes, nudes, and still life; and, of course, nature— smiling and seductive, or veiled and mysterious. Their art is suffused with the magic of a city: Paris in all her allure supplies the setting for their shimmering oils and water colors. People laughed at first: whoever saw grass that's yellow and pink and blue? But the intrepid pioneers persisted and ultimately imposed their vision upon the world. By the end of the century Impressionism had emerged as the leading school in European painting.

The Symbolist Poets

A similar revolt against traditional modes of expression took place in poetry, led by the Symbolists, who aspired to the direct communication of poetic emotion without the intervention of intellectual elements. They used words for the sake of the music contained in them rather than for the meaning. They tried to impart the essence of poetic experience by presenting the symbol rather than stating the fact. As Verlaine's famous quatrain expressed it,

> For we desire above all—nuance,
> Not color but half-shades!
> Ah! nuance alone unites
> Dream with dream and flute with horn.

The French symbolists were strongly influenced by Edgar Allan Poe (1809–1849), whose poetry was introduced into France by his admirer Charles Baudelaire (1821–1867). The end-of-century saw the movement in full course with the rise of three important Symbolist poets: Stéphane Mallarmé (1842–1898); Paul Verlaine (1844–1896); and Arthur Rimbaud (1854–1891). Under their aegis, language achieved something of the elusiveness and subtlety of nuance that had hitherto belonged to music alone.

The Symbolists, like the Impressionist painters, turned away from the pathos of the Romantic movement. They discarded the story element in poetry; they scorned the moral, whether expressed or implied. Rejecting the passionate humanism of Byron and Shelley, Hugo and Lamartine, they turned to nebulous suggestion and dreamlike evocation of mood. Theirs was an exquisite idiom nourished by art rather than by life, whose excessive refinement tended to replace objective reality by the private world of the poet. Symbolism was a hothouse flower that aptly represented the end of the century, with its longing for enchantment and escape.

The new aesthetic doctrines could not but make a deep impression on such musicians as were sensitive to painting and poetry. In consequence, the quest for subtilization of means and refinement of vocabulary soon passed over from painting and poetry to music.

Impressionism in Music

Impressionism in music came as a French—or should one say Parisian?—gesture of revolt against the domination of German Romanticism. For the emotional exuberance of Wagner and his followers Debussy sought to substitute an art that was delicate, subtle, and—to use a favorite word of his—discreet. A pictorial art that wove a web of sensuous allure and conjured up the evanescent loveliness of the world without, rather than the searing conflicts of the world within.

When Debussy, as a young man, submitted his cantata *The Blessed Damozel* to the professors of the Paris Conservatoire, they stated in their report: "It is much to be desired that he beware of this vague impressionism which is one of the most dangerous enemies of artistic truth." Thus was transplanted to the realm of music a label that had already firmly established itself in art criticism. Debussy himself disliked the word and spoke acidly concerning "what some idiots call impressionism, a term that is altogether misused, especially by the critics." Despite him the name stuck, for it seemed to express what most people felt about his music. The Impressionist painters, we saw, tried to capture the movement of color and light. But music is preeminently the art of movement. For this reason the favorite images of Impressionist painting—the play of light on water, clouds, gardens in the rain, sunlight through the leaves—lent themselves readily to musical expression at the hands of a composer who "changed into music every impression his five senses received."

For Debussy, as for Monet and Verlaine, art was a sensuous rather than ethical or intellectual experience. The epic themes of German Romanticism were foreign to his temperament. In the doctrine of art for art's sake he recognized the triumph of Latin *esprit* over the Teutonic love of "deep" meanings. "The French," he wrote, "forget too easily the qualities of clarity and elegance peculiar to themselves and allow themselves to be influenced by the tedious and ponderous Teuton." He counseled his countrymen to turn away from their German models and to rediscover the old masters of France. "Couperin and Rameau—these are true Frenchmen. French music aims above all to please." Debussy here upheld what was the age-old ideal of Gallic art: to charm, to entertain, and to serve—in his phrase—as a "fantasy of the senses."

The Revolt against German Forms

The sonata-symphony, supreme achievement of German constructive genius, had never been altogether congenial to the Latin temperament. Already in the eighteenth century Fontenelle had inquired, "Sonata, what do you want of me?" Debussy's fervent desire to found a genuinely French art inevitably led him away from the grand form of Beethoven. He looked upon sonata form, with its exposition, development, and restatement of musical ideas, as an outmoded formula, "a legacy of clumsy, falsely interposed traditions." The working out of themes and motives he regarded as a species of dull "musical mathematics." It was this Gallic point of view that impelled him, at a concert, to whisper to a friend, "Let's go—he's beginning to develop!"

Even more incisive was his opposition to the Wagnerian music-drama, which at that time held such powerful allure for the intellectuals of France. Debussy's hostility to Wagner is all the more significant in that, in his youth, he had fallen under the spell of the German master and had made, as he put it, "passionate pilgrimages to Bayreuth." He had to free himself from this domination if he was to find his own path, and he was persuaded that French music had to do the same. He aimed some of his choicest barbs at *The Ring of the Nibelung*. "The idea of spreading one drama over four evenings! Is this admissible, especially when in these four evenings you always hear the same thing? My God, how unbearable these people in skins and helmets become by the fourth night!"

From the grandiose architecture of symphony and music-drama

Although Impressionist subject matter did not address the lofty social and political concerns of the Romantics, it nevertheless shared the Romantic taste for lyricism and rich texture. Woman with Chrysanthemums, *1865, by Edgar Degas (1834–1917). The Metropolitan Museum of Art, Bequest of Mrs. H. O. Havemeyer, The H. O. Havemeyer Collection.*

Debussy found his way to the short lyric forms that he used with such distinction—preludes, nocturnes, arabesques. In his hands these became chiseled miniatures whose moods were crystallized in such images as *Reflections in the Water, The Snow Is Dancing, Sounds and Perfumes Turn in the Evening Air*. Significant is his use of names borrowed from the painters: *images, estampes* (engravings), *esquisses* (sketches). These pieces, impregnated with lyricism, reveal him as a true nature poet.

The question remains: was Impressionism a revolt against the Romantic tradition—as its adherents believed—or was it but the final manifestation of that tradition? There can be no question that Debussy raised the banner of revolt against certain aspects of the Romantic heritage. Yet in a number of ways Impressionism continued the basic trends of the Romantic movement: in its allure, its addiction to beautiful sound, its rejection of Classical conceptions of form, its love of lyricism. Romantic too was its emphasis on mood and atmosphere; its fondness for program music and poetic titles; its nature worship and imaginative tone painting; and—most Romantic trait of all—its desire to draw music, painting, and poetry as closely together as possible. What the Impressionists did, really, was to substitute a sophisticated French type of Romanticism for the older German variety.

In any case, the emergence of Impressionism in music went hand in hand with the predominant position that French music assumed after the turn of the century. In 1905 Romain Rolland was able to write about "the sudden change which is being brought about in music. French art, quietly, is in the act of taking the place of German art."

15 Impressionist Methods

"Debussyism was not the work of Debussy alone but a traditionally logical stage of modern evolution."

CHARLES KOECHLIN

Impressionism came to the fore at a time when composers were beginning to feel that they had exhausted the possibilities of the major-minor scale. Debussy's fastidious ear explored subtler harmonic relationships and impelled him to seek new sources of inspiration—specifically, those that lay outside the orbit of German music of the eighteenth and nineteenth centuries. He thus was led to develop his natural affinity with the exotic and the old.

Modal Influences

The medieval modes (see page 27) could not but prove attractive to composers who were seeking to escape the tyranny of the major-minor sound. Consequently, modal harmony began to play an ever more prominent part in twentieth-century works. Debussy emphasized the primary intervals—octaves, fourths, and fifths—which he used in parallel motion. This style of writing somewhat resembled a medieval procedure known as organum, in which a melody was harmonized by another which ran parallel to it at a distance of a fifth or a fourth. (In four-part organum both parts were duplicated an octave

Ninth-Century Organum

higher.) The use of an organum-like style imparted to Debussy's music an archaic effect that was piquant in the highest degree. There is no denying the powerful austerity, the impression of old and remote things conveyed by a passage such as opens *La Cathédrale engloutie* (The Sunken Cathedral). The resemblance to medieval organum is apparent:

For centuries music had centered about the mellifluous intervals of the third and sixth. Debussy's emphasis of the bare intervals of the fourth and fifth was a departure of prime importance for his contemporaries and followers. Notice, in the above example, that the first chord is sustained by the pedal, thereby creating a sonorous haze against which the succeeding harmonies unfold. This use of a pedal point or organ point was an effect prized throughout the Classic-Romantic era. The Impressionists adopted the device and used it with great imagination, deriving a multitude of striking effects from the clash of the transient and the sustained harmony.

The Whole-Tone Scale

In the Exposition of 1889, held in Paris to celebrate the centenary of the French Revolution, Debussy heard the musicians of the Far

East—Java, Bali, Indo-China. He was fascinated by the music of the native orchestra, the gamelan, with its intricate interplay of percussive rhythms and bewitching instrumental colors. Here was a new world of sonority that could be drawn upon to invigorate the traditional patterns of the West.

The music of the Far East makes use of certain scales that divide the octave into equal parts, as does the whole-tone scale popularly associated with Debussy. It should be added that he was by no means the first to employ this scale—we find examples in the music of Glinka, Rimsky-Korsakov, and Liszt; nor did he use it as often as is generally supposed. He did, however, have a strong affinity for it.

The whole-tone scale divides the octave into six whole tones, as in the sequence C, D, E, F-sharp, G-sharp, A-sharp, C.

This pattern lacks the half-tone distances that lend character and direction to the major scale. Hence its expressive scope is extremely limited. Yet its very fluidity made it an excellent vehicle for the elusive melodies and harmonies favored by Impressionism. The following measures from the third act of *Pelléas et Mélisande* illustrate the special magic that Debussy was able to distill from the whole-tone scale.

The Pentatonic Scale

Also favored by the Impressionists was the pentatonic or five-note scale, which is sounded when the black keys of the piano are struck (or the tones C, D, F, G, A). Since this scale too, like the whole-tone pattern, omits the semitones of the major scale, it served the purpose of composers who were seeking a fresh sound.

The pentatonic scale is of very great antiquity and is found throughout the Far East as well as in various parts of Europe. It is popularly associated with Chinese music. Yet it is even more familiar to us through Scottish, Irish, and English folk tunes. *Auld Lang Syne*, for example, and *Comin' through the Rye* are pentatonic melodies.

In his piano prelude *La Fille aux cheveux de lin* (The Girl with the Flaxen Hair), Debussy exploits the quiet charm of the pentatonic

Très calme et doucement expressif

scale to evoke the portrait of a Scottish lassie. In *Pagodes* (Pagodas) he uses themes based on the same scale to create an atmosphere of Chinese ritual music.

etc.

Impressionist Harmony

In the Classical view, the individual chord was considered in terms of its role within the harmonic progression—that is, in relation to what preceded and followed. Impressionism, on the contrary, brought to the fore the twentieth-century tendency to regard the chord as an entity in its own right, a sonorous "thrill" that hit the ear and the nerves with a pungency all its own. What is more, if a single chord made a striking effect, the composer was apt to reinforce that effect by repeating the chord on various degrees of the scale, shifting it up or down without change. The individual chord was intended to arouse a sensation quite apart from any context, even as in Symbolist poetry the picturesque word was removed from its normal environment. In effect, Impressionism released the chord from its function in regard to the movement and goal of the music. Therewith the Impressionists greatly loosened the forms that had been based on the Classical—that is, the functional—concept of harmony.

In the following passage from Debussy's *Soirée dans Grenade* (Evening in Granada), the entire passage consists of a single chord structure which is duplicated on successive tones. We have here the "gliding" chords that become an essential feature of the Impres-

Tempo giusto

sionist style. In a passage such as the above we may even question whether we are dealing with a series of chords at all. Rather we hear a succession of blobs of sound, just as in a melody we hear a succession of individual notes. The harmony here is really a thickening out of the melody; just as, in many an Impressionist painting, the luminous haze is a thickening out of the single line.

Parallel Motion

Harmonies, according to the Classical tenet, resulted from the movement of the several voices. To maximize the tension of this movement, the lines were supposed to proceed as much as possible in *contrary* motion. Impressionism, on the other hand, by viewing the chord as a sonorous entity, severed its relationship to the movement of the individual lines. Indeed, the very concept of shifting chords bodily up or down implies parallel rather than contrary motion, as is apparent from the last musical example. Parallel movement is a prime characteristic of Impressionist music.

Classical harmony specifically forbade the parallel movement of certain intervals such as octaves and fifths, on the ground that this weakened the independent movement of the voice parts. Debussy, contrariwise, used parallel fifths freely, therewith departing from the Classic-Romantic sound. The following example from a passage in *Chansons de Bilitis* creates an atmosphere of mystery and remoteness:

Lento

The harmonic innovations inseparable from Impressionism led to the formation of daring new tone combinations. Characteristic was the use of the five-tone combinations known as ninth chords. These played so prominent a part in *Pelléas* that the work came to be known as "the land of ninths." Here is a typical sequence of parallel ninth chords from *Pelléas.*

A characteristic of Impressionist harmony is the use of what are known as "escaped" chords—harmonies, that is, which give the impression of having "escaped" to another key. Such chords are neither prepared for nor resolved in the conventional sense. They are simply permitted to "evaporate" while the original harmonies are sustained in the lower voices. The following example occurs at the opening of Debussy's *General Lavine—Eccentric* from the second book of *Preludes.* C-major tonality is established in the first measure, against which is heard a series of triads alien to the tonality.

Once the chord became an independent entity, the pull to the tonic naturally was weakened. The composer might even question its need to resolve at all. In the excerpt we quoted from *Soirée dans Grenade* (page 93), the first chord is a dissonance which, by Classical standards, would have to resolve to a consonance. Instead, it is duplicated in a succession of dissonances, none of which displays any tendency to resolve. Thus Debussy, like many of his contemporaries, strengthened the drive toward the "emancipation of the dissonance."

As a consequence of these usages, Impressionist music floated in a borderland between keys, creating elusive effects that may be compared to the nebulous outlines of Impressionist painting. Debussy and his followers contributed decisively to the twentieth-century expansion of the sense of key. By the same token, they broke down the boundaries of the key as an area in harmonic space, and thereby gave impetus to the disintegration of the major-minor system.

Other Aspects of Impressionist Music

The evanescent harmonies of the Impressionist composers called for colors no less subtle. There was little room here for the heaven-storming climaxes of the Romantic orchestra. Instead, we find a veiling of the orchestral sonority, against which the individual timbres stand out with delicate clarity. Impressionist orchestration shimmers with an impalpably pictorial quality. Flutes and clarinets are used in their dark lower register, violins in their luminous upper stage. Trumpets and horns are discreetly muted, and the whole is enveloped in a silvery gossamer of harp, celesta, and triangle, glockenspiel, muffled drum, and—at special moments—a cymbal brushed lightly with a drumstick. We saw that the Impressionist painters, instead of mixing their pigments on the palette, juxtaposed specks of pure color on the canvas. The Impressionist musician similarly juxtaposed pure colors, leaving it to the ear of the hearer to do the mixing.

Instead of the broadly spun melodies of the Romantic style, Debussy cultivated a melody composed of fragmentary phrases, each of which was often repeated. This mosaiclike structure makes for an initimacy of style that is very French. A corresponding modification occurred in rhythm. Debussy and his followers favored a stream of sound that veiled the beat and helped to free music from the "tyranny of the barline." This continuous flow from one measure to the next is most characteristic of Impressionist music. As far as form went, Impressionism moved away from the grand architecture of the Classical heritage, seeking plastic forms that would capture something of the fluidity and charm of improvisation. The avoidance of clear-cut cadences made for an overlapping of phrases, periods, and sections. Structural landmarks as well as the Classical pattern of tension-and-release were veiled in an uninterrupted flow of dreamlike sound.

It would be erroneous to suppose that the historic developments surveyed in this chapter owed their being exclusively to Debussy. The germs of Impressionist procedures are already to be found in the music of Liszt, Musorgsky, Bizet, and other composers. As the nineteenth century drew to its end, new conceptions of melody, harmony, rhythm, color, tonality, and form were in the air, and musicians everywhere sought ways to implement them. What Debussy did was to unite those in a personal style, to reinforce them with a well-reasoned aesthetic doctrine, and to give them the shape in which they won acceptance throughout the world. He forced us, in Constant Lambert's fine phrase, "to listen less with our minds and more with our nerves." In so doing he set his seal upon an era.

16   Claude Debussy (1862-1918)

"The music I desire must be supple enough to adapt itself to the lyrical effusions of the soul and the fantasy of dreams."

His Life

Claude Debussy was born in the town of St. Germain-en-Laye, near Paris. His father, who kept a china shop, wanted him to become a sailor, but the boy's musical talent brought him to the Paris Conservatory when he was eleven. In the next years Claude acquired a reputation as an iconoclast, scandalizing his fellow students and teachers with unconventional harmonies that violated all the rules. "What rules do you observe, then?" one of his professors inquired. "None—only my own pleasure!" "That's all very well," came the reply, "provided you're a genius." Before long, his teachers began to suspect that the daring young rebel was.

At eighteen he was recommended as a pianist in the household of Nadezhda von Meck, the patroness of Tchaikovsky. He played piano duets with the wealthy widow, taught her children, and even proposed—unsuccessfully—to one of her daughters. Madame described him in one of her letters to Tchaikovsky as "Parisian from tip to toe, a typical gamin, very witty and an excellent mimic." His imitations of Gounod were "most amusing."

When he was twenty-two his cantata, *L'Enfant prodigue* (The Prodigal Son), won the top award of the Conservatoire, the Prix de Rome. The scholarship carried with it a protracted residence in the Italian capital at government expense. Debussy looked upon his stay in Rome as a dreary exile: he could not be happy away from the boulevards and cafés that constituted his world. He was required to submit a work each year that would enable the authorities in Paris to judge of his progress. Upon receipt of the first *envoi,* the professors of the Conservatoire reported that "at present M. Debussy seems to be afflicted with a desire to write music that is bizarre, incomprehensible, and impossible to execute." For his third and final piece he submitted what has remained the most successful of his early works, *La Damoiselle élue* (The Blessed Damozel), a lyric poem for solo voices, chorus, and orchestra based on the poem by Dante Gabriel Rossetti. It was this work that elicited the label *impressionism,* which henceforth was attached to Debussy's music.

With his return to Paris his apprenticeship was over. He frequented the salons where the avant-garde gathered; at the famous "Tuesday evenings" of Stéphane Mallarmé he met the leading Impressionist painters and Symbolist poets. Their influence bore rich fruit in 1894, when, at the age of thirty-two, he completed his first major orchestral work, the *Prélude à "L'Après-midi d'un faune"* (Prelude to "The Afternoon of a Faun"), in which the Debussy style appears before us fully formed.

The nineties constituted the most productive decade of Debussy's career. The culminating work of these years was the opera *Pelléas et Mélisande.* Based on the play by the Belgian Symbolist Maurice Maeterlinck, *Pelléas* occupied the composer for the better part of ten years. Debussy continued to polish and revise the score up to the opening night, which took place at the Opéra-Comique on April 30, 1902. Public interest in this premiere was intensified by a bitter feud between the composer and his librettist. Maeterlinck had expected that the role of Mélisande would be created by his wife, Georgette Leblanc, but at the last moment the part was given to a young and practically unknown American—Mary Garden. Infuriated, Maeterlinck made the discovery that every poet does whose verses are set to music: that his creation had lost its independence. He had no ear for music, but he knew enough to suspect that his drama would never again stand on its own feet. In a letter to the press he announced that the operatic *Pelléas* was "a work which is now strange and hostile to me." His drama was "in the hands of the enemy"; he hoped for "its immediate and complete failure." The critics did attack the work as decadent and precious, but the originality and the quiet intensity of the score made a profound impression on the musical intelligentsia. The opera caught on and soon established itself in the international repertory.

Until the success of *Pelléas,* Debussy had been pretty much the bohemian. His existence had been shared by the lovely Gabrielle Dupont—"Gaby of the green eyes"—for the better part of a decade.

A portrait of Claude De-bussy in 1909 by the famous photographer Nadar (Gaspard Felix Tournachon, 1820–1910). Bibliothèque Nationale de Paris.

After her there was Rosalie Texier, a beautiful girl from Burgundy who had come to Paris to work as a dressmaker. Debussy married her in 1899, when he was in such straitened circumstances that he had to give a lesson in order to pay for the wedding breakfast. In 1904 he fell under the spell of Mme. Emma Bardac, wife of a Parisian banker. She was brilliant, worldly, an accomplished musician whose rendition of his songs gave the composer much pleasure. Swept by a consuming love, Debussy and Mme. Bardac eloped. Rosalie tried to kill herself, and was taken to the hospital with a bullet near her heart. After she recovered, a double divorce took place. Debussy was accused by certain of his friends of having been attracted to the glamorous Mme. Bardac because of her wealth. It might be closer the mark to say that she fulfilled the needs of this new phase of his career just as Rosalie had met those of the earlier period. Debussy's second marriage was idyllic. A daughter was born for whom, some years later, he wrote the suite for piano *The Children's Corner* and the ballet for children *La Boîte à joujoux* (The Toy Box). To her mother were dedicated several of the most important works of his final years.

After *Pelléas*, Debussy was the acknowledged leader of the new movement in music, the center of a cult of worshipful disciples who copied his ideas and his mannerisms, and about whom the composer complained, "The Debussyites are killing me!" He appeared in the principal cities of Europe as a conductor of his works and wrote the articles that established his position as one of the wittiest critics of the century. His output slackened toward the end of his life. Although his energies were sapped by cancer, he continued to work with remarkable fortitude. The outbreak of war in 1914 confronted him with the dilemma of the artist amidst universal tragedy. "France," he felt, "can neither laugh nor weep while so many of our men heroically face death. What I am doing seems so wretchedly small and unimportant." Presently, however, he saw that, even as he had led the struggle of French music against German domination, so he must now contribute to the grimmer struggle between the two cultures in the only way he could—"by creating to the best of my ability a little of that beauty which the enemy is attacking with such fury." It was at this time of his country's peril that he assumed the proud title *musicien français*.

The relentless advance of his malady brought the realization that his creative career was over. His last letters speak of his "life of waiting—my waiting-room existence, I might call it. For I am a poor traveler waiting for a train that will never come any more." He died in March 1918, during the bombardment of Paris. The funeral cortege passed through deserted streets while his beloved city was being ripped by the shells of the Big Berthas. It was only eight months before the victory of the nation whose art found in him so distinguished a spokesman.

His Music

"I love music passionately," Debussy wrote, "and because I love it I try to free it from barren traditions that stifle it. It is a free art, gushing forth—an open-air art, an art boundless as the elements, the wind, the sky, the sea! It must never be shut in and become an academic art." This freedom from formula he strove to maintain throughout his life.

His chief orchestral works are firmly entrenched in the concert hall: the *Prelude to "The Afternoon of a Faun,"* a magical score; the three *Nocturnes* (1899)—*Nuages* (Clouds), *Fêtes* (Festivals), and *Sirènes* (Sirens), which show him in his most pictorial vein; *La Mer* (The Sea, 1905); and *Ibéria,* from his last period, which we shall consider in detail. His handling of the orchestra shows a truly French sensibility; his atmospheric writing for flute, clarinet, and oboe displays the traditional French mastery of the woodwinds. French, too, is his economy. There are no superfluous notes in his scores. The lines are widely spaced; the colors stand out in radiant purity. The sound mass is transparent and airy.

Debussy's piano music occupies in the twentieth-century repertory a position comparable to Chopin's in the nineteenth. He was one of the principal originators of the new piano style. With endless subtlety he exploited the resources of the instrument: the contrast of high and low registers, the blending of sonorities made possible by the pedals, the clash of overtones. From among the early works, the two *Arabesques* (1888) are still much played. Also *L'Îsle joyeuse* (The Happy Island, 1904), a luminous evocation of Watteau's make-believe world. The *Suite bergamasque* (1890) contains *Clair de lune* (Moonlight), the most popular piece he ever wrote. *Soirée dans Grenade* (Evening in Granada, 1903) exploits the supple rhythm of the habanera. *Jardins sous la pluie* (Gardens in the Rain, 1903) is an Impressionistic tone painting, as is *Reflets dans l'eau* (Reflections in the Water, 1905). In *Hommage à Rameau* (1905), he pays his respects to the eighteenth-century French master. To his final period belong the two books of twelve *Preludes* each (1910–1913) and the *Etudes* (1915), which he dedicated to the memory of Chopin. We should not be misled by the nebulous outlines of his piano pieces. These seemingly capricious forms bear the imprint of a craftsman who had sovereign command of compositional technique.

Debussy is one of the most important among those who, toward the end of the nineteenth century, established the French art song as a genre independent of the German Romantic lied. Best known among the song sets are the *Cinq Poèmes de Baudelaire* (Five Poems of Baudelaire, 1889); *Ariettes oubliées* (Forgotten Little Tunes, 1888), and *Fêtes galantes* (Courtly Festivals, 1892–1904), to poems of Verlaine; and *Chansons de Bilitis* (1897), to poems of Pierre Louÿs. Debussy's songs are poetic meditations. They demand a special sensitivity on the part of both singer and accompanist, not to mention the listener. Granted this, they are certain to weave their spell.

In chamber music, a field traditionally dominated by the Germans, Debussy achieved some important successes. His *String Quar-*

tet in G minor, written when he was thirty-one (1893), is one of the most engaging in the recent literature. At the end of his career, when he was seeking greater clarity and firmness of structure, he returned to the sonata he had once derided. The three chamber sonatas—for cello and piano; for flute, viola, and harp; and for violin and piano—belong to the years 1915–1917. The critics who heard these works in the twenties described them as indicating an ebbing of the composer's powers, and ever since then commentators have gone on repeating the statement. But one has only to listen to the *Cello Sonata* to feel oneself in the presence of a master. To the last years belongs also the music for Gabriele d'Annunzio's mystery play *Le Martyre de Saint Sébastien* (1911). This unjustly neglected work, with its austere medieval harmonies, possesses both spirituality and power.

Finally, *Pelléas et Mélisande.* This "old and sad tale of the woods," as Debussy called it, captures the ebb and flow of the interior life. It is a tale imbued with all the reticence and lyric charm at its creator's command. Mélisande of the golden hair (and the habit of saying everything twice); Pelléas, overwhelmed by the mystery of a love he never quite fathoms; Golaud, the husband, driven by jealousy to the murder of his half-brother; Arkel, the blind king of this twilight kingdom—they are the victims of a fate "they neither resent nor understand." Yet how compassionately they are conceived, and with what fullness of dimension. Ths music throughout is subservient to the drama. The orchestra provides a discreet framework and creates

The balcony scene from Act II of Pelléas et Mélisande. *In this Metropolitan Opera production, Teresa Stratas and Raymond Gibbs sang the title roles. Copyright © Beth Bergman.*

an atmosphere steeped in nature poetry. The setting of the text is masterly. Perhaps the real conflict of this strangely muted lyric drama is between the transience of human suffering and the eternal impassivity of nature. Listening to it, one understands Debussy's remark, "How much one must first find, how much one must suppress, in order to arrive at the naked flesh of the emotion!" One understands, too, Romain Rolland's description of him as "this great painter of dreams."

Ibéria

Ibéria (1908), the second of three *Images* for orchestra, ushered in the final decade of the composer's career. Those who know Debussy only from earlier scores such as the *Prelude to "The Afternoon of a Faun"* will notice at once the greater sharpness of outline and the brilliance of color that characterize his later orchestral style. Also apparent are a tightening of structure and crystallization of idiom.

With *Ibéria* Debussy joined the line of French composers—Saint-Saëns, Bizet, Lalo, and Chabrier before him, Ravel after—who drew inspiration from Spain. Save for an afternoon spent in San Sebastian, near the border, Debussy never visited the country. For him, therefore, as for Bizet, Spain represented that unknown land of dreams which every artist carries in his heart. However, no less an authority than Spain's greatest composer, Manuel de Falla, wrote of *Ibéria*: "The intoxicating spell of Andalusian nights, the festive gaiety of a people dancing to the joyous strains of a *banda* of guitars and *bandurrias* . . . all this whirles in the air, approaches and recedes, and our imagination is continually kept awake and dazzled by the power of an intensely expressive and richly varied music."

The work is scored for full orchestra. The instruments are treated soloistically and retain their individual timbres throughout, with the luminosity of texture so characteristic of Debussy's style.

I. *Par les rues et par les chemins* (In the Streets and Byways). The movement is marked *assez animé, dans un rythme alerte mais précis* (quite lively, in a rhythm that is tense but precise). The piece opens with a characteristic rhythm set forth by the woodwinds in alternation with pizzicato strings. Debussy is influenced here, as was Scarlatti in the eighteenth century, by the guitar sound that is indigenous to Spain. A plaintive melody emerges on the clarinet, marked "elegant and quite rhythmic." Its subtle syncopations and sinuous contours point to the Moorish element in the popular music of Spain.

The mood is festive, the setting meridional. The steady triple meter is alive with the gestures of the dance. Presently a contrasting idea emerges, *soutenu et très expressif* (sustained and very expressive). Presented by oboe and viola, this is a somber, long-breathed melody that moves languidly within a narrow range, with the frequent repetition of fragments characteristic of the folk style.

Exciting fanfares on the horns and trumpets introduce a slower section. The spirit of the habanera enters the orchestra. The original idea returns in an abbreviated version. The movement dies away.

II. *Les Parfums de la nuit* (Perfumes of the Night). The tempo indication is *Lent et rêveur* (slow and dreamy). Delicate pencilings of color in the opening measures make a characteristic sonority: flutes and oboes against muted violins in high register, a touch of xylophone, clarinet and bassoon silvered by celesta, against the subdued beat of a tambourine. A seductive melody emerges on the oboe, marked *expressif et pénétrant*.

Significantly, Debussy here departs from the purely harmonic writing of his earlier days. Horizontal strands of melody intertwine in a diaphanous counterpoint. This is a tender night song, yet the subjective element is always kept within the bounds of discretion. In the evocative power of its half-lights, this slow movement is indisputably one of Debussy's finest.

III. *Le Matin d'un jour de fête* (The Morning of a Feast Day). The finale follows without a break. It is marked *Dans un rythme de marche lointaine, alerte et joyeuse* (in the rhythm of a distant march, tense and joyous), and is ushered in by a striking rhythm. A light-hearted dance tune is heard in the high register of the clarinet.

(Notice the melodic similarity of the last three examples.)

The music is vividly pictorial—even balletic—in its suggestion of movement. Those who know Debussy only in his twilight moods will be surprised at the percussive dissonance, incisive rhythm, and astringent sonorities that pervade this dance finale.

This view of Rouen Cathedral is one of a series depicting the same subject at different times of day. The subject itself serves as a backdrop for the constantly changing atmosphere and light, which were the artist's chief concerns. Rouen Cathedral, Sunset, 1894, by Claude Monet (1840–1926). The Boston Museum of Fine Arts.

La Cathédrale engloutie (The Sunken Cathedral)

In *La Cathédrale engloutie* (1910), one of the twelve pieces in the first book of *Preludes,* Debussy's pictorial imagination allies itself with the floating sonorities of his favorite instrument. His point of departure was an old Breton legend, according to which the ancient cathedral of Ys rises out of the sea on certain mornings, its bells tolling, its priests intoning their prayers. Then the cathedral sinks back into the deep. Debussy's piano style lent itself admirably to the atmosphere of mystery and enchantment required for such a tale.

The composer's markings indicate the mood: *Profondément calme . . . dans une brume doucement sonore* (in a gently sonorous haze) . . . *doux et fluide* (gentle and fluid). We quoted the opening measures of *La Cathédrale engloutie* to suggest the resemblance between Impressionist harmony and medieval organum (see page 90). The sustained chords shown in that example act as organ points, creating a halo of sounds against which the parallel chords in the upper register unfold in a mystic procession. Debussy subtly exploits the overtones of the piano; the melody has a Gregorian flavor; the music evokes the sound of an organ in a cathedral, but heard as in a dream. Blocklike gliding chords, parallel fourths and fifths, added seconds and sevenths that give the harmony a percussive tang—all the features of the Impressionist style are encountered here. Brief modulations to B major, E-flat major, and later to C-sharp minor contrast with the modal harmony that prevails throughout the piece. The climax comes with bell-like harmonies in a clangorous fortissimo. (Dynamic terms are explained in Appendix l-f.) Debussy intended this to be played *sonore sans dureté* (resounding without hardness). As the cathedral sinks beneath the waves the Gregorian motive is heard *expressif et concentré.* The bell-like motive returns against a rippling accompaniment in the bass, "floating and muffled, like an echo," as if the bells

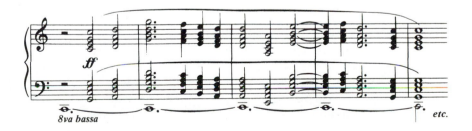

8va bassa

etc.

were still tolling under water. The opening chords return, but with added seconds, as the music dissolves in the mist out of which it came.

We today are so familiar with Debussy's language that it is difficult for us to realize how startlingly original it was in its own time. His music was without antecedents. Like Berlioz and Wagner before him, like Stravinsky and Schoenberg after, he stands among the great innovators in the history of his art.

17   Maurice Ravel (1875-1937)

"I did my work slowly, drop by drop. I tore it out of me by pieces."

Thirteen years the junior of Debussy, Maurice Ravel had to make his way in a milieu dominated by the older master. He imposed the stamp of his own classicist outlook on the Impressionist idiom, and took his place alongside Debussy as a leader of the modern French school.

His Life

Ravel was born in Ciboure, near Saint-Jean-de-Luz, in the Basses-Pyrénées region at the southwestern tip of France. The family moved to Paris shortly after Maurice was born. His father, a mining engineer who had aspired to be a musician, was sympathetic to the son's artistic proclivities. Maurice entered the Conservatoire when he was fourteen. He remained there for sixteen years—an unusually long apprenticeship.

Ravel's career at the Conservatoire was enlivened by his repeated failure to win the Prix de Rome, the official prize that has been held by some of France's most distinguished composers—as well as by a number of nonentities. At his fourth attempt he was eliminated in the preliminary examination, even though his work had already begun to command respect in progressive musical circles. This high-handed action on the part of the professors caused a public scandal. The director of the Conservatoire was forced to resign, and Gabriel Fauré—Ravel's teacher in composition—was appointed in his place. Ravel never forgot the affront. In later life he accepted honors from several foreign states, but refused the decoration of the Legion of Honor from a government that had withheld the Rome prize from a deserving young musician.

Ravel's artistic development was greatly stimulated by his friendship with a group of avant-garde poets, painters, and musicians who believed in his gifts long before those were recognized by the world at large. Youthful enthusiasts, they called themselves the "Apaches." "We had more or less the same tastes in art," wrote Léon-Paul Fargue, "which was lucky for people as hot-headed as we were because, as someone has said, you can't discuss things except with people of your own opinion. Ravel shared our preference, weakness, or mania respectively for Chinese art, Mallarmé and Verlaine, Rimbaud, Cézanne and Van Gogh, Rameau and Chopin, Whistler and Valéry, the Russians and Debussy."

In this rarefied atmosphere the young composer found the necessary intellectual companionship, as had Debussy a decade earlier in the salon of Stéphane Mallarmé. He was affable and detached, presenting to the world a façade of urbanity that covered quivering sensibilities. His biographers are as reticent as was their subject in all that pertained to his personal life. He was enormously attached to his parents and brother; he made a loyal but possessive friend; in all other relationships he was the suave man of the world. There is no evidence that he was capable of romantic love. Beneath his polished surface were limits beyond which he did not care to go.

Ravel's career followed the same course, more or less, as that of almost all the leaders of the modern movement in art. At first his music was hissed by the multitide and cried down by the critics. Only a few discerned the special quality of his work, but their number steadily grew. Ultimately the tide turned and he found himself famous.

Ravel, like Debussy, was profoundly shaken by the outbreak of war in 1914. After making a vain attempt to join the army, he was accepted by the air force, became a driver in the motor transport corps, and was sent to the Verdun sector. To his surprise, the horrors of war aroused no fear in him. On the contrary, they cast a terrible spell. "And yet I am a peaceful person," he wrote from the front. "I have never been brave. But there it is, I am eager for adventure. It has such a fascination that it becomes a necessity. What will I do, what will many others do, when the war is over?"

Maurice Ravel in a painting by Achille Ouvré (1872–1952). André Meyer Collection.

Having fallen seriously ill, he was discharged and returned to Paris just before the death of his mother. Her loss was a heavy blow. In a mood of severe depression he resumed his work with *Le Tombeau de Couperin*. (*Tombeau*, literally a tomb, denotes a lyric form of the age of Louis XIV, offered as homage to a deceased person.) "In reality it is a tribute not so much to Couperin himself," he stated, "as to eighteenth-century French music in general." Grief is here transformed into six serenely graceful dance pieces, each dedicated to the memory of a fallen comrade.

In the years after the war Ravel came into his own. He was acknowledged to be the foremost composer of France and was much in demand to conduct his works throughout Europe. In 1928 he was invited to tour the United States. Before he would consider the offer he had to be assured of a steady supply of his favorite French wines and of French Caporals (he was a chain smoker). Ravel and America took to one another, although he tired first. "I am seeing magnificent cities, enchanting country," he wrote home, "but the triumphs are fatiguing. Besides, I was dying of hunger."

With the passing of the Twenties there began for the composer, as for the world about him, a period of depression. His overrefined, stylized art was not the kind that renews itself through deepening contact with life. Hence he found it increasingly difficult to compose. "I have failed in my life," he had written in a moment of depression. "I am not one of the great composers. All the great ones produced enormously. But I have written relatively very little, and with a great deal of hardship. And now I cannot do any more, and it does not give me any pleasure." In these words we hear the self-induced impotence of an artist who ended as "a prisoner of perfection."

Toward the end of his life Ravel was tormented by restlessness and insomnia. He sought surcease in the hectic atmosphere of the Parisian nightclubs, where he would listen for hours to American jazz. As he approached sixty he fell victim to a rare brain disease that left his faculties unimpaired but attacked the centers of speech and motor coordination. It gradually became impossible for him to read notes, to remember tunes, or to write. Once, after a performance of *Daphnis et Chloé*, he began to weep, exclaiming: "I have still so much music in my head!" His companion tried to comfort him by pointing out that he had finished his work. "I have said nothing," he replied in anguish. "I have still everything to say."

So as not to watch himself "go piece by piece," as he put it, he decided to submit to a dangerous operation. This was performed toward the end of 1937. He never regained consciousness.

His Music

Ravel's is an ultrapolished art. His delicate sense of proportion, his precision of line and ordered grace are in accord with everything we have come to associate with the French tradition. His emotions are controlled by his intellect. In this too he is one with the Gallic spirit. Art for him was created beauty, therefore compounded of artifice: the mirror that reflected his perception of reality, rather than reality itself. "Does it never occur to these people," he remarked, "that I am artificial by nature?" He had a horror of overstatement; he preferred irony and wit to the tragic gesture. Therefore he held on to the crystalline forms that constitute the element of control and "distance" in art. It was his one defense against his own emotions.

The critics of fifty years ago saw his music as a revolt against romantic subjectivity. They emphasized the constructional element in his work. Stravinsky called him a Swiss clockmaker. Ravel himself said, "I make logarithms—it is for you to understand them." We today are in a position to judge more clearly. Ravel was a romantic at heart. Wistful sentiment and tenderness are everywhere present in

In Cézanne's composition, pictorial elements are modified and rearranged according to aesthetic demands. Hence even a landscape painted out of doors is subject to considerations of form and is essentially a work of the imagination; this in contrast to the Impressionist credo of fidelity to nature. Mont Sainte-Victoire *by Paul Cézanne. The Metropolitan Museum of Art, The H. O. Havemeyer Collection, Bequest of Mrs. H. O. Havemeyer.*

his music, albeit at one remove, filtered through a supremely conscious artistry. For this reason he so ably represented the classical orientation, which in France has always been stronger than the romantic. All the same, his pronouncements on music in his later years clearly reveal the romantic origins of his art. "Great music, I have always felt, must always come from the heart. Any music created by technique and brains alone is not worth the paper it is written on. A composer should feel intensely what he is composing."

Ravel stands to Debussy somewhat as Cézanne does to Monet: he was a Postimpressionist. Like Cézanne, he feared that Impressionism, with its emphasis upon the "fantasy of the senses," might degenerate into formlessness. His instinctive need for lucidity and clarity of organization impelled him to return—even as did the painter—to the classical conception of form.

Like Debussy, Ravel was drawn to the scales of medievel and exotic music. He too sought to expand the traditional concept of key. His imagination, like Debussy's, responded to pictorial and poetic titles as a stimulus to creation. (The literary element has always been prominent in French music.) Both men were attracted by the same aspects of nature: the play of water and light, clouds and fountains; the magic of daybreak and twilight, the wind in the trees. Both exploited exotic dance rhythms, especially those of Spain, and leaned toward the fantastic and the antique. Both were influenced by the pure, intimate style of the French harpsichordists: Ravel paid homage to Couperin even as Debussy did to Rameau. Both men admired the Russians, although Debussy responded to Musorgsky while Ravel leaned toward Rimsky-Korsakov and Borodin. Both were repelled by the rhetoric of the nineteenth century. Both felt an affinity for the Symbolist poets, whose verses they set with exquisite taste and nuance. And both suffered from an overdeveloped critical sense that made it difficult for them to work in their later years.

The differences between the pair are no less striking than the similarities. The noontide brightness of Ravel's music contrasts with the twilight gentleness of Debussy's. Ravel's is the more driving rhythm. He is precise where Debussy is visionary. His humor is dryer, his harmony more incisive; the progressions are more cleanly outlined. His sense of key is firmer. He was not attracted to the whole-tone scale as was Debussy; he needed a more solid support for his structure. The voluptuous ambience of Debussy's music is absent from his. He is more daring with respect to dissonance, even as he is more conventional in the matter of form. Where Debussy was evocative and dreamlike, Ravel strove for the chiseled line. Thematic development was never the bugbear to him that it was to Debussy. Through his adherence to the Classical form—in his *Sonatina for Piano*, his *Trio, Quartet,* and the two piano concertos—he achieved the distance he sought between the artistic impulse and its realization.

Ravel's melodies are broader in span than Debussy's, more direct. His orchestral brilliance derives in greater degree from the nineteenth century; he stands in the line of descent from Berlioz and Chabrier as well as Rimsky-Korsakov and Richard Strauss. Where Debussy aimed to "decongest" sound, Ravel handled the Postromantic orchestra with real virtuosity, with special emphasis on what has been called the "confectionary" department—harp glissandos, glockenspiel, celesta, and triangle. Ravel must be accounted one of the great orchestrators of modern times. Stravinsky called him "an epicure and connoisseur of instrumental jewelry." When his creative inspiration began to lag, he found it beguiling to exercise his skill on the music of other men, and orchestrated pieces by Chopin, Schumann, Musorgsky, Chabrier, Erik Satie, and Debussy.

Ravel ranks as one of the outstanding piano composers of the twentieth century. He extended the heritage of Liszt, even as Debussy was the spiritual heir of Chopin. His crisp piano style, with its brilliant runs, its animation and fluency, owns kinship too with the eighteenth-century French harpsichordists. Among his early piano pieces, three attained enormous popularity: *Pavane pour une Infante défunte* (Pavane for a Dead Infanta, 1899); *Jeux d'eau* (Fountains, 1901); and the *Sonatine* (1905). The peak of his piano writing is found in *Gaspard de la nuit* (Gaspard of the Night, 1908), inspired by the fantastic verses of Aloysius Bertrand. The three tone poems of this set—*Ondine, Le Gibet* (The Gallows), *Scarbo*—show Ravel's pictorial imagination at its best.

The French song found in Ravel one of its masters. The witty *Histoires naturelles* (Stories from Nature, 1906), to Jules Renard's prose poems, aroused a storm of hostile criticism and established Ravel's reputation as an *enfant terrible*. The twentieth-century interest in chamber music with voice is exemplified by *Trois Poèmes de Stéphane Mallarmé* for voice, piano, two flutes, two clarinets, and string quartet (1913), and the sensuous *Chansons madécasses* (Songs of Madagascar, 1926). Ravel also cultivated the song with orchestra. *Shéhérazade* (1903), to the poems of his friend Tristan Klingsor, displays his exotic bent. *Deux Mélodies hébraïques* (Two Hebrew Melodies, 1914) was responsible in part for the widespread but erroneous belief that Ravel was Jewish.

It was through his orchestral works that Ravel won the international public. His first important composition in this medium was *Rapsodie espagnole* (Spanish Rhapsody, 1907). *Ma Mère l'Oye* (Mother Goose), originally written as a piano duet, was later orchestrated by the composer (1912). The five pieces of this set are impregnated with that sense of wonder which is the attribute of children and artists alike. *Daphnis et Chloé* we will discuss. *La Valse*, a "'choreographic poem" (1920), came out of the hectic period following the First World War. In this score Ravel deploys the surefire effects that have endeared him to the multitude. The same is true of *Boléro* (1928).

Among his other works are the *Piano Concerto in G* (1931), which fully realizes the composer's dictum that a classical concerto "should be lighthearted and brilliant"; the dramatic *Concerto for the Left Hand* (1931), a masterly composition; *L'Heure espagnole* (The Spanish Hour, 1907), a delicious comic opera in one act concerning an elderly clockmaker and his faithless wife; and *L'Enfant et les sortilèges* (Dreams of a Naughty Boy, 1925), a one-act fantasy on a text by Colette. In the domain of chamber music there is the distinguished *Trio* for piano, violin, and cello (1914); the *Introduction and Allegro* for harp, string quartet, flute, and clarinet (1906), which is much slighter in substance; and the graceful *String Quartet*, written when Ravel was twenty-eight (1903) and dedicated to his teacher Gabriel Fauré. *Tzigane* (1924), a rhapsody for violin and piano (or orchestra), exploits the vein of capricious Gypsyism familiar to us from the *Hungarian Rhapsodies* of Liszt.

Daphnis and Chloé Suite No. 2

The second suite drawn from his ballet *Daphnis and Chloé* is generally accounted Ravel's masterpiece. The work, commissioned by Diaghilev for his Ballet Russe, was produced in Paris in 1912. The action is derived from a pastoral of the Greek poet Longus. Chloé, beloved of the shepherd Daphnis, is abducted by a band of pirates. Daphnis, prostrate with grief, arouses the sympathy of the god Pan. Daphnis dreams that the god will come to his aid. He awakes to find Chloé restored to him. The second suite comprises the final scene of the ballet—Daybreak, Pantomime, and General Dance. The scoring is unusually rich and displays Ravel's mastery of orchestration.

I. *Daybreak.* "Nothing is heard but the murmur of rivulets. Daphnis lies stretched in front of the grotto of the nymphs. Day breaks gradually. The song of the birds is heard. Shepherds discover Daphnis and awaken him. In anguish he looks about for Chloé. She appears, surrounded by shepherdesses. The two rush into each other's arms."

Lent *(slow)*

pp *expressif*   *etc.*

The music paints a morning mood. Woodwinds set up a flickering sound in the upper register. A broadly arching theme emerges in the lower strings. Harp glissandos, celesta, and a violin solo soaring above the harmony create a characteristically Ravelian luminosity. At the point in the action where the lovers embrace, a rapturous outburst sweeps the orchestra. The brass enters, vividly suggesting an upsurge of light.

II. *Pantomime*. "The old shepherd Lammon explains that Pan
saved Chloé in remembrance of the nymph Syrinx whom the god
once loved. Daphnis and Chloé mime the story of Pan and Syrinx.
Chloé represents the young nymph wandering through the fields.
Daphnis represents Pan who declares his love. The nymph repulses
him. In despair he plucks some reeds, fashions a flute, and plays a
melancholy air."

A dialogue between oboe and flute sets the pastoral scene. The
famous flute solo—Pan's melancholy air—is heard against arpeggios
in the strings. This is a rhapsodic melody that Ravel marked "expressive and supple," free in rhythm and unfolding in ornate traceries.
Typical of the many felicities of color is a spot where the flute sus-
tains a high trill while piccolo, harps, and violins outline the harmonic background and are answered by parallel chords on celesta
and divided strings—Impressionism with a vengeance.

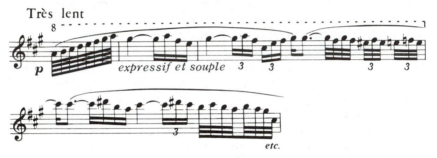

III. *General Dance*. "Before the altar of the nymphs Daphnis
swears his fidelity. Young girls enter dressed as bacchantes and
shaking tambourines. Daphnis and Chloé tenderly embrace. A
group of young men appear. Joyous tumult. A general dance."

The finale abounds in never failing effects. The frequent changes
of meter and the 5/4 time (three plus two) achieve a plasticity of
rhythm that is of the twentieth century. The movement is *Animé*
(lively). There is an unabashed use of chromatic scales to whip up excitement. Behind the façade of Parisian sophistication lurk the
shades of Rimsky-Korsakov and Borodin; the young blades of this
Arcadia have heard the powerful rhythms of *Scheherazade* and the
Polovetsian Dances. Each fragment of melody is heard twice, a
Debussy-like mannerism, and the "confectionary department" is
much in evidence. The hectic climax is an example of Ravel's orchestral wizardry at its calculated best.

Every pronounced trend in art engenders a reaction. Because of
the enormous popularity of Ravel's music in the Twenties and Thir-

ties, it is currently the fashion to deprecate his achievement. True, not all of his music is on the same high level: but whose is? It is important not to underestimate his achievement. Within the limits of his temperament and outlook, he explored a realm of sensibility all his own; and he did so with Gallic taste, wit, and imagination.

18 Other Impressionists

Impressionist music achieved an enormous vogue in the first quarter of the twentieth century. A whole generation of musicians fell under its spell, among them such dissimilar figures as Paul Dukas and Albert Roussel; Isaac Albeniz and Manuel de Falla; Charles Martin Loeffler and Charles Griffes (whom we shall discuss when we come to the Americans). Echoes of its caressing harmonies are to be found in the music of Stravinsky, Schoenberg, and Bartók, Vaughan Williams, Puccini, and Sibelius. In addition, jazz arrangers and Hollywood composers came to be vastly intrigued with its devices, with the result that of all the idioms of twentieth-century music, the Impressionist is the one most familiar to the American public.

Frederick Delius (1862–1934)

"For me music is very simple. It is the expression of a poetic and emotional nature."

Delius's music evokes the English landscape and its seasons: the vernal freshness of spring, the short-lived rapture of summer, the sadness of autumn. His is a gentle lyricism compounded of dreams and longing, a passionate paean to the transience of all earthly things. His countrymen justly regard him as "the most poetic composer born in England."

Delius consistently exalted the emotional aspect of music over the structural. "Music is an outburst of the soul. It is not experimental analysis, like chemistry. There is really only one quality for great music, and that is emotion." One can trace a certain kinship between

Delius's sensibility and that of Debussy. All the same, he evolved his style independently of the French master. He shares certain traits with Debussy, such as a fondness for modal scales and blocklike chords in parallel motion, for poetic landscape and twilight moods. He also shared Debussy's aversion to the complicated thematic work of the German symphony. In all this he is a true Impressionist. Yet one has only to listen to his music to realize how greatly he differs from Debussy, particularly in his liking for a full orchestral sound, his virile handling of the brass, his frank emotionalism, and his subjective approach to nature. His music is suffused with rapture. It represents what his biographer Peter Warlock regarded as "the sunset of that great period of music which is called Romantic." Thence springs

A drawing of Delius in 1932 by Edmond Xavier Kapp (b. 1890).

the retrospective, gently elegiac quality of his music—what has aptly been called his ecstatic melancholy.

Sea Drift (1904), a setting of verses culled from Walt Whitman's *Leaves of Grass,* is a large work for solo baritone, chorus, and orchestra that reveals the composer at his best. From Whitman too he derived the text for his last big choral work, *Songs of Farewell* (1932). *A Mass of Life,* for soloists, chorus, and orchestra (1904–1905), is based on a text drawn from Nietzsche's *Thus Spake Zarathustra.* Among the orchestral works are the nocturne *Paris: The Song of a Great City* (1899); *Brigg Fair,* an English rhapsody in the form of variations on a popular tune (1907); two *Dance Rhapsodies* (1908, 1911); and the fantasy *In a Summer Garden* (1908). The most effective of his operas is *A Village Romeo and Juliet* (1901), ''a lyric drama in six pictures'' on a libretto adapted by Jelka Delius from Gottfried Keller's novel. Presented in recent years by the New York City Opera in an imaginative production based on film projections, the work has proved to be a moving experience in the theater.

On Hearing the First Cuckoo in Spring (1912) can serve as a fine introduction to Delius's art. This lovely minature is for small orchestra, that is, for strings, woodwinds, and horns without trumpets, trombones, tuba, or percussion. The theme is a serene melody whose symmetrical four-measure structure gives it a folklike simplicity. The tune is sung by the violins, its modal harmony imparting to it an unmistakable English character:

Sensuous longing, so richly present in Delius's music, is a quality often associated with English poetry. *On Hearing the First Cuckoo in Spring* captures the same sentiment as Browning's ''Oh, to be in England / Now that April's there,'' or Kipling's ''Give me back one day in England / for it's Spring in England now!'' When Delius wrote the piece he had been living in France for almost a quarter century. One can well understand the nostalgia of the expatriate that found its way into this music.

Delius's tireless champion, Sir Thomas Beecham, regarded him as ''the last great apostle of romance, emotion and beauty in music.'' He cultivated a highly personal idiom of a rather narrow range. But for those who respond to his kind of sensibility, his music speaks eloquently of sweet, wistful things.

Others

A characteristic figure among the non-French Impressionists is Ottorino Respighi (Bologna, 1879–1936, Rome). Respighi produced three symphonic poems that scored international hits: *Le fontane di Roma* (The Fountains of Rome, 1917); *I pini di Roma* (The Pines of Rome, 1924); and *Feste romane* (Roman Festivals, 1929). Among his works were eight operas, three ballets, the one-act "mystery" *Maria egiziaca* (Mary of Egypt, 1932); also a quantity of orchestral and chamber music, concertos, and a number of effective songs. Respighi was a facile composer with a talent for orchestration and a knack for writing music that was infallibly pleasant. He blended Debussyan Impressionism with the sumptuous orchestral panoply of Richard Strauss, added a touch of the exotic which he had imbibed during a brief period of study with Rimsky-Korsakov, and projected the result with the expansive lyricism that was his birthright as an Italian. This novel combination of elements was destined for success, especially since the dazzling colors and surging rhetoric of his music were made to order for virtuoso conductors. He was, in consequence, one of the most frequently performed composers of the second quarter of the century. The chances are that time will not deal kindly with his works except, perhaps, in his homeland. Elsewhere his vogue is on the wane.

That Impressionism could be combined with national elements is demonstrated by the music of the Polish composer Karol Szymanowski (Timoshovka, Ukraine, 1882–1937, Lausanne, Switzerland), who brought to the idiom a Slavic intensity and rich chromaticism all his own. Szymanowski's *La Fontaine d'Aréthuse* (Fountain of Arethusa, 1915), for violin, shows his involvement with the Debussyan idiom. His experiments with atonal and polytonal effects broadened the expressive base of his idiom, as is clear from the *Third Symphony* (1916). While spending some time at a health resort in the Tatras region, Szymanowski heard the ancient songs and dances of the Polish mountaineers. He was struck by the primitive power of the folk melodies, their irregular rhythms and modal turns of phrase. This new interest resulted in the ballet *Harnasie* (1926), and in mazurkas, Polish dances for piano, religious choral works, and songs. In these, as in abstract instrumental works like the *Symphonie concer-tante* for piano and orchestra (1934), Szymanowski struck root in Polish soil and enriched his art by an imaginative use of folk melody. We should mention also his two violin concertos (1922, 1933), the opera *King Roger* (1924), and the *Stabat Mater*. Szymanowski's best music reveals a poetic sensibility. For his countrymen he is a major figure.

Despite the many composers who were attracted to its dreamlike idiom, we are able from our vantage point to see that Impressionism was largely a one-man movement. Debussy's procedures were so special, so easily recognized, that it grew to be practically impossible to write Impressionistic music without sounding like him. The result was that composers were forced to seek other modes of expression.

By excluding pathos and the heroic element, Impressionism narrowed the human appeal of music. But on its own premises it created an enchanting art that opened up a world of dream and fantasy. It introduced harmonic procedures that were of crucial importance to the new music. And it captured a moment of exquisite beauty in a twilight period of European culture.

19 · Away from Impressionism: Erik Satie (1866-1925)

"Am I French? But of course! Why would you want a man of my age not to be French? You surprise me. . . ."

Erik Satie was one of the first to see that Impressionism, despite the significant innovations it had introduced, did not represent the path of the future. He reacted against the element of preciousness in the Impressionist aesthetic, as well as against the luscious complex harmonies cultivated by Debussy and his followers. In raising the slogan of a simple, everyday music, Satie gave impetus to what became one of the most important currents in musical thinking in the years after the First World War.

His Life

Satie was born in the seaside town of Honfleur, on the Normandy coast. His father was a ship broker, his mother a London-born girl of Scottish parentage. The elder Satie subsequently established himself as a music publisher in Paris. Erik entered the Conservatoire when he was thirteen. From the beginning he manifested that deep-rooted hatred of convention which marked him the eternal rebel. The Conservatoire, citadel of tradition, he remembered to the end of his life as "that vast uncomfortable building" which was like "a jail devoid of any attractive features either inside or out." In characteristic fashion he described the opinion that his teachers held of his talent: "My harmony professor thought I had a gift for the piano, while my piano professor considered that I might be talented as a composer."

He was much preoccupied in early manhood with the Rosicrucian sect, which was oriented toward mystical ideas and medieval rites. Also, he officiated as pianist at a famous cabaret in Montmartre, *Le Chat Noir* (The Black Cat). At about this period he met Debussy. He was twenty-four, Debussy four years his senior, when they became friends. During a discussion with Debussy, Satie came forth with a phrase that became famous: "We ought to have our own music—if possible, without sauerkraut!" He influenced the aesthetic behind *Pelléas et Mélisande*. But when he saw the completed manuscript of Debussy's opera, he realized that there was nothing more for him to do in that direction. "I have to seek something else," he wrote to Jean Cocteau, "or I am lost." Dissatisfaction with his technical attainments led him, at the age of forty, to take an unusual step. He entered the Schola Cantorum to study counterpoint with Vincent d'Indy and Albert Roussel. "At your age," Debussy said to him, "one no longer changes one's skin." "If I fail," Satie retorted, "it means that I haven't got it in me to be a composer."

Some years before this Satie had left Montmartre and settled in the working-class suburb of Arcueil. "In this corner," he said, "one senses the mysterious presence of Our Lady of Lowliness." (He wrote a *Mass for the Poor*.) His early Catholic mysticism had long since been supplanted by Radical Socialism. At Arcueil he spent the rest of his life, known as an eccentric and fun-loving bachelor. Nightly he traversed Paris on foot in order to reach his haunts in Montmartre. "Young men," he wrote, "don't go to the cafés. Listen to the grave voice of one who spent much time in them—but who does not regret it!" He lived very humbly, in a single room. Satie was

Erik Satie.
The Bettmann Archive.

completely unworldly when it came to success or wealth. He handed over his works to the publishers for ridiculous prices. Dedicated to music and poverty, he was faithfully attended by both throughout his life.

Satie was drawn into the artistic ferment that centered about Serge Diaghilev's Russian Ballet; he collaborated with Cocteau, Picasso, and Picabia. In the years after the First World War he achieved a certain measure of fame. He became the champion of the new generation of musicians; specifically, he was the mentor of *Les Six*—a group of young composers that included Darius Milhaud, Arthur Honegger, and Francis Poulenc. So too, toward the end of his life, he guided the destinies of four young men—among them Roger Désormière and Henri Sauguet—who took the title of "École d'Arcueil" to show their admiration for the master who had made that suburb famous. A lingering illness carried him off at the age of fifty-nine. "He died as he had lived—without ever quite ceasing to smile."

His Music

Satie is a controversial figure in the art of our time. His music never won a firm place in the repertory. Yet Ravel maintained that Satie had exerted the greatest influence upon him; while Darius Milhaud claims that each work of Satie's foretold the lines along which French music of the last half century developed. As in the case of Busoni, this sprightly Parisian exerted an influence on musical aesthetics extending far beyond the actual performance of his works.

Satie was the apostle of simplicity. All that smacked of pretentiousness was foreign to his temperament. He strove for a forthright, unaffected music, as free from sentimentality as from the pathos of the grand style: a music stripped of nonessentials down to its "bare bones," as he put it. There could be no better statement of his aesthetic doctrine than his description of the "new spirit" in music: "It teaches us to aim at an emotional simplicity and a firmness of utterance that enable sonorities and rhythms to assert themselves clearly, unequivocal in design and accent, and conceived in a spirit of humility and renunciation." It was this kind of impersonal music that the second quarter of the century desired.

During his mystical phase—the Rosicrucian period—Satie was attracted to Gregorian chant and the medieval modes. He was thus one of the pioneers in the movement away from major-minor tonality. Like Debussy, Satie sought to lead French music away from the symphony of Beethoven and the music-dramas of Wagner. Yet he was equally determined to avoid the vagueness and overrefinement of Impressionism. The individual chord, for him, was never the column of magic that it was for Debussy. Always it was subservient to the needs of his chiseled melodic line. Satie's sober, sparse orchestration—"without sauce," as he called it—helped to usher in the style of writing that dominated the Twenties and Thirties. His years of activity in the cafés of Montmartre developed his flair for the popular songs of the French music hall that played a prominent role in his art. As Virgil Thomson has said, Satie realized that the wisest thing music in the twentieth century could do was to stop taking itself seriously. The unpretentious charm of Satie's works in the popular vein pointed out new fields for composers to cultivate. One has but to mention such works as Milhaud's *Le Boeuf sur le toit,* Poulenc's *Mouvements perpetuels,* or Aaron Copland's *El salón México* to realize how rich was the harvest.

Satie is best known to the public for his early piano pieces: the

Sarabandes (1887), *Gymnopédies* (1888), and *Gnossiennes* (1890). Each set contains three dance pieces in the composer's characteristic manner. These works anticipate certain procedures that later became associated with the music of Debussy, notably the unconventional handling of unresolved chords of the ninth, the modal idiom, and the movement of the harmony in parallel, blocklike formations. They also reveal Satie's fondness for unusual titles: *Gymnopédies* and *Gnossiennes* are words coined by himself to suggest that these sculpturesque dance forms were inspired by Greek antiquity. This music has a grave simplicity. It displays certain hallmarks of Satie's style: short, symmetrical phrases repeated over and over; an airy melodic line, with an easy swing; limpid harmony, whose modal character is brought into focus at the cadences; lightness of texture; and establishment at the outset of a rhythmic pattern that persists throughout. In some of his piano music Satie omitted barlines as well as time and key signatures—a daring step in the 1890s.

The works written during and after his studies at the Schola Cantorum, from around 1905 until the eve of the First World War, foreshadow—in their emphasis on contrapuntal texture, economy, and sobriety of style—the Neoclassic orientation that was to establish itself during the Twenties. In these pieces Satie continued to indulge his penchant for droll, mystifying titles. The list includes *Pièces froides* (Cold Pieces, 1897), with its *Airs à faire fuir* (Melodies to Make One Flee); *Trois morceaux en forme de poire* (Three Pieces in the Shape of a Pear, 1903); *Croquis et agaceries d'un gros bonhomme de bois* (Sketches and Annoyances of a Wooden Man, 1913); and *Embryons desséchés* (Dried-up Embryos, 1913). According to Jean Cocteau, Satie's titles were meant "as a good-humored piece of ill-humor, maliciously directed against *Moons Descending on the Temple that Was* and *Sunken Cathedrals.*"

Closely related to the humor of the titles were the admonitions to the performer, now whimsical, now nonsensical, that were strewn throughout the music. Here too we find a desire to parody the poetic directions of the Impressionists. "Like a nightingale with toothache . . . sheepishly and coldly . . . light as an egg . . . with tenderness and fatality. . . ." Rollo Myers, in his perceptive biography of the composer, finds in these sallies "the bitterness of an essentially lonely man who is obliged to camouflage all his serious work in order to forestall the criticism he secretly fears."

Satie possessed a literary gift. His letters, like the essays he wrote throughout his career, abound in a personal brand of humor that ranges from mordant irony to inspired nonsense. A few examples will suffice to give the flavor of his wit. "Although our information is inaccurate, we do not guarantee it. . . . M. Ravel refuses the Legion of Honor, but all his music accepts it. . . . I came into a very young world in a very old time. . . . Before writing a work, I go round it several times accompanied by myself. . . . When I was young they said to me, 'You will see when you're fifty.' I am fifty, and I have seen nothing. . . . Last year I gave several lectures on 'Intelligence and the Appreciation of Music among Animals.' Today I am going to speak to you about 'Intelligence and the Appreciation of Music among Critics.' The subject is very similar. . . ."

The most significant work of Satie's late period is *Socrate,* a "symphonic drama in three parts" based on the dialogues of Plato. This was completed in 1919. It is scored for four soprano soloists and chamber orchestra. For his text Satie drew upon Victor Cousin's translation of the *Symposium,* the *Phaedrus,* and *Phaedo.* This contemplative work embodies the Neoclassic ideal of simplicity and economy of means. The melodic line has the archaic quality that Satie derived from Gregorian chant. The limpid orchestration brings out the lines of the polyphony. The consistent understatement and the absence of any desire to create an effect make for an inner quietude of spirit.

"Only a very remarkable personality," wrote the English critic Wilfrid Mellers, "could attain to the degree of impersonality which makes this music, not one man's loneliness, but an aspect of the modern consciousness transformed into sound." The music of this "forerunner of genius," as he has been called, was amazingly prophetic of much that came after. The music of our time owes much to Erik Satie.

III. *Three Revolutionary Works*

"The secret of the tone must be always pursued anew."

ARNOLD SCHOENBERG

20 Béla Bartók: *Allegro barbaro*

"A genuine peasant melody of our land is a musical example of perfected art. I consider it quite as much of a masterpiece—in miniature—as a Bach fugue or Mozart sonata is a masterpiece in the larger forms."

The New Nationalism

Nationalism in music was a powerful current within nineteenth-century Romanticism. National tensions on the Continent—the pride of the conquering nations and the struggles for freedom of the subjugated ones—gave rise to emotions that found ready expression in music. The German war of liberation against Napoleon inspired Carl Maria von Weber and created a receptive atmosphere for his opera *Der Freischütz*. Poland's struggle for freedom from Czarist rule aroused the national poet in Chopin; Franz Liszt explored the Gypsy idiom of his native Hungary. A united Italy seeking independence from Austria found her national artist in Verdi. Wagner reached the

125

zenith of his career in the newly constituted German Empire, which viewed his epic dramas, based on Teutonic legends, as a monument to national pride. Smetana and Dvořák in Bohemia, Grieg in Norway, the Russian national school—these marked the emancipation of the "younger" nations (musically speaking) from the yoke of the three older musical cultures, Italy, Germany, and France. Musical nationalism retained its vigor into the twentieth century. In the Postromantic era national composers appeared in Finland, Hungary, England, Spain, Poland, Czechoslovakia, and Rumania, to be joined a little later by national schools in the United States and Latin America.

Nineteenth-century Nationalism added a variety of idioms to the language of European music. It exploited the picturesque aspects of local color and fed the Romantic predilection for mood and atmosphere. By associating music with love of country, Nationalism aligned the art with the great social and political movements of the age, so that composers were able to give expression to the deepest aspirations of millions of people. The Romantic composers idealized the life of the folk. They heard peasant tunes through a poetic haze of myth and legend. If these tunes departed from the major-minor scale or from accepted metrical patterns, the composer "corrected" the irregularities. In general, the romantics regarded the folk song as workable material to be embedded—like some piquant flavoring—in an orchestral movement molded to the formulas of Classical symphonism.

Twentieth-century Nationalism, understandably, took a different turn. The new Nationalists were determined to preserve the tunes of the folk singers in as accurate a form as possible. They went into the villages with recording equipment and mastered the techniques of scientific research. And when they used folk tunes in their own works, they took care not to violate the essential character of the ancient melodies. Typical of the new movement was the research of Bartók and Zoltán Kodály in Hungary, of Ralph Vaughan Williams and Gustav Holst in England. "It was not a question," wrote Bartók, "of taking unique melodies in any which way and then incorporating them, or parts of them, in our works, there to develop them according to the traditional formulas. What we had to do was to divine the spirit of this unknown music and to make this spirit, so difficult to describe in words, the basis of our own works." From these expeditions Bartók derived a basic element of his art. "Those days I spent in the villages among the peasants," he recalled later, "were the happiest of my life. In order really to feel the vitality of this music one must, so to speak, have lived it. This is possible only when one

Béla Bartók recording folk songs in a North Hungarian village. (Photograph taken around 1908 by Zoltan Kodály.) Copyright Collection of G. D. Hackett, New York.

comes to know it by direct contact with the peasants." And he summed up his experience in a statement that could serve as a motto for all the twentieth-century Nationalists: "What is the best way for a composer to reap the full benefits of his studies in peasant music? It is to assimilate the idiom of this music so completely that he is able to forget all about it and use it as his musical mother tongue."

Primitivism

The end of Romanticism mirrored the decline of an epoch—of the myriad impulses that had burst into flower with the French Revolution and had brought modern industrial society through its first phase. A great era in Western culture was drawing to a close, its end marked by the First World War.

The spiritual exhaustion of European society at the opening of our century showed itself in an indefinable restlessness. Art sought to escape its overrefinement, to purify and renew itself in fresh streams of feeling. There was a desire everywhere to recapture the spontaneity and the freedom from inhibition that were supposed to characterize primitive life. The fine arts turned for inspiration to the

Twentieth-century artists were strongly influenced by the abstract qualities of primitive sculpture, absorbing elements of these highly schematized yet mysterious configurations into their own abstract compositions. Debating Stool, *New Guinea. The Metropolitan Museum of Art. Michael C. Rockefeller Memorial Collection of Primitive Art.*

magnificent abstraction of African sculpture. Concurrently, musicians discovered the dynamism of African rhythm.

Primitivism was a reaction from the overrefinement of such artists as Debussy and Ravel. Its adherents favored simple, clear-cut tunes of folk character that revolved around a central note and moved within a narrow compass; massive harmonies based on blocklike chords moving in parallel formation with harshly percussive effect; and a strong impulsion to a tonal center. Much in evidence were ostinato rhythms repeated with an almost obsessive effect and a rugged orchestration featuring massed sonorities which contrasted sharply with the coloristic subtleties of the Impressionists.

Twentieth-century composers found inspiration not only in African music but also in the songs and dances of the borderlands of Western culture—southeastern Europe, Asiatic Russia, and the Near East. Out of the unspoiled, vigorous folk music of these regions came rhythms of an elemental power that tapped fresh sources of feeling and imagination. Milestones in this development were such pieces as Bartók's *Allegro barbaro* and Stravinsky's *Le Sacre du printemps* (The Rite of Spring).

Allegro barbaro

Bartók's famous piano piece *Allegro barbaro* (1911) is a milestone in several ways. To begin with, it sums up the new Nationalism in that its wildly unrestrained Magyar spirit is no longer held in check—as in the works of Liszt—by the traditions of Western music. In this astonishing work Bartók assimilated the spirit of true Hungarian music so completely that, to quote his own comment, he was "able to forget all about it and use it as his musical mother tongue."

The *barbaro* of the title sums up the new current of Primitivism that was to invigorate European art on the eve of World War I. The piece caused a furor when it was first performed; Bartók's friend and colleague Zoltán Kodály described the opposition it aroused: "People spoke of a great talent on the wrong path, lost down a blind alley, of morbid tendencies—in short, all the phrases to be expected of dismayed Philistines and slaves of convention." The pulsating vigor of the piece is strengthened by several traits mentioned earlier in this chapter: a simple, clear-cut tune that revolves around a central note within a narrow compass; massive, blocklike chords that create a harshly percussive effect; and an ostinato rhythm repeated with obsessive insistence.

We have here a white-note melody against a predominantly black-note accompaniment; in effect, two independent planes of harmony (polyharmony). Bartók is looking ahead to the use of two or more keys at the same time (a procedure we will discuss in the next chapter). Notable throughout is the primordial power of the rhythm. The nineteenth century, we have pointed out, was so preoccupied with exploring the resources of harmony that rhythm was somewhat left behind. It remained for the early twentieth century to restore the balance.

A second theme is introduced against a syncopated accompaniment. After a big climax dies down, the opening tune returns in a

calmer mood and with a different harmonic background. This time, melody and harmony are part of a single stream, as you can see if you compare both versions:

The second theme returns, gathering force until it erupts in the climactic passage, which is a splendid example of the steely "hammered" chords that introduced a new sound into twentieth-century style. Where nineteenth-century composers used dissonant harmony for sensuous color or emotional expression, the new harmony explored the dissonance as a percussive clang, a jabbing thrust of sound capable of engendering tension. The following example shows Bartók's percussive harmony at its most powerful:

In a passage such as this the single chord is not conceived in relation to what comes before or after. It exists rather as a vertical entity, to be savored for its own color, resiliency, and thrust. This emphasis upon the individual chord is one of the prime traits of twentieth-century harmony. Dissonance, emancipated from the restrictions imposed upon it by functional harmony, has become a value in itself.

The masters of piano style during the Romantic era—Schubert and Schumann, Chopin, Liszt, Franck and Brahms—used the piano as a singing instrument. The new music, on the other hand, cast it in a different role by exploiting its remarkable capacities for percussive rhythm and harmony. Bartók's piece well illustrates this new approach, as a result of which the piano became a self-sufficient percussion instrument.

Allegro barbaro still sounds amazingly fresh and original. In its own day it was nothing short of epoch making.

21 Igor Stravinsky: *Le Sacre du printemps* (The Rite of Spring)

"Very little immediate tradition lies behind *Le Sacre du printemps*. I had only my ear to help me. I heard and I wrote what I heard."

Polytonality

Tonality implies the supremacy of a single key and a single tone center. Composers in the past made the most out of the contrast between two keys heard in succession. Modern composers intensify the contrast by presenting them simultaneously.

The simultaneous use of two keys (bitonality) and of several (polytonality) came to the fore in the music of Bartók and Stravinsky, whence it entered the vocabulary of the age. Toward the end of a polytonal piece, one key is generally permitted to assert itself over the others, and in this way an impression is restored of orderly progression toward a central point. Polytonality is used to bring out the different planes of the harmony. By putting two or more streams of chords in different keys the friction between them is immeasurably heightened. Piano music especially lends itself to this technique, right and left hands playing progressions of chords in different keys. Because the tension comes from the clash of keys, each stream of harmony must be rooted solidly in its own key. Polytonality, then, does not reject the principle of key. It merely extends this principle in a characteristically twentieth-century manner.

During the Twenties, composers were fond of combining three, four, or even five tonalities. However, it soon became apparent that most listeners are incapable of assimilating more than two keys at once with any degree of awareness. When three or more keys are combined, the musics tends to blur into dissonant passages that belong to no key at all. As a result, in recent years composers have written far less music in the polytonal idiom. Bitonality, on the other hand, has remained a most effective procedure.

Here is the famous chord associated with the luckless hero of Stravinsky's ballet *Petrushka*. It is the kernel out of which the work grew: a C-major arpeggio superposed upon one in F-sharp major:

Incidentally, musical terminology being as loose as it is, the term polytonal has come to be applied to any passage that involves more than one key. In other words, it includes bitonality.

Le Sacre du printemps: Scenes of Pagan Russia

"The idea of *"Le Sacre du printemps* came to me while I was still composing *The Firebird.* I had dreamed a scene of pagan ritual in which a chosen sacrificial virgin danced herself to death." Out of this vision grew the work that has remained the most celebrated example of the cult of Primitivism that swept European art in the years prior to World War I. More important, *The Rite of Spring* (1913) set forth the lineaments of a new musical language based on the percussive use of dissonance, polyrhythms, and polytonality. Here Stravinsky's granite-like orchestral sonority takes on the "vibrating transparency," to use Erik Satie's fine phrase, which we associate with it. The work is scored for a large orchestra: 2 piccolos, 2 flutes, flute in G, 4 oboes, English horn, clarinet in E-flat, bass clarinet, 4 bassoons, double basoon; 8 horns, 4 trumpets, trumpet in D, bass trumpet, 3 trombones, 2 tubas; 4 kettledrums, small kettledrums, bass drum, tambourine, cymbals, antique cymbals, triangle, guiro (a Latin American instrument consisting of a serrated gourd scraped with a wooden stick); and the usual complement of strings. Also, in certain passages, a second bass clarinet, second double bassoon, and 2 Wagner tubas.

Part I. *Adoration of the Earth.* The Introduction is intended to evoke the birth of Spring. A long-limbed melody is introduced by the bassoon, taking on a curious remoteness from the circumstance that it lies in the instrument's uppermost register.

The awakening of the earth is suggested in the orchestra. On stage, a group of young girls is discovered before the sacred mound, holding a long garland. The Sage appears and leads them toward the mound. The orchestra erupts into a climax, after which the bassoon melody returns.

Dance of the Adolescents. Dissonant chords in the dark register of the strings exemplify Stravinsky's "elemental pounding"; their percussive quality is heightened by the use of polytonal harmonies:

A physical excitement attends the dislocation of the accent, which is underlined by syncopated chords hurled out by eight horns. A theme emerges on the bassoons, moving within a narrow range around a central tone, with a suggestion of primitive power.

The main theme of the movement, a more endearing melody in folk style, is introduced by the horn. Stravinsky expands this idea by means of the repetition technique so characteristic of the Russian school.

Game of Abduction. The youths and maidens on the stage form into two phalanxes which in turn approach and withdraw from one another. Fanfares on the woodwinds and brass remind us that the composer of these measures studied with the creator of *Scheherazade.*

Spring Dance. A pastoral melody is played by the high clarinet in E-flat and the bass clarinet, against a sustained trill on the flutes. Modal harmonies create on archaic atmosphere. Four couples are left on stage. Each man lifts a girl on his back and with measured tread executes the Rounds of Spring. The movement is *sostenuto e pesante* (sustained and heavy), with blocklike harmonies propelled by ostinato rhythms.

Games of the Rival Cities—Entrance of the Sage—Dance of the Earth. The peremptory beating of drums summons the braves of the rival tribes to a display of prowess. The main idea is presented by two muted trumpets. Notice that the third measure repeats the melodic curve of the two preceding ones, but with a rhythmic dislocation which causes the notes to fall on different beats within the measure:

The orchestration evokes a neolithic landscape. The score abounds in orchestral "finds," such as the braying sound produced by a simultaneous trill in trombones, horns, clarinets, oboes, and flutes over an ostinato in the double bass. The Entrance of the Sage touches off a powerful crescendo rising over several ostinato patterns that unfold simultaneously. An abrupt silence—a pianissimo chord in the strings as the dancers prostrate themselves in mystic adoration of the earth. Then they leap to their feet, and to music of the sheerest physicality perform the Dance of the Earth.

Part II. *The Sacrifice*. The Prelude, a "night piece," creates a brooding atmosphere. The Sage and the maidens sit motionless, staring into the fire in front of the sacred mound. They must choose the Elect One who will be sacrificed to ensure the fertility of the earth. A poignant melodic idea in Russia folk style, first presented by the muted violins in harmonics, pervades the movement. (For an explanation of harmonics see Appendix I-h.)

The music is desolate, but there is nothing subjective about it. This desolation is of the soil, not the soul.

Mystic Circle of Young Girls. The theme of the preceding movement alternates with a melody presented by the alto flute, which

stands out against a dissonant background. The two themes are repeated in various registers with continual changes of color. The major-minor ambiguity goes hand in hand with the soft colors of the orchestration.

The Dance in Adoration of the Chosen Virgin has the Stravinskyan muscularity of rhythm. The eighth note is the metric unit, upon which is projected a series of uneven meters that change continually, sometimes with each measure. The piece develops into a frenzied dance.

Evocation of the Ancestors—Ritual Act of the Old Men. After a violent opening, the movement settles down to a kind of "Scythian blues." An English horn solo presents a sinuously chromatic figure against a background of primordial drums and pizzicato chords in the bass. The music carries a suggestion of swaying bodies and shuffling feet.

Sacrificial Dance of the Chosen Virgin. In this, the climactic number of the ballet, the elected maiden dances until she falls dead. The movement mounts in fury to the point where the Elect One has fulfilled the sacrifice. The men in wild excitement bear her body to the

Sketches by Valentin Hugo of the Sacrificial Dance of the Chosen Virgin for the ballet Le Sacre du printemps. *André Meyer Collection.*

foot of the mound. There is the scraping sound of the guiro, used here for the first time in European orchestral music; an ascending run

on the flutes; and with a fortissimo growl in the orchestra this luminous score comes to an end.

The ballet was presented in Paris in the spring of 1913. The opening night was one of the most scandalous in modern musical history; the revolutionary score touched off a near-riot. People hooted, screamed, slapped each other, and were persuaded that what they were hearing "constituted a blasphemous attempt to destroy music as an art." A year later the composer was vindicated when *Le Sacre*, presented at a symphony concert under Pierre Monteux, was received with enthusiasm and established itself as one of the masterpieces of the new music. Today it is recognized as probably the single most influential score of our century.

22 Arnold Schoenberg: *Pierrot lunaire*

"The great event in my life then was the performance of *Pierrot lunaire* I had heard in December 1912 in Berlin."

IGOR STRAVINSKY

Expressionism

"There is only one greatest goal," wrote Arnold Schoenberg, "towards which the artist strives: to express himself." Expressionism was the German answer to French Impressionism. Where the Latin genius delighted in luminous impressions received from the outer world, the Germanic dug down to the hidden regions of the soul. Where Parisian artists cultivated a refined, highly pictorial nature poetry, those within the middle European orbit rejected the reality about them in order to fasten their gaze on the landscape within. In Vienna, where Sigmund Freud developed the theories of psychoanalysis, artists tried to capture for art the shadowy terrain of the unconscious. *Expressionismus* set up inner experience as the only reality. Through the symbolism of dreams and the glorification of the irrational, it aspired to release the primordial impulses that intellectual man too long had suppressed.

As with Impressionism, the impetus for the Expressionist movement came from painting and poetry. Schoenberg was influenced by the painters Wassily Kandinsky (1866–1944) and Oscar Kokoschka (1886–), Paul Klee (1879–1940) and Franz Marc (1880–1916), by the poets Stefan George (1868–1933) and Richard Dehmel (1863–1920)— even as Debussy had been influenced by Monet and Manet, Mallarmé and Verlaine. The distorted images on the canvases of the Expressionist painters issued from the realm of the unconscious: hallucinated visions that defied the traditional notion of beauty in order to express more powerfully the artist's inner self. In similar fashion, musical Expressionism rejected what had hitherto been accepted as beautiful; this rejection produced new conceptions of melody, harmony and tonality, rhythm, color and form.

Within a twentieth-century framework, Expressionism retained certain attitudes inherited from the nineteenth century. It took over the Romantic love for overwhelming effect and high-pitched emotion, for the strange, the macabre, and the grotesque. Expressionism, actually, may be viewed as the last gesture of a dying Romanticism. Its search for the most powerful means of communication presents certain elements of the Romantic style in their most exacerbated form. Expressionism is familiar to the public through the painting of Kandinsky and Klee, Franz Marc and Kokoschka; the writing of Franz Kafka; the dancing of Mary Wigman (whose aesthetic was acclimated in the United States by the art of Martha Graham); and through such epoch-making films as *The Cabinet of Dr. Caligari* and Fritz Lang's *M*. Expressionist tendencies were already apparent in European opera in Strauss's *Salome* and *Elektra* and reached their full tide in the theater works of Schoenberg and his disciple Alban Berg. Within the orbit of our own culture, Expressionistic elements are to be discerned in the work of such dissimilar artists as James Joyce, William Faulkner, and Tennessee Williams.

Expressionism was the suppressed, the agonized romanticism of an antiromantic age. Its violence was the violence of a world overwhelmed, one that turned to the unconscious and the irrational in its

In contrast to the art of Kandinsky and other prominent German Expressionists, Paul Klee's imagery was strongly rooted in nature. His works created fantasy out of abstract elements such as this precisely drawn fish on a platter surrounded by unidentifiable shapes and objects. Around the Fish, 1926, *by Paul Klee (1879–1940). Collection,* The Museum of Modern Art, *New York. Abby Aldrich Rockefeller Fund.*

flight from a reality no longer to be controlled or understood. The musical language of Expressionism took its point of departure from the ultrachromatic idiom of *Tristan and Isolde.* It favored a hyperexpressive harmonic language linked to inordinately wide leaps in the melody and to the use of instruments in their extreme registers. Previous composers had always set texts in accordance with the natural inflections of the language; Expressionist composers deliberately distorted the normal accentuation of words, just as Expressionist actors distorted the normal pattern of gesture, in order to secure a heightening of tension, a reality transcending the real. Expressionism allied music to "strong" plots replete with violence and unusual behavior, the best example of which is the hallucinatory atmosphere surrounding Wozzeck, the hero of Berg's Expressionist opera. Most important of all, Expressionism aspired to maximum intensity all the time, an unflagging, unrelenting intensity; hence it had to reject those elements—such as the consonance in music—

which represented a slackening of tension. In its preoccupation with states of soul, Expressionism sought ever more powerful means of communicating emotion and soon reached the boundaries of what was possible within the tonal system. Expressionist music was inevitably impelled to push beyond.

Atonality

Tonality in European music, we saw, was based on the principle that seven of the twelve tones belong to a key, while five lie outside it. The whole development of chromatic harmony in the nineteenth century tended to obliterate the distinction between these two groups. Wagner had pushed chromaticism as far as possible while still retaining the sense of a tonic. Schoenberg took the next step. The time had come, he argued, to do away with the distinction between the seven diatonic tones and the five chromatic ones. The twelve tones, he maintained, must be treated as equals. They must be regarded as being freely related to each other rather than to a central tone. By giving them equal importance, Schoenberg hoped to make it possible to exploit fully all the resources of the chromatic scale.

To do away with the sense of the tonic means abandoning a principle that appeared to be as fundamental to the musical universe as gravity is to the physical. (How fundamental becomes apparent if we sing the *do-re-mi-fa* scale and stop on *ti*, resisting the almost physical compulsion to continue to *do*.) Schoenberg maintained that the major-minor system had not existed for more than three centuries, so there was no reason to suppose it could not be superseded. "Tonality is not an eternal law of music," he declared, "but simply a means toward the achievement of musical form." The time had come to seek new means.

The music of Schoenberg and his school has been described by the label atonality. He disliked the term as much as Debussy did impressionism. "I regard the expression *atonal* as meaningless. Atonal can only signify something that does not correspond to the nature of tone. A piece of music will necessarily always be tonal insofar as a relation exists from tone to tone." He suggested that his innovations be described as pantonal, as they aimed at "the synthesis of all tonalities"—the relationship of all tones to one another. But atonality took root, for to most people it summed up the cardinal point of Schoenberg's teaching—his rejection of tonality.

The concept of key, it will be recalled, depends on the distinction

between consonance and dissonance: the dissonant chord constitutes the element of tension which finds resolution in the ultimate
consonance, the tonic. But the consonance, according to Schoenberg,
had become so hackneyed, so obvious, that it could no longer play a
fruitful role in art. Other contemporary composers, faced with the
same problem, sought to inject vitality into consonances by adding
tones that had hitherto been considered foreign to them. Schoenberg
went them one better by discarding consonance altogether. Dissonance now became the norm: his music moves from one level of dissonance to another. He justified this procedure on the grounds that
consonance and dissonance are different not in kind, but only in
degree. "Dissonant tones," he maintained, "appear later among the
overtones, for which reason the ear is less acquainted with them.
Dissonances are only the remote consonances." There could thus be
no "foreign" or chromatic tones. "The alleged tones believed to be
foreign to harmony do not exist. They are merely tones foreign to our
accepted harmonic system."

By eliminating the consonance Schoenberg moved toward a
music that functions always at maximum tension. This circumstance
imparts to it its furious restlessness, what Schoenberg's biographer
Dika Newlin has called "its well-nigh hysterical emotionality." Dissonance resolving to consonance is symbolically an optimistic act, af-
firming the triumph of rest over tension, of order over chaos. Atonal
music appeared, significantly, at a moment in European culture
when belief in that triumph was beginning to be shaken. It is music
that lends itself to moods of convulsive intensity. Inevitably it established itself as the language of German Expressionism.

Pierrot lunaire

Schoenberg's most celebrated work (1912) grew out of a request
by the Viennese actress Albertine Zahm for a piece that she could
recite against a musical background. This commission became the
external stimulus for him to experiment with a problem that had interested him for some time: how to bring spoken word and music as
close together as possible.

In his search for a solution he was led to invent *Sprechstimme* or
"spoken voice" (also known as *Sprechgesang*, "speech-song"), a kind
of declamation in which the vocal melody is spoken, rather than
sung, on exact pitches and in strict rhythm. As Schoenberg explained
it, the reciter sounded the written note at first but abandoned it by

Schoenberg conducting Pierrot lunaire *with soprano Erica Stiedry-Wagner at Town Hall, New York, 1940. Sketch by Dolbin.*

rising or falling in pitch immediately after. There resulted an extraordinarily flexible, weirdly effective vocal line that became a prime vehicle for the moods associated with Expressionism.

In 1884 the Belgian poet Albert Giraud, a disciple of the Symbolists—he was especially influenced by Verlaine—had published a cycle of fifty short poems he called *Pierrot lunaire* (Pierrot in the Moonlight, or Moonstruck Pierrot). His Pierrot was the poet-rascal-clown whose chalk-white face, passing abruptly from laughter to tears, enlivened every puppet show and pantomime in Europe. (In Russia he was Petrushka, in Italy Pagliaccio.) Giraud's poems were liberally spiced with those elements of the macabre and the bizarre that so well suited the taste of end-of-century "decadence." Translated into German by Otto Erich Hartleben, the poems fired Schoenberg's imagination. He selected twenty-one for his Opus 21 (he was a firm believer in numerology), arranged them in three groups of seven, and set them for *Sprechstimme* and an ensemble of five players using eight instruments: piano, flute and piccolo, clarinet and bass clarinet, violin and viola, and cello. The work, he explained, was conceived "in a light, ironical, satirical tone."

Tonality had made possible the development of large instrumental forms in Western music. At this stage in Schoenberg's career, when he was abandoning tonality, he was drawn to small forms within which he could more easily work out the problems of his new atonal language. Giraud's short poems enabled him to create a series of miniatures for which the *Sprechstimme* served as a unifying element. This unity was balanced by the utmost variety of structure, texture, and instrumentation from one piece to the next. Each of the poems is a rondeau, a French verse form of thirteen lines in which the first and second are repeated as the seventh and eighth, and the first reappears again as the last.

1. *Mondestranken* (Moondrunk). For flute, violin, piano, cello. Lively, 2/4. "The wine that only eyes may drink / Pours from the moon in waves at nightfall . . ." (For the complete German-English text, see Appendix II.) The piano announces a motive that will be associated with Pierrot throughout the work. Here it appears as an ostinato figure:

Flute and violin trace delicate patterns against the arabesques of the piano as the *Sprechstimme* creates its eerie atmosphere. At the third stanza, where Pierrot gets drunk on moonlight, there is a change of mood and texture, underlined by the vigorous entrance of the cello.

2. *Colombine*. For flute, clarinet, violin, piano. Flowing, 3/4. Pierrot's longing for Colombine is suggested by a romantic violin solo. It is heard against a piano accompaniment that is more chordal in texture than in the first number. Wide leaps in the *Sprechstimme* underline its pleading character. Flute and clarinet enter toward the end, where Pierrot yearns to tear petals from the roses of moonlight and scatter them on Colombine's auburn hair. The Pierrot motive is heard in the violin in a new version:

The pitches of this motive change with each reappearance. It retains only its overall shape and rhythmic profile.

3. *Der Dandy* (The Dandy). For piccolo, clarinet, piano. Lively,

duple time. Pierrot, "the silent dandy from Bergamo," sits at his dressing table daubing his face in moonlight. His languid mood is indicated by the Pierrot motive in augmentation (longer note values):

The reference to Bergamo suggests the origins of the *commedia dell'arte*. (Debussy paid homage to the town in his *Suite bergamasque*, which includes his own invocation to the moon, the ever popular *Clair de lune*.) In the third stanza, Pierrot racks his brain and wonders, "How shall I make up today?" This is mirrored in the music by a great retard and a slow pace, and at the whispered final line, the music ascends to the highest register.

4. *Eine blasse Wäscherin* (A Pale Washerwoman). For flute, clarinet, violin. Flowing, 4/4. For the first time the piano drops out, which makes a decisive contrast in texture. The moon becomes a pale washerwoman who washes her pale linen in the pale moonlight. The three instruments unfold a quiet, choralelike passage. At the point in the poem where a gentle breeze stirs the stream, the instrumental lines become mobile and break up into small self-generating cells. How subtly the music reflects the poet's pale imagery.

5. *Valse de Chopin*. For flute, clarinet, bass clarinet, piano. Slow waltz, 3/4. Giraud finds a morbid fascination in Chopin's music, which he compares to the pale drop of blood that stains the lips of an invalid. He emphasizes that connection between illness and fierce desire which Thomas Mann projected so powerfully in his *Magic Mountain*. In the second half of the piece the clarinet gives way to the bass clarinet, whose darker sonority underlines the sweet melancholy waltzes that haunt the poet's imagination. Haunting, too, is the short instrumental postlude.

6. *Madonna*. For flute, bass clarinet, violin, cello, piano. Moderately slow, 4/4. A religious mood. "Rise, o Mother of All Sorrows, on the altar of my verses!" The steady stride of pizzicato sounds on the cello underpins the delicate traceries of flute and bass clarinet. We encounter here those enormous leaps in the vocal line that were to become so pronounced a trait of the Schoenbergian school. Characteristic is the leap of almost two octaves when the opening word, *Steig* (Rise), returns:

Violin and piano enter at the end, so that for the first time all five instruments are playing. This fuller texture sets off the three tragic chords with which the piano part ends.

7. *Der kranke Mond* (The Sick Moon). For flute. Very slow, 6/4. Pierrot addresses the moon, who is deathly ill of unappeasable longing. Of the seven pieces in Part One, this shows the lightest texture. Voice and flute unfold in a dolorous counterpoint, with bits of imitation between them. The Pierrot motive is woven into the flute's sad song:

Notice the shuddering intonations with which the voice part ends.

In Part Two, Giraud's poems become more macabre, emphasizing those elements of the satanic and the grotesque that the end-of-century decadents took over from Romantic literature and turned to their own use. To balance this heightened Expressionism, Schoenberg turns to more structural forms. For example, Part Two opens with a passacaglia, a majestic form of the Baroque (seventeenth and early eighteenth century) in slow triple meter. The passacaglia is based on a short phrase in the bass that is repeated over and over while the upper voices weave a continuous variation above it. The ostinato can also be shifted to an upper voice, as in the most famous example of the form, Bach's *Passacaglia and Fugue in C minor*.

8. *Nacht* (Night). For bass clarinet, cello, piano. With motion, 3/2. Night comes, somber and shadowy, as the wings of giant moths blot out the sun. Schoenberg uses the deepest bass register to create an atmosphere heavy with foreboding. The piece grows out of a three-note figure that is announced at the beginning. As a rule, the basic motive of a passacaglia tends to retain its original shape. Here it is subject to variation, as in the following three versions:

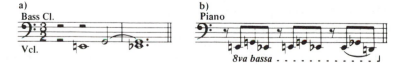

c)
Piano

The piece begins and ends pianissimo, but the middle section rises to a fortissimo climax on the words *Sonne Glanz* (sun's brightness) and moves at a faster pace.

9. *Gebet an Pierrot* (Prayer to Pierrot). For clarinet and piano. Moderate duple meter. The poet begs Pierrot to give him back his laughter; to go back, in other words, to the simple farcical roles of the old Italian comedy. With its sharp profile and forceful thrust, this number makes a vivid contrast with the preceding one. The clarinet tosses off a new, wider-ranging version of the Pierrot motive, on the words *mein Lachen hab ich verlernt!* (I've lost my laughter):

The piano part is remarkably elaborate.

10. *Raub* (Theft). For flute, clarinet, muted violin and cello. Moderate, 4/4. Pierrot commits the ultimate blasphemy. With drunken companions he makes his way into the catacombs to steal the rubies that slumber in dead men's coffins. The blasphemers are paralyzed with fear when the rubies glow at them like so many eyeballs. The tempo accelerates, building up excitement to the point where the would-be robbers abandon their quest. Then it slows down. Schoenberg uses *col legno* (in violin playing, letting the stick of the bow bounce against the strings) to sinister effect. A brief postlude on the piano leads to the next number.

11. *Rote Messe* (Red Mass). For piccolo, bass clarinet, viola, cello, piano. Quite lively, 3/4. Pierrot, at the altar, rips open his priestly vestment and, raising his hand in blessing, holds aloft in his bloody fingers the dripping red Host—his heart! Once again all five instruments play. The piano presents an ostinato figure with trills, against which we hear swelling chords in the low strings and bass clarinet. Special effects include a ghostly arpeggio on the flute, *pppp*, and an equally ghostly chord on the piano when the keys are pressed down without striking (so that the strings will be free to vibrate in

sympathy with sounded notes). With this evocation of the horrible we enter the heartland of Expressionism.

12. *Galgenlied* (Gallows Song). For piccolo, viola, cello. Very fast, 2/4. Pierrot thinks of the scrawny harlot who will embrace him when he is hanged. The shortest piece in the cycle is a bit of gallows humor in which voice and instruments speed up mercilessly to the end. Schoenberg here indulges in some tone painting. The mocking ascent of the piccolo at the end, where Pierrot sees himself swinging on the gallows, reminds one of a similar passage in Richard Strauss's *Till Eulenspiegel,* where that rascal meets his doom.

13. *Enthauptung* (Beheading). For bass clarinet, viola, cello, piano. Moving along, 4/4. Pierrot fantasizes in terror, seeing the moon as a scimitar that is about to behead him. At the end of the first stanza the instruments set up a running figuration that develops into a busy contrapuntal texture. As Pierrot scurries about in deathly fright, his motive appears in inversion (upside down) in the viola, to be imitated very freely in the other parts:

The pace slackens with the instrumental postlude, in which the flute repeats the melody it played in No. 7, *The Sick Moon,* while the melody of the *Sprechstimme* in the earlier number is now divided between bass clarinet and cello.

14. *Die Kreuze* (The Crosses). For flute, clarinet, violin, cello, piano. Slow, 4/4. Part Two ends with a meditation on the fate of poets, whose verses are the holy crosses on which they mutely bleed. The voice recites the first two stanzas to a richly textured accompaniment on the piano. The Pierrot motive is transformed into a nervous flurry:

Another "soundless" chord, for which the keys are pressed down without being struck, is marked with a *fermata* (pause), out of which emerge the other four instruments. The texture is lighter for the third stanza. Notice, in the final measures, the tremolos in the bass register of the piano.

Part Three, much calmer in mood, concerns itself with Pierrot's longing for the old comedy and, ultimately, his homecoming. Schoenberg here turns to structural forms based on counterpoint, notably canon and fugue. (An explanation of both will be found in Appendix I-g.)

15. *Heimweh* (Homesickness). For clarinet, violin, piano. With changing movement, 4/4. A plaintive voice from the old Italian pantomime complains that Pierrot has become too modern, too sentimental. He remembers the distant skies of his native land. The rich instrumental texture includes such special effects as *spiccato* (in violin playing, allowing the bow to bounce on the strings), more "soundless" chords on the piano, and a graphic illustration of the word *sentimental* by a glissando (sliding) in the voice part. The cello enters decisively at the end, with a new version of the Pierrot motive. Its wide-ranging solo serves as a bridge to the next piece.

16. *Gemeinheit* (Meanness). For piccolo, clarinet, violin, cello, piano. Quite fast, 3/4. Another number for the full group. Pierrot drills a hole in Pantaloon's skull and stuffs it with Turkish tobacco. Then he screws his pipe into his victim's bald pate and enjoys a smoke while Pentaloon's screams rend the air. A bit of grotesquerie in which the cello carries the tune, which presents a repeated-note figure as one of its leading motives. (In the German, Pantaloon is Cassander.)

17. *Parodie* (Parody). For piccolo, clarinet, viola, piano. 4/8. An aging, lovesick duenna waits for Pierrot in the arbor, but he never turns up. The moon's bright rays mock her. Schoenberg employs all manner of contrapuntal complexities in this number. The melody of the viola is inverted in the clarinet part and is imitated in a canon by the *Sprechstimme*. Later there is a canonic imitation between voice and piccolo, with an inverted canon between viola and clarinet going on at the same time (that is, the clarinet imitates what the viola is playing but turns it upside down). Whether or not one tries to unravel this *tour de force*, the resulting texture is breathtaking in its gossamer activity.

18. *Der Mondfleck* (The Moonspot). For piccolo, clarinet, violin, cello, piano. Very fast, 3/4. Pierrot, out for fun, is disturbed by a white spot—a patch of moonlight—on the collar of his jet-black

jacket. He rubs and rubs but can't get rid of it. Here the contrapuntal complexities rise to spectacular levels. The piano presents a three-part fugue. Clarinet and piccolo form strict canons in diminution (smaller note values) with the first two voices of the fugue. A third canon is formed independently by violin and cello. At midpoint in the piece clarinet and piccolo, having moved twice as fast as their canonic counterparts in the piano, run out of notes. They therefore reverse their direction, that is, proceed backward (retrograde canon), in diminution with the two voices of the fugue. Meanwhile the independent canon in violin and cello also moves backward from this point. The reversal begins when Pierrot discovers the spot that irritates him so, and concludes when he thinks he has rubbed it out. This incredibly complicated structure looks back to the constructions of the late medieval contrapuntists, who delighted in such dazzling exhibitions of virtuosity.

Here is what retrograde looks like in the clarinet part. At point X you can read the same notes forward or backward:

19. *Serenade.* For flute, clarinet, violin, cello, piano. A very slow waltz, 3/4. Pierrot scrapes away at his viola with a giant-sized bow. Pantaloon objects, whereupon Pierrot grabs him and dreamily draws his bow across Pantaloon's bald pate. In this number Schoenberg revels in the unexpected. Instead of a viola you hear a soaring cello solo. So too, the sad pizzicato mentioned at the end of the first stanza occurs not there but earlier, in the instrumental introduction. The cello part is of a virtuoso character and has a cadenza that begins slowly but accelerates. The other instruments enter at the end to usher in the next piece.

20. *Heimfahrt* (Homecoming). For flute, clarinet, violin, cello, piano. Moving lightly, 6/8. Voice and instruments evoke the gentle flow of a barcarolle (boat song) as Pierrot travels homeward to Bergamo, with a moonbeam for a rudder and a water lily for a boat. Gone is the period of storm and stress. Now all is gentleness and acceptance.

21. *O alter Duft* (O Fragrance of Olden Times). The final piece brings in all eight instruments. At a moving pace, 4/4. Pierrot revels in the fragrant memories of yesteryear. He is happy with the simple pleasures he so long disdained. The agony of night has vanished,

and he looks out with affection on a world bathed in sunlight. This return to an earlier, more innocent time leads Schoenberg to sound the mellifluous thirds and consonant triads of the harmonic system he had abandoned. There are three triads in the final phrase, and the *Sprechstimme* dies away in a pianissimo. Thus ends the work that Stravinsky called "the solar plexus as well as the mind of early twentieth-century music."

Summing Up

In this section we discussed a number of works that date from the first decade and a half of our century. They illustrate the diverse creative currents that made this period so extraordinarily productive: Mahler's *Song of the Earth* (1908); Richard Strauss's *Salome* (1905); Scriabin's *Vers la flamme* (1914); Debussy's *Ibéria* (1908) and *La Cathédrale engloutie* (1910); Ravel's *Daphnis and Chloé* (1912); Delius's *On Hearing the First Cuckoo in Spring* (1912); Bartók's *Allegro barbaro* (1911); Stravinsky's *The Rite of Spring* (1913); and Schoenberg's *Pierrot lunaire* (1912). The last three works reached so far beyond the then accepted norms of rhythm and tonality as to prefigure a new world of sound.

The leaders of the modern movement felt that they represented a beginning. But they were also witnessing an end. European society had moved steadily forward through a century of peace and prosperity, its progress powered by the twin forces of a burgeoning capitalism and an expanding democracy. This period of optimism came to an abrupt end with the First World War. In June 1914 the lamps went out all over Europe. Those who had fought the battles of the new music in the concert halls of Paris, Vienna, and Berlin now had grimmer battles to fight. When the lights went on again four years later, the political, intellectual, and artistic climate of Europe had undergone irrevocable changes. The world would never be the same again. Nor would music.

PART THREE

Between the Wars
(1920–1940)

"There are only twelve tones. You must treat them carefully."

PAUL HINDEMITH

I. *The Central Group*

23 New Trends: The Flight from Romanticism

"Epochs which immediately precede our own are temporarily farther away from us than others more remote in time."

IGOR STRAVINSKY

In rejecting the nineteenth-century heritage, composers turned away from the subjective and the grandiose; from pathos and heaven-storming passion; from landscape painting and the quest for sensuous beauty. The rising generation regarded the Romantic agony as Wagnerian histrionics. It considered itself to be made of sterner stuff. The new music aimed at nothing less than, as the distinguished critic Ortega y Gasset wrote, "to root out private feelings from art, to purify it by exemplary objectification." He considered this "conversion from the subjective to the objective" to be the most important task of the time.

Objectivism

Twentieth-century artists tried to see the world not through the mist of their own illusions but as it actually was. A spirit of detach-

153

ment began to pervade art. The new music aspired to objectivity and directness.

Artists embraced the belief that objects, whether in nature or in art, existed independently of their own personal feelings. They argued that a work of art is not simply a projection of its creator's imagination—as the Romantics had assumed—but is a self-contained organism with a life of its own. Hence the laws that shape the work of art derive not from religion or philosophy or love, but solely from the nature of the artist's material and the principles governing the formal organization of that material. The artist was supposed to set the mechanism going and to see that it reached its destination. He also, according to the new aesthetic, was expected to keep his personal feelings from obtruding upon either the work or the spectator. He had to remain outside his creation, to respect its nature as pure art.

As a result, composers turned from the problem of expression to the problem of formal organization. This emphasis on the structural aspect of art was not limited to music. A similar trend can be observed in painting and sculpture, in the cult of pure form that came to the fore with the Constructivists and Cubists. Under the impact of this movement, musicians abandoned the grandiose themes that had attracted them throughout the Postromantic period. The new matter-of-factness demanded more sober subjects and quieter colors. The emphasis was on restraint and quietness of gesture in every department of musical expression. Once this point was reached, the stage was set for the Neoclassic attitude which in the early 1920s won a dominant position in musical aesthetics.

Urbanism and Machine Music

The Romantics had found an inexhaustible source of inspiration in nature. The new music turned to the imagery of the city. The hectic pace of urban life engendered rhythms that were dynamically expressive of the new age.

With the mechanization of Western society came a widespread feeling that man had surrendered his soul to forces he neither understood nor controlled. The machine became a symbol of power, motion, energy; a symbol too of what was aptly called "the dehumanization of art." In the years after the First World War composers glorified the locomotive, the dynamo, and the turbine in their music. They regarded these as a welcome change from the birds, waterfalls,

The geometrical shapes of Cubism provided a natural basis for Léger's machine iconography. In this painting, robotlike figures mount a staircase in the midst of a modern industrial cityscape. The City, *1919, by Fernand Léger (1881–1955). Philadelphia Museum of Art.*

and twilights of the Romantics, not realizing that they had merely exchanged one set of picturesque symbols for another.

The new tendency produced such works as Honegger's *Pacific 231* (a musical glorification of the locomotive, 1924); John Alden Carpenter's *Skyscrapers* (1926); George Antheil's *Ballet mécanique* (1924), Prokofiev's *Pas d'acier* (Dance of Steel, 1924), Mossolov's *Iron Foundry* (1927), and Carlos Chávez's *HP* (Horsepower, 1932). This trend culminated in the works of one of the most original figures of the century, Edgard Varèse.

The urban spirit found an especially fertile field in opera. The lyric stage for the first time in history witnessed scenes laid in hotel lobbies, bars, nightclubs, transatlantic liners, and city streets. Hindemith's opera *Neues vom Tage* (News of the Day, 1929) contains an aria sung by the heroine in the bathtub, the rhythmic clicking of typewriters, and a business letter recited by the chorus. This was a far cry from the gods, kings, and duchesses of Romantic opera.

The new symbols lent themselves to the spirit of objectivity prized by the Twenties. Even more important, they went hand-in-hand with a music in which movement and action usurped the place of honor formerly occupied by poetic emotion.

Sports and Ballet

In the bitter years after the First World War, emphasis turned increasingly from spiritual values to the physical. Europe found surcease for its shattered nerves in the cult of the body. In ever greater degree sports and athletics became identified with tenacity, endurance, and the will to live.

Sportism became one of the subsidiary themes of the new urban spirit in music. Witness such works as Martinu's *Half-Time* (1925), which sings the joys of football, and Honegger's *Skating Rink* (1922) and *Rugby* (1928). Highly significant was the growing popularity of the ballet, an art which glorifies the body both for its physical allure and its capacities as a precision machine. In the decade after the war the ballet widened its expressive scope and reached new heights of sophistication as an art form. Diaghilev with his Ballets Russes offered composers a platform that came to have prime importance for the new music. Almost every important composer of the day contributed to Diaghilev's repertory.

Under the influence of Primitivism, machine music, sports, and ballet, the Romantic soulfulness of the nineteenth century gave way to the physicality of the twentieth. The shift was well expressed in Stravinsky's dictum that "rhythm and motion, not the element of feeling, are the foundations of musical art."

Humor and Satire

Romanticism had regarded music as inspired utterance: the composer was presumed to be a poet and prophet whose natural habitat was the noble and the sublime. Given such an attitude, it was inevitable that nineteenth-century composers were inclined to what Darius Milhaud called *le sérieux à tout prix* (seriousness at all costs).

Twentieth-century composers increasingly turned to satire, irony, and humor. This tendency was given impetus by the fact that the new dissonant harmony lent itself admirably to humorous effects. Erik Satie was a pioneer in this field with his whimsical parodies of the Impressionist school. His Parisian disciples were determined not to let music take itself too seriously. They rejected all that smacked of what they contemptuously called "rhetoric." During the 1920s Satie's heirs essayed to revive what had been the ideal of French court music in the seventeenth and eighteenth centuries. They wanted to write compositions that were charming, lucid, well ordered, that would entertain and please.

Their aims were shared by a wide variety of composers, among them Hindemith and Weill, Stravinsky and Prokofiev, Shostakovich and Walton. There came into being a witty music that made light of the idols of the past, one in which cleverness and spoofing held the place once preempted by pathos and passion. True, much of this music soon dropped out of sight. But the attitude behind it expressed a real need to bring music down to earth and helped clear the air of much that had outlived its usefulness.

The general disillusion that came in the wake of the First World War impelled artists everywhere to avoid probing or revealing their emotions. The twentieth-century composer, unlike his nineteenth-century forebear, was not going to wear his heart on his sleeve. Introversion of any kind was indissolubly linked to the Romantic ideals which, it was felt, had forever been done away with. By allying music with humor and satire, composers were able to give expression to the bitterness of their time. They felt it necessary to strip their art of the mystique in which both the Romantics and the Impressionists had enveloped it. In line with the new matter-of-factness, composers in the years after the war began to associate their music with deliberately prosaic themes. Milhaud, for example, set to music a *Catalogue of Agricultural Implements* (including the prices). Hindemith turned out music for a comic film called *Felix the Cat*. Such pieces, no matter how fugitive in nature, showed only too clearly that music was moving in a new direction.

The Influence of Jazz

In the years after the First World War the jazz idiom began to claim the attention of serious musicians. The syncopations and polyrhythms of the jazz band could not but appeal to a generation that was finding its way to new rhythmic conceptions. Besides, the vogue of Primitivism made Europeans particularly susceptible to the exotic. They were enchanted by a music whose ancestry went back to the African drums, which mirrored both the dynamic American temper-

The Cowboy, *one of the series of twenty-four* papier collés *entitled* Jazz, 1947, *by Henri Matisse. Collection, The Museum of Modern Art, New York, Gift of the Artist.*

ament and the African genius for rhythm. The kinetic rhythms of the dance band, instinct with the hectic pace of modern urban life, seemed to symbolize the restlessness and hunger for excitement of a war-weary world.

From the technical aspect, the chamber-music character of the jazz band was also appealing. A jazz band of the Twenties was an ensemble of soloists in which the "reeds" (saxophones and clarinets) and the "brasses" (trumpets, cornets, trombones) carried the melody over the steady throb of the "rhythm" (piano, string bass, banjo, or guitar, bolstered by drums and a variety of percussive instruments). The absence of string tone in many bands produced a sonority congenial to twentieth-century ears. Also in accord with contemporary taste was the ambiguity between major and minor typical of jazz music, the frequent polyrhythms, the departure from regular four-measure phrase structure, and the "blue" intonation of certain intervals. After 1917, when a Negro jazz band scored a triumphant success abroad, a number of European musicians became interested in this novelty from America. Among the works that reflected the jazz influence were Erik Satie's ballet *Parade;* Stravinsky's *Ragtime for Eleven Instruments* and *Piano Rag Music;* Darius Milhaud's ballets *Le Boeuf sur le toit* and *La Création du monde;* Hindemith's *1922 Suite for Piano,* with two movements entitled *Shimmy* and *Ragtime;* Honegger's *Concertino* for piano and orchestra; and Ernst Krenek's opera *Jonny spielt auf!* (Johnny Plays!).

Once the jazz idiom and its procedures were absorbed into the language of contemporary music, the vogue passed. Composers turned elsewhere for source material. However, during the 1920s jazz played its part, along with the other influences we have described, in leading European music toward new objectives.

Gebrauchsmusik (Workaday Music)

"It is to be regretted that in general so little relationship exists between the producers and the consumers of music."

PAUL HINDEMITH

The changes in the musical language that occurred in the first two decades of our century could not but bewilder and alienate the mass of music lovers. There resulted an increasing distance between the composer and the majority of his public. Yet even while the leaders of musical advance—Stravinsky, Bartók, Schoenberg, and their compeers—were formulating significant new concepts in style and expression, other forces were at work to effect some sort of rapprochement between "the producers and the consumers" of music.

One such influence, we shall see, emanated from Erik Satie and his disciples, who strove to create an "everyday" music. Another impetus in this direction came from Soviet Russia where the composer, functioning under the control of the state, had to solve the problem of reaching a great mass of listeners who were just discovering music. The fact that the works of the leading Soviet composers—Prokofiev, Shostakovich, Khatchaturian—achieved enormous popularity in the West could not fail to impress composers everywhere; and this reinforced the attempt to bring twentieth-century music closer to the average listener.

The climate that prevailed in Germany in the 1920s, under the liberal Weimar Republic, was especially favorable to "music for everyday living." Encouraged by the large publishing houses, composers sought to create a new public for contemporary music—amateurs, students, and the young. They began to cultivate a simple, practical music designed for use in the home and the community. *Gebrauchsmusik* (literally, "music for use"—that is, workaday music) emerged in a milieu of progressive youth movements, workers' choruses, and the strong desire to foster group activities. Its leading exponents were Paul Hindemith, Ernst Krenek, Kurt Weill, and Hanns Eisler. "The days of composing for the sake of composing are perhaps gone forever," wrote Hindemith in 1927. "A composer should write today only if he knows for what purpose he is writing." This view looked back to the craft practices of preromantic times, when the composer was in the employ of a prince, a church, or an opera house. It was precisely in this way, of course, that the operas of Monteverdi and Lully, the odes of Purcell and the cantatas of Bach came into being.

The trend toward *Gebrauchsmusik* produced Hindemith's "musical game for children," *Wir bauen eine Stadt* (We're Building a City, 1930); his Opus 45, "Music to Sing or Play—for amateurs or music lovers" (1928); his pieces for teaching young violinists the first position; and his music for community singing. Compositions such as these embodied the conviction of the younger generation of German composers that a healthy musical culture depended not on the much publicized virtuoso, but on a broad base of amateurs, young and old, who took part themselves in every phase of musical activity. This attitude, and the works that resulted from it, played a progressive role in the music of the Twenties and Thirties and helped to effect a rapprochement between the modern composer and his public.

24   The New Classicism

"All order demands restraint. But one would be wrong to regard that as any impediment to liberty."

IGOR STRAVINSKY

Twentieth-Century Classicism

When twentieth-century composers turned to the classical ideal, they strove to recapture the spirit of an era when music had not yet begun to call on the other arts for heightened dramatic or pictorial effect; when the art had not yet become preoccupied with personal expression and psychological attitudes. By freeing music from elements alien to it, by building it out of elements derived solely from the nature of sound, they hoped to achieve what Stravinsky called "a wholesome return to the formal idea, the only basis of music." Only in this way, they were persuaded, could they retrieve for the art some of the wholeness that had been lost to it.

Classicism meant different things to different composers. To some it represented a return to the courtly style of the late eighteenth century—the age of Haydn and Mozart (the Classical era proper). To others it meant turning for inspiration to the giants of the first half of the eighteenth century, when the late Baroque was in flower: Bach and Handel, Couperin, Vivaldi, and Scarlatti, in whose contrapuntal writing the new music found the unsurpassable model for linear texture. Others discovered a spiritual kinship with still earlier masters: Monteverdi, Lully, Purcell, Palestrina and Victoria; Marenzio and Gesualdo; the Tudor church composers and Elizabethan madrigalists; and the Flemish polyphonists of the fifteenth and sixteenth centuries. Classicism, in short, came loosely to denote everything that was untouched by the spirit of nineteenth-century Romanticism.

The changes in melody, harmony and rhythm, texture, orchestration, tonality, and form which we described in the first part of this book were so overwhelming that there had to follow a breathing spell during which composers could absorb the new acquisitions of their art. Neoclassicism made this period of consolidation possible. In doing so, it fulfilled a widely felt need for simplification, clarity, and order.

Neoclassicism: The Doctrine

Since Neoclassicism had its most articulate spokesman in Igor Stravinsky, it may be well to examine his utterances as an authoritative summary of Neoclassic doctrine. His evolution as an artist led him from the Postimpressionism of *The Firebird* and the audacities of *The Rite of Spring* to the austerely controlled classicism of his maturity. In the course of it he laid ever greater emphasis upon tradition and discipline. "The more art is controlled, limited, worked over, the more it is free." His own intuitions controlled by a lucid intelligence, Stravinsky consistently extolled the formal above the emotional elements in art. "I cannot compose until I have decided what problem I must solve." But the problem was aesthetic, not personal. "I evoke neither human joy nor human sadness," he wrote. "I move towards an ever greater abstraction." In this, of course, he was one with the other great classicist of our time, his friend Picasso. No less important was Stravinsky's attempt to reestablish the status of music as an autonomous art removed from the experiences of life. "The phenomenon of music is given to us with the sole purpose of establishing an order among things, including above all an order between man and time. To be realized, it needs only a construction. Once the construction is made and the order achieved, everything is said. It would be futile to look for or expect anything else from it."

This view at one stroke rejects the symbolic meanings that composers from Beethoven to Mahler and Strauss associated with their music. Even more, Stravinsky's doctrine represented an effort on a grand scale to purge music of pictorial, literary, and ethical meanings, of the dreams and visions that had attached themselves to it not only during the Romantic period but at other times in the course of its history. Stravinsky's aim was to draw the listener's attention away from his own emotions and reveries and to concentrate it on the tones instead. The emotion aroused by art, he insisted, was of an order that had "nothing in common with our ordinary sensations and our responses to the impressions of daily life."

As a matter of fact, Stravinsky adhered to his thesis less stringently than one might suppose. There is more emotion in his *Symphony of Psalms* than is dreamed of in his philosophy. True, his music of the early and middle twenties exemplifies the artist's sheer delight in making patterns, in playing with the material. But in the later phase of his career he explicitly departed from his doctrine. Speaking of his *Symphony in Three Movements*, which was written during the Second World War, he stated, "During the process of creation in this arduous time of sharp and shifting events, of despair and hope, of tension and at last cessation and relief, it may be said that all these repercussions have left traces in this symphony." Here, obviously, the separation between art and life was no longer upheld with the old finality.

Neoclassicism attracted artists as dissimilar as Schoenberg and Hindemith, Bartók and Milhaud, Honegger and Prokofiev, Aaron Copland and Roger Sessions. Sessions produced what has remained perhaps the best formulation of the Neoclassic ideal. Writing in 1927, he declared: "Younger men are dreaming of an entirely different kind of music—a music which derives its power from forms beautiful and significant by virtue of inherent musical weight rather than intensity of utterance; a music whose impersonality and self-sufficiency preclude the exotic; which takes its impulse from the realities of a passionate logic; which, in the authentic freshness of its moods, is the reverse of ironic and, in its very aloofness from the concrete preoccupations of life, strives rather to contribute form, design, a vision of order and harmony."

Neoclassicism: The Music

One of the prime achievements of the New Classicism was the revival of the absolute forms. Symphony, concerto, sonata, and the various types of chamber music achieved a far greater importance than had been their lot in the first two decades of the century, when they were overshadowed by symphonic poem, ballet, and opera. Equally significant was the return to the forms of preromantic times, such as the suite, divertimento, toccata, concerto grosso, fugue, passacaglia, and chaconne.

The music of the Romantics had adhered to a melodic imagery based on the voice. The New Classicism, contrariwise, favored an instrumental melody that made use of wider intervals and a more extended range. Harmonically, Neoclassicism moved away from the chromaticism of the post-Wagner era. Its music was based on the seven tones of the diatonic scale, although these were used much more freely than ever before. The term pandiatonicism is often used to indicate the new freedom with which the seven tones are combined harmonically and contrapuntally. Pandiatonicism offered a natural medium for the Neoclassicists. In contrast to the multitude of sharps and flats in early twentieth-century music, pandiatonicism favored a sparing use of accidentals and showed a striking affinity for the key of C major. Indeed, it originated as a modern technique of playing the piano on the white keys. Hence the term "white music" that applies to many a page of Neoclassic music, as in the following measures from Stravinsky's *Concerto for Piano and Wind Instruments* (1924):

To the full chordal texture of Romantic and Impressionist music, Neoclassicism opposed a transparent linear texture. The Neoclassic style found its characteristic expression in an agile dissonant counterpoint marked by clarity and freshness and propelled by lithe motor rhythms. In the matter of orchestral color, it need hardly be said, the Neoclassicists veered away from the lush sonorities of the Postromantic period toward sober, sharply defined colors that brought out the interplay of the several lines. Romanticism in music inevitably led to the use of harmony, rhythm, and color for their own sake; the New Classicism—and here perhaps was its most important contribution—ended this lawless independence of the separate elements. It restored these to their true function as parts of the whole, and rendered them strictly subservient to musical idea and design.

The Neoclassic aesthetic rejected the nineteenth-century concept of the Artist in favor of the older craftsman ideal. Stravinsky, significantly, always disliked the term *artist,* which he considered pretentious and romantic. He preferred to regard himself as an artisan. In line with this attitude he welcomed a commission that imposed specific conditions and challenged the craftsman's ingenuity. "When I know how long a piece must take, then it excites me." He repudiated the romantic view of the artist as a being apart, creating out of his loneliness. The aim of art, he pointed out (in a sentence that might have been uttered by one of the art-craftsmen of centuries ago) is "to promote a communion, a union of man with his fellow men and with the Supreme Being."

The New Classicism attracted musicians of a certain taste and temperament—especially those who were fascinated by formal perfection and inclined to separate art from life. Its aesthetic recalled a whole generation to the problems of the craft, focusing their attention on elegance of style and purity of taste. In exalting the *how* over the *what,* it led musicians to the classical virtues of order, discipline, balance, and proportion. At a moment when Western music was unable to proceed further along the romantic path, the New Classicism pointed the way to an athletic musical style, Apollonian in its detachment and serenity, thus upholding the autonomy of music as a self-contained universe in which the artist could grapple with the problem of human freedom in its most abstract and ideal essence.

25 Igor Stravinsky (1882-1971)

"Music to me is a power which justifies things."

It is granted to certain artists to embody the profoundest impulses of their time and to affect its artistic life in the most powerful fashion. Such an artist was Igor Stravinsky, the Russian composer who for half a century gave impetus to the main currents in contemporary music.

His Life

Stravinsky was born in Oranienbaum, a summer resort not far from what was then St. Petersburg, where his parents lived. He grew up in a musical environment; his father was the leading bass at the Imperial Opera. Although he was taught to play the piano, his musical education was kept on the amateur level. His parents desired him to study law. He matriculated at the University of St. Petersburg and embarked on a legal career, meanwhile continuing his musical stud-

Stravinsky, 1957. A drawing by Alberto Gia-cometti (1901–1966). Collection of Mr. and Mrs. Robert D. Graff.

ies. At twenty he submitted his work to Rimsky-Korsakov, with whom he subsequently worked for three years.

Success came early to Stravinsky. His music attracted the notice of Serge Diaghilev (1872–1929), the legendary impresario of the Russian Ballet, who commissioned him to write the music for *The Firebird.* This was produced in 1910. Stravinsky was twenty-eight when he arrived in Paris to attend the rehearsals. Diaghilev pointed him out to the ballerina Tamara Karsavina with the words, "Mark him well —he is a man on the eve of fame."

The Firebird was followed, a year later, by *Petrushka.* Presented with Nijinsky and Karsavina in the leading roles, this production secured Stravinsky's position in the forefront of the modern movement in art. In 1913 came the third and most spectacular of the ballets Stravinsky wrote for Diaghilev, *Le Sacre du printemps* (The Rite of Spring). The work, we saw, caused a riot (Chapter 21), but it spread the young composer's name far beyond the Parisian scene.

The outbreak of war in 1914 brought to an end the whole way of life on which Diaghilev's sumptuous dance spectacles depended. Stravinsky, with his wife and children, took refuge in Switzerland, their home for the next six years. The Russian Revolution had severed Stravinsky's ties with his homeland. In 1920 he settled in France, where he remained until 1939. During these years Stravinsky concertized extensively throughout Europe, performing his own works as pianist and conductor. He also paid two visits to the United States. In 1939 he was invited to deliver the Charles Eliot Norton lectures at Harvard University. He was there when the Second World War broke out, and decided to live in this country. He settled in California, outside Los Angeles, and in 1945 became an American citizen. He died a quarter century later, on April 6, 1971, revered throughout the world.

His Music

Stravinsky throughout his career refused to go on repeating himself. With inexhaustible avidity he tackled new problems and pressed for new solutions. It happened more than once that a phase of his career seemed to move in the opposite direction from the one before. In retrospect, however, his various periods emerge as necessary stages in a continuous evolution toward greater purity of style and abstraction of thought.

Stravinsky issued out of the sound-world of the Russian National school. *The Firebird* displays all the shimmer of Rimsky-Korsakov's orchestra (to which are added the pastel tints of French Impressionism). Here, as in the works that followed, Stravinsky worked within the frame of Russian folklore, drawing sustenance from popular song and dance. All the same, from the beginning he was aligned with those forces in Russian culture that were oriented toward the West—especially those that were receptive to Latin clarity and grace. He thus was free to move toward the universal values that underlie the classical outlook.

The mainspring of Stravinsky's art is rhythm. He was a leader in the revitalization of European rhythm. It is significant that his first great success was won in the field of ballet, where rhythm is allied to dynamic body movement and expressive gesture. As we pointed out in our discussion of *Le Sacre*, his is a rhythm of unparalleled thrust and tension, supple, powerful, controlled. Units of seven, eleven, or thirteen beats, a continual shifting from one meter to another, the dislocation of the accent by means of intricate patterns of syncopation—these and kindred devices revolutionized the traditional concepts.

Stravinsky reacted strongly against the restless chromaticism of the Postromantic era. He found the antidote in a harmonic language that is essentially diatonic. The key supplied him with the necessary framework; it delimited and defined the area of his activity. He achieved excitement by superposing harmonic planes—either melodies or streams of chords—in contrasting keys, obtaining pungent polytonal combinations. Yet no matter how complex the harmony might become, at the point of repose one key emerged triumphant over the rest, reaffirming the principle of law and order.

Stravinsky's subtle sense of sound places him among the master orchestrators. He turned away from the sonorous haze of the nineteenth-century orchestra and led the way to the concertante style of the eighteenth century, in which the instruments stand out soloistically against the mass. His writing is notable for its precision and economy. The nicety of his doublings, his individual way of spacing the harmonies, his use of unconventional registers, and his feeling for the character of the various instruments impart to his orchestration a clean, enameled luster that is unmistakably his. There results a texture based on pure colors, so limpid that, as Diaghilev said, "One could see through it with one's ears."

Stravinsky set great store on melody. "A return to the cult of melody," he stated, "seems to me necessary and even urgent." In the works of his Russian period he was much given to those concise, fragmentary melodies, incisive and direct, that turn about themselves in such characteristic fashion. Later, in his Neoclassic period, he developed the more flowing type of melodic line that is inseparable from a contrapuntal conception of music, finding his model in the self-generating arabesque of Bach. In respect to form, he adhered to the Baroque principle of continuous expansion rather than to the Classical method of "working out" themes and motives, preferring the organic structure of the Baroque to the symmetrical sections of the Classical style. His plastic conception of form exerted a vast influence on the musicians of our time.

With *Petrushka* (1911), Stravinsky found his personal tone. Despite its Russianness, the ballet about the puppet who turns out to have a soul possesses universal appeal. Is not Petrushka, as the com-

In this scene from the 1976 production of Petrushka *by American Ballet Theater, the title role is danced by Mikhail Baryshnikov (right), the Ballerina by Eleanor d'Antuono, and the Moor by Marcos Paredes. Photograph by Martha Swope.*

poser asks, "the immortal and unhappy hero of every fair in all countries?" The carnival scene with which the piece opens is dominated by the "big accordion" sound—a direct echo of the peasant instrument that held Stravinsky spellbound as a child. In *Petrushka* we encounter the laconic melodies, resilient rhythms, and orchestral brightness that are the composer's very own. One of the most original scores of the century, this is the best loved of Stravinsky's works for the theater.

The difficulty of assembling large bodies of performers during the war worked hand-in-hand with his inner evolution as an artist. He relinquished the grand scale of the first three ballets in favor of works more intimate in spirit and modest in dimension. The trend is apparent in *L'Histoire du soldat* (The Soldier's Tale, 1918), for narrator, three characters who speak, dance, and act, and seven instruments. This enchanting piece is based on a Russian folk tale about the deserter who barters his violin—symbol of his soul—for the allurements of the Devil. The works Stravinsky wrote after the First World War show the composer moving away from the Russian style of his first period toward the French-international orientation of his second. Neoclassicism takes over in the ballet *Pulcinella,* which we will discuss. At the same time his "passion for jazz," as he called it, gave rise to the *Ragtime for Eleven Instruments* (1918) and the *Piano-Rag Music* (1919). There followed the "burlesque tale" *Renard* (The Fox, 1916, first performed in 1922), for four vocalists, dancers, and chamber orchestra, based on a folk story that was put into dramatic form by Stravinsky himself. *Les Noces* (The Wedding, 1917, first performed in 1923) is a stylization of a Russian peasant wedding. Four singers and a chorus support the dancers, accompanied by four pianos and a diversified percussion group. This ballet-cantata, with its clear glacial sound and its percussive use of the piano, boasts one of Stravinsky's most powerful scores.

The Neoclassical aesthetic dominates the *Symphonies of Wind Instruments* (1920), dedicated to the memory of Debussy. The instrumental works that followed incarnate the principle of the old concerto grosso—the pitting against each other of contrasting tone masses. This "return to Bach" crystallized in the *Octet,* the *Piano Sonata,* the *Concerto* for piano and wind orchestra, and the *Serenade in A,* all of which date from the years 1923–1925. Stravinsky's writing for the piano derives from the crisp harpsichord style of the eighteenth century rather than from the singing Chopin style of the nineteenth or the shimmering Debussy style of the early twentieth.

His devotion to Neoclassicism was hailed in certain quarters as conclusive proof that the Romantic spirit finally was dead; but the master surprised his disciples by proclaiming his admiration for a number of nineteenth-century composers. He paid homage to Weber and Mendelssohn in the *Capriccio* (1929), a brilliant concert piece for piano and orchestra. The ballet *Le Baiser de la fée* (The Fairy's Kiss, 1928) was "inspired by the Muse of Tchaikovsky." The one-act opera buffa *Mavra* (1922) is dedicated "to the memory of Pushkin, Glinka, and Tchaikovsky." This genial little work is based on Pushkin's tale about the enterprising soldier who makes his way into his sweetheart's house by disguising himself as a maid-servant, only to be discovered in the act of shaving.

Stravinsky's classical period culminates in several major compositions. *Oedipus Rex* (1927) is an "opera-oratorio." The text is a translation into Latin of Cocteau's French adaptation of the Greek tragedy. Stravinsky's comment on his preference for the Latin is revealing. "What a joy it is to compose music to a language of convention, almost of ritual, the very nature of which imposes a lofty dignity! One no longer feels dominated by the phrase, the literal meaning of the words." From the shattering dramaticism of the opening chords, *Oedipus Rex* is an unforgettable experience in the theater. The archaic Greek influence is manifest too in the ballet *Apollon musagète* (Apollo, Leader of the Muses, 1928), which marked the beginning of his collaboration with the choreographer George Balanchine; *Perséphone* (1934), a choral dance drama on a text by André Gide; and the ballet *Orpheus* (1947), a severely classical work that ranks with the master's most distinguished creations.

The *Symphony of Psalms,* which many regard as the chief work of Stravinsky's maturity, we will discuss in detail. The *Symphony in C* (1940), a sunny piece of modest dimensions, pays tribute to the spirit of Haydn and Mozart. With the *Symphony in Three Movements* (1945), Stravinsky returns to bigness of form and gesture. The *Mass* (completed in 1948) is in the restrained, telegraphic style that he favored during his middle years. In 1950 there followed *The Rake's Progress,* an opera on a libretto by W. H. Auden and Chester Kallman, after

The arrival of Baba the Turk. A scene from the American Opera Center's production of The Rake's Progress *at the Juilliard School of Music. Copyright © Beth Bergman.*

Hogarth's celebrated series of paintings. Written as the composer was approaching seventy, this is a mellow, radiantly melodious score.

Stravinsky, imperturbably pursuing his own growth as an artist, had still another surprise in store for his public. In the works written after he was seventy he showed himself increasingly receptive to the procedures of the Schoenbergian school. We will discuss this aspect of his career in a later chapter. Such changes in direction, like those that preceded, naturally alienated some of his admirers and infuriated others. Years earlier, in discussing his progression from Russian Nationalism to Neoclassicism, he explained why he had to follow his own inner development without regard to the wishes of his supporters. Their attitude, he stated in a revealing passage in his *Autobiography*, "certainly cannot make me deviate from my path. I shall assuredly not sacrifice my predilections and my aspirations to the demands of those who, in their blindness, do not realize that they are simply asking me to go backwards. It should be obvious that what they wish for has become obsolete for me, and that I could not follow them without doing violence to myself."

Stravinsky's aphorisms display a gift for trenchant expression. "We have a duty to music, namely, to invent it. . . . Instinct is infallible. If it leads us astray it is no longer instinct. . . . It is not simply inspiration that counts. It is the result of inspiration—that is, the composition." Speaking of his *Mass:* "The Credo is the longest movement. There is much to believe." When asked to define the difference between *The Rite of Spring* and *Symphony of Psalms:* "The difference is twenty years." "How do you know when to end?" an admirer inquired. "Before I begin," was the craftsman's reply. Of the many anecdotes to which his ready tongue gave rise, it will suffice to quote one. After the out-of-town opening of *The Seven Lively Arts,* a revue for which Stravinsky wrote a short ballet, the managers of the show, apprehensive as to how this spare, angular music would be received on Broadway, wired him: "Great success. Could be sensational if you authorize arranger Mr. X to add some details to orchestration. Mr. X arranges even the works of Cole Porter." To which Stravinsky wired back: "Am satisfied with great success."

Granted a long span of life, Stravinsky was aided by that combination of inner and outer factors which makes for an international career. It was his historic role to incarnate a phase of the contemporary spirit. In upholding the Apollonian discipline in art, he revealed an era to itself. He was the representative musician of our time.

26 Two Works by Stravinsky

"When people have learned to love music for itself, . . . their enjoyment will be of a far higher and more potent order, and they will be able to judge it on a higher plane and realize its intrinsic value."

Pulcinella Suite

After the harrowing years of the First World War there was a widespread longing for spiritual renewal through a return to the spirit of an earlier, saner time. Serge Diaghilev, the genius of the Ballets Russes, sensed this need and proposed that Stravinsky write a new ballet based on the music of the eighteenth-century Italian composer Giovanni Battista Pergolesi (1710–1736). In order to interest him in the project, Diaghilev showed him several works by Pergolesi (including some attributed to the short-lived master but actually not by him). Stravinsky fell in love with the music and accepted Diaghilev's commission.

Yet we must not suppose that an external stimulus set the master on the path he was to pursue for the next thirty years. Neoclassicism was very much in the air at the moment; composers all over Europe were turning in this direction. Diaghilev merely provided the immediate spur for an artistic development that would have taken place in any event. Stravinsky himself recognized this. "*Pulcinella* was my discovery of the past, the epiphany through which the whole of my late work became possible. It was a backward look, of course—the first of many love affairs in that direction—but it was a look in the mirror, too."

173

What Stravinsky did was to immerse himself in Pergolesi's music so thoroughly that he could rethink it in his own language. The result was a bridging of the gap that separated him from Pergolesi's world, a blending of two dissimilar temperaments into a unified whole. Stravinsky's sound enfolds Pergolesi's, combines with it, and enriches it, in a score that encompasses humor, fantasy, and sentiment. To paraphrase the biblical phrase, the voice is Pergolesi's voice but the hand is the hand of Stravinsky.

Pulcinella was the traditional hero of Neapolitan *commedia dell'arte*, a figment of the popular imagination who was shrewd, resourceful, warm-hearted, and a bit unscrupulous all at the same time. The scenario of the ballet concerns four young men who are

A seventeenth-century engraving by N. Bonnart of Pulcinella, the commedia dell'arte hero. The Bettmann Archive.

mad with jealousy because all the girls in town are in love with Pulcinella. After a complicated series of disguises and misunderstandings, the four young men win their girls, Pulcinella weds Pimpinella, and all ends happily. The measure of Diaghilev as an impresario may be gauged from the artists he assembled to collaborate with Stravinsky: Picasso did the scenery and costumes, the choregraphy was by Massine, the leading roles were danced by the great Karsavina and Massine himself. The ballet received its premiere in Paris in 1920; Stravinsky was delighted with it. He considered *Pulcinella* to be "one of those productions where everything harmonises, where all the elements—subject, music, dancing and artistic setting—form a coherent and homogeneous whole."

Pulcinella came at a point in Stravinsky's life when, realizing that he could no longer return to Russia, he had exchanged his wartime haven in Switzerland for a permanent abode in France. Musically he exchanged his youthful attachment to Russian folk sources for a Western—that is, European—orientation. In this work he relinquished the grand orchestral panoply of the first three ballets for the chamber orchestra of the early eighteenth century. The score calls for thirty-three players.

Pergolesi flourished at the precise moment in music history when the grandiose Baroque was tapering off to the playful Rococo. When he died the two giants of the late Baroque—Bach and Handel—were still active. Thus the label *Neoclassical* applied to *Pulcinella* might more accurately be *neo-Baroque*. In this score Stravinsky adopted several features of Baroque music: the division of the string section into two groups, solo and accompanying; a concertante style based on vivid contrasts between individual instruments and groups of instruments, underlined by contrasts between soft and loud, between low and high registers; the steady, vigorous beat of Baroque music; and the utmost transparency of texture. From the eighteen numbers of the ballet Stravinsky arranged eleven into a delightful concert suite.

The string group consists of five instruments—first and second violin, viola, cello, and bass. The woodwind section does not include clarinets; its cooler, more objective sound is based on flutes, oboes, and bassoons. There is no percussion group. In its absence, Stravinsky points up the rhythm through his imaginative writing for low strings and brass. Each movement uses a different combination of instruments. The scoring is wholly Stravinskyan in its brightness and wit.

I. *Sinfonia* (Overture). *Allegro moderato,* 4/4, in G major. The slightly pompous air of this introductory number suits perfectly the serio-comic action that is to follow. Winds are contrasted with strings; Stravinsky achieves a lovely harpsichordlike effect by means of oboe and bassoon in high register. The music is propelled by the firm, unwavering rhythm of the Baroque, although not long after the beginning an extra beat sneaks into a 4/4 measure to remind us that, after all, we are in the twentieth century, not the eighteenth. Soft passages set off against loud create those areas of light and shade that were so germane to the early eighteenth-century style.

II. *Serenata. Larghetto* (not quite as slow as *Largo*), 12/8, in C minor. A broadly flowing melody on the oboe unfolds above an accompaniment of flutes and a droning bass in the strings. A muted violin takes over the melody, over plucked strings that suggest a guitar. The flowing 12/8 meter and pastoral mood conjure up memories of the siciliano, that slow-moving, graceful dance of Sicilian origin beloved by Bach, Handel, Scarlatti, Corelli, and other Baroque masters. A characteristic trait of the siciliano was the dotted rhythm in the melody:

Larghetto
Oboe solo

III. *Scherzino*, 4/4 , in C major. This light-hearted "little scherzo" is somewhat more polyphonic in texture, with wonderful contrast between flute and oboe, horns and strings. The movement accelerates to an *Allegro* in 3/8, in A, with the violins presenting an idea in sixteenth-note rhythm that covers an extraordinarily wide span. Notice the guitar sound of the broken chords in the strings toward the end of this section. It is followed by an *Andantino* in 2/4, in F. In this movement Stravinsky has strung together music from several Pergolesi pieces to achieve a twentieth-century pace of contrasts.

IV. *Tarantella*, 6/8, in B-flat major. When 6/8 time is taken at high speed, whether in a tarantella, hornpipe, or jig, it sounds like duple meter—that is, two triplets to a measure. Stravinsky specifies that the movement be played *mezzo forte* (medium loud) and staccato. The strings carry most of the burden of the hectic pace, with brief contrasts and reinforcement from the winds. The tarantella leads directly into the next movement.

V. *Toccata. Allegro*, 2/4, in E major. The Baroque toccata—the term came from the Italian *toccare*, "to touch"—was a composition that exploited the resources of a keyboard instrument, such as organ or harpsichord, with a flittering display of chords, arpeggios, and scale passages. In this toccata the virtuosity is that of the orchestra—and particularly of the trumpet; the winds show off their agility in a short middle section.

VI. *Gavotte with Two Variations. Allegro moderato, alla breve,* in D major. This movement is set entirely for winds. The gavotte, is a stately dance in duple time. The first variation is an *Allegretto* in 6/8. In the second—an *Allegro moderato* in 4/4—the bassoon chatters against the suave traceries of the flute and horn. By changing the contour of the melody, its tempo, meter, and rhythm as well as type of accompaniment, the character of the theme is completely altered. Here are three versions of the tune:

VII. *Vivo.* 2/4, in F major. This brilliant little number depends on a twentieth-century effect, a glissando (slide) on the trombone, which is used with exquisite drollery and imitated by a solo double-bass. The music has a brusqueness of gesture that bears Stravinsky's personal stamp.

VIII. *Minuet. Molto moderato*, 3/8, in F. The piece begins as from afar, with bassoons and horns creating an impersonal sound. They introduce a stately melody that is repeated by the strings. Presently the trombone takes over, and then the trumpet. An exciting crescendo leads into the Finale, an *Allegro assai* (very fast) in 2/4, in C major. The serene gaiety of this music is very much of the eighteenth century, despite the flavoring of syncopations and the powerful rhythmic thrust that propels the movement to its decisive ending, *fff*.

Symphony of Psalms

The *Symphony of Psalms* (1930) was among the works commissioned by the Boston Symphony Orchestra to celebrate its fiftieth anniversary. "My idea was that my symphony should be a work with great contrapuntal development, and for that it was necessary to increase the media at my disposal. I finally decided on a choral and instrumental ensemble in which the two elements should be on an equal footing, neither of them outweighing the other." The result was one of Stravinsky's grandest works, written "for the glory of God" and dedicated to the Boston Symphony Orchestra.

The choice of instruments is unusual. The score omits clarinets and violins—whose seductive tone did not accord with the composer's intention—as well as violas. The woodwind section consists of five flutes (one doubling on the piccolo), four oboes, English horn, three bassoons, and a contrabassoon. The brass includes four horns, five trumpets, three trombones, and a tuba. Stravinsky also calls for two pianos, harp, kettledrums, bass drum, and the darker strings—cellos and double basses. The three movements are performed without a break. The first is the shortest. The slow movement is about twice, and the jubilant finale about three times, as long.

I

Psalmus XXXVIII (Vulgate) Verses 13–14	Psalm XXXIX (King James Version) Verses 12–13

Exaudi orationem meam, Domine,
   et depreciationem meam:
   auribus percipe lacrymas meas.
	Hear my prayer, O Lord,
	   and give ear unto my cry;
	   hold not Thy peace at my tears.

Ne sileas, quoniam advena ego apud te,	For I am a stranger with Thee,
et peregrinus, sicut omnes patres mei.	and a sojourner, as all my fathers were.
Remitte mihi,	O spare me,
ut refrigerer priusque abeam,	that I may recover strength,
et amplius non ero.	before I go hence, and be no more.

The symphony opens with a preludelike section in which flowing arabesques are traced by oboe and bassoon. These are punctuated by an urgent E-minor chord which, spread out across the orchestral gamut, asserts the principal tonality. The altos enter with a chantlike theme consisting of two adjacent notes—the interval of a minor second (semitone) that has structural significance throughout.

This idea alternates with the fuller sound of choral passages as the movement builds to its climactic point on the words *Remitte mihi* (O spare me) over a strong pedal point on E. The modal harmony creates an archaic atmosphere and leans toward the Phrygian (the mode that is sounded by playing the white keys on the piano from E to E). Tension is created by the fact that, although the music seems again and again to be climbing toward the key of C, that tonality will not be reached until the second movement. Toward the end, the semitonal theme is woven into the texture by the inner voices. The sonorous cadence on G serves to launch the slow movement.

II

Psalmus XXXIX (Vulgate) Verses 2, 3, and 4	Psalm XL (King James Version) Verses 1, 2, and 3
Expectans expectavi Dominum,	I waited patiently for the Lord;
et intendit mihi.	and he inclined to me,
Et exaudivit preces meas;	and heard my cry.
et eduxit me de lacu miseriae,	He brought me up also out of an horrible pit,
et de luto feacas.	out of the miry clay,
Et statuit supra petram pedes meos;	and set my feet upon a rock,
et direxit gressus meos.	and established my goings.
Et immisit in os meum canticum novum,	And He hath put a new song in my mouth,
carmen Deo nostro.	even praise unto our God;

Videbunt multi et timebunt: and many shall see it, and fear,
    et sperabunt in Domino.   and shall trust in the Lord.

The slow movement is in fugal style. The subject is announced by the oboe. Wide leaps impart to the melody its assertive character.

The orchestral fugue is in four voices. After a spacious exposition, the sopranos enter with the theme of the choral fugue. The interval of a falling fourth lends expressivity to the words *Expectans expectavi* (I waited patiently).

This theme is taken over by altos, tenors, and basses in turn, to be treated in strict fugal fashion, while the orchestra expatiates upon the opening theme. The movement consequently is in the nature of a double fugue, freely handled, and characterized by a purity of style worthy of its models, the fugues of Bach. The stretto in the choral fugue comes on the words *Et statuit super petram pedes meos* (and set my feet upon a rock), the orchestra dropping out and the theme entering in the different voices at an interval of half a measure. (For an explanation of stretto, see the description of fugue in Appendix I-g.) This is followed by a stretto in the orchestral fugue, the impression of mounting tension being underlined by dotted rhythms. In the final measures elements of the two fugal themes are combined in chorus and orchestra. The climax comes through understatement. In a sudden *piano* the chorus in unison sings *Et superabunt in Domino* (and shall trust in the Lord), while a high trumpet in quarter notes, buttressed by cellos and basses in eighths, reminds us of the subject of the first fugue.

III

Psalmus CL (Vulgate)   Psalm CL (King James Version)

Alleluia.   Praise ye the Lord.
Laudate Dominum in sanctis ejus: Praise God in His Sanctuary:
    laudate eum in firmamento vir-   praise Him in the firmament of
        tutis ejus.   His power.
Laudate eum in virtutibus ejus: Praise Him for His almighty acts:

laudate eum secundum multitu- dinem magnitudinis ejus. Laudate eum in sono tubae:	praise Him according to His excellent greatness. Praise Him with the sound of the trumpet:
laudate eum in psalterio et cith- ara.	praise Him with the psaltery and the harp.
Laudate eum in tympano et choro:	Praise Him with the timbrel and dance:
laudate eum in chordis et organo.	praise Him with stringed in- struments and organs.
Laudate eum in cymbalis bene son- antibus: laudate eum in cymbalis jubila- tionis: omnis spiritus laudet Dominum.	Praise Him upon the loud cymbals: praise Him upon the high sound- ing cymbals. Let everything that hath breath praise the Lord.
Alleluia.	Praise ye the Lord.

The solemn Alleluia serves as introduction. The modal harmony in the chorus is pitted against a C-major pedal point in the orchestra. The *Allegro* proper opens with Stravinskyan rhythms that project the spirit of the Psalm in dancelike measures. The music starts out in a bright C major, with the tonic chord repeated against a driving rhythmic ostinato in the bass, the whole set off by staccato interjections in the orchestra. As so often in Stravinsky's music, the syncopation is underlined by the device of shifting melodic-rhythmic patterns from one beat of the measure to another.

The altos enter on the *Laudate* with the two-note theme of the opening movement. But these notes are now a major instead of a minor second apart. The music gains steadily in power, its forward momentum reinforced by striking modulations. Presently there is a broadening into the slower tempo of the introduction. Then, *subito piano e ben cantabile* (suddenly soft and very songful), the peroration gets under way, on the words *Laudate eum in cymbalis bene sonantibus* (Praise Him upon the loud cymbals), in the key of E-flat. This serene coda, which takes up about one-third of the movement, unfolds over a four-note ostinato in the bass in three-four time, so that the bass pattern begins a beat later with each recurrence. The noble melody of the sopranos reaffirms the semitone interval that has played a fertilizing role throughout the symphony; and the powerful E-flat major tonality rises at the very last to a cadence in C that evokes the *Alleluia* with which the movement opened.

For sheer grandeur of conception there is little in the output of the first half of our century to rival the closing pages of the *Symphony of Psalms*.

27 Béla Bartók (1881-1945)

"I cannot conceive of music that expresses absolutely nothing."

It was Béla Bartók's mission to reconcile the folk melodies and rhythms of his native land with the main currents in contemporary music. In so doing he revealed himself as the greatest composer Hungary has produced, and one of the towering figures in the music of the twentieth century.

His Life

Bartók was born in a district of Hungary that is now part of Rumania. The sensitive, studious lad—he was rather frail in health— soon revealed a serious musical talent. When he was seventeen he was offered a scholarship at the Vienna Conservatory, but he decided instead to follow his friend Ernö Dohnányi to the Royal Academy of Music in Budapest. There young Bartók acquired a reputation as a brilliant pianist. He also came in contact with a strong nationalist movement that strove to shake off the domination of Austro-German culture. His first important work for orchestra was a symphonic poem on the life of the Hungarian patriot Louis Kossuth.

Bartók soon developed an absorbing interest in native folklore. He became aware that what passed for Hungarian folklore in the eyes of the world was either the Gypsy music that had been romanticized

*Portrait sketch of Bartók
by B. F. Dolbin, 1944.
André Meyer Collection.*

by Liszt or the popular tunes of the café musicians, which were overlaid with elements of Austro-German music. Impelled by what he later described as "an urge towards the unknown, a dim inkling that true folk music was to be found only among the peasant class," he undertook to collect the native songs before they died out. In company with his fellow composer Zoltán Kodály, and armed with the indispensable recording equipment, he set out on a series of investigations that took him to the remotest villages of the country. From these expeditions Bartók derived the basic element of his art. "Those days I spent in the villages among the peasants," he recalled later, "were the happiest of my life. In order really to feel the vitality of this music one must, so to speak, have lived it. And this is possible only when one comes to know it by direct contact with the peasants." He also explored the folk music of neighboring countries—Slovakia, Rumania, Bulgaria, and what is now Yugoslavia—and subsequently extended his investigations to include Turkish and Arab folk song. Bartók later published a great deal on ethnomusicology and became one of the leading authorities in this field—a rare example of artistic creativity going hand-in-hand with a gift for scientific research.

His attainments as a pianist were recognized when, in 1907, he was appointed professor of piano at the Royal Academy in Budapest. His compositions, however, were much too advanced for a public accustomed to the standard German repertory. In 1911, along with Kodály and other young musicians, Bartók formed the New Hungarian Musical Society, which was dedicated to the goal of disseminating modern music. The project was defeated by the apathy of the public and the hostility of the critics. Bartók became so discouraged that for a time he gave up composing.

The tide turned when Hungary was declared independent of Austria at the end of World War I. The resultant upsurge of national feeling created a favorable climate for Bartók's music. His ballet *The Wooden Prince* was presented with great success at the Budapest Opera and was followed by his opera *Duke Bluebeard's Castle*. However, when Admiral Horthy came to power, Bartók's librettist—who had been active in the short-lived regime of Béla Kun—had to flee Hungary. The two works were dropped from the repertory. *The Miraculous Mandarin*, a ballet, was rejected by the authorities because of what they regarded as its immoral subject. Bartók undertook no further works for the stage.

In the ensuing years he was acclaimed throughout Europe as one of the leading figures of his generation. But he was less successful in his own country. Bartók was out of sympathy with the Horthy regime and did nothing to ingratiate himself with those who might have furthered his career. The alliance between Horthy and Nazi Germany confronted the composer with issues that he faced without flinching. His physical frailty had no counterpart on the moral plane. He spoke out against Hitler in a political climate where it was inexpedient to do so, protested the playing of his music on the Berlin radio, and lost no opportunity to make clear his abhorrence of Nazism. "In Hungary," Bartók wrote, "the 'civilized' Christian folk are almost entirely devoted to the Nazi system. I am really ashamed that I come from this class." To go into exile meant surrendering the official status he enjoyed in Hungary and the economic security that went with it. But he would not compromise. "He who stays on when he could leave may be said to acquiesce tacitly in everything that is happening here." Bartók's friends, fearing for his safety, prevailed upon him to leave the country while there still was time. He arrived in the United States in 1940 and settled in New York City.

He embarked on a concert tour, playing two-piano music with his wife and onetime pupil, Ditta Pasztory-Bartók. He also received an honorary doctorate from Columbia University and an appointment there to do folklore research. (Bartók throughout his life refused to teach composition.) Despite this fair beginning, his life in America yielded little in the way of happiness. His retiring personality was not one to make an impact on the American public. He felt increasingly isolated in his new surroundings. His letters, some of them written in English, trace a mounting curve of discouragement. "Concerts are few and far between. If we had to live on those we would really be at the end of our tether. Our situation is getting daily worse and worse. I am rather pessimistic. I lost all confidence in people, in countries, in everything. Until now we had two free pianos, a baby grand and an upright. Just today I got the news the upright will be taken from us. So we will have no possibility to study two-piano works. And each month brings a similar blow. I am wondering and asking myself what next?" With the entry of the United States into the war, such income as Bartók still received from Hungary was cut off. "At Columbia," he wrote at the end of 1942, "I am 'dismissed' from Jan. 1 on. They seem to have no more money for me. Otherwise my career as a composer is as much as finished: the quasi boycott of my works by the leading orchestras continues; no performances either of old works or new ones. It is a shame—not for me, of course."

The onset of leukemia made it impossible for Bartók to appear in public any longer. Friends appealed for aid to ASCAP (American Society of Composers, Authors and Publishers). Funds were made available to provide the composer with proper care in nursing homes and to enable him to continue writing to the end. A series of commissions from various sources spurred him to the composition of his last works. They rank among his finest. When he realized that he was dying he worked feverishly to finish his *Third Piano Concerto,* in order to leave his wife the only inheritance within his power. The *Viola Concerto* was left unfinished, to be brought to completion from his sketches by his friend and disciple Tibor Serly. "The trouble is," he remarked to his doctor shortly before the end, "that I have to go with so much still to say." He died in the West Side Hospital in New York City at the age of sixty-four.

The tale of the composer who dies in poverty only to be acclaimed after his death would seem to belong to the romantic past, to the legend of Mozart, Schubert, Musorgsky. Yet it happened in our time. Bartók had to die in order to make his success in the United States. Almost immediately there was an upsurge of interest in his music that soon assumed the proportions of a boom. As though impelled by a sense of guilt for their previous neglect of his works, conductors, performers, record companies, broadcasting stations, and even his publishers rushed to pay him the homage that might have brought him comfort had it come in time.

His Music

Bartók set out from the world of Wagner and Liszt, Brahms and Richard Strauss. In the course of his development he assimilated and outgrew the devices of French Impressionism. He was influenced by Stravinsky and Schoenberg, some of whose procedures he somewhat anticipated. Like them, he disclaimed the role of revolutionary. "In art there are only fast or slow developments. Essentially it is a matter of evolution, not revolution."

Despite the newness of his language he was bound by vital ties to the beauty and logic of form which are the essence of the classical heritage. "In my youth my ideal was not so much the art of Bach or Mozart as that of Beethoven." He espoused the Beethovenian vision of music as an embodiment of human experience. The quotation at the head of this chapter indicates an attitude altogether at variance with the formalist aesthetic of Stravinsky. His art recaptures the heroic lyricism of an earlier age. In the introspective slow movements of his larger works is to be found the hymnic quality of the Beethovenian adagio.

The study of Hungarian folklore, he wrote, "was of decisive influence upon my work because it freed me from the tyrannical rule of the major and minor keys." The peasant tunes, based on old modes and pentatonic scales, were as liberating for Bartók as the sonorities and rhythms of the Balinese gamelan had been for Debussy. From the songs of southeastern Europe, he states, "we could learn how best to employ terseness of expression, to cultivate the utmost excision of all that is nonessential. And it was this very thing, after the excessive grandiloquence of the romantic period, that we thirsted to learn."

Bartók's idiom is concentrated, reticent, austere. The powerful melodic line is peculiarly his own. At times it loosens into freely flowing arabesques that suggest the rhapsodical improvisations of east European (and all Eastern) music. Yet it can also be angular, taut. Characteristic are melodies which, like those of Stravinsky in his Russian period, move within a norrow range and circle about a single note. Bartók too is fond of repeating fragments on different beats of the measure, producing the primitive effect of a melody turned in upon itself. The influence of Hungarian folk songs is manifest in the abundance of intervals of the second, fourth, and senventh. The melody line often proceeds scalewise. Within the limits he imposes upon himself, Bartók achieves an astonishing diversity of effect.

He loosened the old modes through a species of chromatic ornamentation. He also experimented in combining different modes (*polymodality*). Therefrom came his fondness for the simultaneous use of major and minor. Characteristic are his bold superimposing of independent streams of chords upon one another; his use of chords built in fourths instead of thirds; his addiction to cluster chords that take on a rude strength from the bunching together of the tones; and the use of parallel seconds, sevenths, and ninths which gives his music an extraordinary impact. He is a master of percussive dissonance. In the *Allegro barbaro*, we found the hammer-blow treatment of astringent chords that reached its full vogue some years later with Stravinsky's *Rite of Spring*. (See musical example, page 34.) Although Schoenberg's thinking held a great attraction for him, Bartók never abandoned the concept of tonality. His frequent use of pedal points and of a drone bass—a feature of peasant instruments everywhere—binds together the harmony and emphasizes its tonal character. Given Bartók's free use of keys and modes, it would be difficult to describe a work of his as being in E major or minor. But we can say with assurance that it centers around E.

Bartók's is one of the great rhythmic imaginations of modern times. His pounding, stabbing rhythms are instinct with elemental force and tension. Fom the folk dances of southeastern Europe he developed a rich store of asymmetrical formations. Typical is his fondness for repeated notes and for passages based on alternating patterns, such as triple and duple, or a group of five beats and one of three—a procedure taken from Bulgarian folk dance. Like Stravinsky, he played a major role in the revitalizing of Western rhythm, achieving a freshness and an eruptive force that were unheard of before his time.

Bartók was much preoccupied with formal unity and coherence, which he attained through the cumulative development of themes and motives. His music is imbued with the spirit of continuous variation; the material is made to reveal new facets of its nature throughout. There results a form that is thoroughly consonant with the twentieth-century concept of dynamic symmetry, marked by a sense of relentless growth, tension, and forward thrust.

Bartók's fugal texture is a masterly example of modern dissonant counterpoint and incarnates the urge of his era for abstraction of thought, tightness of structure, and purity of diction. Counterpoint led him, as it did Stravinsky, to simplification of style and compression. His orchestration exemplifies the contemporary tendency to use color for the projection of ideas rather than as an end in itself. He ranges from brilliant mixtures to threads of pure color that bring out the interweaving melody lines; from a hard, bright sheen to characteristically Bartókian flickerings of color traced against a luminous haze. A somber light permeates his slow movements, those brooding "night pieces" which, to use Beethoven's famous phrase, are "more an expression of feeling than tone painting." Bartók's personal way of handling such familiar effects as glissandos, trills, tremolos, and harmonics, and his arresting use of divided strings and of the percussion group—indeed, his whole approach to sound—bespeak a prodigious orchestral imagination.

A virtuoso pianist himself, Bartók typifies the twentieth-century treatment of the piano as an instrument of percussive rhythm. The frequent cluster chords are hammered with the full weight of shoulder and arm. The dissonant seconds are frequently played with one finger—by the thumb or the fifth.

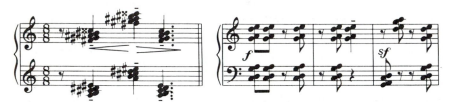

Bartók was devoted to the miniature. The *Bagatelles* and *Elegies* (1908), *Burlesques* and *Sketches* (1910), *Hungarian Peasant Songs* (1906), and *Romanian Dances* (1910) are intimate genre pieces. There are also several volumes of children's pieces. The most important piano work of his later years is *Mikrokosmos* (1926–1937), a collection of one hundred and fifty-three pieces ranging from the simplest grade to virtuoso level. The *Sonata for Two Pianos and Percussion* (1938) is a remarkably original work which the composer later transcribed as the *Concerto for Two Pianos and Orchestra*.

The six string quartets (1910–1939) rank among the major achievements of our century. In their breadth of vision and profound humanity these quartets are the legitimate progeny of Beethoven's. The two *Sonatas* for violin and piano (1921–1922) stem from the period when Bartók stood closest to Viennese atonalism. The *Sonata for Unaccompanied Violin* (1944) is a tightly knit work in the difficult medium made famous by Bach. Bartók reached his creative peak in the final decade of his life. Turning to the chamber orchestra, he produced in 1936 the *Music for String Instruments, Percussion and Celesta.* Tonal opulence and warmth of expression characterize the *Concerto for Orchestra.* The master's final testament, the *Third Piano Concerto* (1945), is a work of vehemence and breadth. Its three movements are in turn dramatic, contemplative, and satanic. The last mood, a favorite with the Romantics, constitutes a link between Bartók and his nineteenth-century compatriot Franz Liszt. The opera *Duke Bluebeard's Castle* (1911), the ballet *The Wooden Prince* (1914–1916), and the ballet-pantomime *The Miraculous Mandarin* (1919) exemplify the modern trend toward concise dramatic works: each is in one act.

Bartók differs from Stravinsky in one respect. Each of the Russian master's works is homogeneous in style, no matter how much he may change from one work to the next. A piece by Bartók, contrariwise, is apt to incorporate diverse elements, these being held together by the sheer force of his personality. Bartók encompassed the various trends of his time, from polytonality to the atonal, from Expressionism to the Neoclassical, from folk song to the constructivist, from lyricism to the purely dynamic, from a rough Primitivism to the intellectual, from racy humor and grotesquerie to the tragic; and—the ultimate step—from Nationalism to the universal. And he reconciled all these with the high aim of a former time—to touch the heart.

Bartók's prime quality was an unflinching integrity that informed every act of the artist and the man. He was one of the great spirits of our time.

28 Two Works by Bartók

"What we had to do was to divine the spirit of this unknown folk music and to make this spirit, so difficult to describe in words, the basis of our works."

Music for String Instruments, Percussion and Celesta

This piece (1936), a landmark in the twentieth-century cultivation of chamber-music textures, was written for Paul Sacher and the Basel

Chamber Orchestra, which gave it its first performance. The unusual combination of instruments indicates the composer's intent to explore the sonorous possibilities of such an ensemble. Bartók's conception called for two string groups to frame the percussion. He carefully specified the arrangement of the players on the stage:

	Double Bass I	Double Bass II	
Cello I	Timpani	Bass Drum	Cello II
Viola I	Side Drums	Cymbals	Viola II
Violin II	Celesta	Xylophone	Violin IV
Violin I	Piano	Harp	Violin III

I. *Andante tranquillo.* The movement is based on a single crescendo that grows inexorably from *pp* to a *fortissimo* climax and then subsides. We hear a fugue based on an undulating chromatic theme that moves within the range of a fifth, from A to E, and includes all the semitones between. This subject is introduced by the muted violas. Each time the subject enters it appears a fifth higher or lower, fanning out from the central tone A—first on E (a fifth above A), then on D (a fifth below A); on B (a fifth above E), G (a fifth below D), F-sharp

(a fifth above B)—growing steadily in power until the climactic point is reached on E-flat. Thereupon the theme is inverted and the movement returns to the central A. Thus, the crescendo-decrescendo pattern is combined with ascending-descending motion. Since the entire movement is woven out of the generating theme, this *Andante* achieves an extraordinary concentration of thought and consistency of texture.

II. *Allegro.* The main idea is a taut, imperious subject, whose chromatic character relates it to the germinal theme of the preceding movement. This *Allegro* is a closely knit sonata form that draws its impetus from the gestures of the dance. The development section

contains an exciting passage in fugal style. In the recapitulation, the main idea returns in Bartók's favorite alternation of 3 and 2 time, then settles into 3/8. The two groups of strings are used antiphonally, in question-and-answer formation.

III. *Adagio*. This "night piece" reveals Bartók's gift for evoking a magical landscape through instrumental color. The eerie repetition of the high F on the xylophone ushers in a rhapsodic cantillation of the viola. The main theme of the movement is presented by celesta and violin. Bartókian flickerings of sound—runs on the celesta mingled with glissandos on harp and piano—provide a background for the free development of a chromatic idea born of the germinal theme. The climax of the movement is based on a tense five-tone motive that is bandied about among the instruments. This is the central point of the movement. The measures that follow it (at measure 49) are an exact replica—but backward—of those that came before.

IV. *Allegro molto*. The finale combines the passionate abandon of Magyar folk dance with contrapuntal processes that are tossed off with sheer virtuosity. The movement opens with plucked chords that conjure up the sound of folk instruments.

The central idea of this expanded rondo form outlines the Lydian mode (see page 27). The rhythm is a Bulgarian dance pattern of 8/8 in groups of 2, 3, and 3:

The middle part of the rondo theme goes back to the sinuous contours of the germinal theme. In the contrasting sections Bartók deploys his propulsive rhythms, which at times take on a jazzlike animation, and his powerful cluster chords on the piano. Each recurrence of the rondo theme brings fresh variation. The movement

builds up to a climax that leads to the triumphal return of the germinal theme, now purged of its chromaticism. This diatonic version is presented with expanded intervals. The coda leads to a clangorous, affirmative cadence.

Fourth String Quartet

Bartók's *Fourth Quartet* (1928) rests on an architectonic conception that welds the five movements into an organic unity. The third or central movement is placed between two scherzos, which are related in thematic material, as are also the two outer movements. German theorists liken this kind of musical structure to an arch. The formal scheme of the quartet is reinforced by the key relationships, even though these are treated very freely. The first and last movements center around C; the second around E (a major third above C); and the fourth around A-flat (a major third below C).

The musical tissue is fashioned out of motivic cells which lead into one another with that inevitableness which is the essence of Classical form. The contrapuntal texture is closely woven, with an abundance of canonic and free imitation (although, interestingly, neither fugue nor fugato is present in the work). The writing throughout is of virtuoso caliber and makes the highest technical demands upon the players.

I. *Allegro*. The first movement grows out of a compact germinal motive which pervades the entire work, generating rhythms and themes. Introduced by the cello in the seventh measure, this basic idea moves along the chromatic scale from B to D-flat, them down to B-flat:

We hear it almost immediately in inverted form:

It is taken up by the viola in a diatonic version, its intervals expanded, and from then on undergoes a searching development. The music for the most part has a chromatic sound. The rhythmic patterns overlap, imparting to the movement its relentless drive. Notice the percussive effect of the cluster chords, the inexorable growth of the basic idea, the glissandos on all four instruments that make so striking a sonority, and the intensification that comes with the *Più mosso* (faster) at the end.

II. *Prestissimo*. The instruments play *con sordino* (with mutes). The germinal motive, now expanded to include the eight semitones from E to B, is introduced by viola and cello playing in octaves. This idea is developed through variational procedures as the music slithers up

and down the chromatic scale in a fleet *perpetuum mobile*. Its ghostly quality links it to the *scherzo fantastique* of the nineteenth century. A second motive emerges, consisting of a tone preceded by its upper and lower neighbors, which is presented in canonic imitation at the second. Ostinato rhythms, syncopation, and glissandos contribute to the effect of this movement, which vanishes as mysteriously as it began.

III. *Non troppo lento*. The brooding slow movement is the centerpiece of the work. The cello launches a long-breathed melody whose florid arabesques evoke the rapturous improvisation of Hungarian folk musicians on the *tárogató* (a woodwind instrument of the clarinet family). Much in evidence is the characteristic rhythm of Hungarian folk song, a sixteenth followed by a dotted eighth (♪♩.)—a pattern resembling the Scotch snap. The Bartókian flickerings of sound in the middle part suggest the "night music" that the master loved to write. The *tárogató* melody returns and is rounded off by a pianissimo allusion to the nocturnal music on the first violin.

IV. *Allegretto pizzicato*. Bartók desired, for the second sherzo, "a strong pizzicato, so that the string rebounds off the fingerboard." Both motives of the earlier scherzo return. The second is again treated in canonic imitation, this time at the ninth. Notice the violent dynamic contrasts between *ppp* and *ff*, and the folk quality of the plucked-string sound. For all its thematic relationship to the second movement, this scherzo has a quite different expressive content.

V. *Allegro molto*. Widely spaced fortissimo chords conjure up a rude peasant instrument of the drone-bass type. The ostinato rhythms have a primitive force, as have the open fifths of the accompaniment. The germinal theme reappears in its diatonic form and is soon presented in inversion, then with expanded intervals. The movement builds to a coda of immense power.

The *Fourth String Quartet* unites abstract thought and searching emotion within a convincing form. It is an extraordinary achievement in respect to imaginative handling of the string quartet medium, the achievement of organic unity through motivic coherence, sustained tension, and impassioned expressivity.

29 Paul Hindemith (1895-1963)

"One can still learn much from 'Papa' Haydn."

The artist endowed with a strong historic sense is impelled to affirm his kinship with the past. In the late nineteenth century it was Brahms who played this retrospective role. In the second quarter of our century it was Paul Hindemith who found in his heritage the point of departure for his own work.

His Life

Hindemith was born in Hanau, a city near Frankfurt, of a working-class family. His father being opposed to his choice of a musical career, the boy left home when he was eleven and made his way playing in dance bands, motion picture houses, cafés, and theaters. He managed to receive a sound musical training at the Conservatory of Frankfurt and became concert master, ultimately conductor at the opera house of that city. A virtuoso on the viola, he played in the Amar Quartet, a group that won fame in the early 1920s for its performances of contemporary chamber music.

Hindemith was the most substantial figure among the composers who came into prominence in Germany in the years after the First World War. His music embodied the boldly experimental spirit that flourished under the Weimar Republic and was widely performed at the various festivals for contemporary music. It was at one of these that Richard Strauss, after hearing his more advanced compositions,

Hindemith in a pencil sketch by Rémusat. André Meyer Collection.

remarked to the young man, "*You* don't have to write like that—you have talent!"

In 1927 Hindemith was made professor of composition at the Berlin Hochschule. Here, and at the Volksmusikschule—a project for the dissemination of musical knowledge among the masses—he put into practice his progressive theories of musical education. His aim was to produce versatile craftsmen in the sense of the eighteenth century, rather than the overspecialized virtuoso that had been brought into fashion by the nineteenth. He encouraged his students to learn to play a number of instruments, to perform each other's compositions, and to participate in a many-faceted musical experience based on group activity. In 1935 Hindemith found a more extensive laboratory for his theories when the Turkish government commissioned him to organize the musical activities of the country. He drew up the blueprint for a complete system of education, from elementary school level to teachers' training schools; founded symphony orchestras along the most advanced Western lines; and in the course of three visits to Turkey put the plan into effect.

Although the Nazi regime was eager to encourage artists of German blood, Hindemith was much too modern for a regime that recognized the Wagnerian as the proper path for contemporary German music. Propaganda Minister Goebbels accused him not only of "atrocious dissonance" but also of "cultural Bolshevism" and "spiritual non-Aryanism," and Hindemith's music was banned as being "unbearable to the Third Reich." The composer came to the United States shortly before the outbreak of the Second World War and joined the faculty of Yale University. Many young Americans came under his influence there and at the summer school of the Berkshire Music Center in Tanglewood, Massachusetts. In 1949 Hindemith was invited to deliver the Charles Eliot Norton lectures at Harvard University. He subsequently expanded these into a book, *A Composer's World*, which in lively fashion gives the essence of his artistic creed.

Hindemith exerted a strong influence on the American scene during the decade and a half he spent here. With the restoration of peace he felt the need of returning to the pattern of life in which he had his roots. In 1953 he went to live in Zurich. During the ensuing years he was ever more active as a conductor. In 1959 he came back to the United States for a series of concerts and conducted several works, the most important of which was *Pittsburgh Symphony—1958*, written for that city's two-hundredth anniversary. He died in Zurich at the age of sixty-eight.

His Music

Hindemith was German to the core. His heritage manifests itself in his love of florid counterpoint, his Gothic luxuriance of invention, and the ample curves of melody that revive the arabesque of Bach. German, too, are his love for the wind instruments, for which he writes with such mastery; his solid orchestral sound; his respect for workmanship; and his occasionally heavy-handed humor. "What I like about him," Francis Poulenc once remarked, "is that lyricism, at once heavy and agile, like mercury."

Like the masters of the German Baroque, Hindemith was rooted in the Reformation. His art was nurtured by the Lutheran chorales and the old songbooks; by the masters of sixteenth-century counterpoint; by the cantatas and fugues of Bach. For Hindemith, as for the medieval philosophers whom he liked to quote, the greatness of music lay in its moral significance. Sounds and forms, he maintained "remain meaningless to us unless we include them in our own mental activity and use their fermenting quality to turn our soul towards everything noble, superhuman and ideal." Equally exalted was his conception of the composer's function. "A composer's horizon cannot be far-reaching enough; his desire to know, to comprehend, must incite, inspire, and drench every phase of his work. Storming the heavens with artistic wisdom and practical skill must be his least ambition."

Hindemith took his point of departure from the music of Brahms, Max Reger—who influenced him strongly—and Richard Strauss. From a harmonic conception of music he moved steadily to the contrapuntal art inherited from Bach and the polyphonists of the Renaissance. He played an important part in the development of dissonant counterpoint, which constitutes a basic element of his style. Hindemith's melody, rooted in the popular song of medieval Germany, emphasizes the fundamental intervals of a fourth and a fifth. Now orante and discursive, now terse and muscular, it lends itself well to contrapuntal combination. It is personal, but not subjective.

Hindemith's harmony is based on the free use of the twelve tones around a center. Certain daring combinations result from a counterpoint of chord against chord instead of note against note (polyharmony). He steadfastly adhered to the principle of tonality, which he regarded as an immutable law. (Hence his opposition to the Schoenbergian school.) His use of simple triads as points of repose imparts to his music a serenity that is one of its outstanding traits. His harmony can be dry and dissonant; or, as in his later works, it may take on a mellow chromaticism. It often has a modal coloring, as is to be expected from a composer with so strong an affinity for old music.

In the matter of rhythm Hindemith was markedly less spectacular then either Stravinsky or Bartók. In his less inspired moments the counterpoint jogs along with a steady pulsation that reminds one of the music of the Baroque. But at his best, his emotion transforms itself into motion; he arouses himself to a rhythmic nervosity marked by diversified metrical patterns. There results a driving, motoric music that is entirely contemporaneous in spirit.

In respect to form Hindemith was a traditionalist. His models were the great contrapuntal forms of the Baroque: concerto grosso, passacaglia and chaconne, toccata and fugue; also the balanced form of the Classical sonata. He was partial to dance forms and was one of the first Europeans to show an interest in jazz. His instrumental forms reveal qualities at the same time Hindemithian and German: clarity of design, spaciousness of architecture, and sturdiness of construction.

The Neoclassic attitude pervades his handling of the orchestra (although he blends it with a somewhat romanticized Baroque). Color, he felt, should be subordinated to texture and form. In this, of course, he stands alongside Stravinsky, Schoenberg, and Bartók. By nature inclined to sobriety, he mistrusted the modern emphasis on striking timbres. "Music as an agent of moral elevation seems to have lost its position. Sound and its effect on our auditory nerves apparently is the only factor considered essential. Symphony orchestras have degenerated into mere distributors of superrefined sounds, and the more sparkling and alluring the sounds appear, the higher is an orchestra's rating." This love of sensation, he warned, is inimical to true musical understanding. "It is the curse of virtuosity that it can beget nothing but virtuosity."

Chamber music occupies a central place in Hindemith's output. The compositions entitled *Kammermusik,* for various combinations of instruments, are flanked by a long list of solo sonatas, duos, trios, quartets, quintets, and concertos. He wrote copiously for his own instrument. Especially well known is *Der Schwanendreher* (The Swan Catcher, 1935), a concerto for viola and small orchestra based on traditional folk songs, as well as the *Trauermusik* (Funeral Music, 1936) for viola and strings.

His vocal works range from solo song to cantata and oratorio. In the first category the weightiest item is *Das Marienleben* (The Life of Mary, 1923; revised, 1948), a song cycle for soprano and piano to poems of Rainer Maria Rilke. Memorable too is *Die junge Magd* (The Young Maid, 1922), a set of six somber songs for contralto accompanied by flute, clarinet, and string quartet. Of his choral works, mention should be made of his setting of Walt Whitman's *When Lilacs Last in the Dooryard Bloom'd* (1946).

Two of Hindemith's scores have won success as ballets—*Nobilissima Visione* (1937) and *The Four Temperaments*, a theme and four variations for piano and strings (1944). His most substanial achievement in the lyric theater is *Mathis der Maler* (Matthias the Painter, 1934), based on the life of the painter Matthias Grünewald. The symphony he derived from *Mathis* became one of his best-known works. A decade and a half later he embarked upon another opera about a famous personage, the astronomer Kepler: *Die Harmonie der Welt* (The Harmony of the Universe), from which he also derived a symphony

(1951). But the later work did not make nearly the same impact on the musical world as did *Mathis*.

Hindemith's formative period fell in the decade following Germany's first defeat. In his youthful rebellion against Romanticism he captured the nihilism of the 1920s. Sardonic humor and parody drove their way through his scores. His need to share in the life of his time brought him to the social viewpoint embodied in *Gebrauchsmusik*, the aims of which we described in an earlier section. At the same time his commitment to Neoclassicism made itself felt in an emphasis upon linear writing and an objectivism that frequently verged on matter-of-factness. With the passing of the years he grew gentler. The harshness and the irony receded, the expressive element came to the fore. His poetic lyricism was allowed to assert itself in ever greater degree, ultimately bringing about a reconciliation with the romantic emotion which he began by rejecting. He himself summed up this development: "Nothing is more wearisome or more futile than the most antiquated of all manias: the rage to be modern. With all the appreciation that one may reasonably bring to technical innovations, we should nevertheless minimize the word *new* in the term 'new art' and emphasize rather the word *art*."

In his first theoretical work, *Unterweisung im Tonsatz* (2 volumes, 1937, 1939, published in English as *The Craft of Musical Composition*, 1941), Hindemith made a comprehensive attempt to establish a modern theory of harmony. His teaching activities at Yale resulted in two books that have been widely used as texts—*A Concentrated Course in Traditional Harmony* (2 volumes, 1943, 1953) and *Elementary Training for Musicians* (1946). Like Stravinsky and Schoenberg, Hindemith gave much thought to the problems of contemporary music. The observations scattered through *A Composer's World* and other writings reveal a positive temperament and an incisive intellect. Almost every page yields characteristic utterances. "People who make music together cannot be enemies, at least not while the music lasts. . . . The proclamation of one's modernity is the most efficient cover for a bad technique, unclear formulations, and the lack of personality. . . . The reactions music evokes are not feelings but they are the images, memories of feelings. Dreams, memories, musical reactions—all three are made of the same stuff. . . . Genius seems to be the ability to retain the keenness of the first vision until its embodiment in the finished piece is achieved." Against the tendency to formalism in contemporary writing: "If music written on this basis has any message for others, it is the crassest order, 'You have to believe in my constructions,' in a time when we all are so terribly in need of some shiny little reflection of that other message, the one that Schiller and Beethoven gave to mankind: *Seid umschlungen, Millionen*—be embraced, ye millions." Finally: "If there is anything remaining in this world that is on the one hand basically aristocratic and individualistic and on the other as brutal as the fights of wild animals, it is artistic creation."

Kleine Kammermusik, Opus 24, No. 2

Hindemith was one of a number of composers who revived the spirit of Classical chamber music in unpretentious works that could be played by amateurs at home as well as by professionals on stage. A fine example of this development is his *Kleine Kammermusik* (Small Chamber Music), Opus 24, No. 2, for five winds, which he wrote in 1922. The five instruments are flute, oboe, clarinet, horn, and bassoon. The score carries the statement, as a kind of dedication, "Written for the Wind Chamber-Music Society of Frankfurt." In this respect, too, Hindemith was looking back to the practice of Classical and Preclassical times, when a piece was written for a specific occasion, purpose, or group.

I. The first movement, in common time (4/4), is marked *Lustig, Mässig schnelle Viertel* (Joyous, fairly fast quarter notes) and boasts a strong energetic rhythm. The opening melody, marked by the broad, undulating curves so dear to this composer, is rich in motives that are capable of growth and development. The first measure contains three of these: motive *a*, a repeated-note figure; motive *b*, a descending arpeggio that will lend itself to expansion and inversion; and motive *c*, which dominates the movement:

Hindemith weaves a closely knit tissue in which each of the three motives, as it is tossed from one instrument to another, has full opportunity to work out its destiny. For an age that was seeking to escape the overly sensuous sonority of the strings, these lean and pleasant woodwind textures must have come as a welcome change. The sound is somewhat impersonal, athletic, objective, with an outdoor quality that from time to time takes on a humorous cast.

A contrasting theme emerges on the oboe. Based on triplet rhythm, it flows more smoothly than the first. It too has an undulating line:

This idea is repeated ever more broadly before the return of the first. It returns as a fleeting reminiscence at the very end.

II. *Walzer. Durchweg sehr leise* (Very soft throughout). This is a kind of parody-waltz with a roguish lilt. The main idea is a wide-ranging melody introduced by clarinet and echoed a tone lower (in sequence) by the piccolo, which in this movement replaces the flute. The repeated-note figure heard at the opening of the first movement flowers into an idea that serves both as a melody in its own right and as accompaniment to a tune on the horn. Since there are no drums in this piece, the lower wind instruments mark the waltz rhythm and do so with surprising effectiveness. The repeated-note figure comes to the fore in the final measures.

III. *Ruhig und einfach* (Calm and simple). This slow movement grows out of a lyrical phrase of great simplicity:

Notice the syncopated pattern in the second measure. This is the "snap" popularly associated with Scottish folk song. It takes on a quite different quality in these Teutonic surroundings. We encounter here a structural pattern very typical of Hindemith: a slow movement that encloses a faster, more eventful middle section. Hindemith cautions against too abrupt a change of mood by marking the middle section *nicht scherzando!* (not too light-hearted), with an exclamation point to boot. A hushed ostinato rhythm, repeated over and over again beneath a flowing melody, *ppp*, imparts dramatic tension to these measures:

The first melody returns and in the final measures is combined with the ostinato rhythm.

IV. *Schnelle Viertel* (Fast quarter notes). In this brief interlude the repeated-note figure flowers into new patterns, alternating with solo passages in free rhythm—like cadenzas—on each of the instruments. The result is a dialogue between strict rhythm and free rhythm, between multicolored sound and solo sound.

V. *Sehr lebhaft* (Very lively). Hindemith was one of a number of modern composers who were fascinated by the rhythmic flexibility of the old masters, which they tried to recapture through the use of syncopated patterns and the subtle shifting of accents within the measure. This *Allegro* is a splendid example. Beyond that, it serves as a fitting close to this charmingly extravert little work that pays homage so gracefully to the golden age of chamber music.

Hindemith's influence on the international scene reached its peak during the Forties. His music is considerably less in evidence at present, but this probably is only a temporary phenomenon. His contribution has been too substantial to be affected by the vagaries of fashion or the fluctuations of taste. In the art of the twentieth century Paul Hindemith was a prime factor for order, stability, and the continuity of the great tradition.

30   *Les Six*

"Enough of clouds, waves, aquariums, nymphs, and perfumes of the night. We need a music that is down to earth—an everyday music."

JEAN COCTEAU

The Heritage of Satie

We discussed Erik Satie's strong stand against Debussyan Impressionism. This trend merged in the 1920s with the general reaction against Romanticism and found a witty spokesman in the French writer Jean Cocteau. In a little work entitled *Le Coq et l'arlequin* (The Rooster and the Clown), Cocteau launched an all-out attack against the music of the nineteenth century, "the kind one listens to with one's head in one's hands." He called for "music with a punch" and proclaimed the era of "the circus and the music-hall"— that is, an aesthetic rid of Romantic soulfulness. So it was that Satie became the spiritual godfather and Cocteau the literary prophet of a group of six young musicians—*Les Six*—who were attracting much attention in Paris at the time.

Of the six, two—Louis Durey and Germaine Tailleferre—soon dropped from sight. A third, Georges Auric, made his reputation outside France mainly as a film composer. The other three—Darius Milhaud, Arthur Honegger, Francis Poulenc—became leaders of the modern French school.

Darius Milhaud (1892–1974)

"A composer should do everything with application, with all the resources of contemporary technique at his disposal. He can then hope that, after a life of hard work, he will see some works survive."

"I am a Frenchman from Provence," Milhaud began his autobiography, "and by religion a Jew." This sentence points up the two poles of the composer's heritage. He came from a distinguished, well-to-do family that had lived in Aix-en-Provence for centuries and received his training at the Paris Conservatory. Paris remained the center of his activities throughout his life, except for the years during World War II, when he found a refuge in the United States. After the war he divided his time between that city, where he taught at the Conservatory, and the United States, where he was active at several schools: Mills College, the Berkshire Music Center at Tanglewood, the Music Academy of the West at Santa Barbara, and the summer school at Aspen, Colorado.

Milhaud's is the music of a lyricist. His melodies are rooted in the soil of his native Provence. There is a simplicity and directness about them, a quietude of spirit and modesty of bearing that constitute the hallmark of his style. From the point of view of harmonic language he was one of the foremost proponents of polytonality, in the evolution of which he played a leading role. His attempt to expand the language of comtemporary harmony by combining different tonalities was pursued with all the logic of a keen, inquiring mind. His orchestral writing has the French clarity of texture. He experimented with small groups of instruments treated in chamber-music style. At the same time he was capable of those massive effects for full orchestra and chorus which have attracted French composers since Berlioz to "the big machine."

Milhaud was one of the most prolific composers of our time. His

Darius Milhaud, seated, with the pianist Menahem Pressler, looking at a score. (Ben Greenhaus Photography.)

list of works reached well above the three-hundred mark, including operas, children's operas, ballets, incidental music for plays, film music, choral works—cantatas, psalms, and settings of various poems and Hebrew prayers—symphonies, concertos, string quartets, piano pieces, and songs.

La Création du monde (The Creation of the World), one of his best-known works, offers a delightful introduction to his music. This ballet depicts the creation of the world from the point of view of Negro folk legends. Milhaud, on a visit to New York in 1922, was fascinated by the jazz he heard in Harlem. In this piece, he stated, "I made wholesale use of the jazz style to convey a purely classical feeling." He expanded the customary jazz ensemble into a chamber orchestra. His evocation of the nostalgic blues, his simultaneous use of major and minor, and his intricate counterpoint—so close in spirit to the dissonant counterpoint of Dixieland—resulted in a work that captured the improvisational quality of the jam session; yet the jazz elements were infused with the elegance and wit of a sensibility that is wholly French. Coming two years before Gershwin's *Rhapsody in Blue*, *La Création du monde* was a landmark in the music of *Les Six*. How well the following tune from the Overture evokes the mood of the Twenties. It is the theme of a jazz fugue that is introduced by the double bass and presented in turn by trombone, saxophone, and trumpet:

Milhaud's music, urbane and distinguished, bears the imprint of a master craftsman. Its creator was a *musicien français* who traced his lineage from Couperin and Rameau, Berlioz, Chabrier, and Satie.

Arthur Honegger (1892–1955)

"My desire and my ambition have always been to write music that would be accessible to the great mass of listeners, yet sufficiently free from banality to interest the music lover."

Although he became one of *Les Six,* Arthur Honegger (who was born in Le Havre of Swiss parents) was far less receptive to the doctrines of Cocteau and Satie than were his comrades. His Swiss-German background was not to be sloughed off that easily. His profession of faith, uttered in his early twenties, made it inevitable that he would be the first to break away from the group: "I do not follow the cult of the fair and the music-hall, but on the contrary, that of chamber music and symphony in their most serious and most austere aspect." In 1921 Honegger's oratorio *Le Roi David* (King David) won a sensational success, which was equaled three years later by that of *Pacific 231,* a symphonic poem glorifying the locomotive.

Much of Honegger's music is monumentally conceived, grandiose. It suggests the out-of-doors and lends itself to performance in the open. He succeeded in projecting the force of a manly temperament into dramatic oratorios—one may call them choral operas—such as *King David, Judith* (1926), and *Jeanne d'Arc au bûcher* (Joan of Arc at the Stake, 1935), which became one of his most widely performed works. The great mass of listeners who felt themselves left behind by the new music found in Honegger's works the pathos and grandeur they had missed since the eclipse of Romanticism. This was the secret of his success.

By the same token, once the tide of Stravinskyan Neoclassicism swept across Europe Honegger's music lost some of its impact. Toward the end of his life he could not help feeling that the world had

An early portrait sketch of Honneger by Fernand Ochsé.   André   Meyer Collection.

somehow slipped away from him. A vast disenchantment breathes from the pages of *Je suis compositeur* (I Am a Composer), a little book of reminiscences that appeared in 1951, when he was approaching sixty. "The métier of a composer," he wrote, "has the distinction of being the activity and the preoccupation of a man who exerts himself to produce a product that no one wants to use. I would compare it to the manufacture of Cronstadt hats, shoes with buttons, or Mystère corsets." In the same vein were the words of advice he addressed to his students at the École Normale: "Gentlemen, you absolutely wish to become composers? Have you reflected on what awaits you? If you write music no one will play it, and you will not be able to earn your living. If your father can support you, nothing prevents you from covering paper with black dots. You will find plenty of paper, but what you put down will have only a secondary importance for your fellows. They are not at all impatient to discover you and your sonata. Composing is not a profession. It is a mania, a gentle form of madness. . . ."

Like his friend Milhaud, Honegger was fascinated by American jazz. This preoccupation makes itself felt in the finale of his *Concertino for Piano and Orchestra*. Composed in 1920, the piece reveals the Parisian side of Honegger's oeuvre. Here he is still one of *Les Six*, writing for the sheer delight of weaving patterns into a music that is tasteful, simple, and direct. The term *concertino* (little concerto) implies a compact structure and unpretentious manner. The piece is in three movements that take about ten minutes to play. First is a moderate *Allegro* that commences as a dialogue between piano and orchestra. It is followed by a *Larghetto* (not as slow as *Largo*) in which the piano unfolds a broadly flowing melody rich in unexpected turns. The finale, an *Allegro* in 4/4, thrusts us abruptly into the jazz sound of the 1920s. Woodwinds moan, trumpets and trombone seem to be improvising a rapturous blues, and the piano executes complex patterns that look like the "breaks" in a piano piece by Zez Confrey. Honegger wrote the *Concertino* in 1924, two years after Milhaud's *La Création du monde* and the same year as Gershwin's *Rhapsody in Blue*, which would seem to indicate that European composers were quicker than their American colleagues to recognize the possibilities of jazz as a basis for serious works of lasting value.

Francis Poulenc (1899–1962)

"I have sought neither to ridicule nor to mimic tradition, but to compose naturally as I felt impelled to."

Francis Poulenc was so completely the Frenchman that in order to express the Gallic spirit he needed only to be himself. It was precisely then that this Parisian achieved the clarity and elegance we have come to recognize as the enduring traits of French art.

Poulenc's precocious talent manifested itself in the *Mouvements perpétuels* for piano, which he wrote when he was nineteen. These unpretentious miniatures, imbued with humor and charm, established him as the natural heir of Satie. In his vocal and piano music, however, he revealed himself as a lyricist possessed of the gift of fresh, spontaneous melody. The *Mass in G* (1937), *Salve Regina* (1941), and *Stabat Mater* (1951) stand with the finest examples of twentieth-century choral music. Equally distinguished is the cantata *Figure humaine* (1943), on poems of Paul Éluard, a moving work inspired by France's suffering during the German occupation.

Poulenc was an outstanding exponent of the modern art song. He wrote over one hundred and thirty songs. "I find myself able to com-

A caricature of Poulenc by his friend Jean Cocteau (1889–1963). André Meyer Collection.

pose music," he stated, "only to poetry with which I feel total contact—a contact transcending mere admiration." Poulenc felt this contact mainly with contemporary poetry. His song cycles include *Le Bal
masqué* (The Masked Ball, 1932), a "secular cantata" on the surrealist
verses of Max Jacob; a setting of Paul Éluard's *Telle Jour telle nuit*
(Night Is Like Day, 1937); *Banalités*, on poems of Guillaume Apollinaire (1940); and the brilliantly executed *Le Travail du peintre* (The
Painter's Work, 1956), on a set of seven impressions of contemporary
painters by Éluard. Poulenc's songs place him in the tradition of
Fauré, Duparc, Debussy, and Ravel.

The ways of talent are unpredictable. At the age of fifty-four the
"apostle of the Parisian café-concert" undertook a tragic piece in the
grand-opera tradition. *Dialogues des Carmélites* (Dialogues of the Car-

melites, 1953–1955) is Poulenc's weightiest work. The play, by the Catholic poet Georges Bernanos, concerns a group of Carmelite nuns who refuse to disband during the French Revolution and suffer martyrdom. Here the composer was able to call upon his mastery in writing for women's voices. *La Voix humaine* (The Human Voice, or, simply, The Voice, 1958), a "lyric tragedy in one act," is a *tour de force*—an opera with a single character. A woman sings a forty-five-minute monologue into the telephone bidding farewell to the lover who is abandoning her in order to marry another woman. Based on a play by Jean Cocteau, the work runs the gamut from tender recollection to unbearable anguish, mounting in an implacable line to the final outburst when, the conversation having come to its inevitable end, the woman falls on the bed sobbing "Je t'aime! Je t'aime!" It testifies to Poulenc's continuing popularity in this country that in recent years both works were presented to the public in new productions— *Carmelites* at the Metropolitan Opera and *La Voix humaine* by the New York City Opera, in English versions by the present writer. Poulenc himself felt that these were dramas of the interior life and should always be presented in the language of the audience.

Banalités

No discussion of Poulenc can be complete without consideration of his songs, for it was in these that he made his most personal contribution. He set thirty-four poems by Apollinaire, of whom he said, "I heard the sound of his voice. I think that's essential for a musician who does not want to betray a poet. The sound of Apollinaire, like all his work, is at the same time melancholy and joyous." It was this duality that Poulenc, himself an ambivalent man, was particularly equipped to express in music.

At the beginning of the Second World War Poulenc enlisted in an antiaircraft unit. He was demobilized during the "phony" armistice on the Franco-German front. Back in his country home at Noizay, near Amboise, he began the song cycle he called *Banalités*, on five poems of Apollinaire from the period of the First World War, when the Surrealist and Dadaist movements were expanding the frontiers of literature. The five songs of Poulenc's cycle, ranging in mood from the absurd to the whimsical to the profoundly lyrical, bear no trace of the ominous time in which they were written. France was not yet aware of the tragedy that was about to befall her.

I. *Chanson d'Orkenise* (Song of Orkenise). Poulenc's tempo direction is *Rondement, dans le style d'une chanson populaire* (Briskly, in the style of a popular song).

> Through the gates of Orkenise
> A wagoner wants to enter;
> Through the gates of Orkenise
> A vagabond wants to leave.
>
> And the guard of the town
> Falling on the vagabond:—
> "What are you carrying out?"
> "I left my heart there."
>
> And the guards of the town
> Falling on the wagoner:—
> "What are you bringing in?"
> "My heart, in order to marry."

The music captures the naive charm of the poem, its folk-song quality underlined by the regular phrases of the first section. This includes the stanzas just quoted. The dialogue is highlighted by dynamics: the questions of the guards are loud, the answers of romantic vagabond and wagoner are soft. In the second section, which includes the final two stanzas, Poulenc introduces some charming irregularities. The guards warn the two young men that love, like the road ahead of them, is gray. (For the complete French-English text of the cycle, see Appendix II.)

II. *Hotel. Très calme et paresseux* (Very calm and lazy).

> My room has the shape of a cage
> The sun stretches his arm through the window . . .
> I don't want to work
> I want to smoke

The languid vocal line, marked *piano, très lié et expressif* (soft, very smooth and expressive), delicately evokes the mood and atmosphere of Apollinaire's poem. Notice the upward leap that highlights the key word of the opening line, *cage:*

Sluggish harmonies in the background caress the ear. This music is perfumed with the bittersweet lyricism that constitutes Poulenc's very personal brand of sophistication.

III. *Fagnes de Wallonie* (Wallon Heaths). The third poem is in a darker, more surrealistic vein then the first two:

> So many deep sorrows
> Bear my heart to the desolate heaths

Poulenc's instructions, *Très vite, d'un seul élan* (Very fast, in a single rush), suggest the most remarkable feature of this song: a forward surge, an irresistible momentum that never falters, carrying the song to its high point on the word *mort* (death). An eloquent postlude on the piano allows the emotion to cool.

IV. *Voyage à Paris* (Journey to Paris). "Anyone who knows me will think it quite natural that I should have snapped up with eager mouth the deliciously stupid verse of *Voyage à Paris*." The deliberate banality of Apollinaire's poem, which is not far above doggerel, gave its name to the cycle, Poulenc's use of *Banalités* being a subtle way of drawing attention to the skill with which he avoided it.

> Ah, what a charming thing
> To leave the dull country
>   For Paris
>   Darling Paris
>   That one day
> Love must have created . . .

This charming little number, dedicated to Poulenc's other favored poet, Paul Éluard, is cast in the form of a swinging waltz whose tempo indication is *allant* (bustling) and *gai*. The mood is suggested by several indications scattered throughout the piece: *avec charme, très naturel, très amiable*.

V. *Sanglots* (Sighs). The final piece of the cycle is at the other end of the emotional spectrum—a deeply felt lament for the misery that is part of the human condition:

> My poor heart my wounded heart
> Like the heart of all men . . .

Here is an outpouring of feeling in the Romantic tradition of Fauré and Duparc. Remarkable is the breadth of the melodic line, the sustained lyricism, the shattering modulations, and the controlled tension that mounts inevitably to the impassioned climax:

> Then tear your heart out too
> For nothing will be free till the end of time

No-tre a-mour est ré-glé par les cal-mes é - toi-les   Or nous sa-vons qu'en nous

A dark resignation broods over the final measures:

> Let us leave all to the dead
> And let us hide our sobs.

Poulenc began by being fashionable with the chic audience that desires above all to be amused. But the underlying honesty of his music, its melodic distinction and refinement, caused it to make its way with the larger public. He had the wisdom to attempt only what lay within his reach. The result is music with a style and a sound of its own. You will never mistake it for anyone else's.

31 The Russians

"Can the true artist stand aloof from life and confine his art within the narrow bounds of subjective emotion? Or should he be where he is needed most, where his words, his music, his chisel can help the people live a better, finer life?"

SERGEI PROKOFIEV

The Soviet View

The Russian attempt to bridge the gap between contemporary composers and their listeners differs, in one fundamental respect, from similar attempts in our society. With us the decision is left to the individual. In the Soviet Union, on the other hand, the matter is considered to be a concern of the State. The notion that the individual artist creates as a form of self-expression is as alien to the Communist view as the notion that the individual entrepreneur is free to invest in and develop his own business. Art is held to be created for the nation as a whole. It is supposed to reflect Marxist ideology and to educate the public in the Communist way of life.

The musicians of the West, accustomed to complete freedom of choice in all matters pertaining to their art, would find it well-nigh impossible to function within such a frame. Yet the leaders of the Soviet school not only have added a number of significant works to the present-day repertory, but have won immense popularity precisely in the two countries that are farthest removed from the political ideology of their homeland—the United States and England.

The question arises: may we accept their music as a sincere expression of their artistic convictions, or are their works written to please the commissars? It must be remembered that the composers who found it impossible to accept the Soviet regime—Rachmaninov, Stravinsky, Glazunov—left Russia and pursued their careers in exile. On the other hand, musicians like Shostakovich and Khatchaturian, Tikhon Khrennikov and Dmitri Kabalevsky grew up under the Soviet regime. They are products of Soviet education and culture. They have received enormous admiration from their countrymen, honors and rewards from their government. As Virgil Thomson pointed out in a perceptive analysis, "Soviet music is the kind of music it is because the Soviet composers have formally and long ago decided to write it that way, because the Communist party accepts it that way, and because the people apparently take it. Russians mostly, I imagine, believe in their government and country. Certainly these great, official public figures do. They could not, in so severe and censored a period, have become national composers by mere chicanery."

The Soviet composer has to write music that will communicate its meaning to a large circle of listeners. This can be quite a problem. On the other hand, he is sustained in his task by the knowledge that he is needed and that, as long as he writes the kind of music that is expected of him, it will be published, performed, discussed, and listened to eagerly by his compatriots.

Socialist Realism

The aesthetic path officially approved by the Soviet government is known as socialist realism. This theory of art stresses the connection between music and the imagery of life and tends to link musical expression with a strongly emotional content. As Shostakovich explains it, "Bringing into being a work that must be permeated with great ideas and great passions, that must convey through its sounds tragic suspense as well as deep optimism and must reaffirm the beauty and dignity of man—this is the difficult and complicated task demanded by realism."

The artistic oeuvre of Ernst Barlach (1870–1938) was decisively influenced by a trip he made to Russia in 1906. This bronze, dating from 1908, bespeaks his dedication to social realism. Russian Lovers. *Gustrow, Barlach-Archiv.*

The emphasis upon art as socially significant communication rather than individual self-expression has its roots in the intellectual climate of nineteenth-century Russia. One has but to read Tolstoy's *What is Art?* to realize how far he stood from the doctrine of art for art's sake that was beginning to conquer the Western world. Musorgsky's letters reveal the same preoccupation. "Art is a means of communicating with mankind," declared this most Russian of composers. "Let us look life boldly in the eye!" Dostoevsky's creed was similar: "My function is to portray the soul of man in all its profundity." And even earlier, Glinka had maintained that "It is the people who create, we composers only arrange."

A similar continuity is to be observed in the music itself. The first generations of Soviet composers studied at the conservatories of Moscow and Leningrad with the pupils and heirs of Rimsky-Korsakov, Musorgsky, Tchaikovsky, and Anton Rubinstein. Despite the great changes that separated them from the Russia of the Czars they retained the chief characteristics of their forebears: brilliant orchestral coloring; a flair for exciting rhythms; a fondness for direct forms based on repetition and sequence, rather than on the intricacies of thematic-motivic development so dear to the German mind; an exuberant use of folk and popular elements; and exploitation of exotic themes drawn from Asiatic Russia.

If socialist realism is the proper path for the Soviet artist to follow, all that he must not do is summed up under the label of *bourgeois formalism*. This, in Soviet parlance, is always a term of reproach. It implies "an excessive observance of form," or "obedience to stock formulas." Formalists are those who "sacrifice the *substance* of the musical thought for the sake of its *form*." They use their technical skill and mastery "for the sole purpose of disguising the fact that they, for the moment, have no worthy musical thought to express." Soviet opposition to bourgeois formalism has been aimed equally at Stravinskyan Neoclassicism and the twelve-tone school of Arnold Schoenberg. Both, with their emphasis on abstract technical procedures, were considered to reject the emotional imagery that relates music to life. Both were regarded as representing all that the Soviet composer is supposed to avoid.

The Composer and the Government

If the members of the twentieth-century Russian school had dutifully followed the path of socialist realism and avoided that of bourgeois formalism, there would be no problem. Soviet composers, however, are like composers everywhere. They are vitally interested in exploring the technical resources of their art. They cannot remain altogether oblivious of the experiments of their Western colleagues. As a result, despite every wish on their part to serve the regime, some of them have inevitably come into conflict with the authorities.

As a matter of fact, there was a brief period in the Twenties when modernism in art—in music, poetry, and painting—was made welcome in the Soviet Union. It was not until the Thirties that a wall was erected to shut out foreign influences. This rejection was made manifest in 1936 when *Pravda*, official organ of the Communist Party, launched a scathing attack on Shostakovich's opera *Lady Macbeth of Mzensk*. "The listener is from the very first bewildered by a stream of deliberately discordant sounds. Fragments of melody, beginnings of a musical phrase appear on the surface, are drowned, then emerge again to disappear once again in the roar. To follow this 'music' is difficult; to get anything out of it, impossible. The composer apparently does not set himself the task of listening to the desires and expectations of the Soviet public. He scrambles sounds to make them interesting to formalist aesthetes who have lost all good taste."

The problem was in abeyance during the period of the Second World War, when Soviet composers duly expressed in their music their love of country and their joy in its victory. Shortly afterward, however, they again aroused the ire of the government because of their susceptibility to the influence of the West. In January 1948, they were summoned to a conference by the Central Committee of the Communist Party, at which they were taken to task by Andrei Zhdanov, one of the leading Soviet theoreticians on art, philosophy, and music. In his address to the composers Zhdanov exhorted them to emulate the classical masters, who were able "to obtain unity of brilliant artistic form with profound content, to combine great mastery with simplicity and comprehensibility." He urged them to base their works upon folk song, to concentrate on operatic and program music, admonishing them not to allow their interest in rhythm to tempt them away from the primacy of melody. "The government," he stated, "has given many of you, including those who erred along formalistic lines, Stalin prizes. In doing so, we did not believe that your work was free of shortcomings, but we were patient, expecting our composers to find the strength to choose the proper road. We want you to overcome as quickly as possible the lag from which you are suffering and to develop into a glorious cohort of Soviet composers who will be the pride of the entire Soviet people."

The government point of view was embodied in the Decree of 1948, which criticized Shostakovich, Prokofiev, and others for their formalist tendencies. It accused them of having "torn themselves away from the ideals and artistic tastes of the Soviet people" and took them to task for having "cloistered themselves in a narrow circle of specialists and musical epicures." The Decree went on to combat the notion that the artist creates for posterity and must therefore leave his contemporaries behind. "In our country, composers are given unlimited opportunities. They have a listening audience such as no composer ever knew in the past. It would be unforgivable not to take advantage of all these opportunities, and not to direct one's creative efforts along the correct realistic path."

Despite all this, the problem was not solved. Soviet composers continued to be alternately praised and blamed by the government until the end of the Stalin era, when a more permissive attitude came into being. The new orientation was apparent in an editorial in *Pravda* in November 1953, which warned against the dangers of uniformity: "One of the most terrible evils for art is leveling, trimming everything according to one pattern, even if it is the best pattern. Such an approach to creative work obliterates all individuality, gives rise to clichés, imitations, deters the development of creative thought, deprives art of the joy of searching. That is why it is so important sometimes to support an artist in his daring . . . to respect the artist's right to independence, courage, and experimentation." The new line of thought culminated in the statement of the Central Committee of the Communist Party of May 1958, which was elucidated in a lengthy article in *Pravda*. The government admitted that the criticisms launched in 1948 against its leading composers had been "unfounded and unjust" and blamed these on "Stalin's subjective attitude to art." The *Pravda* editorial went on to state that "in questions of literature and art it is necessary to be high-principled, considerate, and attentive to artists, and helpful in supporting their creative initiative."

It is against this background that we must understand the music of the Soviet school.

32 Sergei Prokofiev (1891-1953)

"The cardinal virtue (or, if you like, vice) of my life has always been the search for originality. I hate imitation. I hate hackneyed methods. I do not want to wear anyone else's mask. I want always to be myself."

Sergei Prokofiev was one of those fortunate artists who achieve popularity with the mass public and at the same time retain the admiration of musicians. The brilliance and versatility of his gifts won him a place among the foremost composers of his time.

His Life

Prokofiev composed his first piece, a *Hindu Gallop*, when he was five and a half. He entered the St. Petersburg Conservatory at the age of thirteen, arriving for the entrance examination armed with the manuscripts of four operas, two sonatas, a symphony, and a number of piano pieces. Rimsky-Korsakov, who was one of the examiners, exclaimed "Here is a pupil after my own heart."

At nineteen Prokofiev made his first public appearance in St. Pe-

A drawing of Prokofiev by Michel Larionov (1881–1964). André Meyer Collection.

tersburg. He played a group of his piano pieces, among them the *Suggestion diabolique*. The dynamism of this music revealed at once a distinctive personal style. The works that followed—particularly the *Second Piano Concerto*, the *Second Piano Sonata*, and the *Sarcasms* for piano—established Prokofiev as the *enfant terrible* of Russian music. He rather enjoyed the role. In May 1914, he completed his course at the Conservatory. Over the opposition of Alexander Glazunov, the conservative director of the school, he was awarded the first prize in piano playing.

Exempt from military service, Prokofiev during the war years composed with unflagging productivity. The Revolution of 1917 caught him unawares, since politics was outside his sphere of interest. As the conditions of life grew ever more difficult, he began to think seriously of emigrating to the United States, where he would be able to work in peace. The *Classical Symphony* was given its premiere in Petrograd in April 1918, and made a strong impression on the new People's Commissar of Education, Anatole Lunacharsky. When Maxim Gorky introduced Prokofiev to Lunacharsky, the composer spoke of his desire to go to America. The Commissar replied,

"You are a revolutionary in music, we are revolutionaries in life. We ought to work together. But if you wish to go, I shall place no obstacles in your way." In May 1918, Prokofiev set out for Vladivostok. He gave two concerts in Tokyo and one in Yokohama; in September he arrived in New York.

His first recital in Aeolian Hall drew praise for his playing and invective for his music. The critics spoke of "a carnival of cacophony," "Russian chaos in music," "Bolshevism in art." Prokofiev fared better in Chicago, where his *Scythian Suite* met with success. More important, the head of the Chicago Opera Company, Cleofonte Campanini, decided to produce his new opera, *The Love for Three Oranges,* as soon as Prokofiev had finished the score. Campanini's sudden death caused the production to be postponed. "This put me in a most awkward position. I had been engaged on the opera for almost a year and had completely neglected my concerts." Prokofiev tried to retrieve his position by giving recitals; but he was doomed to fail. Audiences at that time were avid for foreign pianists who played Beethoven, Chopin, and the rest. A modern composer performing his own works was definitely not a drawing card. It became clear to him that the conquest of the new world was not going to be as easy as he had imagined. "I wandered through the enormous park in the center of New York and, looking up at the skyscrapers that bordered it, thought with cold fury of the marvelous American orchestras that cared nothing for my music, of the critics who balked so violently at anything new, of the managers who arranged long tours for artists playing the same old hackneyed programs fifty times over." There was nothing for it but to admit defeat and try Paris.

Things looked up immediately he reached the French capital. Diaghilev produced his ballet *Chout* (The Buffoon), which had a resounding success. In the meantime Mary Garden had assumed the direction of the Chicago Opera Company and decided to honor the contract with Prokofiev. *The Love for Three Oranges* received its premiere in Chicago on December 30, 1921, with Prokofiev conducting, and was warmly received. In New York, on the other hand, the opera met with hostility. "The production cost 130,000 dollars," one critic quipped, "which is 43,000 dollars per orange. But the opera fell so flat that its repetition would spell financial ruin." New York made amends a quarter century later, when *The Love for Three Oranges* became one of the most popular works in the City Opera repertory.

For the next ten years Prokofiev made Paris his headquarters, with frequent journeys to the musical centers of Europe and the United States to perform his music. Yet the sense of being uprooted grew within him. An encounter with Maxim Gorky in Naples could not but sharpen his longing for his native land. He continued for another few years, composing and touring; but his return to Russia presented itself to him more and more as an inescapable necessity. To his devoted friend Serge Moreux he wrote, "I've got to live myself back into the atmosphere of my native soil. I've got to see real winters again, and Spring that bursts into being from one moment to the next. I've got to hear the Russian language echoing in my ears. I've got to talk to people who are of my own flesh and blood, so that they can give me back something I lack here—their songs, my songs. Here I'm becoming enervated. I risk dying of academicism. Yes, my friend—I'm going back!"

The sixteen years of wandering between 1918 and 1934 were followed by nineteen years spent for the most part in his homeland. During this period he consolidated his position as the leading composer of the Soviet school. As one who had voluntarily rejoined the Soviets when he might have made a career abroad, he was sought out by the regime, laden with honors and financial rewards. In 1943 he received the Stalin Prize for his *Seventh Piano Sonata*. The following year he was given the Order of the Red Banner of Labor for outstanding services in the development of Soviet music.

At the same time, of all the Soviet composers he was the one who, due to his long residence abroad, was most closely associated with the Western influences which the regime considered inimical to socialist art. What was worse, he had worked in close collaboration with Diaghilev, whom the Soviet press described as "the degenerate, blackguard, anti-Russian lackey of the Western bourgeoisie," and had been friendly with such "servile and corrupt musical businessmen as Stravinsky." As a result, when the Central Committee of the Communist Party in 1948 accused the leading Soviet composers of bourgeois formalism, Prokofiev was one of the principal targets of criticism.

The government showed its displeasure with its recalcitrant composers by ordering the works of Prokofiev to be removed from the repertory, along with those of Shostakovich, Khatchaturian, and Miaskovsky. However, as these men happened to be the Big Four of Soviet music, the prohibition could not very well be maintained. After a few months Prokofiev's works—first his ballets, then his symphonies—began to be performed again. His next compositions, the *Sixth Symphony* and the opera *A Tale of a Real Man*, on a subject drawn from contemporary Soviet life, were attacked in the official press as being formalistic. *Izvestia* called the opera an example of "impractical, ivory-tower workmanship"; *Pravda* doubted whether one could expect anything "to satisfy the needs of the great Soviet people" from a composer whose work was penetrated to the core by "Western formalist decay." Prokofiev, who had sincerely tried to meet the requirements of socialist-realist art, was taken aback by the severity of the criticism. His answer was the *Seventh Symphony,* which received its premiere in Moscow in October 1952. This work of his ripest maturity quickly established itself, both within the Soviet Union and abroad, as one of his finest.

He died five months later, at the age of sixty-two. His death came one day after that of Josef Stalin. The Soviet Government withheld the news for forty-eight hours, presumably so that the one event would not overshadow the other.

His Music

Prokofiev appeared at a twilight moment in the history of Russian music, when the mysticism of Scriabin and the introverted romanticism of Rachmaninov dominated the scene. Into this atmosphere his youthful works—audacious, earthy, gloriously alive—came like a burst of fresh air. The wholesome athleticism of his music—what Russian critics called its "football" quality—went hand in hand with a rare knack of capturing in music the vivid gesture, the mocking grimace; he epitomized the revolt against Romanticism.

In his middle or "Western" period Prokofiev came under the influence of Diaghilev and tried to function within the Stravinskyan aesthetic of abstract art that dominated the Parisian scene. But the constructivist approach, natural to Stravinsky, was not at all suited to Prokofiev's particular gifts. After the failure of his *Fourth Symphony* in Paris, Prokofiev found his path by moving toward the romanticism that he had so long repressed in himself. "Music," he wrote, "has definitely reached and passed the greatest degree of dissonance and of complexity that it is practicable for it to attain. Therefore I think the desire which I and many of my fellow composers feel, to achieve a more simple and melodic expression, is the inevitable direction for the musical art of the future."

Hence it need not be concluded that Prokofiev wrote as he did in his final years because of his return to Soviet Russia. We may be closer the mark in supposing that it was the other way around. He returned to Soviet Russia because he felt that he would find there a favorable environment for the kind of music he wanted to write. The point has been well taken by the British critic Gerald Abraham: "Why should Prokofiev, who was continuing a brilliant career outside Russia, have voluntarily returned to a land where he knew certain limitations would be imposed on his work, unless he felt that these limitations would be unimportant? The truth is, I think, that he had already been tending in this direction for some time." The melodic appeal of his music, his fondness for Russian themes, his mastery of operatic and choral writing, his avoidance of introversion, and his prevailing optimism were precisely the traits that accorded with the dominant trends in Soviet art.

Prokofiev himself has provided us with an analysis of the elements of his style. "The first is Classical, originating in my early infancy when I heard my mother play Beethoven sonatas. It assumes a Neoclassical aspect in my sonatas or concertos, or imitates the Classical style of the eighteenth century." In the *Classical Symphony* (1917), composed "as Haydn might have written it had he lived in our day," Prokofiev came as close as anyone in the twentieth century to recapturing the gaiety of Haydn's effortless *Allegros*. The second element in his style he identified as the search for innovation. "At first this consisted in the quest for an individual harmonic language, but was later transformed into a medium for the expression of strong emotions." This strain is manifest in such early works as *Sarcasms* (1914); *Visions fugitives* (1917) for piano; and the *Scythian Suite* (1915) with its deliberate Primitivism.

"The third is the element of the toccata, or motor element, probably influenced by Schumann's *Toccata*, which impressed me greatly at one time." The toccata is associated with a strong rhythmic drive, generally of the "perpetual motion" type that is so much to the fore in the music of our century. "The fourth element is lyrical. Since my lyricism has for a long time been denied appreciation, it has grown but slowly. But at later stages I paid more and more attention to lyrical expression." This element understandably dominated the final phase of his work.

"I should like to limit myself to these four elements, and to regard the fifth, that of the grotesque which some critics try to foist on me, as merely a variation of the others. In application to my music, I should like to replace the word grotesque by 'Scherzo-ness' or by the three words giving its gradations: *jest, laughter, mockery*." Prokofiev stood in the forefront of those who attempted to broaden musical expression to include the comic and the mischievous. In his later years the grotesquerie mellowed into a compassionate humor.

The bold thrust of his melody, with its wide leaps and unexpected turns of phrase, is no less characteristic of his style than are his athletic, marchlike rhythms. His orchestration possesses all the brilliance of the earlier Russian masters. His harmonic language is remarkably varied and expressive. It can be pungently dissonant, but is essentially diatonic. Typical are the sudden changes of key that add excitement to his scores. (See the example from *Peter and the Wolf* on p. 27.) Also characteristic is his fondness for the bright C major, as striking a preference as, say, that of Mendelssohn for E minor. His compositional method was based on the clear-cut definition of key. Although there are atonal passages in his works, these are used, as he said, "mainly for the sake of contrast, in order to bring tonal passages to the fore." To fashion a work without tonality was, to him, "like building on sand." In his devotion to the large forms Prokofiev was a traditionalist. His classicism derived from Scarlatti, Haydn, and Mozart rather than, as in the case of Stravinsky, from Bach. "I want nothing better, nothing more flexible or more complete than the sonata form, which contains everything necessary to my structural purpose."

Both because of the nature of his gifts and of the aesthetic philosophy that he embraced, Prokofiev became one of the most popular of all twentieth-century composers. A greater number of his works have established themselves as "classics" than those of almost any other of his contemporaries save Stravinsky. Among them we find *Lieutenant Kije* (1934), a suite arranged from his music for the film; *Peter and the Wolf* (1936), a "symphonic fairy-tale for the young and old," in which each of the characters, animal and human, is represented by a distinctive instrumental color and theme; *Alexander Nevsky* (1939), a cantata arranged from the music for the celebrated Eisenstein film; the ballets *Romeo and Juliet* (1936) and *Cinderella* (1944); the *Scythian Suite;* and the *Classical Symphony.* The two *Violin Concertos* (1917, 1935) have found favor with music lovers the world over, as has the *Third Piano Concerto,* which we will discuss. The nine piano sonatas (1909–1947) are a contribution of prime importance to the modern repertory for the instrument. Especially popular with pianists are the sets of short pieces, such as the *Sarcasms* and *Visions fugitives.* Prokofiev, himself a virtuoso, wrote for the piano with profound insight; his powerful rhetoric helped to create the twentieth-century piano style.

In his later symphonies Prokofiev sought to recapture the heroic affirmation of the Beethovenian symphony. This is especially true of

A scene from the NBC television production of War and Peace (1957) *showing General Kutuzov conferring with his staff.*

the *Fifth* (1944), dedicated "to the spirit of Man," and the last, the *Seventh* (1952). Of his operas, two in particular found favor outside his homeland: *The Love for Three Oranges* (1919) and *The Duenna* (1940), a sprightly work based on Sheridan's comedy. *The Flaming Angel* (1927) and *War and Peace* (1941–1942, later much revised) were introduced to this country in English versions by the present writer, the first by the New York City Opera in 1966 and the second in a television performance by the NBC Opera Theater in 1957. *War and Peace* is Prokofiev's major effort in the lyric theater. He and his second wife, the poet Mira Mendelssohn, fashioned the libretto from Tolstoy's epic novel. The opera is conceived in the grand tradition. Among its highlights are the moonlit scene during which Prince Andrei is first attracted to Natasha; Natasha's first ball in St. Petersburg; the heroic war scenes centering about Marshal Kutuzov; and the affecting scene of Andrei's death. When first presented, the work received a lukewarm reception from critics and public alike. It has since established itself as one of the strongest productions in the Bolshoi Opera repertory.

Piano Concerto No. 3

The elements that Prokofiev enumerated as basic to his style are abundantly present in his most celebrated work for the piano (completed in 1921).

I. *Andante—Allegro.* "The first movement," Prokofiev wrote, "opens with a short introduction. The theme is announced by an unaccompanied clarinet and is continued by the violins for a few measures.

Soon the tempo changes to *Allegro*, the strings having a passage in sixteenths, which leads to the statement of the principal subject by the piano." This driving theme exemplifies—as does the entire work—Prokofiev's skill in achieving rhythmic diversity within the traditional meters.

"Discussion of this theme is carried on in a lively manner, both the piano and the orchestra having a good deal to say on the matter." Prokofiev exploits the contrast between piano and orchestral sonority with great élan. "A passage in chords for the piano alone leads to the more expressive second subject, heard in the oboe with a pizzicato accompaniment."

"This is taken up by the piano and developed at some length, eventually giving way to a bravura passage in triplets. At the climax of this section the tempo reverts to *Andante* and the orchestra gives out the first theme, fortissimo. The piano joins in, and the theme is subjected to an impressively broad treatment." The *Allegro* returns, the two main ideas are treated with great brilliance, and the movement ends with an exciting crescendo.

II. *Andantino.* The second movement consists of a theme with five variations. The theme, strongly Russian in character, is announced by the orchestra.

"In the first variation," the composer explained, "the piano treats the opening of the theme in quasi-sentimental fashion, and resolves into a chain of trills as the orchestra repeats the closing phrase. The tempo changes to *Allegro* for the second and third variations, and the piano has brilliant figures, while snatches of the theme are introduced here and there in the orchestra. In Variation Four the tempo is once again *Andante,* and the piano and orchestra discourse on the theme in a quiet and meditative fashion. Variation Five is energetic (*Allegro giusto*) and leads without pause into a restatement of the theme by the orchestra, with delicate chordal embroidery in the piano." This embroidery is colored by a spectral chromaticism that embodies the composer's love of the fantastic.

III. *Allegro ma non troppo.* The Finale displays the gradations that Prokofiev assigned to "scherzo-ness"—jest, laughter, mockery. Also present is that spirit of grotesquerie so vital to his expression. The mood is established at the outset by the staccato theme for bassoons and pizzicato strings:

This is interrupted by what Prokofiev called the blustering entry of the piano, played in chordal textures of great propulsive force. "The orchestra holds its own with the opening theme and there is a good deal of argument, with frequent differences of opinion as regards key." The solo part carries the first theme to a climax.

The melodist in Prokofiev is represented by the second theme, in his finest vein of lyricism, introduced by the woodwinds. "The piano replies with a theme that is more in keeping with the caustic humor of the work." Then the lyric theme is developed in the grand manner. An exciting coda brings the work to a close on a dazzling C-major dissonance:

Despite his difficulties with the doctrine of socialist realism, Prokofiev appears to have remained faithful to the aesthetic he espoused upon his return to Russia. A year before his death he wrote the following lines, which may be taken as a final affirmation of his creed: "When I was in the United States and England I often heard discussions on the subject of whom music ought to serve, for whom a composer ought to write, and to whom his music should be addressed. In my view the composer, just as the poet, the sculptor, or the painter, is in duty bound to serve man, the people. He must beautify human life and defend it. He must be a citizen first and foremost, so that his art may consciously extol human life and lead man to a radiant future. Such, as I see it, is the immutable goal of art."

33 Dmitri Shostakovich (1906-1976)

"I consider that every artist who isolates himself from the world is doomed. I find it incredible that an artist should wish to shut himself away from the people, who in the last analysis form his audience. I always try to make myself as widely understood as possible; and if I don't succeed, I consider it my own fault."

Dmitri Shostakovich belonged to the first generation of artists who grew up under the Soviet regime. He was entirely a product of Soviet training and may be regarded as the representative artist of the new order in Russia.

His Life

He was born and raised in what was then St. Petersburg. His parents and relatives were close to the revolutionary underground, and for them the overthrow of the monarchy in 1917 signaled the dawn of a new era. Dmitri made his way to school through streets crowded with fiercely debating soldiers and civilians. "I met the October Revolution on the street," he later remarked. Among the lad's first efforts at composition were a *Hymn to Liberty* and a *Funeral March for the Victims of the Revolution.*

His youth came in a bitter time. Civil war, inflation, and famine shook the social order to its foundations. The death of his father left the family exposed to privation. It was his mother who, in the face of almost insurmountable difficulties, made it possible for the boy to continue at the St. Petersburg Conservatory, where he studied with Alexander Glazunov and Maximilian Steinberg, the two favored disciples of Rimsky-Korsakov.

The severe conditions under which he grew up took their toll. For a time he was threatened with tuberculosis. At the lowest point in his fortunes he earned a few rubles by playing the piano in a movie house. Fortunately he did not have to wait long for success. His *First Symphony,* written as a graduation exercise when he was not yet nineteen, made an extraordinary impression and blazoned his name throughout the musical world.

Shostakovich began his career at a propitious moment. The defection to the West of such major figures as Rachmaninov and Stravinsky, who subsequently were joined by Glazunov himself, left a void which it became almost a matter of national honor to fill. Of the musicians of the rising generation, Shostakovich was clearly the most gifted. His star rose rapidly.

Shostakovich's *Second Symphony* (1927) commemorated the October Revolution. The *Third* was the *First of May Symphony* (1929). Each was "a proletarian tract in tones," as the composer later expressed it. Neither was successful. This phase of Shostakovich's career culminated in the four-act opera *Lady Macbeth of Mzensk.* Produced in Leningrad and Moscow in 1934, the work scored an immediate hit with the Russian public. The following year *Lady Macbeth* was presented with great éclat at the Metropolitan Opera House as well as in Cleveland and Philadelphia. The sensational theme of the opera—the heroine kills both her husband and her father-in-law for the sake of her lover—and the ultrarealistic handling of the material attracted a

A sketch of Shostakovich by Rémusat, bearing the composer's signature. André Meyer Collection.

great amount of attention, with the result that Shostakovich at thirty was one of the best-known composers of his generation.

For two years *Lady Macbeth* ran in Leningrad to packed houses. Then, in January 1936, *Pravda*, official organ of the Soviet government, printed its scathing attack upon the opera. We quoted a paragraph in our discussion of the Soviet musical scene. The article went on to state: "The author of *Lady Macbeth* was forced to borrow from jazz its nervous, convulsive, and spasmodic music in order to lend 'passion' to his characters. While our music critics swear by the name of socialist realism, the stage serves us, in Shostakovich's work, the coarsest kind of naturalism. The music quacks, grunts, and growls, and suffocates itself in order to express the amorous scenes as naturalistically as possible. And 'love' is smeared all over the opera in the most vulgar manner."

The article made it clear that the government did not call into question either Shostakovich's talent or his ability "to depict simple and strong emotions in music." What was questioned was only the use to which he put his talent. Nor could it escape the attention of his countrymen that a *Pravda* editorial—a space customarily reserved for political matters of the gravest import—had been turned over to the doings of a thirty-year-old musician. To be singled out so, even in a negative way, could not but add to Shostakovich's fame.

As for the composer himself, he went through a period of stern self-examination; he was too deeply committed to the Soviet view to question the directives of the rulers of his country. His *Fourth Symphony* (1936), a gloomy and introspective work, was already in rehearsal. He withdrew it. A year later, he was reinstated when the Leningrad Philharmonic presented his *Fifth Symphony* (1937). Across the score was written, "Creative reply of a Soviet artist to just criticism." The work was a triumphant success. *Pravda* praised the "grandiose vistas of the tragically tense *Fifth Symphony*, with its philosophical seeking." Shostakovich's personal victory was followed by a greater one when, in 1940, his *Piano Quintet* was awarded the Stalin Prize of a hundred thousand rubles, probably the largest sum ever paid for a chamber-music work.

The Nazi invasion of Russia released a surge of patriotism in the composer. "I volunteered for service at the front, and received the reply: 'You will be called when required.' So I went back to my duties at the Leningrad Conservatory." (He was professor of composition at his alma mater.) His *Seventh* or *Leningrad Symphony* (1941) was inspired by the militant spirit of his native city when it was besieged by the Germans, and at this critical moment Shostakovich inevitably assumed the role of poet laureate. "He rested his ear against the heart of his country," wrote the novelist Alexei Tolstoi, "and heard its mighty song." The *Seventh Symphony* marked the high tide of Shostakovich's popularity in the United States. It was introduced by Arturo Toscanini in a much heralded broadcast in the summer of 1942 and was subsequently played throughout the country. A writer in *Life* magazine facetiously pointed out that it was almost unpatriotic, even for Americans, not to like the piece.

When *Pravda* launched its attack on formalism in 1948, Shostakovich was again one of the principal targets. His reply to the charges showed that even when he himself was assailed, he remained an unofficial spokesman for the government's "stern but paternal solicitude for us Soviet artists." "Work—arduous, creative, joyous work on new compositions that will find their path to the heart of the Soviet people—this will be a fitting response to the Resolution of the Central Committee."

A year later, in March 1949, he was sent to the United States as delegate to the Cultural and Scientific Conference for World Peace. Had he come five years earlier he would have been acclaimed and feted. Now, however, the cold war was in full swing. He was not allowed to travel outside New York City; his visa was limited to the duration of the conference. After a stay of ten days, during which one caught a glimpse of him at a concert of the New York Philharmonic, he took his leave. His second visit, in November 1959, was a much happier one.

In the final decades of his life Shostakovich added steadily to a catalogue whose opus numbers passed well beyond the hundred-mark. His position as the musical spokesman of his country was officially acknowledged when, on the occasion of his fiftieth birthday, he was awarded the Order of Lenin. He died in Leningrad in 1976, at the age of seventy.

His Music

If the art of Prokofiev was based on vocal melody, that of Shostakovich derived from the language of the instruments. His themes stride over a wide range; he writes for the orchestra with real flair. Certain devices are pushed to the length of mannerism: the use of instruments in their extreme registers, mischievous leaps from low to high, the "hollow" ring of widely separated orchestral lines, unison and octave passages; glissandos on the strings, unexpected contrasts of sound, long melodies traced by a single woodwind, and rhythmic patterns repeated relentlessly. Purple passages abound in his works; but his music always "sounds," and his effects are surefire.

Shostakovich handles the large forms of instrumental music with great assurance. He has the capacity for sustaining and developing a musical line that marks the born symphonist. His way of foreshortening the recapitulation section is in line with twentieth-century musical aesthetics, as are his transparent orchestration, his fondness for linear texture, and his contrapuntal technique.

Shostakovich is given to black-and-white contrasts of mood. On the one hand, impudent satire, mocking gaiety, and a humor verging on the boisterous; on the other, a lyric strain that is meditative and impregnated with sentiment. His orchestral cantilena can be diffuse

Like Shostakovich, the Lithuanian sculptor Jacques Lipchitz (1891– 1973) favored forms that are enormous in conception and execution. Joie de vivre, 1927–1960. Courtesy The Albert Einstein College of Medicine.

and sometimes lacks distinction. At its best, however, it achieves power, unfolding in a broad recitative that builds up into impassioned climaxes. His resilient rhythms bound along with gusto. His pungent harmonies lean toward the chromatic, as might be expected in a style that shows the influence of César Franck and Mahler. Indeed, Mahler's music holds such attraction for him that his Moscow colleagues used to say he suffered from an attack of Mahleria. Withal, Shostakovich's music rests on a firm diatonic base.

His model was Beethoven, whom he regarded as the orator of an era no less turbulent than his own. "Only Beethoven," he wrote, "was a forerunner of the revolutionary movement." The epic quality of Beethoven's art was exemplary for him. "I see our epoch," he stated, "as heroic, spirited, and joyous." The Beethovenian concept of victory through struggle was basic to his thinking. "Good music lifts and heartens people for work and effort. It may be tragic but it must be strong."

Shostakovich's *First Symphony* (1925), a work bursting with creative vigor, is a wonderful piece for a youth of nineteen to have written. The *Fifth* we will examine in detail. The *Sixth* (1939) exemplifies the composer's attempt to condense and simplify his style; it has never achieved the popularity of its predecessor. The *Seventh* or *Leningrad Symphony* is an uneven work, and too long; but it captures the immediacy of the stirring events that inspired it. The *Eighth* (1943) displays the winding melodies in which Shostakovich recreates the arabesque of Bach. It is the outpouring of a sensitive spirit still tormented by memories of the war. The *Ninth* (1945), on the other hand, is a happy work, classical in its simplicity and its espousal of the chamber music ideal. In the *Tenth* (1953) Shostakovich adopted the emotional tone of the late nineteenth-century symphony to depict his own drive for inner harmony. Among the final group of symphonies, special interest attaches to the *Thirteenth* (1961), in which Shostakovich antagonized his government by setting a poem by Yevgeny Yevtushenko memorializing the Jews who were massacred by the Nazis at Babi Yar. The work was banned in the Soviet Union for several years. In the *Fourteenth* (1969) he used the verses of three poets whose works have attracted a number of Western composers—García Lorca, Apollinaire, and Rilke. Although the poems ostensibly concerned themselves with death, the text was slanted as a thinly veiled denunciation of all forms of tyranny over the minds of men. The symphony was dedicated to the English composer Benjamin Britten. With the *Fifteenth* (1971), Shostakovich brought his symphonic labors to a close on a note of bitterness and disillusion.

In the *Concerto* for piano, trumpet, and strings (1933) the composer pays homage to the Neoclassic spirit. The dry toccatalike passages show Shostakovich's predilection for grotesquerie. The *Violin Concerto* (1955) is a work of the composer's maturity, projecting the moods of struggle and aspiration that have occupied him in recent years. Shostakovich's fifteen string quartets (1938–1974) show his serious approach to the problem of contemporary chamber music. The later quartets are preoccupied with the same moods of inner struggle as figure in the *Tenth Symphony*. The *Quintet* for piano and strings (1940) displays the composer's ingenuity in handling what has always been a difficult combination; it is a most satisfying work. Shostakovich has written a quantity of film and ballet music, as well as incidental music for plays; but these, because of the themes they handle, are hardly for export. One little item, the Polka from *The Age of Gold* (1930), has been much played. The *Twenty-Four Preludes* (1933) for piano show his idiomatic writing for the instrument and are full of ideas. He has also written songs and choral pieces; but these are the least important part of his output.

Symphony No. 5, Opus 47

Shostakovich's attempt to recapture the epic tone of Beethovenian symphonism is most successfully realized in his *Fifth Symphony* (1937). "The theme of my symphony," he wrote, "is the stabilization of a personality. In the center of this composition, which is conceived lyrically from beginning to end, I saw a man with all his experiences. The finale resolves the tragically tense impulses of the earlier movements into optimism and the joy of living."

I. *Moderato.* The opening subject is announced in antiphonal imitation between low and high strings. It is a tense, lofty idea that establishes the D-minor tonality of the work. The widely striding intervals of the first phrase are balanced by stepwise movement in the second.

From this idea grows another which is sung by the first violins. The movement unfolds in flowing lines, embodying the singing polyphony that Shostakovich took over from Mahler. Mahlerian too is the elevated pathos that pervades this broadly conceived sonata form. The writing exploits the warmly emotional tone of the strings, which is pitted against the cooler timbres of the woodwinds. The second theme, introduced by first violins against chords on the harp and strings, is a soaring melody marked by expressive leaps, which is subsequently taken over by the cellos. The development is character-

ized by a steady quickening of tempo and an ever greater reliance on the brass. The themes are manipulated chiefly by means of imitative procedures and rhythmic transformation (diminution, augmentation), with a relentless buildup of tension. Dramatic use is made of trumpet fanfares and dotted-note patterns, against the tumultuous kind of figuration in the strings that Tchaikovsky used so effectively. Thematic transformation results in a resolute march, *poco sostenuto*. The opening motive is again presented antiphonally, but this time in a rapid tempo. The recapitulation is ushered in by an overpowering proclamation of this motive, *largamente, fff*, by woodwinds, horns, and strings in unison. The second theme, now transposed into D major, is presented in canonic imitation by solo flute and horn. The coda has a gently retrospective quality. A solo violin soars above the orchestra, silvered by the tones of the celesta, as the movement dies away.

II. *Allegretto*. The Scherzo evokes that spirit of the Austrian *Ländler* so prominent in Mahler's symphonies. The element of grotesquerie, a favorite mood with Shostakovich in his younger years, is established at the outset. Tonality is handled very freely, the music rotating between A minor and C major. The main theme, redolent of the "scherzo fantastique" of the Romantic period, is in C minor.

The movement is in A-B-A form (actually a Scherzo and two Trios), with repetition of sections and an overall symmetry that goes hand in hand with the popular character of the material. At least one of the melodies verges on the deliberately banal. When the main theme returns, *da capo*, it is shifted up a half tone to C-sharp minor, for intensification. The movement as a whole gives an effect of freshness, earthiness, and rhythmic élan.

III. *Largo*. The centerpiece of the symphony is the slow movement in F-sharp minor, which unfolds in great arcs of self-propelling, songful counterpoint. This is in the great tradition of the Romantic *Adagio*, introspective, "tragically tense," as the composer

called it, and is suffused with personal lyricism. The test of such a movement is its capacity to sustain tension. Shostakovich succeeds— this is incomparably the most fully realized of his *Adagios*—because of his ability to shape purely lyrical material into large, continuous structures.

In even greater degree than the first movement, the *Largo* is based on the emotive power of string tone, which is pitted against the woodwinds. The brass is silent throughout. The tracing of a single line by a solo woodwind against a curtain of string sound—a practice that Sibelius taught those who listened to him—comes off effectively in the middle of the movement. The massively sonorous climax that Shostakovich achieves without recourse to trumpets, horns, or trombones must be accounted a real feat of orchestration. One has a sense throughout the movement that he previsioned every combination of timbres with the utmost vividness. The pianissimo F-sharp major chord at the close makes for an effect of utter serenity.

IV. *Allegro non troppo.* Massed trumpets, trombones, and tuba present the theme of a "satanic" march against the beating of the ket-

tledrums. The key is D minor. The music is dark in color, full of propulsive energy and tension, and with a touch of the bizarre. The movement is a rondo; the references to the earlier movements make the symphony an example of cyclical form. The progression from tumult and strife to triumphal fulfillment hinges on the shift from minor to major—a time-honored device that can be carried off only if it is managed without self-consciousness, which is precisely how Shostakovich does it. He handles the Classical procedures of thematic-motivic development, as he does the palette of the Romantic orchestra, with all the customary exuberance of the Russian school. This finale is rooted in the surging rhetoric of Tchaikovsky's symphonies. It is a heritage that Shostakovich comes by honestly and uses well. The grandiose coda in D major brings the symphony to its end on a note of heroic affirmation.

The problem of the individual in a collective society formed the central drama of Shostakovich's life. He moved along a difficult path, sustained in equal degree by passionate conviction and a big talent. We shall never know what direction Shostakovich's gift would have taken had it been exercised in a society different from his own. There is no conditional in history. Given the time and place in which he appeared, his role was cut out for him. In fulfilling it, he became a leader in the attempt to adapt the language of contemporary music to the emotional needs of the common man.

34 Twelve-Tone Music

"I believe composition with twelve tones is not the end of an old period but the beginning of a new one."

ARNOLD SCHOENBERG

In the chapter on *Pierrot lunaire* we traced Arnold Schoenberg's abandonment of the traditional system of major-minor keys. Tonality had supplied the framework within which had evolved the great forms of Classical music, but Schoenberg felt himself impelled, for expressive reasons, to use sounds that had no place in the tonal system. Without the framework of the Classical forms, he was forced at first to limit himself to short pieces, or to vocal music in which the text constituted a unifying factor. More and more he felt the need of a new musical principle that would take the place of tonality and enable him to develop large-scale forms. This he found in the technique he evolved in the years after the First World War. He named it "the method of composing with twelve tones."

The Twelve-Tone Method

"I was always occupied," Schoenberg declared, "with the desire to base the structure of my music *consciously* on a unifying idea." The twelve-tone technique made it possible for him to achieve coherence and unity in a musical composition without recourse to traditional procedures such as literal repetition, symmetrical phrases, resolution of dissonance into consonance, and a hierarchy of notes around a central tonic. At the same time, the use of traditional features or forms was not precluded by the technique, should the composer wish to emply them. When Schoenberg explained the method to his students in 1923, he concluded by saying: "You should use the row and compose as you had done it previously." That meant, he explained, "Use the same kind of form or expression, the same themes, melodies, sounds, rhythms as you used before."

As that statement suggests, the twelve-tone technique does not dictate a particular musical style. For some time, however, its only adherents were Schoenberg and his pupils, and so the technique was at first regarded as inextricably associated with their basically Expressionistic style. Not until after the Second World War, when composers as diverse as Igor Stravinsky and Aaron Copland began using Schoenberg's method, did it become clear that the technique was adaptable to any style. It wasn't a method for composing Expressionistic music; like the tonal system, it was a framework within which one could compose many kinds of music.

In the tonal system, a scale of seven notes, and the chords built from them, form the basic materials from which the composer shapes his melodies and harmonies. The other five notes are also used, but in a subsidiary role. The tonal system is so structured that a central function is assigned to one of those seven notes, the tonic. Schoenberg's method abolished the special role of the tonic; all twelve notes of the octave were to be equally important. The unifying and organizing principle of each piece would be a particular arrangement of the twelve notes—a tone row, or, as Schoenberg preferred to call it, a *basic set*. (Recent writers also call it a series, and refer to the serial technique.) All the musical structures in the piece would be derived from that particular ordering of the twelve notes: melodies, harmonies, counterpoints.

This was a logical step for Schoenberg, who was greatly concerned that his new method of organizing music be closely related to the principles of the great German masters whom he revered: Bach, Mozart, Beethoven, Wagner, and Brahms. These men had varied and developed their themes in ways that could be seen as forerunners of a technique in which a succession of notes would be varied and transformed to produce different but related ideas. Schoenberg cited as an example the fourth movement of Beethoven's last string quartet (F major, Opus 135). The slow introduction of this movement is based on this three-note motive—a third down, a fourth up:

The main motive of the *Allegro* section contains the same intervals turned upside down (inverted):

And the second phrase of the *Allegro* theme consists of that motive, turned backward (retrograde: *a*), then upside down (retrograde inversion: *b*), and with the intervals between the notes filled in (*c*):

The twelve-tone method extended such techniques (which were also a common feature of fugal writing as used by all the great composers) until they permeated every corner of the musical work.

As Schoenberg declared, "The main advantage of this method of composing with twelve tones is its unifying effect. I believe that when Richard Wagner introduced his Leitmotive—for the same purpose as that for which I introduced my basic set—he may have said, 'Let there be unity!'" The basic set establishes, of course, not merely a series of pitches but—even more important—a series of intervals. Through all the transformations to which the set can be subjected (similar to those shown in the Beethoven example), that succession of intervals remains, and its persistence in the melodies, harmonies, and counterpoints of a piece cannot but result in the closest possible relationship among these different dimensions of the musical fabric. (A more detailed account of the method will be found in Appendix I-k.)

Unlike the scale of traditional tonality, which remains the same in many different pieces, a fresh tone row is created for each piece—that is, a new arrangement of the twelve notes. And although every row will contain the same twelve notes, each one will have a distinctive pattern of intervals.

If a row is not like a scale, it is also not like a theme. The theme of a piece or movement may incorporate the basic set of the piece, as, for example, does Schoenberg's *Fourth String Quartet:*

But equally often, the basic set may be divided between melody and accompaniment, or between contrapuntal lines. It provides a framework that need be no more evident to the beholder than the steel skeleton that holds up a building.

Schoenberg and Stravinsky

During the lifetime of the two giants of twentieth-century music, their respective followers felt that there was a good deal of opposition between the two camps. People spoke of Stravinsky vs. Schoenberg, Paris vs. Vienna, Neoclassicism vs. dodecaphony (another name commonly used for the method, derived from the Greek word for twelve-tone). Yet we see today that the Schoenbergian method came out of the same need for order and clarity as Stravinskyan Neoclassicism. Both schools of thought focused attention on the constructivist aspects of art. Both returned to the kind of thematic-motivic work to which the Impressionists and Postimpressionists were so bitterly opposed. And both returned to absolute forms of eighteenth-century music such as the suite and concerto. The ultimate reconciliation between the two points of view came about when, as we shall see in a later chapter, Stravinsky in his final years embraced the Schoenbergian discipline. Whereupon scores of his followers who for years inveighed bitterly against the twelve-tone method were suddenly converted to it. This was an about-face without parallel in the aesthetic wrangles of our time.

There was, however, a basic difference between the two masters. Stravinsky's Neoclassicism sprang out of a fundamentally antiromantic trend. He desired above all to subordinate the emotional, expressive aspects of music to formal-constructive values. Music for him was essentially an abstract art which he strove to free from the literary symbols that had attached themselves to it. Schoenberg, on the other hand, was a product of German Romanticism. "The composer today without some trace of romanticism in his heart," he wrote, "must be lacking something fundamentally human." Where Stravinsky rejected the concept of art as personal expression, Schoenberg adhered to it fervently. "I write what I feel in my heart—and what finally comes on paper is what first coursed through every fibre of my body." Where Stravinsky regarded art as a hermetic experience separated from the experiences of life, Schoenberg upheld their connection. "What else can I do than express the original word, which to me is a human thought, a human word, a human aspira-

Schoenberg's credo that a work of art should transmit the turbulent emotions of the artist was fundamental to the German Expressionists. The structure of this characteristic portrait is jagged and geometric, the space confined, the figure eerily distorted. Ernst Ludwig Kirchner (1880–1938), Frauenkopf Gerda, 1914. The Solomon R. Guggenheim Museum, New York.

tion." Stravinsky saw himself as a spokesman for the classic view of life, the die-hard reaction against romanticism. "The old romanticism is dead; long live the new!" Stravinsky recoiled in distaste from any attempt to attach metaphysical meaning to music. For Schoenberg the mystical approach was highly congenial. "My personal feeling is that music conveys a prophetic message revealing a high form of life towards which mankind evolves. There is only one content which all great men wish to express: the longing of mankind for its future form, for an immortal soul, for dissolution into the universe."

It can be seen why Schoenberg resented it when analysts followed the peregrinations of the tone row in much the same spirit as they would solve a crossword puzzle. The technique of twelve-tone writing, he maintained, was "a family affair." That is, it concerned the composer but not the listener, who had to be moved by the music rather than to concern himself with how it was put together. So much has been written about the tone row, its retrograde, inversion, and retrograde-inversion, that the impression is often given of the twelve-tone composer as one who constructs musical crossword puzzles. What is forgotten is that the artist always follows a set of procedures which he has mastered, just as each one of us has mastered the rules of grammar, in order to be able to express himself freely. We do not accuse Shakespeare of subordinating poetic expression to technique because his sonnets are written in iambic pentameters and follow an intricate rhyme scheme. In any case, composers for generations had to master the rules of the game—an intricate set of technical procedures in harmony and counterpoint, form and orchestration—before they could achieve artistic expression. The artist masters the rules in order to rise above them, to shake them off. Almost everything Schoenberg wrote was created in a fury of inspiration, with lightning speed, and with an almost clairvoyant envisioning of all the possibilities of the material. "The most important capacity of a composer," he pointed out, "is to cast a glance into the most remote future of his themes or motives. He has to be able to know beforehand the consequences which derive from the problems existing in his material and to organize everything accordingly. The theme consists not of a few notes but of the musical destinies of those notes."

To Schoenberg's adherents twelve-tone music became a concept of truth and beauty to which they were dedicated with an almost religious fervor. All the same, many musicians had great difficulty in forming a connection with it, as they suddenly found themselves in a realm where all the customary landmarks of music had been swept away. Some, like Hindemith, opposed the twelve-tone style because it repudiated what they regarded as the immutable law of any organized musical art—gravitation to the tonic. Others rejected it because it was completely unrelated to the melody of folk and popular song, and because its jagged melody lines, with their enormous leaps, bore no relation to what the human voice can do. They maintained that the formal procedures of twelve-tone music had no real validity because the ear could not hear them; that dissonance unrelieved by consonance became monotonous; that twelve-tone music moved within an extremely narrow expressive range; and that, whereas the procedures of fugue and cantata, symphony, chamber music and opera sprang out of the common practice of generations of composers all over Europe, the twelve-tone method was the creation of a single mind from which it sprang fully armed like Athena from the brain of Jove.

Despite these strictures, the devotees of the twelve-tone method gradually gained tremendous influence. If their music did not reach the big public (any more than did *Finnegans Wake*), it did challenge the musical intelligentsia and exerted a fruitful influence even upon those composers who did not accept its ideology *in toto*. For it opened up exciting new ways of utilizing the resources of the twelve-tone scale. In the decades after World War II dodecaphonic thinking emerged as the most advanced line of thought in musical aesthetics, and made a durable, profoundly significant contribution to the language of contemporary music.

35 Arnold Schoenberg (1874-1951)

"I am a conservative who was forced to become a radical."

It is significant that, like Stravinsky, the other great innovator of twentieth-century music disclaimed revolutionary intent. The reader may recall Schoenberg's remark on this point: "I personally hate to be called a revolutionist, which I am not. What I did was neither revolution nor anarchy." Quite the contrary; his disciples regard him as having carried to its logical culmination the thousand-year-old tradition of European polyphony.

His Life

Arnold Schoenberg was born in Vienna. He began to study the violin at the age of eight and soon afterward made his initial attempts at composing. Having decided to devote his life to music, he left school while he was in his teens. The early death of his father left him in straitened circumstances. For a time he earned his living by

A portrait of Schoenberg by Oskar Kokoschka (b. 1886) Collection, Mrs. Annie Knize. (Photo courtesy The Bettmann Archive)

working in a bank and meanwhile continued to compose, working entirely by himself. Presently he became acquainted with a young musician two years older than himself, Alexander von Zemlinsky, who for a few months gave him lessons in counterpoint. This was the only musical instruction he ever had.

Through Zemlinsky young Schoenberg was introduced to the advanced musical circles of Vienna, which at that time were under the spell of *Tristan* and *Parsifal*. In 1899, when he was twenty-five, Schoenberg wrote the string sextet *Verklärte Nacht* (Transfigured Night). The following year several of his songs were performed in Vienna and precipitated a scene. "And ever since that day," he once remarked with a smile, "the scandal has never ceased."

It was at this time that Schoenberg began a large-scale work for voices and orchestra, the *Gurrelieder*. For the huge forces, choral and instrumental, required for this cantata he needed music paper double the ordinary size. Work on the *Gurrelieder* was interrupted by material worries. To earn a livelihood, Schoenberg turned to orchestrating popular operettas. In 1901, after his marriage to Zemlinsky's sister, he moved to Berlin and obtained a post in a theater, conducting operettas and music-hall songs. He even wrote cabaret songs himself.

Upon his return to Vienna Schoenberg became active as a teacher and soon gathered about him a band of disciples, of whom the most gifted were Alban Berg and Anton Webern. The devotion of these advanced young musicians sustained Schoenberg in the fierce battle for recognition that lay ahead. At this time too he came under the influence of the abstract painter Wassily Kandinsky and began to paint. An exhibition of his pictures in 1910 revealed a striking talent and a starkly Expressionist style.

An important adherent was Gustav Mahler, who exercised considerable influence upon Schoenberg's development. When Schoenberg's *Chamber Symphony*, Opus 9, was first presented and the audience responded by whistling and banging their seats, Mahler sprang up in his box to command silence. He recognized the creator in Schoenberg. But he knew too that the younger man—they were separated by fourteen years—belonged to a future in which he himself had no part. To his wife Alma he confided, "I do not understand his work. But then he is young and may well be right. I am old, and perhaps I do not have the ear for his music."

Despite the hostility of the public, Schoenberg's music and doctrines slowly made their way. The tide turned in 1913 with the first performance of the *Gurrelieder*, which was received with wild enthusiasm by the Viennese. In this long-delayed moment of triumph Schoenberg was unable to forget the years of rejection that had been inflicted on him by his native city. Called to the stage again and again, he bowed to the conductor Franz Schreker and to the orchestra, but would not acknowledge the ovation tendered him by the public. "For years those people who greeted me with cheers tonight refused to recognize me. Why should I thank them for appreciating me now?"

With each new work Schoenberg moved closer to the point where he would have to reach out beyond the tonal system. "I already feel," he wrote in 1909, "the opposition that I shall have to overcome. I suspect that even those who have believed in me until now will not be willing to see the necessity of this development. It is not lack of invention or of technical skill that has urged me in this direction. I am following an inner compulsion that is stronger than education, and am obeying a law that is natural to me, therefore more powerful than my artistic training."

The war years interrupted Schoenberg's creative activity. Although he was past forty, he was called up for military service in the Vienna garrison. He had reached a critical point in his development. There followed a silence of seven years, between 1915 and 1923, during which he clarified his position in his own mind and prepared for as bold a step as any artist has ever taken—the rejection of tonality. True, there already had been stirrings in this direction before him. But it was he who set the seal of his personality upon this development and who played the crucial role in creating a new grammar and syntax of musical speech.

The goal once set, Schoenberg pursued it with that tenacity of purpose without which no prophet can prevail. His "method of composing with twelve tones" caused great bewilderment in the musical world. All the same, he was now firmly established as a leader of contemporary musical thought. His fiftieth birthday was marked by a performance of his *Friede auf Erden* (Peace on Earth, 1907) by the chorus of the Vienna Opera, an address by the burgomaster of the city, and a "birthday book" of appreciative articles by his disciples and by leading figures in the world of art. In 1925 he was appointed to succeed Ferruccio Busoni as professor of composition at the Berlin Academy of Arts. The uniquely favorable attitude of the Weimar Republic toward experimental art had made it possible for one of the most iconoclastic musicians in history to carry on his work from the vantage point of an official post.

This period in Schoenberg's life ended with the coming to power of Hitler in 1933. Like many Austrian-Jewish intellectuals of his generation, Schoenberg had been converted to Catholicism. After leaving Germany he found it spiritually necessary to return to the Hebrew faith. He arrived in the United States in the fall of 1933. After a short period of teaching in Boston, he joined the faculty of the University of Southern California and shortly afterward was appointed professor of composition at the University of California in Los Angeles. In 1940 he became an American citizen. He taught until his retirement at the age of seventy, and continued his musical activities till his death six years later. A seeker after truth until the end, to no one more than to himself could be applied the injunction he had written in the text of his cantata *Die Jacobsleiter* (Jacob's Ladder, 1913): "One must go on without asking what lies before or behind."

His Music

Schoenberg stemmed out of the Viennese past. He took his point of departure from the final quartets of Beethoven, the richly wrought piano writing of Brahms, and the orchestral sonority of Bruckner and Mahler—behind whom, of course, loomed the un-Viennese figure of Wagner.

Schoenberg's first period may be described as one of post-Wagnerian Romanticism; he still used key signatures and remained within the boundaries of tonality. The best known work of this period is *Verklärte Nacht*, Opus 4. *Pelleas und Melisande*, Opus 5, after Maeterlinck's Symbolist play, was written in 1902, the year in which Debussy's opera on the same subject was first produced. Lasting almost an hour, this fervid symphonic poem exploits to the full the expressive possibilities of the mammoth orchestra of the Strauss-Mahler period. The Postromantic orchestral style is carried to its furthest limits in the *Gurrelieder*, a work that occupied Schoenberg intermittently from 1900 until 1911. This gigantic cantata, on a cycle of lyrics by the Danish poet Jens Peter Jacobsen, centers about the tragic love of King Waldemar IV of Denmark and the beautiful Tove, who is subsequently poisoned by Waldemar's jealous queen. The work, cast in a hyperemotional post-*Tristan* idiom, calls for an orchestra of about a hundred and forty players; five soloists; and four choruses—three male choirs singing in four parts and a mixed choir in eight parts: all in all, almost four hundred performers.

During these years Schoenberg also produced works along quite different lines. The songs of Opus 2 and Opus 3 set forth the vein of lyricism in Schoenberg's art. The *Eight Songs* of Opus 6 (1905) already display the dislocation of the vocal line through the use of wide intervals which became one of the hallmarks of his school. The *First String Quartet* in D minor, Opus 7 (1904-1905) embodies the preoccupation with chamber-music style that came to have an ever greater influence on Schoenberg's orchestral writing. This tendency comes to the fore in the *First Chamber Symphony* for fifteen instruments, Opus 9 (1906), in which the polyphonic cast of Schoenberg's thought made necessary the utmost individualization of the instrumental lines. The tonal period ends with the *String Quartet No. 2* in F-sharp minor, Opus 10 (1907-1908), the last work in which Schoenberg used a key signature. He introduced a voice in the final movement which sings—significantly—Stefan George's *Ich fühle Luft von anderen Planeten* (I feel the air of other spheres).

Schoenberg's second period, the atonal-Expressionist, gets under way with the *Three Piano Pieces,* Opus 11 (1909), in which he abolishes the distinction between consonance and dissonance, and also the sense of a home key. He is moving from a harmonic-vertical mode of thought to a contrapuntal-horizontal one; from romantic subjectivity to an objective, classical orientation in which lyric emotion is controlled by thematic logic, and in which formal procedures such as canonic imitation play an ever more important role. During this period too Schoenberg turns to the utmost condensation of utterance. His output centers about the short lyric forms—piano and orchestral pieces, and songs. On the one hand he was reacting against the overextended forms of the Mahler-Strauss period as well as his own *Pelleas* and *Gurrelieder.* On the other, the new atonal idiom was so concentrated and intense, its future direction as yet so uncertain, that he could best work out its structural problems in abbreviated forms.

The fifteen songs to Stefan George's Expressionist poems *Das Buch der hängenden Gärten,* Opus 15 (1908), show the increasing complexity of Schoenberg's vocal writing. The voice is no longer supported by the accompaniment but must negotiate the zigzag vocal line on its own, sustained only by the singer's stout heart and (a prerequisite!) absolute pitch. To this phase of Schoenberg's career belong two Expressionist works for the theater—they can hardly be called operas. *Erwartung* (Expectancy, 1909), on a libretto by Marie Pappenheim, is a "monodrama": it has a single character, requires a huge orchestra, and is about half an hour in length. The action, which runs the gamut from tenderness to jealous rage, concerns a woman who wanders through a wood at night seeking the lover who has abandoned her for another. She relives the relationship in memory and finally stumbles upon the dead man's body. *Die glückliche Hand* (The Lucky Hand, 1913) has a libretto by Schoenberg himself. The action is extremely symbolic, revolving around such matters as the quest for happiness and the struggle between man's higher and lower impulses. In one scene Schoenberg the painter-composer calls for a crescendo in both sound and color, from red through brown, green and blue-gray to purple, red, orange, yellow, finally white: the Viennese-Expressionist counterpart of Scriabin's attempt to correlate sound and color.

The *Five Orchestral Pieces,* Opus 16, constitute one of the high points of this period. Another is *Pierrot lunaire,* which we discussed in Chapter 22. This was the first composition to carry Schoenberg's name beyond his immediate circle. Its moonstruck hero, a Pierrot far removed from his Russian counterpart Petrushka, remains one of the most striking creations of German Expressionism.

The atonal-Expressionist phase of Schoenberg's career ended with the *Four Songs* for voice and orchestra, Opus 22 (1914). Schoenberg's third period, that of the twelve-tone method, was ushered in—after the long silence we referred to—by the *Five Piano Pieces* of Opus 23 (1923). In the last of the set the new technique is revealed in all its features. It should not be supposed that Schoenberg completely changed his musical language when he adopted the twelve-tone method. The serial manner of writing merely enabled him to organize the intuitions that had been present in his earlier works, to systematize the aims toward which he had been moving for years. There is much less difference in sound between the pre–twelve-tone works and those that followed than one might imagine. Seen in retrospect, the third period stemmed naturally out of the second; the evolution was as continuous as it was inevitable.

The twelve-tone method is in evidence in the *Serenade* for seven instruments and bass voice, Opus 24 (1923). The third and fourth movements, the Variations and Sonnet, are based on tone rows. The classical objectivity that informs this phase of Schoenberg's work is manifest in a work such as the *Suite for Piano,* Opus 25, which we will discuss. The constructive logic of the twelve-tone method made it possible for him to undertake longer works than those written in his atonal period, and to reconcile the new technique with the Classical sonata form. This rapprochement is effected in the *Quintet* for flute, oboe, clarinet, bassoon, and horn, Opus 26 (1924); and the *String Quartet No. 3*, Opus 30 (1926), in which the serial technique is used in a somewhat freer manner. To this period also belong the one-act opera *Von Heute auf Morgen* (From Today till Tomorrow, 1929); *Begleitungsmusik zu einer Lichtspielszene* (Accompaniment to a Film Scene, 1930), in which Schoenberg used the twelve-tone idiom to project moods of anxiety and fear; and the *Variations for Orchestra,* Opus 31 (1927–1928), one of his most powerful works. The fourth and last period of Schoenberg's career—the American phase—we will consider in a later section.

Schoenberg was a tireless propagandist for his ideas, a role for which his verbal gifts and his passion for polemics eminently fitted him. From his *Treatise on Harmony* (1911), which begins with the famous "This book I have learned from my pupils"—he dedicated the work to the memory of Gustav Mahler—essays and articles flowed from his pen conveying his views in a trenchant, aphoristic style which, late in life, he transferred from German to English. The following observations are characteristic: "Genius learns only from itself, talent chiefly from others. . . . One must believe in the infallibility of one's fantasy and the truth of one's inspiration. . . . If it is art it is not for all, and if it is for all it is not art. . . . Creation to an artist should be as natural and inescapable as the growth of apples to an apple tree. . . . The twelve tones will not invent for you. When you find that something you have written is very complicated, you should at once be doubtful of its genuineness." (It cannot be said that he always adhered to this maxim.) "No art has been so hindered in its development by teachers as music, since nobody watches more closely over his property than the man who knows that, strictly speaking, it does not belong to him. . . . It is said of many an author that he has indeed technique, but no invention. That is wrong: either he also lacks technique or he also has invention. . . . Mannerism is originality in subordinate matters. . . . An apostle who does not glow preaches heresy. . . . The laws of nature manifested in a man of genius are but the laws of the future."

His belief in the ineluctable necessity and the rightness of his doctrines sustained him and gave him the strength to effectuate his revolution. His doctrine focused attention on basic compositional problems and has profoundly affected the course of musical thought in the twentieth century. Now, as during his lifetime, Arnold Schoenberg continues to be—as the critic Paul Rosenfeld once called him—"the great troubling presence of modern music."

36   Two Works by Schoenberg

"Time is a great conqueror. He will bring understanding to my works."

Suite for Piano, Opus 25

The *Suite for Piano*, Opus 25, dating from 1924, was the first work to be written completely in the twelve-tone idiom. It came after the years of silence during which Schoenberg was perfecting his method and belonged to the first group of works in which he found his new voice. "I find myself," he wrote, "positively enabled to compose as freely and fantastically as one does only in one's youth, and nevertheless subject to a precisely definable esthetic discipline." In other words, the very rigor of the method freed his imagination. How close this statement is to Stravinsky's, "The more art is controlled, limited, worked over, the more it is free." And how close both credos are to Hegel's "Freedom is the recognition of necessity."

We have alluded to the fact that the new language did not represent as complete a break with the past as most people imagine. Schoenberg himself was explicit on this point. "I usually answer the question why I no longer write as I did at the period of *Verklärte Nacht* by saying, "I do, but I can't help it if people don't yet recognize the fact." Already he foresaw that his twelve-tone method would be accused of stifling inspiration. For him the very opposite was true, for which reason he again and again emphasized the importance of impulse, intuition, sponteneity. "A composer must not compose two or eight or sixteen measures today and again tomorrow and so on until the work seems to be finished, but should conceive a composition as a totality, in one single act of inspiration, intoxicated by his idea, he should write down as much as he could, not caring for little details. They could be added or carried out later."

We mentioned his dislike of rigid analyses that reduced twelve-tone works to a species of musical acrostics. He inveighed against this repeatedly. "I can't utter too many warnings against overrating these analyses, since after all they only lead to what I have always been dead against: seeing how it is *done*, whereas I have always helped people to see what it *is!* I can't say it often enough: my works are twelve-tone *compositions*, not *twelve-tone* compositions."

The suite, a favorite form throughout the first half of the eighteenth century, was cultivated by such masters as Bach and Handel. In reviving it Schoenberg affirmed his kinship with them. Consisting as it did of a series of short song or dance forms, the suite was useful to Schoenberg at this stage, for within its compact movements he could experiment with his new language without having to sustain the burden of organizing extended forms.

The piano, capable of melody, harmony, and counterpoint, attracted Schoenberg throughout his career, especially at those points when he planned an advance into uncharted regions. From a practical point of view, he stood a much better chance of having a piano piece performed—at a time when his music aroused bitter opposition on the part of the Establishment—than was the case with an orchestral score. On five occasions, each marking a crucial point in his thinking, he wrote for the piano. Of these five works, the *Suite for Piano*, Opus 25, is certainly the best known. Glenn Gould, one of its memorable interpreters, said of it, "I can think of no composition for solo piano from the first quarter of this century which can stand as its equal."

The suite consists of six brief movements: Prelude, Gavotte, Musette, Intermezzo, Minuet, and Gigue. All of these save the intermezzo figure in the suites of Bach. The six movements are derived from a single tone row, which is used in four versions: the original series, its inversion, and two transpositions of these. We shall heed Schoenberg's admonition against tracing in detail the wanderings of the row. The listener will get much more out of following the flow of the music. (The row forms are given in Appendix I-k; observe how they relate to the music examples below.)

I. *Prelude. Rasch* (Fast), 6/8. The look of the notes on the page brings to mind the preludes of Bach. At the start, there is imitation between right- and left-hand parts, resulting in a rich contrapuntal texture.

The music takes its momentum from heavily accented rhythms, with repeated-note figures traveling throughout the polyphonic web. Harmonically the piece depends for its bite on the dissonant intervals favored by the dodecaphonic style—major sevenths, major ninths, diminished fifths. Despite the twelve-tone method, this Prelude speaks the same post-*Tristan* language as Schoenberg's earlier piano works. It runs a wide gamut over the keyboard and ends with a brusque gesture.

II. *Gavotte. Etwas langsam, nicht hastig* (Somewhat slow, not hurried), 2/2. Notice that the pitches of this theme are the same as those of the right hand at the beginning of the first movement—but in different octaves.

The rhythm changes subtly within the measure, lending the music a flexible, even capricious quality akin to the rubato that was so inseparable a part of nineteenth-century piano style. Repeated-note figures persist. Note that, according to twelve-tone procedure, the repetition of a note is regarded simply as its extension and does not count in the unfolding of the row.

III. *Musette. Rascher* (Faster), 2/2. A musette is a dance form of pastoral character with a drone bass, which was popular in the early eighteenth century. Bach's *English Suites Nos. 3* and 6 contain two well-known examples. Schoenberg's Musette is a graceful little piece that derives its light-hearted quality from staccato notes in the upper register. It is structured in the regular four-measure phrases that are rarely found in Schoenberg's music, but which serve here to create the atmosphere of an eighteenth-century dance form. The first section is repeated, an interesting circumstance in view of his later opposition to all unvaried repetition. ("Never do what a copyist can do!") The piece is in the two-part or A-B form favored by the Baroque. The final section of the second part repeats the material of the first in altered form. At the end of the Musette Schoenberg asks that the Gavotte be repeated, so that these two pieces together constitute an A-B-A form: Gavotte-Musette-Gavotte.

IV. *Intermezzo.* 3/4, $\downarrow$ = 40. (This metronome marking indicates forty quarter notes a minute.) Schoenberg here invokes one of the great types of late Romantic piano music, the intermezzo of Brahms. Several features recall Brahms: the heavy chordal texture, the use of triplets against eighth notes ("three against two"), the use of the richly sonorous lower register; above all, the Romantic introspection, the "soulfulness" of the music. This, in fine, is a lyric meditation that moves much closer to the sound-world of Schoenberg's earlier music than did the preceding pieces. Its position among a series of dance movements is analogous to that of the Aria in Bach's *Third Suite for Orchestra.* Mostly the left hand carries the main line while the right supplies background. They exchange roles about half way through the piece. There are frequent rests and pauses, so that the Intermezzo seems to be stopping and starting again, creating a curious impression of hesitation. This effect is strengthened by the fact that Schoenberg in this music moves completely away from traditional phrase structure. A long-drawn-out crescendo is powered by tension-building chords that culminate in a fortissimo climax, after which the music returns to the mood of reverie.

V. *Minuet. Moderato,* 3/4. Schoenberg follows the form of the Classical minuet as developed by Haydn and Mozart: an A-B-A structure in which the middle section is the Trio, after which the minuet is repeated from the beginning (da capo). The Classical symphony retained the triple meter of the court dance but stylized it into an orchestral movement marked by aristocratic grace and charm. Schoenberg carries the process of stylization much further. The triple meter is thoroughly disguised through syncopated patterns and smaller time values (sixteenth and thirty-second notes).

In Classical usage the trio was quieter than the minuet and often took on an outdoor quality through the use of woodwinds and horns. Schoenberg's Trio thins out the texture to two voices, with the tone row transformed into an inverted canon:

Each section of the Trio is repeated, after which the Minuet is repeated da capo. Needless to say, even while he adheres to the Classical form, Schoenberg fills it with a thoroughly non-Classical content.

VI *Gigue. Rasch* (Fast), 2/2. The gigue developed from the Irish or English jig into a constituent member of the Baroque dance suite. This ebullient dance was generally in 6/8 time. However, when taken rapidly the six beats are heard as two groups of three (triplets); hence Schoenberg's use of 2/2 (duple meter) is not a radical departure from traditional usage. What is radical is his treatment of the rhythm, which alternates duple and triple patterns or uses them simultaneously throughout.

This Gigue is propelled forward by remarkable rhythmic tension, which derives its power from complex interlocking rhythms—patterns, that is, based on the rapid alternation of right and left hand.

Variations for Orchestra, Opus 31

Schoenberg's Opus 31 (1928), the first twelve-tone work for orchestra, signals the master's return to orchestral writing after a decade and a half. Having achieved a continuous texture in the short forms, he was ready to apply his method to a more ample structure. For this attempt, significantly, he chose variations rather than symphony. This accorded with his goal of "perpetual variation," whereas the symphony—with its contrasting key areas—he naturally regarded as the citadel of tonal thinking.

The work calls for a large orchestra that includes madolin, harp, celesta, and a full percussion section. The ensemble is handled for the most part in the manner of a chamber orchestra, with the tutti passages standing out, by sheer weight, against soloistic textures. The large orchestra was made necessary by Schoenberg's technique of fragmenting the contrapuntal lines and distributing them among various instruments. Besides, he needed a full orchestra to support the spacious architecture of the *Variations*.

Introduktion. Mässig, ruhig (moderate, calm), 2/2. Schoenberg's conception that every passage in a work should have its own structural function is well exemplified in the opening portion of the work. The mysterious pianissimo of the opening tremolos, fraught with expectancy, is in the nature of an introduction. Schoenberg introduces the motive B–A–C–H (B-flat, A, C, B-natural), which plays a unifying role in the piece. Significantly, this motive is never transposed, but always appears in its original form. Elements of the theme are presented in the introduction; but it accords with the transitory character of this passage that a clear-cut statement is postponed until the next section.

Thema. Molto moderato, 3/4. The vagueness is dispelled. The theme, composed of four distinct phrases, is introduced by the cellos. The first phrase contains the basic set:

(The remaining three phrases set forth the retrograde inversion, the retrograde, and the inversion, while the accompanying harmonies are equally derived from the forms of the row. The basic set and its variants are given in Appendix I-k.)

Variation I. *Moderato*, 3/4. Oboes, violins, then horns, harp, violas, and cellos set up a light nervous movement in which sixteenth notes predominate. The theme unfolds in the bass against a counterpoint composed largely of thirds and sixths. The prevalence of these intervals contributes to the gentle atmosphere that envelops this variation.

Variation II, marked *Langsam* (slow), in 9/8 time, introduces a complex polyphonic tissue articulated by eighteen instruments used soloistically. The texture is based on a triple canon between cello and bassoon, bass clarinet and flute, muted violin and oboe. The last two present the theme against the contrapuntal intricacies of the other instruments, intricacies which involve all four versions of the row and canonic imitation in contrary motion.

In the next five variations the theme is relegated to a subordinate position, emphasis being placed on new countersubjects and fresh rhythmic structures. Variation III, marked *Mässig* (moderate), in 3/4, is presented as an orchestral tutti. The virile tone is implemented by energetic rhythms and the prominence of the brass. The theme is in the horns. In Variation IV, a *Walzertempo* (waltz-time), the theme is presented by harp, celesta, and mandolin as an accompaniment to new contrapuntal lines. The instrumental writing is light and mobile, in the nature of a chamber orchestra. Variation V, *Bewegt* (agitated), in 3/4, opens with a grandiose tutti. The theme is mostly in the bass, in the cello part. Schoenberg dissolves it in the orchestral tissue so as to focus our interest on other matters.

Variation VI, an *Andante* in 4/8, returns to the concertante style. Three solo cellos, a viola, and a double bass are pitted against the mass and are joined by the full string section. The dissolution of the theme proceeds, it being almost wholly confined to the first cello and the middle register. Variation VII, marked *Langsam* (slow), in 4/4 time, expounds several new ideas in a richly polyphonic texture. The theme, presented by piccolo, glockenspiel, and solo violin, *ppp*, dissolves into a series of isolated points; yet it occupies a more important position than in the preceding variation. Schoenberg, in effect is preparing to bring it back into the limelight.

Variation VIII, marked *Sehr rasch* (very lively), in 2/2, involves the entire orchestra. The theme dominates the musical discourse. The variation unfolds as a kind of free canon in contrary motion between the theme and a counterpoint against a rhythmic ostinato in eighth notes punctuated by chords. Variation IX is marked bilingually: *L'istesso tempo; aber etwas langsamer* (same tempo, but somewhat slower). This variation has a more complex structure than those that preceded. The different parts of the theme are superposed upon one another, so that what has been heard in succession is now presented simultaneously. The theme, introduced by the piccolo, is imitated in contrary motion by the clarinets.

The Finale opens with a recitative that evokes the same air of gentleness which characterized the Introduction. The first section, marked *Mässig schnell* (fairly fast), introduces the B–A–C–H motive with pianissimo fluttertonguing on the flutes. The *Grazioso* that follows, first in 2/4, then 3/4, presents new aspects of the theme and new countersubjects. An accelerando leads into the *Presto,* which combines the B–A–C–H motive with the theme; a canon in contrary motion on the B–A–C–H motive is played by two trumpets. The climax of the movement is reached in the *Pesante* (heavy); this interrupts the *Presto* and presents the B–A–C–H motive as a kind of motto theme. An extraordinary *Adagio* of six measures—one of the most beautiful passages, in regard to sonority, that Schoenberg ever wrote—leads back into the *Presto* that completes the work. The final chord appropriately unites all twelve tones of the chromatic scale—Schoenberg's affirmation of the all-embracing unity that underlies all diversity.

37 Alban Berg (1885-1935)

"Not a measure in this music of ours—no matter how complicated its harmonic, rhythmic, and contrapuntal texture—but has been subjected to the sharpest control of the outer and the inner ear, and for the meaning of which, in itself and in its place in the whole, we do not take the artistic responsibility."

It was the unique achievement of Alban Berg to humanize the abstract procedures of the Schoenbergian technique and to make them more accessible to listeners. Upon a new and difficult idiom he imprinted the stamp of a lyric imagination of the first order.

His Life

Berg was born in Vienna. He came of a well-to-do family and grew up in an environment that fostered his artistic proclivities. The urge to write music asserted itself during his adolescence. At nine-

Alban Berg.
Photograph courtesy of BMI Archive.

teen he made the acquaintance of Arnold Schoenberg, who was sufficiently impressed with the youth's manuscripts to accept him as a
pupil.

During his six years with Schoenberg he acquired the consummate mastery of technique that characterizes his later work. Schoenberg was not only an exacting master, but also a devoted friend and
mentor who shaped Berg's whole outlook on art; in a sense, Schoenberg filled a void that had been left by the early death of Berg's father. The young musician was shy and introverted, a dreamer who
did not find it easy to pass from intention to deed. Schoenberg's
forceful nature supplied the necessary antidote to the uncertainties of
the artist and the man.

Berg's letters give evidence of the strong ties that bound him to his teacher. In 1910—he was then twenty-five—he wrote to his friend Webern: "How despondent you must be again, far away from all these divine experiences, having to forgo the walks with Schoenberg and miss the meaning, the gestures and cadence of his talk. Twice a week I wait for him at the Karlsplatz, before teaching begins at the Conservatory, and for the fifteen to thirty minutes' walk amidst the hubbub of the city, which is drowned out by the 'roar' of his words. But to tell you about all this is only to increase your suffering and sense of deprivation." Only a talent of the first order could outgrow such a hold. Of the fairly large group of students that surrounded Schoenberg in Vienna, only two—Berg and Webern—emerged as creative personalities in their own right.

Berg's *Piano Sonata*, Opus 1, the early songs of Opus 2, and *String Quartet*, Opus 3, were presented at concerts of Schoenberg's pupils and elicited a certain amount of appreciation among the musical intelligentsia; but they did not yet indicate his true stature. The outbreak of war in 1914 hurled him into a period of depression. "The urge 'to be in it'," he wrote to Schoenberg, "the feeling of helplessness at being unable to serve my country, prevented any concentration on work." A few months later he was called up for military service, despite his uncertain health (he suffered from asthma and attacks of nervous debility). He was presently transferred to the War Ministry in Vienna. Already *Wozzeck* occupied his thoughts; but he could not begin writing the music until the war was over. He then worked assiduously at the opera and completed it in 1921. Three excerpts were performed in Frankfurt in 1924. In December 1925, *Wozzeck* was presented at the Berlin State Opera. At one stroke Berg was lifted from comparative obscurity to international fame.

In the decade that remained to him he produced only a handful of works; but each was a significant contribution to his total output. During these years he was active as a teacher. He also wrote about music, propagandizing tirelessly on behalf of Schoenberg and his school. Although after *Wozzeck* he was admired all over the world, he remained a prophet without honor in his own country. In a letter to Webern concerning his nomination to the Prussian Academy of Arts in 1930, he writes ironically: "It pleased me very much, especially on account of Vienna, that is, of Austria, which—as it well known—has virtually overloaded us for years with honors and appointments."

With the coming to power of Hitler, the works of Schoenberg and his school were banned in Germany as alien to the spirit of the Third Reich. The resulting loss of income was a source of worry to Berg, as was, to a far greater degree, the rapid Nazification of Austria.

Schoenberg's enforced emigration to the United States in the fall of that year was a bitter blow, especially as the master could not readily accept the fact that both Berg and Webern were remaining behind.

Exhausted and ailing after the completion of the *Violin Concerto*, Berg went to the country for a short rest before resuming work on his opera *Lulu*. An insect bite brought on an abscess that caused infection. Upon his return to Vienna he was stricken with blood poisoning. He was taken to the hospital and given a transfusion. On catching sight of the donor, a typical young Viennese, he remarked jokingly, "Let's hope I don't become a composer of operettas." During the final delirium his mind was occupied with *Lulu;* he went through the motions of conducting the music, exhorting the orchestra to play more firmly. He died on Christmas Eve, 1935, seven weeks before his fifty-first birthday.

His Music

Berg's art issued from the world of German Romanticism—the world of Schumann, Brahms, Wagner, Richard Strauss, and Mahler. The romantic streak in his temperament bound him to this heritage even after he had embraced the dodecaphonic style. His tendency to incorporate tonal elements into the twelve-tone language makes him the most accessible of the composers of Schoenberg's school, consequently the one with the widest public.

Berg's was the imagination of the musical dramatist. For him the musical gesture was bound up with character and action, mood and atmosphere. The natural outlet for this kind of imagination is, of course, the opera house. Yet even in his abstract instrumental works, the shaping of the material into self-contained forms took on psychological overtones. In the *Lyric Suite,* for example, the titles of the various movements clearly indicate the composer's relationship to romantic tone poetry: I. *Allegro gioviale.* II. *Andante amoroso.* III. *Allegro misterioso; trio estatico.* IV. *Adagio appassionato.* V. *Presto delirando.* VI. *Large desolato.*

Where Berg showed himself the true Schoenbergian was in his penchant for intricate contrapuntal structures, his mastery of the principles of perpetual variation, and the extreme condensation of his forms. Like his teacher, he leaned toward the formal patterns of the past—fugue and invention, passacaglia, variations, sonata, and suite. (Interestingly, the symphony for full orchestra is absent both from his and Schoenberg's output.) His use of the classical molds in-

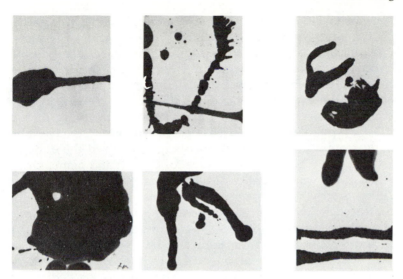

In 1965, the American artist Robert Motherwell (b. 1915) executed a series of paintings on paper entitled Lyric Suite. *They are based on his impressions of Berg's composition, which he knew and admired. Collection the artist.*

dicates how clearly he felt the need for a firm structural framework to compensate for the loss of the unifying power of tonality.

Like so many of his contemporaries, Berg favored the interval of the fourth as a constructive element in melody and harmony. He used the seventh as a prime source of melodic and harmonic tension. He was master of an imaginative orchestral palette, which he employed with classical economy and precision. We find in his works the rarefied sonorities of the dodecaphonic school, and all the devices native to it—the evanescent glissandos, trills, fluttertonguings, harmonics, and muted passages. Characteristic was his exploitation of what he called "constructive rhythm," in which a rhythmic pattern was allotted the same decisive role in the unfolding of a movement as would ordinarily be given a distinctive melodic figure. These and kindred devices were synthesized into an extremely personal style marked by lyric feeling and dramatic élan.

The list of his published works begins with the *Piano Sonata*, Opus 1 (1907–1909), a highly charged work in a post-Wagnerian idiom. The four songs of Opus 2 (1909) reveal the composer in a period of transition from Mahlerian Romanticism to the Expressionist tendencies of his later years. In the last of the four, the young composer abandons key signatures. The *String Quartet*, Opus 3, in two movements (1910), shows the ambiguity of key that was native to Berg's thinking. Opus 4 consists of *Five Songs* for voice and orchestra (1910), on picture-postcard (literally) texts by the Viennese poet Peter Altenberg. These texts were pithy utterances that Altenberg was in the habit of dashing off to his friends. In this work Berg profited from the experiments of Schoenberg and Webern in new orchestral sonorities and in the unconventional handling of the voice. The last piece of the set, a Passacaglia, contains a twelve-tone row. Berg wrote it years before Schoenberg formalized the dodecaphonic technique. The set of four pieces for clarinet and piano, Opus 5—the first of the works Berg dedicated to his teacher—was written in 1913. In his striving for the utmost condensation of material Berg was influenced by the short piano pieces of Schoenberg. The *Three Orchestral Pieces*, Opus 6 (1913–1914), consisting of a Prelude, Round, and March, date from a period of severe inner crisis when Berg was seeking his way as an artist. They show affinity with Mahler rather than with Schoenberg, to whom they were dedicated. With the third piece of this set we find ourselves in the atmosphere of *Wozzeck*.

We shall discuss Berg's masterpiece in detail. This milestone in operatic literature was followed by the *Chamber Concerto* for piano, violin, and thirteen wind instruments, which was dedicated to Schoenberg on the latter's fiftieth birthday. The work is notable for its use of contrapuntal procedures associated with the twelve-tone school: strict canonic imitation, inversion, and retrograde motion. It displays, too, Berg's love of musical anagrams; the basic theme consists of all the letters in the names Arnold Schoenberg, Anton Webern, and Alban Berg that have musical equivalents. (In German usage, *S* and *H* are respectively E-flat and B-flat.)

Berg's most widely known work, after *Wozzeck*, is the *Lyric Suite*, written in 1925–1926. The first and last movements follow strictly "the method of composing with twelve tones." The slow movement contains an allusion to the Prelude of *Tristan and Isolde*. Originally written for string quartet, the *Lyric Suite* achieved such popularity that in 1928 the composer arranged the three middle movements for string orchestra.

Berg spent the last seven years of his life on the opera *Lulu*. The composer fashioned the libretto himself from two dramas by Frank Wedekind—*Earth Spirit* (1893) and *Pandora's Box* (1901). Lulu is the eternal type of *femme fatale* "who destroys everyone because she is destroyed by everyone." Berg's opera is strong stuff as a libretto. Murder, blackmail, sexual perversion, and imprisonment enter into a tale that takes us from Berlin to a gambling den in Paris, and to the final degradation of the aging heroine on the streets of London. The choice of such a subject for an opera accorded with the social and intellectual climate that prevailed in central Europe in the Twenties. Berg was in the midst of orchestrating *Lulu* when he interrupted the task to write the *Violin Concerto*. The opera remained unfinished at his death, and for years his widow withheld permission for another musician to complete the work from Berg's sketches. These obstacles were removed by her death in 1976, and as of the present writing (1978) the musical world eagerly awaits the premiere of the complete *Lulu*.

Alban Berg is today one of the most widely admired masters of the twelve-tone school. His premature death robbed contemporary music of a major figure.

Wozzeck: Opera in Three Acts

"When I decided to write an opera, my only intention was to give to the theater what belongs to the theater. The music was to be so formed that at each moment it would fulfill its duty of serving the action."

In 1914 Berg saw the play that impelled him to the composition of *Wozzeck*. He finished the draft of the libretto by the summer of 1917. Most of the music was written from 1918 to 1920 and orchestrated the following year. The vocal score was published in 1923 with the financial help of Alma Mahler, to whom *Wozzeck* was dedicated.

The author of the play, Georg Büchner (1813–1837), belonged to the generation of intellectuals who were stifled by the political repressions of Metternich's Europe. His socialist leanings brought him into conflict with the authorities. After his death at twenty-four, the manuscript of *Danton's Tod* (The Death of Danton) and the unfinished *Woyzeck* (this was the original spelling) were found among his papers. In the stolid infantryman Wozzeck he created an archetype of "the insulted and the injured" of the earth. Though it issued from the heart of the Romantic era, Büchner's stark drama is surprisingly contemporary in thought and feeling. Above all—as Berg, with the intuition of genius, immediately recognized—the play was ideally suited to the emotional atmosphere of the Expressionist theater and the atonal music of the twentieth century.

Berg's libretto tightened the original play. He shaped the material into three acts, each containing five scenes. These are linked by brief orchestral interludes whose motivic facture serves to round off what has preceded as well as to introduce what follows. As a result, Berg's "opera of protest and compassion" has astonishing unity of texture and mood.

The action centers around Wozzeck's unhappy love for Marie, by whom he has had an illegitimate child. Wozzeck is the victim of the sadistic Captain and of the Doctor, a coldly scientific gentleman who uses Wozzeck for his experiments—to which the soldier submits because he needs the money. (Wozzeck is given to hallucinations. The Doctor is bent on proving his theory that mental disorder is related to diet.) Marie cannot resist her infatuation with the handsome Drum Major. Wozzeck slowly realizes that she has been unfaithful to him. Ultimately he kills her. Driven back to the death scene by guilt and remorse, he drowns himself. The tragedy unfolds in three acts. The first is the exposition of the theme: "Wozzeck in relation to his environment." The second is the development of the theme: "Wozzeck becomes more and more convinced of Marie's infidelity." The third act is the catastrophe: "Wozzeck murders Marie and atones by suicide."

The vocal line sensitively portrays characters and situations. Harmonically, the greater part of the opera is cast in an atonal-Expressionist idiom. Berg anticipates certain twelve-tone procedures; he also looks back to the tonal tradition, puts a number of passages in major and minor keys, and uses leitmotifs in the Wagnerian manner. The snatches of popular song in the score create an effective contrast to their atonal surroundings. Appearing in so special a context, they take on a strange wistfulness.

In the opening scene, Wozzeck is shaving the Captain. From the hysterical Captain's opening remark—"Langsam, Wozzeck, langsam" (Slow, Wozzeck, go slow!)—the jagged vocal line, with its wide leaps and brusque inflections, projects the atmosphere of German Expressionism. Wozzeck's music is more sustained in manner. His reply introduces the chief motive associated with him, on the words "Wir arme Leut! Sehn Sie, Herr Hauptmann, Geld, Geld! Wer kein Geld hat!" (Poor folk like us! You see, Captain, money! Without money . . .).

Wir ar-me Leut'! Seh'n Sie, Herr Haupt-mann, Geld, Geld! Wer kein Geld hat!

This motive in various guises underlines the key statement of the scene, beginning with "Ja, wenn ich ein Herr wär": "Yes indeed, if I

Wozzeck (Peter Glossop) and Marie (Janis Martin) in Act 1, Scene 3, of the Metropolitan Opera's production of the opera. Copyright © Beth Bergman.

were a fine gentleman and had a silk hat and watch and an eyeglass, and could talk fancy, I would be virtuous too. But I'm a poor nobody."

Scene 2, in which Wozzeck and his friend Andres are seen cutting branches in a field, is one of several in which Berg conjures up an atmosphere of fear through his handling of the orchestra. Flickerings of sound on piccolos, oboes, and clarinets admirably prepare Wozzeck's "Du, der Platz ist verflucht!" (Man, this place is cursed). In this scene we have the first of the songs, that of Andres: "Das ist die schöne Jägerei" (Hunting is a good sport). This is in 6/8, a meter traditionally associated with hunting scenes; the song illustrates Berg's way of evoking popular elements, although in a somewhat distorted form. The following scene, which takes place in Marie's room, shows her growing interest in the Drum Major. Berg here uses military music in a most poignant way. Marie's enthusiastic "Soldaten sind schöne Burschen" (Soldiers are handsome fellows!) brings with it a suggestion of A-flat major despite the shifting chromatic harmonies. The lullaby that follows, in 6/8 time—"Mädel, was fängst du jetzt an?" (Girl, what song shall you sing? You've a little child but no husband!)—is a hauntingly lovely bit. When the child falls asleep, Marie remains lost in thought. The scene ends with the strings intoning a motive of fifths closely associated with her:

"Their harmonic immobility," Berg wrote, "expresses, as it were, her aimless waiting, which is only terminated with her death."

Scene 4, between Wozzeck and the Doctor, takes place in the latter's study; we return to the atmosphere of obsession. The music takes the shape of a passacaglia. How better to express the Doctor's *idée fixe*—the connection between nutrition and insanity—than by twenty-one variations on a theme? The theme of the passacaglia is a twelve-tone row that is first played by the clarinet at the end of the orchestral interlude. Here it is presented by the cellos and basses, ex-

tending over eight measures, and followed by the variations. The final scene of Act I, a street in front of Marie's door, brings the climax of the action thus far: Marie yields to the Drum Major.

The first scene of Act II, again in Marie's room, involves another motive of fear, this time felt by the child, when Marie bursts out impatiently "Schlaf, Bub!" (Go to sleep, boy!): a minor second on the xylophone, which returns in various forms throughout the scene.

When Wozzeck enters, suspicious, this motive (*x*) reappears in a sudden slow tempo as a canon on the muted trombones:

The second scene takes places on a street where the Captain and the Doctor meet. The Doctor feeds the Captain's neurotic fears about his health. A passage "in slow waltz time" adds an ironic touch to this obsessive dialogue. When Wozzeck appears they torment him with veiled references to Marie's infidelity. The music for this scene is based on two forms of the Baroque: an invention (which, it will be remembered, was associated with Bach's keyboard music); and a fugue based on three themes, each associated earlier in the opera with one of the three men.

The scene culminates in Wozzeck's agonized outcry, "Gott in Himmel! Man könnte Lust bekommen sick aufzuhängen!" (God in Heaven! A man might want to hang himself!). The orchestral interlude that follows is a brooding *Largo* scored for chamber orchestra. In the third scene, in front of Marie's dwelling, Wozzeck threatens her. When he raises his hand against her, Marie's words point to the tragic outcome: "Rühr mich nicht an"—"Don't touch me. Better a knife in my flesh than a hand on me. My father didn't dare when I was ten." Scene 4, which takes place at the inn, is introduced by a slow Ländler (an Austrian popular dance in the style of a rustic waltz). Various elements—a song of two young workingmen, a waltz, a chorus, a song by Andres, Wozzeck's rage at seeing Marie dance with the Drum Major, and a mock sermon by a drunken young fellow—are welded into a vivid scene in which Berg skillfully exploits the clash between the band onstage and the orchestra. Noteworthy is the guitar sound that accompanies the waltz of Marie and the Drum Major. Scene 5, which takes place in the guard house, opens with the snores of the sleeping soldiers. The Drum Major boasts of his new conquest. Wozzeck throws himself at the Major, but is beaten down by his burly opponent.

Act III opens with Marie's reading of the Bible, a profoundly moving scene. She tells her child about a poor orphan who had no one in the world, who was hungry and wept. . . . The passage stands out against its atonal surroundings because it is in F minor. A fugue unfolds as she reads about Mary Magdalen and pleads that the Lord forgive her frailty. The scene of the murder, which takes place along a forest path by a pond, abounds in ominous sonorities, as at Marie's words "Wie der Mond rot aufgeht" (How red the moon is!), where the strings hold a B natural spread out over five octaves against muted trombones and fluttertonguing on muted trumpets. Unforgettable is the repeated stroke on two timpani, going from a whisper to a spine-chilling *fff* as Wozzeck cries "Ich nicht, Marie! Und kein Andrer auch nicht!" (If not me, Marie, then no other!) just before he kills her. The drum strokes become softer and return to a pianissimo. In the interlude that follows, the note B is sustained by the orchestra for thirteen measures in a dramatic crescendo, punctuated by the brutal rhythm that symbolizes the catastrophe.

In Scene 3 Wozzeck returns to the tavern and dances with Marie's friend Margaret, who notices blood on his hands. The scene opens with a wild polka accompanied by an out-of-tune piano.

The haunted atmosphere returns as Wozzeck, in Scene 4, goes back to the pond. How poignant is his "Marie! Was hast Du für eine rote Schnur um den Hals?" (Marie, what is that red string around your neck?) His last words as he drowns, "Ich wasche mich mit Blut . . ." (I wash myself in blood—the water is blood . . . blood . . .), usher in a series of ascending chromatic scales that pass in a ghostly pianissimo from the strings to the woodwinds and brass.

There follows a symphonic meditation in D minor, a passionate lament for the life and death of Wozzeck. This inspired fantasy indicates how richly Berg's art was nourished by the Romanticism of Mahler. The final scene takes place in the morning in front of Marie's house. Children are playing. Marie's little boy rides a hobbyhorse. Other children rush in with news of the murder, but Marie's son does not understand. The children run off. The little boy continues to ride and sing. Then, noticing that he has been left alone, he calls "Hopp, hopp" and rides off on his hobbyhorse, to the sound of clarinet, drum, xylophone, and strings, *ppp*. For sheer heartbreak the final curtain has few to equal it in the contemporary lyric theater.

Wozzeck envelops the listener in a hallucinated world in which the hunters are as driven as the hunted. It could have come only out of central Europe in the Twenties. But its characters reach out beyond time and place to become eternal symbols of the human condition.

38 Anton Webern (1883-1945)

"With me, things never turn out as I wish, but only as is ordained for me—as I must."

In the 1950s and 1960s, the music of Anton Webern came into its own. Inevitably, his brief, evanescent works will never bulk large in the repertory, but they have made a firm place for themselves. And they have decisively shaped the music of many younger composers.

His Life

Anton von Webern (he dropped the prefix of nobility in later life) was born in Vienna. His musical gifts asserted themselves at an early age. In addition to his work in composition he studied musicology at the University of Vienna under Guido Adler and received his doctorate in that field. He was twenty-one when he met Schoenberg and, with Alban Berg, formed the nucleus of the band of disciples who gathered around the master. Webern studied with Schoenberg from 1904 till around 1910. Although he worked independently thereafter, he maintained the closest contact with both Schoenberg and Berg,

269

and participated directly in the shaping of the new atonal language.

After leaving the university in 1906, Webern conducted at various German provincial theaters and in Prague. But Vienna was the hub of his world. In 1918, when Schoenberg founded his Society for Private Musical Performances, at whose concerts many important works were presented for the first time, Berg and Webern were his trusted aides in preparing the programs. Webern soon began to conduct the Vienna Workers' Symphony Concerts organized by the authorities of the then socialist city. But as the years passed he found public activity less and less congenial to his retiring disposition. After the First World War he settled in Mödling, a suburb of Vienna, where he lived quietly, devoting himself to composition and teaching.

Anton Webern. A lithograph by Hildegard Jone, 1946. André Meyer Collection.

Webern suffered great hardship after Austria became part of the Third Reich. The Nazis regarded his music as *Kulturbolshevismus,* forbade its performance, and burned his writings. He was permitted to teach only a few pupils, and had to give his lectures—in which he expounded the Schoenbergian point of view—in secret. In order to avoid forced labor during the war, he worked as proofreader for a Viennese publisher. To escape the Allied bombings of Vienna, Webern and his wife sought refuge at the home of their son-in-law in Mittersill, a small town near Salzburg. But fate awaited him there. On September 15, 1945, as he stepped out of his house in the evening to smoke a cigarette (the war had ended five months before, but Mittersill was still under a curfew), he failed to understand an order to halt and was shot by a trigger-happy sentry of the American occupying forces. "The day of Anton Webern's death," wrote his most celebrated admirer, Igor Stravinsky, "should be a day of mourning for any receptive musician. We must hail not only this great composer but also a real hero. Doomed to total failure in a deaf world of ignorance and indifference, he inexorably kept on cutting out his diamonds, his dazzling diamonds, of whose mines he had such a perfect knowledge."

His Music

Webern responded to the radical portion of Schoenbergian doctrine, just as Berg exploited its more conservative elements. Of the three masters of the modern Viennese school, he was the one who cut himself off most completely from the tonal past. Indeed, he has been called the only real atonal composer, as he never accepted even the limited coexistence of tonal and atonal elements which is to be found in the works of Schoenberg and Berg. Webern developed an extremely novel and personal style, yet one that was neither capricious nor arbitrary, for it represented the most minute working out of the principles upon which he based his art.

This style evolved toward an ideal of the utmost purity and economy in the articulation of musical thought. Building upon the Schoenbergian doctrine of perpetual variation, Webern suppressed all repetition of material. "Once stated, the theme expresses all it has to say," he wrote. "It must be followed by something fresh." This belief embodied his desire for continual renewal in the creative process and his attempt to achieve ever fresh invention. The Schoenbergians, we saw, abandoned the spacious Classical forms in favor of

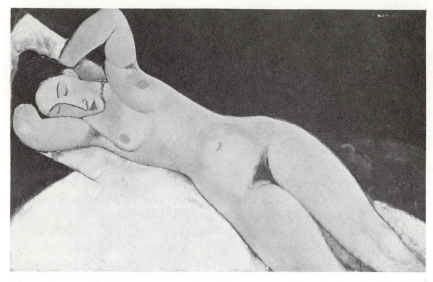

The economy and purity of style which characterizes Webern's music may also be found in the elegant simplicity of Modigliani's work. A supreme draftsman, his elongated figures are linear yet sculptural in the impression of roundness and volume which they convey. Nude, 1917, by Amadeo Modigliani (1884–1920). The Solomon R. Guggenheim Museum, New York.

extreme compression. Webern carried this urge for brevity much farther than either of his comrades.

Such conciseness seems to nullify the very notion of time as we have come to understand it in music. The composition is over almost before we are aware that it has begun. This economy of utterance, which carried to hitherto unimagined extremes the twentieth-century desire for the exclusion of nonessentials, answered a real need of Webern's temperament. The *Six Bagatelles for String Quartet*, Opus 9, have been well characterized as "melodies in one breath." Arnold Schoenberg wrote of them: "Think of the concision which expression in such brief forms demands! Every glance is a poem, every sigh a novel. But to achieve such concentration—to express a novel in a single gesture, a great joy in a single breath—every trace of sentimentality must be correspondingly banished."

Hardly less novel is the musical fabric in which Webern clothed his ideas. His inordinate sensitivity to sound went hand in hand with what Henry Cowell has called "an almost frighteningly concentrated interest in the possibilities of each individual tone." This caused him to place the utmost expressive value on each sonority.

His scores call for the most unusual combinations of instruments. Each tone is assigned its specific function in the overall scheme. The instruments, used in their extreme registers, frequently play one at a time, and very little. This technique results in an extreme attenuation—one might call it atomization—of the musical fabric, which confers upon the individual sonority an importance it never had before. A four-tone chord will be distributed among as many instruments playing in four different registers. Webern applied Schoenberg's principle of the nonrepetition of pitches to color. There are passages in his works where each tone in a melodic line is played by a different instrument. This procedure, of course, can be traced back to the Schoenbergian concept of *Klangfarbenmelodie* or "tone-color melody." When no instrument is allowed to play more than one or two notes of a theme in succession, the changing timbre takes on almost a melodic value; indeed, in such passages the color is at least as important as the pitch.

This preoccupation with sound for sound's sake is, of course, one of the hallmarks of the contemporary approach to music. Webern's works abound in the most delicate effects, with much contrast between muted and unmuted instruments, the division and sub-division of strings, pianissimo trills and tremolos, and the most precise instructions as to how the individual tone is to be produced. His sensitivity to timbre is matched by the subtle dynamic level at which he pitches his discourse. There are passages that are no more than a whisper. A superabundance of rests serves to set off the individual tones. This is music in which silence is hardly less expressive than sound. The rhythmic designs through which the material is presented are of the most elusive. The single phrases have their special character and coherence; but the metrical scheme is not readily apparent. Webern's deliberate avoidance of strongly accentuated patterns, his way of placing the weightier sounds on the offbeat and of perpetually varying the rhythmic phrase imparts to his music its indefinable quality of "hovering suspension," of immobility. The effect of discontinuity is strengthened by the wide leaps in the melodic lines of both his vocal and instrumental music. A pointillism so rarefied needed a strong structural sense to sustain it if it were not to degenerate into the flimsiest impressionism. From his earliest works Webern displayed a constructive sense whose logic and power grew with each successive composition. Underlying the disembodied sound is a firmly knit architecture based on interval proportion and projected in musical space by the most careful ordering of all its elements. The interval became the basic structural element in Webern's music, ultimately taking the place of the theme. Major sevenths and minor ninths, major and minor thirds and their derivatives are the most important intervals in his music. Beneath the evanescent sound is the hard core, the cutting edge. Hence the aptness of Stravinsky's comparison with diamonds.

The music of Webern's formative period shows the influence of Schoenberg; yet he took only what could nourish his personal style, and soon diverged from his master in order to enter a domain uniquely his own. A number of early works have recently been discovered and published, but Webern's official debut was the *Passacaglia for Orchestra*, Opus 1. This was followed by a number of significant works: *Five Movements for String Quartet*, Opus 5 (1909); *Six Orchestral Pieces*, Opus 6 (1910); *Six Bagatelles for String Quartet*, Opus 9 (1913); and *Five Orchestral Pieces*, Opus 10 (1913). These were flanked by the poetic songs—some with piano, others with instrumental accompaniment—in which Webern's essentially lyric gift found a congenial outlet.

Once he had carried the art of aphorism to a limit beyond which there could be only total silence, Webern had to turn back in the direction of more extensive forms. He found the answer to his structural problem in the twelve-tone method. He adopted this in his Opus 17, the *Three Sacred Folk Songs* for voice, clarinet, bass clarinet, and violin (1924); and he remained faithful to it for the rest of his life. Within the framework of the dodecaphonic system he evolved a style of writing based upon the most intellectual disciplines of the art of counterpoint. The close-knit texture of his music represents the summit of musical economy. In this motivic fabric, concentration of thought and purity of style are carried to the furthest point. The devices of canonic writing are handled with true virtuosity. Double canons in contrary motion are common occurrences in Webern's music. His fondness for structural abstraction led him into intricacies which rival those of the medieval contrapuntists.

With his *Symphony*, Opus 21 (1928) Webern came into his fully matured style. In this and the works that followed, the twelve-tone technique is used with unprecedented strictness; the material is made to create its own forms. To this last period belong the *Quartet* for violin, clarinet, tenor saxophone, and piano, Opus 22 (1930); the songs of Opus 23 (1934) and Opus 25 (1935); the *Concerto for Nine Instruments*, Opus 24 (1934); and *Das Augenlicht* (The Light of Our Eyes), Opus 26 (1935), for mixed chorus and instrumental ensemble. From these years date also the *Piano Variations*, Opus 27 (1936); *String Quartet*, Opus 28 (1938); and Webern's last three works: two cantatas for solo voices, chorus, and orchestra, Opus 29 (1939) and Opus 31 (1943); and the *Variations for Orchestra,* Opus 30 (1940). These reveal a master who has vanquished the most complex problems of counterpoint, and who uses his mastery to achieve the Schoenbergian goal of deriving "an abundance of thematic forms from the least possible musical material in the smallest possible space, while at the same time holding these forms to a strict unity."

Schoenberg had contented himself with an organization based upon fixed series of pitches. Webern extended this concept to include timbre and rhythm. Therewith he moved toward complete control of the sonorous material—in other words, total serialization. His disciples, for instance Pierre Boulez and Karlheinz Stockhausen, have carried the implications of Webern's music to its furthest consequences by applying the serial technique to pitches and rhythms, timbres, dynamics, and densities. As a result, Webern emerged as the dominant figure in dodecaphonic thinking at the middle of our century.

Webern's mature output was thirty-one works, all recorded on four long-playing records. This is not much to show for a creative activity that extended over thirty-five years, but the music is so carefully calculated that it impresses one as having been written at the rate of a few notes a day. Many of the inner relationships that hold it together—the canons, retrograde forms, and inversions—are hardly discernible to the ear. They concern the twelve-tone initiate rather than the ordinary listener. However, one need not be aware of the technical complexities to savor the eerily beautiful sonorities that flow from this strange, lonely music. They evoke the remote region inhabited by Webern, a region that only a few will choose to enter. "They alone will understand these pieces," wrote Schoenberg, "who hold the faith that one expresses in tones what can be said only in tones. . . . Subtle, indeed, are the senses that can differentiate here. Fine is the mind capable of finding pleasure in things so recondite!"

Four Songs for Voice and Instruments, Opus 13

Essentially a lyricist, Webern was attracted to vocal music throughout his career. Indeed, in the twelve years between 1915 and 1927 he wrote only music based on words. The short lyric poem offered atonal composers a valuable framework at a time when they

were abandoning traditional notions of form and structure; and Webern, like his master Schoenberg, took full advantage of the circumstance. Like most of the leading song composers of the twentieth
century, he was particularly responsive to the poetry of his own time.
Among his favorite poets were Georg Trakl and Stefan George; also
Hans Bethge, whose *Chinesische Flöte* (Chinese Flute)—a series of
free adaptations from old Chinese poets—supplied the texts also for
Mahler's *Song of the Earth*.

The four songs of Opus 13 (1914–1918) take about seven minutes
to sing. Thus, while they are somewhat longer than several of Webern's works that immediately preceded, they are still short by conventional standards and well illustrate his aphoristic style.

I. *Wiese im Park* (Lawn in the Park), on a poem by Karl Krause.
Sehr ruhig (Very calm), 3/4. Accompanied by thirteen solo instruments: flute, clarinet, bass clarinet; horn, trumpet, trombone;
celesta, glockenspiel, harp; violin, viola, cello, bass. The vocal line
unfolds in a series of tiny motives charged with tension, punctuated
by rests; Webern was one of the composers who fully understood the
dramatic power of silence in music.

These fragments alternate with ampler curves of melody at the points
of climax. Characteristic are the wide leaps, the abundance of dissonant intervals such as major sevenths and ninths that generate expressive tension, and the manner in which the motivic cells in the
voice part are echoed by the instruments. The melody is instrumental in character rather than vocal. In this regard Webern followed the
practice of Bach. As in *Pierrot lunaire,* we are here squarely in the
orbit of atonal Expressionism; but Webern has filtered the influence
of Schoenberg through his own intensely personal vision.

Notice the rarefied texture of the accompaniment, based on a kind
of instrumental pointillism in which individual notes and groups of
notes stand out with maximum clarity. Webern's sensitivity to poetic

image is matched by his uncanny ability to place a key word within the phrase in such a way as to endow it with maximum expressiveness. For example, the upward leap of a major seventh to F-sharp on *Sonntag* (Sunday) in the second stanza, or the upward leap of a major seventh to a high A on *Wunder* (wonder)—the climactic point of the melody line—in the third. (For the complete German-English text see Appendix II.)

Tempo picks up at the second stanza. The mention of bluebells turns the composer's mind to the bell sounds that he so loved. Striking too is the threatening rasp of muted brass—horn, trumpet, trombone—that comments on *Nicht weiter will ich* (I'll go not further) at the beginning of the third stanza. Tension winds down in the last line, *Und alles bleibt so alt* (And everything is old), with a widely spaced chord for strings and bass, *ppp*, at the end.

II. *Die Einsame* (The Lonely Girl), on a poem by Wang-Seng-Yu from Bethge's *Chinese Flute. Bewegt* (With movement), 2/4. The same instrumental group as in I, except that the flute is replaced by a piccolo. The melody moves in a more sustained fashion, as befits the mood of loneliness projected by the poem. The instruments are strongly individualized here and play a more expressive role. In the opening phrase the melody rises to a climax on the key word *Himmel* (sky):

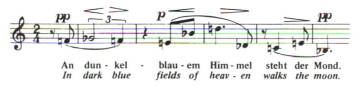

| An | dun - kel - | blau - em | Him - mel | steht der Mond. |
| *In* | *dark blue* | *fields of* | *heav - en* | *walks the moon.* |

The setting of emotional words like *weine* (weep) and *Tränen* (tears) prepares the way for the climax on a high B-flat, fortissimo, on the central word of the poem, *Sehnsucht* (longing). From there tension unwinds rapidly, as in the first song, on the final thought: *weil du es nie begreifen wirst, wie weh mir ist, wenn ich nicht bei dir bin* (because you'll never understand how great my pain when I am not with you). The voice sings alone the final word on a spectral high G-flat, *ppp*. Webern throughout uses triplet patterns in various speeds and combinations, alongside the traditional divisions of the beat into duple patterns. The procedure imparts to his music a plasticity of rhythm that is very much his own.

III. *In der Fremde* (In a Strange Land), on a poem by Li-Tai-Po, from Bethge's *Chinese Flute. Fliessend* (Flowing), 2/4. Nine instruments: piccolo, clarinet, bass clarinet, trumpet, celesta, harp;

muted violin, viola, and cello. This song is a miniature; it lasts one minute. The flowing legato line stands far closer to traditional concepts of melody than is usually the case with Webern. The instruments establish an exotic atmosphere that is silvered by the tinkle of celesta and harp. Notice the striking projection of the two key words: *Mond* (moon) and *Heimat* (homeland).

IV. *Ein Winterabend* (A Winter Evening), on a poem by Georg Trakl. *Sehr ruhig* (Very calm), 4/4. Ten instruments: clarinet, bass clarinet; trumpet, trombone; celesta, harp; violin, viola, cello, double bass. The poem contrasts the cosiness of a winter evening, for those who can repair to a brightly-lit room and well-stocked table, with the sorrow of the homeless wanderer. It takes a firm sense of pitch to execute a passage such as the following, with its tricky dissonant intervals:

The vocal line bristles with such dissonances, which many musicians branded as unsingable until a few contemporary artists proved the contrary. The melody ends with a highly charged interval, a diminished octave. The instruments comment with a dissonant harmony, *ppp,* and the cycle ends on a single note—a harmonic on the harp.

Symphony for Small Orchestra, Opus 21

The *Symphony,* Opus 21—for clarinet, bass clarinet, two horns, two harps, violins, violas, and cellos—ushered in the most important phase of Webern's career, when his desire for absolute purity of language led him to his own completely original style. With this composition he became the first of the modern Viennese school to undertake the grand form of the Classical period. (As we saw, neither Schoenberg nor Berg cultivated the symphony.) It goes without saying that Webern's piece is as far removed from the expansion-and-development techniques traditionally associated with symphonic style as it is from the tonic-dominant polarity that made the symphony the embodiment of tonal thinking. Webern's *Symphony* takes just under ten minutes to play, and shows the same concentration of thought and sparseness of writing as do his other scores. The single-

Webern, *Symphony*, Opus 21, I

note texture, punctuated now and again with two-note chords, is of the utmost refinement. The lines are shaped in such a fashion as to place maximum emphasis upon the individual tone, its placement and color. This music, as René Leibowitz remarked, is "stripped to its barest essentials." (The row forms will be found in Appendix I-k.)

I. *Ruhig schreitend* (Moving quietly). The first movement unfolds as a double canon for four voices—that is to say, two canons running simultaneously, each for two voices, with the answering voices imitating the leaders in contrary motion. Notice, in the opening passage of the *Symphony*, how Webern departs from the usage of traditional counterpoint by continually crossing the voices. Notice too the wide leaps in each melodic line due to octave displacement. Webern's extraordinarily delicate use of color serves to set off not only the several voices but also the different motives within the row. Taking the upper canon first, we see that the first motive (tones 1–2–3–4) is played by second horn and answered by first horn. The second motive (5–6–7–8) is played by clarinet and imitated by bass clarinet. The third motive (9–10–11–12) is stated by cellos and answered by violas. Thus the relationship between the leading voice and the answering voice is underlined by the use of homogeneous tone color—brass, woodwind, and string respectively. (See example on page 279.) A similar individualization of timbre obtains in the second or lower canon.

The movement is divided into two parts, each of which is repeated (measures 1–24, and 25–66). The first ten measures of part two (25–34) are immediately repeated backward (35–44). Throughout the first part the prevailing rhythmic values are whole notes, halves, and quarters. The second part brings a quickening of the movement: eighth notes appear. The first part ranges from low to medium-high register; the second climbs to high. The first part, except for one solitary *forte*, moves between *pianissimo* and *mezzo-piano;* the second builds to a *forte* passage, whose intensity is reinforced by the various members of the string group playing successively in unison, and by a high open D in the first horn—its highest note throughout the movement. There is a quick subsiding; the Coda unfolds a canon in contrary motion for two voices. A muted solo violin plays for three consecutive measures—a continuity of color not often found in Webern. The movement ends *pianissimo.*

II. *Variationen* (Theme and Variations). The second—and last —movement, consisting of a theme, seven brief variations, and a coda, injects into the symphony the element of perpetual variation so dear to the Schoenbergian school. The theme, marked *Sehr ruhig*

THEME

(very quiet), is a musical sentence of eleven measures. Measure 6 is the turning point; after it the first half of the theme is transposed and repeated backward. The theme as a whole, read backward, is the same as the forward version transposed up an augmented fourth.

Each variation, like the theme, is eleven measures long. The first, marked *lebhafter* (livelier), is a double canon for four voices in contrary motion, played by the muted strings. This continuity of a single color, a feature of this movement but otherwise unusual in Webern's music, is relieved by an alternation of pizzicato notes and those played with the bow. As in the theme, the second half of the variation repeats the first half backward, and this symmetry is maintained in the following variations. Variation 2, *sehr lebhaft* (very lively), is a trio for clarinet, bass clarinet, and horn, with chords on the harp and occasional interjections by the strings. Clarinet and bass clarinet play a canon, while the horn plays a continous line of eighth notes. Variation 3, *wieder mässiger* (again more moderately), is a kind of diminutive toccata movement in which Webern returns to his usual style of pointillist instrumentation.

The fourth variation is the slowest. Marked *äusserst ruhig* (extremely quiet), it occupies the central position in the movement. The texture increases in density at this point. For the first time in the symphony five tones are sounded simultaneously. The complex canonic writing links this section to the first and last variations. The fifth variation, *sehr lebhaft* (very lively), corresponds to the toccata movement of Variation 3. Based on an ostinato in the strings, this variation proceeds in a steady crescendo from *ppp* to *pp*, *p*, *mp*, and *mf*. The rhythm is based on groups of sixteenth notes that form symmetrical patterns of their own. Despite the rapidity of movement, this variation strongly gives the impression of turning around itself. There results that special effect of near-immobility which is so germane to Webern's style.

Variation 6, *marschmässig* (like a march), is a trio for clarinet, bass clarinet, and horn, like Variation 2, but without any string color.

Clarinet and bass clarinet again play a canon, while the horn this time plays sustained notes. Variation 7, *etwas breiter* (somewhat broader), is a double canon in contrary motion. The overall scheme of the variations is therefore revealed to be as symmetrical as the theme itself: Variations 1 and 7 are double canons, 2 and 6 are trios, 3 and 5 are toccatalike movements, and Variation 4 is the keystone. The Coda maintains the reversible form of the variations. It consists of twenty-four tones which spell out the theme and its retrograde fragmented and distributed among clarinet, harp, first violin, and cello. The *Symphony* ends with two single notes on the harp.

The composer of this exquisitely controlled, concentrated work was content to go his way, an obscure figure in the musical circles of his time, overshadowed by those who made a bigger noise in the world. Selflessly dedicated to his austere vision of sonorous beauty, he was sustained only by an inner faith in the ultimate rightness of his intuitions. He had no way of knowing that, little over a decade after his death, avant-garde musicians in Europe and America would think of themselves as belonging to "the age of Webern."

I. *Other Significant Figures*

39 Leoš Janáček (1854-1928)

"What matters is uncompromising truthfulness, in life as in art."

Fifteen years ago Leoš Janáček was all but unknown in this country. Little by little, recordings and performances of his works began to increase from year to year. As was the case with Mahler, his time finally came.

His Life

Janáček was born in Hukvaldy, a village in Moravia (the eastern part of Czechoslovakia). His father and grandfather were school-master-organists and Leoš, who grew up in poverty, expected to follow in their footsteps. He was educated in the Augustinian Abbey of Brünn, now Brno, where music was very much a part of the curriculum, and went on to a teachers' training school. The director of the school recognized his talent and made it possible for the young man to complete his musical education in Prague, Munich, and Vienna. Upon his return Janáček married his benefactor's daughter and became active as organist, choral director, and organizer of musical events in Brno. His career unfolded within the framework of this provincial town.

Janáček matured very slowly as an artist. The first work that fully revealed his gifts, the opera *Jenufa*, was completed in 1903 when he was almost fifty. He wrote it in the shadow of a personal tragedy—the death of his young daughter Olga, to whose memory he dedicated the opera. *Jenufa* achieved a local success in Brno, but its path in Prague was blocked by the enemies that Janáček's outspoken tongue and pen had created for him. Finally all obstacles were overcome and the opera conquered Prague in 1916. Two years later it

A pencil sketch of Janáček by B. F. Dolbin. André Meyer Collection.

reached Vienna, with the glamorous Maria Jeritza in the title role. The work created a sensation and disclosed the existence of a musician of European stature. (The great soprano, nearly ninety, was present to take a bow on a memorable night in 1976, almost sixty years later, when after a long absence from the repertory *Jenufa* returned to the Metropolitan.)

Janáček was a highly emotional man with what one of his biographers called "a big loving heart": impetuous, explosive, an earthy, elemental being who recognized no separation between life and art. His dynamic personality struck those around him like a force of nature. He never recovered from the deaths of his young son and daughter. With the passing of years he grew further and further away from his wife, a woman of the upper class who had no understanding either of his peasant background or his egalitarian ideals. His last years were brightened by a passionate friendship with a woman almost forty years his junior. To the happiness that she brought him he ascribed the creative energy that carried him from one major work to the next during the last two decades of his life. At the age of seventy-four he was able to write Kamilla Stoesslova with all the ardor that we mistakenly associate only with youth: "I have begun to compose something marvelous. Our life will be contained in it. I shall call it *Love Letters*. How many treasured experiences we have had together! Like little flames, these will light up in my soul and become the most beautiful melodies. In this work I shall be alone with you. No one besides us . . ." The work was his *Second String Quartet*.

He died that summer of a pulmonary infection, at the end of a happy vacation in his native village with Kamilla and her children, and was buried in Brno.

His Music

Janáček had to outgrow his traditional training before he could find his own voice. He freed himself from the classical past through his identification with east-Moravian folk song. Twenty years before Bartók went into the villages of Hungary, Janáček began the scientific study of the folk songs of his homeland. From them he derived the modal harmonies, irregular rhythms, and unconventional melodic patterns that give his idiom its freshness and strength. His art was rooted in the soil, nurtured equally by Slavonic folklore and nature mysticism; and he recognized the source of its power: "Folk song—I have lived with it since childhood. In folk song the entire man is enshrined, his body and soul, his milieu—everything. He who is rooted in folk song becomes a complete man."

Like Musorgsky, whose ideas strongly influenced him, Janáček aspired to a musical realism—what he understood as truth—derived from the inflections of his native tongue. He was inordinately sensitive to the cadence of spoken language, to the psychological nuances buried in everyday speech. These nuances he translated into what he called "speech-motives," melodic cells alive with psychological meaning. "It happened that, when someone spoke to me, I did not always understand his words but I did understand the melodic cadences of his speech. I knew at once whether that person lied or was inwardly agitated. Sometimes, during a most ordinary conversation, I felt and indeed heard that my companion was inwardly weeping. The inflections of human speech—and indeed of the voices of all living creatures—became to me a source of profound truth, a life-necessity, as it were. Speech-motives are my windows into the soul." It is these "speech-motives" that impart such emotional validity to the melody line in his operas and vocal works and that in sublimated form echo as well through his instrumental works.

Janáček's musical language is of the Postromantic period. His harmony is extremely mobile and expressive. In his later works he dispensed with key signatures. He had little interest in the traditional forms, preferring a mosaic structure based on the continual variation of a few basic motives. He has been compared to Musorgsky for his unconventionality of thought, his rough-hewn and original harmonies, the compassion and love of humble folk that inform his art. In his operas Janáček emphasizes the orchestra, which wreathes the action in a flood of luminous sound. He avoids expansive lines in the vocal writing, as he does thematic development in the orchestra. The texture unfolds as a series of thematic nuclei which, because of the homogeneity of the style, combine in larger units and give a vivid musical characterization of the people on stage. The result is an extremely concentrated idiom marked by dramatic truth and sustained intensity.

These elements are fused in a powerful synthesis in Janáček's masterpiece *Jenufa*. The opera, based on Gabriella Preissova's drama of Moravian peasant life, centers about the murder of an illegitimate child, a theme familiar to English readers through such works as George Eliot's *Adam Bede* and Thomas Hardy's *Tess of the D'Urbervilles*. In this instance the crime is carried out by Kostelnicka, Jenufa's strong-willed guardian, who is motivated by her frantic desire to shield her ward from shame. This situation, one of the great nineteenth-century parables of the conflict between the individual and society, afforded Janáček wide scope for a music-drama that lifts the action to the highest plane of compassion and forgiveness.

The Czech half of his homeland—Bohemia—was urban, industrialized, Germanized. Janáček identified himself with the Slovakian half, which was rural, backward, poverty-stricken. Musically he leaned toward the Slavonic heritage of Dvořák rather than the Bohemian heritage of Smetana (although in later life he overcame his antipathy to the latter). His pan-Slavic sympathies led him toward Russia in the east rather than Germany in the west, with important results for his art. His dramatic vision was nurtured by the images of spiritual redemption through suffering and expiation that abound in nineteenth-century Russian literature. Janáček's *String Quartet No. 1* (1923) was inspired by Toltoy's *Kreuzer Sonata*. Ostrovsky's moving drama *The Storm* provided the libretto for *Katya Kabanová* (1921), an opera that ranks with *Jenufa* in dramatic power. Also Dostoevsky, the poet of "the insulted and injured," was a seminal influence on the Czech composer. The great novelist's memoirs of prison life in Siberia served as the basis of Janáček's last opera, *House of the Dead* (1928).

The Makropoulos Case (1925) is based on Karel Capek's fantastic play about a beautiful woman who is three hundred years old. *The Cunning Little Vixen* (1923) is an exquisite fantasy steeped in nature mysticism, in which the little fox becomes the personification of the eternal feminine. It should be noted that the five operas just mentioned have all been presented in this country, four in various theaters and *House of the Dead* in a powerful television production, in English, under the direction of Peter Hermann Adler.

A number of Janáček's works are heard increasingly on our concert programs and are available on records: *Diary of a Young Man Who Vanished*, for voices and piano (1919); *Suite for Wind Sextet* ("Youth," 1924), inspired by memories of his early years in the Augustinian Abbey at Brno; *Concertino for Piano and Chamber Orchestra* (1925); *Capriccio for the Left Hand*, for piano and chamber orchestra (1926); *Sinfonietta*, which we will discuss; *Slavonic Mass*, also known as *Glagolitic Mass* (1926); and *String Quartet No. 2* ("Love Letters," 1928).

Sinfonietta

Janáček was profoundly stirred when Czechoslovakia achieved its independence at the end of the First World War. He expressed with characteristic exuberance what it meant to him to watch the new nation grow. "I am filled with the young spirit of our republic, with a young music. I do not belong to those who have stayed behind, but to those who would rather look forward. We are a people that must take their place in the world. We are the heart of Europe. And the beating of this heart should be audible to Europe." It was his aim as an artist to help bring this about.

The "young music" of the seventy-two-year-old composer took shape as a *Sinfonietta* (1926), which he dedicated to the Armed Forces of his country. In it he tried to express, as he wrote Kamilla, "the contemporary free man, his spiritual beauty and joy, his strength, courage, and determination to fight for victory." This radiant work is a suite for orchestra in five movements in which Janáček recaptured, in twentieth-century terms, the spirit of one of the most attractive forms of eighteenth-century entertainment music—the divertimento.

The *Sinfonietta* harks back to the outdoor sound of a military band, a sound that would be a treasured memory for anyone who spent his youth in a central European town. Indeed, the first impulse toward the work came on a summer day in a park, when Janáček and Kamilla sat listening to such a band. The composer was delighted by the fanfares and by the fact that each trumpeter stood up to play his solo (a practice that still obtains in jazz bands). Shortly thereafter, when asked to write a piece for a mass rally of the national sports movement *Sokol* (Falcon) in Prague, Janáček composed a fanfare for brass that became the point of departure for the *Sinfonietta*. The outdoor sound is suggested by the scoring: four flutes and clarinets instead of the usual three; two each of oboes, English horns, and clarinets; a really expanded brass section—four horns, fourteen trumpets, four trombones and three tubas; percussion and strings. Each movement is scored for a different combination of instruments.

I. *Allegretto*, 2/4. For trumpets, tubas and kettledrums. The opening movement illustrates Janáček's mosaic method of composition, based on the repetition or variation of short melodic fragments that are incorporated into a larger structure. This method is as typical of the Russian school (Musorgsky, Rimsky-Korsakov, Stravinsky) as the process of expansion through thematic-motivic development is typical of the German. Like Prokofiev, Janáček has a way of plunging directly from one tonality into the next, omitting the transitional modulations that added spaciousness to the classical architecture. By excluding the formal-intellectual elements of musical construction he achieves the simplicity, spontaneity, and elemental vigor of folk song. As a result, the emotional content of the music is kept at white heat throughout.

The first movement is based on asymmetrical phrases of three, five, and seven measures that bear the imprint of Slavonic folk song. Characteristic are the sudden changes of tempo from *Allegretto* to *Allegro* to *Maestoso* (majestic). Seven variations lead the opening motive from its initial pronouncement—through subtle accretions in rhythmic and melodic detail—to its brilliant "apotheosis" at the end.

This process of accretion leaves the listener with an overall impression of inevitable growth.

II. *Andante*, 4/8. For woodwinds, four trombones, and strings. The second movement begins with a rotating accompanimental figure in the clarinets, over which emerges a guileless little tune played by two oboes. Although of Janáček's mintage, it bears the marks of Slavic folk song. Janáček, incidentally, uses no key signatures, but indicates the sharps and flats as he goes along. The procedure implies a flexible concept of tonality that is very much of the twentieth century. Each fragment of melody is heard twice, the fragments gradually building up into a long line:

This movement too is marked by the sudden changes of tempo that abound in Balkan popular music. The accompanimental figure presently becomes a melody in longer notes (augmentation). So certain is Janáček's handling of form that the movement gives an overall impression of large-scale construction even though it is based on fragments. There is nothing miniature about this music.

III. *Moderato*, 2/2. For woodwinds, brass, harp, and strings. This impassioned song for orchestra is based on a melody of noble pathos introduced by muted violins and cellos. It captures the dramatic ten-

sion of a folk ballad, but it is a wholly personal expression. Incidentally, Janáček, like Falla, never used folk tunes in his works. His concept was akin to the Spanish master's doctrine of "truth without
authenticity." A composer might create in the spirit of the folk, but
always with his own voice.

The opening section, in moderate tempo, contrasts with two
faster ones. The first of these begins as a dialogue between chords on
the brass in low register and flickerings on flutes and piccolo in high
(the kind of flickering sound that later came to be associated with
Bartók.) The scoring here, of instruments used in extreme high and
low register without any middle ground, is typical of Janáček. The
second episode derives its material from accompanimental figures in
the first, but transformed in regard to instrumental color, tempo, dynamics, and interval relationships. The orchestra works up a climax
of symphonic proportions; then the opening melody returns, round-
ing off this "night piece" in the mood of lyric meditation with which
it began.

IV. *Allegretto*, 2/4. For woodwinds, brass, harp, bells, strings.
This movement consists of a set of variations on a folklike theme that
exemplifies Janáček's fondness for building a melody from short
phrases. In this case a phrase of three measures is repeated and followed by a two-measure codetta. Although the overall length of this
tune is eight measures (3+3+2), the same as in melodies of the
Classic-Romantic period, the layout is different:

Used in the manner of an ostinato, the theme is heard fourteen
times, in the course of which Janáček changes its scoring, rhythm,
register, and dynamics, together with those abrupt changes of tempo
and key to which we have referred. Noteworthy is the graceful way
in which he combines the basic idea with countermelodies.

V. *Andante con moto*, 2/4. For woodwinds, without bassoons;
brass, including all the trumpets; percussion, and strings. The movement opens with a plaintive melody in the flutes. Melody and accom-

paniment expand into a spacious section, with both elements assuming new forms. A scherzolike middle section marked *Più mosso* (faster) prepares the way for the return of the theme. The steady buildup of tension soon reveals the real goal of the movement—the return of the fanfares with which the *Sinfonietta* opened. These broaden into a burst of orchestral splendor in which trills throughout the orchestra fill the air with excitement. And the piece ends on a note of affirmation worthy of a national poet who had a heroic vision of man.

40 Ralph Vaughan Williams (1872-1958)

"The art of music above all other arts is the expression of the soul of a nation. The composer must love the tunes of his country and they must become an integral part of him."

Until Edward Elgar appeared on the musical scene at the end of the nineteenth century, England had produced no major composer for two hundred years. The rise of a native school in the Postromantic period consequently fulfilled a deep need in that music-loving nation. The English renascence was heralded by an awakening of interest in native song and dance. The folk-song revival centered about the work of Cecil Sharp and his disciples, who went into the villages and hamlets and took down the traditional tunes from the lips of folk singers. The movement toward a national music was strengthened by the revival of interest in the masters of Tudor church music, in the Elizabethan madrigalists, and in the art of Purcell. Out of this ferment came a generation of composers. The most important figure among them was Ralph Vaughan Williams, who succeeded Elgar as the representative of English music on the international scene.

His Life

Ralph Vaughan Williams was born in Down Ampney, Gloucestershire, the son of a well-to-do clergyman. At the age of eighteen, he

Ralph Vaughan Williams. A photograph from the Bettmann Archive.

entered the Royal College of Music where he studied with the elder statesmen of the English renascence, Sir Charles Hubert Parry and Sir Charles Villiers Stanford. Two years later, Vaughan Williams entered Trinity College, Cambridge, where he took both a musical and general degree. There followed a short stay abroad, during which he studied in Berlin with Max Bruch, a composer in the Romantic tradition. He then returned to Cambridge, and in 1901 recieved his doctorate in music, the most respectable appendage a British musician can have.

A decisive influence at this time was Vaughan Williams's involvement with the folk-song revival. He worked along the lines laid down by Cecil Sharp, going into the villages of Norfolk to collect traditional melodies. In 1904 he undertook to edit the music of a hymnbook, and enriched the hymnology with some simple tunes of his own. "Two years of close association with some of the best (as well as some of the worst) tunes in the world was a better musical education than any amount of sonatas and fugues."

Despite this activity, in 1908—he was then thirty-six—Vaughan Williams came to the conclusion that he was "lumpy and stodgy, had come to a dead-end, and that a little French polish" would do him good. He decided to study with Ravel, his junior by three years, and went to Paris for that purpose. There could hardly have been a stranger choice of master for the bluff, homespun Englishman than the elegant Parisian. "When I had shown him some of my work he said that, for my first lesson, I had better *écrire un petit menuet dans le style de Mozart*. I saw at once that it was time to act promptly, so I said in my best French, 'Look here, I have given up my time, my work, my friends and my career to come here and learn from you, and I am *not* going to write a *petit menuet dans le style de Mozart.*' After that we became great friends and I learned much from him."

The outbreak of war in 1914 relegated music to a secondary place in the composer's life. Although he was forty-two, he enlisted, was commissioned as a lieutenant in the Royal Garrison Artillery, and saw combat duty in France throughout 1918. The war over, he resumed his career. He became professor of composition at the Royal College of Music, in which post he helped train many gifted musicians of the new generation. He was the most active of the so-called "folk-song school of composers," and after Cecil Sharp's death in 1933 he guided the destinies of the English Folk-Song Society. In 1935 Vaughan Williams, having refused official honors on earlier occasions, accepted the Order of Merit. These are the external landmarks of an intense inner life whence issued a steady stream of works, vocal and instrumental, in all genres. In the last years of his life Vaughan Williams was the unofficial composer laureate of his native land. This aspect of his career was underlined when the Credo and Sanctus of his *Mass in G minor* were performed in Westminster Abbey at the coronation of Queen Elizabeth II. He completed his *Ninth Symphony* at the age of eighty-five, and died a year later.

His Music

Vaughan Williams stood at the furthest possible remove from the "art for art's sake" doctrine of an aesthete like Delius. Basic to his view was the desire to bring art into the most direct relationship to life. "The composer," he wrote, "must not shut himself up and think about art: he must live with his fellows and make his art an expression of the whole life of the community." But life is not lived in the abstract. It is experienced in a certain place and shared with a certain group of people. Hence Vaughan Williams took his stand as an advocate of national music. "Art, like charity, should begin at home. It is because Palestrina and Verdi are essentially Italian and because Bach, Beethoven and Wagner are essentially German that their message transcends their frontiers. The greatest artist belongs inevitably to his country as much as the humblest singer in a remote village."

In the ancient tunes of the peasantry Vaughan Williams found the living expression of the English spirit. Having assimilated the character of popular melody to his personal thinking, he wrote music that sounded national whether he quoted actual folk songs or not. As a matter of fact there are fewer quotations of folk song in Vaughan Williams's music than is commonly supposed. What is decisive in his art is the fact that in the English folk-song revival he found his spiritual habitat. "This revival," he wrote, "gave a point to our imagination; far from fettering us, it freed us from foreign influences which weighed on us."

He was devoted to all manifestations of the English spirit. His numerous settings of hymns and carols exemplify his dictum that the traditional tunes must be treated "with love." Basic ingredients of his style derive from the Elizabethan madrigalists and the polyphonists of the Tudor era. His homage to the golden age of English music took shape in one of his most successful works, the *Fantasia on a Theme by Tallis* (1910). Even more, it shows itself in his flair for choral music. "A massive, broad, bare choral style like his," one of the leading British critics wrote, "has not been heard among English musicians since Purcell."

The English language powerfully affected Vaughan Williams's vocal line. He ranged wide in his choice of poets, from Chaucer, Shakespeare, and Milton to Coleridge, Shelley, Tennyson, and Hardy. His democratic leanings found a sympathetic echo in Walt Whitman, whose poetry he set in *Towards the Unknown Region*, a cantata for chorus and orchestra (1905), and *A Sea Symphony*, for soprano, baritone, chorus, and orchestra (1910). The Bible was an abiding influence, as was Bunyan. *Job*, "a masque for dancing" (1930), was inspired by William Blake's illustrations for the Book of Job. Most important in this category is his symbolic opera or "morality" *The Pilgrim's Progress* (1949), on a text by his wife, the poet Ursula Wood, after Bunyan. These, like his religious works, are imbued with the spirit of English Protestantism. True, his finest piece of church music, the *Mass in G minor* (1922), uses the text of the Roman Catholic rite. But the spiritual provenance of this music is the Anglican service.

Vaughan Williams's response to the English landscape is projected in the *London* (1914) and *Pastoral* (1922) symphonies; *The Lark Ascending*, a romance for violin and orchestra based on a poem of George Meredith (1914); and the song cycle *On Wenlock Edge*, for tenor, string quartet, and piano, to lyrics drawn from A. E. Housman's *A Shropshire Lad* (1909). Of his nine symphonies, the most dramatic is the *Fourth* in F minor (1935), a somber, uncompromising work of great impact. Vaughan Williams's operas are not for export; they speak to the English mind. *Hugh the Drover*, a ballad opera (1914), is in the tradition of those nationalist works which glorify the life and virtues of the folk. *Sir John in Love* (1929), based on Shakespeare's *Merry Wives of Windsor*, suffers from inevitable comparison with one of the most luminous of all operas, Verdi's *Falstaff*. If any stage work of Vaughan Williams ever succeeds in establishing itself outside his homeland it will probably be *Riders to the Sea* (1937), on Synge's powerful one-act play about Irish fishermen; the work shows his expressive declamation and his ability to sustain a mood.

Vaughan Williams was primarily a melodist. His love of folk tunes was part of an essentially melodic approach to music. He shied away from chromatic harmony. His natural expression was diatonic, with strong leanings—encouraged by his interest in old music—toward modal harmony and counterpoint. Characteristic is his great fondness for the flatted seventh step, an effect found in folk tunes based on old scales, and for modal cadences. Common chords figure prominently in his writing, and he also liked to use strings of triads in parallel motion. In his later works he adopted daring harmonic procedures, building up simple chord formations into complex dissonances of great expressivity. His preoccupation with the Elizabethan madrigal liberated him from the four-square rhythms of the Classic-Romantic period; his rhythmic flexibility is especially noticeable in his sudden shifts from duple to triple patterns. He favored old forms—the passacaglia, fugue, and concerto grosso; also the Elizabethan fantasia, with its flowing counterpoint. Like Sibelius, whom he very much admired—he dedicated his *Fifth Symphony* to the Finnish master—Vaughan Williams held the attention of the world largely because of his command of the grand form. His nine symphonies are ample of gesture and noble in tone.

Vaughan Williams's huge output runs the gamut of his art. His music is fresh, cool, wholesome. It has strength and lyricism, yet the emotion is held in check by natural reticence. It retains a certain roughness and directness of manner despite the composer's long years of schooling; these traits were part of his personality. His honesty in all that regarded his art was as engaging as the humility with

The art of the distinguished English sculptor Henry Moore (b. 1898) lends itself to descriptive phrases equally applicable to the music of his countryman Vaughan Williams: fresh and cool, strong yet lyrical; at times direct, but also subtle and restrained. The King and Queen, 1952–1953. *Hirshorn Museum and Sculpture Garden, Smithsonian Institution, Washington, D.C.*

which he spoke of his achievements, as when he wrote, "I have struggled all my life to conquer amateurish technique and now that perhaps I have mastered it, it seems too late to make any use of it." One is reminded of Haydn's touching remark: "I have only just learned in my old age how to use the wind instruments, and now that I understand them I must leave the world."

Serenade to Music

Vaughan Williams's *Serenade to Music* (1938) was written as a tribute to the British conductor Sir Henry J. Wood "on the occasion of his Jubilee, in grateful recognition of his services to music." It became the composer's gesture of homage to the glory of music, projected through the verses of England's greatest poet. The piece is based on Shakespeare's invocation to music in the "love duet" of Lorenzo and Jessica in Act V, Scene 1 of *The Merchant of Venice* (with a few lines of Portia added). Vaughan Williams wrote it for sixteen solo singers who had been associated with Sir Henry during his long career, and orchestra.

Shakespeare is not easy to set to music. His verse has so powerful a music of its own that it defies anyone else's. All the greater is Vaughan Williams's achievement in having unlocked in so inevitable a fashion the music hidden in the Bard's verse. *Serenade to Music* should be required listening for those benighted souls who go around saying that English is difficult to sing.

The orchestral introduction—harp, clarinet, horns, strings—establishes the proper mood of nocturnal enchantment. As one of Vaughan Williams's admirers put it, "the work is all silver and moonlight." A solo violin, soaring aloft, announces a little motive that recurs as a motto throughout the work:

p *cantabile*

The music picks up momentum with a change to triplet rhythm that prepares for the entrance of the voices, singing in eight-part harmony.

> How sweet the moonlight sleeps upon this bank!
> Here will we sit, and let the sounds of music
> Creep in our ears. Soft stillness and the night
> Become the touches of sweet harmony.

We are adrift in a luminous world of musical music and harmonious harmony. The opening section unfolds within a spacious D-major tonality, with a brief excursion to F. Vaughan Williams took full advantage of the contrasts inherent in the major-minor system as well as the heightened expressivity made possible by shifting suddenly from one key to another. This approach stemmed, of course, from his reliance on diatonic rather than chromatic harmony.

The voices take over:

> Look how the floor of heaven
> Is thick inlaid with patines of bright gold . . .

The words are given a special magic by modulations from F major to G, and thence to B-flat. (For the complete text see Appendix II.) The

triplet rhythm persists, building up tension against the central statement of this section, which is divided between solo voices and the
entire group:

> Such harmony is in immortal souls;
> But whilst this muddy vesture of decay
> Doth grossly close it in, we cannot hear it.

The mood changes with discreet fanfares on trumpets and horns
resounding against tremolos in the strings.

> Come, ho, and wake Diana with a hymn!
> With sweetest touches pierce your mistress' ear,
> And draw her home with music.

The orchestra gives full-throated utterance to the basic motive.
An *Andante con moto* in 3/4 prepares the way for Shakespeare's celebrated pronouncement on the uplifting power of music, perhaps the
most eloquent tribute ever penned to the art of sound. Vaughan
Williams underlines its importance by setting it as a bass solo that
moves from the home key of D major to E, then to G, B-flat and D-
flat, with the chorus joining in on the final line.

> The man that hath no music in himself,
> Nor is not moved with concord of sweet sounds,
> Is fit for treasons, strategems and spoils;
> The motions of his spirit are dull as night,
> And his affections dark as Erebus.
> Let no such man be trusted!

The music finds its way back to the basic motive in the home key and
original tempo, although somewhat more animated. Triplet rhythm
reappears as a tension-building device, with a modulation to F major
that is brightened by glissandos on the harp.

> Peace, ho! The moon sleeps with Endymion
> And would not be awak'd!

Vaughan Williams achieves a sweet serenity here. The passage leads
naturally into the final appearance of the basic motive and the beautiful cadence, *ppp*, in D.

One senses the manly personality and the warm heart behind this
music. "He looks like a farmer," Stephen Williams wrote of him. "A
big, heavy, lumbering figure, usually dressed in rough tweeds, who
looks as though he is on his way to judge the shorthorns at an agricultural fair." Vaughan Williams in extraordinary fashion met the

needs of his time and place. He was, as one of his compatriots called him, "the most English of English composers."

41 Kurt Weill (1900-1950)

"I write only to express human emotions."

Kurt Weill was one of the most original figures to emerge in Germany in the period after the First World War. He was a child of his time, but he managed also to transcend it. For this reason his best theater works are not only vivid documents of the 1920s that produced them, but continue to have meaning for us today.

His Life

Weill's father, a cantor of the Jewish community in Dessau, recognized the boy's talent and saw to it that he received a thorough musical education. After several years at the Berlin Hochschule with Engelbert Humperdinck, the composer of *Hansel and Gretel*, Weill acquired practical experience as a coach and conductor in provincial opera houses. He returned to Berlin when he was twenty-one and spent three years studying with Ferruccio Busoni, whose classical teachings bore fruit in Weill's lifelong devotion to economy of means, directness of statement, and clarity of texture.

The young composer responded to the artistic ferment that was centered in Berlin. His early works, such as the *String Quartet*, Opus 8 (1923), and the *Concerto for Violin and Wind Band*, Opus 12 (1924), show his experimental bent as well as his imaginative response to the chief influences about him: Mahler, Richard Strauss, Hindemith, Schoenberg. It was in the theater that Weill found his personal style. Borrowing elements from the political cabaret and the satiric review, he fused these into a new kind of topical opera that pungently hit off the temper of the time. He found his ideal librettist in the Communist poet-playwright Bertolt Brecht (1898–1956), with whom he pro-

Kurt Weill. Photo Karsh-Canada.

duced his masterpiece *Die Dreigroschenoper* (The Three-Penny Opera), which we will discuss. There followed *Aufstieg und Fall der Stadt Mahagonny* (Rise and Fall of the City of Mahagonny, 1930), which ministered to the vogue of jazz then prevailing in Europe. Brecht placed the action in a legendary city vaguely resembling Chicago in the heyday of Al Capone: a city founded by three gangsters and in the throes of a gold rush. The plot gave Brecht every opportunity to satirize the evils he associated with capitalism—greed, political corruption, prostitution, and a philosophy of life based exclusively on the pursuit of money.

Already in 1929 Hitlerite students were creating disturbances when Weill's music was played, both because of the political content of his operas and because he was Jewish. He left Germany in 1933, accompanied by his wife, the actress Lotte Lenya, who had won fame as the foremost interpreter of his songs. After two years in Paris and London they came to the United States. Weill adapted himself to his new environment with amazing flexibility. Given his unerring sense of theater, he could not but conquer Broadway. There followed a series of scores that rank high among American musicals: Paul Green's *Johnny Johnson* (1935), Franz Werfel's *The Eternal Road* (1937), Maxwell Anderson's *Knickerbocker Holiday* (1938), Moss Hart's *Lady in the Dark* (1941), *One Touch of Venus* with S. J. Perelman and Ogden Nash (1943), Elmer Rice's *Street Scene* (1947), and Anderson's *Lost in the Stars* (1949), based on Alan Paton's novel on the white-black confrontation in South Africa, *Cry the Beloved Country*. Weill also transplanted the *Gebrauchsmusik* ideal to the American scene in *Down in the Valley*, a folk opera for young people based on a Kentucky mountain song (1948). The piece has been widely performed by college workshops. He had just completed plans to collaborate with Maxwell Anderson on an operatic version of Mark Twain's *Huckleberry Finn* when, at the age of fifty, he died in a New York hospital of a heart attack. Lotte Lenya dressed his body in his favorite pullover and a pair of working trousers. "He will be very busy up there," she said, "and I want him to be comfortable."

His Music

Weill wanted to rejuvenate opera by freeing it from the Wagnerian conventions that, he felt, were stifling it; to transform it into a living theater that would communicate directly with a mass public. In doing so he became one of a number of modern composers who were seriously concerned with the growing gap between those who wrote music and those who listened to it. Actually he was reverting to a type of *Singspiel* that was part of the German tradition—the play with spoken dialogue, enlivened by humorous situations, topical references, songs, and dances, that reached its supreme embodiment in Mozart's *Magic Flute*. Weill aimed for a new relationship between stage and music, achieved through lyrical numbers that had popular appeal but at the same time were the handiwork of a thoroughly schooled musician.

He did not hesitate to use jazz rhythms, brash orchestral combinations, and pungently dissonant harmonies in support of bitter-sweet tunes that had a nostalgic charm all their own. Those chiseled melodies of his wrapped themselves around Brecht's ferocious lyrics to form, as in certain chemical reactions, a compound more powerful than either of its constituents. The result was a remarkable kind of theater piece that has been well described as "the weightiest possible lowbrow opera for highbrows and the most full-blooded highbrow musical for lowbrows." In these works the Romantic symbols of nineteenth-century operetta were replaced by the sights and sounds of modern big-city life, projected through a whole new set of images—luxury hotels, bars, airplanes, motor cars—and a whole new set of characters—gangsters, prize-fighters, lumberjacks, prostitutes—who were both products of the system and in revolt against it.

Brecht's theater presented ideas of social protest in the simplest possible terms. His need for direct expression—a directness that at times verged on the brutal—conformed ideally to the aesthetic of simple, direct statement that Weill had inherited from Busoni. After history had parted them—Brecht went from Paris to Scandinavia while Weill chose New York—the stringent requirements of the Broadway theater again imposed simplicity and directness on Weill's stage works. Thus, throughout his career, his melodic gift was shaped by the practical requirements of the theater.

Weill influenced a whole generation of composers. Among his operatic progeny may be counted such diverse works as George Gershwin's *Of Thee I Sing*, Marc Blitzstein's *The Cradle Will Rock*, Gian Carlo Menotti's *The Consul*, Benjamin Britten's children's operas, and the Bavarian "plays with music" of Carl Orff. Especially influential was the chamber-music texture of his orchestration and the informal, intimate tone that struck an altogether fresh note in the lyric theater.

The Three-Penny Opera

In 1728 London was enchanted by John Gay's *The Beggar's Opera*, a satire on English life for which the idea had been suggested by Jonathan Swift. Politically, the work was a thinly veiled attack on the Prime Minister, Horace Walpole, and his government. Musically, its popular songs ("airs"), arranged by the Anglicized German musician Johann Pepusch, offered London theater goers an antidote to the Italian opera seria, the stylized, artificial type of opera that was the favorite entertainment of the aristocracy. *The Beggar's Opera* was so successful that it ended the reign of opera seria in London and forced a bankrupt impresario named George Frideric Handel to turn from opera in Italian to oratorio in English—and immortality.

Exactly two hundred years later, in 1928, Brecht and Weill transformed Gay's piece into a metaphor of their own time. Set in the underworld against a background of social decay and hunger, rich in satire and gallows humor, the work caught the bleak mood of a Germany racked by postwar disillusionment, inflation, corruption, unemployment, and a Weimar Republic increasingly menaced by Hitlerism. The savagery of Brecht's lyrics was matched by the power of Weill's melodies and the jazz-band sound of his orchestration. The piece created a sensation. Within five years it was translated into eleven languages and rang up ten thousand performances in all the major cities of Germany and central Europe.

Kurt Weill's jazz was, of course, neither the authentic folk jazz of New Orleans and St. Louis, nor the commercialized but thoroughly American product of Tin Pan Alley. Neither was it the Europeanized jazz of Stravinsky, Milhaud, and Honegger. It stood somewhere in between, bearing the imprint of a man of the theater whose ear was thoroughly attuned to the vernacular. Brecht advanced the action of Gay's play by a century, to London on the eve of Queen Victoria's coronation—the London that we know from the novels of Dickens and Thackeray. The cast of characters is as sleazy a group as was ever assembled—and how vividly they come to life in the theater.

Mr. Jonathan Jeremiah Peachum is the "King of the Beggars" in London. He controls the begging industry, fits out his clients in the rags and bandages necessary for their calling, assigns them their routes, shares in their profits, and sends his strong-arm men to deal with anyone who dares beg without his permission. Mrs. Peachum drinks a bit, but otherwise shares in all the social ambitions of a tycoon's wife. These naturally center on a proper marriage for their pretty daughter Polly. Macheath, better known as Mack the Knife, is the leader of the city's most notorious gang of thieves and cut-throats. The action takes place in Soho, a neighborhood that is at the opposite end of the social spectrum from Mayfair and Picadilly. Peachum and his lady are horrified to discover that Polly has fallen in love with Mack and wants to marry him. Such a marriage would upset their plans on every level. Polly defies her parents, and the marriage takes place in the stable in Soho that serves as Mack's hangout. His friends contribute a variety of wedding presents—from a harpsichord to a magnificent dinner set—that have just come from some of the finest homes in London.

The rest of the action centers about the parents' attempt to rid themselves of their inconvenient son-in-law. For this they seek the assistance of Tiger Brown, the corrupt Chief of Police who was a buddy of Mack's in the army and receives a percentage of his profits in return for giving advance notice of police raids. Tiger Brown is reluctant to betray Mack; but when it comes to the crunch he will look the other way. Mrs. Peachum finds another helpful ally in Gin Mill Jenny (in the latest New York revival, rechristened Low-Dive Jenny), who for a time was Mack's paramour. She informs the police

A scene from the original production of The Three-Penny Opera *(1928). Lotte Lenya and Rudolph Forster created the roles of Jenny and Macheath.*

when he returns for a visit to her somewhat unsavory establishment. Her light passing of forefinger across throat as she hands over her former lover became a standard gesture in Germany for underworld (or any other world) betrayal.

Macheath, imprisoned in Old Bailey, settles in for a brief stay. He can afford to pay for special privileges, and he knows he will soon buy his way out. Lucy, daughter of the Chief of Police, is Polly's rival for Mack's affections and helps him plan his escape. Much as Mack likes Polly, he realizes that in this tight squeeze Lucy will be more useful; so, when the two girls fight over him, he favors her. Tiger Brown, who feels somewhat ashamed at having done in his friend, is delighted when Mack escapes. But Mr. Peachum has the last say. He threatens to marshall the thousands of beggars under his control and turn them loose over London at the Queen's coronation. Tiger Brown has no choice but to rearrest Mack, and this time in earnest. Mack is rushed to the death house in preparation for his hanging.

While Mack eats his last meal, his so-called friends take leave of him. Tiger Brown is in tears, Mr. and Mrs. Peachum are triumphant, Polly and Jenny are sorry that he has to go so soon. The gallows are up, the crowd is waiting for the execution. But when Macheath has reached the gallows, Mr. Peachum steps forward and informs the audience that, even though in real life no one is spared a thing, in this play the author has thought up a different ending. "So that you might witness, at least in the opera house, how for once mercy and not justice carries the day." A messenger arrives from the Queen to announce that, in honor of her coronation, she not only has decided to set Macheath free but confers upon him a title, a castle, and a pension of ten thousand a year for the rest of his life. Mrs. Peachum muses, "How lovely and peaceful life would be, if the royal messenger on horseback would always arrive." The moral? There is none. Brecht has shown us human beings at their worst, and we are amazed at how closely they resemble the people we know.

Weill's orchestration projects the brassy jazz sound of the 1920s. His score calls for eleven musicians playing twenty-three instruments, among which are saxophones, harmonium (a reed-organ), accordion, banjo, and guitar. The inclusion of guitar is interesting in view of the attention its concentrated timbre was receiving from Schoenberg and his disciples. The best way to enter the world of *The Three-Penny Opera* is to listen to the complete German recording with German-English text. There are also several fine recordings in English. It will suffice here to mention the high spots.

The Overture opens with pungent dissonances and a majesty that parodies Handel's overtures. The curtain rises on a fair in Soho, whose unsavory denizens are out in full force. The Streetsinger launches into the *Ballad of Mack the Knife,* one of the unforgettable tunes of our century, impudent, cynical, haunting. For several years it was blared forth by every radio and juke box in our land. The hit tune of the play, it was an afterthought; Brecht and Weill decided they needed one more number and stayed up the night before the dress rehearsal.

> And the shark has teeth,
> Which he wears in his face.
> And Macheath has a knife,
> But the knife you cannot see . . .

Peachum and his wife, discussing Polly's infatuation, mock the notion of romantic love with the *Instead of Song.*

> Instead of,
> Instead of staying home in their warm beds,
> They have to have fun, they have to have fun,
> Just as if they were somebody.
>
> There's that moon over Soho,
> There's that damn "D'you feel my heart beating" line,
> There's that "Where you go I go, Johny!"
> When love begins and the moon is still rising . . .

The romantic love song of Polly and Mack has a cynical under-pinning:

> Love may last, or it may not;
> If not here, then some place else . . .

This is followed by Polly's touching explanation to her parents of why she fell in love with Mack, the *No and Yes Song:*

> I once believed, when I was quite innocent,
> And that I was, just the same as you,
> That some day someone would surely come along,
> And then I would know what to do . . .

And if he had money, and was nice, and had a clean collar even on workdays, and did the right thing when he was with a lady, she would say No! to egg him on. But then someone came along who had no money, was not nice, had no clean collar, and didn't care about the right thing with a lady—and she said Yes.

The finale, sung by Peachum, his wife, and Polly, teaches us the moral of Act I:

> The world is poor and man is vile,
> And that's about it!

In Act II, Jenny sings what is perhaps the greatest Brecht-Weill song, *Pirate-Jenny* or *Dreams of a Kitchen Maid:*

> Gentlemen, today you see me washing the dishes
> And making up each bed,
> And you give me a penny and I thank you kindly,
> And you see my rags in this crummy hotel.
> And you don't know whom you're talking to,
> And you don't know whom you're talking to.

But one day she'll stand by the window smiling, because a ship with eight sails and fifty cannons will draw up at the dock. And people still won't know who she is. But the fifty cannon will be bombarding the town, and the laughter will stop, and the walls will come tumbling down, and the pirates will round up everyone, put them in chains, and bring them before Jenny:

And they'll ask me, Which one shall we kill?
And they'll ask me, Which one shall we kill?
And a deathly silence will cover the harbor,
And you'll hear me say: All!
And when the heads begin to roll
I'll say: Hoppla!
  And the ship with eight sails
  And fifty cannon
  Will sail off with me.

In 1954 *The Three-Penny Opera* was revived in New York's *Theatre de Lys,* where it ran for six years. It was presented in Marc Blitzstein's beautiful translation, with Lotte Lenya singing the role of Jenny that she had created a quarter century before. No one who heard her will ever forget that fragile figure of doom with the chalk-white face and black stockings, the haunted eyes and throaty voice, as she sang this ballad. Between the first Berlin production and the revival the world had come to know about Auschwitz and Buchenwald, and the sound of that *Hoppla!* froze your blood. Listen to her on the recording, and it still will.

It is sometimes given to an artist to capture a moment in time, and by an act of imagination to endow it with meaning for all who come after. Kurt Weill did precisely this in *The Three-Penny Opera.* The moment he was fated to illumine—when butter cost a hundred thousand marks a pound and the Brown Shirts were beginning to march—can never cease to have meaning for our century.

42   Other European Composers between the Wars (I)

Manuel de Falla (1876–1946)

"Our music must be based on the natural music of our people. In our dance and our rhythm we possess the strongest of traditions that no one can obliterate."

The musical renascence in Spain at the end of the nineteenth century followed lines similar to those we have traced in England and

*Manuel de Falla and
Wanda Landowska. The
Bettmann Archive.*

Hungary. On the one hand, there was a revival of interest in the sixteenth-century masters, such as Tomas Luís de Victoria, Morales,
and Cabezón. On the other there was a turning to authentic folk
music based on modes that antedated the major-minor. Prime mover
of the renascence was Felipe Pedrell (1841–1922). As a composer Pedrell is all but forgotten. But his teachings fell on fertile ground; he
raised a generation of composers. Albéniz and Granados profited
from his pioneering. His most distinguished pupil, Manuel de Falla,
became the leading figure of the modern Spanish school.

   Fame came to Falla when he was in his late thirties, with the
premiere of his opera *La Vida breve* (Life is Short) in 1913. In the two
decades that followed he enjoyed something of the status of a national artist. The years of the Spanish Civil War were a time of intense anguish for the sensitive composer, for he had strong ties on
both sides. After Franco's victory the government was eager to honor
him, but he found it difficult to accommodate himself to the new
order. When an opportunity arose to conduct an orchestra in Buenos

Aires he eagerly accepted the invitation, and spent the last seven years of his life in voluntary exile in Argentina. He lived in the town of Alta Gracia, in the heart of the "New Andalusia" that could never mean as much to him as the old. There he died in November 1946, at the age of seventy.

Falla's was not a sustained kind of creativity. His reputation rests on half a dozen works, most of them composed when he was in his forties or earlier. *La Vida breve* abounds in lovely sounds that evoke the landscape of his native Andalusia. The Andalusian style, which most people identify as "Spanish," is continued in the one-act ballet *El Amor brujo* (Bewitched by Love, 1915); *Noches en los jardines de España* (Nights in the Gardens of Spain, 1911–1915), three "symphonic impressions" for piano and orchestra, in which the Spanish idiom is combined with French Impressionism; and *El Sombrero de tres picos* (The Three-Cornered Hat, 1919), a humorous ballet based on Alarcón's *The Magistrate and the Miller's Wife*. The national element is less prominent in Falla's last works, the most important of which is the *Concerto for Harpsichord* with flute, oboe, clarinet, violin, and cello (1926). Here the Spanish idiom is refined and stylized, in the process rising above the realm of the picturesquely local to the universal.

In *El Amor brujo* Falla conjures up the rapturous melodic line of the Andalusian Gypsies, with its oriental coloring and fanciful ornamentation. The action revolves about the theme of exorcism that is to be found in the folklore of all countries. The beautiful Candelas has been in love with a dissolute Gypsy who, now that he is dead, returns to haunt her. The spell is broken when Carmelo, who is truly devoted to her, is able to convince Candelas that his love for her is stronger than the power of the dead man.

Falla's colorful rhythms and evocative melodies continue to delight a worldwide audience. In Spanish lands he is regarded—like Delius in England and Sibelius in Finland—as a major figure.

Ernest Bloch (1880–1959)

"I am a Jew. I aspire to write Jewish music because it is the only way in which I can produce music of vitality—if I can do such a thing at all."

Ernest Bloch, who was born in Switzerland and settled in the United States when he was thirty-six, found his personal style through mystical identification with the Hebraic spirit. His response

Ernest Bloch.

to his heritage was on the deepest psychic level. "It is the Jewish soul that interests me, the complex, glowing, agitated soul that I feel vibrating throughout the Bible: the freshness and naiveté of the Patriarchs, the violence of the books of the Prophets, the Jew's savage love of justice, the despair of Ecclesiastes, the sorrow and immensity of the Book of Job, the sensuality of the Song of Songs. It is all this that I strive to hear in myself and to translate in my music—the sacred emotion of the race that slumbers deep in our soul."

Given in equal degree to sensuous abandon and mystic exaltation, Bloch saw himself as a kind of messianic personality. Yet the biblical vision represented only one side of Bloch's art. He was also a modern European and a sophisticate, member of an uprooted generation in whom intellect warred with unruly emotion. Ultimately the inner struggle became greater than even so strong a personality could sustain. In his mid-fifties, when he should have been at the height of his powers (and when, ironically, he had achieved the leisure of which every artist dreams), there was a marked slackening of his creative energy. Bloch continued to work into his seventies. Yet with the exception of the *Sacred Service* (1933), the works on which his fame rests were almost all written between his thirtieth and forty-fifth years.

Bloch's "Jewish Cycle" includes his most widely played work, *Schelomo* (Solomon, 1916); the *Israel Symphony* (1912–1916); *Trois Poèmes juifs* (1913); *Psalms 114* and *137* for soprano and orchestra, and *Psalm 22* for baritone and orchestra (1914); *Baal Shem,* on Jewish legends, for violin and piano (1923, subsequently arranged for orchestra); and *Voice in the Wilderness* for cello and chamber orchestra (1936). Several of Bloch's works lie outside the sphere of the specifically national. The best known of these is the *Concerto Grosso* for strings with piano obbligato, which Bloch wrote in 1925 as a model for his students in the Neoclassic style. To this category belong also the noble *Quintet* for piano and strings (1923) and the *String Quartets Nos. 1* (1916) and *2* (1946). In these nonprogrammatic compositions we see the tone poet refining the picturesque national elements in

The art of the painter Marc Chagall (b. 1889) draws its inspiration from Russian-Jewish folktales and from his attachment to the Jewish religion and traditions. Like Bloch, Chagall reveals a deep commitment to this background and its representation in art. The Green Violinist, *1924–1925.* The Solomon R. Guggenheim Museum, *New York.*

his idiom, sublimating them in order to achieve greater abstraction and universality of style. Mention should also be made of Bloch's only opera, *Macbeth* (1909), an unjustly neglected work that made a very strong impression when it was presented in New York by the Juilliard School.

In *Schelomo* (Solomon), a "Hebraic Rhapsody" for cello and orchestra, Bloch evokes a biblical landscape now harsh and austere, now lush and opulent; an antique region wreathed in the splendor that attaches to a land one has never seen. This musical portrait of King Solomon is projected with all the exuberance of a temperament whose natural utterance inclined him to the impassioned and the grandiose. The music conjures up the image of Solomon in all his glory—king and warrior, poet and lover, sage and prophet; the builder of the Temple, the sensualist of the Song of Songs, the keen wit of the Proverbs, finally the disenchanted Preacher proclaiming that all is vanity.

Bloch's kind of music is not in fashion at the moment. But fashions change more quickly than we suspect. If he seems to be cut off from the mainstream of contemporary musical thought right now, it is quite likely that, as his distinguished pupil Roger Sessions prophesies, "the adjustments of history will restore to him his true place among the artists who have spoken most commandingly the language of conscious emotion."

Albert Roussel (1869–1937)

"I have always pursued the design of the construction and the rhythm. The search for form and its proper development have been my constant preoccupations."

At a time when Debussy, Ravel, and Satie revealed anew the grace of Gallic art, Albert Roussel pointed the way to the discipline and logic inherent in the large-scale forms of absolute music. Therewith he effected a union between twentieth-century French music and the spirit of Classical symphonism.

Roussel started out as a composer of highly pictorial music. For a time he was seduced, as he put it, by the allure of Impressionism; but he realized that it would only lead him to an impasse. He found his true path by giving full play to his sense of form and construction—a sense based on a solid contrapuntal technique. "What I want to realize," he wrote, "is a music satisfying in itself, a music which seeks to eliminate all picturesque and descriptive elements."

A portrait of Albert Roussel, 1935, by Jules Joëts (1884–1959). André Meyer Collection.

Paris in the Twenties considered both Impressionism and the symphony outmoded. It was in this climate that Roussel espoused the cause of a French Neoclassicism oriented to the cultivation of the large forms—symphony, concerto, sonata, suite, trio, quartet, and the like. He had a varied ancestry within the French tradition. His melodic imagery was nurtured by the old chansons; he responded to the charm of French folk song. He was influenced by the eighteenth-century suite, with its elegant pattern making, and by the decorative opera-ballets of Rameau. The Baroque concerto grosso was congenial to his own rhythmic vitality, while his years at the Schola Cantorum related him to the tradition of Franck and d'Indy. From Satie he learned to appreciate the delights of the café-concert and music hall, whose spirit informs the saucy tunes of his scherzos. His experience in the Orient sensitized him to subtleties of melodic and rhythmic inflection unfamiliar in the West, nor was he left untouched by the rhythmic innovations of his younger contemporary, Stravinsky. All these influences were assimilated to an idiom that was essentially lyrical, and that bore the imprint of a fastidious musical personality.

Roussel's three "classical" symphonies—the *Second* (1921), *Third* (1930), and *Fourth* (1934)—stand as the centerpiece of his output. These works manifest the vigorous thought and carefully wrought detail characteristic of the composer. Closely related is the *Suite in F* (1926), which is based on three eighteenth-century forms, Prelude, Sarabande, and Gigue. The Classical orientation is paramount in a varied list of chamber and orchestral works. As a ballet composer Roussel is best known to the public through the two concert suites derived from *Le Festin de l'araignée* (The Spider's Feast, 1912) and *Bacchus et Ariane* (1930). The latter work is notable for its powerful rhythmic thrust.

Nowhere did Roussel give freer play to his purely musical impulses than in the sunny *Third Symphony*, a work that marks the high point of his commitment to the Classical point of view. The first movement, an *Allegro vivo*, has that continuous forward impulsion which gives Roussel's music its *élan*. The second, an *Adagio*, shows his ability to spin out a long melodic line. Third is a scherzo marked *Vivace*, a kind of rustic waltz that captures the atmosphere of the country fair. The finale is an *Allegro con spirito*, a gay movement that has something about it of the circus and the music hall, but at the same time is stamped with refinement.

"It is really marvelous," observed Francis Poulenc of this symphony, "to combine so much springtime and maturity." The composer of this delightful work is one of the distinguished figures in modern French music.

Zoltán Kodály (1882–1967)

"To become international one must first be national, and to be national one must be of the people."

"If I were asked," Béla Bartók wrote, "in whose music the spirit of Hungary is most perfectly embodied, I would reply, in Kodály's. His music is indeed a profession of faith in the spirit of Hungary. Objectively this may be explained by the fact that his work as a composer is entirely rooted in the soil of Hungarian folk music. Subjectively it is due to Kodály's unwavering faith in the creative strength of his people and his confidence in their future."

For ten years, from 1906 on, Kodály and Bartók spent their summers together, traveling through the villages of their homeland with recording equipment and taking down the ancient melodies exactly as the peasants sang them. The two young composers, acutely aware

Zoltán Kodály. A pencil sketch by B. F. Dolbin. André Meyer Collection.

that in musical matters Budapest had become a colony of Vienna and Berlin, perceived it as their lifework to create an autochthonous art based on authentically Hungarian materials. Armed with the energy of youth and the zeal of the missionary, they persisted despite the carping of critics and the indifference of the musical establishment. Fortunately, what they advocated made too much sense for it to be rejected indefinitely. After a time their ideas caught on.

History separated the two comrades-in-arms. As the regime of Admiral Horthy moved closer to Hitler, Bartók, we saw, left for the United States. Kodály remained behind, his more adaptable nature choosing "internal emigration"—that is, an increasing aloofness from the Nazi tide and the expression of his antifascist sentiments in subtle ways: for example, his *Variations for Orchestra* on the patriotic song *The Peacock,* his choral setting of which the authorities had already banned. When Hitler's troops occupied Hungary in 1944, Kodály's situation became precarious, for his wife was Jewish. They found refuge in the air-raid shelter of a convent, where Kodály completed a chorus for women's voices, *For St. Agnes's Day,* dedicated to the Mother Superior who had been instrumental in saving their lives.

Kodály's enormous impact on the artistic life of his homeland was the result of his functioning as a total musician: composer, ethnomusicologist—that is, scholar and scientific folklorist—critic, educator, and organizer of musical events and institutions. Each of these activities was related to the rest, and together they represented a total commitment to the ideal of freeing Hungarian music from German domination through the spirit of its folklore. From his absorption in the Hungarian folk idiom he distilled a musical language all his own. His melodies are often pentatonic or minor, with sparing use of chromatic inflection. They seem to have been made up on the spur of the moment. This improvisational quality manifests itself in extravagant flourishes, of a kind that are deeply embedded in Hungarian music. Typical are the abrupt changes of tempo, sudden shifts in mood, and a fondness for repetitive patterns based on simple rhythms.

Colorful orchestration and infectious rhythms have established Kodály's chief orchestral works in the international repertory. Chief among these are the *Dances from Galanta* (1933), *Variations on "The Peacock"* (1939), and *Concerto for Orchestra* (1939). Among the important vocal works are the *Psalmus hungaricus* (1923) and *Missa brevis* (Short Mass, 1952). The most important of his works for the stage is *Háry János*, whose hero was well described by the composer: "Háry is a peasant, a veteran soldier, who day after day sits in the tavern, spinning yarns about his heroic exploits. Since he is a real peasant, the stories produced by his fantastic imagination are an inextricable mixture of realism and naiveté, of comic humor and pathos. That his stories are not true is irrelevant, for they are the fruit of a lively imagination, seeking to create for himself and for others a beautiful dreamworld." The work is best known through an orchestral suite that scored an international success.

It was Kodály's high achievement to achieve a fine synthesis of personal style and national expression. As a result, he spoke not only to his own people but to the world.

William Walton (1902–)

"I seriously advise all sensitive composers to die at the age of thirty-seven. I know I've gone through the first halcyon period, and am just ripe for my critical damnation." (1939)

William Walton is the most striking figure of the generation of English musicians who came to maturity in the decade after the First

Sir William Walton at his home in Ischia, Italy. The Bettmann Archive.

World War. He moved slowly but steadily from the exuberant cleverness of his youthful works to the unashamed romanticism of his later ones. In so doing he found his true bent and managed to win for himself a substantial place in the musical life of our time.

Considering the reputation he enjoys with the public, Walton has written surprisingly little. He is known outside England by a handful of works: the witty *Façade* (1922), for chamber ensemble accompanying abstract poems by Edith Sitwell; the *Viola Concerto* (1929); the oratorio *Belshazzar's Feast* (1931); and the *Violin Concerto* he wrote for Jascha Heifetz (1939), an amply designed piece compounded of soaring lyricism and technical fireworks. He is very much appreciated as a film composer. His score for Laurence Olivier's production of *Henry V* abounded in the bright, virile sounds that stir the British heart. Distinguished too were his scores for Laurence Olivier's *Hamlet* and *Richard III*, and Bernard Shaw's *Major Barbara*. Walton's opera *Troilus and Cressida* is admired in England but has not yet established itself elsewhere.

Walton's style at its best is characterized by sensuous lyricism, spontaneity, and charm of sentiment. His ability to spin out a long melodic line is one that musicians regard with respect. Walton's music is tonal, generously spiced with dissonance. His harmonic idiom, based on the free use of the twelve tones around a center, is overlaid with chromaticism. He favors the major-minor ambiguity that has attracted so many contemporary composers. He feels at home in the large instrumental forms. As regards rhythm, Walton belongs to the generation that was deeply influenced by Stravinsky. He also had a passing interest in jazz. From these two sources derive the changes of meter, the syncopations, and the percussive-rhythm effects that energize his music.

Filled with the tumult and vitality of youth—Walton was twenty-nine when he wrote it—*Belshazzar's Feast* adapts the English oratorio tradition to the requirements of twentieth-century style. Based on massive choral writing—"perhaps the only compositional technique that English composers are heir to," as the British critic Peter Heyworth observed—it is a concentrated piece which in thirty-five minutes of music presents a series of vivid choral frescoes. The text, by Sir Osbert Sitwell, drawn from the Psalms and the Book of Daniel, moves swiftly to the incident that constitutes the dramatic climax—the handwriting on the wall and the subsequent destruction of Babylon. The Narrator is a baritone whose florid recitatives not only introduce the choral episodes but also evoke the savage intensity of the biblical tale. Yet this is no drama of individuals. The emphasis, as in many of Handel's oratorios, is on the crowd. The action is presented through the collective view, through voices massed in sorrow, gaiety, or exultation. The chorus at times comments on the action, at times participates. It has no fixed identity. In the first section of the work it speaks for the Jews, in the second for the Babylonians, in the third again for the Jews.

Walton's setting of the text is molded to the natural inflections of the English language. The orchestration matches the choral writing in vividness and dramatic suggestion. The score calls for a full-sized orchestra augmented by piano, organ, and—in the manner of Berlioz—by two extra brass bands, each consisting of 3 trumpets, 3 trombones, and tuba.

The composer of this broadly designed work is a prophet with honor in his own country; he is now known as Sir William Walton. The title accords well with a virile music that is rooted in tradition and British to the core.

Carl Orff (1895–)

"Melody and speech belong together, I reject the idea of a pure music."

The twelve years of Nazi rule, which bound composers to a post-Wagnerian ideology, were a period of retrogression for German music. In that time Germany lost the commanding position she had occupied in the modern movement throughout the Twenties. However, since the Second World War several German composers have succeeded in winning an international reputation. Among them is Carl Orff, a thoroughgoing conservative.

Orff took his point of departure from the clear-cut melody, simple harmonic structure, and vigorous rhythm of Bavarian popular song. (He is a native of Munich.) His music derives its emotional appeal from the *Gemütlichkeit* of the Munich *Bierstube,* from the glow that envelops the heart after enough steins have been emptied in a low-ceilinged, smoke-filled room. He is of the twentieth century in that he regards rhythm as the form-building element in music (as distinct from the nineteenth-century musicians, who found that element in harmony). His rhythm draws its strength from the simple patterns of folk tune and peasant dance: patterns which he at times repeats with a ferocity bordering on obsession. Orff's melodies are born of this rhythmic impulse. He avoids harmonic complexity and the intellectual attitudes inherent in contrapuntal writing. The themes are repeated without any attempt at variation; for contrast, they are shifted

A sketch of Carl Orff by B. F. Dolbin. André Meyer Collection.

to other keys. As one would expect, Orff's writing is strongly tonal, despite an occasional admixture of clashing polytonal chords. In the absence of thematic and contrapuntal elaboration, the impression is one of an almost primitive simplicity and forthrightness.

Orff's desire to reach the public goes hand in hand with his affinity for the theater, which by its very nature appeals to a mass audience. A theater based almost exclusively on rhythmic dynamism is apt to be very exciting; and that, at its best, Orff's theater certainly is. Moments of comedy in his operas alternate with lyrical passages; the music supports and illumines the action without ever embarking on any expansion of its own. And always there is the rhythm, relentless and irresistible, to keep the action moving and the tension high.

Orff's two best-known theater pieces, *Der Mond* (The Moon, 1937–1938, revised 1941) and *Die Kluge* (The Wise Woman, 1942) are based on Grimm fairy tales. They have Orffian rhythm and tunefulness in abundance. This is also true of *Carmina burana*, his most celebrated work (1936); *Catulli Carmina* (Songs of Catullus, a "scenic cantata," 1942); *Antigonae,* on Hölderin's adaptation of the Sophoclean tragedy (1947–1948); and *Trionfo di Afrodite* for soloists, large and small chorus, and orchestra (1951).

Orff called *Carmina burana* a "dramatic cantata." It can be given in a stage version, with dancing and pantomime, and has been so presented. Actually, it is a concert piece for solo singers, chorus, and orchestra. The choral forces are in three groups—a large chorus, a small one, and a boys' chorus. The supporting body is an orchestra of the usual size augmented by two pianos, five kettledrums, and a large percussion group.

The text is drawn from the famous thirteenth-century collection of Goliard songs and poems that was discovered in the ancient Bavarian monastery of Benediktbeuren in 1803. Hence the name *Carmina burana* (Songs of Beuren). These *cantiones profanae*, or secular songs, were written in a mixture of medieval Latin, low German, and French by wandering students, minstrels, vagabond poets, and runaway monks—the rascals, artists, dreamers, and bohemians who stood outside the pale of respectable society. Their poems hymn nature and love, the joys of the tavern and the free life; yet they contain also an undercurrent of protest against the cruel fate of those who do not fit in. From this extraordinary document of the late middle ages Orff selected twenty-four lyrics, in which earthy humor and mockery mingle with moods of rebellion, bittersweet joy, longing, and sorrow.

The composer of this dynamic piece is a personality with a view and an approach of his own. His music does not wear well with those who respond to the intellectual aspects of music. But to those who hear it for the first time *Carmina burana* is apt to bring an excitement all its own. One can understand why it became one of the hits of the 1950s.

43 Other European Composers between the Wars (II)

Jacques Ibert (Paris, 1890–1962) was a facile composer who combined Impressionist and Neoclassic techniques. He is best known for *Escales* (Ports of Call, 1922), a set of three symphonic sketches; the *Concertino da camera* for alto saxophone and small orchestra (1934); and the amusing *Angélique* (1927), the most successful of his six operas.

Henri Sauguet (Bordeaux, 1801–), a disciple of Erik Satie, wrote incidental music for Giraudoux's *The Mad Woman of Chaillot*. He has been influenced by Erik Satie's aesthetic of a simple, unpretentious music, melodious, graceful, and pleasing in character. The romantic element is more prominent in his weightier compositions such as *La Chartreuse de Parme* (The Charterhouse of Parma, 1927–1936), a grand opera based on Stendhal's novel—the most important of his five operas.

André Jolivet (Paris, 1905–1974) studied with Edgard Varèse and was strongly influenced by Schoenberg and Alban Berg. His conception of music as a kind of magical incantation is implicit in certain of his orchestral works: for instance, the prelude entitled *Cosmogonie* (1938); the *Cinq Danses rituelles* (Five Ritual Dances, 1939); *Suite delphique* (Delphic Suite, 1942); and the symphonic poem *Psyché* (1946), in which he tries to picture the struggle of the soul to free itself from material bonds.

Jean Françaix (Le Mans, 1912–) studied composition with Nadia Boulanger. The *Concertino* for piano and orchestra, written when he was twenty, shows his Neoclassic bent. Among his works are the *Trio* for violin, viola, and cello (1933); *String Quartet*, and *Quintet* for violin, viola, cello, flute, and harp (1934); *Quartet* for saxophones (1935); and *Divertissement* for bassoon and string quartet (1942).

Reinhold Glière (Kiev, 1875–1956, Moscow) belonged to the older generation of Russian composers who bridged the transition from Czarist to Soviet Russia. An enormously successful ballet, *The Red Poppy* (1927), carried his name all over the world. Its most popular number, *Russian Sailors' Dance,* shows what excitement music can generate when it gets steadily louder, faster, and moves up in pitch. Glière was an extremely prolific composer who turned out operas, ballets, symphonies, symphonic poems, overtures, chamber music, about two hundred songs, and a like number of piano pieces.

Nikolai Miaskovsky (Novogeorgievsk, near Warsaw, 1881–1950, Moscow) is one of those composers who achieve fame within the borders of their homelands without ever winning comparable eminence elsewhere. He was the most prolific symphonist of the first half of the twentieth century, with twenty-seven symphonies (1908–1950) to his credit. He also wrote choral and orchestral pieces, nine string quartets, piano music, and songs.

Aram Khatchaturian (Tbilisi, Georgia, 1903–1978) was an Armenian who stood far closer to the Romantic heritage than either Prokofiev or Shostakovich. His use of folklore material accorded, on the one hand, with the Soviet desire to build a melodious music accessible to the masses, and on the other, with the government's attempt to draw into the sphere of art the songs and dances of the national minorities within its borders. He is known abroad for his *Piano Concerto* (1936), which derives from the bravura style of Liszt; the expansive *Violin Concerto* (1940); and the ballets *Gayane* (Happiness, 1942) and *Spartacus* (1953).

Dmitri Kabalevsky (St. Petersburg, 1904–), a pupil of Miaskovsky, comes out of the tradition of Musorgsky and Borodin, Tchaikovsky and Scriabin. Kabalevsky is best known in the West for the overture to his opera *Colas Breugnon* (1937), based on Romain Rolland's novel, and for *The Comedians,* a suite for small orchestra (1940). His writing is strongly rhythmic and tonal.

The Italian school had the difficult task of creating a base for modern instrumental music in a land where Verdi and Puccini reigned supreme. A leader in this development was Alfredo Casella (Turin 1883–1947, Rome). Advocating a "return to the pure classicism of our ancestors," Casella attempted to lead Italian music away from the nineteenth century; away, too, from the Beethovenian symphony, whose processes of thematic development he considered alien to the Italian tradition, and from Impressionism, which he thought had exhausted its force. His Neoclassic orientation is apparent in the works of his maturity: the *Partita* for piano and orchestra (1924), based on old instrumental forms such as the passacaglia, gagliarda, and giga; the *Concerto romano* of 1926; and *Scarlattiana* for piano and orchestra (1927).

Gian Francesco Malipiero (Venice, 1882–1973, Treviso) ably seconded the efforts of his friend Casella to revive the traditions of the Italian Baroque. His monumental edition of the complete works of Claudio Monteverdi, in sixteen volumes, was a labor of love that left an indelible mark upon his own music. Equally significant is his edition of the complete works of Antonio Vivaldi. Malipiero moved away from the thematic development and recapitulation that is the basic technique of German symphonism, adopting instead the Baroque interplay of contrapuntal lines within a continuous texture. His huge output includes over twenty operas, eleven symphonies, a dozen choral works of ample dimension, four ballets, four piano concertos, seven string quartets, piano music, and songs.

Lennox Berkeley (Boar's Hill, near Oxford, 1903–) studied in Paris with Nadia Boulanger, from whom he imbibed the Stravinskyan aesthetic that strongly influenced his thinking. His graceful writing inclines toward the miniature; hence his affinity for the short forms. His comic chamber opera *The Dinner Engagement*, presented at the Aldeburgh Festival in 1954, is a more fully realized work than is his grand opera, *Nelson* (1951). The *Stabat Mater* for six solo voices and chamber orchestra (1940) shows Berkeley's lyricism and his sensitive ear for tone colors. His orchestral works include the *Serenade for Strings* (1939), *Symphony No. 1* (1940), *Divertimento in B-flat* (1943), the lyrical *Nocturne* (1945), and *Symphony No. 3* (1969). Berkeley has also written theater and film music, concertos, chamber music, works for various instruments, a quantity of piano music, and songs.

Carl Nielsen (Nørre Lyndelse, Denmark, 1865–1931, Copenhagen) spent most of his life as a performer and conductor with various musical organizations in Copenhagen. Although his works enjoyed only local celebrity during his lifetime, they have shown signs in recent years of becoming part of the international repertory. His major achievement is a series of six symphonies which follow a basically Brahmsian ideal, but in a distinctly personal manner. In the words of the British critic Robert Simpson, "Most of his mature works treat a chosen key as a goal to be achieved or an order to be evolved, and his final establishment of the key has all the organized inevitability . . . with which the flower appears at a plant's point of full growth." In addition to the symphonies, his catalogue includes a

Violin Concerto (1912), *Flute Concerto* (1926), *Clarinet Concerto* (1928), and chamber music.

In the twentieth-century concert of nations, Georges Enesco (Liveni, Rumania, 1881–1955, Paris) was the accredited representative of Rumania. He received a solid grounding at the Vienna Conservatory, then went to Paris where he studied with Massenet and Fauré. He was primarily a concert violinist; but in his compositions he went beyond the sphere of his chosen instrument. Piano music, chamber music, songs, and three symphonies are included in his output. Enesco's imagination was captured by the Gypsy fiddlers of his homeland, whose melodies shaped the imagery of his two *Rumanian Rhapsodies* (1901, 1902). These vastly successful pieces, which have passed into the repertory of the "pop" concert, are tuneful and full of dash. More serious in character is the opera *Oedipus,* after the drama of Sophocles, which was produced at the Paris Opera in 1936; but this work failed to win the acceptance accorded his less ambitious compositions. In his later years Enesco became interested in teaching. Yehudi Menuhin is one of several distinguished violinists who owe much to his guidance.

Frank Martin (Geneva, 1890–1974, Maarden, Holland) is the most important representative of the modern Swiss school. He began as a traditionalist; his early works show the influence of Franck, Fauré, and the Impressionists. There followed a transitional period (1925–1932) during which he experimented with oriental and ancient meters, emulated Bartók in exploiting the unequal rhythms of east European song and dance, and enriched his style with elements drawn from folk music. An intensive study of Schoenberg's music impelled him, between 1932 and 1937, to compose in the strict twelve-tone style. He then found his way to a personal language that combined twelve-tone and tonal elements. This reconciliation of dodecaphonic with the older harmonic functions has been Martin's specific contribution to contemporary style.

Le Vin herbé (The Bleached Wine, 1938–1941), a "dramatic oratorio" based on an excerpt from Joseph Bédier's version of the Tristram and Iseulte story, for twelve solo voices, seven string instruments, and piano, is a full-length work in Martin's Neoromantic vein. The massive *Golgotha,* on texts drawn from the New Testament and the writings of St. Augustine, for five solo voices, chorus, organ, and orchestra (1945–1948), revives the tradition of the Passion-oratorio of Bach. Among Martin's instrumental compositions are *Petite Symphonie concertante,* for harpsichord, harp, piano, and double string orchestra (1945), his most widely played work; *Concerto* for seven wind instruments, kettledrums, and strings (1949); the *Violin Concerto* of 1951, and the *Concerto* for harpsichord and small orchestra of 1952. The list also includes *The Tempest* (1955), after Shakespeare, an opera in which Romantic and Impressionist elements freely intermingle; and the oratorio *La Mystère de la nativité* (1960), in which the seventy-year-old composer returned to certain of the influences that dominated his youth.

PART FOUR

The American Scene

"The way to write American music is simple. All you have to do is to be an American and then write any kind of music you wish."

VIRGIL THOMSON

44 Music in America

"A true musical culture never has been and never can be solely based upon the importation of foreign artists and foreign music, and the art of music in America will always be essentially a museum art until we are able to develop a school of composers who can speak directly to the American public in a musical language which expresses fully the deepest reactions of the American consciousness to the American scene."

AARON COPLAND

The Background

It is our nation's great achievement to have created, out of elements inherited from Europe, something completely new and fresh; something specifically un-European. We all recognize what is American in music, although we should be hard put to it to define exactly what that quality is. Having been shaped by a wide variety of factors, the American quality is not any one thing.

Conditions in a pioneer country did not foster the emergence of music as a native art. Consequently, throughout the nineteenth century we imported Italian opera and German symphony. The great American composer of the pre–Civil War period issued neither from the tradition of Haydn and Mozart nor from that of Rossini and Bellini. He came out of the humbler realm of the minstrel show, and his name was Stephen Foster.

In the second half of the nineteenth century, a native school of serious composers emerged. First to achieve more than ephemeral fame was John Knowles Paine (1839–1906), who for thirty years was professor of music at Harvard. Paine was the mentor of the so-called Boston or New England group that included the leading American composers at the turn of the century. Among them were George W. Chadwick (1854–1931), Edgar Stillman Kelley (1857–1944), Horatio Parker (1863–1919), and Mrs. H. H. A. Beach (1867–1944). Arthur Foote (1853–1937) and Henry F. Gilbert (1868–1928) also belonged to this generation. These composers, musically speaking, were German colonists. They studied in Leipzig, Weimar, Munich, or Berlin, and worked in the tradition of Schumann and Mendelssohn or Liszt and Wagner. It was their historic mission to raise the technical level of American music to the standards of Europe. But their music, weakened by their genteel outlook on art and life, bore no vital relationship to their milieu. It has not survived.

A more striking profile was that of Edward MacDowell (1861–1908), the first American composer to achieve a reputation abroad. His four piano sonatas and two concertos for piano and orchestra show him to have been at home in the large forms. MacDowell was at his best, however, in the small lyric pieces which are still favorites with young pianists. The *Woodland Sketches*, whence the perennial *To a Wild Rose;* the *Fireside Tales* and *New England Idyls* are the work of a miniaturist of charm and poetic sensibility. MacDowell was well aware that a new age was dawning for the American composer and foretold its coming in a striking passage: "Before a people can find a musical writer to echo its genius it must first possess men who truly represent it—that is to say, men who, being part of the people, love the country for itself: men who put into their music what the nation has put into its life. What we must arrive at is the youthful optimistic vitality and the undaunted tenacity of spirit that characterize the American man. That is what I hope to see echoed in American music."

The composers we have mentioned, although they lived in the Postromantic era, were really Romanticists who had come too late. In the world arena they have been overshadowed by their European contemporaries, compared to whom they unquestionably take second place. Yet comparisons are hardly in order. The European Postromantics were the heirs of a rich past. The Americans were building for a rich future. They were pioneers dedicated to a lofty vision. We have every reason to remember them with pride.

Emergence of an American School

The first generation of the modern American school—composers born in the 1870s and '80s—faced a difficult task. They had to effect the transition from the Postromantic era to the modern, and they had to discover what an American music would be like. Some of them continued more or less in the path of their predecessors. Frederick Shepherd Converse (1871–1940), Henry Hadley (1871–1937), Daniel Gregory Mason (1873–1953), and David Stanley Smith (1877–1949) carried on the genteel tradition of the earlier New England group. Although they and their fellows had an occasional success, the fact remains that during the first quarter of our century the serious American composer was something of a stepchild in his own country. His music faced a twofold handicap: it was contemporary, and it lacked the made-in-Europe label that carries such weight with our public. He had no powerful publishers to champion his cause, no system of grants and fellowships to give him the leisure to compose, no famous conductors to bring him the performances he needed. On the rare occasions when a work of his was played, as like as not it was sandwiched between two masterpieces of the ages, almost as if to point up the fact that we had no Bach or Beethoven in our midst. As we follow the careers of the older generation of modern American composers, we cannot help feeling that they appeared upon a scene which was not quite ready for them. Yet, even if the immediate circumstances were not propitious, the country could not remain forever indifferent to its creative musicians. It is against this background that we must trace the emergence of the modern American school.

45 American Impressionists

"It is only logical that when I began to write I wrote in the vein of Debussy and Stravinsky; those particular wide-intervalled dissonances are the natural medium of the composer who writes today's music.

CHARLES T. GRIFFES

The Influence of Impressionism

The enormous popularity of Impressionism in this country during the first quarter of our century broke the grip of the German conservatory. The new generation of American musicians went to Paris, even as their predecessors had gone to Leipzig or Weimar. This trend, strengthened by the boycott of all things German during the First World War, engendered one of the most significant developments in American musical life—the turning from German to French influence.

The devices of Impressionist music figured prominently in the works of the Alsatian-born Charles Martin Loeffler (Mulhouse, 1861–1935, Medfield, Massachusetts). Loeffler came to this country

American painters of the late nineteenth century were as deeply influenced by the French Impressionists as the composers were. El Jaleo, *1882, by John Singer Sargent (1856–1925). Isabella Stewart Gardner Museum.*

when he was twenty and played in the first-violin section of the Boston Symphony Orchestra for eighteen years. He is remembered chiefly for *A Pagan Poem* (1905–1906), an evocative work for thirteen instruments, which he subsequently rewrote for piano and orchestra. Loeffler was a recluse and a mystic. His was a music of shadowy visions; it showed his affinity for Gregorian chant, medieval modes, and Impressionist harmonies. All the same, his feeling for line and clarity of form sets him apart from the French Impressionists, with whom he is often grouped. He was a fastidious workman and highly critical of his work, which he subjected to repeated revisions. His music bears some resemblance to the style that came to be associated with Debussy; yet he found his way to it in the 1890s, before he could have heard much of the Frenchman's music.

Several other Americans were receptive to French influence. Among them were John Alden Carpenter (1876–1951), Edward Burlingame Hill (1872–1960), Arthur Shepherd (1880–1958), and Deems Taylor (1885–1966). Carpenter achieved a vogue in the Twenties with two ballets that sought to incorporate the rhythm and tempo of American life: *Krazy Kat* (1922) and *Skyscrapers* (1926). Taylor's two operas, *The King's Henchman* (1926) and *Peter Ibbetson* (1930), were produced at the Metropolitan Opera House with great fanfare, but soon dropped out of sight. Many other Americans took to Impressionism. Indeed, a young American beginning to compose in the Twenties turned as naturally to Debussy's idiom as his successors twenty years later turned to Stravinsky's, or forty years later to Webern's.

Charles Tomlinson Griffes (1884–1920)

The most gifted among American Impressionists was Charles Tomlinson Griffes. Born in Elmira, New York, he went to study in Germany at the age of nineteen. His four years in Berlin brought him into contact with a rich musical culture. Upon his return he accepted a teaching job at a boys' preparatory school in Tarrytown, New York. His chores at the Hackley School interfered seriously with his composing, but he was never able to escape; he remained there until his death.

Recognition finally came to Griffes in the last year of his life, when his works were accepted for performance by the Boston, New York, and Philadelphia orchestras. *The Pleasure Dome of Kubla Khan,* presented by the Boston Symphony in its home city and in New York, scored a triumph. A few days later, the accumulated strain of years took its toll; Griffes collapsed. The doctors diagnosed his illness as pleurisy and pneumonia; the deeper cause was physical and nervous exhaustion. He failed to rally after an operation on his lungs and died in New York Hospital at the age of thirty-six.

Griffes represents the current in American music most strongly oriented to foreign influence. His dreamlike art could not be nurtured by indigenous folk song. A nostalgic yearning, a gently elegiac quality informs his music. Stimulated by far-off places and remote times, his imagination turned to moods and fancies rooted in romantic longing. He admired the composers who at that time were attracting the attention of progressive musicians—Debussy, Ravel, Musorgsky and Scriabin, Busoni, Stravinsky, Schoenberg. Another liberating influence was his preoccupation with the music of the Far East.

Griffes's fame rests on a comparatively small output. He favored the short lyric forms. Songs like *By a Lonely Forest Pathway* and *The Lament of Ian the Proud* reveal a lyricist of exquisite sensibility. He was no less successful with the short piano piece and brought to

American piano music a subtlety of nuance that had hitherto been found only among the French composers. Characteristic are the *Three Tone Pictures—The Lake at Evening, The Night Winds,* and *The Vale of Dreams* (1910–1912); and the *Four Roman Sketches—The White Peacock, Nightfall, The Fountain of Acqua Paola,* and *Clouds* (1915–1916). Of the orchestral works, the most important are *The Pleasure Dome of Kubla Khan* (1912), the *Poem* for flute and orchestra (1918), and *The White Peacock,* which Griffes transcribed for orchestra.

The Pleasure Dome of Kubla Khan was inspired by the visionary poem of Coleridge: "In Xanadu did Kubla Khan / A stately pleasure-dome decree. . . ." Griffes gave his imagination free rein, he stated, in the description of Kubla Khan's strange palace. "The vague, foggy beginning suggests the sacred river, running 'through caverns measureless to man down to a sunless sea.' The gardens with fountains and 'sunny spots of greenery' are next suggested. From inside come sounds of dancing and revelry which increase to a wild climax and then suddenly break off. There is a return to the original mood suggesting the sacred river and the 'caves of ice.' "

The composer of this haunting music did not live to fulfill the rich promise of his gifts. But the vision of beauty which formed the substance of his art, and the fastidious craftsmanship he attained in the projection of that vision, were of prime importance to the evolution of our native school.

46 Charles Ives (1874-1954)

"Beauty in music is too often confused with something that lets the ears lie back in an easy chair. Many sounds that we are used to do not bother us, and for that reason we are inclined to call them beautiful. Frequently, when a new or unfamiliar work is accepted as beautiful on its first hearing, its fundamental quality is one that tends to put the mind to sleep."

Charles Edward Ives waited many years for recognition. Today he stands revealed as the first truly American composer of the twentieth century and one of the most original spirits of his time.

His Life

Ives was born in Danbury, Connecticut. His father had been a bandmaster in the Civil War and continued his calling in civilian life. George Ives was the ideal father for anyone who was to become an experimental composer. He was a singularly progressive musician with endless curiosity about the nature of sound. He listened carefully to church bells; and when he found that he could not duplicate their pitch on the piano, he built an instrument that would play the tones "in the cracks between the keys"—that is, quarter tones. Or he made his family sing *Swanee River* in the key of E-flat while he played the accompaniment in the key of C, "in order," his son later wrote, "to stretch our ears and strengthen our musical minds."

Charles at thirteen held a job as church organist and already was arranging music for the various ensembles conducted by his father. At twenty he entered Yale, where he studied composition with Horatio Parker. Ives's talent for music asserted itself throughout his four years at Yale; yet when he had to choose a career he decided against a professional life in music. "Assuming a man lives by himself and with no dependents, he might write music that no one would play prettily, listen to or buy. But—but if he has a nice wife and some nice children, how can he let the children starve on his dissonances? So he has to weaken (and if he is a man he *should* weaken for his children) but his music more than weakens—it goes 'ta-ta' for money! Bad for him, bad for music!" Ives thus began by assuming that society would not pay him for the kind of music he wanted to write. He was not mistaken.

He therefore entered the business world. Two decades later he was head of the largest insurance agency in the country. The years it took him to achieve this success—roughly from the time he was twenty-two to forty-two—were the years when he wrote his music. He composed at night, on weekends, and during vacations, working in isolation, concerned only to set down the sounds he heard in his head.

The few conductors and performers whom he tried to interest in his works pronounced them unplayable. Some smiled, persuaded that such writing could come only from one who was ignorant of the rudiments. Others, accustomed to the suavities of the Postromantic period, concluded that the man was cracked. He was indeed, as Aaron Copland called him, "a genius in a wasteland." After a number of these rebuffs Ives gave up showing his manuscripts.

Charles Ives.

When he felt the need to hear how his music sounded, he hired a few musicians to run through a work. Save for these rare and quite inadequate performances, Ives heard his music only in his imagination. He pursued his way undeflected and alone, piling up one score after another in his barn in Connecticut. When well-meaning friends suggested that he try to write music that people would like, he could only retort, "I can't do it—I hear something else!" Or, in a moment of frustration, "Are my ears on wrong?"

Ives's double life as a business executive by day and composer by night finally took its toll. In 1918, when he was forty-four, he suffered a physical breakdown that left his heart damaged. The years of unrewarded effort had taken more out of him emotionally than he had suspected. Although he lived almost forty years longer, he produced nothing further of importance.

When he recovered he faced the realization that the world of professional musicians was irrevocably closed to his ideas. He felt that he owed it to his music to make it available to those who might be less hidebound. He therefore had the *Concord Sonata* for piano privately printed, also the *Essays Before a Sonata*—a kind of elaborate program note that presented the essence of his views on life and art. These were followed by the *114 Songs*. The three volumes, which were distributed free of charge to libraries, music critics, and whoever else asked for them, caused not a ripple as far as the public was concerned. But they gained Ives the support of other experimental composers who were struggling to make their way in an unheeding world. Henry Cowell, Wallingford Riegger, and Nicolas Slonimsky espoused his cause, as did the critic Paul Rosenfeld. Significantly, Ives's music first won attention in Europe. Slonimsky conducted three movements from *Holidays* in Paris, Budapest, and Berlin. Anton Webern presented his work in Vienna. The tide finally turned in this country when the American pianist John Kirkpatrick, at a recital in Town Hall in January, 1939, played the *Concord Sonata*. Ives was then sixty-five. The piece was repeated several weeks later by Kirkpatrick and scored a triumph. The next morning Lawrence Gilman hailed the *Concord Sonata* as "the greatest music composed by an American."

Ives had already begun to exert a salutary influence upon the younger generation of composers, who found in his art a realization of their own ideals. Now he was "discovered" by the general public and hailed as the grand old man of American music. In 1947 his *Third Symphony* achieved performance and won a Pulitzer Prize. This story of belated recognition was an item to capture the imagination and was carried by newspapers throughout the nation. Ives awoke at seventy-three to find himself famous. Four years later the *Second Symphony* was presented to the public by the New York Philharmonic, exactly half a century after it had been composed. Leonard Bernstein, who conducted the piece, remarked, "We have suddenly discovered our musical Mark Twain, Emerson and Lincoln all rolled into one." The prospect of finally hearing the work agitated the old man; he attended neither the rehearsals nor the performances. He was, however, one of millions who listened to the radio broadcast.

He died in New York City three years later, at the age of eighty.

His Music

Charles Ives, both as man and artist, was rooted in the New England heritage, in the tradition of plain living and high thinking that came to flower in the idealism of Hawthorne and the Alcotts, Emerson and Thoreau. The sources of his tone imagery are to be found in the living music of his childhood: hymn tunes and popular songs, the town band at holiday parades, the fiddlers at Saturday night dances, patriotic songs and sentimental parlor ballads, the melodies of Stephen Foster, and the medleys heard at country fairs and in small theaters.

This wealth of American music had attracted other musicians besides Ives. But they, subservient to European canons of taste, had proceeded to smoothe out and "correct" these popular tunes according to the rules they had absorbed in Leipzig or Munich. Ives was as free from subservience to the European tradition as was Walt Whitman. His keen ear caught the sound of untutored voices singing a hymn together, some in their eagerness straining and sharping the pitch, others just missing it and flatting; so that in place of the single tone there was a cluster of tones that made a deliciously dissonant chord. Some were a trifle ahead of the beat, others lagged behind;

Grant Wood (1892–1942) drew his imagery from a wealth of indigenous material and established a style distinctly rooted in American history. Daughters of the Revolution, 1932. Cincinnati Art Museum—The Edwin & Virginia Irwin Memorial. (Courtesy Associated American Artists, N.Y.)

consequently the rhythm sagged and turned into a welter of poly-rhythms. He heard the pungent clash of dissonance when two bands in a parade, each playing a different tune in a different key, came close enough together to overlap; he heard the effect of quarter tones when fiddlers at a country dance brought excitement into their play-ing by going a mite off pitch. He remembered the wheezy har-monium at church accompanying the hymns a shade out of tune. All these, he realized, were not departures from the norm. They *were* the norm of popular American musical speech. Thus he found his way to such conceptions as polytonality, atonality, polyharmony, cluster chords based on intervals of a second, and polyrhythms. All this in the last years of the nineteenth century, when Schoenberg was still writing in a post-Wagner idiom, when neither Stravinsky nor Bartók had yet begun their careers, when Hindemith had just been born. All the more honor, then, to this singular musician who, isolated alike from the public and his fellow composers, was so advanced in his conceptions and so accurate in his forecast of the paths that twen-tieth-century music would follow.

Ives's melodies represent the least revolutionary part of his canon. He is fond of quoting hymn tunes or popular songs, relying upon such allusions to establish the emotional tone. He is partial to procedures that later came to be associated with the Schoenbergian school—inversion, retrograde, rhythmic augmentation, and diminu-tion. Although he was addicted to greater dissonance than almost any composer of his time, his harmonic progressions give an impres-sion of unity because of the strong feeling of key behind them. His use of polychords is most original. He will set two streams of har-mony going, treating them like single lines in counterpoint. There is imaginative polytonal writing in his music and an occasional atonal passage. Ives was no less inventive in the domain of polyrhythms. Patterns of three, four, five, or six notes to the measure are pitted against units of seven, eleven, thirteen, or seventeen notes. He went from one meter to another with the flexibility that was later to be as-sociated with Stravinsky and Bartók; and he anticipated Stravinsky in his use of dissonant chords repeated as a percussive-rhythm ef-fect. He also created jazzlike rhythms long before jazz had emerged in its familiar form. Ives was one of the first musicians to write with-out regular barlines or time signatures, simply placing the barline wherever he desired an accented beat. He rebelled against the nin-teenth-century habit of writing within the capacities of each in-strument. He sought rather to transcend those capacities. The sound, for him, had to serve the musical idea. He moved away from symmetrical repetition to an off-balance freshness in the arrangement of the material, achieving a plasticity of form that was very much of the twentieth century.

The central position in his orchestral music is held by the four symphonies. The *First* (1896–1898) dates from the period when he was evolving his style. The *Second* (1897–1901) is a romantic work in five movements. The *Third* (1901–1904) quotes the old hymn *Take It to the Lord,* as well as the Welsh battle song known as *All Through the Night,* and is the most fully realized of Ives's symphonies. Fourth is the *Symphony for orchestra and two pianos* (1910–1916), in which the composer introduces the hymn tune *Watchman, Tell Us of the Night.* Of similar dimension is *A Symphony: Holidays,* of which we will speak later in the chapter.

Among his orchestral works are *Three Places in New England* (1903–1914) and *Three Outdoor Scenes* (1898–1911), consisting of *Hallowe'en, The Pond,* and *Central Park in the Dark,* the last-named for chamber orchestra; also *The Unanswered Question* (1908). The *Sonata No. 2* for piano—*Concord, Mass., 1840–1860*—we will discuss. The *114 Songs* (1884–1921) range from works in folk style to those which express passion, anger, and poetic feeling. Ives chose texts from Keats, Stevenson, Browning, and Landor, as well as from modern poets. Some of the texts he wrote himself; others are by his wife. The songs are as unequal in quality as they are diverse in character. But the collection as a whole, which includes such striking things as the rugged cowboy ballad *Charlie Rutlage* and the evocative *Serenity, Evening,* and *Ann Street,* vividly reflects the personality behind it. Ives also wrote a great number of chamber, choral, and piano compositions, including two string quartets and four violin sonatas.

There are crudities and rough spots in Ives's style, as there are in the prose of Theodore Dreiser, in the verse of Whitman. These are traceable on the one hand to Ives's temperament, on the other to the fact that since he never heard his music, he was not impelled to limit himself to what an audience could readily assimilate. His desire to express all the facets of life precluded his developing a homogeneous style. Nor did he ever acquire that solidity of technique which marks the professional composer. Aaron Copland, in a perceptive essay on Ives, has well summed up his predicament: "He lacked neither the talent nor the ability nor the metier nor the integrity of the true artist—but what he most shamefully and tragically lacked was an audience. 'Why do you write so much—which no one ever sees?' his friends asked. And we can only echo, 'Why indeed?' and admire the courage and perseverance of the man and the artist." Perhaps the most moving tribute to Ives came from a contemporary of his who knew only too well what it meant for an artist to be rejected by his time—Arnold Schoenberg: "There is a great man living in this country—a composer. He has solved the problem of how to preserve one's self and to learn. He responded to negligence by contempt. He is not forced to accept praise or blame. His name is Ives."

In 1974 the musical world celebrated the centenary of Ives's birth. Throughout that season practically every note he wrote was performed somewhere, and recorded as well. Would he have been surprised!

The Fourth of July

"A set of pieces for orchestra called *Holidays,*" Ives recalled, "had its career from 1897 to 1913. These four pieces, movements of a *Holiday Symphony,* take about an hour, and although they were first called together a symphony, at the same time they are separate pieces and can be thought of and played as such." The four pieces emulate Vivaldi's *The Seasons: Washington's Birthday* (winter); *Decoration Day* (spring); *The Fourth of July* (summer); and *Thanksgiving* (autumn). Ives called the work "Recollections of a boy's holidays in a Connecticut country town." But, as with every significant artist, this "recapture of things past" is much more than an exercise in personal nostalgia. Rather are these memories rooted in the life that flowed about him as he was growing up, so that the roots of this music reach down to the life-style of a nation. The point is made in the eloquent program notes that Ives wrote for each movement. The one for *The Fourth of July* is particularly vivid in its evocation of what this day meant to a young American of Ives's generation:

"It's a boy's 4th—no historical orations—no patriotic grandiloquences by 'grown-ups'—no program in his yard! But he knows what he's celebrating—better than most of the county politicians. And he goes at it in his own way, with a patriotism nearer kin to nature than jingoism. His festivities start in the quiet of the midnight before, and grow raucous with the sun. Everybody knows what it's like—if everybody doesn't—Cannon on the Green, Village Band on Main Street, fire crackers, shanks mixed on cornets, strings around big toes, torpedoes, Church bells, lost finger, fifes, clam-chowder, a prize-fight, drum-corps, burnt shins, parades (in and out of step), saloons all closed (more drunks than usual), baseball game, . . . the pistols, mobbed umpire, Red, White and Blue, runaway horse—and the day ends with the sky-rocket over the Church-steeple, just after the annual explosion sets the Town-Hall on fire.''

It testifies to the haphazard way in which Ives's music was preserved that the manuscript of *The Fourth of July*, now one of his best-loved works, was almost lost. Ives's partner in the insurance business, Julian Myrick, told how in 1914, when they were moving their office, they cleaned out the safe. ''Ives had one part, and I had another—and he'd cleaned out his part, and I went to clean out my part—and there's a stack of music. And I said, 'Charlie, you want me to throw this away?' And he came over—he said, 'Why, Mike! God, that's the best thing I've written'—and it was *The Fourth of July*, about to be thrown away!'' Ives dedicated the piece to Myrick.

He felt that with this work he had fully evolved his style. ''I remember distinctly, when I was scoring this, that there was a feeling of freedom as a boy has, on the Fourth of July, who wants to do anything he wants to do, and that's his one day to do it. And I wrote this, feeling free to remember local things etc., and to put in as many feelings and rhythms as I wanted to put together. And I did what I wanted to, quite sure that the thing would never be played, and perhaps *could* never be played.'' Here Ives touched upon the one advantage that accrues to the artist who lacks a public. Since there is no one he must please, he is quite free to experiment.

The piece follows one of the most familiar patterns in music: the gradual progression from soft and slow to loud and fast—in this case from an orchestral pianissimo marked *Adagio molto*, which is very, very slow, to a furious *Allegro* and fortissimo. What is original is the meaning that Ives injected into this pattern, and the personal quality of imagination that he brought to the handling of it. The music, extraordinarily dense in texture, presents a mosaic of popular and patriotic songs, among them such favorites as *The Battle Cry of Freedom*, *Marching through Georgia*, *The Battle Hymn of the Republic*, *The Girl I Left Behind Me*, *London Bridge*, *Yankee Doodle*, and *Dixie*. But the central position is reserved from Ives's favorite melody, *Columbia, the Gem of the Ocean*, which serves as the main theme of the piece and becomes a source of motivic, harmonic, and contrapuntal material. The tunes are transformed into Ivesian melodies through the addition of ''wrong'' notes, changes in meter and rhythm, free variation, and dropped beats. Ives explains the latter in characteristic fashion: ''The uneven measures that look so complicated in the score are mostly caused by missing a beat, which was often done in parades.''

Here is his version of *Columbia, the Gem of the Ocean,* whose opening phrase is buried in the lowest register, played pianissimo by tuba and double bass as a foundation for the orchestral harmony:

The music flows forward through all the intermediate degrees of tempo and dynamics: *Adagio* to *Andante* to *Allegretto* to *Allegro moderato* to *Allegro con spirito,* thenceforward to the hair-raising climax. At the beginning of the *Allegro con spirito* trumpets and trombones play a distorted version of *Columbia, the Gem of the Ocean.* Meanwhile clarinets and cornet are playing Ives's version of *The Battle Hymn of the Republic.* They play the verse while the flutes play the chorus. At the same time the xylophone is playing *Yankee Doodle,* as is the piano against an accompaniment of formidably dissonant chords:

And, to add to the dissonance tension, first and second violins are playing cluster chords in contrary motion:

The explosion comes soon after. It is marked *Allegro con fuoco*—fast, with fire. Whether Ives intended a bilingual pun here we have no way of knowing. In any case, orchestral pandemonium breaks loose. The passage bristles with Ivesian polyrhythms and polymetrics: winds and brass cope with thirteen simultaneous rhythms, interlaced with no less than seven patterns in the percussion. Tone clusters and tremolos on the piano thicken the texture, while violins and violas continue their cluster chords in contrary motion, sub-divided into twenty-four parts. Ives obviously is having a great time remembering the boy who exploded the firecrackers and skyrockets that set the Town Hall on fire.

John Kirkpatrick, who edited Ives's scores, calls a passage like this—there are several in Ives's works—"phantasmagoria." Yet terms like *pandemonium* or *phantasmagoria* are inaccurate in one re-spect: the sound, so unprecedented in Ives's day, was conceived with the utmost clarity and control. As he put it, "In the parts taking off explosions, I worked out combinations of tones and rhythms very carefully by kind of prescriptions, in the way a chemical compound which makes explosions would be made."

In this piece Ives anticipated present-day composers of aleatory or chance music, who give the performer a greater freedom of choice than he ever had before. "It is not absolutely essential that these notes or rhythms be kept to literally. . . . It is the underlying gist that is really the important thing. If one player should get to the end of an explosion-period first, he steadily holds until everybody reaches him, and the conductor wipes them out together." Ives can never resist a dig at the conventional listener who prefers "nice" music: "Or, in other words, the worse these places sound to Rollo, the better it is."

A brief coda of two measures, pianissimo, winds down the ex-citement.

Concord Sonata: Hawthorne and The Alcotts

The *Piano Sonata No. 2—Concord, Mass. 1840–1860*—is Ives's ges-ture of homage to his spiritual heritage. The work, which occupied him from 1909 to 1915, is in four movements that are named for the leaders of New England transcendentalism—Emerson, Hawthorne, the Alcotts, and Thoreau. (Their basic doctrine, derived from the anti-materialism of German idealist philosophers like Hegel and Kant, upheld the innate goodness of man.) The Sonata, we saw, was the first work of Ives to make an impact on the public.

II. *Hawthorne.* Without key or time signature. Ives explained his purpose: "Any comprehensive conception of Hawthorne, either in words or music, must have for its basic theme something that has to do with the influence of sin upon the conscience—something more than the Puritan conscience, but something which is permeated by it. . . . This fundamental part of Hawthorne is not attempted in our music (the 2nd movement of the series) which is but an extended fragment trying to suggest some of his wilder, fantastical adventures into the half-childlike, half-fairylike phantasmal realms."

Liszt or Berlioz would have entitled this kind of movement *Scherzo fantastique*. It presents abrupt changes of mood and violent contrasts of fast and slow, loud and soft, high and low. The dense writing, like Schoenberg's, descends from the tightly woven texture of Brahms's piano style. The movement requires a formidable technique. Since Ives was able to play it, he must have been quite a pianist. It is marked *Very fast* and begins with running passages that vividly suggest "fantastical adventures into phantasmal realms." There follows a lyrical passage that shows Ives's ability to wreathe a melody in Impressionistic harmonies. Never before did piano music look like this:

These pianissimo chords are tone clusters designed to release the overtones and sympathetic vibrations of the piano strings. As in the music of Debussy, such floating columns of sound are used as a source of sonic enchantment rather than as functional harmonic entities.

Ives loved to combine disparate elements into a formal unity. Scraps of popular song and ragtime unite in astonishing fashion with a beautiful hymnlike passage and a fantastic march whose resilient dotted rhythms anticipate Prokofiev but soon move over into the homelier regions of Sousa. The following passage anticipates the tone clusters with which, a generation later, Henry Cowell astonished the world:

There is passing reference to the opening rhythm of Beethoven's *Fifth Symphony*, the "three-shorts-and-a-long" that runs like a unifying thread through the *Concord Sonata*. Further on Ives transforms *Three Cheers for the Red, White, and Blue* into a canonic passage in which the left hand imitates the right. The peroration is marked "From here on, as fast as possible," which is followed somewhat later by "Faster" (Robert Schumann did the same thing). Ives reminds us of the hymn, *ppp*, and the movement ends with a typical Ivesian upsurge, very fast and *fff*:

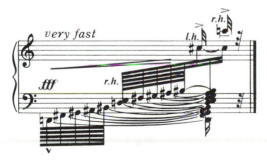

III. *The Alcotts*. No key, time, or tempo indication. Shortly after the opening passage, the music is bitonal: B-flat major in the right hand, A-flat in the left. Ives suggests the setting in a memorable passage: "Concord village, itself, reminds one of that common virtue lying at the height and root of all the Concord divinities. As one walks down the broad-arched street, passing the white house of Emerson—ascetic guard of a former prophetic beauty—he comes presently beneath the old elms overspreading the Alcott house. It seems to stand as a kind of homely but beautiful witness of Concord's common virtue—it seems to bear a consciousness that its past *is living,* that the 'mosses of the Old Manse' and the hickories of Walden are not far away. . . . . And there sits the little old spinet-piano Sophia Thoreau gave to the Alcott children, on which Beth played the old Scotch airs, and played at the Fifth Symphony." This was written at a time when Louisa May Alcott's *Little Women* was still read by thousands of American children. Emerson's house, incidentally, was occupied for a time by Nathaniel Hawthorne, who wrote most of his *Mosses from an Old Manse* there. Ives was indeed invoking divinities.

After the complexities of *Hawthorne, The Alcotts* is simplicity itself. This slow movement reveals Ives in a lyrical, reflective mood. How nostalgic is the opening theme, to which the bitonal harmony of the passage that follows imparts a refreshing tartness. The climax

of the movement consists of an extended fantasy on the "three shorts and a long" of Beethoven's *Fifth,* which turns out to be a transformation of Ives's opening theme:

A series of Impressionist harmonies reveals the piano sound at its loveliest, and leads into the section in which he tenderly evokes the "old Scotch airs." The music works up to the triumphal pronouncement of Beethoven's motto theme, from which it subsides to a beautiful cadence in C (with a B-flat).

Ives related this movement to "the memory of that home under the elms . . . and the family hymns that were sung at the end of each day." Underlying it was his attempt "to catch something of that common sentiment—a strength of hope that never gives way to despair—a conviction in the power of the common soul which, when all is said and done, may be as typical as any theme of Concord and its transcendentalists."

Charles Ives holds a unique place in our musical life. Certainly no other composer so vividly captured the transcendental quality of the New England heritage. He is our great primitive. Like the writers he admired most, he has become an American classic.

47 The Twenties

"Our musical alphabet must be enriched. Speed and synthesis are characteristic of our epoch. We need twentieth-century instruments to help us realize those in music."

EDGARD VARÈSE

The Second Group

The composers whose works attracted some attention in the 1920s did not fare much better than their predecessors. They had to wait many years before they received some measure of the recognition that was due them. Several fell silent, even as Ives did, when they should have been at the height of their powers.

At the same time the forces were slowly gathering that would make this country a little more hospitable to American music. To begin with, the composers who represented European modernism began to come here more and more frequently to conduct and propagandize for their works. Their activities could not but create a somewhat more favorable climate for their American colleagues. In addition, the emergence of a strong native school became a matter of national pride and found support in various quarters. The era of prosperity in the Twenties encouraged private patronage in the form of grants and fellowships. Of enormous value to the members of this generation were the Guggenheim fellowships, the Prix de Rome (which gave the recipient three years at the American Academy in Rome), the Pulitzer Prize, and the grants of the National Academy of Arts and Letters. Equally helpful were the commissions for new works offered by the League of Composers, the Alice M. Ditson Fund of Columbia University, the Elizabeth Sprague Coolidge Foundation, and, somewhat later, the Koussevitzky Foundation. Increased opportunities were offered the composer to see his work in print, through the publication awards of the Eastman School of Music, the Juilliard School, the Society for the Publication of American Music, and similar organizations.

Confronted by a public that listened eagerly to the older music but steadfastly ignored their own, American composers began to band together in associations expressly designed to foster the new music. In 1921 was founded the International Composers' Guild. There followed the League of Composers, the United States section of the International Society for Contemporary Music (I.S.C.M.), the American Composers' Alliance, and the National Association of American Composers and Conductors. Out of this ferment came the magazine *New Music,* founded in 1927 by the composer Henry Cowell and his associates, which for several decades served as a clearing ground for progressive ideas on musical aesthetics, theory, and practice.

Of great help was the forward-looking policy of conductors like Serge Koussevitzky, Leopold Stokowski, and Dimitri Mitropoulos, who made a point of giving the American composer a hearing. The conservatories, too, which had hitherto concentrated on the training of instrumentalists and singers, began to turn their attention to the needs of young composers. This was accompanied by a significant change in the administration of our music schools. It had been the custom to appoint celebrated performers as the directors of conservatories. For example, the concert pianist Josef Hoffman became head of the Curtis Institute in Philadelphia, and was followed by the violinist Efrem Zimbalist. The pianist Ossip Gabrilowitch (son-in-law of Mark Twain) directed the Cincinnati College of Music, and the pianist Ernest Hutcheson occupied a similar position at the Juilliard School in New York. Now it began to be recognized that a composer was perhaps a more appropriate figure to supervise the training of musicians. The appointment of Howard Hanson as director of the Eastman School of Music in Rochester set a precedent that was followed with increasing frequency in the following decades. Hanson made an invaluable contribution to the cause of American music by presenting annual festivals where the Eastman-Rochester Symphony Orchestra, under his direction, played the newest works of his fellow composers. Coming at a time when the American composer desperately needed exposure to the public, these festivals were a milestone in the history of our native music.

During the Twenties, too, the music departments in our colleges and universities took on new importance as centers of progressive musical activity. The widespread policy of hiring composers to teach composition opened up a much wider sphere of influence to our creative musicians. It also provided them with a means of livelihood that did not entirely interfere with their creative work. (One wishes that the last statement were a little truer than it is. In many colleges the teaching and administrative load is so heavy as to reduce the composer to weekend and summer writing.) The fact that American composers began to occupy chairs at our leading universities further underlined the growing prestige of the modern American school.

We have referred to the shift, in our music, from German to French influence. Where Americans had previously gone to study in Munich, Leipzig, or Weimar, they now flocked to Paris. In this connection we must mention Nadia Boulanger, the extraordinary teacher who guided several generations of American composers to Stravinskyan Neoclassicism. The list of her pupils, beginning with Aaron Copland, reads like a Who's Who of American composers. Among them were Roy Harris, Walter Piston, Douglas Moore, Virgil Thomson, Quincy Porter, and Marc Blitzstein. These men did not come into prominence until the Thirties, but the foundation for their future eminence was established a decade earlier.

F. Scott Fitzgerald immortalized the 1920s as the Jazz Age. American composers, like their European confreres, realized increasingly

During the 1920s, the French influence on painting techniques was still evident in American art, but more and more, artists drew upon the characteristics of life around them for their subject matter. Lower Manhattan, 1920, by John Marin (1870–1953). *Collection, The Museum of Modern Art, New York, The Philip L. Goodwin Collection.*

that jazz could serve as the basis for serious music. This trend resulted in a variety of works, most of which are now forgotten. Three, however, achieved international fame and a secure position in the repertory: George Gershwin's *Rhapsody in Blue, An American in Paris,* and *Piano Concerto in F.* Composers through the ages had nourished their art with elements drawn from folk and popular music. Gershwin was following in their footsteps when he wrote, "Jazz I regard as an American folk music; not the only one but a very powerful one which is probably in the blood and feeling of the American people more than any other style of folk music. I believe that it can be made the basis of serious symphonic works of lasting value."

Thus, gradually, the situation was becoming more favorable for the American composer. Unfortunately, the composers whom we will now discuss were still too experimental to profit from the change. Their time had not yet come.

48 Edgard Varèse (1883-1965)

"I refuse to submit myself only to sounds that have already been heard."

Edgard Varèse is one of the truly original spirits in the music of our time. The innovations of Stravinsky, Schoenberg, and Bartók unfolded within the frame of the traditional elements of their art, but Varèse went a step further: he rejected certain of those elements altogether.

His Life

Varèse was born in Paris of Italian-French parentage. He studied mathematics and science at school, since his father intended him for an engineering career. But at eighteen he entered the Schola Cantorum, where he worked with Vincent d'Indy and Roussel, and later was admitted to the master class of Charles-Marie Widor at the Paris Conservatoire. In 1909 he went to Berlin, where he founded a chorus devoted to the performance of old music. During this time he became a close friend of Busoni, who strongly influenced his thinking.

With the outbreak of war in 1914 Varèse was mobilized into the French army, but was discharged the following year after a serious illness. He came to the United States in December, 1915, when he was thirty, and lost no time in making a place for himself in the musical life of his adopted land. He organized an orchestra in New York City that devoted itself to contemporary works, but became increasingly aware that there was no audience for new music in this country. Accordingly, in 1921 he and Carlos Salzedo founded the International Composers' Guild, for the express purpose of presenting the music of living composers. In the six years of its existence the Guild presented works by fifty-six composers of fourteen nationalities, including the first performances in this country of Schoenberg's

*Edgard Varèse. Robin
Carson photograph.*

Pierrot lunaire and Stravinsky's *Les Noces,* and introduced to America
such composers as Webern, Berg, Chávez, and Ruggles.

The greater part of Varèse's music was written during the Twenties and early Thirties. He found a champion in Leopold Stokowski, who performed his scores despite the violent opposition they aroused in conventionally minded concert goers. Then, like his colleagues Ives and Ruggles, Varèse fell silent when he should have been at the height of his powers. During the next twenty years he followed the new scientific developments in the field of electronic instruments, and resumed composing in 1952, when he began to work on *Deserts.*

By that time the scene had changed; there existed a public receptive to experimental music. When an enterprising record company made available four of his works, Varèse was enabled to reach an audience that had never before heard his music. He was invited by the State Department to conduct master classes in composition in Darmstadt, Germany. The younger generation of European composers who were experimenting with tape-recorded music suddenly discovered him as one whose work had been prophetic of theirs. The long-neglected master finally came into his own.

He died in New York City at the age of eighty-two.

His Music

Several important currents within the mainstream of contemporary music came together in Varèse's works: the desire to root out private feelings from art and to achieve a completely objective style; the spirit of urbanism and the attempt to evoke the imagery of a machine civilization; the rejection of tonal harmony; the interest in Primitivism, with its revitalization of rhythm and its attendant emphasis on the percussive instruments; the attempt to return music to its pristine sources and to mold it into architectural forms as pure sound. Given Varèse's early training in science and his mathematical turn of mind, it was almost inevitable that he would be sensitive to these trends. He adopted a frankly experimental attitude toward his art that placed him among the extreme radicals of our time.

The abstract images that brood over Varèse's music are derived from the life of the big city: the rumble of motors, the clang of hammers, the shriek and hiss and shrilling of factory whistles, turbines, steam drills. His stabbing, pounding rhythms conjure up the throb and hum of the metropolis. There is a steely hardness, a cutting edge to Varèse's music. Its tensions result from the collision of sound masses. Its sense of distance comes from the superposition of sonorous planes. Understandably, Varèse's expressive goal led him away from melody and harmony, the principal elements of the Classic-Romantic style. The ingredients of his music are pure sonority and pure rhythm. The harmonic texture as such is strongly dissonant, consisting mainly of minor seconds or ninths and major sevenths. Hence the glitter and tension of this music, which is animated by his intricate counterpoint of rhythms. In this area Varèse is one of the prime innovators of our time. His powerfully kinetic rhythms recall the complex percussive patterns of African and Far Eastern music. It follows that his attention is focused on that group in the orchestra which stands closest to sheer sonority and rhythm, the percussion, which he handles with inexhaustible invention.

It goes without saying that his music does not lend itself to the conventional procedures of thematic-motivic development. Varèse works with rhythmic-sonorous cells that continue to be transformed as long as the music lasts. His sound pieces have a surprising unity.

*The colliding sound mass-
es of Varèse's music
find plastic expression in
the Cubist decentraliza-
tion of imagery.* Guitar
and Flowers, *1912, by
Juan Gris (1887–1927).
Collection, The Museum
of Modern Art, New
York. Bequest of Anna
Erickson Levene in
memory of her husband,
Dr. Phoebus Aaron
Theodor Levene.*

They are precisely calculated, written in a stripped, laconic style that
makes for economy and refinement of means. He rejects the Romantic interest in timbre for its own sake. "I do not use sounds impres-
sionistically as the impressionist painters used colors. In my music
they are an intrinsic part of the structure." This lapidary music unfolds in geometrical patterns based on the opposition of sonorous
planes and volumes—patterns which, in their abstraction, are the
counterpart in sound of the designs of cubist painting. Varèse's
music was utterly revolutionary in its day. It sounded like nothing
that had ever been heard before.

The fanciful names Varèse gave his works indicate the connection
in the composer's mind between his music and scientific processes.
Amériques (1922), a symphonic poem making use of a large orchestra,

is "a symbol of discovery: new worlds on earth, in the stars and in the minds of men." *Hyperprism* (1923) is for a chamber orchestra of two woodwinds, seven brass, and sixteen percussion instruments. The title, Varèse stated, "has a geometrical connotation and implies a fourth-dimensional significance." It is a neatly organized piece that communicates even to those who, like the present writer, know nothing about the fourth dimension. *Arcana* (1927), for orchestra, is one of the few works by Varèse that follow a trditional formal procedure. The piece develops a basic idea through melodic, rhythmic, and instrumental variation, somewhat in the manner of a passacaglia.

Octandre (1924) is a chamber work for eight instruments—flute, clarinet, oboe, bassoon, horn, trumpet, trombone, and double bass—whose lines interweave in a polyphonic texture of freshness and brilliancy. *Intégrales* (1925) we will discuss in detail. *Ionisation* (1931) is Varèse's best-known work as far as the big public is concerned. It is scored for thrity-five different instruments of percussion and friction, played by thirteen performers. Achieving a daring liberation of percussion and bell sounds from their traditional subservience to melody and harmony, *Ionisation* is an imaginative study in pure sonority and rhythm.

Intégrales

"*Intégrales*," Varèse wrote, "was conceived for a spatial projection. I constructed the work to employ certain acoustical means which did not yet exist, but which I knew could be realized and would be used sooner or later." In *Intégrales* Varèse became aware of what he considered a third dimension in music. "I call this phenomenon 'sound projection,' or the feeling given us by certain blocks of sound. Probably I should call them beams of sound, since the feeling is akin to that aroused by beams of light sent forth by a powerful searchlight. For the ear—just as for the eye—it gives a sense of prolongation, a journey into space." This metaphor explains the term *spatial music* that was first used in connection with *Intégrales*. (The title is the French word for integers. In mathematics, an integer is a whole number, not a fraction; by extension, an entire thing, a whole.)

The inner tension of the piece derives from the conflict between the sounds that Varèse heard in his imagination and the limitations of the conventional instruments within which those sounds had to be realized. For his purpose the wind instruments, with their clean, focused timbres and somewhat impersonal quality, were vastly preferable to the strings, whose tone can be shaded according to the personal whim of the player. *Intégrales* is scored for winds and percussion. The wind group consists of eleven instruments: two piccolos, two clarinets, an oboe, horn, piccolo (very high) trumpet, and regular trumpet; three trombones in different registers—tenor, bass, and the rarely used contrabass trombone. This group consequently extends from very high register (piccolos, clarinets, piccolo trumpet) to very low (bass and contrabass trombones).

The percussion group consists of seventeen instruments handled by four players: I, suspended cymbal, side drum, tenor drum, snare drum; II, castanets, cymbals, high, medium, and low Chinese blocks; III, sleighbells, chains, tambourine, gong; IV, triangle, tam-tam (a larger, deeper-toned gong), crash cymbals (small, thin cymbals commonly used in jazz bands), rute (a brush of bristles used for special effects on the bass drum), and slapstick (consisting of two sticks of wood which, when slapped together, produce a sharp, crackling sound).

In rejecting the traditional makeup of the orchestra Varèse at the same time rejected the traditional concepts that such an orchestra was supposed to serve. His harmony combines not only different pitches but, more important, different timbres together with their overtones. His polyphony consists of layers of sound added one above the other. "Taking the place of the old fixed linear counterpoint," he explained, "you will find in my works the movement of masses, varying in radiance, and of different densities and volumes. When these masses come into collision, the phenomena of penetration or repulsion will result. Here you have again as a point of departure the same devices that are found in classical counterpoint, only now adapted to new necessities, but still acting as a basic discipline for the imagination."

The piece opens *Andantino*, with a theme on the E-flat clarinet that is like a summons. Since it consists mainly of a repeated note, it obviously owes its power to the element of rhythm rather than pitch:

This becomes a kind of motto theme that is repeated in the upper register by various instruments, with all kinds of subtle variation both in melodic outline and rhythm. It is presently engaged in a dialogue with forceful dissonances in the brass. Three measures of percussion lead into the second section, a *Moderato* in which the material is restated in the bass register by the horn, against a curtain of sound set up by trombones and percussion. The tenor trombone introduces a new version of the motto theme:

Section three, an *Allegro*, takes its point of departure from a trumpet call that features the dissonant interval of a major seventh (indicated by an asterisk):

This section unfolds with abrupt changes from very slow (*Lento*) to very fast (*Presto*). The final section is ushered in by percussion alone. There follows an oboe solo that introduces a theme of two notes. This again illustrates Varèse's way of giving profile to his themes by means of rhythm and dynamics rather than pitch. Yet through some mysterious alchemy he is able to inform this simple pattern with all the pathos of a lamentation:

The continuation of this idea bristles with dissonant intervals such as a diminished octave and major seventh. These impart to the music its highly emotional quality:

Intricate counterpoints of rhythm work up a tension that is interrupted briefly by the return of material from the preceding section. From there on the music builds steadily to the terrifying explosion—as of sounds hurtling through space—at the end.

In *Intégrales,* as in his other works of the Twenties, Varèse pushed to the outermost boundary of what could be done with conventional instruments. There remained for him only one course: to take the next step into the world of electronic sound. We will follow him on that course in a later chapter.

49 Carl Ruggles (1876-1971)

"Music which does not surge is not great music."

Carl Ruggles, like Charles Ives, came into an environment that was not prepared to receive him. The circumstance affected him no less profoundly than it did his fellow New Englander. Although he had a long life, he produced only a handful of works. There was no public to stimulate him, to demand that he write. After the Thirties he fell silent.

His Life and Music

"The Cape Cod composer" was born in the town of Marion, Massachusetts, near Buzzard's Bay. When the time came for him to prepare for a profession, he went to Boston intending to study the art of ship design. He ended up at Harvard, studying composition with John Knowles Paine. After eleven years of conducting an orchestra in Winona, Minnesota, Ruggles went to New York and became active in the affairs of the International Composers' Guild, which at that

Carl Ruggles. (Photograph courtesy of Carl Fischer, Inc.)

time represented the most advanced tendencies in American music. From these exciting years date the four works on which his reputation rests—*Men and Angels* (1920), *Men and Mountains* (1924), *Portals* (1926), and *Sun-Treader* (1926–1931).

"In all works," Ruggles maintained, "there should be the quality we call mysticism. All the great composers have it." Music for him had a symbolic meaning, in terms of poetic suggestion and emotion, over and above the notes. This is apparent both from the titles of his works and the literary mottoes he associated with them. *Men and Mountains* derives its title from a line of Blake: "Great things are done when men and mountains meet." *Portals* bears on its score a quotation from Walt Whitman: "What are those of the known but to ascend and enter the Unknown?" Similar titles are *Men and Angels*, *Sun-Treader*, and *Vox clamans in deserto* (A Voice Crying in the Wilderness, for solo voice, chorus and orchestra). There is a visionary quality in Ruggles's music, a burning intensity. He has well been called an apostle of ecstasy.

His need to communicate emotion found its natural outlet in a harmonic language based on chromatic dissonance, which he regarded as the element of expressive tension. Hence we find that, as in the case of the Schoenbergians, his music draws its forward impulsion from varying levels of dissonance rather than from the contrast of dissonance and consonance. The chromatic element in Ruggles's writing derives from his desire to exploit to the full the capacities of the twelve tones of the scale. As a result, he never repeated a tone, or any octave of it, before nine or ten others have intervened. His reluctance to empahsize a central tone led Ruggles away from traditional tonality. Like the composers of Schoenberg's school he was fond of the devices of sixteenth-century counterpoint—canonic imitation, inversion, and retrograde. He wrote a bold melodic line, full of thrust and rhythmic vigor, and capable of sustained flight. His melodies are marked by sweeping outlines, chromatic inflection, and wide leaps. He was essentially an orchestral composer. Characteristic is the monumental effect he achieved by making the instruments play in unison, especially the brass.

Ruggles's music may be characterized as atonal; it bears a certain relationship to that of the Viennese school. Nonetheless, he issued from an environment totally different from that of Schoenberg and his disciples. He found his way to certain principles that resembled theirs, because these principles were in the air. But his music moves in another world of feeling and has its own expressive goal. The point has been well made by the English critic Wilfrid Mellers: "It is improbable that Ruggles knew Schoenberg's music well, though, discounting their opposed backgrounds, there is much in common between the two men. Both were amateur painters who, in their visual work, sought the expressionistic moment of vision. Both, in their music still more than in their painting, found that the disintegrated fragments of the psyche could be reintegrated only by a mystical act. Schoenberg, as Viennese Jew, had an ancient religion and the spirit of Beethoven to help him; Ruggles had only the American wilderness and the austerities of Puritan New England. For this reason he sought freedom—from tonal bondage, from the harmonic straitjacket, from conventionalized repetitions, from anything that sullied the immediacy and purity of experience—even more remorselessly than Schoenberg. . . . In Schoenberg's 'free' atonal music and in Ruggles's chromatic polyphony there is a minimum of repetition, for each piece is a new birth. Self-consciousness is lost as the polyphony sings and wings."

"Wiry, salty, disrespectful, and splendidly profane," Virgil Thomson wrote about the ninety-four-year-old composer, "he recalls the old hero of comic strips Popeye the Sailor, never doubtful of his relation to sea or soil." Of the many anecdotes connected with Ruggles—"the very quintessence of New Englandism," as one admirer described him—it will suffice to repeat one told by his friend Henry Cowell that gives the flavor of both the man and artist: "One morning when I arrived at the abandoned school house in Arlington (Vermont) where he now lives, he was sitting at the old piano, singing a single tone at the top of his raucous composer's voice, and banging a single chord at intervals over and over. He refused to be interrupted in this pursuit, and after an hour or so, I insisted on knowing what the idea was. 'I'm trying over this damned chord,' said he, 'to see whether it still sounds superb after so many hearings.' 'Oh,' I said tritely, 'time will tell whether the chord has lasting value.' 'The hell with time!' Carl replied. 'I'll give this chord the test of time right now. If I find I still like it after trying it over several thousand times, it'll stand the test of time, all right!'

He died in Bennington, Vermont at the age of ninety-five.

Sun-Treader

Generally regarded as Ruggles's magnum opus, this work was completed in 1931 after he had spent years in bringing it to its final form. Although it was performed in Paris the following year (under the baton of Nicolas Slonimsky, who performed yeoman service in propagating the music of Ives and Ruggles in Europe in the Thirties), the piece was not heard in the country of its origin until thirty-four years later. The upsurge of interest in Ives spilled over on his equally neglected colleague sufficiently to inspire a Ruggles Festival in Portland, Maine in 1966, under the auspices of Bowdoin College, at which the Boston Symphony Orchestra gave *Sun-Treader* its American premiere. By this time Ruggles was ninety. He never heard a live performance of *Sun-Treader*, although he did hear the recording that had appeared the year before.

The title comes from a line in Robert Browning's poem on the death of Shelley: "Sun-Treader, Light and Life be thine forever." Browning was responding to the luminous quality of Shelley's poetry, and it is this striving for luminosity that gives Ruggles's music its pictorial quality, its sense of vast open space. Whether these relate to sun, sea, sky, and mountains or to some vaster—because immaterial—landscape of the soul, each listener must decide for himself. The piece was dedicated to Harriette Miller, a patroness of the arts whose generosity made it possible for Ruggles to compose and paint in his retrat in Vermont, undisturbed by the world.

The work vaguely follows Classical sonata form. There is an exposition based on two contrasting themes, a development, and a re-capitulation of the material. Like a number of twentieth-century composers, Ruggles combines this form with the more modern concept of a continuous development unfolding freely out of generative cells of melody, harmony, or rhythm. Sections seething with emotion alternate with short lyrical passages; the form thus unfolds as a series of dramatic contrasts. Ruggles's score calls for a large orchestra with a specially large brass section: six horns, five trumpets, five trombones, and two tubas. The writing is extremely dense, with woodwinds, brass, and strings continually doubling—that is, reinforcing each other. The contrapuntal lines interweave in great clashes of sound, propelled by the same dissonant intervals that are prominent in the music of Schoenberg: minor seconds and ninths, major seconds and sevenths, augmented and diminished octaves, fifths and fourths. Orchestration, harmony, counterpoint, rhythm, dynamics, and the continually shifting densities of sound all complement one another in sustaining the dramatic urgency of the music, its surge—to use Ruggles's favorite word—from beginning to end. The painter in Ruggles is never far removed from the composer. Witness his instruction at one point in the score that the cymbals are to be struck with soft sticks, pianissimo, "like a shimmer of gold."

The opening theme unfolds against the peremptory throb of kettledrums—like the pounding of a heart—in a striking metrical pattern: seven beats, five, three, one. Thus drama enters at the very outset. Now the idea takes off in a great jagged line that soars crazily higher and higher, the equivalent of what is known in the symphonies of Haydn and Mozart as a "rocket theme." The mood is what German writers of the Romantic school used to describe as *himmelsturmend,* heaven-storming. Notice the prevalence of dissonant intervals (under the brackets).

By contrast, the second theme flows smoothly, by half step or narrow leap, within a narrow range. It is introduced by a solo oboe and clarinet backed by second violins:

The main theme reappears in the course of the exposition, shifted down a major third. There are passages of imitative counterpoint here that establish the kinship of this music with the great tradition, as in the following passage, where the second violins take over a motive of the violas and are in turn imitated by the first violins:

A sudden *Allegro* brings in a third idea, what might be considered the equivalent of a "closing theme" in the Classical scheme. It undulates but ultimately strides downward as resolutly as the opening theme climbed up:

The passage of imitative counterpoint toward the end of the development section is exceedingly close-knit in texture. The recapitulation is ushered in by the opening theme, which is now shifted half a step down. The second theme is heard at the same pitch as before. It is now marked "Serene, but with great expression." The principal theme triumphs when trumpets and trombones proclaim it in unison, while the upward-leaping melody is heard against a countermelody. A short brilliant coda—the final surge—leads to the closing chord, which is marked *ff–p–fff*.

The composer of these poetic measures was a natural-born musician; yet untoward circumstances cheated him of the full flowering of his gifts. His admirer Charles Seeger suggested this in an apt passage: "Here is a man who has an unusual number of the attributes of genius: might it not be that if he had been born at another time or in a different place he would have been able to make his grandiose dreams more palpable, turn out a bulk of work that would compel the acceptance of his notions of beauty as the standard of his day, and fix him in the honored position of the first great musician of an epoch?" We shall never know.

50 Experimental Composers of the Twenties

Henry Cowell (1897–1965)

"I want to live in the *whole world* of music!"

Henry Cowell was the first of several composers born in California who branched out in new directions during the 1920s and '30s. There is a twofold significance in this circumstance. First, it meant that our musical culture now encompassed the whole country, so that our westernmost states were producing creative musicians who could take their place alongside their colleagues from the Eastern seaboard and the Middle West. Second, and equally important, these men would not be as apt to look across the Atlantic for guidance but would rather seek inspiration from the regions across the Pacific, specifically the musics of the Far East. Cowell played a leading part in this development.

While still in his early teens, Cowell, without anyone to guide him but his intuition and totally uninhibited by any awareness of musical tradition, found his way to the tone clusters that became the hallmark of his early piano style. *Tone clusters* are groups of adjacent notes played simultaneously, as when a pianist presses down a group of keys with the palm of his hand, his forearm, or a ruler. They may be thought of as chords based on the interval of a second rather than on a third, as in traditional harmony, or a fourth or fifth, as in twentieth-century harmony. (See page 22 for examples of secundal, quartal, and quintal harmony.) Actually, the tone cluster, as Cowell used it, was an agglomeration of sounds rather than a chord. It was a sonority somewhere between fixed pitch and noise and functioned as an impression or "thrill" (somewhat like Debussy's parallel chords) rather than as a functional harmony. Here Cowell anticipated the interest in sheer sonority that was to become a major preoccupation of music after World War II.

In several other respects he was years ahead of his time. He investigated the serial organization of rhythmic values that we will find in the music of post-Webern composers. He anticipated the random music of John Cage by writing pieces in which the performer could choose the order of musical events. And within his own idiom, which was based on a dissonant chromaticism, he found his way to atonality, polytonality, and the new linear counterpoint.

Listen to Cowell's two best-known piano pieces—*The Banshee* and *Aeolian Harp*—which vividly illustrate his exploration of what was then a new world of sound. In *The Banshee* (1925) he sent the pianist's hand into the entrails of the piano to pluck, strike, and scrape the strings directly, a precedent that has been followed in many piano pieces written since 1950. *The Aeolian Harp* (1923) exploits the shimmering cloud of sympathetic vibrations that are unique to the piano. Music has moved so rapidly and so far in the past three decades that it is almost impossible for us to appreciate the originality of Cowell's innovations of half a century ago. He has been unjustly neglected, for there is so much in his output that can be listened to today with interest and enjoyment. He may well be the next of our half-forgotten masters to be rediscovered.

Wallingford Riegger (1885–1961)

"When I undertook to create, it was in spite of my environment."

Wallingford Riegger's music made its way slowly, for its qualities were not such as impress the crowd. It was not until he reached his sixties that he was recognized as one of the substantial figures of his generation.

A native of Albany, Georgia, Riegger grew up in New York. After several brief teaching stints he returned to the city, and spent the major part of his career there. He became friendly with the pioneers of the modern movement in America—Charles Ives, Carl Ruggles, Edgard Varèse, and Henry Cowell. "We had rejected the neo-classicism of a war-weary Paris and had struck out for ourselves, each in his own way. We formed the Pan-American Association of Composers and gave, at a tremendous expense of time and energy, numerous concerts both here and abroad."

Riegger found his style through the Schoenbergian technique, which freed him from dependence on the Classic-Romantic heritage. He used the twelve-tone language in an altogether personal way, combining it freely with elements drawn from the Classical tradition. He well described his attitude: "The idiom to me is secondary, depending on the nature of the musical idea. A man who writes dry music in the twelve-tone technique will do so in any style."

Riegger's mature period opens with the *Study in Sonority* (1927) and the witty *Canons for Woodwinds* (1931). *Dichotomy*, for chamber orchestra (1932), is based on two opposing tone rows; hence the title. It is one of Riegger's strongest works. *New Dance* (1932) won popularity not only as an orchestral piece but also in its two-piano version. (The composer arranged it for other combinations as well.) *Music for Brass Choir* (1949) comes out of a bold instrumental imagination, as does the powerful *Symphony No. 4* (1957). These are outstanding items in a varied list that centers about orchestra, chamber, and choral pieces.

Study in Sonority, for ten violins or any multiple of ten, sets forth Riegger's approach to the problems of texture, harmony, rhythm, and form. In this piece he speaks the language of atonal Expressionism that foretells his subsequent commitment to twelve-tone music. The ten violins (or twenty, thirty, or forty) are divided into three groups. Four carry the melodic material, four the harmonies, counterpoints, and rhythmic figures, and two the bass line. The functions of the three groups naturally overlap, opening up manifold possibilities in the interplay of lines, textures, and pungently disso- nant harmonies on which the architecture rests.

The piece unfolds in free form from an intense four-note motive that moves upward by half steps, suggesting the highly chromatic nature of Riegger's language. Notice the dynamic markings through which he underlines the dramatic nature of this fragment:

Riegger takes full advantage of the dynamic contrasts inherent in string tone. Low register is pitted against high, soft against loud, pizzicato against regular bowing, solo passages against the group. The score calls for a number of special effects that have since become part of the vocabulary of the string instruments.

With its fertility of invention and integrity of style, this music bespeaks an independent and original mind. It reveals Wallingford Riegger as one of our truly important composers.

Ruth Crawford (1901–1953)

Serious music is a cooperation of head and heart, of feeling and thinking.
CHARLES SEEGER ON RUTH CRAWFORD

Ruth Crawford was born in East Liverpool, Ohio and grew up "in that traditional cradle of Americanism, a minister's household." She composed along traditional lines until, in her late twenties, she came to New York. There she studied with her future husband, the musi- cologist Charles Seeger, who along with Henry Cowell and others was active in what was then the avant-garde. Crawford's writing took a boldly experimental turn, and she produced a series of strik- ingly original works. She was the first woman to hold a Guggenheim fellowship in composition, which made possible a year in Berlin. It was during this year that she wrote her most important work, the *String Quartet 1931.*

There was, however, no audience in America for what she had to say. Like Ives and Ruggles, she gave up composing when she should have been at the height of her creativity. After her marriage to Seeger she collaborated with him in editing collections of American folk songs. This activity played its part in determining the career of her stepson, the talented folk singer Pete Seeger. She died in Chevy Chase, Maryland in 1953, her music practically forgotten. It is only in recent years that she has been recognized as belonging to that small group of innovative American composers who in remarkable fashion anticipated developments that became current only several decades later.

Crawford's *String Quartet 1931* is a concise, arresting work that displays her style at its best. The first movement, in 3/4 time and moderate tempo, opens with a melody marked by the wide leaps that became increasingly characteristic of twentieth-century music. Notice the dissonant interval of a major seventh at the outset:

Rhapsodic in nature, the movement is unified by motivic-rhythmic cells that pervade the entire work. They reappear in an entirely fresh context in the Scherzo, a snappy movement in 2/4 time marked *Leggiero* (light). Third is the slow movement, an *Andante* in 4/4, which Charles Seeger called "an experiment in dynamic counterpoint. Each part has a different alternation of crescendo and diminuendo, or else the same alternation but beginning and ending at different times."

It is the fourth movement, an *Allegro possibile* (as fast as possible) in 2/2, that is the most remarkable in its anticipation of present-day procedures. This finale consists of two lines that answer one another antiphonally. The upper line is carried by the first violin, the lower by the other three instruments playing in octaves, muted. The upper line begins with a single note that—with each succeeding phrase, one note at a time—grows into a grand unit of twenty notes. This point is reached in the middle of the movement. Then the process is reversed: the music is played backward (in retrograde), but shifted up a half step, with the units growing progressively shorter until we return to the single note at the end. This goes hand in hand with a rigorous control of dynamics. The violin starts out fortissimo, gradually decreases its volume until it reaches a pianissimo in the middle of the movement, then increases the volume until it returns to fortissimo in the final measures.

The lower part is organized just as rigorously. It is based on an ostinato pattern of ten notes that serves as a tone row, in which—as in the Schoenbergian row—no single pitch is repeated. This is repeated to make a twenty-note pattern that is decreased one note at a time until it reaches a single-note unit in the middle of the movement, whereupon the process is reversed a half tone higher. Each statement of the row begins on the next note of the series and is subject to the kind of permutation that we associate with twelve-tone technique. Here the dynamic scheme is from pianissimo to fortissimo and back to pianissimo.

The opening line of the movement shows how all this works. Notice that the second half of the ostinato (the last ten notes) duplicates the pattern of the first ten beginning with the second note of the series instead of the first, which entirely changes the disposition of the phrase.

Allegro possibile

What we have here is an attempt to achieve total control over all the elements involved—pitch, rhythm, and phrase structure. In this movement Ruth Crawford foreshadowed in remarkable fashion what became a major preoccupation of composers after the Second World War. One can only conjecture how she might have developed if the time and place had been ready for her.

Others

John J. Becker (Henderson, Kentucky, 1886–1961, Wilmette, Illinois) has been called the "forgotten man" of modern American music. He was in the forefront of the innovators who, in the years between the wars, sought new paths. "Laws," he wrote, "are made for imitators; creators make their own laws." And to the same point: "It is every composer's duty to add to the already existing musical resources. The true creative artist must never be satisfied. He must seek new paths constantly, for only by seeking will he find for himself the way to musical truth and beauty."

Becker was an innovator in harmony and orchestration. In such stage works as *Dance Figure* (1933), on a poem by Ezra Pound, for solo voice, dance group, and large orchestra, and *A Marriage with Space* (1934), for solo and mass recitation, solo and group dancers, and large orchestra, he anticipated certain procedures of today's multimedia theater. And in his sacred music he united the pure a cappella style of Palestrina with twentieth-century dissonance. Only two works of his have found their way into the record catalogues: *Symphony No. 3* (*Sinfonia brevis*, 1929) and the *Concerto Arabesque*, for piano and orchestra (1930).

Adolph Weiss (Baltimore, 1891–1971, Van Nuys, California) was the first native-born American to study with Schoenberg at the Berlin Academy of Fine Arts (1924–1927). He was also one of the first to move away from the limitations of conventional notation: he wrote his music in columns of figures which he then transcribed into notes. Weiss used the dodecaphonic technique to express an outlook on life which, as Henry Cowell put it, "is quite different from Schoenberg's and is philosophically American." His best-known work is the "scherzo jazzoso" for orchestra, *American Life* (1929). Weiss achieved a wide reputation as a teacher and did yeoman work in the 1930s in introducing young Americans—among them John Cage—to the Schoenbergian aesthetic.

Leo Ornstein (Krementchug, Russia, 1892–) came to this country with his parents when he was fifteen. In his early twenties he appeared as a concert pianist both in the United States and Europe, playing his own works as well as the then moderns—Debussy, Ravel, Schoenberg, and Scriabin. Ornstein helped organize the League of Composers in 1923. Audiences, startled by the unprecedented dissonance and rhythmic complexity of his idiom, came to think of him as "the Wild Man of Music." He anticipated many of the procedures that later were accepted as part of the legitimate musical vocabulary. Overshadowed by later innovators, Ornstein was relegated to the role of a precursor and forgotten, but his music is now enjoying an overdue revival.

George Antheil (Trenton, New Jersey, 1900–1959, New York City) began his career as a composer by embracing what he called "an anti-expressive, anti-romantic, coldly mechanistic aesthetic." This culminated in the sensational *Ballet mécanique*, which created a furor in Paris in 1927. "I scored the ballet for eight pianos, a pianola and an airplane propeller." When the piece was presented in New York the number of pianos was doubled; anvils, bells, automobile horns, and buzzsaws were added. The audience responded with cheers and hisses; Antheil leaped into international fame as "the Bad Boy of music," a role he thoroughly enjoyed. In 1929 he had another success with his opera *Transatlantic,* on his own libretto, a work of an almost tabloid realism, whose action unfolds in an ocean liner, in a Child's restaurant, in a nightclub that is raided. The heroine sings an extended aria while in her bathtub. Antheil in later years settled down to writing Hollywood film scores and amply designed instrumental music. His last symphonies—he wrote six—are grandiose works in a Postromantic style.

As can be seen from this meager account, the bold experimenters in our music during the 1920s and '30s were like voices crying in a wilderness. It would please them to know that half a century later the freedoms they envisaged and fought for can be taken for granted by their successors.

51 The Thirties

"Because we live here and work here, we can be certain that when our music is mature it will also be American in quality."

AARON COPLAND

The American School Moves Forward

The Thirties were the years of the Great Depression. A somber mood prevailed in the country, leading to increasing awareness of its spiritual resources, of which music was one of the most rewarding. A strong current of populism made itself felt as the decade unfolded. The government undertook patronage of the arts through the WPA and Federal Theater Project. This was the period of the "proletarian" novel, which came to fruition in a number of significant works such as Michael Gold's *Jews without Money* (1930), James T. Farrel's trilogy about Studs Lonigan (1932–1935), John Steinbeck's *The Grapes of Wrath* (1939), and Pietro di Donato's *Christ in Concrete* (1939). A comparable spirit shaped the canvases of several painters who caught the mood of the Depression, among them Philip Evergood, Ben Shahn, and Raphael Soyer.

During the Thirties, political commitment became an important element in art. Ben Shahn (1898–1969) conveys the eerie atmosphere surrounding a trial which aroused enormous social protest. The Passion of Sacco and Vanzetti, 1931–1932. *Collection of the Whitney Museum of American Art, New York, Gift of Edith and Milton Lowenthal in memory of Juliana Force.*

Hard times made our musicians ever more appreciative of the rich store of folk and popular songs, spirituals and work songs that surrounded them. This aspect of the Thirties made itself felt in a variety of compositions. One thinks immediately of Marc Blitzstein's *The Cradle Will Rock* (1936), Virgil Thomson's *The Plough that Broke the Plains* (1936) and *The River* (1937), George Gershwin's *Porgy and Bess* (1935), Aaron Copland's *Billy the Kid* (1938), Douglas Moore's *The Devil and Daniel Webster* (1938), and Roy Harris's *Folksong Symphony* (1939).

Conditions surrounding the publication and performance of American music steadily improved. The larger radio networks, such as the National Broadcasting Company and Columbia Broadcasting

System, adopted the imaginative policy—soon unhappily discontinued—of commissioning new works. An ever wider network of grants, fellowships, and prizes continued to encourage the creative musician. Gradually, too, the powerful organizations of the writers of popular music—ASCAP (American Society of Composers, Authors and Publishers) and BMI (Broadcast Music, Incorporated)—began to take an interest in the composer of serious music and awarded him his share (in most cases not very large) of the revenues accruing from the public performance of copyrighted works.

The political upheavals in Europe in the years preceding the Second World War influenced our musical development in the most immediate way. There was an influx of European musicians seeking a haven from Nazism and war, as a result of which this country during the thirties became the musical center of the world. The presence in our midst of Stravinsky, Schoenberg, Bartók, Hindemith, Milhaud, Ernst Krenek, Bohuslav Martinu, and their confreres had an enormous impact on our musical life. These leaders of the modern movement were active as teachers, conductors, and performers of their works. Many young musicians studied with Hindemith at Yale and Tanglewood, with Schoenberg at UCLA, with Milhaud at Mills College and Aspen, with Krenek at Vassar and Hamline University, with the other Europeans whose activities we will discuss in a later chapter—and came directly under their influence. It was no longer necessary for a young American musician to study abroad. He could receive the best training in the world in the United States.

During this time our composers were actively experimenting with the techniques of contemporary musical speech. In craftsmanship their scores began to bear comparison with the best of Europe's. Most important of all, a new public emerged that was interested in hearing and supporting American music. For their part, composers went forth to meet this public halfway. The spirit of *Gebrauchsmusik* that had played so important a part in the milieu of Hindemith and Kurt Weill found its counterpart here, as did the "everyday music" toward which the youthful *Les Six* had aspired. Composers began to write film music, ballets, music for high school students, music for civic celebrations. Little by little the gulf that had separated American composers from their public narrowed. Thus it came about that those born at the turn of the century and after found an incomparably more favorable climate for their work than had their forebears. By the end of the 1930s the American composer was fairly well established as a working artist within the frame of his own country.

Toward an American Music

As American composers became more sure of themselves, they aspired in ever greater measure to give expression to the life about them. At first they concentrated on those features of the home scene that were not to be found in Europe: the lore of the Indian, the Negro, and the cowboy. They became increasingly aware of a wealth of native material that was waiting to be used: the songs of the southern mountaineers, which preserved intact the melodies brought over from England three hundred years ago; the hymns and religious tunes that had such vivid associations for Americans everywhere; the patriotic songs of the Revolutionary period and the Civil War, many of which had become folk songs; the tunes of the minstrel shows which had reached their high point in the songs of Foster. There were, in addition, the work songs from various parts of the country—songs of sharecroppers, lumberjacks, miners, river men; songs of prairie and railroad, chain gang and frontier. Then there was the folklore of the city dwellers—commercialized ballads, musical-comedy songs, and jazz: a world of melody, rhythm, and mood.

Certain composers, on the other hand, resisted this kind of local color. They preferred the international idioms of twentieth-century

Some artists were concerned with city life on a more intimate scale. Edward Hopper (1882–1967) takes typical elements of the urban landscape—all-night diners, store fronts, street corners—and captures the sense of loneliness and isolation generated by the modern city. Nighthawks, *1942. The Art Institute of Chicago. Friends of American Art Collection.*

music which had been stripped of folk elements: Impressionism, Neoclassicism, atonality, and twelve-tone music. Others managed to reconcile the two attitudes. They revealed themselves as internationally minded in certain of their works, but employed folklore elements in others. It was gradually realized that Americanism in music was a much broader concept than had at first been supposed: American music could not but be as many-faceted as America itself. A work did not have to quote a Negro spiritual, an Indian harvest song, or a dirge of the prairie in order to qualify for citizenship.

The music of the American school follows no single formula. Rather, it reflects the contradictory tendencies in our national character: our jaunty humor, and our sentimentality; our idealism, and our worship of material success; our rugged individualism, and our wish to look and think like everybody else; our visionary daring, and our practicality; our ready emotionalism, and our capacity for intellectual pursuits. All of these and more are abundantly present in a music that has bigness of gesture, vitality, and all the exuberance of youth.

52   George Gershwin (1898-1937)

"Porgy and Bess is a folk tale. Its people naturally would sing folk music. When I first began work on the music I decided against the use of original folk material because I wanted the music to be all of one piece. Therefore I wrote my own spirituals and folksongs. But they are still folk music—and therefore, being in operatic form, *Porgy and Bess* becomes a folk opera."

George Gershwin's career, cut short at its peak by his untimely death, has become something of a legend among us. In terms of native endowment he unquestionably was one of the most gifted musicians this country has produced.

His Life

Gershwin was born in Brooklyn of Russian-Jewish parents who had immigrated some years before. He grew up on the teeming East

Side of New York City. The dynamic, extrovert youngster was about ten when he began to study the piano. Given his intensity and his eagerness to learn, he might have gone on to a conservatory, but his future direction already was clear to him. The sixteen-year-old boy, discussing jazz with his teacher, said, "This is American music. This is the kind of music I want to write."

He took the first step toward his ultimate goal when he became a song plugger for Remick's, a well-known publisher of popular music. His first published song, *When You Want 'Em You Can't Get 'Em* (1916), netted him five dollars. From these modest beginnings Gershwin's career moved rapidly forward. In 1919 he wrote his first musical comedy score, *La La Lucille,* and his first hit, *Swanee,* which was brought to fame by Al Jolson. In the ensuing decade he produced a substantial number of the memorable songs associated with his name, among them *Somebody Loves Me* from the *Scandals of 1924;*

George Gershwin, a self portrait, 1921. (The Bettmann Archive)

Oh Lady Be Good and *Fascinating Rhythm* from *Lady Be Good* (1924); *The Man I Love* from *Tip Toes* (1925); and *'S Wonderful* from *Funny Face* (1927).

In these show tunes we encounter the distinctive profile of the Gershwin song: fresh lyricism; the subtle rhythms, now caressing, now driving; the chromatic harmony; and the sudden modulations. Gershwin's imagination impelled him to transcend the limitations of what was a stereotyped commercial form. He found his lyricist in his brother Ira, whose unconventional word patterns perfectly suited his notes. Together they helped to bring into being a sophisticated type of popular song that caught the pulse of the Twenties.

In the meantime Gershwin established himself in the field of orchestral music. His first major effort in this direction was the *Rhapsody in Blue*, which Paul Whiteman presented at an eventful concert at Town Hall on February 12, 1924. The piece was the high point of Whiteman's attempt to make jazz respectable. The *Rhapsody* was a fantastic success and carried Gershwin's name round the globe. The *Concerto in F* received its premiere at Carnegie Hall in 1925, with the composer playing the solo part and Walter Damrosch conducting the New York Symphony Orchestra. In this work Gershwin continued his efforts to "make a lady out of jazz," to the satisfaction of all concerned. During his last trip abroad in 1928 he heard the European premiere of the Concerto at the Paris Opera, where it scored a resounding success.

To the final group of musicals belong *Strike Up the Band* and *Girl Crazy* (1930), *Of Thee I Sing* (1931), and *Let 'Em Eat Cake* (1933). Meanwhile he had made several additions to his list of orchestral works, chief of these being *An American in Paris*. By now he was ready for the crowning task of his life, the opera *Porgy and Bess*, which we will discuss.

Physically attractive and endowed with a magnetic personality, George Gershwin was the center of an adoring circle of friends. He played his own music with enormous flair and thoroughly enjoyed doing so. He fell in love frequently, but never married. In his early thirties he became interested in painting and turned out a number of canvases that show talent. The last year and a half of his life was spent in Hollywood, where he wrote the music for several movies—*Shall We Dance?*, *A Damsel in Distress* (both with Fred Astaire), and *Goldwyn Follies*. He was not happy working in pictures, for the conventions of Hollywood were even less tractable than those of Broadway; besides, he missed the excitement of New York. But he never returned. After a brief illness, he was found to have a brain tumor. He did not survive the operation.

His Music

Gershwin took the three ingredients that went into the folk song of the streets of New York—jazz, ragtime, and the blues (to which, in *Porgy and Bess,* he added the Negro spiritual)—and out of these wove a characteristic popular art. He was able to do so because of his spontaneous lyric gift. As he himself said, he had more tunes in his head than he could put down on paper in a hundred years.

His aim was to reconcile jazz and "classical"; or, as it used to be put in those days, to bring Tin Pan Alley to Carnegie Hall. Composers before him had seen the possibilities of jazz as a basis for serious works. Witness Stravinsky's *Ragtime* and Milhaud's *La Création du monde,* both of which antedated the *Rhapsody in Blue;* also the experiments of Debussy and Satie. But for these men jazz was an exotic dish, which they served up more or less self-consciously. For Gershwin, on the other hand, jazz was a natural mode of expression. Thus he was able to reveal to the world the charm and verve of our popular music.

In his forays from Times Square to 57th Street Gershwin encountered serious technical problems, which he solved within the limits of his time and place. For his forms he turned to the nineteenth century, using them in rather artless fashion. The rhapsody, the concerto, and the symphonic poem of Liszt were his models. The rhapsody, being the freest of Romantic forms, lent itself best to his purpose. The *Rhapsody in Blue* is a dashing work in which is consummated the union of Lisztian pianism and jazz. The *Concerto* and *An American in Paris* are less secure from a formal standpoint. They are carried along by the sheer verve of the melodies that constitute their themes.

In *Porgy and Bess* (1935), on the other hand, Gershwin had everything in his favor—the tenderness and compassion, the instinct of the musical dramatist, the lyrics of his brother Ira, and the wonderful tunes to go with them. And so he captured, as Lawrence Gilman put it, "the wildness and the pathos and tragic fervor that can so strangely agitate the souls of men." A dozen operas launched at the Metropolitan with recitative and arias in the most approved German or French manner have fallen into oblivion, while this "folk opera"—

as Gershwin called it—goes on to new triumphs with the years and has been hailed the world over as an American classic.

Porgy and Bess

It was in 1925 that DuBose Heyward wrote his novel about Negro life in his native Charleston, South Carolina. The book was an instant success, as was the play adapted from it two years later. Gershwin was immediately impressed by the story and its possibilities for musical treatment. However, it was not until seven years later that he was ready to begin work on the opera. He spent the summer of 1934 with the Heywards at Folly Beach near Charleston, where he was able to observe at first hand the life, customs, and singing of the Gullahs, an isolated community of blacks on one of the islands outside the city. They were his models for the inhabitants of Catfish Row. He had the advantage of working directly with Heyward, who transformed the play into a libretto. The lyrics were by Heyward and Ira Gershwin.

One of the first problems Gershwin had to solve was the recitative, which constitutes the narrative element in opera, the dialogue that advances plot and action (as opposed to aria, which is the songful, the lyrical element). Recitative by its very nature contains a lot of information that does not demand to be sung, and a number of literary men throughout the history of opera—among them Voltaire and Rousseau, Addison and Steele—ridiculed the singing of it as being contrary to nature and good sense. Heyward, as might be expected, sided with them. "I feel more and more," he wrote Gershwin, "that all the dialogue should be spoken. This will give the opera speed and tempo."

Gershwin, reaching out beyond the traditions of the Broadway musical theater, was determined that his opera be sung throughout. This was one of the factors that contributed to the modest run of the first production—124 performances, a disappointingly low figure for a Gershwin show. As in the case of Bizet's *Carmen* sixty years before, which reached out similarly beyond the traditions of opéra-comique, *Porgy and Bess* was more than the public was ready for. Both works conquered only after their composers were dead, *Porgy and Bess* in a shortened version produced by Cheryl Crawford in 1941, in which the recitatives were all but eliminated in favor of spoken dialogue.

Gershwin's fine ear made it possible for him to create a musical line deftly shaped to the vernacular. "The recitative I have tried to

A view of Catfish Row on a summer's night. Act I, scene 1 of the Houston Grand Opera production (1976) of Porgy and Bess. *Photograph by Martha Swope.*

make as close to the Negro inflection in speech as possible, and I believe my song-writing apprenticeship has served invaluably in this respect, because the song writers of America have the best conception of how to set words to music so that the music gives added expression to the words." Instead of tackling the extended lyric flight of the operatic aria, he wrote the songs that spread the fame of *Porgy and Bess* throughout the globe. "Because *Porgy and Bess*," he wrote, "deals with Negro life in America it brings to the operatic form elements that have never before appeared in opera and I have adapted my method to utilize the drama, the humor, the superstition, the religious fervor, the dancing and the irrepressible high spirits of the race. If, in doing this, I have created a new form, which combines opera with theater, this new form has come quite naturally out of the material."

Black artists were quick to point out that the opera, like the book and play on which it was based, represented a white man's view of the Negro and was not free of some of the stereotypes associated with that view. Duke Ellington was eager "to debunk Gershwin's lampblack Negroisms"; Hall Johnson described the work as "an opera about Negroes rather than a Negro opera." The civil rights movement of the 1950s and '60s, and its attendant upsurge of racial pride, could not look favorably on the "Uncle Tomism" embodied in Porgy. On the other hand, the black community could not overlook the fact that Gershwin's work opened up extraordinary opportunities for black singing actors at a time when such opportunities were severely limited, or that the roles of Porgy and Bess launched a number of brilliant careers for black artists, from Todd Duncan and Anne Brown, to Leontyne Price, William Warfield, and, more recently, Clamma Dale. Thus, despite its reservations, the black community could not but participate in the success of the work.

These pros and cons can be argued on an intellectual level. Once you are in the theater they fade before the irresistible vitality and melodic invention of Gershwin's score, the compassion with which he viewed his protagonists, and the pathos and nobility with which his music invests their joys and sorrows. You need only a recording—there are several—to be transported into the magic world of this vibrantly alive work.

George Gershwin, like Bizet after *Carmen*, died as he stood on the threshold of important advances in his art. Because he was so close to us we are prone to view him within the framework of the Broadway musical theater. It is well to remember that so severe a judge as Arnold Schoenberg said at the time of his death, "I grieve over the deplorable loss to music, for there is no doubt that he was a great composer."

53 Aaron Copland (1900-)

"I am hopelessly a musician."

It has been Aaron Copland's preoccupation, for over half a century, to express "the deepest reactions of the American consciousness to the American scene." Composer, teacher, writer on musical topics, and organizer of musical events, he is one of the most important figures of the modern American school.

His Life

"I was born on a street in Brooklyn that can only be described as drab. Music was the last thing anyone would have connected with it." Thus begins the autobiographical sketch in Copland's book *Our New Music*. His father was a Russian-Jewish immigrant who, like many of his generation, found his opportunity in the new world. An older sister taught Aaron the piano. When he was fifteen he decided to become a composer. As the first step toward this goal he tried to learn harmony through a correspondence course. After a few lessons he realized the need for more substantial instruction and became a pupil of Rubin Goldmark. The latter, a thoroughgoing conservative, warned his pupil against having any traffic with the "moderns," which only whetted the young man's curiosity. "By the time I was eighteen I already had something of the reputation of a musical rebel—in Goldmark's eyes, at any rate."

In the summer of 1921 Copland attended the newly founded school for Americans at Fontainebleau, where he came under the influence of Nadia Boulanger. Her classes opened up a new world to him. He decided to stay on in Paris and became Boulanger's first full-time American student in composition. As we indicated in an earlier chapter, the influence of this remarkable woman on Copland's generation can hardly be overestimated. In later years the "Boulangerie" (a pun on the French word for bakery) included some of our leading composers.

Copland spent three years in Paris. He came in contact with the most significant developments in the modern movement and took delight in following frankly experimental paths. He returned to New York in 1924, with an impressive commission: Nadia Boulanger had asked him to write a concerto for organ for her American appearances. Copland composed the piece while working as the pianist of a hotel trio at a summer resort in Pennsylvania. The *Symphony for Organ and Orchestra* was given that season by the New York Symphony under the baton of Walter Damrosch. The genial conductor sensed that his audience would be shocked by the acerbity of the piece. When it was over, he turned round and said, "If a young man at the age of twenty-three can write a symphony like that, in five years he will be ready to commit murder."

It was Copland's good fortune that his gifts unfolded in an environment ready for them. He was helped by private patronage, fellowships, commissions, and prizes such as the five-thousand-dollar

Aaron Copland. Photograph by John Ardoin, courtesy of Boosey and Hawkes, Inc.

award he received in 1929 from the RCA Victor Company for his *Dance Symphony*. At the same time he played a leading role in making his environment receptive to the music of the modern American school. With Roger Sessions he organized the Copland-Sessions Concerts, which functioned from 1928 to 1931 and featured the works of American composers. He was active in inaugurating the festivals of American music at Yaddo, in Saratoga Springs, New York. He was a moving spirit in the League of Composers throughout its existence. His concern for the composer's economic plight led to activity in that sphere, too: he was one of the founders of the American Composers' Alliance and served as president of that organization for seven years.

This unremitting activity went hand in hand with his writing and teaching. In numerous magazine articles he ludicly advocated the cause of modern music. The courses he presented at the New School for Social Research in New York City brought him an awareness of what the layman should be told about music. His books—*What to Listen for in Music* (1939) and *Our New Music* (1941)—found a wide public both here and abroad. He taught at Harvard University in 1935 and 1944 and returned to give the six Charles Eliot Norton lectures in 1951–1952, which were published in his book *Music and*

Imagination. He taught at Tanglewood from the time the Berkshire Music Center was founded and took an active part there in training the younger generation of American musicians.

Copland's interest in Mexico, originally that of a tourist, deepened to a genuine appreciation of Latin-American culture. During the decade of the Second World War, when it was impossible to travel in Europe, he found congenial sources of inspiration below the Rio Grande. This predilection took a somewhat official turn when the Office of Inter-American Relations sent him, in 1941, on a goodwill tour of nine Latin-American countries. The State Department subsidized a similar journey in 1947.

These activities are the exterior landmarks of Copland's steady inner growth as an artist. Both together have made him a major force in American music for the past fifty years.

His Music

Copland belongs to a generation of Americans who were nurtured by the Parisian view of life and art. As a pupil of Nadia Boulanger he found his point of departure in the Neoclassicism of Stravinsky. He passed through a number of phases as he responded to one or another of the dominant forces in his milieu. After he completed his *Symphony for Organ and Orchestra* (in 1928 he reworked it, without organ, into his *First Symphony*), he became eager to write a work that would above all be American. "I had experimented a little with the rhythms of popular music in several earlier compositions, but now I wanted frankly to adopt the jazz idiom and see what I could do with it in a symphonic way." He encompassed this aim in *Music for the Theater* (1925), in which jazz was assimilated to the polytonal language of Neoclassicism. Copland continued this line of thought in the *Concerto for Piano and Orchestra,* which he played with the Boston Symphony in 1927. "This proved to be the last of my 'experiments' with symphonic jazz. With the *Concerto* I felt I had done all I could with the idom, considering its limited emotional scope. True, it was an easy way to be American in musical terms, but all American music could not possibly be confined to two dominant jazz moods: the 'blues' and the snappy number."

The first phase of Copland's development culminated in the *Symphonic Ode* of 1929. This important score brought into focus the chief elements of his early style: the rhetorical bigness of gesture—what Paul Rosenfeld called his "grandiosity"; the stylization of jazz polyrhythms; and the polytonal language he had learned in Paris. The works that followed the *Ode* were no longer so grand or, to use Copland's adjective, so fulsome. The *Piano Variations* (1930) and *Short Symphony* (1933) are more spare in sonority, more lean in texture, as are the orchestral *Statements,* which we will discuss. To the same period belong *Vitebsk* (Study on a Jewish Theme, 1928) for violin, cello, and piano, the one piece in which Copland made use of Jewish material; and the *Sextet,* a reduced version of the *Short Symphony* for string quartet, clarinet, and piano. During this austere and frankly esoteric period Copland was much influenced by Stravinsky as well as by the "objectivism" that was in the air in those years.

At this time he became increasingly aware of a curious contradiction in his thinking. He was writing for the orchestra—a medium that by its very nature has to address itself to the big public. Yet he was turning out pieces couched in an idiom that could not possibly reach the average listener. He had to ask himself for whom he was writing. "During these years I began to feel an increasing dissatisfaction with the relations of the music-loving public and the living composer. The old 'special' public of the modern music concerts had fallen away, and the conventional concert public continued apathetic or indifferent to anything but the established classics. It seemed to me that we composers were in danger of working in a vacuum. Moreover, an entirely new public for music had grown up around the radio and phonograph. It made no sense to ignore them and to continue writing as if they did not exist. I felt that it was worth the effort to see if I couldn't say what I had to say in the simplest possible terms."

Copland's third style period was notable for his imaginative use of folklore elements—cowboy songs, New England and Quaker hymns, Latin-American rhythms—and for his preoccupation with media that communicate with a large public. Works such as *The Second Hurricane* (1936), a "play-opera" for high school children, and the *Outdoor Overture* (1941), written for the orchestra of the High School of Music and Art in New York City, subserve the goal of functional music. From his Latin-American travels came two of his most popular works, *El Salón México* (1936) and *Danzón Cubano,* a two-piano piece based on Cuban dance rhythms. In this category of *Gebrauchsmusik* are also pieces like *Music for Radio* and the five film scores that brought him to the attention of broad segments of the American public: for John Steinbeck's *Of Mice and Men* (1939), Thornton Wilder's *Our Town* (1940), Lillian Hellman's *The North Star* (1943), Steinbeck's *The Red Pony* (1948), and Henry James's *The Heiress* (1948). The score for *The Heiress* won an Academy Award.

The three ballet scores of this period combined vivid rhythms and brilliant orchestral textures with a tender feeling for the rural American scene. *Billy the Kid* (1938) we will consider in detail. *Rodeo* (1942) continues the use of Americana in a somewhat lighter vein, based as it is on the efforts of an overly energetic cowgirl to get her man. The third work in this group, *Appalachian Spring,* which he wrote for Martha Graham (1944), is unquestionably one of Copland's most distinguished scores. Related to these in intent are several patriotic works that reflect the travail of the war years, such as *A Lincoln Portrait* (1942) for speaker and chorus, on a text drawn from the Great Emancipator's speeches. At the same time Copland continued to cultivate the more serious aspects of his art. The *Piano Sonata* (1941), *Sonata for Violin and Piano* (1943), *Concerto for Clarinet and String Orchestra* that was commissioned by Benny Goodman (1948), and *Quartet for Piano and Strings* (1950) are more mellow works than his earlier essays in the large instrumental forms. The intervening years of experience with the mass media had humanized Copland's art. The most important composition of these years is the *Third Symphony* (1944–1946). Mention should be made too of the *Twelve Poems of Emily Dickinson* for voice and piano (1948–1950), in the composer's characteristic vein of contemplative lyricism.

To these years belong Copland's single foray into the realm of opera. *The Tender Land,* on a libretto by Horace Everett (1954), was commissioned by Richard Rodgers and Oscar Hammerstein 2nd for the thirtieth anniversary of the League of Composers. The work is tender, and it is about land; but it lacks the dynamic conflict of personalities, the projection of human motives in musico-dramatic terms which is of the essence in opera. There was little likelihood that Copland would make his mark in the lyric theater. Opera, like love, is best discovered before one is fifty.

Copland's personality inclines him to lucidity, order, and control. He was setting forth his own aesthetic when he wrote, "The typical contemporary composer prefers an objective, impersonal approach; a complex, contrapuntal texture; a concentration on perfection of line and beauty of proportion." This classicist creed does not rule out either emotional expression or a direct relationship between music and life. "What, after all, do I put down when I put down notes? I put down a reflection of emotional states: feelings, perceptions, imaginings, intuitions. An emotional state, as I use the term, is compounded of everything we are: our background, our environment, our convictions."

Copland's harmonic language is essentially diatonic. He needs the key center if only because of his assiduous exploration of polytonal relationships. The triad is basic to his thinking. Characteristic is his wavering between major and minor (or his simultaneous use of both), which lends an attractive ambiguity to many a passage. An archaic modal flavor ofttimes pervades his music, imparting to it the inner quietude that emerges from the slow movements of his larger works.

Copland has the temperament of the lyricist, a fact that was somewhat obscured during the earlier phases of his development. His melodies are simple and direct, relying on stepwise movement along the scale and basic intervals such as thirds, fourths, and fifths. He builds up his melodic forms through the use of motivic fragments that are repeated over and over, each time with accretions, in a process of cumulative growth. There results the long line which he regards as the prime requisite for musical architecture. His preoccupation with folk material greatly benefited his melodic sense. The use of folk melodies, he points out, ought never to be a mechanical process. "They can be successfully handled only by a composer who is able to identify himself with, and re-express in his own terms, the underlying emotional connotations of the material."

Copland's music has a strong rhythmic impulse. In fast movements it thrusts forward with a motoric, toccata-like propulsion that generates excitement. He is much given to the use of ostinato and percussive rhythm, especially in his earlier works. The frequent changes of meter make for supple and vivacious movement. The accents are distributed with artful asymmetry, resulting in syncopations that possess the charm of the unexpected. His meticulous workmanship is evident in his orchestral texture. Like Stravinsky, he uses as few notes as possible. The careful spacing of the chords is a delight to those who examine his scores. His spare instrumental writing emphasizes the high registers, particularly of the trumpets and violins. This helps him achieve the clean, transparent sound that is one of the hallmarks of his style.

In his later works, such as the *Piano Fantasy* (1958), Copland has shown himself receptive to the serial techniques of the twelve-tone school. Yet his adoption of Schoenbergian procedures by no means implies abandonment of the key principle. Rather, he assimilates the serial technique to his own harmonic language, using it as a means of achieving maximum abstraction of thought and refinement of texture. This direction is apparent in *Connotations for Orchestra* (1961–1962) and the orchestral piece entitled *Inscape* (1967). The *Duo* for flute and piano (1970–1971), on the other hand, reverted to his earlier tonal style. Copland has not found the musical climate of the

Seventies conducive to further composition, and he has become increasingly active as a conductor, both of his own and other composers' music. He has done his work.

Statements

Statements (1934–1935), a suite for orchestra consisting of six short movements, dates from what is generally described as Copland's austere period. The works of that period were considered to be, as Copland himself described them, "difficult to perform and difficult for an audience to comprehend"; so much so that *Statements* had to wait seven years before Dimitri Mitropoulos and the New York Philharmonic gave the piece its first complete performance. Yet today this music sounds so tuneful and accessible that one finds it difficult to explain some of the criticisms leveled at it forty years ago. Thus do our ears change from one generation to the next.

"The word *statement*," Copland wrote, "was chosen to indicate a short, terse orchestral movement of a well-defined character, lasting about three minutes. The separate movements were given evocative titles as an aid to the understanding of what I had in mind when writing these pieces."

I. *Militant*. In a marked and bold style throughout, 4/4. The first statement is based on a single theme, announced at the beginning by flutes, oboes, bassoon, and strings in unison. This is a concise idea in the composer's prevalently diatonic idiom, wide of range and forceful of stride:

Copland directed that it be played *marcato* (marked) and *non legato*. Notice the conflict between the E-flat in the second and fourth measures and the E-naturals in the third, an ambiguity that gives the theme its inner tension. The downward leap of a fourth in the second measure becomes part of a basic motive, either alone, as at *A*, or in connection with the broken chord that precedes it (at *B*).

The movement unfolds through the repetition and accretion of fragments in the French manner rather than the thematic-motivic type of development dear to the Germans. This is a lithe, athletic kind of music whose decisive character reinforces the militant mood suggested by the title.

II. *Cryptic.* Fairly slow, 4/4. By way of contrast, the second movement is to be played *dolce* (soft, sweet) and *misterioso.* It is scored for brass and flute, with an occasional use of bass clarinet and bassoon. The opening idea, presented by solo flute, is of the utmost simplicity, for it consists of two adjacent notes. In other words, a minimum of movement:

The interval of a second figures also in the accompanying parts, especially in inversion—that is, moving down instead of up. This motive is presently expanded into a rhetorical pronouncement by flute and trumpets. Dotted rhythm and upward leaps of a fourth give this idea urgency and character:

Horns, trumpets, and trombones unite to produce the spare, open sonorities so characteristic of Copland's music. The sense of power in these sounds is accentuated by the wide spacing of the chords, a procedure that young Copland may have taken over from Stravinsky, but which he made entirely his own. After this powerful upsurge the music subsides, and the movement ends as cryptically as it began, *dolce, misterioso, ppp.*

III. *Dogmatic.* Lively, 3/4. We have no clue as to what Copland is being dogmatic about; but whatever that is, it leads him to explore the enormous tensions inherent in dissonant harmony. A little ascending motive on strings and brass, to be played *pesante* (heavy) and staccato, is punctuated by explosive chords and is followed by a brilliant passage for the violins in the upper register. This is a three-part piece (A-B-A). The middle section (B) quotes the angular theme of Copland's *Piano Variations,* which he had written in 1930. This theme, here divided between horn and trumpet, again exploits the ambiguity—and tension—between a sharp and a natural; in this case, between F-sharp and F-natural:

Then the first section (A) returns, but shifted down, first a fourth, then a fifth.

IV. *Subjective*. For violins, violas, and cellos. Calm and expressive, 3/4. Copland here utilizes the richly emotional sound of the string instruments to make a personal statement. This is a lonely music that unfolds in long, flowing lines. Copland's is a typically modern sensibility responding to the sense of aloneness that is part of a big-city environment. The mood is subtly suggested in the drooping line of the opening measures:

Noteworthy are the plangent sonorities that Copland extracts from the string choir. It is almost as if the various instrumental lines were rubbing against each other, producing an extremely intense sound. Original too is the way in which the violas and cellos move in great upward sweeps against the violins, darkening the texture.

V. *Jingo*. Fast, cut time, for full orchestra. In the fifth statement Copland approaches the popular manner of his next period, but with one difference. There he will derive his inspiration from rural America and the vast open spaces of the West. Here he hymns the jazzy rhythm of the big city in which he grew up, a tribute that is brought into focus when piccolo and first violins present the opening measures of *The Sidewalks of New York*. The first phrase is lifted out of its waltz time in a kind of rhythmic dislocation characteristic of the composer, while the second phrase of Copland's version hints at rather than quotes the original tune:

The mood of the piece is best summed up by the adjective Copland wrote into the score: *perky*. Charming is a little trumpet solo further on, marked *poco sentimentale*, echoed by a wailing trombone. The

Sidewalks tune returns briefly after a *fff* climax, and the music dies away, *pppp*.

VI. *Prophetic*. In varying tempos, beginning slow, and in various meters: 7/4, 4/4, 3/4, 3/8, 4/4, and so on. For full orchestra. The final statement is, in Copland's description, "rhapsodic in form and centers around a chorale-like melody sung by the solo trumpet." (A *chorale* is a hymn, or a melody in the style of a hymn.) An impressive orchestral introduction sets the epic mood. The choralelike melody is marked *mezzo piano, cantabile, dolce, nobilmente* (fairly soft, songful, sweet, nobly). The opening phrase leaps up along an interval that gradually diminishes in size, a formation occuring quite frequently in Copland's melodies:

Gong, cymbals, and bass drum add drama—and a sense of space—to the climax. At the end of the piece the opening phrase of the chorale is combined with a later phrase, so that what we first heard in succession we now hear simultaneously. Copland does not tell us what this visionary music is prophetic of. But one of the things it prophesizes—which he could not have known when he wrote it—is the prairie music that opens *Billy the Kid*. In short, he was here unconsciously foretelling his future development.

Billy the Kid

Art is the grand illusion. It creates a world that, from the moment we enter it, seems more real to us than reality itself. Thus it happens that the musical sound most widely associated with the cowboy and the West was created by the son of Russian-Jewish immigrants who grew up in Brooklyn. He fashioned this sound not out of memories of a life he had known, but through that act of will and imagination which is the essence of artistic creation.

For the ballet based on the saga of Billy the Kid Copland produced one of his freshest scores. In it are embedded, either in whole or in part, such cowboy classics as *I Ride an Old Paint*, *Great Grand-Dad*, and *The Dying Cowboy*. They are not quoted literally. What Copland does is to use these melodies as a point of departure for his own; they flavor the music but are assimilated to his personal style.

A scene from Billy the Kid *in a recent American Ballet Theater production.*
Photograph by Fred Fehl.

Billy the Kid—the Brooklyn-born William Bonney—had a brief
but intense career as desperado and lover, in the course of which he
became one of the legends of the Southwest. The ballet touches on
the chief episodes of his life. We see him first as a boy of twelve
when, his mother having been killed by a stray bullet in a street
brawl, he stabs the man responsible for her death. Later, during a
card game with his cronies, he is accused of cheating and kills the ac-
cuser. Captured after a running gun battle, he is put in jail. He
murders his jailer and gets away. A romantic interlude ensues when
he rejoins his Mexican sweetheart in the desert. But the menacing
shadows close in on him. This time there is no escaping. At the close
we hear a lament for the death of the dashing outlaw.

The concert suite contains about two-thirds of the music of the
ballet. *The Open Prairie,* which serves as a prologue, evokes a spacious landscape. The theme, announced by oboe, then clarinet,

creates an outdoor atmosphere, while modal harmonies in parallel motion give a sense of space and remoteness:

This prelude unfolds in free form, woven out of the opening theme through a process of repetition and expansion. It reaches a fortissimo climax and is followed by a scene that conjures up "a street in a frontier town." A theme derived from the cowboy song *Great Grand-Dad* is presented by piccolo "nonchalantly." Copland slightly changes the melody and gives it a sophisticated harmonic background:

The A-flat major tonality of this meolody persists while a contrasting tune, in the key of F, is thrust against its last note. There results a striking polytonal effect:

The contrasting melody takes over. The following example shows how Copland sets it off through the use of dissonant harmony:

Polyrhythm results when the melody, in 4/4 time, is presented against an accompaniment in 3/4. A dance performed by Mexican

women is based on *I Ride an Old Paint*. Copland changes the familiar
tune, giving it a more distinctive profile:

This episode builds from a quiet beginning to a *fff* climax. The next,
Card Game (Molto moderato), has the quality of wistful lyricism so
characteristic of Copland. The setting is a starry night in the desert.
The music projects a mood of gentle contemplation. In violent contrast is *Fight (Allegro)*—the pursuit of Billy and the gun battle—with
its overtones of brutality. The *Celebration* that follows Billy's capture
is properly brassy and gay. Copland presents a jaunty tune in a striking polytonal passage: the melody, in C major, is heard against a
pedal point on C sharp and G sharp that suggests C-sharp major. The
clash between the two keys points up the tune and makes it stand out
against its background. Notice how the dotted rhythm heightens the
melody; notice also the asymmetrical structure: a phrase of four
measures is answered by one of three.

Altogether lovely is the Epilogue (*Lento moderato*), in which the
prairie music of the opening returns. The physical landscape is transformed into a poetic symbol of all that is vast and immutable. It is in
passages such as this that Copland's art shows itself to be rooted in
our soil. For the world at large he is the repesentative American composer of the mid-twentieth century.

54 Roger Sessions (1896-)

"I am not trying to write 'modern,' 'American' or 'neo-classic' music. I am seeking always and only the coherent and living expression of my musical ideas."

Roger Sessions stands high in the regard of the musical fraternity. He concerns himself with problems fundamental to contemporary musical thought and does so on the highest level of artistic responsibility.

His Life

Sessions was born in Brooklyn, New York, of an old New England family. His parents returned to Massachusetts shortly after the future composer was born. He gave early evidence of his talent and wrote an opera, *Launcelot and Elaine,* at the age of twelve; he entered Harvard when he was fourteen. After graduating from Harvard, Sessions continued his musical studies with Horatio Parker at Yale. In 1917, when he was twenty-one, he was appointed to the faculty of Smith College and taught there for four years. He had already begun

Roger Sessions.

to compose, but was dissatisfied with the results. At this point he found an inspiring teacher in Ernest Bloch, under whose guidance he discovered his own creative path. "It would be impossible," he has said of Bloch, "to exaggerate what I owe to him."

When Bloch became head of the Cleveland Institute of Music he brought his pupil there as his assistant. Sessions remained in Cleveland for four years. From this period dates the music for Leonid Andreyev's symbolic drama *The Black Maskers;* the score is dedicated to Bloch. In 1925, when Bloch was dismissed from his post by the directors of the Institute, Sessions resigned in protest. He spent the next eight years in Europe: three in Florence, three in Rome, and two in Berlin. He returned to the United States in 1933; taught for a time at various schools in the Boston area and at the New School in New York; and in 1935 joined the music faculty of Princeton University, where he remained for a decade. He then became head of the music department at the University of California in Berkeley. In 1953 he returned to Princeton, where he taught until his retirement.

Sessions has taken an active part in the propagation of the new music. With Aaron Copland he organized the Copland-Sessions concerts, one of the first sustained attempts to bring contemporary music to the New York public. He was on the board of directors of the League of Composers and for eight years was president of the United States section of the International Society for Contemporary Music. His writings include "The Composer and his Message," in a collection of essays assembled by Augusto Centero under the title *The Intent of the Artist* (1941); *The Listening Experience of Composer, Performer, Listener* (1950); a textbook, *Harmonic Practice* (1951); and *Questions About Music* (1970).

His Music

Sessions is one of our internationally minded composers. The deliberate search for a nationalist music implies, for him, a limiting of the artist's freedom of choice. Americanism in music, he maintains, "is bound to come only from within, a quality to be discovered in *any* genuine and mature music written by an American." The classical approach is fundamental to his view of art and life. In an earlier chapter we quoted a paragraph of his that became the prime formulation of the Neoclassic creed (pp. 162–63). Sessions upholds the classical primacy of pure musical form and ideas. "For me, and I believe for nearly all composers, musical ideas have infinitely more substance, more specific meaning, and a more vital connection with experience than any words by which they can be described." All the same, there is a romantic strain in his thinking that sets him apart from the Stravinskyan aesthetic. The German Romantic tradition—the heritage of Wagner, Bruckner, Richard Strauss—played a seminal part in his development. If he was influenced by the Neoclassic aesthetic of Stravinsky, he responded in no less degree to the visionary romanticism of Bloch. As his pupil Mark Schubart has pointed out, his thinking "follows the German conception of music as a grandly expressive art, rather than the French conception of it as a sensuous or coloristic one."

Sessions my be regarded as an Expressionist. "My music," he writes, "is always expressive in intent, and often has very concrete associations for me. In composing, however, I follow not the associations but the impulsion of the musical ideas themselves." Music reaches down "to the energies which animate our psychic life. It reproduces for us the most intimate essence, the tempo and the energy of our spiritual being. It reproduces these far more directly and more specifically than is possible through any other medium of human communication."

The large, geometric sculptures of David Smith's late period are highly formalistic, ordered compositions built of abstract elements. Sessions, too, has created grandly expressive works through essentially non-emotive vocabularies. Cubi XXVII, 1965, by David Smith (1906–1965). The Solomon R. Guggenheim Museum, New York.

Sessions has been profoundly influenced by Schoenbergian thought. His music lies in the area between atonal chromaticism and the twelve-tone system; he prefers to remain on the periphery of the dodecaphonic school. The complexity of his music is inseparable from the complexity of his thinking. His is a subtle, allusive mind that sees all the ramifications of an idea and delights in tracing them to their ultimate consequences. Sessions is not one to try to make things easy for the listener. Yet his music, he feels, is not unduly difficult for those who take the trouble to familiarize themselves with it. "Experience has shown me over and over again that the 'difficulty' of my music is anything but insuperable. This is, of course, true of all new music if it is genuine, if it really has something to say. I have had ample occasion to observe that a work which was 'difficult,' say, ten or twelve years ago is no longer so. Both for performer and listener these difficulties have meanwhile cleared up, with results that have been surprising to all concerned. What the listener needs is familiarity with the language—sufficient familiarity to be able to respond to the tones, melodies, harmonies and rhythms it contains."

The simplest introduction to Sessions's music is through *The Black Maskers* (1923). Written when he was twenty-seven years old, the incidental music to Andreyev's Symbolist play dates from the period when he was most susceptible to Romantic influences. The sumptuous orchestral writing (quite Straussian in spots) foreshadows Sessions's later mastery in this domain. His mature output centers about the large forms of instrumental music. The *First Piano Sonata* (1930) is a deeply felt piece that shows his ability to discipline his emotions, as does also the *First String Quartet* in E minor (1936). A milestone in Sessions's development is the *Violin Concerto* (1935), which we will discuss. The *Second Piano Sonata* (1947) combines the dissonant texture of Neoclassicism with a chromatic idiom and violent contrasts of moods.

The central place in Sessions's output is held by his eight symphonies, which extend across four decades (1927–1968). With the exception of the *First*, a sunny, unproblematic piece that sums up Sessions's Neoclassic period, these bear the imprint of profound thought and concentrated emotion characteristic of the composer. The *Third* (1957) belongs to a group of works marked by a more personal lyricism and a more accessible style. This group includes the *Second String Quartet* (1951), the brilliant *Concerto for Piano and Orchestra* (1956), the *Idyll of Theocritus* for soprano and orchestra (1954), and the *Mass* (1958). In the *Third Symphony* Sessions adapts the serial techniques of twelve-tone music to his own ends. As he points out, he is not among the composers who commit themselves to the twelve-tone system as a value in itself, preferring to regard it "as a tool to be used in the forging of music valid on quite different and perennially vital grounds."

Sessions has written a one-act opera, *The Trial of Lucullus* (1947); the libretto is based on a play by Bertolt Brecht in which the celebrated Roman general stands trial after his death, his jury consisting of the little people whose lives were shattered by his triumphs. The work has been presented by our more venturesome opera workshops and is a moving experience in the theater. Sessions's full-length opera *Montezuma* (1941–1962), on a libretto by G. A. Borghese, received its premiere in Berlin in 1964 and its first American performance in Boston in 1976, by Sarah Caldwell's company. The opera requires a sumptuous production and its music makes heavy demands on both performers and listeners. As a result, our major opera houses have not yet undertaken to mount it.

Age has not withered Sessions's creative drive. At present a vigorous octogenarian, he has during the past decade added a number of important works to his list. Among them are *When Lilacs Last in the Dooryard Bloom'd*, a cantata for soloists, chorus, and orchestra on Walt Whitman's lines (1969); *Rhapsody for Orchestra* (1969); *Concerto for Violin, Cello, and Orchestra* (1971); and *Concertino* for chamber orchestra (1971).

Concerto for Violin and Orchestra

The Classic-Romantic concerto was based on the opposition between solo instrument and orchestra—a symbolic opposition of one against the many, the individual against the mass. Certain twentieth-century composers such as Prokofiev and Shostakovich adhered to this conception, in which the two masses of sound take turns in dominating the action. Others, on the contrary—among them Stravinsky, Hindemith, and Berg—turned back to the Baroque concerto in which the soloist plays almost continually, becoming the dominant factor, while the orchestra serves principally to amplify, illumine, and add intensity to the solo part. It is this conception that shapes the *Violin Concerto* of Sessions (1935). The brilliant orchestration gives the accompaniment a vivacity all its own, but this is never allowed to overshadow the violin, which carries the brunt of the thematic material.

To assure the primacy of the solo instrument Sessions excluded violins from the orchestral score; the string section consists of violas, cellos, and double basses. These are teamed with a fairly large complement of winds—three flutes, one oboe, four clarinets, three bassoons, four horns, and two each of trumpets and trombones. The concerto combines Neoclassic elements with a powerful Expressionism. It is a strongly tonal work despite the free use of chromatic harmonies. The singing nature of the violin impelled Sessions to spin out sweeping lines of melody. Pronounced unplayable at first, the piece gradually established itself as one of the most significant concertos of our time.

I. *Largo e tranquillo, con grande espressione*. B minor, 3/4. The movement opens with two motives, divided between trombone and trumpets, that play a seminal part throughout. Motive *A* consists of five steps along the B-minor scale, rising from tonic to dominant, while motive *B* twists and turns over a wider range along dissonant intervals—augmented fourth, major seventh, and diminished octave:

With the entrance of the solo instrument Sessions combines both motives. The violin traces a songful line derived from motive *B* while the violas in the accompaniment recall the scalewise motion of *A*, moving upward and then down:

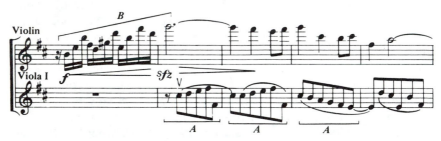

The movement illustrates his method of building continuity. An idea comes to the fore, is given profile and direction so that the listener's attention is focused on it, then submerges into the overall flow, to be replaced by a new idea or the original idea in a new version. The following example sounds for a moment like a second theme intended as a foil for the first, since it is notably more serene. On closer inspection it turns out to be based on an inversion, in longer notes, of motive *A* followed by elements derived from *B:*

A gradual heightening of tension in harmony, texture, and rhythm builds up to the climactic point of the movement, which is reached when the violin plays a series of repeated major sixths fortissimo over sustained harmonies in the orchestra. An elaborate cadenza on the violin, with plenty of double stops, leads to a quiet ending.

II. *Allegro*, A major, 2/4. The second movement is an A-B-A form whose opening section combines the rhythmic energy of the Classical scherzo with the spirit of the *fantastique* that Berlioz and Liszt imparted to its Romantic successor. In the opening two measures motive *A* is transformed into an upward-leaping figure while *B*, extended, retains the twists and turns along with the interval relationships of its original version:

Colored by the somewhat mischievous sound that woodwinds assume when they play rapid staccato notes in high register, the movement rushes forward with great rhythmic élan, powered by nimble figuration in both solo part and accompaniment. Brief forays into foreign keys help sustain the harmonic tension. The violin part calls for supreme virtuosity, of the kind in which technical display is never an end in itself but always serves the musical expression.

The middle section in G major, marked *Più tranquillo*, is an area of relaxation. An oboe presents the two basic motives in a new context:

This section is a fine example of Sessions's singing counterpoint, which draws inspiration from the polyphonic art of the sixteenth century, with its gently undulating lines, rather than from the more profiled counterpoint of the age of Bach. Here the meaning lies in the sum total of all the parts rather than in any single one of them. When the first section returns to round out the form, Sessions is not content to repeat the material but varies it freely in regard to melody, harmony, rhythm, texture, and orchestration. What he retains is the fantastic character of the opening section, and the virtuosity.

III. *Romanza.* The third movement unwinds in the relaxed flow characteristic of six beats to a measure in slow tempo. Embedded in the melody line are the two basic motives, but so transformed as to be barely recognizable:

Here, as elsewhere in the Concerto, Sessions allows both motives to permeate the texture not so much through direct quotations as in more subtle ways, so that they direct the musical flow even when scarcely retaining their original shape. Soon after, they approximate more closely their original form:

The violin part is kept well above the orchestral background; it is an impassioned voice soaring ever higher. This melodious *Andante,* which illustrates Sessions's capacity for singing lines that unfold in a broad arc, descends from the great slow movements of the Classic-Romantic period. But it lifts their outpouring of sentiment into a twentieth-century frame, allying the expression of feeling with profundity of thought. Noteworthy is the tranquil ascent to the emotional high point of the movement, a sustained F-sharp in the upper register, from which the violin line falls away in a flowery cadenza-like passage that leads directly into the finale.

IV. *Molto vivace e sempre con fuoco* (Very lively and always with fire). The cadenza settles down to the driving rhythm of a tarantella (that fast and furious Neapolitan dance in rapid 6/8 that took its name from Taranto in South Italy, or—according to legend—from the spider *tarantula* whose poisonous bite the dance was believed to cure). The soloist is given every opportunity to display his prowess in double stops, trills and leaps, staccato and pizzicato, various types of bowing, and intricate figuration that hurtles across the entire range of the instrument. Momentum never flags, with the main theme propelled by syncopated rhythm and a succesion of bold upward leaps:

The music is touched by the spirit of grotesquerie we associate with such twentieth-century masters as Mahler and Prokofiev. Six-eight time is punctuated by occasional shifts to nine-eight, imparting flexibility and caprice to the forward flow. Brief areas of relaxation slacken the tension, only to heighten it when the original tempo is restored. The most important of these is an excursion into triple meter in which the music takes on the charm of a waltz. The bold upward leaps, filled in by glissandos, become coquettish:

These changes in tempo and mood are underlined by frequent changes of key, with a very free approach to tonality throughout. The concerto ends, as it began, in B minor.

This music, both subtle and strong, shows the rather special cast of Roger Sessions's mind. It underlines his position as one of the most distinguished representatives of the modern American school.

55 Other Composers between the Wars

Douglas Moore

"The particular ideal which I have been striving to attain is to write music which will not be self-conscious with regard to idiom, and will reflect the exciting quality of life, traditions, and country which I feel all about me."

Douglas Moore (Cutchogue, Long Island, 1893–1969, Greenport, Long Island), had to shake off the French influence before he could find his true bent. This he was able to do only by going back to his roots. "I cannot believe," he wrote in the Twenties, "that the fashions decreed by such elegant couturiers as the Parisian Stravinsky or Ravel, successful as they are in permitting a post-war Europe to express herself in music, are likely to be appropriate or becoming for us."

Moore was a romantic at heart. He regarded romanticism as a characteristic American trait. "We are incorrigibly sentimental as a race, and our realism in the drama and literature usually turns out to be meltingly romantic in execution. The best of what we accomplish is usually achieved by dint of high spirits, soft-heartedness, and a great deal of superfluous energy." Moore favored American themes in both his instrumental and vocal works. Of his six operas, two caught on in a big way. *The Devil and Daniel Webster* (1938) has a fine libretto by Stephen Vincent Benet, based on his celebrated short story. This exuberant one-acter, which shows Daniel Webster matching his wits and eloquence against the Devil's, soon established itself as an American classic.

Equally successful was *The Ballad of Baby Doe* (1956), based on an American legend that really happened: the rise and fall of Horace Tabor, who struck silver in Leadville, Colorado, became one of the wealthiest men of his time, and was ruined when the United States abandoned the silver standard for gold. The action unfolds in a tur-

A scene from Act II of the 1958 production of The Ballad of Baby Doe. *Beverly Sills (center) created the title role with the New York City Opera.*

bulent period of American history against the background of a Colorado mining town. The eternal triangle involves Horace; Augusta, his domineering and straitlaced wife, who accompanied him from his humble beginnings to wealth and power; and Baby Doe, as she was known among the miners—a twenty-year-old beauty with an uncertain past, for whose sake the middle-aged magnate divorced Augusta. John La Touche provided a dramatically compelling libretto. The story line is one that has been infallible in the drama ever since the Greeks—the destruction of the hero through the fatal flaw he carries within him. In the final scene of the opera we see Tabor as a crushed old man, and Baby Doe keeping her promise to him to guard the Matchless Mine. (The real Baby Doe guarded the mine, a solitary eccentric wearing castoff men's clothing, with gunnysacks wrapped around her feet, until she was found frozen to death on the floor of her shack in March, 1935.)

The Devil and Daniel Webster and *Baby Doe* came at a time when our lyric theater did not have many viable works. American opera goers have every reason to remember Douglas Moore with gratitude.

Walter Piston

"Is the Dust Bowl more American, than, say, a corner in the Boston Athenaeum?"

Walter Piston (Rockland, Maine, 1894–1976, Boston) represented the international point of view in our music. His Neoclassic aesthetic transcended the local and reached out toward universal values of craftsmanship and formal beauty.

Piston was an academic composer in the same sense that Brahms was. Like the German master he tried to hold on to the great Classical forms of absolute music—symphony, concerto, sonata, string quartet—at a time when other composers were turning away from them. Like Brahms too, he felt that the traditional forms could be revived by fresh content and a highly personal approach. Thus, his was the Classical aim of conveying purely musical thoughts within beautifully rounded forms.

Such an attitude precluded programmatic or descriptive intent. It also precluded a nationalistic style based on literary or anecdotal elements. He argued forcefully for the international point of view: "If a composer desires to serve the cause of American music he will best do it by remaining true to himself as an individual and not by trying

Walter Piston.

to discover musical formulas for Americanism." And to the same point: "If the composers will increasingly strive to perfect themselves in the art of music and will follow only those paths of expression which seem to take them the true way, the matter of a national school will take care of itself. The composer cannot afford the wild-goose chase of trying to be more American than he is." Piston accordingly advocated the broadest possible interpretation of what is American. "The plain fact," he observed, "is that American music is music written by Americans."

This is not to say that Piston's music bears no relationship to his environment. He assimilated elements of the American popular idiom, especially of the jazz that figured so prominently in his youthful experiences as a musician. But he subjected these elements to a process of stylization, so that they became organic parts of a total expression whose chief goal lay elsewhere. Piston spoke the international language of Neoclassicism, which was understood with equal readiness in Paris, London, Berlin, or New York. His style was admired no less for the distinction of its ideas than for the perfection of its workmanship. His art was based on linear counterpoint. Although he adhered to the principle of tonality, Piston was intrigued by certain aspects of Schoenbergian thinking. He favored the intricate devices of fugal and canonic writing which to many contemporary musicians represent the ultimate refinement of thought. His was the consolidating type of mind that assimilates the most significant trends in the art of an epoch, welds them into a personal language, and sets upon them the seal of stylistic unity.

Piston's list includes eight symphonies (1937–1968), three string quartets, the *Violin Concerto* of 1939, and a *Quintet* for piano and strings (1949). Among the later works we should mention the *Variations for Cello and Orchestra* (1966), the *Clarinet Concerto* of 1967, and the *Flute Concerto* of 1971. In 1938 he wrote a ballet called *The Incredible Flutist,* from which he extracted a tuneful orchestral suite that became his most popular work.

The *Second Symphony* (completed 1943) shows the composer at his best. The first movement is a broadly designed *Moderato* in 6/4. There is something Brahmsian about the way the opening theme floats up out of the lower register in the dark resonance of violas and cellos:

The slow movement, an *Adagio* in 8/8, displays a full-throated lyricism that grows quietly out of a kernel of melody introduced by the bassoon. Third is an *Allegro* in *alla breve* (cut time: four-four counted rapidly as two). This movement combines the light-hearted spirit and forward drive of the classical scherzo with the ample dimensions of a symphonic finale.

Young musicians today find Piston's art irrelevant to their concerns. Given the ebb and flow of popular taste, this eclipse may well prove to be temporary. Piston's works are elegant, mature, architecturally clear, and self-contained. It is inconceivable that the best of them will not find a permanent place in our concert life.

Virgil Thomson

"I wrote in Paris music that was always, in one way or another, about Kansas City. I wanted Paris to know Kansas City, to understand the ways we like to think and feel on the banks of the Kaw and the Missouri."

Virgil Thomson (Kansas City, 1896–) belongs to that group of American artists who found themselves through their contact with

Virgil   Thomson.   A photograph   taken   in 1949 by Maurice Grosser.

French civilization. Paris revealed to them the fine reserve of the Gallic spirit, its worship of clear and lucid expression, its impeccable taste and urbane wit. Residence abroad served to make them more aware of their native inheritance. At the same time it purged them of all remnants of provincialism and forced them to measure themselves against the craftsmanship and esprit of a great tradition.

Thomson in his early writing followed the Neoclassic style that prevailed in Paris during the Twenties. His *Sonata da chiesa* for five instruments (1926) marks the high point of his attempts in this direction. After a time, however, dissonant counterpoint and the striving for intellectual detachment became less and less congenial to a temperament that was essentially warm and lyrical. He found his true path through contact with Erik Satie and *Les Six.* Indeed, he became the link between Satie's aesthetic and the contemporary American school, preaching a return to a simple idiom that would be free alike from the grandiloquent rhetoric of the Postromantic era and from what he has called "our own century's rigidly modernist neo-classicism." Like Satie, Thomson sought a musical language that would be elegant, precise, and not above spoofing itself. Music had been taking itself too seriously, he maintained. Now it must learn to relax. Behind this attitude was Thomson's conviction that modern music had become too complex, too intellectual. He became one of the most articulate proponents of the new romanticism, and sought to recapture the lyric tradition in twentieth-century terms. "The new romanticism," he asserted, "strives neither to unify mass audiences nor to impress the specialists of intellectual objectivity. Its guiding motive is the wish to express sincere personal sentiments with a maximum of directness and of spontaneity. It tends consequently to avoid impersonal oratory; and it is wary about the conventionalistic tendencies bound up with consistent and obligatory dissonance."

In Paris he met Gertrude Stein. Their friendship led to an important decision: an opera. This was *Four Saints in Three Acts* (1928), with a cryptic libretto worthy of the "Mother Goose of Montparnasse." The work reached New York in 1934 and catapulted Thomson to fame. The collaboration with Miss Stein produced a second opera, *The Mother of Us All* (1947), dealing with the life and career of the feminist leader Susan B. Anthony. An odd assortment of characters from different periods of American history are fancifully juxtaposed in various scenes. General Grant, expressing himself in excellent Steinese, declares bravely, "As long as I sit I am sitting." Miss Anthony sings persuasively, "You're entirely right but I disagree with you," and is informed that "a Cause is a Cause because." *The Mother of Us All* is a vivid bit of Americana that proved to possess ample vitality when it was revived in New York in 1959 and at the Santa Fé Opera in 1976. The collaboration with Miss Stein came to an end with her death. One wonders what their next would have been like.

Thomson pioneered too in another important genre—film music. American film makers were notably behind their European confreres when it came to film music. European directors were accustomed to commission scores from the top composers of their country—Milhaud, Honegger, Hindemith, Walton, Prokofiev, Shostakovitch. Hollywood, on the other hand, developed a breed of craftsmen who supplied a neutral kind of music that "warmed" the screen without attracting undue attention to itself—that is, without distracting the audience from the action. What resulted was a series of scores sumptuously orchestrated in the manner of Ravel or Richard Strauss but, except for the inevitable "love theme," without any particular musical profile. Thomson's scores for Pare Lorentz's documentary about soil erosion, *The Plow that Broke the Plains* (1936), and, a year later, for Lorentz's *The River*, set a new standard for film music in this country and paved the way for such distinguished scores as Copland's *Of Mice and Men* and *The Red Pony*, as well as Thomson's for

Robert Flaherty's memorable film about oil prospecting, *Louisiana Story* (1948). Like Copland, Thomson extracted concert suites from his film scores so that the music would live on in the concert hall after the film had disappeared. Listen to one of these or to the complete recording of *The Mother of Us All* for a fine introduction to the art of this profoundly American romantic.

Howard Hanson

"I recognize of course that romanticism is at the present time the poor stepchild without the social standing of her elder sister, neoclassicism. Nevertheless I embrace her all the more fervently, believing as I do that romanticism will find in this country rich soil for a new, young, and vigorous growth."

The achievement of Howard Hanson (Wahoo, Nebraska, 1896–) extends beyond his activities as a composer. It may be safely said that in the second quarter of the twentieth century no individual in the United States did more for the cause of American music than he.

As director of the Eastman School of Music and teacher of composition, Hanson influenced a generation of young American musicians. But this, he knew, was not enough. A public had to be created for American music. In 1925 he inaugurated the American Composers' Orchestra Concerts, under the auspices of the Eastman School. These were supplemented by annual festivals of American music given by Hanson with the Eastman-Rochester Symphony Orchestra, at which some of the most important works of the past quarter century received their first performance.

In his own music Hanson is traditional and eclectic. He has cultivated the symphonic poem as perfected by Liszt and the "poematic" symphony as practiced by Franck and Sibelius. Of his six symphonies the most important are the *First*, the *Nordic* (1922), and the *Second*, the *Romantic* (1930). His aim in the *Romantic Symphony*, he wrote, was to create a work "young in spirit, romantic in temperament, and simple and direct in expression." The composition, in three movements, opens with a motto theme of Franckian vintage that recurs in various guises. The music abounds in sweet violin tone in high register, proclamatory trumpets and horns, and shattering climaxes. In an age opposed to sentiment and rhetoric, this Symphony is unashamedly sentimental and rhetorical. Hanson's symphonic poems include *Lux aeterna* (1923) and *Pan and the Priest* (1926). We should mention too his chief choral work, *The Lament for*

Beowulf (1925), and his opera *Merry Mount* (1934). In addition to a varied list of orchestral and choral works, Hanson produced a substantial amount of chamber, piano, and organ music, and songs.

Hanson's works spoke persuasively to a generation of music lovers brought up on Franck, Brahms, and Sibelius, assuring them that twentieth-century music had something to say that they could understand. This needed doing in the Twenties and Thirties, and Hanson filled the need. No less important was his championing of our native composers at a time when they needed someone to plead their cause.

Roy Harris

"I am trying to write a music which expresses our time and period in America, and which is serviceable to our musical life. What I am trying to say in music is related principally to the region of the West where I was born and where I understand life best."

Roy Harris (Lincoln County, Oklahoma, 1898–) came out of the West almost as if he had been sent to answer the need for an American composer. He exploded on our scene as a kind of Carl Sandburg in music, a homespun and outspoken young man who boldly upheld his heritage. With his spare frame, soft drawl, and inexhaustible energy, looking "like a mid-Western farmer in city clothes," Harris captured the imagination of his countrymen as no twentieth-century composer had done. During the Thirties he was the most frequently performed and most widely admired of contemporary American musicians. Then his star went into an eclipse from which it never emerged. By the time the mid-century arrived, Harris—who only fifteen years before had been hailed as the white hope of American music—was outside the maintream of significant advance. All the same, in his freshest and most meaningful work he made a genuine contribution to our music.

The American quality in his work goes deeper than the quotation of popular material—whether cowboy ditty, Civil War song, or hymn tune—that often serves him as a point of departure. His music is American in its buoyancy and momentum, its expansiveness and manly strength. He has identified himself so closely with the American dream that he expresses its temper best when he is most himself. "One would think, to read his prefaces," quipped Virgil Thomson, "that he had been awarded by God, or at least by popular vote, a monopolistic privilege of expressing our nation's deepest ideals and highest aspirations.''

Harris's epic-dramatic gift is at its best in the large forms of abstract instrumental music. Fourteen symphonies, extending over four decades of creative activity, form the core of his output. The *Third*, his most frequently performed work (1938), is in one movement made up of contrasting sections. The composer's description indicates the emotional content of the piece. ''Section I: *Tragic*—low string sonorities. Section II: *Lyric*—strings, horns, woodwinds. Section III: *Pastoral*—emphasizing woodwind color. Section IV: *Fugue*—dramatic. *A.* Brass, percussion predominating. *B.* Canonic development of Section II material, constituting background for further development of fugue. *C.* Brass climax. Rhythmic motif derived from fugue subject. Section V: *Dramatic-Tragic*. Restatement of violin theme of Section I.''

The opening motive expands into a long-breathed line of the cello that accords with Harris's goal of a self-generating melody. The even

quarter-note movement is spaced at the end of the phrase by a longer note or a rest—a rhythm derived, of course, from the imagery of the congregational hymn. (This is one of several American symphonies—Ives's *Third*, Copland's *Third*, and Virgil Thomson's *Symphony on a Hymn Tune* are other examples—whose opening theme is derived from our heritage of psalmody.) The full orchestra then presents a kind of chorale. In the section identified by Harris as lyric, his songful counterpoint asserts itself in the fluent, overlapping lines and in his antiphonal treatment of strings and winds. The pastoral section evokes the ''nature sound'' of the Romantic era in a twentieth-century environment. The warbling of the strings and the mounting animation of the brass conjure up a lovely landscape.

The fugue subject is a commanding idea, with a sharp melodic profile and rhythmic urgency:

The elaborate fugal development builds up into what Harris calls the ''brass climax.'' The restatement of the choralelike theme broadens into a spacious coda based upon the steady beat of the drum. Although Harris thinks of the mood as "dramatic-tragic," this processional strikes the epic tone, and justifies those of Harris's admirers who find in his *Third Symphony* echoes of "the dark fastness of the American soul, of its despair and its courage, its defeat and its triumph."

Roy Harris was a vital force in our musical coming of age. His *Third* is still one of the finest symphonies yet produced by an American.

Randall Thompson

"A composer's first responsibility is, and always will be, to write music that will reach and move the hearts of his listeners in his own day."

Randall Thompson (New York, 1899–) is a moderate by nature and conviction. It has been his goal to create an art grounded in the needs of the American scene, expressing "our own genuine musical heritage in its every manifestation, every inflection, every living example."

Thompson owes his popularity to a variety of qualities, chief among which is his ability to use melodic materials rooted in the inflections and rhythms of American popular song. His most successful orchestral piece, the *Second Symphony* (1931), with its jazzy rhythms, the blues of the slow movement, and the spacious melody of the finale, exemplify the essentially American quality of his music.

Thompson's flair for choral writing is manifest in his smooth counterpoint, broad overall effects, and exemplary setting of English text. His choral pieces are enlivened by flashes of humor and whimsy. Among his most impressive achievements in this medium is *The Testament of Freedom*, for chorus and orchestra. Written in 1943 to commemorate the two-hundredth anniversary of the birth of Thomas Jefferson, the piece was based on four excerpts from Jefferson's writings that were relevant to the critical time our nation was passing through. The opening *Largo* is set to "The God who gave us life gave us liberty at the same time; the hand of force may destroy but cannot disjoin them." Thompson's strong diatonic harmonies are eminently suited to the emotional content of the words. The text of the final movement, a *Lento tranquillo*, is drawn from one of Jefferson's letters to Adams, written almost half a century after the great revolutionary period of their youth. "I shall not die without a hope

that life and liberty are on steady advance. . . ." This pronouncement of ripe old age impels Thompson to a flowing canon that is
maintained for the greater part of the piece. The climax is built on a
reprise of the opening text, which at the end eloquently identifies
liberty with life. It is all very grand, and very American.

Others

Among the Americanists of the older generation we should mention Arthur Farwell (St. Paul, Minnesota, 1872–1952, New York City),
who used Indian melodies in a number of his works; John Powell
(Richmond, Virginia, 1882–1963, Charlottesville), who achieved a
success with his *Rapsodie Nègre;* and Louis Gruenberg (Brest-Litovsk, Russia, 1884–1964, Beverly Hills, California). Gruenberg,
whose parents immigrated to this country when he was a child, is
best known for his opera *Emperor Jones,* based on the play by Eugene
O'Neill. The work made quite a stir when it was presented at the
Metropolitan Opera House in 1933.

Frederick Jacobi (San Francisco, 1891–1953, New York City) produced a number of works in which the Hebraic influence was paramount. Most important of these is the *Sabbath Evening Service* of
1952. Certain of his compositions were inspired by the songs and ritual dances of the Pueblo Indians of New Mexico and Arizona: the
String Quartet on Indian Themes (1924) and *Indian Dances* for orchestra
(1928). Jacobi for many years taught composition at the Juilliard
School.

Richard Donovan (New Haven, Connecticut, 1891–1970, Middletown, Connecticut) was professor of music theory at Yale University.
Characteristic of his precise, pithy style are the *Symphony for
Chamber Orchestra* (1936); *Design for Radio,* for orchestra (1945); and
the lively *Suite for String Orchestra and Oboe* (1955).

Bernard Rogers (New York City, 1893–1968, Rochester) was head
of the composition department of the Eastman School of Music, in
which post he influenced many of our younger composers. His four
symphonies follow the ideal of intense, personal expression. Rogers
also wrote a variety of shorter pieces of a programmatic nature. His
most important work is *The Passion,* for solo voices, mixed chorus,
and organ (1942), an impressive, deeply felt version of the last hours
and death of Christ.

Leo Sowerby (Grand Rapids, Michigan, 1895–Port Clinton, Ohio,
1968) was the first American composer to hold the Prix de Rome. His

best-known works are *Prairie* (1929), an Impressionistic orchestral piece inspired by Carl Sandburg's poem; and *Canticle of the Sun,* for chorus and orchestra (1945), which won him a Pultizer Prize.

William Grant Still (Woodville, Mississippi, 1895–) is the dean of our black composers. A dedicated proponent of Negro nationalism, he based his music on the folk songs of his people, expressing their sorrows and aspirations. This goal is fully realized in such works as the *Afro-American Symphony* (1931); the cantata *And They Lynched Him on a Tree* (1940); and *In Memoriam: The Colored Soldiers Who Died for Democracy* (1943).

Leroy Robertson (Fountain Green, Utah, 1896–1971, Salt Lake City, Utah), widely known as "the Mormon composer," was for many years head of the music department at the University of Utah. His works include the *String Quartet* of 1940, *Rhapsody* for piano and orchestra (1944), and the symphonic piece *Trilogy* (1947).

Quincy Porter (New Haven, Connecticut, 1897–1966, Bethany, Connecticut) was a string quartet performer on the viola all his life. Hence his special affinity for chamber music. His ten string quarters (1923–1965) represent four decades of steady growth toward the Neo-classic ideal of impeccable craftsmanship, clarity, and beauty of form. Mention should be made too of his *Viola Concerto* (1948), with its meditative first movement and whimsical second, an important addition to the recent literature for that instrument; and the *Concerto concertante* for two pianos and orchestra, which won him a Pultizer Prize in 1954.

Ernst Bacon (Chicago, 1898–) describes himself as "an ardent believer in indigenous American music." He is a regionalist with a keen ear for musical dialect and an affinity for the Anglo-Celtic heritage manifest in our southern mountain tunes. His songs, of which he has written more than two hundred, show his sensitivity to the inflections of American speech. His works include two symphonies (1932, 1937); two orchestral suites—*Ford's Theater* (1943) and *From These States* (1943); two operas in folk style—*A Tree on the Plains* (1942) and *A Drumlin Legend* (1949); and *The Last Invocation,* a Requiem for chorus and orchestra on poems by Whitman and Emily Dickinson (1968–1971).

In an age that too often identifies quality with size, Theodore Chanler (Newport, Rhode Island, 1902–1961, Boston) made a special place for himself as a master of the miniature. He adapted the art song to twentieth-century needs, making of it a sophisticated epigrammatic form in which technical adroitness accompanied carefully wrought detail. Typical of his style are the settings of the verses of

Walter de la Mare, such as the *Eight Epitaphs* (1937), *Three Epitaphs* (1940), and *Four Rhymes from Peacock Pie* (1940). His music is marked by pungent harmony and an abundance of dissonant tension. His affinity for the large instrumental forms is manifest in a variety of works, among them the *Concerto for Violin and Orchestra* (1941), *Variations and Epilogue* for cello and piano (1946), and the *Concerto for Two Pianos* (1950). Chanler taught at the Longy School of Music in Cambridge, Massachusetts.

Vittorio Giannini (Philadelphia, 1903–1966, New York City) inherited the tradition of Verdi and Puccini, to which he added an admixture of the rhythmic vigor and sumptuous orchestral panoply of Richard Strauss. *The Scarlet Letter* (1938), after Hawthorne's masterpiece, suffered from the combining of American story material with an essentially European style. In *The Taming of the Shrew* (1953), on the other hand, Giannini found a capital vehicle for his gifts. Shakespeare's lusty tale, with its picturesque Italian setting, lent itself to a delightful opera buffa, and the composer adroitly utilized all the possibilities offered by the plot. Equally successful was *The Servant of Two Masters*, after Goldoni's comedy (1967). Giannini tried his hand at orchestral, choral, and chamber music; but his natural habitat unquestionably was the opera house.

The four decades of American music that we have traced in these chapters formed a crucial period in American music. When it began, our composers were a tiny group concentrated along the Eastern seaboard, most of whom still looked to Leipzig and Munich for guidance. Uncertain of themselves and their future, they wrote for a public that was only too ready to ignore them. When it ended, the American school—its members active throughout the land—consisted of a varied group of thoroughly schooled musicians who had discovered their language and whose scores technically were on a par with anything produced abroad. Into the works of the modern American school were woven the chief tendencies of our time—Nationalism, Neoclassicism, Neoromanticism, Impressionism, Expressionism, expanded tonality, polytonality, atonality, twelve-tone method. And binding all these together was an indefinable quality, a product-of-America flavor that, ranging in mood from mystic exaltation to exuberant vitality, was as subtle as it was irresistible.

56 Latin America

"A truly creative musician is capable of producing, from his own imagination, melodies that are more authentic than folklore itself."

HEITOR VILLA-LOBOS

The twenty republics of South and Central America boast a flourishing musical life. Their governments adhere to the European notion that art should be fostered by the state. Each of them has a ministry of fine arts or a music section within the ministry of education that supports conservatories, grants subsidies to orchestras and radio stations, organizes music festivals, and encourages native composers with prizes, fellowships, and performances.

In eighteen of the twenty republics the language and culture are Spanish: Argentina, Bolivia, Chile, Colombia, Costa Rica, Cuba, Dominican Republic, Ecuador, Guatemala, Honduras, Mexico, Nicaragua, Panama, Paraguay, Peru, El Salvador, Uruguay, and Venezuela. In Brazil the language is Portuguese; in Haiti it is French. The European influence in all these countries has been superimposed upon native Indian and Negro elements. Thus, Latin American civilization amalgamates the racial and cultural strains of three conti-

421

nents: Europe, South America, and Africa. The mixture of the elements varies according to the population of each republic. The Indian influence is strong in Mexico, Peru, Bolivia, Ecuador, and Central America. The Negro element, more pronounced in the West Indies, makes itself felt in the Latin-African character of Haiti's art, as well as in Afro-Cuban melodies and rhythms. The music of Brazil, on the other hand, is an admixture of all three strains. This fascinating diversity is being consolidated in each of the countries with the emergence of native schools of music with a strongly nationalist point of view.

Heitor Villa-Lobos

"I compose in the folk style. I utilize the themes and idioms in my own way and subject to my own development. An artist must do this. He must select and transmit the material given him by his people."

Heitor Villa-Lobos (Rio de Janeiro, 1887–1959, Rio de Janeiro), the foremost composer of Latin America, was a figure of international reputation. He left his imprint on every facet of Brazilian music and in the process added a number of picturesque works to the twentieth-century repertory.

Villa-Lobos's lyricism favored improvisational forms rather than the carefully planned architectonics of the symphony. He did some of his best writing in the chôros, which was his original contribution to twentieth-century music. The chôros, as Villa-Lobos defined it, "represents a new form of musical composition in which a synthesis is made of different types of Brazilian music, Indian and popular, reflecting in its fundamental elements the rhythm and characteristic melodies of the people." His fourteen essays in this form are for various combinations of instruments. The first (1920) is for guitar, the second (1921) for flute and clarinet, the third (1925) for male chorus and seven wind instruments. The later chôros employ larger forces. Villa-Lobos was much preoccupied with what he called *sincretismo*—the fusion of native with outside influences. In his *Bachianas brasileiras* he created a form intended to forge a link between the art of his homeland and the Western tradition. There is very little true counterpoint in these nine suites that were written "in homage to the great genius of J. S. Bach." But their easy tunefulness has recommended them to a wide public.

The fifth of the *Bachianas brasileiras,* for soprano and eight cellos,

Heitor Villa-Lobos.

is the most popular of the series. It consists of two parts—*Aria* (1938) and *Dansa* (1945). In Brazilian usage, Villa-Lobos explained, an aria "is a kind of lyric song." This aria, subtitled Cantilena, is marked *Adagio*. The pizzicato of the cellos suggests the guitar sound, thereby evoking the atmosphere of the serenade so frequently met with in Latin American music. Over a string background there unfolds one of those self-generating melodies for which the model was provided for all time by the famous Air from the *Suite No. 3* of Bach. The vocal

line recaptures the flowing cantilena of the Baroque. Yet this "return to Bach" has nothing in common with Stravinskyan Neoclassicism, for it derives almost wholly from an orientation based upon nine-teenth-century Romanticism.

The *Dansa* is an *Allegretto* in 2/4 whose powerful accents are suggested in the subtitle *Martelo* (hammered). This movement, Villa-Lobos wrote, "represents a persistent and characteristic rhythm much like the *emboladas*, those strange melodies of the Brazilian hinterland. The melody suggests the birds of Brazil." The text, by the Brazilian poet Manuel Bandeira, apostrophizes the lovebird of the forest, Irere. As often happens with Villa-Lobos, the ecstatic mood is projected in an atmosphere of unbridled Primitivism. Music such as this bespeaks a national poet for whom art was synonymous with the expression of spontaneous emotion.

Villa-Lobos's music possesses both the virtues and the faults of a young culture. His collected works, whenever that project is put through by a grateful nation, will cover a wall in the library at Rio de Janeiro. Out of that mass of notes enough should survive to keep his memory green.

Carlos Chávez

"We have had to work for fifteen years in Mexico to free outselves from the stuffy conservatory tradition, the worst kind of academic stagnation. We have found ourselves by going back to the cultural traditions of the Indian racial stock that still accounts for four-fifths of the people of Mexico."

Carlos Chávez (Mexico City, 1899–1978, Mexico City) played the same decisive role in the musical life of Mexico as Villa-Lobos did in that of Brazil. Profoundly affected by the social upheaval about him, Chávez—along with his friend Diego Rivera—became a leading figure among the dedicated band of musicians, painters, and poets who captured the spirit of the revolution in their work. They directed Mexican art away from a pallid imitation of foreign models to a vigorous Nationalism rooted in the native soil.

Chávez's journeys to the outlying mountain regions of his homeland revealed to him the power and richness of Mexico's folk music. In those formative years he assimilated both Indian and *mestizo* (Spanish-Indian) elements into his art. As a result he succeeded in creating music which, as Aaron Copland expressed it, "caught the spirit of Mexico—its native, stolid, *mestizo* soul." His works, as Copland aptly describes them "are stoic, stark, and sombre like an Orozco drawing." Chávez adheres to the Neoclassic point of view. His writing is lean, virile, hard, like the tribal tunes from which he drew inspiration. In this connection one may quote the composer's perceptive remark: " 'Primitive' music is really not so primitive. It is ancient and therefore sophisticated."

Chávez's best-known work, *Sinfonía India* (1936) was composed during one of his visits to New York. The work, in one movement,

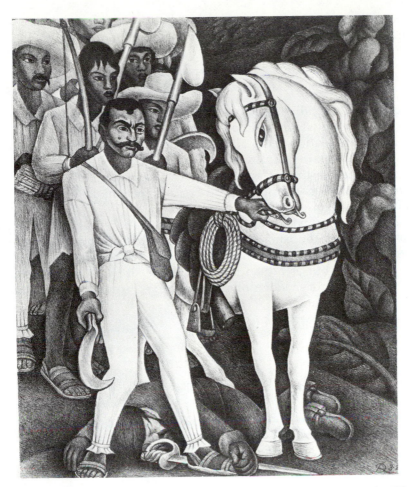

The vivid Nationalism and revolutionary spirit reflected in this fresco by Diego Rivera (1886–1957) has its musical counterpart in the works of Chávez. Agrarian Leader Zapata, 1931. Collection The Museum of Modern Art, New York.

adapts the Classical sonata form to the requirements of the indigenous material on which it is based. The opening section, marked *Vivo*, is in 5/8 time with brief excursions to 2/4 and 3/4. After a short introduction, oboes and violins present a strongly rhythmic melody of the Huichole Indians of Nayarit:

The idea is expanded with vigor. Then, in an *Allegretto cantabile,* the clarinet sings a melody of the Yaqui Indians of Sonora:

Another Sonora Indian melody forms the basis of the *Adagio* section. It is presented by flutes and horn, whence it passes to the strings.

The recapitulation of the *Allegro* themes follows in the usual manner. The finale introduces a dance theme of the Seri Indians in 6/8 time, with interesting cross rhythms. The melody unfolds against a *perpetuum mobile* background, in an exciting coda marked by steadily mounting tension.

This music is wiry and lithe. Its quality has been admirably summed up by the composer's friend Aaron Copland: "Chávez's music is extraordinarily healthy. It is music created not as a substitute for living but as a manifestation of life. It is clear and clean-sounding, without shadows or softness. Here is contemporary music if there ever was any."

Others

Francisco Mignone, one of Brazil's most distinguished composers, was born in São Paulo in 1897. Most of his major works are on Brazilian subjects, such as the opera *O Contractador dos diamantes* (The Diamond Merchant, 1924); the *Fantasias brasileiras* for piano and orchestra, of which he wrote four (1931–1937); *Suite brasileira* for orchestra (1933); and the ballet *Quadros amazonicos* (Amazonian Pictures, 1949).

Camargo Guarnieri was born in Tiété in the State of São Paulo in 1907, and received his training first at the Conservatory of São Paulo then in France. Guarnieri is a prolific composer. Among his works are two piano concertos; the *Symphony No. 1,* which was given its premiere by the Boston Symphony Orchestra in 1946, the composer conducting; the orchestral suite *Brasiliana* (1951); and *Chôros* for piano and orchestra.

The gifted Mexican composer Silvestre Revueltas was born in Santiago Papasquiaro on the last day of 1899 and died in Mexico City on October 5, 1940. It was Chávez who encouraged him to devote himself seriously to composition. In 1937 Revueltas went to Spain, where he worked in the music section of the Loyalist government.

After his return to Mexico he continued his career as composer and conductor. His health undermined by years of poverty, heavy drinking, and an irregular life, he succumbed to pneumonia in his forty-first year.

Revueltas's warmly romantic temperament found its best expression in short, flexible forms. His melodic imagery is steeped in Mexican folklore, although he never quoted existing melodies. As he himself said, "Why should I put on boots and climb mountains for Mexican folklore if I have the spirit of Mexico deep within me?" The power of his music derives from compact melodic ideas of an almost primitive directness, which are woven into a vibrant texture of dissonant counterpoint and free polyrhythms. Among his orchestral works are *Cuauhnahuac*—this is the Indian name for Cuernavaca—(1932); *Esquinas* (Corners, 1930); *Ventanas* (Windows, 1931); *Caminos* (Roads, 1934); and *Planos* (Planes, 1934). Revueltas also wrote chamber music, songs, and several film scores. His premature death robbed Mexican music of one of its finest talents.

PART FIVE

The Second Revolution

"Composing music once meant to me writing the music I like. Now it means to me writing out of a deep concern for new music and for the cause of new music."

LUKAS FOSS

57 After World War II

"It may well be—I take it upon myself to predict it—that the apotheosis of the machine age will demand a subtler tool than the tempered scale, capable of setting down arrangements of sounds hitherto neglected or unheard. . . ."

LE CORBUSIER

The Postwar Scene

When the lights went on again at the end of the Second World War, they illumined a different world. The musical scene was as radically changed as were its social-political surroundings.

The first musical revolution of our century, which had taken wing some thirty years earlier, had run its course. Its implications had been broadly explored in the years between the wars; its protagonists were now older men. A new revolution—or should one call it evolution?—was in the making. Like the first, it had its roots in the past even as its gaze was on the future. A new generation, with new interests and a new outlook, gradually came into prominence.

In Europe, musical life had been severely disrupted by the war. In

431

many cities, bombs had destroyed the opera houses and concert halls, so the first step was that of rebuilding, while performers and composers started to work in makeshift quarters. In London, Vienna, Berlin, Hamburg, Milan, and other cities that had borne the brunt of the air raids, new auditoriums arose, with modern equipment, sometimes built into precise replicas of historic buildings, sometimes into striking examples of modern architecture and design. This process took many years and was eventually matched by a spate of new theaters and arts centers in parts of the world that had been undamaged by the war—American cities such as New York and Washington, Atlanta, Los Angeles, and Minneapolis, Canadian cities such as Toronto and Montreal, even distant Sydney, Australia. While the repretory presented in these new halls was heavily weighted toward the past, they were also symptomatic of a broadening musical public, which gradually accepted the masterpieces of the earlier twentieth century and began to take an interest in the music of its contemporaries.

The presence in America, at war's end, of Europe's most eminent composers—Stravinsky, Schoenberg, Bartók, Hindemith, Milhaud, Krenek, Martinu, and others—could not but have a profound effect on our musical life. And their absence, equally, was an important feature of the musical scene in their native countries. The great exodus in the face of Hitler had left a vacuum behind. In Germany, especially, the new generation of composers had no immediate past to which they could relate automatically, for many of the older men who had remained were compromised politically as well as dated musically. Young European composers in the late Forties and early Fifties had to find fresh models, and they turned to hitherto neglected figures—among them Anton Webern, Edgard Varèse, and younger men such as Olivier Messiaen and John Cage.

In Europe, the radio played a significant role in this second revolution. The state radio stations allotted time and performing resources to new music on a generous scale. In addition, they became the focus for experimentation with electronic sound production; the studios attached to the radio stations of Paris, Cologne, and Milan were centers for the diffusion of avant-garde works and the exploration of new technology. Of comparable importance, in the United States, were the universities, which began to invite composers of the most advanced tendencies to teach composition and theory. As a result, American colleges became centers of contemporary musical thought and activity. Whereas in the past the term *academic* had carried a somewhat pejorative connotation, implying as it did a hide-

The Sydney Opera House, which opened its doors amid much fanfare in 1973, is a spectacular multipurpose complex superbly sited at Bennelong Point on Sydney Harbour. (Photograph courtesy Qantas Airlines.)

bound conservatism, academic figures now emerged as leaders of musical experimentalism. Since music departments in colleges reach considerable numbers of students, who later become teachers and leaders of opinion in communities throughout the land, it can be seen that this new academic orientation played an important role in disseminating the new musical styles. Furthermore, the composer as college professor became far more directly involved in the presentation of his ideas and his music than had been the case before.

Worldwide, an enormously influential fact was the development of the long-playing record and the tape recorder. Before the war, new music could only be heard through infrequent performances in the concert hall, or studied in score (if—and it was a rather big if—the work was even published). The tape recorder brought down the cost of making recordings, and the long-playing record brought down the cost of distributing them. Soon after its introduction in 1948, the LP record began broadening musical horizons, and the record catalogues expanded to include early music, Baroque music—and new music as well. Eventually, the record collector had access to more music than even the most assiduous concert goer, and he became a more adventurous listener thereby. No longer restricted to the

Classic-Romantic repertory that had dominated musical life for so long, the modern listener has become receptive to novelty from the present as well as from the distant past and from other lands and cultures.

This was not without its effect on composers as well, for LP records and tapes vastly speeded up the dissemination of new musical ideas. Within hours of its premiere, a new work could be heard by its composer's colleagues thousands of miles away; they no longer had to wait years for the score to be published or a performance to take place locally. Each new development in composition was quickly known everywhere, its implications studied and discussed, and the next step prepared, with a speed unprecedented in musical history. As a result, the years since 1950 have been one of the most active, diverse, and exciting periods of musical invention and development, marked by a kaleidoscopic succession of new techniques and inspirations, trends and movements, works and personalities.

But before turning to the new figures who emerged after the war, we should look first at the great composers from Europe who concluded their work here in America—in particular, the three men whose careers began respectively, in St. Petersburg, Budapest, and Vienna, bestrode the first half of the century, and ended in the United States.

58 European Masters in America

"One has to practice one's art with a knowing sense of its radical nature."

STEFAN WOLPE

Bartók, *Concerto for Orchestra*

The increasing sophistication of the new music engendered one of the most serious problems in the musical life of our time—the gap between composer and public, which appeared to be very large by mid-century. Many music lovers were increasingly disturbed by the fact that they could not enjoy the new music as much as they did the old. Composers were disturbed too, and from time to time made a special effort to write a work that would be accessible to the big public. One of the finest examples is Béla Bartók's *Concerto for Orchestra* (1943), which was commissioned by Serge Koussevitzky for the Boston Symphony Orchestra and received its first performance in 1944, the year before Bartók died. He was already gravely ill when he received the commission, but the knowledge that a great orchestra was waiting to perform his music spurred him on to a magnificent effort. "The general mood of this work," he wrote, "represents, apart from the jesting second movement, a gradual transition from the sternness of the first movement and the lugubrious death-song of the third to the life-assertion of the last." He called the piece a concerto because of its tendency, as he put it, "to treat the single instruments in a *concertante* or soloistic manner." The use of the term in this early eighteenth-century sense implies that the element of virtuosity prevails; but the virtuoso in this case is the entire orchestra. Of symphonic proportions, the piece exemplifies Bartók's mastery of the grand form, his highly personal use of folklore elements, and his wonderful sense of sound. The *Concerto* was his first work to establish itself with the general public.

I. *Introduzione. Andante non troppo—Allegro vivace.* The Introduction is spacious of gesture. It prepares the listener for a large work. In the composer's best vein are the sonorities of the opening passage, a solemn statement by cellos and basses set off by tremolos on upper strings and flute. The theme is based on the interval of the fourth (indicated by brackets), which occupies a prominent position in the melodic formations of this composer.

The first subject of the *Allegro vivace* consists of a vigorously syncopated figure that ascends to a climax and as briskly subsides:

Here too the fourth is prominent. A contrasting idea in folklore style consists mainly of two notes. The development builds up tension through contrapuntal imitation. The restatement is abbreviated, as is customary in twentieth-century works. The movement has the quality of inevitable progression that is the essence of symphonic style.

II. *Giuoco delle coppie* (Game of Pairs). So called because the wind instruments are paired at specific intervals, bassoons in sixths, oboes in thirds, clarinets in sevenths, flutes in fifths, muted trumpets in seconds. This "jesting second movement," as Bartók called it, is marked *Allegretto scherzando*. The side drum, without snares, ushers in music of a processional nature that is filled with teasing ideas. In

evidence is the element of the bizarre that appealed to Berlioz and Mahler no less than to Bartók. The form is a "chain" of five little sections, each featuring another pair of instruments. There is a chorale for brass. The five sections are then restated with more elaborate instrumentation.

III. *Elegia. Andante non troppo.* This movement is the "lugubrious death song." An oboe traces a long line of lamentation against Bartókian flickerings of clarinet, flute, and harp tone. The music is rhapsodic, visionary; it rises to a tragic climax. This is a heroic canvas in the great line of the hymnic adagios of Beethoven.

IV. *Intermezzo interrotto* (Interrupted Intermezzo). A plaintive tune in folk-song style is introduced by the oboe and continued by the flute. The nonsymmetrical rhythm, an alternation of 3/4 and 5/8,

imparts to the movement a wayward charm. There follows a broadly songful theme on the strings, one of the great melodies of the twentieth century. The mood is interrupted as the music turns from folk lyricism to the sophisticated tone of the cafés. The return of the lyric

theme on muted strings makes a grandly poetic effect. The movement is replete with capriciousness and tender sentiment.

V. *Finale. Pesante—Presto.* There is an introduction of seven measures marked *pesante* (heavily), in which the horns outline the germinal theme. The movement of "life-assertion" gets off to a whirl-
wind *perpetuum mobile* (perpetual motion) in the strings. The fugue
that follows parades intricate devices of counterpoint; yet so lightly
does Bartók wear his learning that there is nothing here to tax the untutored ear. The fugue subject is presented by the second trumpet.
Notice again the decisive role played by the interval of a fourth.

The answer, played by the first trumpet, is an inversion of the theme.
The folk tune as Bartók uses it here has nothing in common with the
prettified peasant dances of the nineteenth century. Its harmonies
are acrid, its rhythms imbued with primitive strength. The movement rises to a mood of heroic affirmation.

Schoenberg, *A Survivor from Warsaw*

The cantata *A Survivor from Warsaw* (1947) sprang out of one of
the most profound experiences of Schoenberg's life. As we saw, he
had grown away from his Jewish origins and ultimately became a
Catholic. The rise of Hitlerism reminded him that he was a Jew. After
he left Germany he found it spiritually necessary to return to the
Hebrew faith. He was deeply shaken when, at the end of the war, the
world learned how the Nazis had transported millions of Jews from
all over Europe into the Warsaw Ghetto and then herded them into
the gas chambers of Dachau, Buchenwald, Auschwitz. The world
learned too how the final remnant of Jews in the Ghetto decided to
die fighting rather than be slaughtered, and organized the first upris-
ing in Occupied Europe. Emotionally involved as he was in these
historic events, Schoenberg in *A Survivor from Warsaw* produced one
of his most dramatic works.

We pointed out how well the atonal idiom lent itself to the moods of fear and suspense that were native to German Expressionism. These moods predominate in *A Survivor*, a six-minute cantata marked by the utmost emotional intensity. Here the fear and suspense are brought into dramatic focus through the text, which was written by Schoenberg himself in English. He was no literary craftsman, and he was writing in a language that he had learned late in life; yet the blazing sincerity out of which he wrote more than makes up for a certain crudity of style.

A narrator recounts how a group of Jews were conducted to their death by a detachment of Nazi soldiers. The Germans order the Jews out of the camp and line them up for the final march. They urge them on with blows and curses, shooting those that fall behind. Finally the order comes to count off, so that the sergeant may know how many to deliver to the gas chamber. They begin to count, first slowly, then faster. Finally, as by a common impulse, they begin to sing the *Shema Yisroel*—the ancient prayer that is the central creed of the Hebrew faith.

The grim tale is told by one who survived because he was left among the dead. At two points narration gives way to action. First, when the narrator quotes the sergeant, imitating his brutal manner of barking commands. Here Schoenberg uses the percussion instruments—bass drum, snare drum, xylophone, cymbals—to underscore the text. Second, at the dramatic climax of the piece, the grandiose moment, as Schoenberg called it, when in the face of death the Jews begin to sing. At this point, when the narrator is replaced by male chorus, the full orchestra enters for the first time. (Hitherto the orchestra has played only in groups.)

From the suspenseful fanfare of the trumpets at the outset, the score abounds in remarkable strokes. For example, the high trill on the trombones in the orchestral introduction. Or the unusual effects on the string instruments, produced by tapping the strings with the stick of the bow or by scratching the strings with the stick. In the same category are the high trills on the woodwinds, fluttertonguing on the muted brass, and the snarling sound produced by forcing the tone of muted trumpets and horns. Extraordinary too is the crescendo, accelerando, and breathless intensification of rhythm (based on a pattern of two against three) when the Jews count off, faster and faster, until "it finally sounded like a stampede of wild horses."

Although in several works of his American years Schoenberg returned to writing tonal music, in *A Survivor from Warsaw* all the material is derived from a twelve-tone row (see Appendix I-k), which appears in its definitive form only at the entrance of the chorus, though it is suggested softly by the muted horn when the narrator speaks of "the old prayer they had neglected for so many years":

Here is the melody to which the *Shema Yisroel* is sung:

She-ma   Yis-ra-el   A-do-noy   el-o-he-noo   A-do-noy   e - hod

Despite the formal intricacies of his method, Schoenberg maintained again and again that the prime function of a composer was to move the listener. "I write what I feel in my heart—and what finally comes on paper is what first coursed through every fibre of my body. A work of art can achieve no finer effect than when it transmits to the beholder the emotions that raged in the creator, in such a way that they rage and storm also in him." In *A Survivor from Warsaw* Schoenberg fashioned a work of art that fully transmits to us the emotions that raged in him.

Stravinsky: *Agon*

Agon occupies a special place in Stravinsky's output. The earliest parts of it date from December, 1953—from the period, that is to say, when he was becoming increasingly interested in dodecaphonic music. Parts of the ballet were written in 1954, before *Canticum sacrum;* the rest during the next three years. The first numbers of the ballet recapture the rhythmic dynamism of his earlier works, and contain stylistic references to *Petrushka, Le Sacre, L'Histoire du soldat,* and other compositions of his Neoclassic period. The later parts of *Agon* show the master's more consistent use of serial technique and his growing preoccupation with the procedures of Webern. The opening and closing fanfares, like the interludes that set off the main divisions of the work, are not in the twelve-tone style. The harmonic language ranges from diatonic to bitonal, from polytonal and atonal to out-and-out dodecaphonic. Thus the score literally shows Stravinsky in the process of taking possession of his final style period. What welds the twelve-tone and non-twelve-tone elements in *Agon*

A scene from the New York City Ballet production of Agon. *Photograph by Fred Fehl.*

into a stylistic unity is the unmistakable personality behind the music.

Agon consists of twelve short pieces (the work lasts just over twenty minutes) modeled on court-dance sequences of the time of Louis XIII and XIV, as set forth in a French dance manual of the mid-seventeenth century. The work consequently takes its place in the series of classical ballets which includes *Apollon musagète* and *Orpheus*. Unlike those, it has no central theme, but consists instead of a series of abstract patterns belonging to no specific period, for four male and eight female dancers. Stravinsky uses the Greek word *agon* to signify a dance contest. The first performance took place in Los Angeles in June, 1957, in celebration of the composer's seventy-fifth birthday.

Although the score of *Agon* calls for a fairly large orchestra, the ensemble for the most part is not used in its entirety. This makes for a chamber-music texture of extraordinary refinement, each dance being conceived for a contrasting group of instruments used soloistically. The score is notable for unusual combinations—solo violin, xylophone, tenor and bass trombone in one number; trumpets, mandolin, harp, and cello solo in another. The intimate, pointed tone of the mandolin is pitted against the other instruments in most novel fashion. The individualization of timbre throughout, in combination with the highly concentrated idiom, makes this one of the most tightly wrought of Stravinsky's scores, in which careful calculation exists side by side with brilliancy of sound and vivacity of movement.

The work is divided into three parts. The first consists of a *Pas de quatre* for four male dancers, who advance from the rear with their backs to the audience; a double *Pas de quatre;* and a triple *Pas de quatre* for the entire company. The music for the third dance is a variation of the second. Part Two begins with a short orchestral prelude. The first *Pas de trois* begins with a Saraband-Step for solo male dancer, followed by a Galliard for two female dancers and a Coda for all three. A brief orchestral interlude leads into the second *Pas de trois,* consisting of a *Bransle Simple* for two male dancers, a *Bransle Gay* for solo female dancer, and a *Bransle de Poitou* for all three dancers. The third part begins, after a few measures of orchestral stretto, with four duos (quartet of four couples). There follow the last two numbers—a dance of three trios, each consisting of one male and two female dancers, and the Coda for three groups of four: that is, the entire group. Near the end, where the music returns to the fanfares of the opening, the female dancers leave the stage and the male dancers resume their positions with their backs to the audience, as at the beginning.

The pattern, then, is identical in all three parts: first a male dancer or dancers, then female, then both together, with the full ensemble appearing only near the beginning and at the end. The music subtly indicates the difference between male and female dances; those for the men are more dynamic in rhythm, bolder in contrapuntal line and instrumentation. Trumpets, xylophone, trombones underline the character of the male dances, as flutes, mandolin, and castanets do for the female numbers.

The score abounds in "finds," such as the extraordinary passage in the Prelude to the first *Pas de trois* where a G-major triad is sounded in the treble by three basses playing harmonics; the single-note writing for the piano; the combination of violin solo, xylophone, tenor and bass trombones in the Saraband-Step; or of trumpets, mandolin, harp, and cello solo in the Coda of the first *Pas de trois.* Rhythm plays a formative role throughout. For as the texture grows more and more attenuated, the darting specks of sound are firmly held together by the rhythmic impulsion. The interplay of lines shows that desire to penetrate the uttermost secrets of counterpoint which was the preoccupation of so many great composers in their ripest years. What emerges from almost every measure of the score is the fact that when a creative artist takes over a new system, he becomes its master, and not the other way around. In its enameled sonorities, its concision and rhythmic intensity, its vitality and wit, *Agon* is wholly Stravinsky's. It could have come from no one else's pen.

Stefan Wolpe

Stefan Wolpe (Berlin, 1902–1972, New York City) was a thoroughgoing original whose music bears the imprint of a powerful personality. He assimilated the major influences of his youth—Busoni, Bartók, Schoenberg, Webern, Stravinsky—into a terse, intense idiom uniquely his own. Wolpe left Nazi Germany in 1933, spent several years in what was then Palestine, came to the United States in 1938, and ultimately settled in New York. He based his art on a technique of developing variation of a highly concentrated nature, the material generated from basic interval relationships within a severely contrapuntal texture powered by asymmetrical meters and rhythms. He aimed for what he called "a decomposition of tonality" through the use of triadic and nontriadic chords combined with harmonies to which they were only distantly related.

For a few years under the Weimar Republic—the late 1920s and early '30s—Wolpe responded to the same social currents that generated the *Gebrauchsmusik* of Hindemith and the political theater of Brecht and Kurt Weill. He simplified his dense, atonal idiom so that it would be accessible to a larger circle of performers and listeners. With the collapse of political liberalism in Germany his creativity turned back to the mainstream of contemporary musical thought. During his years in Palestine his consciousness as a Jew was to the fore; the works he wrote there show the rhythmic and melodic configurations of Semitic song and dance. These influences were absorbed into a mature style that shows his preoccupation with the distribution of musical space and his love of juxtaposing contrasting elements such as long lines moving within a narrow compass against short notes leaping over several registers, or densely bunched chords against linear expansion several octaves above or below.

All those who came under his influence at Black Mountain College in North Carolina or C. W. Post College of Long Island University agree that Wolpe was a great teacher, a man of extraordinary intellect and erudition whose view of Western culture—not in the least limited to his own aesthetic predilections—was exhilarating in the highest degree. He was a major figure for a wide circle of admirers and as more of his works become available on records, his influence will assuredly grow. Available at present are several important works, among them the *Trio* (1963), the *String Quartet* (1969), *Form for Piano* (1959), and the *Quartet* for trumpet, tenor saxophone, percussion, and piano (1950).

Ernst Krenek

Ernst Krenek (Vienna, 1900–) leaped into fame in 1927 with his jazz opera *Jonny spielt auf!* (Johnny Plays!). He found his mature style in the twelve-tone idiom, which for him represented "a very high degree of logical coherence and intelligible significance." He felt that the twelve-tone technique, like any other technical means, was sensible in so far as it increased the mastery of the human mind over natural resources. His first work in this idom, the grandiose opera *Karl V* (Charles V), was banned by the Nazis because they considered the composer guilty of *Kulturbolshevismus*. He came to the United States in 1938, the year of Hitler's annexation of Austria. One of the most prolific composers of our time, Krenek gave up using opus numbers after his ninety-sixth work. His list includes eleven operas, three ballets, six piano sonatas, five symphonies, four piano concertos, and eight string quartets; also several books, among which *Music Here and Now* (1939) is the best known. A severely intellectual composer who makes no concessions to the public, Krenek is an authoritative exponent of certain advanced tendencies in twentieth-century musical thought.

He is also the hero of a delightful anecdote included in Hans Heinsheimer's book *Menagerie in F-sharp*. After the first performance of a Krenek piano concerto in Boston, a little old lady sitting next to Heinsheimer turned to her husband and said, "You know, dear, conditions must be terrible in Europe."

Others

Alexander Tcherepnin (St. Petersburg, now Leningrad, 1899–1977, Paris) assimilated a number of disparate elements into his style. From his father, the composer Nicolas Tcherepnin (one of Prokofiev's principal teachers), he inherited the Russian Postromantic tradition. From a sojourn in the Caucasus immediately after the revolution—his father became director of the conservatory in Tbilisi, in Georgia—he carried away a love of Georgian folk music. When civil war reached the Caucasus, the Tcherepnin family settled in Paris, where the young composer completed his studies and absorbed the prevailing aesthetic of Neoclassicism. His tours as a concert pianist took him to the Far East and brought him into direct contact with the music of China and Japan. In Shanghai he met the Chinese pianist

Hsien Ming Lee, who subsequently became his wife. After the war he taught at De Paul University in Chicago, and in later years divided his time between New York and Paris.

Tcherepnin handled the large forms with a sovereign command of contrapuntal and variation techniques. His transparent orchestral texture bespeaks the influence of Parisian Neoclassicism. He explored new harmonic possibilities through a nine-tone scale (C–D♭–E♭–E–F–G–A♭–A–B–C) that combined the major–minor ambiguity so dear to the contemporary mind with a modal flavor. Equally distinctive was his use of a type of polyphony that he christened *interpoint*, which he described as "note between notes, replacing the classical counterpoint (point against point or note against note). The interpoint may be vertical or horizontal, when the barline is not the same for each of the voices of the polyphony . . ." Six piano concertos and five symphonies are the principal items in a varied list of piano, chamber, and orchestral works, operas, ballets, and theater pieces that illustrate the secure art of a composer who was in every sense a musical citizen of the world.

Erich Itor Kahn (Rimback-im-Odenwald, Germany, 1905–1956, New York City) showed his talent at an early age. His discovery of Schoenberg's music, at a time when the master was virtually unknown outside a small circle, marked a turning point in his development. He left Germany when Hitler came to power and settled in Paris, where he was active as pianist, teacher, and composer until the outbreak of the Second World War brought another dislocation. (Frida Kahn's *Story of a Generation* vividly evokes the wanderings shared by so many thousands during those desperate years.) In 1941 the Kahns made their way to the United States.

To the structural logic and concentrated thought of twelve-tone writing Kahn brought the warmth of a lyric temperament. His was a highly personal music in which refined craftsmanship was joined to subtlety of feeling and expression: a music suffused with the composer's total dedication of his vision of artistic truth. From his fairly limited but varied list one may single out the *Ciaccona dei tempo di guerra* (Chaconne in Time of War, 1943), a monumental work for piano in which he handled the variation procedure with Baroque richness of invention and mastery of contrapuntal device; *Actus tragicus* (Tragic Deed, 1947), for ten instruments, in which the lyric elements native to Kahn's style exist side by side with declamatory passages of a more dramatic nature; and the *String Quartet* of 1953, one of his profoundest works.

Vittorio Rieti (Alexandria, Egypt, of Italian parents, 1898–) represents that segment of modern Italian music which is oriented toward French Neoclassicism. His long residence in Paris imparted to his music its cosmopolitan character. Rieti's copious output includes operas, ballets, choral works, orchestral and chamber music, concertos, piano pieces, and a number of extremely effective songs. The *Second Avenue Waltzes* for two pianos (1944), *Fifth Symphony* (1945), *Third String Quartet* (1953), and *Quintet for Woodwinds* (1958) display the elegance of his instrumental writing. His is a refined art that avoids the rhetorical, seeking to charm rather than to impress. Behind it stands a composer who is irresistibly drawn to whatever is subtle, witty, and urbane.

Karol Rathaus (Tarnopol, Poland, 1895–1954, New York City) taught at the Berlin Hochschule from 1925 until the coming of Hitler and, after several years in London, emigrated to the United States in 1938. He was the first professor of composition at Queens College of the City University of New York, a post he occupied until his death. He combined the song and dance patterns of his native Poland with a strain of brooding mysticism that stemmed from the spiritual climate of east-European Jewry, asserting itself in ecstatic dance moods and lyricism of a rhapsodic cast. These two elements he assimilated to the tradition of Austro-German Postromanticism. His *Third Symphony* (1942), *Polonaise symphonique* (1944), *Twenty-Third Psalm* for chorus and orchestra (1945), and *Diapason,* a cantata for baritone solo, mixed chorus, and orchestra on texts of Dryden and Milton (1952), stand out in a varied list that includes ballets, operas, film, theater, piano and chamber music, and extremely expressive songs.

Bohuslav Martinu (Politchka, Czechoslovakia, 1890–1959, Prague), who spent the war years in the United States, belonged to a new generation of Czech musicians who looked for inspiration to Paris instead of Vienna. The Neoclassic influence is manifest in such works as the *Partita for Strings* (1931), *Sinfonia* for two orchestras (1932), and *Piano Concerto* (1935). As time went on Martinu's classical outlook was tempered by the romantic strain that was at the core of his nature. In works such as the *Double Concerto* for two string orchestras, piano, and kettledrums (1940), which was written after the betrayal of his country at Munich, he echoed the mood of a tragic time. Out of the same current of feeling came the *Mass at Camp* for baritone, male chorus, wind, and percussion (1939), and *Memorial to Lidice* (1943). Martinu belonged to the spontaneous type of musician we associate with Bohemia. He produced a vast amount of music in all the forms and genres of his art, including ten operas, ten ballets, six symphonies, and much chamber music. He succeeded in amalgamating Czech musical traditions with contemporary Western trends. His clean, compact writing abounds in spontanous melody and kinetic rhythms. He consistently upheld the primacy of expression over technique. In this, as in his carefully wrought music, he was a worthy representative of one of the most musical nations in Europe.

59 New Trends

"A masterpiece is more likely to happen to the composer with the most highly developed language."

IGOR STRAVINSKY

The years since World War II have brought forth many new ideas about music—its nature, its purpose, its structure, its techniques. We are, probably, still too close to these developments to sort out those that will ultimately prove, in the view of history, to have been the most important and influential. However, some general impulses can be observed as common to the work of many composers.

Toward Stricter Control

The basic tenet of Schoenberg's twelve-tone method, as we have seen, was that all the pitch material of a piece—melody, harmony, counterpoint—should be derived from a single source: the row, or series, as it was sometimes also called. After the war, various composers in America and Europe perceived the possibility of extending this principle to other musical dimensions, such as rhythm, dynamics, and tone color. This, it was felt, would produce still greater unity and coherence. Extending the principle of the series to these other dimensions, these composers evolved the idea of "total serialization," whereby every element of the work would represent the central idea of the series.

As one spokesman put it, "Our aim is an art in which proportion is everything—a *serial art*." The strongest influence was the music of Anton Webern—neglected in his lifetime but in the 1950s brought to the forefront by performances and a complete recording of his music. To some European composers, indeed, it appeared that Webern himself had taken the initial steps along the path of serially organizing

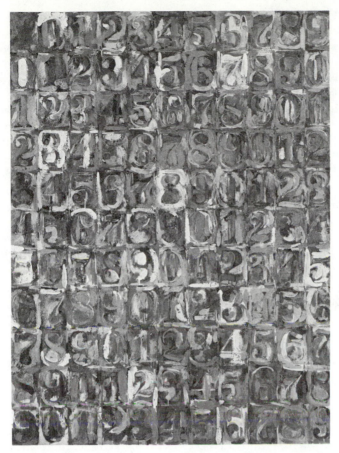

Serialism was a characteristic feature of Pop Art. A familiar object or idea from everyday life represented repeatedly gradually loses its associative qualities, becoming instead simply lines, colors, and texture. Jasper Johns (b. 1930), Numbers in Color, *1959. Albright-Knox Art Gallery, Buffalo, New York. Gift of Seymour H. Knox.*

such elements as dynamics and rhythm. Others, though more skeptical, found suggestions in his work of a music that, unlike Schoenberg's, was composed without reference to formal ideas inherited from the past, that drew its symmetries and proportions directly from the structure of the row.

Whether historically correct or not, these views of Webern were enormously stimulating to younger composers, offering a precedent for what they wanted to do. The decade of the Fifties became "the age of Webern." And there was an unexpected ally in this cause. Before the war, the leader of the composers opposed to Schoenberg and his method had been Igor Stravinsky; like Wagner and Brahms in the previous century, these two men seemed to be at opposite poles. But Stravinsky, too, as the leading Neoclassicist of the age, sought law and order in music. One need only recall his remark, "The more art is controlled, limited, worked over, the more it is free"; and, to the same point, "Music is given to us with the sole purpose of establishing an order in things." His conversion to the twelve-tone system in the early Fifties caused nothing short of a sensation in the world of music. Opponents of the Schoenberg method had long insisted that you could not use it without sounding like Schoenberg; Stravinsky's about-face demonstrated conclusively that it was nothing like so constricting a tool, for he assimilated the new technique to his own style and continued to sound like himself. Significantly, of the three Viennese masters, Stravinsky singled out Webern as the object of his special admiration (you may recall his eloquent tribute, on p. 271). Even though Stravinsky's treatment of serial technique was wholly individual, and quite unlike that of the younger followers of Webern, his advocacy could not but add to the authority of the hitherto neglected Austrian and the ideas that seemed to stem from him.

A variety of methods was devised for carrying out "total serialization." In general, they involved taking the intervals of the row—the distances between the pitches—and interpreting them by analogy as distances in time (to determine rhythmic relationships) and in loudness (to determine dynamics). This could be done with greater or less sensitivity to the actual musical results; today, a number of works composed in those years seem to be nothing more than laboratory experiments—and unsuccessful ones at that, mere mechanical workings-out of numerological schemes. But the ideas and techniques of serialization have proved persistent, and talented composers have put them to fruitful use. Furthermore, the impulse to control the musical material was joined to the possibilities made available by the new technology of electronic music, which we will discuss in the next chapter; now a composer could not only plan every detail of his work with the strictest precision, but also construct an absolutely correct electronic performance that would match his intentions in every respect.

Toward Greater Freedom

Alongside these developments were others of different import. Counterpoised against those whose ideal was of strictly organized music were others who sought less control over the musical material, or proposed a greater role for the performer in determining the progress of the musical work. Traditionally, there has been much latitude in the performance of music. Tempo markings such as *Allegro* and *Adagio* are not precise, but merely indicate a range of possibilities; dynamic indications such as piano and forte are merely relative, not absolute. Even the more precise metronome marks for tempo that came into use during the nineteenth century were rarely intended to be rigidly interpreted; indeed, composers often put notes in the score explaining that they were only "suggestions," subject to modification depending on such factors as the acoustics of the particular concert hall. Flexibility of tempo, too, was often taken for granted. In the seventeenth and eighteenth centuries, performers were expected to decorate melodic lines, to improvise details of accompaniments (figured bass), to supply cadenzas of their own. And of course American jazz was a vital and continuing tradition in which the role of the performer is often more important than that of the composer—or, in fact, equivalent to it in important respects.

Thus there were ample precedents for the reaction that set in after

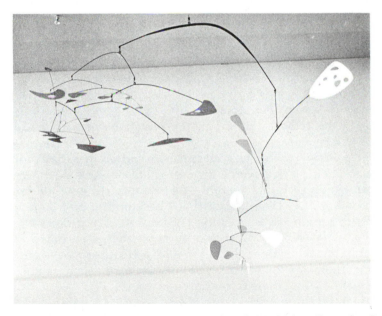

Part of the charm of the mobile, as invented and refined by Alexander Calder (1898–1976), lies in its constantly changing configurations, reached entirely by chance. International Mobile, *1949. The Museum of Fine Arts, Houston. Gift from Dominique and John de Menil in memory of Marcel Schlumberger.*

World War II to the increasing tendency on the part of composers (going back at least to Beethoven, who in his *Fifth Piano Concerto* took over the soloist's traditional role of supplying a cadenza) to leave less and less of the detail of their music up to performers. This reaction, too, may have been directed against the increasing prevalence of recordings, which never change at all (whereas even the same performer will never play the same piece exactly the same way twice). So the aesthetic concept of indeterminacy came into play in concert music, as it did in other performing arts. Not only in the performing arts of dance and theater, in fact, for it can be seen in such works as the mobiles of Alexander Calder, which move around to form a variety of shapes, or in the canvases of Jackson Pollock, where the paint was splashed on the surface almost at random.

Three general types of musical indeterminacy may be distinguished. In improvisation the performers agree beforehand on certain general procedures and on the type of material, and then give free rein to their fantasy within these limitations. The most familiar example is the jazz improvisation on the melodies and harmonies of a familiar song, with the order of solos determined in advance. In *aleatory* music—the term is derived from the Latin word for dice—the overall course of the work is fixed, with the details left up to the performers' choice or to chance. Conversely, open form indicates music in which the details are fixed but the sequence of the larger formal events is determined by choice or chance. In practice, of course, these categories may overlap, and the range of possibility is enormous. Some examples of indeterminate music will sound no more different in several performances than, say, Beethoven's *Fifth Symphony* in the radically different interpretations of two conductors; others will be more or less unrecognizable in different performances.

The principle of indeterminacy can be carried into the act of composition itself, so that even a precisely notated work may have been written without rational thought—for example, the notes determined by throwing dice. Here, the aesthetic background is still more radical, for the composer is rejecting the idea of art as a rational, structured activity, conceiving it as a more playful, less exalted activity than it has been regarded during most of the course of Western civilization. There are precedents for this attitude, such as the Dada movement, which came to the fore during the First World War, rejecting all traditional standards of what art was supposed to be; or the Italian Futurists who, a few years earlier, had proclaimed that one sound or noise was as good as any other. This kind of artistic anarchism has its role in extending the boundaries of art, engender-

The Dada artists had a particular penchant for surprise and the unexpected. In this work, Jean Arp (1887–1966) employs his familiar organic forms in chance arrangements. Objects Arranged According to the Laws of Chance or Navels, 1930. *Varnished wood relief. The Museum of Modern Art, New York.*

ing a healthy skepticism toward outmoded traditions, and—as we shall see in the chapter on John Cage—exerting an invigorating influence even upon those artists who do not accept its basic premises.

The interplay of these two basic impulses brought about a period of intense musical activity—and also intense aesthetic strife. Equally important in understanding the development of recent music is the role of techniques and technology, which exerted an important shaping force on these crucial decades.

60 New Sounds

"Composers are now able, as never before, to satisfy the dictates of that inner ear of the imagination."

EDGARD VARÈSE

It is a truism that each stage of social and cultural evolution engenders its own artistic forms and media. Thus it was inevitable that the great scientific advances of the past century, specifically in the field of electronics and acoustics, would have a profound effect on the course of music, both directly and—through the stimulus they gave to composers working along more traditional lines—indirectly.

Electronic Sound

Strictly speaking, the term *electronic music* is a misnomer, a catch-all term for many different kinds of music involving sounds generated electronically. Electronic sound may be used by the composer in any way he wishes. Traditional music may be performed electronically, as for example the music of Bach in the famous *Switched-*

On Bach recording. But the electronic techniques also make available a range of sounds far beyond that of traditional instruments, a precision of pitch, rhythm, dynamics, and tone colors, and—if the composer so desires—the possibility of supervising down to the most minute detail the "performance" of his work.

There were several milestones in the conquest of this new potential: the invention of the electronic tube in 1906; the building of electrophonic concert instruments such as the Theremin in the years after the First World War; and the development of practical machines for recording sound on magnetic tape during the late Thirties and early Forties (based on the work of the Danish engineer Vladimir Poulsen, as far back as 1889). Technical advances, however, have significance only when they answer human needs in the domain of the intellect and imagination. Even as these inventions were being developed, the signs were not wanting that new conceptions were taking shape whose ultimate implications led beyond the resources of traditional instruments. The "emancipation of the dissonance" effectuated by Debussy and his generation was one such sign. Busoni's desire for an "uninterrupted continuity" of the musical material was another. He spoke of the possible fissure of sounds, experimented with microtonal scales (based, that is, on intervals smaller than a semitone), and in his *Sketch of a New Esthetic of Music* described an instrument that could transform electrical current into a controlled number of sound vibrations. A more immediate precursor was Edgard Varèse, who already in the Twenties was exploiting percussion and bell sonorities in unprecedented ways. Varèse's assumptions formed one of the points of departure for the experimental composers who emerged a quarter century later.

None of these initiatives led to any conclusive results until the middle of the century, when magnetic tape recorders became generally available. Because it permitted sounds to be recorded separately and then spliced together in the sequence desired by the composer, tape had great advantages over the disc-recording methods previously in use. In fact, the French composers who first experimented with what they called *musique concrète* ("concrete"—that is, real—"music," because they took the sounds they worked with from nature) started with disc recording, but they quickly switched to tape when its advantages became evident. They recorded sounds from the world around them—sounds that would, in earlier days, have been dismissed as "noise"—and then manipulated them. By making a tape loop, a sound could be repeated again and again in an ostinatolike pattern. By speeding up or slowing down the tape, the character of the sounds could be changed—low roars changed into shrill whines, for example. The tape could be reversed, changing a decreasing sound into a crescendo. And by rerecording, all these sounds could be superimposed one on the other to create the final work. The process was cumbersome, but the results attracted much attention.

While these experimentalists were working in the studios of the French radio under the direction of Pierre Schaeffer, two Americans had begun to experiment along similar lines. Otto Luening and Vladimir Ussachevsky, at Columbia University, used more conventional musical sounds as source material, but by the time these had been manipulated on tape they sounded just as novel and striking as the French *musique concrète*. The first public concert of compositions for tape recorder in the United States was given at New York's Museum of Modern Art in October 1952; the program included Ussachevsky's *Sonic Contours* and Luening's *Low Speed, Invention,* and *Fantasy in Space.*

A third group of composers worked at the studio of the West German Radio in Cologne, under the direction of Herbert Eimert; its leading figure was the young Karlheinz Stockhausen. The Cologne studio used sounds derived from an electronic generator—sine tones, as pure sounds without overtones are known. These were then built up into more complex sounds. Despite the disparity in sound sources, all three schools of early electronic composition had in common the need to assemble their music through the painstaking and time-consuming expedient of tape manipulation and splicing, and they all ended up with the same kind of finished product: a tape containing a definitive "performance" of their work.

During the early 1950s, technology took another step forward when scientists working at RCA developed the RCA Electronic Music Synthesizer, an elaborate system that could generate electronically any tone specified by the composer—any pitch, any duration, any dynamic, any type of attack and decay. An improved model of this instrument was installed in 1960 at the joint studio set up by Columbia and Princeton Universities, alongside the enlarged laboratory that Luening and Ussachevsky had developed. Though it was too expensive to be widely duplicated, the undoubted advantages of the RCA Synthesizer stimulated other inventions and techniques of producing electronically generated sounds. Much smaller synthesizers became available in the 1960s, some of them reasonably portable and usable for live performance. (Technically, they were not the first such instruments—indeed, the familiar electronic organ is

The RCA Electronic Music Synthesizer at the Columbia-Princeton Music Center, New York.

among their precursors; rather than trying to imitate an existing instrument, however, the new portables produced sounds never before heard in concert halls.) Today, the wide availability of such synthesizers has meant that many colleges and universities can offer facilities for work with electronic sounds, and of course there are commercial studios as well.

One important distinction began soon to appear among the users of electronic sounds. Some composers preferred to create a finished product on tape. Others were more interested in using the new sounds in something like the conventional performance situation. Electronic tools that could amplify and distort the sounds of voices and conventional instruments were brought into use, as well as multitrack sound systems that could make sounds appear to "move" around a hall. Such devices could also be used to bring the element of chance into play, transforming sounds made by a live musician in unpredictable ways before they were amplified for the audience to hear. Whatever a composer's aesthetic persuasion, there would be some form of electronic sound of interest to him. And there was the possibility of combination between tape and live performers, which restored the element of unpredictability that tape suppressed, adding as well the sense of competition between the fixed, unyielding progress of the taped sounds and the flexibility and virtuosity of the live performers. (In a later chapter, we will discuss a work of this type by Milton Babbitt, synthesized on the RCA machine.)

A further stage of development began in the Sixties: the use of the electronic computer to synthesize sounds. Just as the shape of a sound wave is represented by the innumerable microscopic wiggles of a record groove, it can also be represented by a series of numbers. So computer programs have been developed that will compute series of numbers equivalent to a composer's specifications of pitch, duration, tone color, and dynamics, and these number series can then be converted into electronic signals that will activate a loudspeaker. With suitably flexible programs, computers have become a widely used source of musical sounds. (In the situation we have just described, the computer has nothing to do with the *composition* of the music, merely with its realization in sound. But computers have also been used in the composing process—to calculate possible sound combinations, to generate random number of series for chance music, even to "compose" music according to carefully phrased instructions. The results thus achieved can be played on ordinary instruments or synthesized electronically.)

The use of electronic sounds is, of course, by no means limited to concert-style music. They have become an integral part of rock music, television commercials, and film scores. They have, in just a few years, become an accepted part of the musical landscape. They offer boundless possibilities to the composer—but no panaceas, for the composer must still have musical ideas to begin with.

Varèse, *Poème electronique*

"I have been waiting a long time for electronics to free music from the tempered scale and limitations of musical instruments. Electronic instruments are the portentous first step toward the liberation of music."

In 1958 Philips, a Dutch electrical company, commissioned Le Corbusier to design a pavilion at the Brussels Fair that would be "a poem of the electronic age." The French-Swiss architect invited Varèse to write the music for an eight-minute fantasy of light, color, rhythm, and tone designed to put its audience "in the presence of the genesis of the world." The sounds were to be distributed over four hundred loudspeakers, so arranged as to create a sense of spatial dimension. No matter when the spectator arrived, he heard the piece in its entirety as he passed through the pavilion. The *Poème électronique* has been made available on records.

Varèse composed most of the music directly on tape. Some of the drum sounds were created by a pulse generator. The human element is represented by a girl's voice, but one that has been treated elec-

The Philips Pavilion, Brussels World Fair, 1958. Architect: Le Corbusier. Photo-graph courtesy The Museum of Modern Art, New York.

tronically. Drum sounds, bell sounds, sirens, and persistent rhyth-mic patterns unfold in a continuum whose curiously depersonalized quality grips the imagination and conjures up visions of a strange new world. There is something almost terrifying about the ac-cumulation of energy in this music; yet its inner tensions are un-folded within the bonds of a form that has a rigorous logic all its own.

Thus, at the age of seventy-three, the intrepid explorer was still pursuing new paths, bringing back to his less venturesome fellows the shapes and sounds of the music of the future.

New Sounds from Old Instruments

Perhaps stimulated in part by the novel sounds emerging from the electronic studios, a new cycle of coloristic invention has marked recent writing for traditional instruments. Composers and performers have worked together in experimenting with possibilities, developing new playing techniques that yield new colors, wider ranges, even multiple sounds (chords) from instruments that used to produce only one note at a time. Many composers today work with performing ensembles—indeed, are often themselves part of such groups, as instrumentalists or conductors—and this close contact has been mutually stimulating, as composers set new challenges for players, or players discover new sounds for which composers then seek out musical uses.

Much of this adventurous growth has taken place in the context of the mixed chamber ensemble, which has become the predominant medium for new music. Usually comprising one each of the standard string and wind instruments, plus percussion and piano, the contemporary chamber ensemble may range from three or four to as many as twenty players, from which the composer will select a particular instrumentation for each piece. Such ensembles have sprung up in many major cities and university communities here and abroad. Their members specialize in the particular virtuosity demanded by the new techniques, and they have no inhibitions about trying out something simply because "it was never done before." Composers still write for the symphony orchestra when the opportunity arises, but the chamber ensemble, because of its greater experience in modern idioms, is likely to be the medium in which they try out their newest ideas.

In no area has the new vocabulary of tone colors grown faster than in the percussion. Once limited to emphasizing climaxes, underlining rhythms, or delicately coloring melodies, these instruments have multiplied in number and increased in variety to the point where entire pieces are written for them alone. The historical landmark in the development of percussion was Varèse's *Ionisation* (1931), which demonstrated that an all-percussion ensemble could be put to musically effective use. At times during the Sixties, it seemed as if anything that could be struck or hammered—even, perhaps, the proverbial kitchen sink—would be mustered into the concert hall, while the widespread interest in music of other cultures brought to the fore the many percussion instruments of Africa, Asia, and Latin America.

Today, instead of a single gong, the composer may ask for three or four, of different sizes and pitches; a similar range of drums and cymbals is often required. The xylophone, marimba, and vibraphone have become independent melody instruments of considerable versatility and virtuosity. And traditional percussion instruments are now used in new and unconventional ways. Those formerly only

The Fifties brought great innovations in the materials and methods of painting. One stunning development of this period was the "big picture"; another, the experiments in ways of throwing and pouring paint over the canvas to achieve richness of color and texture. Grayed Rainbow, 1953, *by Jackson Pollock (1912–1956). Courtesy of the Art Institute of Chicago. Gift of the Society for Contemporary American Art.*

struck are also scraped, tapped, brushed. A bass drum will "groan" if rubbed with hard rubber or a finger. A double-bass bow, heavily rosined, makes a capital effect when drawn across a cymbal or gong. John Cage and others have called in their scores for a "water gong": a gong is struck and then lowered into a tub of water, which changes its pitch as it is immersed.

Such developments have extended to other departments of the orchestra. New kinds of woodwind articulations have been borrowed from jazz, such as the "slap-tongue" effect, in which the player strikes his tongue against the mouthpiece. The "whistle tone" of the flute (an ethereal sound in the upper register produced by relaxing the embouchure and lowering the breath pressure) and the muted "echo tone" of the clarinet (in which the reed is partially stopped with the tongue) are examples of new coloristic resources.

Multiple stops—ways of playing more than one note at a time—have been discovered, and even the clicking of an instrument's keys have been put to use. Similar effects have been devised on brass instruments, naturally including the whole range of color-altering mutes borrowed from jazz.

String instruments are now not only bowed and plucked; the body of the instrument may be tapped or rapped with the fingers or the bow. Bowing the body of the violin brings forth a memorable hiss. The strings may be slackened, or bowed on the "wrong" side of the fingers on the fingerboard; both procedures yield a pale, wraith-like sound. Electronic amplification can be used, often in conjunction with such special effects, which may be too delicate to be heard more than a few feet from the player. Contact microphones placed on instruments not only amplify them, but also exaggerate the "noise" component of their sound.

The oldest, and most celebrated, of novel effects from a traditional instrument is the "prepared piano," first introduced by John Cage in the Forties. The "preparation" consists of inserting between the piano's strings a variety of nuts, bolts, screws, pieces of rubber, felt, wood, and metal. The result is a miniature percussion orchestra, each note acquiring a different color or resonance, depending on the object attached to its strings. Beyond this, contemporary pianists must be prepared to reach inside the instrument's case and strike the strings with mallets or fingers; to pluck the strings; to scrape them with rubber erasers; to slam down the piano lid; or to rap on the case. If other instruments are played into the piano's entrails while the dampers are raised, an interesting halo of resonance is stimulated (this, too, is so delicate as to require occasional amplification).

Nor has the human voice been exempt from this wave of experimentation. Singers are asked to produce percussive sounds by clicking the tongue, popping sounds with the lips or cheeks, exploding consonants, and hissing sibilants. Almost any sound from a whisper to a howl may be required, as well as giggles, screams, whistles, heavy breathing, and whining. No longer is the classical legato, the firm rounded tone and smooth phrasing of the Italian school, the ideal of vocal technique; it is merely one choice among many possible vocal sounds.

Clearly, the third quarter of our century has been a time of rich and fruitful experimentation on the part of composers and performers. At first, performers were reluctant to undertake such music, for which their basically nineteenth-century training had hardly prepared them; improvisation, in particular, was foreign to their background and experience. But gradually the more adventurous spirits showed that it could be done, and others have followed, while the teaching of performers has also begun to catch up with the needs of modern composers. The "new virtuosity" of today's performers has become one of the exciting aspects of the contemporary musical scene, stimulating to both composers and listeners.

The New Notation

Traditional musical notation, a system evolved over many centuries, served adequately as long as music was based on the diatonic scale and major-minor harmony, on regular beats grouped simply in twos or threes or multiples thereof, and on standard instruments played in standard ways. Once composers went beyond these limitations, new ways had to be found of writing music down. Complex rhythmic groupings and transitions and microtonal pitches called for refinements of the existing system. Music in which the different players were not strictly coordinated had to be laid out in a new way. A whole range of graphic notation has grown up to guide or stimulate improvisatory performance without unduly restricting the players. And symbols were devised to represent all the new playing techniques—at first in bewildering and contradictory variety, though now some degree of standardization is coming about.

61 Aspects of New Music

"How can you make a revolution when the revolution before last has already said that anything goes?"

CHARLES WUORINEN

Until about 1950, the hope was often expressed by composers and critics that the various techniques and aesthetic viewpoints of modern music would coalesce into a new "common practice"—similar to the shared musical language of previous centuries. However, instead of assimilating the diverse styles of Stravinsky, Bartók, Schoenberg, and their contemporaries into the heritage of Bach and Handel, Haydn, Mozart, and Beethoven, Brahms and Wagner, composers have gone on inventing new techniques, forms, and styles. A common language now seems further away than ever. Instead of one common practice, there are many different practices. Even the essential elements of older music have been called into question and re-evaluated by composers of today, many of whom think in terms of "time" rather than rhythm, of "pitch" instead of melody and harmony.

Time in New Music

Before the twentieth century, virtually all music was based on regular meters—the steady alternation of strong and weak beats. Within this framework, the use of different rhythmic patterns, tempos, dynamics, and types of phrasing provided composers with a seemingly endless range of expressive possibilities. As we have seen, in the early part of the new century the use of irregularly spaced accents (changing meters) and of simultaneous but different rhythmic patterns (polyrhythms) brought a new vitality and fresh potential to this aspect of music.

But these innovations by Stravinsky and others did not overthrow the concept of an underlying pulse; they merely made it less regular, more complex. Only after mid-century did composers begin to take seriously the possibility of music without any pulse at all. Such music was arrived at independently from two directions. On the one hand, John Cage and his disciples were seeking to do away with the predictability in music—and what could be more predictable than a steady beat? They planned their music so that the sounds would occur at random, at unspecified intervals of time. On the other hand, the complex patterns developed by some of the serialists yielded music so asymmetrical in rhythm that it could no longer be heard in terms of any regular pulse. The realization that these two approaches led to similar results brought about much theorizing and experimentation. Even more conservative composers, such as Benjamin Britten, found that free rhythm could be used as an effective contrast to a regular pulse. A whole range of new possibilities was opened up.

Still another approach was the use of a regular but constantly changing pulse, exploited most extensively in the music of Elliott Carter. Though this can be done through the traditional devices of accelerando and ritardando, more complex procedures are also possible. If, for example, a regular flow of eighth notes is first accented on every sixth note and then on every fifth one, the flow of the notes remains the same but the accented notes come more frequently and thus the tempo is faster. With similar and more elaborate procedures, the changing flow of time can become an essential element of musical structure.

Still another liberating element in thinking about this dimension of music was brought about by electronic music and its use of tape. In working with tape, a composer needs to decide precisely how long—in terms of seconds or microseconds—a note is to be, rather than merely thinking of it as, say, "two beats long"; that is, he must think in absolute rather than relative terms, in "real time" rather than "musical time." It is perfectly possible to synthesize music with a regular pulse—but also possible to avoid a pulse—more easily than with live performers, who are accustomed by training and habit to thinking of music in terms of pulse.

Related to these new approaches to music and time, naturally, are philosophical overtones. The use of regular pulse has been a basic element in the sense that uninterrupted movement toward a goal has characterized Western music through much of its history, and this sense surely expresses something basic about Western man's view of the world. The static quality of pulseless music has much in common with other cultures, notably those of the Orient, and it is not surprising to find that many of the composers in pursuit of such a quality in their music are also much influenced by Eastern modes of thought and behavior.

Pitch in New Music

Western music's sense of movement and destination is, of course, also created by its use of harmony and melody: the phrase coming to a cadence, the movement returning to the home key. But these are not necessary characteristics of music, as other cultures demonstrate and as composers since World War II have discovered. The primacy of melody in music, already much weakened in the earlier part of the century, is no longer taken for granted. Much of today's music is "athematic"—made of colors, harmonies, textures, rhythms that are

The athematic quality of much modern music finds a parallel in the notion of "all over" or "action" painting, in which a canvas has no prescribed borders or obvious representational intention. Composition, 1955, by Willem de Kooning *(b. 1904). Collection The Solomon R. Guggenheim Museum, New York.*

held together without the clearly defined thread of a single line that we call a melody.

During the Fifties and early Sixties, the term "pointillism" (derived from the name given to the school of French Postimpressionist painters, such as Seurat and Signac, who built up their pictures with individual dots of color rather than larger brushstrokes) came to be used in connection with a certain type of serial music. In this style, whose musical ancestor was Anton Webern, the individual notes were often so far apart, either in time or space, that they could not be heard as forming melodies or harmonies; each was a "point," an individual event.

Later came the idea of "clouds" of pitches—a great many notes in the same general pitch area played very close together, so quickly that the individual sounds could not easily be distinguished. The effect could be likened to a large blurry mass, quite different from the precise, distinct notes of yesteryear. The Greek-French composer Iannis Xenakis and the Pole Krzysztof Penderecki, whose works made much use of this and related devices, also revived the tone clusters of Henry Cowell, now produced by an entire orchestra instead of by the arms of one pianist.

Another form of experimentation involves the use of microtones—division of the octave into more than twelve intervals. Earlier in the century, a few composers had occasionally used quarter-tones (notes halfway between the notes of the chromatic scale) for coloristic effects, and the Czech Alois Hába wrote entire pieces using such scales. Now the possibilities of more refined subdivisions are being explored—an effort greatly facilitated by the use of electronic music, which can produce these refinements of pitch rather more easily than can live performers (although some adventurous and skilled players have become remarkably adept at this difficult technique).

With these and other techniques, composers have discovered how to make music without melody, replacing lines with blocks of sound, blocks of tone color that could change imperceptibly or dramatically. Yet at the same time others continue to write music in terms of lines and counterpoints, and to many all these possibilities seem useful at one time or another. Today, in fact, every piece makes its own rules, defines its own vocabulary of sounds, makes its own assumptions about what is musically logical or interesting. There is no longer a central vocabulary of materials and procedures shared in common, and every new piece must explain itself from scratch.

Musical Theater Today

Contemporary composers have been vitally concerned with developing a new kind of music theater that would be as germane to our epoch as traditional opera has been to former times. This trend has given rise to what is sometimes described as multimedia theater, or the theater of mixed media.

These terms are somewhat misleading, since opera has always been a theater of many media, involving as it does music and drama, singing, acting, and dancing, presented with all the allure of the theater arts—costumes, scenery, and lighting. From Monteverdi to Verdi, from Handel to Wagner and beyond, opera composers tried to avail themselves of all the resources open to them and to combine those with all the ingenuity of which they were capable. Contemporary composers have done the same, which means that they take advantage of all the new resources available to them. These include electronic and live music; mime, dance, speech, song, and chant; movement, light, and film projections. Included too are aleatory procedures, improvisation, situations based on performer choice or indeterminacy, and audience participation. In short, Wagner's nineteenth-century dream of a total art work—what he called the *Gesamtkunstwerk*—has been expanded to involve all the new resources made possible by mid-twentieth-century musical technology. There results a total kind of theater using an unrestricted environment that encourages complete interaction with the audience, rather than the formal proscenium-and-stage that separates the players from the spectators.

The Audience Gap

For many decades now, the general musical audience has lagged in its understanding of contemporary music. In the nineteenth century, new developments were always presented within the framework of the central musical language, and listeners could always, even in the most apparently "revolutionary" works, find familiar elements. Although a new piece might contain unusual sounds or develop in unexpected ways, still the basic language was similar to that of older and familiar pieces.

In the twentieth century, this has no longer been so. Audiences accustomed to the familiar concert repertory found the absolute novelty of some contemporary works violently offensive. Today, however, listeners are becoming used to this situation. Younger generations have grown up surrounded by music from all over the world and from all periods of the past, and they have fewer preconceptions about what music "ought to be." Composers, too, have learned that, in this new, less monolithic state of affairs, it sometimes helps to give verbal clues to their listeners, in the form of descriptive titles, programmatic narratives, or analyses that suggest ways of hearing their music. And, as a composer's work becomes well known, his particular language becomes familiar to more and more people, who—understanding what he is trying to do—are better able to follow his next step.

In the following chapters, we will consider works by eight composers, prominent and representative figures of the postwar period. Their music is very different, and they exemplify something of the variety of styles now being practiced. The fact that eight such disparate works (not to mention many others that might have been added if space permitted) can be found in one relatively brief span of time attests that this is a unique moment in the history of music. And, if we keep our minds open and approach the music of our contemporaries with sympathetic attention, we are likely to find it also an uncommonly stimulating moment.

62 Four Representative European Composers

Olivier Messiaen (1908–)

"I consider rhythm the prime and perhaps the essential part of music."

In the years after the Second World War Olivier Messiaen emerged as one of the most influential musicians in Europe. Among the young composers whose aesthetic he helped shape were three future leaders of contemporary music—Iannis Xenakis, Karlheinz Stockhausen, and Pierre Boulez.

Messiaen, who was born in Avignon, received his musical training at the Paris Conservatory, where he won most of the available prizes. At twenty-three he became organist of the Church of the Trinity and five years later professor at both the École Normale de Musique and the Schola Cantorum. He was drafted into the army shortly after the outbreak of war, was captured by the Germans in June 1940, and for two years was a prisoner of war. On his release he was appointed to the faculty of the Paris Conservatory. He sub-

Olivier Messiaeu in his garden transcribing bird songs for one of his compositions. Copyright Collection G. D. Hackett, New York.

sequently taught in Tanglewood, Darmstadt, and various centers of contemporary music in North and South America.

Messiaen has steadfastly adhered to his conception of art as the ideal expression of religious faith. Early in his career he placed his music, as he put it, "at the service of the dogmas of Catholic theology." He considers his religious feeling to be the most important aspect of his art, "the only one perhaps that I will not regret at the hour of my death." He is a mystic and a visionary, for whom the three most important elements of man's experience on earth—love of God, human love (as exemplified by Tristan and Isolde), and love of nature "are summed up in one idea: divine love!" What he had to teach his pupils went far beyond the notes. As Pierre Boulez summed it up, for Messiaen "music was more than a work of art, it was a way of existing, an inextinguishable fire."

Works inspired by religious mysticism occupy a central position in his list, from *Apparition de l'Église éternelle* (Apparition of the Eternal Church) for organ and *Hymne au Saint Sacrement* (Hymn to the Sacred Sacrament) for orchestra of 1931, to *Et exspecto resurrectionem mortuorum* (And I expect the Resurrection of the Dead) for woodwinds, brass, and metal percussion of 1964 and *La Transfiguration de Notre Seigneur Jésus-Christ* for piano, flute, clarinet, cello, xylorimba, vibraphone, marimba, chorus, and orchestra (1965–1969). Such dedication to religious mysticism on the part of a musician is uncommon in our time.

Many streams commingle in Messiaen's music. His love of nature has centered about his interest in bird songs, in which he has found an inexhaustible source of melody. From this preoccupation stem such works as *Oiseaux exotiques* (Exotic Birds, for piano and orchestra, 1956) and *Catalogue d'oiseaux* (Catalogue of Birds, for piano, 1956–1958). Of his notation of bird songs he says, "For the melody and the rhythm I have always tried to notate with the utmost precision except for very small intervals and very short durations, which are replaced by slightly larger intervals and durations, the others being impractical. But I always respect the scale of the different durations; the relations between pitches and durations stay the same with a slight change in tempo and register which, I repeat, does not destroy the relations." Messiaen has also been strongly influenced by the undulating melodic line of Gregorian chant, the quiet remoteness of the medieval modes, the subtle, asymmetrical rhythms of Indian music, and the delicate bell-sounds of the Javanese gamelan. All these strands are woven into the colorful tapestry of his *Turangalîla-Symphony* (1948), a monumental orchestral work in ten movements.

Messiaen has made a contribution of unparalleled importance to the contemporary literature of the organ. He has also written piano music that abounds in novel sonorities, the exploitation of the instrument's extreme registers, and a thoroughly original approach to piano technique. Here he has found his ideal interpreter in his wife, the pianist Yvonne Loriod. "Melody first and foremost," he declared with romantic exuberance while still in his twenties, and he has never relinquished this conviction. In harmony he took his point of departure from the innovations of Debussy, as in rhythm from those of Stravinsky. His harmonies, like Debussy's, are used primarily for their color rather than for their functional value. In his emphasis on the individual harmony he is very much of the age. It imparts to certain of his works a static element that suits the ecstatic quality of the music. His harmonies are often conceived in their relation to timbre. In this he follows the lead of Varèse, who, as he points out, replaced the concept of chords "by sound complexes designed for maximum color and intensity." Hand in hand with this goes a plasticity of form based on melodic-rhythmic cells that expand or contract irregularly, their unfolding enlivened by free and continuous variation.

As the quotation at the head of this chapter suggests, it is in the field of rhythm that Messiaen has made his most original contribution. His development in this area fits the mid-century trend toward nonsymmetrical patterns. "A rhythmic music is one that disregards repetition, squareness, and regular division, a music that is, in short, inspired by the movement of nature, a movement of free and uneven durations." His rhythmic language, he explains, combines a number of elements, among which he mentions "durations distributed in irregular numbers, an absence of even beats and of symmetrical measures, love for prime numbers . . ." In line with the climate of the post-Webern era, he extended Schoenberg's serialization of pitch to include also durations, types of attack, and intensities. He has experimented also with "tempo modulations" in which an accelerando or ritardando may serve to alter the quality of a rhythm.

On all these levels Messiaen has been a pathfinder. But perhaps his most important role was to reaffirm the power of music to express human emotion and to embody man's profoundest aspirations. This needed doing in our time, and Messiaen did it boldly, imaginatively, with unshakeable conviction.

Quartet for the End of Time

The winter of 1940 found Messiaen in the German camp Stalag VIIIA, in Saxony. Among the prisoners were three French musicians: a violinist, cellist, and clarinetist. Messiaen began to write a chamber-music piece for them, to which he soon added a piano part. It was a monumental work in eight movements that helped to sustain the composer through this terrible time. When he completed it, Messiaen and his friends decided to organize a performance of the quartet. The violinist and clarinetist had managed to hold on to their instruments. A cello was found in the camp, with one of its strings missing, and an old upright piano, "badly out of tune, with some keys sticking periodically." The concert took place on a bitter cold night in January 1941, in front of five thousand prisoners from France, Belgium, Poland, and other countries. Messiaen prepared this polyglot audience of peasants, workers, intellectuals, soldiers, by explaining to them what he had tried to say in the music. In later years he declared that he had never had so attentive and understanding a public.

The work that was given to the world under such dramatic circumstances was the *Quatuor pour la fin du temps* (Quartet for the End of Time). It was inspired by a wonderful passage in the Revelation of St. John, Chapter X: "I saw an angel full of strength descending from the sky, clad with a cloud and having a rainbow over his head. His face was like the sun, his feet like columns of fire. He set his right foot on the sea, his left foot on the earth and, standing on the sea and on the earth, he raised his hand to the sky and swore by Him who lives in the centuries of centuries, saying: *There shall be no more Time,* but on the day of the seventh Angel's trumpet the mystery of God shall be accomplished."

1. *Liturgy of Crystal. Bien modéré* (quite moderate), 3/4. "Between three and four in the morning, the awakening of the birds: a blackbird or a nightingale improvises, surrounded by a sonorous cloud of dust, by a halo of trills lost high up in the trees." The solo parts—clarinet and violin—are marked "like a bird." Messiaen directs that the chords on the piano, legato and pianissimo, should be "enveloped in pedal." The movement unfolds at a pianissimo, and ends *ppp*.

2. *Vocalise for the Angel who Announces the End of Time.* "The first and third sections, very short, evoke the power of this mighty angel. . . . On the piano, soft cascades of blue-orange chords envelop in their distant chimes the song of the violin and cello, which is almost like plainchant." The movement, in 3/4, alternates between *Robuste, modéré* (vigorous, moderate) and *Presque vif, joyeux* (fairly lively, joyous). Its "impalpable harmonies" are marked *ppp* and *Presque lent* (fairly slow). Messiaen compares them to "drops of water in the rainbow." These are surrounded at either end by incisive chords on the piano, *fff*.

3. *Abyss of the Birds.* "For clarinet solo. The abyss is Time, with its sorrows and lassitudes. The birds are the opposite of Time: our desire for light, for stars, for rainbows and jubilant vocalises!" This movement is marked *Lent, expressif et triste* (slow, expressive, and sad). A broad arc of desolate melody alternates with passages that are

to be played, according to Messiaen's directions, in a gay, capricious manner, evoking the birds that are "the opposite of Time."

4. *Interlude.* "A Scherzo, more extrovert than the other movements, but attached to them by several melodic reminiscences." *Décidé, modéré, un peu vif* (decisive, moderate, somewhat lively), 2/4. This was the first of the movements to be written, before Messiaen decided to add the piano part. The opening passage, which returns toward the end of the movement, has a dancelike character. The middle section, with its rapid runs and trills on the clarinet and a lovely melodic phrase in the upper register of the violin, evokes birds.

5. *Praise to the Eternity of Jesus. Infiniment lent, extatique* (infinitely slow, ecstatic). "Jesus is here considered as the Word. A long and infinitely slow phrase on the cello magnifies, with love and reverence, the eternity of this powerful and mild Word, 'whose years shall not be consumed.' " This rapturous meditation deploys all the expressive capacities of the cello. The melody is accompanied by soft chords on the piano:

6. *Dance of Fury, for the Seven Trumpets. Décidé, vigoureux, granitique, un peu vif* (decisive, vigorous, granitic, somewhat fast). "Rhythmically this is the most characteristic movement. The four instruments in unison imitate the charm of bells and trumpets. . . . Listen especially to the terrible fortissimo of the theme in augmentation and changed register toward the end of the movement."

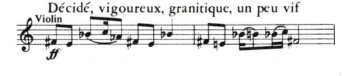

7. *Glow of Rainbows for the Angel who Announces the End of Time. Rêveur, presque lent* (dreamily, fairly slow), 3/4. "Certain passages

from the second movement return here. . . . In my dreams I hear and see groups of chords and melodies, colors and familiar shapes. Then, after this transitory stage, I pass into the unreal and experience with ecstasy a whirling, a dancing interpenetration of superhuman sounds and colors. These swords of fire, these streams of blue-orange lava, these sudden stars—this is the glow, these are the rainbows!" Certainly no other composer of the twentieth century has described in such vivid detail the visionary, almost hallucinatory character of the creative act—better, the creative act as he experienced it.

8. *Praise to the Immortality of Jesus.* "This praise is love. Its slow rise towards the climax traces the ascent of men toward God, of the Child of God toward His Father, of the human-made-God toward Paradise." *Extrêmement lent et tendre, extatique* (extremely slow and tender, ecstatic), 4/4. When the violin soars into the upper regions of its highest string we have a romantic atmosphere, whether the composer is singing of divine or earthly love. Thus the listener can enjoy this music whether or not he shares the theology behind it.

It testifies to the couarage of the human spirit that Messiaen was able to rise above the squalor, hunger, and cold of that dreadful winter in Stalag VIIIA to conceive and execute so bold a work. This need to soar above the immediacies of life to a higher plane of experience imparts to all his music its quality of aspiration, its essential spirituality.

Benjamin Britten (1913–1976)

"I believe that it is possible and desirable to develop a kind of British opera that will explore the vital native qualities of the English voice and language."

Benjamin Britten was a musician of great invention, technical mastery, and charm. He was undoubtedly the most important English composer of his generation.

Britten was born in Lowestoft, in Suffolk, the son of musical parents. By the time he was fourteen the boy had produced ten piano sonatas, six string quartets, three suites for piano, an oratorio, and dozens of songs. After several years of study with the composer Frank Bridge, he won a scholarship to the Royal College of Music, where he soon distinguished himself both in piano and composition.

He had his first public performance shortly after his nineteenth birthday, when the *Phantasy for String Quintet* and some part-songs were presented at a concert of contemporary music. His *Sinfonietta* for chamber orchestra was heard a few weeks later. His schooling over, Britten went to work for the G. P. O. Film Unit, a politically progressive group that produced documentary films. "The company I was working for had very little money. I had to write scores not for large orchestras but for six or seven instruments, and to make these instruments make all the effects that each film demanded." He could not have served a more valuable apprenticeship.

His work for the films, radio, and theater brought him into contact with the forward-looking young poets of the day—Auden, Isherwood, Spender, C. Day Lewis, and Louis MacNeice. These writers were affected by the political ferment of the times—this was the period of the Spanish Civil War—and they played an important part in Britten's intellectual development. On the musical front he scored his first big success with *Variations on a Theme of Frank Bridge* for string orchestra.

The European situation continued to deteriorate, and early in 1939 Auden left for the United States, having decided that only there would he find the proper conditions for his work. Britten decided to follow his friend's example. He left England in the summer of 1939, and settled in New York. The American sojourn saw the production of a number of major works: the *Violin Concerto* (1939); *Les Illuminations* (1939), a song cycle in which with rare felicity he caught the bitterness of Rimbaud's poems; *Diversions on a Theme* for piano and orchestra (1940); and *Sinfonia da Requiem* (1940). By this time England was taking the punishment of the Luftwaffe raids. Britten, although a pacifist, felt more and more that his rightful place was in his homeland. While in California he read a British magazine in which his attention was caught by the opening line of an article by E. M. Forster: "To think of Crabbe is to think of England." This reference to the poet of his native Suffolk, who was born two centuries before at Aldeburgh, not far from his own birthplace, filled him with homesickness. His decision was taken forthwith.

It was no easy matter to cross the Atlantic in the fall of 1941. He waited in New York for almost six months before he could obtain passage. The delay made it possible for him to hear his *Sinfonia da Requiem* conducted by Serge Koussevitzky in Boston. The conductor, struck by the dramatic quality of Britten's music, offered him a commission for an opera. Thus Britten was able to go ahead with a project that already had taken shape in his mind—the writing of an opera based on material from George Crabbe's poem *The Borough*. In March 1942 he returned to England.

A drawing of Benjamin Britten in 1964 by B. F. Dolbin. Collection André Meyer.

Exempted from active service as a conscientious objector, Britten was permitted to aid the war effort in his own way. He appeared as a pianist all over England and continued to compose. A number of new works were completed during the war, among them *Peter Grimes,* on a libretto by Montague Slater based on Crabbe's poem. The work received its premiere in June, 1945, was presented in practically all the opera houses of the world, and established Britten as an international figure.

In 1947 he settled in Aldeburgh, in a house overlooking the sea. The village immortalized by Crabbe became the center of his activities, which included frequent appearances as conductor and pianist both in England and abroad. Britten was instrumental in organizing the Aldeburgh Festival, which has been held every summer since 1948. His involvement with the scene of his labors was well described by the composer when, in the summer of 1951, he was made an Honorary Freeman of the Borough of Lowestoft: "Suffolk, the birthplace and inspiration of Constable and Gainsborough, the loveliest of English painters; the home of Crabbe, that most English of poets; Suffolk, with its rolling, intimate countryside; its heavenly Gothic churches, big and small; its marshes, with those wild seabirds; its grand ports and little fishing villages. I am firmly rooted in this glorious country. And I proved this to myself when I once tried to live somewhere else." He died in Aldeburgh in 1976, at the age of sixty-three.

Britten was essentially a lyricist. Whether for voices or instruments, his art drew its imagery and its melodic line from that most personal of instruments, the human voice. It follows that the grand forms of instrumental music—the sonata and symphony—attracted Britten far less than they did the majority of his contemporaries. Much more to his taste was the theme and variations which, because it is less architectonic than the sonata, permits the shorter flights of fancy that appeal to the lyricist. Hence his devotion to the passacaglia. He also assiduously cultivated the three forms in which a series of numbers adds up to a large-scale work: the suite, the song cycle, and the opera.

Britten was devoted to the classical view of the artist as a master craftsman. For him, as for Stravinsky, each composition represented a particular problem that had to be solved. He enjoyed working on a commission, and readily shaped his inspiration to conditions imposed from without. The classicist in Britten demanded a certain distance between the raw emotion and its sublimation into art. Hence his addiction to formal procedures such as canon and fugue. His operas display a number of devices for creating distance between the action and the audience: the male and female chorus in the *Rape of Lucretia,* or the framework in *Billy Budd,* whereby Captain Vere in his old age reflects upon the tragedy of Billy.

Like every artist of clasical persuasion, Britten was keenly aware of his heritage. The art of the Elizabethan madrigalists, of the Tudor church composers, and of Purcell was a living reality to him. Even as Purcell did in the seventeenth century, Britten assimilated important influences emanating from the Continent and adapted them to the English taste. He responded to the rhythmic élan of the early Stravinsky (he did not care for the Russian's later works); to the orchestral lyricism of Mahler, who influenced him profoundly; and to the operatic Expressionism of Alban Berg.

Britten had the imagination of the musical dramatist. He was adept at the delineation of character through music, at suggesting a mood or an atmosphere with a few telling strokes. He exemplified the modern trend back to the Classical conception of opera. "I am especially interested," he wrote, "in the general architectural and formal problems of opera." He therefore rejected the Wagnerian concept of "endless melody" in favor of the Classical practice of separate numbers which, as he said, "crystallize and hold the emotion of a dramatic situation at chosen moments." Nor did he always set the text in accordance with the natural inflections of the words, adhering rather to the doctrine that it is permissible to distort the prosody in the interest of heightened expression.

Peter Grimes announced to the world that a musical dramatist of stature had arrived upon the scene. This impression was in no way belied by *The Rape of Lucretia* (1946), even though Britten's second opera, on a libretto by Ronald Coleman, has none of the earthy vitality of the first. Intead, it is a highly stylized treatment of the Roman story and shows true elegance in its classical restraint. *Albert Herring* (1947) represents Britten's solitary venture into the field of comic opera. The libretto by Eric Crozier was freely adapted from a story by Maupassant. In 1948 Britten came forth with a new version of *The Beggar's Opera*. The following year he wrote *The Little Sweep*, a poignant children's opera which, together with its prologue, is known as *Let's Make an Opera*, and allows for audience participation.

In *Billy Budd* (1952), the libretto of which was adapted by E. M. Forster and Eric Crozier from Melville's famous story, the symbols of good and evil implicit in the tale of the ill-fated sailor inspired the composer to a somber work that is powerful musically no less than dramatically. This was followed by *Gloriana* (1953), an opera about Elizabeth and Essex, written in honor of the coronation of her namesake, which received its premiere in the presence of the Queen. Certainly no Englishman present on that occasion could fail to be moved. All the same, *Gloriana* is strictly for home consumption. *The Turn of the Screw*, first presented at the Venice Festival of 1954, captures in uncanny fashion the atmosphere of evil that so subtly permeates Henry James's celebrated tale. *Noye's Fludde*, a one-acter for children (1958), was followed by *A Midsummer Night's Dream*, which was given its premiere at the Aldeburgh Festival of 1960. *Owen Wingrave* (1971), based on another James story, was originally written for television. Britten's final stage work was an operatic version of Thomas Mann's *Death in Venice* (1973).

Britten's operas are an outgrowth of the music-festival movement, which offers the contemporary composer a much more hospitable platform than does the traditional opera house. He found a congenial medium in chamber opera, a genre whose small cast and modest orchestra allow subtleties that would be lost in the larger frame of grand opera. Here Britten's classical economy of means, transparency of texture, and flair for supple rhythms show to their best advantage, as does his predilection for harmonic directness and a light, radiant sound.

To the works we have mentioned may be added *A Ceremony of Carols* (1942), a cycle for treble voices and harp; the lovely *Serenade* for tenor solo, horn, and string orchestra (1953); the *Spring Symphony* for soloists, chorus, and orchestra—a cycle of lyric poems in praise of spring by twelve English poets (1949); the *Nocturne* for tenor and chamber orchestra (1958); and numerous song cycles written for his close friend and musical associate, the tenor Peter Pears. The *Young Person's Guide to the Orchestra*, a set of variations and fugue on a theme by Purcell (1946), is both entertaining and instructive. Among the later works we may also mention three "parables for church performance," for soloists, chorus, and chamber ensemble, that have been much played in the United States: *Curlew River* (1964), *The Burning Fiery Furnace* (1966), and *The Prodigal Son* (1967).

War Requiem

Two major English poets died in World War I. Rupert Brooke, whose poems adhered to Rudyard Kipling's "manly" view of war, became the symbol of golden-haired British youth marching gallantly to a warrior's death. The opposite, unpopular view of the war as a brutal slaughter without purpose or meaning was expressed by Wilfrid Owen, who, after winning the Military Cross, was killed at the age of twenty-five just before the Armistice of 1918. Owen's poetry, which tried to explode what he called "the Old Lie," had to wait longer for acceptance than Brooke's, but it is now apparent that he rather than Brooke was the outstanding English poet of the war. For Britten, a conscientious objector in World War II, the use of Owen's verses in a major work was a statement of the highest emotional and intellectual import. He quoted three lines of Owen as the motto of the *War Requiem:*

> My subject is War, and the pity of War.
> The Poetry is in the pity . . .
> All a poet can do today is to warn.

Britten dedicated the Requiem (1961) to the "loving memory" of four friends killed in the Second World War. The passionate tenderness of the poet inspired the composer to what many regard as his masterpiece.

Throughout his career Britten was fascinated by the union of opposites, the combining of widely contrasting elements within the frame of a single work. Out of this came his decision—a boldly imaginative stroke!—to combine Owen's lines with the Latin text of the Mass for the Dead. Thus the sacred text, in which grief is filtered through a hieratical expression and lifted to the universal plane, became a frame for Owen's intensely personal vision.

There are three sonorous levels within the structure of the work. Owen's poems are sung by two soldiers, tenor and baritone, accompanied by a chamber orchestra. Theirs is the world of actual combat, of fear, tension, grief, and questioning. Around them are ranged the larger forces of the Latin Mass—soprano solo and full chorus supported by orchestra—representing the world of religious faith and ritual, and the age-old plea for mercy and peace. Third is the boys' chorus, whose pure, disembodied sound is equally far removed from the travail of the battlefield and the dogma of the Church. This chorus is accmpanied by an organ. As is traditional in choral music, individual words, phrases, and lines are repeated over and over again in order to allow room for musical expansion of the concise Latin text.

I. *Requiem aeternam.* The first words of the text float out of a dark pianissimo marked "Slow and solemn":

Requiem aeternam dona eis, Domine: Rest eternal grant them, O Lord:
et lux perpetua luceat eis.   and let eternal light shine upon them.

(For the complete Latin-English text see Appendix II.) The chorus murmurs these lines against a melody that is intoned by the strings in unison, in a tense, striding rhythm. It grows throughout the movement by a process of accretion, serving as a unifying thread:

Bells toll as a solemn processional unfolds, rising steadily to the radiance of strings and woodwinds in upper register to suggest the "eternal light" of the text. Soon the procession returns to the dark pianissimo whence it came.

Boys' chorus:

Te decet hymnus, Deus, in Sion.   Thou, O God, art praised in Sion.

The pure sonority of boys' voices wreathes the text in a flutelike resonance. Then the processional (*Requiem aeternam*) is repeated, building as before to an upsurge of light on *lux perpetua*. Mood and tempo change abruptly on the final chord; arpeggios on the harp usher in the next section, "Very quick and agitated." The tenor, supported by chamber orchestra, enters almost at once:

> What passing-bells for those who die as cattle?
>   Only the monstrous anger of the guns,
> Only the stuttering rifles' rapid rattle
>   Can patter out their hasty orisons . . .

How distinctive is Britten's way of setting text, and how nobly it fulfills what he called one of his chief aims—"to try and restore to the musical setting of the English language a brilliance, freedom, and vitality that have been curiously rare since the death of Purcell." The instrumental texture is of the utmost transparency and variety. Harp arpeggios recur again and again, and an oboe recalls the theme of the boys' chorus (*Te decet*). Bells toll gently as the movement ends in a mood of supplication: *Kyrie eleison, Christe eleison* (Lord have mercy, Christ have mercy).

II. *Dies irae*

Dies irae, dies illa,   Day of wrath and doom impends,
Solvet saeclum in favilla,   Heaven, earth in ashes ends!
Teste David cum Sibylla.   David's words and the Sybil's.

Quantus tremor est futurus,   What fear men's bosoms rends
Quando Judex est venturus,   When the Judge from heaven descends,
Cuncta stricte discussurus!   On whose sentence all depends!

Unlike Mozart, Berlioz, and Verdi, who began their vision of Judgment Day with a mighty gesture, Britten's canvas opens with fanfares on the brass that are none the less dramatic for being pianissimo. The whispering of the chorus has a quality of awe and fear. Staccato rhythm, based on an asymmetrical meter—7/4—adds urgency to the movement, which leaps up to a blazing fortissimo at the *Tuba mirum:*

Tuba mirum spargens sonum	The trumpet flings a wondrous sound
Per sepulchra regionum,	Through the earth's sepulcher,
Coget omnes ante thronum.	Summoning all before the Throne.

All nature quakes as heaven and earth prepare to answer to the divine Judge. The chamber orchestra sets the scene for the baritone solo:

> Bugles sang, sadd'ning the evening air;
> And bugles answer'd, sorrowful to hear . . .
> The shadow of the morrow weighed on men.

The fanfares of the *Dies irae* echo sadly as the baritone sings of young soldiers who do not know what the morning may bring them. Deeply moving is the ascending-descending scale pattern with which Britten concludes Owen's stanza:

Britten's way of letting accented syllables fall on unaccented beats makes for great rhythmic flexibility. We have encountered this separation of word accents and musical accents in the Expressionistic settings of Schoenberg and Berg.

Liber scriptus (Lo! the book has been brought forth in which all has been recorded, according to which the world will be judged). A soprano, supported by the orchestra, unfolds a boldly profiled melody marked "Slow and majestic." Wide leaps and dotted rhythm give the vocal line its bite:

Quid sum miser (What shall I, miserable one, plead? Who will intercede for me when even the just need mercy?). The semichorus asks these life-and-death questions against the steady beat of the kettledrum, like the beating of a heart.

Rex tremendae majestatis (King of tremendous majesty, who freely saves those worthy of it, Fount of pity, save me!). The soprano's melody inverts the first two measures of her previous solo:

This section leads into the duet of the two soldiers (tenor and baritone):

> Out there, we've walked quite friendly up to Death;
> Sat down and eaten with him, cool and bland . . .
> We whistled while he shaved us with his scythe.
> Oh, Death was never enemy of ours!

There is mordant irony in the contrast between this talk of Death and the music, which is marked "Fast and gay." The gaiety is underlined by triplets in the strings, the marchlike rat-tat-tat of the snare drum, and a devil-may-care whistling that sweeps through the orchestra, to which the piccolo contributes its share.

"We laughed, knowing that better men would come / And greater wars . . ." It is a bitter laughter.

Recordare (Remember, kind Jesus, that I am the cause of your sacrifice. Do not leave me on that Day). A women's chorus in four parts continues the plea for redemption.

Confutatis maledictis (When the wicked are confounded and cast to the flames, summon me with the blessed ones). The basses enter with an assertive melody in 5/4 and are answered by the tenors. Six horns and three trombones suggest, by their snarling, the terror of those doomed to eternal damnation.

There follows a baritone solo marked "Very broad":

> Be slowly lifted up, thou long black arm,
> Great gun towering t'ward Heaven, about to curse . . .
> But when thy spell be cast complete and whole,
> May God curse thee, and cut thee from our soul!

The poet's malediction is punctuated by the fanfares of the *Dies irae*. When he finishes his curse the shattering music of the *Dies irae* returns in all its fury. As before, the meter is 7/4.

Lacrimosa (Ah! that day of tears and mourning!). Accompanied by chorus and orchestra, the soprano sings one of those wide-ranging, infinitely poignant tunes of which Britten knew the secret:

Her music is interrupted four times by a tenor solo, a song of mourning for youth doomed to die. Thus the two polarities of the work—the ritual text in Latin and the poems in English—are drawing ever closer to one another.

> Move him,
> Move him into the sun—
> Gently its touch awoke him once . . .
> If anything might rouse him now
> The kind old sun will know.

Bells toll again, and the chorus ends this part with the same chords that ended the first movement.

III. *Offertorium. Domine Jesu Christe, Rex gloriae* (Lord Jesus Christ, King of Glory, deliver the souls of all the faithful dead from the pains of hell and the deep pit). Against arpeggios on the organ, the boys sing as in the distance. Their undulating melodic line suggests the gentle rise and fall of Gregorian chant.

Sed signifer (But let the standard-bearer Saint Michael lead them into the holy light). A twittering of woodwinds enlivens this prelude to a fugue, the subject of which Britten—emulating the practice of Bach and Handel—drew from an earlier work. The fugue subject is heard on the main thought, *Quam olim Abrahae promisisti et semini ejus* (which of old Thou didst promise to Abraham and his seed). Introduced by tenors and basses, this is a resilient theme that takes on suppleness from the syncopated rhythm in the second and third measures:

The fugue musters all the traditional devices of counterpoint, but Britten wears his learning lightly. His is the art that conceals art, and what comes through to the listener is the lovingkindness of God's promise to His children. There is a crescendo at each repetition of the key thought *et semini ejus* (and his seed), as if to emphasize the promise to unborn generations.

The mention of Abraham in the sacred text leads Britten, by a natural association, to Owen's poetic version of the Abraham and Isaac story, in which the patriarch disregards the word of God and slays his young son. The switch from Abraham to Abram—one of the most dramatic strokes in the Requiem—is effectuated as the chorus is replaced by solo tenor and baritone, and the full orchestra by the chamber group. The transition is made by a solo clarinet playing a lighthearted version of the fugue theme.

> Then Abram bound the youth with belts and straps,
> And builded parapets and trenches there,
> And stretched forth the knife to slay his son.

Arpeggios on the harp herald the angel who tells the Patriarch that God will accept a ram in place of Isaac.

> But the old man would not so, but slew his son,—
> And half the seed of Europe, one by one . . .

The two solo voices repeat "half the seed of Europe, one by one" while, as a background, the boys' chorus sings the *Hostias* (We offer unto Thee, O Lord, sacrifice of prayer and praise), their young voices suggesting the slaughter of the innocents. And now Britten's poetic scheme stands revealed. The two antipodes of his Requiem—the ritual Latin text and Owen's poem of senseless sacrifice—are heard simultaneously, brought together in an emotional and musical unity.

The preceding chorus is repeated, but now sopranos and altos instead of basses and tenors bring in the theme, which is heard upside down (see example on facing page).

Also inverted is the dynamic scheme. This time there is a diminuendo with each repetition of *et semini ejus* (and all his seed),

Quam o - lim A - bra - hae pro-mi-si - sti, et se-mi-ni e - jus.

reminding us that in the modern sacrificial rite the young were no longer spared.

IV. *Sanctus*

Sanctus, Sanctus, Sanctus Dominus   Holy, Holy, Holy, Lord God of
   Deus Sabaoth   Hosts

Against the luminous sound of vibraphone, glockenspiel, antique cymbals, and bells, the soprano traces a melismatic line (a single syllable extending over a series of notes). This is a song of praise in free rhythm.

Hosanna in excelsis (Glory to be Thee, O Lord most high). This eight-part chorus opens with sopranos introducing a theme of Handelian concision. Reinforced by brass and woodwind instruments, the voices build layer upon layer to a great outpouring of sound. For Britten, as for Purcell and Handel, the idea of glory is inseparable from the golden sonority of massed horns, trumpets, and trombones. The glory subsides as the soprano, against a background of chorus and orchestra, sings the *Benedictus* (Blessed is he that cometh in the name of the Lord); whereupon the chorus of praise is heard again. Out of it emerges the voice of the baritone, the voice of despair after joy and courage and hope have died:

> After the drums of Time have rolled and ceased,
> And by the bronzed west long retreat is blown,
> Shall life renew these bodies?

A weary Earth replies in accents of ineffable sorrow:

> "My fiery heart shrinks, aching. It is death.
> Mine ancient scars shall not be glorified,
> Nor my titanic tears, the sea, be dried."

V. *Agnus Dei.* In this movement two disparate bodies of sound—tenor solo supported by the chamber orchestra and full chorus supported by the orchestra—interweave. Owen's lines—

> One ever hangs where shelled roads part,
> In this war He too lost a limb,
> But His disciples hide apart;
> And now the Soldiers bear with Him—

merge in mood and spirit with the burden of the *Agnus Dei:* O Lamb of God, Who takest away the sins of the world, grant them rest. Marked "Slow," the music flows in a relaxed 5/16 rhythm. At the end, in the nature of a summation, the tenor sings a plea for peace. The phrase follows an ascending scale pattern that is as unusual as it is moving:

VI. *Libera me.* The final movement begins with the menacing sound of tenor and bass drums solo, *ppp.* We hear a slow march that moves into a gradual accelerando. Double basses enter with a distorted version of the theme that opened the first movement:

Soprano and chorus sing some of the most moving lines of the Latin text: *Libera me, Domine, de morte aeterna in die illa tremenda* (Deliver me, O Lord, from death eternal on that fearful day). Crescendo and accelerando fortify each other as tension-begetting elements. The music mounts in intensity to the entrance of the soprano with a melody whose downward leaps reflect the supplication of the words, "I stand in fear and trembling . . ."

There follows the emotional high point of Owen's lines, the *Strange Meeting* of the two dead soldiers:

> I am the enemy you killed, my friend,
> I knew you in this dark; for so you frowned
> Yesterday through me as you jabbed and killed.
> I parried; but my hands were loath and cold,
> Let us sleep now . . .

In this final section all the forces join for the first time—soloists, boys' chorus, and full chorus, organ, chamber orchestra, and full orchestra—in one encompassing resolution. The soloists repeat over and over again "Let us sleep now," while the boys and chorus sing *In Paradisum* (May the Angels lead thee into Paradise). The chorus ends with *Requiescant in pacem* (May they rest in peace) as churchbells ring and the chords that ended Parts I and II are heard again, leading through the Amen to a serene final cadence on an F major chord.

Thus ends one of the outstanding works of our century.

Karlheinz Stockhausen (1928–)

"First you make the music, and then the music changes you."

Karlheinz Stockhausen was born in Modrath, near Cologne. His boyhood fell in the high noon of Nazi indoctrination; he was eleven when the Second World War began. In the last years of the war, since he was too young for the army, he was sent to various youth camps to help build the Western Wall against the Allied forces, and later served in a military hospital. Having played the piano from the age of six, he continued his musical studies after the war, first at the Musikhochschule in Cologne, under Frank Martin, then with Olivier Messiaen in Paris. Somewhere along the line he managed to become an expert jazz pianist. He pursued his interest in physics and acoustics at the University of Bonn, became associated with the Studio for Electronic Music at the West German Radio in Cologne, and produced the first published score of electronic music in his *Electronic Studies* (1953–1954). Important too in his development was his study of phonetics and communication science at the University of Bonn.

Stockhausen's career shows a propitious coincidence of the forces that make for success in the musical world. He appeared on the scene at a time when, after the years of Nazi regression, the German public was receptive to the progressive movement in art. This favorable climate was further strengthened by the political and economic resurgence of West Germany. Stockhausen became one of the editors of *Die Reihe* (The Row), the quarterly review of serial music published by Universal Edition of Vienna, whose powerful resources were marshaled behind the propagating of his ideas. Gifted both as an organizer and polemicist, Stockhausen propagandized for his music as eloquently as he played and conducted it. He taught seminars in composition at the International Summer Courses for New Music in Darmstadt, lectured at the University of Pennsylvania in Philadelphia and at the University of California at Davis, traveled

Karlheinz Stockhausen

Stockhausen. A sketch by B. F. Dolbin in 1964. André Meyer Collection.

widely, spent time in Mexico and Japan, and—an ardent advocate of combining live and instrumental sounds—formed a group that gave hundreds of concerts of his electronic instrumental music. As a result of these far-flung activities he became one of the best-known among the leaders of the European avant-garde.

Stockhausen took his point of departure from the music of Webern. He continued the Viennese master's attempt to achieve minute control over all the elements of composition. He expanded the concept of the series to include not only pitch but also rhythm, timbre, dynamics, and density, in this way achieving total serialization. At the same time he was fascinated by the possibility of combining total control with total freedom, thereby—according to the Hegelian doctrine of "the unity of opposites"—reconciling two seemingly irreconcilable goals into a higher synthesis. In Stockhausen's music total control, attained through elaborate precompositional calculations, becomes a frame within which the performer can exercise his choice. "Even in the early completely predetermined compositions," he wrote, "there's a lot of randomness in different degrees." The degree of randomness increased steadily as he went along. "The relativity that entered determinism gave more and more aleatory tasks to the performer. This new situation allows a choice, and I think *choice* is the only thing which gives dignity to the human being."

Stockhausen recognized five basic dimensions as constituting the uniqueness of each individual sound—pitch, volume (intensity), duration, timbre, and position in space. From these five parameters were derived all the other elements of music—color (instrumentation), density of texture, melody, harmony, register, tempo, rhythm, and meter. He regarded total serialization as the best way of achieving full equality among the basic five dimensions, and by making them ever more independent of one another he was able to draw them into new kinds of relationships. He expanded the tight architecture of Webern, which was based on tiny motivic cells, into larger units or groups, a group being a segment of musical time (whether a few seconds or a few minutes long) that was unified by a specific process. This process might embody one of a number of factors—the fact that the music stayed within a certain register, or that the volume increased or decreased at a specific rate, or that in a certain passage long notes prevailed, or dense textures or woodwind timbres or augmented fourths. In effect, group composition, as he named it, depended on the way each group related to all the other groups. The concept allowed an expansion of musical form far beyond the concentrated structures of Webern. For example, *Momente* for soprano, four choral groups, and thirteen instrumentalists (1962–1964), in which groups of various durations function on several levels, takes almost two hours. In this and other works Stockhausen imparted to serial music a dimension of length which Schoenberg, Berg, and Webern had abjured.

He began his career with works for conventional instruments, such as *Kontra-Punkte* for flute, clarinet, bass clarinet, horn, trumpet, trombone, piano, harp, violin, and cello (1952–1953). The piece displays all the lineaments of Stockhausen's style—the meticulous craftsmanship, the flexible rhythms, the placement of each note so as to maximize its significance and its power to surprise, and the joy of weaving sound patterns for their own sake. The *Piano Pieces I–X* were written between 1952 and 1954. *Piano Piece XI* (1956) has aroused widespread interest. The work, as Stockhausen's publishers put it, is available in three forms. It comes in a roll packed in a cardboard carton; or with a wooden stand to put on the piano; or on a board. When the roll is unfurled it measures 37 x 21 inches. The piece consists of nineteen fragments which the pianist is permitted to play in whatever order his eye falls on them, with any of six different tempos, dynamics, and types of touch (staccato, legato, and the like). This offers the performer a vast number of possible versions. "When he has played one fragment three times, the piece must end." By exercising his choice the pianist has become a collaborator of the composer instead of being exclusively his interpreter.

Stockhausen believes that the new concepts in music can no longer be expressed through an orchestral apparatus inherited from the nineteenth century. The masterpieces of the past, as far as he is concerned, no longer have to be listened to at concerts; they can be heard just as well at home through recordings or radio. Electronic music, on the other hand, embodies new conceptions of time and space that can be projected properly only in concert halls specially designed for this purpose. "What's important is that for the first time in the history of mankind we have the means to make sound travel." He envisions a spherical auditorium with walls studded with loudspeakers, equipped with a platform in the center for the listeners, who will hear the music coming from all directions, stereophonically. "I want to be able to bring sounds from every surface area of the room." He compares this kind of listening, in which the perspective changes continually, to the painting of Paul Klee, in which one object "is seen from five, six or seven different perspectives at the same time—the multiple perspective within one composition." It is the dynamic quality of multilevel seeing or hearing that fascinates him. He is similarly attracted to the painting of Franz Kline, Willem de Kooning, Jackson Pollock, and Robert Motherwell, "in which the action of the painting itself," as he puts it, "the traces of brush movements are what we call aleatory." Such painting, he points out, results in completely new textures.

"What I'm interested in is to see how form and material become completely one." Stockhausen's later works reveal his preoccupation with ways of leaving the material free to mold the form. He allows the form to be shaped by the reaction of the performers to one another, or sometimes indicates the processes involved rather than the sounds that are to result from those. As examples of this tendency we may mention *Carré* for four orchestras and four choruses (1959–1960); *Kontakte* for electronic sounds, piano, and percussion (1960); and *Hymnen* (Anthems) for electronic and concrete sounds (1966–1967). He has elucidated his goal in these works in a rather dramatic fashion: "What I'm trying to do, as far as I'm aware of it, is to produce models that herald the stage after destruction. I'm trying to go beyond collage, heterogeneity and pluralism, and to find unity; to

"Action painting" was a term coined to describe the muscular, energetic art of the New York School. Bold strokes across huge canvasses resulted in new textures and conveyed the intensity behind the conception and execution of these works. Mahoning, 1956, by Franz Kline (1910–1962). Collection of the Whitney Museum of American Art, New York.

produce music that brings us to the essential ONE. And that is going to be badly needed during the time of shocks and disasters that is going to come." He envisions a catastrophe that will kill "hundreds of millions of the human race," followed by the kind of rebirth that "can only happen when there is death. A lot of death!" Behind the facade of the sophisticated man of the twentieth century there lurks an apocalyptic, Wagnerian imagination.

Gesang der Jünglinge

Gesang der Jünglinge (Song of the Youths, 1955–1956), Stockhausen proudly announced, "is the first work to use the direction of the sounds and their movement in space as aspects of the form." The piece, then, embodies his view that the shifting aural perspectives made possible by stereophonic listening can become dynamic, form-building elements. "With *Gesang der Jünglinge*," he recalls, "I had five speakers surrounding the audience. And the sound moved from one speaker to the next, sometimes in circles around the public, or made diagonal connections moving from speaker three to five, let's say. The speed of the sound, by which one sound jumps from one speaker to another, now became as important as pitch once was. And I began to think in intervals of space, just as I think in intervals of pitches or durations. I think in chords of space."

In *Gesang* Stockhausen combined sung sounds with electronically produced ones. This desire to humanize synthetic sounds with live ones has been an interesting trend in new music. He did not regard the two types of sound as irreconcilably opposed. On the contrary, he considered the sung sounds to be "individual *organic* members of the more comprehensive *synthetic* sound family." In other words, he was transforming the two opposing elements into that "unity of opposites" which, as a philosophical concept, is so dear to the German mind.

The vocal material was drawn from a canticle in the Apocrypha to the Book of Daniel, the third chapter of which tells of the men whom Nebuchadnezzar ordered thrown into a fiery furnace. Sustained by their faith, they walked in the midst of the fire unscathed. The canticle consists of a series of acclamations in praise of God. In turn, the elements—sun, moon, and stars, winds, fire and heat, ice and snow, night and day, light and darkness—are exhorted to praise the Lord.

Stockhausen knew that the German text would be familiar to his audience. He therefore concluded that its fundamental character as a hymn of praise would not be altered no matter how he rearranged the sentences and phrases, individual words and syllables, or even vowels and consonants of the canticle. In short, he felt free to treat the text as purely sonorous material. He had a twelve-year-old boy sing and speak the text on tape, which was then electronically manipulated by splicing and superimposed upon itself to form ensemble effects, the murmuring and shouting of a crowd, canonic forms spoken and/or sung, tone clusters, and similar effects. These were then combined with the electronic sounds. "At certain points in the composition," he explained, "the sung sounds become comprehensible words. At others, they remain pure sound values. Between these extremes there are various degrees of comprehensibility of the word. Whenever speech momentarily emerges from the sound-symbols in the music, it is to praise God."

In order to achieve total control of the material—that is, total serialization—Stockhausen analyzed and classified all the phonetic properties and color components of the sung or spoken words. Not only were pitch levels, durations, dynamics, and densities organized in series, but also the varying degrees of intelligibility of the words, the type of rendition—whether spoken or sung—and the stereophonic distribution of the sounds in regard to their being near or far, on the right or the left. The sung tones were blended with the electronic ones to form what the composer called "a mutual sound-continuum." Serial organization determined "how fast, how long, how loud, how soft, how dense, how intricate the tones must be, and how great or small the proportions of pitch and timbre must be in which the tones are audible." With German thoroughness Stockhausen published several articles in *Die Reihe* in which he minutely analyzed his procedures, hoping thereby to clarify his artistic goal—"first of all to arrange everything separate into as smooth a continuum as possible, and then to extricate the diversities from this continuum and compose with them." The result of all this activity confirms, as do all his works, his basic conviction that "the structure of a work and its material are one and the same thing." In effect, he is one of many contemporary musicians for whom the traditional dichotomy between form and content has been transformed into the conviction that the form *is* the content.

What interests the listener, in all this, is not the manner of organization but its results. The ear is held by ululating sonorities out of which an isolated word—*Sonne* (sun), *Mond* (moon), *Regen* (rain), *Tau* (dew)—emerges now and again with arresting suddenness, followed as often as not by a sonic explosion. Mysterious passages alternate with dramatic ones. At times the sound leaps hither and yon in dizzying swirls, like a character in an animated cartoon. The interaction between voice and electronic sounds produces some eerie effects; the fragmentation of text, in which the composer sets words with regard not to their meaning but solely to their phonetic components, has become one of the hallmarks of the new style. The music abounds in striking sonorities. One understands why *Gesang der Jünglinge* quickly won an international reputation.

Stockhausen's writings on music are the counterpart of his experiments in composition. They reveal a mercurial mind endowed with a plenitude of imagination and a penchant for scientific (according to some, pseudoscientific) terminology, which he uses freely in his attempts to come to grips with the problems of contemporary music. In any case, he is without question one of the most arresting figures to have emerged in Germany since the Second World War.

Pierre Boulez (1925–)

Pierre Boulez is the most important French composer of the avant-garde. He is also the best known because of his widespread activities as a conductor, in which capacity he has propagandized tirelessly in behalf of contemporary music. The American public grew familiar with his name and work through his five-year stint as music director of the New York Philharmonic.

At the Paris Conservatory Boulez studied with Messiaen, who exerted a powerful influence upon him. He subsequently fell under the spell of Debussy and Stravinsky; and, more significantly, under that of Schoenberg's disciple Anton Webern, whose influence was at its height in the years after the war. Taking his point of departure from Webern's later works, Boulez extended Schoenberg's serial technique to control not only pitch but the other elements of music as

Boulez in a drawing by Rémusat, 1966. André Meyer Collection.

well. Despite his total commitment to serial procedures, Boulez became aware that the advances of the modern Viennese school in melody, harmony, and counterpoint had not been equaled by advances
in rhythm. He tried to overcome this disequilibrium by taking over
the plastic rhythms of his teacher Messiaen and putting them to his
own use within the twelve-tone idiom. Already in his *Sonatine for
Flute and Piano*, an early work (1946), he tried, he tells us, "for the
first time to articulate independent rhythmic structures, of which
Messiaen had revealed to me the possibilities, upon classical serial
structures."

The emotional content of Boulez's music extends from a gentle
lyricism to a furious Expressionism that ranged him with the "angry
young men" of our time. Boulez himself has stated, in an essay on
rhythm, "I think that music should be collective magic and hyste-
ria." His violent emotions find their necessary compensation in the
mathematical rigor with which his structural schemes are worked
out. His writing is marked by extreme concentration of thought, as
by the great freedom with which he employs the serial technique.
From Messiaen he has taken over a fondness for bell and percussion
sounds that evoke the Balinese orchestra known as the gamelan. His
limpid orchestral texture is based on the clearest possible differentiation of timbres. Because of his extensive activities as a conductor, his
output has not been large. Among his chief works we should mention two piano sonatas (1946, 1948) and a still incomplete third; *Le
Marteau sans maître* (The Hammer without a Master), which we will
discuss; and *Pli selon pli* (Fold upon Fold, 1960), which includes the
three *Improvisations sur Mallarmé*.

Le Marteau sans maître

Boulez's best-known work, *Le Marteau sans maître* (1953–1954),
presents the chief traits of his style within a compact frame. It is a
suite of nine movements based on three short poems of René Char.
We will discuss three movements—the setting of the first poem (No.
3), its prelude (No. 1, *Before*) and postlude (No. 7, *After*).

The piece is for contralto and a group of six instruments, of which
the alto flute, viola, and guitar are most in evidence. These are supported by a xylorimba (an instrument combining the metallic sonority of the xylophone with the gentler wood sound of the marimba)
and a vibraphone, which lends a touch of magic to the ensemble. The

sixth "instrument" is a varied group of percussion manipulated by a single player. The full group never plays. Instead, each movement presents another combination of instruments from the ensemble.

The overall sound, of the bell and percussion variety, is limpid, brilliant, perhaps evoking the music of the Far East. The transparent texture, rarefied sound, and occasional immobility of this music places it in the line of descent from the late works of Webern. The vocal line shows the wide leaps we associate with twelve-tone music. As might be expected, Boulez does not try to make clear the words of a poem. "If you want to 'understand' the text," says he, "read it!" He believes that music should heighten the meaning of a text rather than set it realistically. This approach establishes a kinship between *Le Marteau sans maître* and Schoenberg's *Pierrot lunaire*. Certainly the later work would have been inconceivable without the earlier.

Char's poetry is thoroughly surrealist in the violence—and disconnectedness—of its images. The reader may find the translation more than a little mystifying. Rest assured, the original is as obscure.

L'Arisanat furieux	*Furious Artisans*
La roulotte rouge au bord du clou	The red caravan at the edge of the prison
Et cadavre dans le panier	And a corpse in the basket
Et chevaux de labours dans le fer à cheval	And work horses in the horseshoe
Je rêve la tête sur la pointe de mon couteau le Pérou	I dream, head on the point of my Peruvian knife

1. *Before "L'Artisanat furieux."* For alto flute, vibraphone, guitar, and viola. This prelude introduces the attenuated sonority of the post-Webern world. The tempo marking is *rapide;* yet despite the speed of the movement, single notes stand out with extreme clarity. The wide spacing of the instrumental lines contributes to this effect, as do the wide leaps in the flute and viola parts.

The tense plucked-string sound of the guitar here corresponds to the sound of the mandolin in certain works of Schoenberg and Webern. Together with the bell-like sonority of the vibraphone, it forms a backdrop for the gyrations of flute and viola. The dark hue of the viola contrasts ideally with the brighter timbre of the flute. Boulez's serial technique, with its emphasis upon dissonant intervals such as the augmented and diminished octave, makes for a highly integrated texture. Yet the listener is aware not so much of the concentrated thought as of an overall impression of extremely light and luminous sound.

3. *L'Artisanat furieux* (Furious Artisans). This duet between con-tralto and flute is marked *Modéré sans rigueur* (moderate, without strictness). The meter changes practically with every measure, result-ing in a free rhythmic flow of the utmost plasticity. Hence the music unfolds in that free, improvisational manner, both ornate and rhap-sodical, that twentieth-century composers have taken over from the music of the East. One receives an impression of great delicacy and refinement of style.

The words dissolve in music, an effect heightened by the fact that time and again a single vowel is extended for several notes. Here is an example of Boulez's conviction that we should listen not for the words but for what the composer has done with them. In effect, he handles the voice as if it were another instrument. The vocal part therefore becomes pure sonorous material, even as the flute part is. The enormous range of the vocal line and the devilish intervals that the voice has to execute call for a special kind of singer, one prefera-bly with absolute pitch. Voice and instrument complement each other, now echoing, now answering one another. Notice the flut-tertonguing on the flute, an effect dear to Mahler, Schoenberg, and Berg. It occurs at three points in the course of the piece and is espe-cially prominent after the first line of text.

7. *After "L'Artisanat furieux." Rapide.* A brief postlude, related to the prelude both in its intervallic structure and sound texture. Boulez here uses three instruments instead of four: flute, vibraphone, and guitar, omitting the viola. Since it does not follow *L'Artisanat* in the score, it is a postlude that serves also as a reminiscence.

Boulez has shrewdly assessed the role of his type of composer. "I think that our generation will give itself to synthesizing as much as—if not more so than—discovering: the broadening of techniques, generalising of methods, rationalisation of the procedures of writ-ing—in sum, a synthesis of the great creative currents that have manifested themselves principally since the end of the nineteenth century." To this synthesis he has made a very personal contribu-tion.

63 Four Representative American Composers

John Cage (1912–)

"My purpose is to eliminate purpose."

John Cage represents the type of eternally questing artist who no sooner solves one problem than he presses forward to another. "I am more like a hunter or inventor," he has said, "than a lawmaker." A native of Los Angeles, he is one of several West Coast artists who found nourishment in Oriental music and philosophy, particularly Hindu thought and Zen Buddhism. He studied with Henry Cowell and Schoenberg, each of whom exerted a strong influence upon his thinking. He began his career with a strong interest in non-Western scales and, by his own evidence, in "chromatic composition dealing with the problem of keeping repetitions of individual tones as far apart as possible (1933–34)." There followed "compositions with fixed rhythmic patterns or tone-row fragments (1935–38)," along with music for the dance, film, and theater.

John Cage, 1976. Photograph by Rhoda Nathans.

Cage was persuaded that the path of advance lay through rhythm rather than pitch. He therefore relinquished the tone-row technique of Schoenberg, based as that was on the serial ordering of pitches. For the next fifteen years he was preoccupied with the overall structuring of time—that is, of absolute (physical) rather than relative (musical) time—as the essential form-building element in music. As he summed it up, "I devise a rhythmic structure based on the duration, not of notes, but of spaces of time." It was of course precisely this sort of structure that was to come to the fore in tape and electronic music.

An abiding interest in rhythm inevitably leads a composer to explore the possibilities of the percussion instruments. Cage soon realized that the traditional dichotomy between consonance and dissonance had given way to a new opposition between music and noise, as a result of which the boundaries of the one were being pushed back to include more of the other. In a lecture on the future of music delivered in 1937 he prophesied that "the use of noise to make music will continue and increase until we reach a music produced through the aid of electrical instruments, which will make available for musical purposes any and all sounds that can be heard." In fine, he was continuing from where Varèse had left off two decades earlier. Meanwhile he announced that "any sound is acceptable to the composer of percussion music: he explores the academically forbidden 'nonmusical' field of sound insofar as it manually possible."

Out of this period of percussion music came *Construction in Metal* (1939), which was scored for an "academically forbidden nonmusical" combination of orchestral bells, five thundersheets, twelve-gong gamelan, three Japanese temple gongs, eight cowbells, four automobile brake drums, eight anvils, four Turkish and four Chinese cymbals, four muted gongs, water gong, suspended gong, and tam-tam, abetted by a piano muted by metal cylinders. The rhythmic structure of the piece was based on "the whole having as many parts as each unit has small parts, and these, large and small, in the same proportion." In other words, to repeat Cage's formula, a structure based on the duration not of notes but of spaces of time.

Cage's exploration of percussive rhythm led him to invent, in 1938, what he named the "prepared piano." The "preparation," we saw, consisted of inserting nails, bolts, nuts, screws, and bits of rubber, wood, metal, or leather at crucial points between the strings of an ordinary grand piano. There resulted, as Virgil Thomson expressed it, "a gamut of delicate twangs, pings, and thuds" whose overall sound resembled that of the Javanese gamelan. Cage described his invention as having "a decibel range comparable to that of the harpsichord. In effect, the prepared piano is a percussion ensemble under the control of a single player."

He wrote a number of works for this instrument, the major one being *Sonatas and Interludes* (1946–1948). Each of the sixteen sonatas and four interludes that make up the series is an autonomous unit whose rhythmic organization is based on fixed phrase lengths within a given span of time. The music reflects the composer's preoccupation with Oriental philosophy. "After reading the work of Ananda K. Coomaraswamy, I decided to attempt the expression in music of the 'permanent emotions' of Indian tradition: the heroic, the erotic, the wondrous, the mirthful, sorrow, fear, anger, the odious, and their common tendency toward tranquility." The striving for tranquility was to become a pervasive element in Cage's life and work.

The emphasis in European art since the Renaissance had been on the individuality of the creator. A number of twentieth-century artists—Stravinsky, for one—had already espoused the view that the continual striving for self-expression and originality at all costs was ultimately inimical to art, since it subjugated the artist to his own egoism. As an adherent of both Zen and Hindu philosophy, Cage could not but frown on the "cult of personality" so indigenous to our Western, highly competitive society. " 'Art' and 'music,' when anthropocentric (involved in self-expression) seem trivial," he declared, "and lacking in urgency to me." He was turning back to the medieval conception of a depersonalized anonymous art in which the individual work existed apart from its creator and even—like those statues in Gothic cathedrals placed where no one would ever see them—of its perceiver.

Cage also overturned the traditional distinction between sound and silence. He pointed out that in a normal environment there was no such thing as total silence. What we thought of as silence was really a medley of random sounds floating all around us. Hence the distinction between sound and silence was relative rather than absolute: music consisted of sounds that were intended, whereas silence consisted of sounds that were unintended. Awareness of silence, like meditation, is one of the disciplines of the contemplative life. We can therefore understand why Cage eagerly embraced the notion, traditional in India, that the purpose of music is "to quiet the mind, thus making it susceptible to divine influences." Out of this current of thought comes Cage's statement, "If you want to know the truth of the matter, the music I prefer, even to my own and everything, is what we hear if we are just quiet." More and more his music strove for quietude of spirit. In this context one can understand his admiration for Erik Satie, whose music aspires to the same goal. Cage's most striking effort in this direction was the composition he called 4' 33" (1952). His friend the pianist David Tudor sat silently at the piano for the specified amount of time, indicating by the dropping and raising of his arms that the nonpiece was in three nonmovements. Cage's intention was to structure four minutes and thirty-three seconds of silence so that the audience would become aware of the silent music in the auditorium, the random sounds floating all around them. His detractors thought of it as just another publicity stunt. Here is Cage's rebuttal: "I have never gratuitously done anything for shock, though what I have found necessary to do I have carried out, occasionally and only after struggles of conscience, even if it involved actions apparently outside the 'boundaries of art'."

By this time he had rejected the development of themes, the arousal of emotion, and the buildup of architectural forms that constitute the great tradition of Western music. He was moving toward a concept of music as a dynamic process, a continual becoming rather than a fixed object or form. His concentration on unfamiliar relationships of space and time, instead of on new melodies and chords, persuaded him that all musical relationships were worth considering, whether they had been arrived at by chance or by design. "A

John Cage's interest in the random sounds of silence is shared by his friend Robert Rauschenberg (b. 1925). This large construction consists of five elements, each of which contains moving parts which periodically emit a medley of sounds from everyday life: traffic, low-volume radio hum, news bulletins, bits of conversations, hum of machinery. Where Cage allows his audience to create similar sounds each time 4'33" is performed, Rauschenberg creates a permanent composition on the same theme. Oracle, 1965. *Collection: Musée National d'Art Moderne, Paris.*

sound does not view itself," he wrote, "as thought, as ought, as needing another sound for its elucidation; it has no time for any consideration—it is occupied with the performance of its characteristics: before it has died away it must have made perfectly exact its frequency, its loudness, its length, its overtone structure." This emphasis on the individual sound, we saw, was one of the great preoccupations of the post-Webern generation. "One may give up the desire to control sound," Cage concluded, "clear his mind of music, and set about discovering means to let sounds be themselves rather than vehicles for man-made theories or expressions of human sentiments." The attempt to discover these means led him to become one of the most fervent advocates of music of choice and chance.

Cage's approach to indeterminacy is based on the position that all sounds available to the ear can be music, and that these do not need to have a purpose in order to be enjoyed. "I try to arrange my composing means so that I won't have any knowledge of what might happen. And that, by the way, is what you might call the technical difference between indeterminacy and chance operations. In the case of chance operations, one knows more or less the elements of the universe with which one is dealing, whereas in indeterminacy, I like to think that I'm outside the circle of a known universe, and dealing with things that I literally don't know anything about." Cage's chance operations include compositional choices determined by throwing dice (*aleatory*, you will recall, comes from *alea*, the Latin for chance or dice). He has also relied on the *I Ching* (Book of Changes), an ancient Chinese method of throwing coins or marked sticks for chance numbers, from which he derived a system of charts and graphs governing the series of events that could happen within a given structural space. By superposing one chart or graph upon another he could ensure that all the parameters of his music—tempo, duration, pitch, dynamics—would be unforeseen. "I believe that by eliminating purpose, what I call *awareness* increases. . . . Now I don't bother to use the word form, since I am involved in making processes the nature of which I don't foresee."

Music had begun, in the dawn of civilization, with random cries, calls, tappings, and other noises. It had gradually developed, along with the other arts, to a point where for thousands of years a musical composition embodied the conscious selection of certain details and exclusion of others, the shaping of sounds into rational forms based on predictable procedures, the result being a work of art that embodied creative intelligence and reasoning will. Now the circle had come full: it was back to the primal randomness whence it came. To the ultrarationality of the total serialists Cage opposed an indeterminacy that freed the performer—and the music—from the composer's control. For example, in *Imaginary Landscape No. 4* (1951), twelve radios were set going simultaneously, tuned to different stations. The material, consequently, was completely random. The only predetermined element was the time span within which this assemblage of sounds and noises took place.

To set up a framework within which unpredictable events will take place is relatively simple to do in the realm of live performance. But to transfer this indeterminacy to tape, which by its nature is a fixed medium, requires considerable ingenuity. Cage solved the problem in *Fontana Mix*, which became the first tape-recorded work to establish conditions whose outcome could not be foreseen. The piece, it goes without saying, had an enormous influence on subsequent developments.

Fontana Mix

Composed in the Studio di Fonologia of the Italian Radio in Milan, *Fontana Mix* (1958) calls for "parts to be prepared from the score for the production of any number of tracks of magnetic tape, or for any number of players, any kind and number of instruments." The material consists of a set of ten transparent sheets with points, ten drawings having six differentiated curved lines, and a graph each of whose units equals a unit of time. By superposing these one upon the other, they can be combined in innumerable ways to produce patterns that suggest specific activities to the performer (or performers). Such a program allows chance to operate in every conceivable way. As a result, *Fontana Mix* sounds different with each performance.

The three recordings that have been made represent three totally different realizations of the material. The version for magnetic tape alone is animated, consisting of a montage of disassociated events—hissings, whisperings, groanings, gurglings, twitterings, and rumblings woven into a tapestry of sounds as varied as the free association of ideas when the mind is permitted to wander. These ever-shifting images at times give the same sense of randomness as when one turns the knob of the radio and hears successive fragments of music or speech from various stations. Here then is a perfect realization of Cage's desire to create "indeterminate music" through discontinuous works that unfold random events within a fixed span of time.

The second, and liveliest, of the three recordings combines *Fontana Mix* with *Aria*, sung by Cathy Berberian. This version focuses interest on Miss Berberian's remarkable performance. The *Aria* is notated in such a manner as to allow the performer to share with the composer in creating the work. "The notation," Cage explains, "represents time horizontally, pitch vertically, roughly suggested rather than accurately described." The vocal line is drawn in black or in one or more of eight colors, each representing another style of singing; jazz, contralto and contralto lyric, *Sprechstimme*, dramatic, Marlene Dietrich, coloratura and coloratura lyric, folk, Oriental, baby, and nasal. The text employs vowels and consonants and words from five languages: Armenian, Russian, Italian, French, and English. The composer concludes his instructions by pointing out that all aspects of the performance not notated (such as dynamics, type of attack, and the like) may be freely determined by the singer. Miss Berberian makes the most of this program, the result veering from nonsense singing to satire and parody of a rather delicious kind.

The third recording, by the percussionist Max Neuhaus, represents "the interaction and mixture of feedback channels set up by resting contact microphones on various percussion instruments that stand in front of loudspeakers." (Feedback is the acoustical phenomenon that occurs when a microphone picks up the sound from a loudspeaker and "feeds it back" into the same loudspeaker: the result is a howling noise.) This realization consists of a series of signals each of which is sustained for so long a time as to approach—at least for sensitive ears—the threshold of physical pain. The impression of absolute immobility is akin to that in certain yoga exercises which tend to empty the mind of all thought. Toward the middle of the record the sustained noises take on the relentless quality of an electric drill, ending as abruptly as they began.

So serious a critic as Peter Yates has called Cage "the most influential living composer today—whatever opinion you or I may hold about his music." He was the mentor of a group of younger Americans, among them Morton Feldman, Earle Brown, Gordon Mumma, LaMonte Young, and Christian Wolff. He worked in closest collaboration with the dancer Merce Cunningham. He formed strong bonds of personal friendship with painters like Jasper Johns and Robert Rauschenberg. The Rauschenberg-Cage-Cunningham collaboration resulted in the production at Black Mountain College of Cage's *Theater Piece*, probably the first "happening" in the United States. And he pointed the way for several Europeans, notably Boulez and Stockhausen. Whether as composer, writer, amateur philosopher, or aesthetician, Cage has been a seminal force in the artistic life of our time.

Elliott Carter (1908–)

"I like music to be beautiful, ordered, and expressive of the more important aspects of life."

Of the composers who came into prominence in the mid-Forties, none is more widely admired by musicians than Elliott Carter. His works are not the kind that achieve easy popularity. But their sureness of line, profundity of thought, and maturity of workmanship bespeak a musical intellect of the first order.

Elliott Cook Carter is a native of New York City. When he entered

Harvard he majored in English literature. It was not until his last year there that he decided to be a musician. He stayed on as a graduate student and studied with Walter Piston.

In 1932 Carter went to Paris, where for three years he worked with Nadia Boulanger. From this period dates the first of his works to be heard in public, incidental music for a performance of the *Philoctetes* of Sophocles by the Harvard Classical Club. For the same group he wrote, after his return to the United States in 1935, the music for Plautus's *Mostellaria*. One number from this score, the *Tarantella*, was widely performed by the Harvard Glee Club. Carter settled in New York City in 1936. His articles on modern music published in various periodicals won him a reputation as a thoughtful critic. In 1940 he accepted an appointment to the faculty of St. John's College in Annapolis, Maryland, where the philosopher Scott Buchanan had inaugurated a "great books" program.

His duties at St. John's interfered with his composing, however; so Carter relinquished his post and went to Santa Fé, New Mexico, where, in the winter of 1942, he completed his *First Symphony*. He served during the war as music consultant at the Office of War Information. Since then, he has taught frequently—at the Peabody Conservatory in Baltimore, Columbia University, Queens College, Yale University, and the Juilliard School—but his main activity has been composing.

Carter's chief concern has been with the expressive and imagina-

Elliott Carter.

tive elements of his art. His music has grown more intricate as he has found his own voice and cut away those things that are not essential to his vision. His concern is never with technique as an end in itself; he uses it only to focus what he wishes to say. His is an elaborate kind of music that exists on many levels and reflects an original and subtle mind. It requires careful listening, for it is as concentrated in thought as it is complicated in facture. To those who make the effort, it reveals a sensibility that, although quite special, is as germane to the American scene as anything being written in this country today.

Carter started out with a musical idiom rooted in diatonic modal harmony. His gradual assimilation of a dissonant chromaticism went hand in hand with his response to the many influences that directed his development. He absorbed dodecaphonic no less than Stravinskyan elements; but he uses both in an independent fashion. His contrapuntal writing shows secure workmanship and constructive logic. His language is abstract, his style is one of extreme control. Withal, he achieves a personal tone.

Carter inherited the rhythmic suppleness that was the legacy to his generation of both Stravinsky and Bartók. He has listened carefully to the madrigals of the Renaissance, whose elastic cross-rhythms follow the natural accentuation of the language rather than a fixed meter. From jazz he took over the concept of a regular metrical bass with free rhythms above it, a device he uses both in his *String Quartet No. 1* and the *Sonata for Cello*. He made a novel attempt to use fluctuations in tempo and meter as form-building elements. Through the use of shifting accents and irregular scansion of phrases he achieved the polyrhythmic counterpoint that gives his music its plasticity. From this point he arrived at the concept he calls "metrical modulation," a technique whereby he passes from one metronomic speed to another by lengthening or shortening the value of the basic unit. In the past such changes involved changes in speed based on simple metrical proportions: for example, a quarter-note unit in one passage equaled a half-note unit in another. Carter has carried such "modulations" to the utmost refinement and exactitude in terms of metronomic timing. In the *Adagio* of his *Cello Sonata*, to cite one case, he begins with the eighth note at 70 and, through a subtle "modula tion," emerges with the eighth note at 60. This lengthening of the unit note in the irregular proportion of 7:6 is carried out within a frame of strict meter, and with such fine gradation that the effect is utterly smooth.

Carter is a slow worker; his reputation rests on a comparatively small number of works that occupy an extremely important place in

Louise Nevelson (b. 1899) assembles metal or wood fragments that interest her—volumes and curves that make for marvelously subtle rhythmic harmonies—and organizes them into totally controlled architectonic shapes. Moon Garden Wall II, *1975. The Pace Gallery, New York.*

the contemporary repertory. Preeminent among these are the *Variations for Orchestra* (1955), a work that exploits the resources of the orchestra in virtuoso fashion; the *Double Concerto* for harpsichord, piano, and two chamber orchestras, which we will discuss; the dramatic *Piano Concerto* (1965); the brilliant *Concerto for Orchestra* (1969); and the *Symphony of Three Orchestras* (1976). Of equal moment are the three *String Quartets* (1951, 1960, 1971); these are bold, uncompromising works that constitute the most significant contribution to the genre since Bartók. Both the *Second* and *Third Quartets* were awarded the Pulitzer Prize. Other works for smaller forces include a *Piano Sonata* (1946); a *Cello Sonata* (1949); a *Sonata for Flute, Oboe, Cello, and Harpsichord* (1952); a *Duo for Violin and Piano* (1974); a *Brass Quintet* (1974); and a cycle of songs to poems by Elizabeth Bishop, *A Mirror on Which to Dwell* (1975).

Double Concerto for Harpsichord and Piano

One of Carter's most important and imaginative works, the *Double Concerto for Piano and Harpsichord with Two Chamber Orchestras* (1961) embodies concerns that preoccupied him for many years. This is one of a series of twentieth-century works in which composers combined two or more dissimilar bodies of sound so as to achieve directional contrasts. (We heard two others—Bartók's *Music for Strings, Percussion and Celesta* and Britten's *War Requiem*). Characteristic is Carter's interest in the chamber rather than traditional orchestra.

"The idea of writing this Double Concerto," the composer stated, "was suggested to me by the harpsichordist Ralph Kirkpatrick. As my thoughts took shape, the matter of reconciling instruments with different responses to the finger's touch became a central concern." The basic contrast was between the plucked strings of the harpsichord and the struck strings of the piano. "A concept had to be found that made this instrumental confrontation vivid and meaningful." Carter is here reviving, in twentieth-century terms, the Baroque concerto grosso, which was based on the confrontation between two groups of players. This concept, he goes on to say, "gave rise to the devising of elaborate percussion parts, the choice of instruments for the two orchestras, and a musical and expressive approach that affected every detail. Various relationships of pitched and non-pitched instruments, with the soloists as mediators, and the fragmentary contributions of the many kinds of tone colors to the progress of the sound events were fundamental."

The players are arranged on stage according to the following plan:

Percussion I	Percussion II		Percussion III	Percussion IV
	Trombone		Bassoon	
	Trumpet		Horn II	
	Horn I		Clarinet	
	Flute		Oboe	
	Double Bass		Cello	
	Viola		Violin	
	Harpsichord		Piano	

Significant, in view of contemporary trends, is the central role assigned to the unusually rich percussion section. The first percussionist handles slapstick (two pieces of wood), anvil, cowbells, wood blocks, triangle, two suspended cymbals, tambourine, gong, and tam-tam (a larger gong). The second plays temple blocks, triangle, cymbal, snare drum, tambourine, military drum, and tam-tam. In the third group are crotales (small cymbals of thick metal that can be tuned to a definite pitch), claves (Latin-American round hardwood blocks that are struck together), maracas (gourds filled with dry seeds, a Latin-American instrument), cymbal, two snare drums, military drum, and bass drum. In the fourth group are crotales, bongos (a vertical curved drum, of Latin-American origin, slapped with the hand or tapped with the fingers), two tom-toms, cymbal, snare drum, guiro (a notched gourd scraped with a stick), and a very large bass drum. Several of these come in different sizes and ranges—soprano, alto, tenor, bass, contrabass. All the drums, Carter specifies, "must form a continuous 'scale' of clearly distinguishable pitch levels, as evenly spaced as possible, starting from the highest available Bongo to the lowest available Bass Drum."

Considering the strong trend among twentieth-century composers to free music from all literary associations, it is interesting that Carter did have such associations in mind, although perhaps more as a metaphor than as a description of content. "After a time, I began to think of a literary analog to the concerto's expected form—Lucretius' *De Rerum Naturae,* which describes the formation of the physical universe by the random swervings of atoms, its flourishing and its destruction. Bit by bit, however, a humorous parody of Lucretius in Alexander Pope's *Dunciad* took over in my thoughts, in lines like:

> "All sudden, Gorgons hiss, and Dragons glare,
> And ten-horn'd Fiends and Giants rush to war;
> Hell rises, Heav'n descends, and dance on earth;
> Gods, imps, and monsters, music, rage and mirth,
> A fire, a jig, a battle, and a ball,
> Till one wide conflagration swallows all.

"The beautiful end of Pope's poem seemed to articulate in words the end of the work I had already composed:

> "—the all-composing hour
> Resistless falls; the Muse obeys the power.
> She comes! She comes! the sable throne behold
> Of Night primeval, and of Chaos old! . . .
> Lo! thy dread empire, Chaos! is restor'd;

Light dies before thy uncreating word:
Thy hand, great Anarch! lets the curtain fall;
And universal Darkness buries all."

Carter constructed the work in an architectural form that in music
is analogous to an arch: seven sections, of which the first three balance the last three with a centerpiece between. The work follows an
overall principle of perpetual variation. As Carter put it, each section
consists of "a series of short, usually overlapping episodes, mosaics
of fragments that derive from parts of the basic material in different
ways."

I. *Introduction.* The percussion instruments open the proceedings
in a pianissimo that grows in volume as other instruments join in.
The two groups present themselves as contrasting bodies of sound in
an ever more clearly defined way. The interval of a second, both
major and minor, presented in short tremolos, takes on structural
significance. The two protagonists are presented, squaring off
against one another, as it were. The opening statement of the piano
combines consonant and dissonant intervals: on the one hand, major
sixths, perfect fourths and fifths; on the other, major seconds and
sevenths:

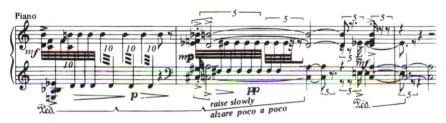

The harpsichord responds with a rapid flourish in which the perfect
fourth stands out among the dissonances that surround it:

These intervals, used percussively, are associated with specific patterns of acceleration and retardation that embody Carter's system of
ever so flexible, continually changing metrics. Such intervallic
schemes provide the work with a firm substructure from which

Carter derives, as he puts it, "ideas of many degrees of interrelationship on several different levels at once." The Introduction reaches a climax of rhythm-and-dissonance tension, whence it quickly subsides and leads into the next section.

II. *Cadenza for Harpsichord.* A wide-ranging passage in the shape of an arpeggio ushers in this part:

Harpsichord

The various speeds and their associated intervals unite to produce polyrhythmic patterns that, not as dense as in the preceding section, take on a greater mobility and articulation. The cadenza presents a distillation of the rhythms and intervals typical of the harpsichord and its ensemble. Hence its epigrammatic character.

III. *Allegro scherzando.* This section is given over mainly to the piano and its group, with brief interjections and comments by the harpsichord group. The scoring is remarkably economical, the instrumental lines being so distinct and well aerated that, as one of Stravinsky's admirers once said about the Russian master's orchestration, one can practically see through the sound with one's ears. Carter keeps the two solo instruments well in the foreground and specifically requests that they predominate whenever they play. "The dynamic inflections, accents, and crescendi in the piano part should be emphasized by the performer and not be obscured by the orchestra." The opening notes of the piano set the playful mood implied in *scherzando:*

sempre scherzando e non troppo forte

Piano

IV. *Adagio.* This section, the centerpiece of the arch, is preceded by a passage in which the metrical unit changes from measure to measure. In this type of "modulation" the music becomes faster or slower not according to the whim of the player, but because the value of the basic unit has been lengthened or shortened according to the specifications of the composer. Here is how Carter indicates this procedure:

The *Adagio* proper is mainly for the winds, which are centrally located in each orchestra. They play slow music against more rapid figuration from the two soloists, who are supported by percussion and occasionally strings. The slow music of the winds remains steady, rhythmically independent of the patterns of acceleration and retard that involve the outer circle of players, patterns that run clockwise around the orchestra when the music slows down—piano, cello, double bass, harpsichord, percussion—and counterclockwise when it speeds up.

Save for a few brief passages, the two solo instruments have hitherto played separately. Now they engage in a lengthy duet in which first one, then the other predominates, while at certain points they meet as equal partners. The contrast between them in tone color is presently underlined by a contrast in tempo: the piano observes a gradual accelerando while the harpsichord, along with the other instruments, embarks on a gradual ritardando. The piano reaches maximum speed even as harpsichord and percussion arrive at the opposite pole. After a breathless moment, punctuated by the ringing of the crotales, the next movement begins.

V. *Presto.* Balancing the piano's role in the *Allegro scherzando* (Section III) the harpsichord is to the fore in the *Presto*, accompanied by all the instruments except percussion. The piano interrupts twice with material drawn from the *Adagio.* Its opening statement, marked *Maestoso* (majestic), highlights three intervals that have played a form-building role—perfect fifth, major seventh, and minor second:

(Maestoso)

In the piano's second interruption this material becomes a point of departure for an extended passage that leads into the next section.

VI. *Cadenzas for Piano.* The two cadenzas in this section balance the cadenza for harpsichord in Section II. The first presents intricate figuration broken up between both hands and follows the traditional role of cadenzas in displaying the virtuosity of the performer. The harpsichord, as if accepting the challenge, responds with a brilliant series of arpeggios. The second cadenza is more complex rhythmically and leads into a section which, as Carter puts it, "amplifies the questioning inflections of the Presto by all the instruments." The percussion predominates as cymbals and drums beat out a series of patterns in arresting counterrhythm to the two soloists, recalling the atmosphere of the opening passage of the work.

VII. *Coda,* balancing the *Introduction.* There could be no better description of this section than the composer's: "The work concludes with an extended *Coda,* using the entire ensemble in a series of long-phased oscillations (that include many short-phased ones) from one group to the other, during which previous ideas are recalled in new contexts. Reversing the general plan of the *Introduction* (although not the musical one), these fragments lose their definition gradually, become shorter, sometimes more condensed, sometimes more dispersed, merging more and more into the slow waves of percussion rolls that rise and fall according to the basic polyrhythmic structure of the whole work."

Elliott Carter's *Double Concerto for Harpsichord and Piano* has established itself in our concert life as a masterpiece of the new music. It confirms his position as probably the most important composer in America today.

Milton Babbitt (1916 –)

"Anyone who hears well can be educated to appreciate my music. The more you listen to serial music, the better able you are to recognize its grammar, its configurations, its modes of procedure."

Just as composers of the nineteenth century related their music to Romantic poetry and painting, several among the avant-garde composers of our time tend to relate their work to the exact sciences, thereby exalting the intellectual-rational element in art over the intuitive-emotional one. A leading proponent of this ultrarational attitude is Milton Babbitt, a native of Philadelphia. "Some people say my music is 'too cerebral,' " he states. "Actually, I believe in cerebral music—in the application of intellect to relevant matters. I never choose a note unless I know precisely why I want it there and can give several reasons why it and not another."

Babbitt studied with Roger Sessions. When Sessions was asked to form a graduate department of music at Princeton University he in-

Milton Babbitt at the RCA Synthesizer.

vited his brilliant pupil, then twenty-two, to join its faculty. Babbitt has taught at Princeton ever since, and as professor of composition has had a strong influence on musicians of the younger generation. Given his kind of mind, he was inevitably attracted to the almost scientific logic of the twelve-tone method, which for him represented a revolution in musical thought "whose nature and consequences can be compared only with those of the mid-nineteenth-century revolution in mathematics or the twentieth-century revolution in theoretical physics." He soon realized the possibilities for further development inherent in Schoenberg's system. It became his conviction that "the twelve-tone set must dominate *every* aspect of the piece."

As a result, he led the way toward an ultrarational music in which the composer would control every dimension of the musical fabric. His *Three Compositions for Piano* (1947) and *Composition for Four Instruments* (1948) were the first examples of total serialization. He applied the principle of the series not only to pitch but also to rhythm, dynamics (including not only the soft-loud element but also the attack and decay of the sound), and timbre. Therewith he developed the premises of Schoenberg's method into an all-inclusive system in which the basic row—or set, as Babbitt calls it—totally controlled the relationships and processes within a particular piece.

By the same token Babbitt was one of the first to evaluate the possibilities of electronic music, not because of the new sonorities it made possible—"Nothing," he holds, "becomes old as quickly as a new sound"—but because it offered the composer complete control over the final result. At the Columbia-Princeton Electronic Music Center in New York City he was able to work out his ideas on the RCA Synthesizer. "When you live through as many bad performances of your music as I have, I must confess that I look forward to walking into the electronic studio with my composition in my head and walking out with the performance on the tape in my hand." Out of this "unique and satisfying experience," as he calls it, came two important works in which he explored the possibilities of the new medium: *Composition for Synthesizer* (1960–1961) and *Ensembles for Synthesizer* (1962–1964).

All the same, it has never been Babbitt's intention that the Synthesizer should supplant the live musician. "I know of no serious electronic composer who ever asserts that we are supplanting any other form of music or any other form of musical activity. We're interested in increasing the resources of music." The next step, Babbitt saw, was to combine electronic music with live performers. This new area he explored in *Vision and Prayer* (1961), for soprano and synthesized accompaniment; *Philomel* (1964), which we will discuss; *Correspondences* (1966–1968), for string orchestra and synthesized accompaniment; and *Reflections* (1975), for piano and tape. Nor did he forsake the field of live music: two connected works, *Relata I* (1965) and *Relata II* (1968), are for orchestra, and two string quartets, his *Third* and *Fourth*, date from 1970.

Philomel

Philomel (1964) offers the listener an excellent introduction to Babbitt's music. The work is for live soprano and tape. The tape contains a synthesized accompaniment and also the recorded voice of a soprano (Bethany Beardslee, for whom the piece was written). The text, by the poet John Hollander, is based on Ovid's version—in the *Metamorphoses*—of an ancient myth concerning the origin of that favorite bird of poets, the nightingale. This indeed is one of those gory Greek myths that impelled Freud to investigate the darker corridors of human nature. Pandion, King of Athens, had two daughters, Procne and Philomel. Procne married Tereus, King of Thrace, by whom she had a son, Itys. After several years she longed to see her younger sister, and prevailed upon her husband to sail to Athens and bring back Philomel. On the return journey Tereus developed a consuming passion for his sister-in-law. When they reached his kingdom he led her into a forest, raped her, and cut out her tongue to silence her. For a year Philomel was held captive; but she managed to communicate her terrible story by weaving it into pictures and sending the tapestry through a servant to Queen Procne. The queen understood the message. She found Philomel and during the annual Bacchic rites brought her back to the palace disguised as one of the celebrants. Aroused to a frenzy by the Bacchanalian celebrations, Procne decided to avenge her sister. She killed her son Itys and cooked his remains, which she served to her husband as a delectable dish. (This theme, interestingly, persists in folklore through the centuries.) When Tereus asked after his son, Philomel took Itys's severed head and hurled it at him. The two sisters fled into the woods, pursued by Tereus. But before he could overtake them the gods transformed him into a hoopoe, an unclean bird that befouls its own nest. Procne was turned into a swallow, and Philomel became a nightingale.

Babbitt's *Philomel* begins just after the transformation has taken place. The piece falls into three sections. In the first, the newly created nightingale tries stutteringly to find her voice. She can sing only isolated notes or small groups of notes as she struggles incoherently to express the agony through which she has passed. This section ends with Hollander's felicitous stanza, "Oh, men are sick: The gods are strong . . . What is this humming? I am becoming / My own song . . ." Second is the *Echo Song.* In a dialogue with the birds of the forest, Philomel accepts her new existence. In the third section, like Keats's nightingale, she pours forth her soul "in full-throated ease." (For the complete text of *Philomel,* see Appendix II.)

The live soprano is echoed by the recorded soprano on the tape, who is heard against an electronic background. This recorded voice, which has been modified by electronic devices, represents, in Hollander's words, what Philomel "heard in the woods, what she thought she heard there, what she fancied she heard inside her own head, and so forth." The live sound and the synthesized sound intertwine to become a completely integrated whole. As a number of composers discovered, the combination of a live performer with tape humanizes the electronic sound and gives it another dimension.

The text of the *Echo Song* recalls a device of seventeenth- and eighteenth-century poetry, in which the echoing voice picks up the final sounds of a question and transforms them into an answer:

Philomel

O thrush in the woods I fly among,
Do you, too, talk with the forest's tongue?

Echo

Stung, stung, stung,
With the sting of becoming
I sing.

Here, the echo attaches the final "s" of "forest's" to the sound of "tongue," thus creating the word "stung." Philomel addresses herself successively to the thrush, the hawk, the owl, the raven, the gull, and finally to the green leaves of the forest. In the dialogue, the urgent lyricism of the live voice contrasts vividly with the distant, electronically dehumanized singing and whispering of the echo voice. The contrast is underlined by the glittering sonority—at times suggesting plucked strings—of the synthesized sounds.

Philomel is based on a series, from which Babbitt derives not only the twelve-tone pitch material of the work but also the layout of rhythms, dynamics, and tone colors. Yet this strict underlying unity clearly does not preclude enormous variety and expressivity. We quoted Stravinsky's remark that "the more art is controlled, limited, worked over, the more it is free." The rules within which an artist works (like the rules within which people play a game such as bridge or poker) do not hamper him. On the contrary, they stimulate his imagination. What Stravinsky is saying, and what artists have learned through the ages, is that you could not have the game without the rules, because then you would have total freedom, which is chaos. This explains why a work like *Philomel*, despite the elaborate structural procedures that control its course, can give the listener a sense of utter buoyancy and freedom.

The significant artist is one who incarnates the significant impulses of his time. Milton Babbitt is such a one. His music embodies important intellectual currents in the contemporary scene.

George Crumb (1929–)

George Crumb, a native of Charleston, West Virginia, studied with Ross Lee Finney at the University of Michigan and with Boris Blacher at the Berlin Hochschule für Musik. He has won numerous honors and awards and is currently professor of composition at the University of Pennsylvania.

In recent years Crumb has forged ahead to a notable position among the composers of his generation. He owes this preeminence partly to the emotional character of his music, allied to a highly developed sense of the dramatic. His kind of Romanticism is unusual among the advanced composers of our time. Crumb uses contemporary techniques for expressive ends that make an enormous impact in the concert hall. The influence of Webern is apparent in the sparseness of his textures and the economy of the writing; also in the placement of single sonorities so that they will achieve maximum effect: Yet Crumb departs from this part of his heritage in the sweep of his melodic lines, which are not infrequently underpinned by modal harmonies or Impressionistic parallel chords that look back to Debussy. Like many musicians of his generation he has been attracted to the gentle bell-sounds of Asiatic music, a predilection apparent in his highly personal handling of the percussion section. His music often gives the listener a sense of rapturous improvisation, an impression strengthened by the passages of chance and performer choice that punctuate his scores.

Crumb has shown an extraordinary affinity for the poetry of Federico Gracía Lorca, the great poet who was killed by the Fascists during the Spanish Civil War. Besides *Ancient Voices of Children*,

George Crumb.

which we will discuss, his Lorca cycle includes several important works: *Night Music I,* for soprano, piano, celesta, percussion (1963); *Songs, Drones and Refrains of Death,* for baritone, electric guitar, electric double bass, electric piano (doubling an electric harpsichord), and two percussionists (1968); *Madrigals, Book III,* for soprano, harp, and percussion (1969); *Madrigals, Book IV,* for soprano, flute (doubling alto flute, piccolo), harp, double bass, and percussion (1969); and *Night of the Four Moons,* for mezzo-soprano, alto flute (doubling piccolo), banjo, electric cello, and percussion (1969). In the domain of orchestral music his most important work is *Echoes of Time and the River,* four processionals (1967). Two volumes of *Makrokosmos* (1972, 1973) exploit all the resources of the amplified piano, while *Music for a Summer Evening* (subtitled *Makrokosmos III,* 1974) is scored for two amplified pianos and percussion. Most of Crumb's recent music has been made available on records; it is important to remember, however, that the visual element is an essential aspect of his music's theatrical character, and it makes its strongest impression in live performance.

Ancient Voices of Children

Ancient Voices of Children (1970) is a cycle of songs for mezzo-soprano, boy soprano, oboe, mandolin, harp, electric piano, and percussion. The texts are fragments of longer poems which Crumb grouped into a sequence so as to achieve musical continuity. There are two movements for instruments alone. These, along with one of the vocal movements, are imbued with the spirit of dance. Indeed, the composer suggests that they can be performed by a dancer as well.

Endowed with an aural imagination of remarkable vividness, Crumb tirelessly explores new ways of using voice and instruments. Like many contemporary composers he uses the voice like an instrument, in a vocal style which he describes as ranging "from the virtuosic to the intimately lyrical." He has found his ideal interpreter in the mezzo-soprano Jan DeGaetani, whose recording of the work remains an example for all other interpreters.

The score abounds in unusual effects. The soprano opens with a fantastic vocalise (a wordless melody, in this case based on purely phonetic sounds) which she directs at the strings of an electrically amplified piano, thereby arousing a shimmering cloud of sympathetic vibrations. The pitch is "bent" to produce quarter tones. Included in the score are a toy piano, harmonica, and musical saw. The percussion players use all kinds of drums, gongs and cymbals, Tibetan prayer stones, Japanese temple bells, and tuned tom-toms (high-pitched drums of African origin); also a marimba, vibraphone, sleighbells, glockenspiel plates, and tubular bells.

I. *El niño busca su voz.* Very free and fantastic in character. "The little boy was looking for his voice. (The king of the crickets had it.) In a drop of water the little boy was looking for his voice. I do not want it for speaking with; I will make a ring of it so that he may wear my silence on his little finger." The soprano part offers a virtuoso exhibition of what the voice can do in the way of cries, sighs, whispers, buzzings, trills, and percussive clicks (Crumb specifies *not* a clucking sound). There are even passages marked "fluttertongue"—an effect we have hitherto associated only with instruments. Throughout, Crumb captures the rapturous, improvisational spirit of flamenco song. The passion is here, the sense of mystery and wonder—but in a thoroughly twentieth-century setting.

The boy soprano answers, singing offstage through a cardboard speaking tube. His "after-song" should sound "simple and unaffected, even naive." The boy's part ends *pppp*, "timidly." (For the complete Spanish-English text, see Appendix II.)

Dances of the Ancient Earth. Very rhythmic. An ecstatic oboe solo is supposed to sound "raw, primitive, shawm-like." (The shawm was an early ancestor of the oboe, which was introduced into Europe from Asia Minor around the twelfth century.) The music conjures up the atmosphere of the Near East, of that highly charged, florid melody that entered the Spanish soul through the Moors. "Bended" pitches on mandolin, harp, and oboe produce the quarter-tones that are an integral part of Oriental song. The percussion instruments reinforce the Levantine atmosphere. The piece ends with a joyous outburst on the oboe. Notice throughout the remarkable plasticity of the rhythm.

II. *Me he perdido muchas veces por el mar.* "I have lost myself in the sea many times with my ear full of freshly cut flowers, with my tongue full of love and agony. I have lost myself in the sea many times as I lose myself in the heart of certain children." The soprano whispers the text through a speaking tube, phrase by phrase, against an extraordinary background. A musical saw, played with a cello or double-bass bow, gives forth a haunting sound. No less striking is the glissando produced by moving a chisel along a string of the amplified piano, or the scraping of a fingernail along the metal winding of a harp string, which produces a nasal whistling sound. Each timbre stands out with unusual clarity. All in all, this movement is a tour de force in atmosphere and sonority.

III. *¿De dónde vienes, amor, mi niño?* Freshly, with dark, primitive energy. In this poem Lorca uses the question-and-answer pattern that is found in folklore throughout the world. A mother questions her unborn child. "From where do you come, my love, my child? From the ridge of hard frost. What do you need, my love, my child? The warm cloth of your dress. . . . When, my child, will you come? When your flesh smells of jasmine-flowers. Let the branches ruffle in the sun and the fountains leap all around!" Lorca here reaches down into what Jung would have called the racial unconscious. The music matches the poet's intention with shattering eloquence. The song opens with birdlike calls to a primitive cry on the words "mi niño" (my child). Now the drums establish an ostinato rhythm: the deliberate, ceremonious pattern of the bolero with which Ravel electrified the world fifty years ago. Crumb adapts it to his own expressive needs in a compact, intense form that avoids the obvious overextension of Ravel's concert piece. The drums beat a powerful crescendo as the mother exuberantly hails her child. A gradual diminuendo extends to the last measure. The final chord, *fff*, is a kind of primal scream.

IV. *Todas las tardes en Granada, todas las tardes se muere un niño.* Hushed, intimate; with a sense of suspended time. "Each afternoon in Granada, a child dies each afternoon." This heart-rending lament has the quality of a primitive mourning ritual. The voice part unfolds in a toneless murmur, supported by harmonica, marimba, and percussion. Then, in the upper register of a toy piano, we hear Bach's *Bist du bei mir*—an echo of life-affirmation triumphant over death. Crumb explains the intrusion, which is wonderfully effective: "In composing *Ancient Voices of Children,* I was intrigued with the idea of juxtaposing the seemingly incongruous: a suggestion of Flamenco with a Baroque quotation (*Bist du bei mir,* from the Notebook of Anna Magdalena Bach), or a reminiscence of Mahler with a breath of the Orient. It later occurred to me that both Bach and Mahler drew upon separate sources in their own music without sacrificing 'stylistic purity.' " What matters, in such cases, is the extent to which the composer absorbs such elements into his personal style. Given a strong creative personality, he is certain to do so.

Ghost Dance. To the accompaniment of maracas and whispered syllables from the percussion players, the mandolin is made to produce an "eerie, spectral" dance with the help of a glass rod and a metal plectrum.

V. *Se ha llenado de luces mi corazón de seda.* Luminous. "My heart of silk is filled with lights, with lost bells, with lilies, and with bees, and I will go very far, farther than those hills, farther than the seas, close to the stars, to ask Christ the Lord to give me back my ancient soul of a child." The metallic clang with which this movement opens is indeed luminous, combining the timbres of metallic plates, antique cymbals, harp, electric piano, tubular bells, vibraphone, and suspended cymbals. A wraithelike passage leads into an ornate Mahlerian melody marked "timidly, with a sense of loneliness." Soprano and oboe alternate, the instrument taking on a remote quality when it moves offstage.

A powerful crescendo leads into the impassioned music for the last line of the poem. This suddenly stands revealed as the climax toward which Crumb has been working from the very beginning. "It is sometimes of interest to a composer," Crumb writes, "to recall the original impulse—the 'creative germ'—of a compositional project. In the case of *Ancient Voices* I felt this impulse to be the climactic final words of the last song: '. . . and I will go very far . . . to ask Christ the

Lord to give me back my ancient soul of a child.' " The music subsides as soprano and boy soprano remember the birdlike calls of the
opening.

In *Ancient Voices* Crumb has found the right music for the dark in-
timations of Lorca's poetry. The work has justly established itself as a
prime example of contemporary imagination and feeling.

Postscript

We have traced the course of contemporary music through the
first eight decades of the twentieth century. We have chronicled the
flux and reflux of musical forces that began with the revolt against
the Romantic heritage. It is clear that the changes which took place in
the past eighty years are as momentous as any that the history of
music has witnessed, and as dislocating to those who lived through
them as any revolution is apt to be.

A survey of music in the early eighteenth century would have
revealed a homogeneous picture of musical practice, in spite of the
individual differences between Bach and Handel, Vivaldi and Scarlatti. The same would have been true a century later, even though
one might have discovered much greater divergence between Chopin and Mendelssohn, Wagner and Verdi. This book presents an infinitely greater variety of aesthetic goals and harmonic idioms. What
common denominator can be applied to a scene that contains
Schoenberg and Prokofiev, Webern and Poulenc, Menotti and Stockhausen? The absence of a common practice among composers, of a
universal tradition and homogeneous language, makes for a diversity that is fascinating, but that is also apt to be more than a little
bewildering. All the more important, then, to pause and take stock of
what our century has achieved thus far.

What emerges from such stock taking at that twentieth-century
music does not represent so drastic a break with the past as listeners
of sixty years ago supposed. The leaders of the modern movement, as
we have seen, disclaimed revolutionary intent. They viewed the upheaval that they inaugurated as part of the dynamic process of evolu-

tion to which all human endeavor is subject. Their innovations have become part of the vocabulary of music. The areas of thought and expression that they opened up are being further explored by their disciples and heirs. The turbulent half century against which their lives unfolded is taking its place in history as the latest—and, because closest to us, the most exciting—chapter in that eternal process of change which attends the growth of a living art. The works of Stravinsky, Schoenberg, Berg, Webern, of Britten, Carter, Boulez, and Crumb, issue out of the great tradition of Western music and eloquently affirm the continuity of that tradition. At the same time they represent the next step forward, one made inevitable by what came before.

Readers who have perused these pages have glimpsed the vast musical panorama of our time. One can but hope that they will pursue their investigations farther. They will find in the appendices a list of books that will assuredly expand their understanding and enjoyment of the heady musical art of the twentieth century. Yet they must remember that there is only so much that can be written or read about sounds. The magic, the true meaning, lies in the sounds themselves. Let them therefore use the books as an introduction to what is, finally, the one valid thing we can do about music—to listen to it! Let them listen carefully, perceptively, over and over again: with curiosity, with eagerness, with joy.

Dictionary of
Contemporary
Composers
and their
Recorded Works

It has been said that there are more composers alive today than were known in all the centuries preceding our own. The number has been estimated at about three thousand. How could one hope to choose a representative group!

The guiding principle in assembling this dictionary has been the availability of the composer's works on record, since there is no point in discussing music that cannot be heard by the reader. This book is an introduction rather than a history; therefore, it does not try to be comprehensive. Within this context, the following list, incomplete though it is, is more than sufficient to show the reader the multiplicity of styles and viewpoints to be found in today's music.

The record catalogues change from month to month as certain works are deleted, others added, and still others reissued. In addition, record shops that deal in the unusual stock many items, especially works of European composers on European labels that are not listed in the American catalogues. Those have not been included here because of their limited availability. Still, the list of recorded compositions is impressive and can serve as the basis for an excellent contemporary collection.

It is my hope that the reader will explore, listen with open ears, and—above all—enjoy!

I should like to express my thanks to Verna Fine Gordon *of* CRI *and to the* American Music Center *for their unfailing cooperation in the preparation of this Dictionary.*

S AMUEL A DLER (Mannheim, Germany, 1928–) studied, among others, with Walter Piston, Paul Hindemith, Aaron Copland, and Randall Thompson. He teaches at the Eastman School of Music. Adler's works include four symphonies, two operas, and numerous chamber and choral works. He has also been active in the field of Jewish synagogue music, using a diatonic-linear style marked by freedom of voice leading and dissonance. On records: *Sonata for Horn and Piano* (1948); *Southwestern Sketches,* for wind ensemble (1961); *Quartet No. 4* (1963); *Canto II,* for bass trombone (1970); and *Xenia, A Dialogue for Organ and Percussion* (1972).

H U GH A I TK E N (New York, 1924–) studied at the Juilliard School with Vincent Persichetti, Bernard Wagenaar, and Robert Ward. He teaches at Paterson College. Aitken's is a varied list of instrumental and vocal works. He has also written on aesthetics in relation to the new music. On records: *Cantatas No. 1* (1958), *No. 3* (1960), *No. 4* (1961); *Piano Fantasy* (1967); *Montages,* for solo bassoon (1968); and *Suite* for solo bass (1968).

WILLIAM ALBRIGHT (Gary, Indiana, 1944–) attended the Juilliard School and continued his composition studies with Hugh Aitkin, Ross Lee Finney, and Olivier Messiaen. He is associate director of the Electronic Music Studio at the University of Michigan. The popular element in his music, stemming from jazz, is prominent in his theater and film scores. His recorded works include several for organ: *Juba* (1965), *Pneuma* (1966), *Organbooks I* and *II* (1967–1969), and a piece for percussion, *Take That* (1972).

JOSEF ALEXANDER (Boston, 1910–) studied at the New England Conservatory and Harvard. A Neoromantic orientation is immediately evident in his three symphonies and several works on records: *Songs for Eve* (1958), *Three Pieces for Eight* (1966), *Burlesque and Fugue for Trumpet and Piano* (1970).

DAVID AMRAM (Philadelphia, 1930–) studied various instruments at Oberlin Conservatory and the Manhattan School of Music, but is primarily self-taught in composition. His music has a spontaneous quality that goes hand in hand with his experience as a jazz musician, his talent for improvisation, and his affinity for theater music. The latter quality had full scope during the years he spent as music director of the Phoenix Theater, the Lincoln Center Repertory Theater, and the New York Shakespeare Festival. Among his recorded works is the *Quintet for Winds* (1968).

THOMAS JEFFERSON ANDERSON (Coatsville, Pennsylvania, 1928–), one of the leading black composers, studied with Darius Milhaud and Richard Hervig. He teaches at Tufts University. His music shows the adaptation of pluralistic values whose range reflects the influence of primitive, jazz, post-Webern, and avant garde music. On records: *Squares,* for orchestra (1965); *Chamber Symphony* (1968); *Variations on a Theme by M. B. Tolson,* for soprano and chamber ensemble (1969).

EDWARD APPLEBAUM (Los Angeles, 1937–), who teaches at the University of California at Santa Barbara, studied with Henri Lazarof. He is one of a growing group of composers who are returning to the Classical forms, as is attested by his *Symphony No. 1.* On records: *Piano Sonata* (1965); *Montages* (1968); *Shantih,* for cello and piano (1969); *Foci,* for viola and piano (1971); *Piano Trio "Reflections"* (1972).

JON APPLETON (Los Angeles, 1939–), who studied with Andrew Imbrie, Henri Lazarof, and Vladimir Ussachevsky, teaches at Dartmouth College. A leading figure in electronic and computer music, he is the developer of the Dartmouth Digital Synthesizer. His music reflects diverse influences, but is always interesting in terms of pure sound. Recorded music includes: *Georganna's Farewell* (1975), and *World Music Theater,* an album containing the following electronic works: *Chef d'oeuvre* (1967); *CCCP* (1969); *Times*

Square Times Ten (1969); *Apolliana* (1970); *Sones de San Blas* (1970); *Neusehir* (1971); and *Ofa atu Tonga* (1973).

BÜLENT AREL (Istanbul, Turkey, 1919–), began his career as a sound engineer at Radio Ankara. After some years as a composer in the Neoclassic style, he adopted twelve-tone techniques. Arel, who teaches at the State University of New York at Stony Brook, has produced a number of important electronic pieces. These consist, as he puts it, "of mostly individually composed sounds" subjected to classic electronic-studio techniques. Recorded: *Electronic Music No. 1* (1960); *Music for a Sacred Service,* on tape (1961); *Stereo Electronic Music No. 1,* on 5-, 4-, or 2-track tape (1961); *For Violin and Piano* (1966); *Mimiana II* and *Frieze* (1969); *Stereo Electronic Music No. 2* (1970).

DOMINICK ARGENTO (York, Pennsylvania, 1927–), who teaches at the University of Minnesota, studied with musicians as diverse as Hugo Weisgall, Luigi Dallapiccola, and Howard Hanson. Argento's flair for the theater was enriched by his work with Tyrone Guthrie in Minneapolis, for whose productions he wrote a number of scores. His operas include *The Boor,* after Chekhov (1957); *A Water-Bird Talk* (after Chekhov and Audubon, 1974); and *The Voyage of Edgar Allen Poe* (1976). On records: *Letters from Composers,* a song cycle for tenor and guitar (1969); *Postcard from Morocco,* an opera (1971); and *To Be Sung upon the Water,* a song cycle for high voice and instrumental ensemble (1973).

ROBERT ASHLEY (Ann Arbor, Michigan, 1930–), together with the composer Gordon Mumma, headed the Cooperative Studio for Electronic Music in Ann Arbor; worked with the painter-sculptor Milton Cohen on "Space Theater" programs that coordinated projections with amplified sound; and was one of the founders of the ONCE Group, an informal association of composers, performers, filmmakers, theatrical designers, architects, and other artists aiming at a synthesis of visual, verbal, and electronic elements in combination with movement and gesture, often within an aleatory structure. Ashley helped organize the ONCE Festivals that took place from 1961 to 1968, and now directs the Mills College Center for Contemporary Music. He has produced sound tracks for films and has been strongly influenced by "the manner of film production (group effort toward an abstract goal)." His works on records include: *She Was a Visitor,* for chorus (1967); and *Purposeful Lady Slow Afternoon,* electronic music theater (1968).

LARRY AUSTIN (Duncan, Oklahoma, 1930–), director of systems complex for the Studio of Performing Arts at the University of Southern Florida, began as an improviser of modern jazz on the trumpet and string bass. He is one of the founders of the New Music Ensemble, a group of seven performer-composers whose free improvisations rely on the ensemble's "compositional feeling for structure from the smallest musical gesture to the total composition." Austin's works in what he calls "open style" combine tape music with improvisational procedures. His most ambitious work to date is *The Mage: A*

Theater Piece in Open Style for Three Percussionists, Tape, Projections, and Conductor (1965). The New Music Ensemble has issued several recordings under its own label (NME) that set forth its "spontaneous composition" in a contemporary, provocative idiom. Also on records: *Piano Variations* (1960); *Piano Set* (1964).

JACOB AVSHALOMOV was born in Tsingtao, China in 1919, of Russian-Jewish parents. Among his teachers were his father, the composer Aaron Avshalomov, Ernst Toch, Bernard Rogers, and Aaron Copland. His music combines Oriental elements, undoubtedly the result of his boyhood in China, with influences derived from Preromantic music, especially the madrigals and motels of the Renaissance. On records: *How Long, Oh Lord . . .* , a cantata (1948–1949).

DAVID BAKER (Indianapolis, Indiana, 1931–) studied with Gunther Schuller, among others, and made his reputation as jazz trombonist and arranger-composer for Stan Kenton, Lionel Hampton, and Maynard Ferguson. He has emerged as one of the leading black composers; his music combines jazz, blues, and gospel with twelve-tone techniques and other styles. Baker is chairman of the Department of Jazz Studies at Indiana University. His major works include the cantata *Black America* (1968), dedicated to Martin Luther King, and the *Cello Sonata* (1973), which has been recorded. He had written several books on jazz improvisation. Also available on records: *Le Chat qui pêche*, for soprano, jazz quartet and orchestra; *Contrasts* for piano trio; and *Sonatina* for tuba and string quartet.

LEONARDO BALADA (Barcelona, Spain, 1933–) studied, among others, with Aaron Copland and Vincent Persichetti. He teaches at Carnegie-Mellon University. Balada combines his Spanish heritage with contemporary trends, as in his *Guernica* (1966) and *Steel Symphony* (1972). On records: *Sonata* for violin and piano (1960); *Cumbres* for band (1960); *Guernica* (1966); *Geometrias No. 1* (1969); *Cuartis* for four instruments (1969).

DON BANKS (Melbourne, Australia, 1913–) is active in London as a composer of film and television scores. He has been strongly influenced by Milton Babbitt's music and thought. His experience as a jazz pianist and arranger is reflected in several third-stream compositions. On records: *Concerto for Horn and Orchestra* (1966).

SAMUEL BARBER (West Chester, Pennsylvania, 1910–) studied at the Curtis Institute of Music in Philadelphia. He is one of the very few composers who was trained as a singer. This may help to account for the essentially lyrical nature of his music, which issues from a genuinely creative impulse. It is deeply felt, has a distinctive profile, and bears the mark of a poetic imagination. A large public was attracted to Barber's assured handling of large forms, his elegant craftsmanship, and his refined taste. As a result, throughout his career Barber has been one of the most frequently performed composers of the American school. Most of his important works are available on records. Among these are *Dover Beach,* on a poem by Matthew Arnold, for voice and string quartet (1931), *Adagio for Strings* (1936), *Symphony No. 1 in One Movement* (1936), *Essay No. 2,* for orchestra (1942), *Capricorn Concerto,* for orchestra (1944), *Medea's Meditation and Dance of Vengeance* (1946), *Violin Concerto* (1947), *Knoxville: Summer of 1915,* for soprano and orchestra (1948), the opera *Vanessa* (1958), *Piano Concerto* (1962), and the opera *Antony and Cleopatra* (1966, revised 1973).

ELAINE BARKIN (New York City, 1932–), who teaches at the University of Michigan, studied at Queens College with Karol Rathaus, at Brandeis University with Irving Fine, and in Berlin with Boris Blacher. Among her works are *Refrains* (1968), *String Quartet* (1969), and *Plus ça change* (1972). The *Quartet* is recorded.

WAYNE BARLOW (Elyria, Ohio, 1912–) attended the Eastman School and absorbed the Neoromantic aesthetic that prevailed there. Subsequently, he worked with Schoenberg at the University of Southern California. He is now director of the Electronic Music Studio at Eastman. On records: *Rhapsody for oboe, The Winter's Past* (1938); *Trio* for oboe, viola, and piano (1964); *Dynamisms,* for two pianos, and *Elegy,* for viola and piano (1967).

LESLIE BASSETT (Hanford, California, 1923–) studied with Ross Lee Finney at the University of Michigan, with Honegger and Nadia Boulanger in Paris, and electronic music with Mario Davidovsky. He teaches at the University of Michigan. Chamber music is prominent in a list that includes piano, orchestral, and choral works as well as music on tape. On records: *Variations for Orchestra* (1962–1963); *Music for Cello and Piano* (1968); *Music for Saxophone and Piano* (1968); *Sextet* for piano and strings (1972); *Sounds Remembered,* for violin and piano (1972).

IRWIN BAZELON (Evanston, Illinois, 1922–) studied with Paul Hindemith and Darius Milhaud. Bazelon is a prolific composer whose works show a variety of influences ranging from rock and jazz to the symphonic tradition. He has written quantities of music for television commercials and industrial films. Also, according to his own account, he has a talent for playing the horses. His list includes six symphonies (1960–1970), *Brass Quintet* (1963), and *Churchill Downs Concerto* (1972). On records: *Duo* for violin and piano (1963); *Brass Quintet; Symphony No. 5* (1968); *Propulsions,* a percussion concerto for 7 players.

JACK BEESON (Muncie, Indiana, 1921–), professor of music at Columbia University, has made his mark primarily as an opera composer, but has also written orchestral works. His best known opera is *Lizzie Borden* (1965), based on the famous Boston murder of 1892, with a libretto by Kenward Elmslie, who also wrote the libretto of Beeson's earlier opera *The Sweet Bye and Bye* (1956). Two other operas have texts by the composer: *Hello Out There* (1953) and *My Heart's in the Highlands,* after the play by William Saroyan (1969). On records: *Hello Out There, The Sweet Bye and Bye, Lizzie Borden,* as well as *Symphony No. 1 in A* (1959).

JACK BEHRENS (Lancaster, Pennsylvania, 1935–) studied, among others, with Peter Mennin, Vincent Persichetti, and Roger Sessions. He teaches at California State College. Behrens favors the large instrumental forms, as in his *Triple Concerto* for clarinet, violin, and piano. On records: *Feast of Life* for piano (1975).

DAVID BEHRMAN (Salzburg, Austria, of American parents, 1937–) studied, among others, with Wallingford Riegger, Walter Piston, and Karlheinz Stockhausen. He was cofounder of the Sonic Arts Union, a group that included Robert Ashley, Alvin Lucier, and Gordon Mumma, who presented programs of individual and collaborative music using electronics in combination with photography, film, and theater. Their music has been recorded. Also on records: *Runthrough,* an electronic piece.

PAUL BEN HAIM (Munich, 1897–), one of the leading composers of Israel, left Germany at the beginning of the Nazi regime. He has been strongly influenced by the folkloristic musical tradition of the Jews and Arabs in the lands of the Near and Middle East. Ben Haim is best known in the United States for *The Sweet Psalmist of Israel* (Three Symphonic Movements, 1953). Recorded are *Three Songs without Words,* for voice with chamber orchestra or piano (1952).

RICHARD RODNEY BENNETT (Broadstairs, Kent, England, 1936–), a pupil of Lennox Berkeley and Pierre Boulez, lives in London, where he has earned his living mainly as a composer of film, radio, television, and theater music. Bennett is a twelve-tone composer whose serial techniques do not exclude tonal structures and strongly patterned rhythms. His vivid orchestration is highly expressive, underlining the communicative quality of his music. Among his recorded works are *Calendar,* for chamber ensemble (1960), *Concerto* for guitar and chamber ensemble (1970), and *Commedia IV,* for brass (1973).

WARREN BENSON (Detroit, 1924–) studied at the University of Michigan and teaches at the Eastman School of Music. His works combine Neoromantic elements with large-scale forms, and show his distinctive handling of the wind instruments. On records: *Marche* (Encore for woodwind quintet, 1951); *Transylvania Fanfare* (1953); *Trio* for percussion (1957); *Symphony for Drums and Orchestra* (1962); *Star-Edge,* for saxophone (1964); *Helix,* for solo tuba and concert band (1966); *Recuerdo Solo* for oboe-English horn (1966); *Helix,* for tuba (1976).

ARTHUR BERGER (New York City, 1912–) was the leading figure of a group of Harvard-trained composers whom Aaron Copland dubbed a "Stravinsky school," several of whom, including Berger, had been pupils of Walter Piston at Harvard and of Nadia Boulanger in Paris. Typical of the Neoclassic aesthetic that prevailed in this group were such works as Berger's early and extremely witty *Woodwind Quartet* (1941). *Ideas of Order* (1952), for orchestra, represents one of the high points of Berger's first period. With the *Chamber Music for 13 Players* (1956) Berger proved himself increasingly receptive to twelve-tone procedures, which he adapted to his earlier style with consummate craftsmanship and control. This important composer is inadequately represented on records by the aforementioned *Chamber Music for 13 Players,* one of his most distinguished works, and *Three Pieces for 2 Pianos* (1962).

WILLIAM BERGSMA (Oakland, California, 1921–) attended the Eastman School, where he studied with Howard Hanson and Bernard Rogers. He taught for more than twenty years at the Juilliard School and in 1963 became director of the School of Music at the University of Washington. His three-act opera *The Wife of Martin Guerre* attracted much attention when it was presented in 1956. Among Bergsma's recorded works are a *Suite* for brass quartet (1945); *Tangents,* for piano (1951); *Concerto* for wind quintet (1958); and *Concerto* for violin and orchestra (1966).

LUCIANO BERIO (Oneglia, Italy, 1925–) is a leading figure among the radicals of the post-Webern generation in Italy. Together with Bruno Maderna, he founded the electronic studio in Milan that became a center for the Italian avant-garde, and for several years taught composition at the Juilliard School in New York. Berio's music exemplifies major trends on the contemporary scene—serialism, electronic technology, and indeterminacy. In his earlier works he used a strict serial technique, into which he injected the lyricism that was his birthright as an Italian. A strong sense of theater pervades his music, particularly in such works as *Passaggio,* an opera for solo soprano, two choruses, and orchestra; and the *Sinfonia* for orchestra, organ, harpsichord, piano, chorus, and reciters (1968), the second part of which pays homage to Martin Luther King. Berio's interest in linguistics has led him to a highly original treatment of language sounds. He has also been in the forefront of those composers who experimented with combining live music and tape. He found his ideal interpreter in the soprano Cathy Berberian, who for some years was his wife and for whom he wrote a number of important works, among them *Chamber Music* (1952), *Omaggio a Joyce* (1958), and *Visage* (1961). Berio is well represented on records. All the aforementioned works are available, as well as *Differences,* for five instruments and tape (1958–1959), and *Circles,* for soprano, harp, and two percussion ensembles, on poems by e. e. cummings (1962).

LEONARD BERNSTEIN (Boston, 1918–) has had a spectacular career as composer, conductor, pianist, lecturer, author, and television personality. He was the first American-born musical director of the New York Philharmonic and the youngest ever appointed to the post. His serious works include the *Jeremiah Symphony* (1942); *The Age of Anxiety,* for piano and orchestra, based on W. H. Auden's poem of that name (1949); *Serenade* for violin, strings, and percussion (1954); the widely discussed *Mass,* composed for the opening of the John F. Kennedy Center for the Performing Arts in Washington (1971); and *Songfest,* for six solo voices and orchestra (1977). In his scores for Broadway, Bernstein achieved a sophisticated kind of musical theater that exploded with energy. The list includes *On the Town,* a full-length version of his ballet *Fancy Free* (1944); *Wonderful Town* (1953); *Candide* (1956), whose Overture has become a staple of the present-day repertory; and *West Side Story* (1957), which remains a masterpiece of our popular lyric theater. Practically everything Bernstein has written is available on records.

WALLACE T. BERRY (La Crosse, Wisconsin, 1928–) teaches at the University of British Columbia. He studied with Halsey Stevens at the University of Southern California and with Nadia Boulanger in Paris. He is author of *Form in Music* and *Structural Functions in Music,* and coauthor of a book on imitative counterpoint. On records: *String Quartet No. 2* (1964); *Canto Lirico* (1965); *Duo for Flute and Piano* (1972).

CHARLES L. BESTOR (New York City, 1924–) teaches at the University of Utah. He studied, among others, with Paul Hindemith, Peter Mennin, and Vincent Persichetti. Bestor is one of a number of composers who have combined electronic music with live performance. On records: *Piano Sonata* (1962, rev. 1974).

THOMAS BEVERSDORF (Yoakum, Texas, 1924–), who teaches at Indiana University, studied with Bernard Rogers, Kent Kennan, and Howard Hanson at the Eastman School and absorbed the Neoromantic aesthetic that prevailed there. He subsequently worked with Arthur Honegger and Aaron Copland. Beversdorf is partial to the large Classical forms; his list includes four symphonies. On records: *Sonata* for horn and piano (1945); *Sonata* for violin and piano (1963); and *Sonata* for cello and piano (1969).

GORDON BINKERD (Lynch, Nebraska, 1916–) studied with Bernard Rogers at the Eastman School and with Walter Piston at Harvard. For more than two decades he was professor of composition at the University of Illinois. In music, he is a "centrist," attempting to reconcile the radical innovations of the present with the classical traditions of the past. Among his recorded works: *Cello Sonata* (1952); *Violin Sonata* (1974).

HARRISON BIRTWISTLE (Accrington, Lancashire, England, 1934–) in recent years has emerged on the international scene as one of the most important British composers of his generation. With Peter Maxwell Davies he formed the Pierrot Players in London, for the performance of new chamber music that lent itself to theatrical presentation. His music is marked by temperament, a lyric gift, massive sonorities, and a dramatic tension that commands the listener's attention. On records: *Ring a Dumb Carillon,* for soprano, clarinet, and percussion (1965), *Tragoedia,* for wind quintet, harp, string quartet (1965); *Nenia—The Death of Orpheus,* for soprano, three bass clarinets, piano, crotales (1970); and *The Triumph of Time*, for orchestra (1972).

BORIS BLACHER (Newchang, China, of German-Russian parentage, 1903–1975, Berlin) was one of the important German composers after World War II. Within the frame of tonality he experimented with polyharmony, polytonality, and a rhythmic process based on systematic changes of meter which he called "variable meters." At the Berlin Hochschule, of which he was director from 1953 to 1970, a large number of present-day composers studied with and were influenced by him. On records: *Divertimento*, for trumpet, trombone, and piano (1946); *Ornaments*, based on "variable meters," for orchestra (1953); *Orchestral Fantasy* (1956); *Blues—Espagnola-Rumba Philharmonica*, for twelve solo cellists (1972).

EASLEY BLACKWOOD (Indianapolis, Indiana, 1933–), who teaches at the University of Chicago, studied with Paul Hindemith, Nadia Boulanger, Olivier Messiaen, and Bernard Heiden. Blackwood's work is traditional in form, while his harmony hovers on the dividing line between tonality and atonality. Blackwood's oeuvre includes three symphonies, two string quartets, and the *Piano Concerto* of 1970. On records: *Sonata* for flute and harpsichord (1962); *Concerto* for violin and orchestra (1966).

MARC BLITZSTEIN (Philadelphia, 1905–1964, Fort-de-France, Martinique) studied at the University of Pennsylvania and the Curtis Institute, as well as with Nadia Boulanger in Paris and Arnold Schoenberg in Berlin. During the Depression he turned his energies toward the creation of a leftist musical theater that would offer a satirical comment on our society as the Bert Brecht–Kurt Weill musicals had done for theirs. (It was, incidentally, in the Blitzstein adaptation that their *Three-Penny Opera* triumphed in this country.) Blitzstein achieved his goal in *The Cradle Will Rock* (1936), a landmark in our musical theater, that dealt with the conflict between a steel baron and a labor union. His lyrics for this extraordinary work were as pungent as the music. So too the *Airborne Symphony* (1945) captured the spirit of the war years. Both works are available on records, though Blitzstein's masterpiece, *Regina*, an opera on Lillian Hellman's *The Little Foxes* (1948–1949), unfortunately is out of print.

KARL-BIRGER BLOMDAHL (Vaxjo, Sweden, 1916–1968, Stockholm) is best known for his "space-ship opera," *Aniara*, which combines twelve-tone, pop, and electronic elements. He is represented on records by his *Third Symphony, Facetter* (Facets, 1950), in which he modified Schoenbergian procedures by infusing them with tonal-rhythmic elements related to the music of Bartók.

WILLIAM BOLCOM (Seattle, Washington, 1938–) studied, among others, with Milhaud and Messiaen, and now teaches at the University of Michigan. His music incorporates a variety of influences from serialism to popular music; these influences are assimilated to a style peculiarly his own. For example, his *Session 2,* for violin and viola (1966), uses, as he has described it, "everything from B. Marini to Beethoven to wild chromatic-1960s to bits of waltzes." Among his recorded works are *Black Host,* for organ, percussion, and tape (1967); *Frescoes,* for piano, harmonium, and harpsichord (1971); and *Open House,* a song cycle for tenor and chamber orchestra (1975).

BENJAMIN BORETZ (New York City, 1934–) has been strongly influenced by Schoenberg, Sessions, and Milton Babbitt. He teaches at Bard College and is active as a writer as well as composer. Boretz is editor of *Perspectives of New Music,* which since its inception in 1962 has been the most important outlet for contemporary musical thought. On records: *Group Variations II,* for computer-synthesized tape (1968–1970).

MARTIN BOYKAN (New York City, 1931–), who teaches at Brandeis University, studied with Walter Piston, Paul Hindemith, and Aaron Copland. His works include two string quartets and the *Concerto* for 13 players. On records: *String Quartet No. 1* (1967).

HENRY BRANT (Montreal, 1913–), who teaches at Bennington College, has experimented, to quote his phrase, with "space as an essential aspect of musical composition." His music is based on the sharpest possible contrast between two or more instrumental groups in the same piece, "each of which keeps to its own style, highly contrasted to the styles of the other groups, retains its own rhythmic, harmonic, and instrumental scheme consistently throughout, and is assigned to its own specific, isolated position in the concert hall." He thus anticipated the spatial concepts that came to the fore in the '60s with Stockhausen and others. His works on records include *Hieroglyphics 3,* for instruments, optional voices, and organ (1957); *Millennium 4,* for brass quintet (1963); and *Angels and Devils,* for solo flute and an orchestra of flutes (1931).

EARLE BROWN (Lunenberg, Massachusetts, 1926–) has been one of the most consistently innovative composers of his generation. Along with John Cage and pianist David Tudor, he was an associate member of the Music for Magnetic Tape project in New York from 1952 to 1955, and has since been active as a recording producer and teacher, as well as composer. His music has been strongly influenced by his association with visual artists; especially relevant were the improvisatory quality of Jackson Pollock's paintings and the free form of Alexander Calder's mobile sculptures. Brown pioneered the exploration of "open form," in which the sounds are specified but the sequence of events is not determined in advance; also a type of graphic notation based on the concept of proportional notation, in which time is divided into relative units whose duration is suggested by the spacing of the notational signs. This results in a variable kind of form in the creation of which the performer plays an active part. Thus performer's choice and the randomness attendant upon it are essential elements of Brown's art. His ideas have been widely influential. On records: *December,* for piano (1952); *Four Systems,* for four amplified cymbals (1954); *Hodograph,* for piano (1959); *No-*

vara, for nine instruments (1962); *Corroboree,* for piano (1964); *String Quartet* (1965).

NEWEL K. BROWN (Salt Lake City, 1932–) studied, among others, with Leroy Robertson at the University of Utah and with Bernard Rogers, Howard Hanson, and Wayne Barlow at the Eastman School. He teaches at North Texas State University. Brown's chamber music and songs show his lyrical bent. On records: *Poetics* (1970).

HERBERT BRÜN (Berlin, 1918–) studied, among others, with Stefan Wolpe. He teaches at the University of Illinois. Brun's list includes instrumental and electronic works; in recent years he has been interested in computer music. He has also become increasingly aware of the socio-political significance of musical ideas, an awareness, as he puts it, "that keeps growing the more I teach, the more I hear and listen, the more I compose." On records: *Gestures for Eleven* (1964).

HAROLD BUDD (Los Angeles, 1936–) studied, among others, with Ingolf Dahl and Gerald Strang. He teaches at the California Institute of the Arts. Budd has a flair for unusual combinations of instruments, as in his *"—only three clouds—"* for trombone quintet. Budd was influenced by jazz and the music of Morton Feldman and John Cage, and is one of several composers who have transferred to music the aesthetic of the minimalist painters of the 1960s. "Much of my music is extremely quiet, and very little happens in terms of old-time virtuosity—but it does, I think, call for a lot of spiritual virtuosity." On records: *"—only three clouds—"* for trombone quintet (1969), and the electronic pieces *Coeur d'Orr* (1969) and *Oak of Golden Dreams* (1970).

DAVID BURGE (Evanston, Illinois, 1930–) studied at Northwestern University and the Eastman School of Music. He teaches at the University of Colorado. Burge has been a champion of the new piano music both as performer and composer. He uses serial procedures in his compositions, which include chamber works and pieces in which live music is combined with tape. On records: *Sources IV,* for piano (1969).

SYLVANO BUSSOTTI (Florence, Italy, 1931–) has been a pioneer in the use of graphic scores. His larger forms are built cumulatively out of fragments whose subtle interrelationships create a sense of structure. Influenced alike by post-Webern serialism and the experiments of John Cage, he has incorporated the innovations of our time in an expressive personal style. On records: *Coeur* (Heart, 1959), for percussion and electronic equipment; *Frammento* (Fragment, 1959), for voice and piano; *Positively Yes,* for the same medium (1965).

FRANK CAMPO (New York City, 1927–) studied with Ingolf Dahl, Arthur Honegger, and Leon Kirchner. He teaches at California State University at Northridge. His list includes orchestral works, string quartets, piano music, and a one-act opera, *The Mirror;* he has a special affinity for the winds, for which he writes in a novel manner. On records: *Kinesis* (1950); *Five Pieces for*

5 Winds (1958); *Sonata* for violin and piano (1959); *Concertino* for three clarinets and piano (1965); *Madrigals,* for brass quintet (1970); *Commedie,* for trombone and percussion (1971).

NICCOLO CASTIGLIONI (Milan, Italy, 1932–) was trained at the Verdi Conservatory in Milan and continued his studies with Boris Blacher in Berlin. He was also active in the summer courses at Darmstadt. He has concertized extensively in Europe as a pianist and taught at several universities in this country. Castiglioni was strongly influenced by Pierre Boulez. On records: *Tropi,* for chamber ensemble (1959); *Gymel,* for flute and piano (1960).

NORMAN CAZDEN (New York City, 1914–), who teaches at the University of Maine, began his career as a concert pianist. It is not surprising that piano music occupies a prominent place on his list, which includes chamber music, a symphony, and a considerable amount of theater music. On records: *Piano Sonata No. 3* (1950).

ROBERT CEELY (Torrington, Connecticut, 1930–), who teaches at the New England Conservatory, studied with Sessions, Kirchner, Babbitt, and Milhaud. To the influences emanating from these musicians, he has added a terse, compact idiom of his own. On records: *Stratti,* for tape (1963); *Vonce,* for tape (1967); *Logs,* for two double basses (1969); *Hymn,* for cello and double bass (1970).

JOEL O. CHADABE (New York City, 1938–) is a pupil of Elliott Carter. He teaches at SUNY/Albany and has worked extensively in electronic music. On records: *Street Scene,* for English horn and tape (1967); *Daisy,* for colored shadows and tape (1972); and two electronic pieces, *Ideas of Movement at Bolton Landing* (1971) and *Echoes* (1972).

DAVID CHAITKIN (New York City, 1938–) studied, among others, with Seymour Shifrin and Luigi Dallapiccola. He teaches at New York University. Chaitkin's list includes film music as well as orchestral, chamber, and piano works. On records: *Etudes* for piano (1974).

THEODORE CHANLER (Newport, Rhode Island, 1902–1961, Boston) studied at the Cleveland Institute with Ernest Bloch and in Paris with Nadia Boulanger. He made his mark as a composer of songs that revealed his uncanny ability to capture the mood and atmosphere of a poem. These qualities were coupled with a discriminating literary taste. On records: *Epitaphs* (1940).

JOHN E. CHEETHAM (Taos, New Mexico, 1939–) teaches at the University of Missouri. He has an affinity for the brass instruments, as is manifest in his best-known piece, *Scherzo for Brass Quintet,* which has been recorded.

PAUL SEIKO CHIHARA (Seattle, Washington, 1938–) studied, among others, with Nadia Boulanger and Gunther Schuller. He teaches at U.C.L.A Chihara, who is of Japanese background, is receptive to Zen thinking. This may account for the unusual serenity of his music, a serenity that some listeners associate with Oriental attitudes toward life and art. Wholly contemporary is Chihara's preoccupation with sound as such. Along with pieces for orchestra and various instrumental groups, Chihara has availed himself of the Moog and Buchla synthesizers. He is very well represented on records: *Symphony in Celebration* (1957); *Redwood,* for viola and percussion (1968); *Grass* (concerto for double bass and orchestra, 1972); *Wind Song,* for cello and orchestra (1972); *Ceremony II (Incantations),* for amplified flute, two amplified cellos, and percussion (1973); *Piano Trio* (1974); *Missa Carminum* (1975).

BARNEY CHILDS (Spokane, Washington, 1926–) studied, among others, with Carlos Chávez, Aaron Copland, and Elliott Carter. He teaches at the University of Redlands. Childs moved from a Neoclassic idiom based on the use of contrapuntal designs within conventional forms to an increasing reliance on continuous motivic expansion. He has a strong interest in American Indian melodies and in recent works has introduced indeterminacy and performer choice into larger fixed forms. In his tape music he likes to use "real-life material" culled from radio announcements and musical advertisements. His works on records do not do justice to his many-faceted activity. They include *Sonata* for solo trombone; *Trio* for clarinet, cello, and piano; *Thirty-seven Songs; Music for Two Flute Players; Duo* for flute and bassoon.

CHOU WEN-CHUNG (Chefoo, China, 1923–) is a disciple and biographer of Edgard Varèse. He combines Oriental and Western elements in a personal style that has been compared to "a tonal brushwork in space." Like John Cage, Chou has applied to his works principles drawn from *I Ching,* Chinese calligraphy, and ancient Chinese instrumental music. On records: *Willows Are New,* for piano (1957); *Cursive,* for flute and piano (1963); *Yu Ko,* for nine players (1965); *Pien,* concerto for piano, winds, and percussion (1966).

ARTHUR COHN (Philadelphia, 1910–) has combined his composing career with a number of administrative posts. He was head of the music division of the Philadelphia Free Library, directed the University of Pennsylvania Museum Concerts, and at present is music editor at Carl Fischer Company in New York. He is the author of several books on music. His compositions includes six string quartets and a variety of chamber and orchestral works. On records: *Kaddish,* for orchestra (1964).

MICHAEL COLGRASS (Chicago, 1932–), who studied mainly with Wallingford Riegger and Ben Weber, is a free-lance percussionist. His experience with theater orchestras, dance groups, and jazz bands has contributed to the development of a style that takes into account the needs of both performers and listeners. This awareness on his part, coupled with a lively tonal imagination and a flair for lyrical melody, makes him one of the most frequently performed composers of his generation. On records: *Percussion Music* (1953); *Fantasy-Variations for Percussion* (1961); *The Earth's a Baked Apple,* for orchestra and chorus (1968).

PAUL COOPER (Victoria, Illinois, 1926–) studied, among others, with Roger Sessions and Nadia Boulanger. He teaches at Rice University. Cooper's Neoclassic orientation is manifest in the four symphonies and five string quartets that occupy the central position in his list of works, which also includes large pieces for chorus and orchestra. He has combined the large Classical forms with aleatory and improvisational elements. Cooper has been active as a music critic and is the author of a widely used textbook. On records: *Sonata* for flute and piano (1964); *Variants* for organ (1971–1972); *String Quartet No. 4: Landscape* (1975); *String Quartet No. 5: Umbrae* (1975).

DAVID COPE (San Francisco, 1941–) was a pupil of George Perle, Ingolf Dahl, and Halsey Stevens. He teaches at Miami University of Ohio. Cope's affinity for the theater manifests itself also in the dramatic intensity of his large instrumental works. He is one of the growing group of composers who combine electronic music with live performance. Cope is the author of a stimulating survey of the contemporary scene, *New Directions in Music*. For a composer still in his thirties he is unusually well represented on records. Available are *Variations* for piano and wind orchestra (1966); *Cycles*, for flute and double bass (1969); *Bright Angel*, for trumpet and tape (1971); *Margins*, for trumpet, cello, percussion, and two pianos (1972); *Arena*, for cello and tape (1974).

ROQUE CORDERO (Panama, 1917–) was assistant director of the Latin-American Music Center at Indiana University and now teaches at Illinois State University. In recent years he has composed almost exclusively in the twelve-tone idiom. He is represented on records by a *Quintet* for flute, clarinet, violin, cello, and piano (1949) and a *Violin Concerto* of unusual virtuosic brilliance (1962).

JOHN CORIGLIANO (New York City, 1938–), while making imaginative use of contemporary techniques, has written works of unusual accessibility. Hence his success with the public, who find his music novel enough to be exciting but not so unfamiliar in style as to be beyond comprehension. Corigliano teaches at Herbert Lehman College. On records: *Poem in October*, for tenor and chamber ensemble (1970), and *Oboe Concerto* (1975).

PAUL CRESTON (New York City, 1906–) is a prolific composer, largely self-taught, whose opus numbers reach well over a hundred. Included are five symphonies, concertos for various instruments, and a variety of chamber, piano, choral, and orchestral pieces. Creston has adhered to a Neoromantic aesthetic that stresses the expressive elements of music. His recorded works include *Concertino for Marimba and Orchestra* (1940); *Concerto for Alto Saxophone and Band* (1944); *Prelude and Dance for Band* (1959); and *Corinthians XIII*, for orchestra (1963). He teaches at Central Washington State College.

INGOLF DAHL (Hamburg, Germany, 1912–1970, Frutigen, Switzerland) studied at the Music Academy in Cologne and the University of Zurich, then with Nadia Boulanger. He lived in Europe until the outbreak of the Second

World War and later taught at the University of Southern California. Dahl combined a Neoclassic orientation with serial procedures. Among his works on records: *Allegro and Arioso*, for woodwind quintet (1942); *Music for Brass Instruments* (1944); *Concertino a tre*, for clarinet, violin, and cello (1946); *Divertimento*, for viola and piano (1948); *Sonata pastorale*, for piano (1959).

Luigi Dallapiccola (Pisino, Istria, now Yugoslavia, 1904–1975, Florence) emerged in the 1940s as the outstanding Italian composer of his generation. He assimilated the thinking of the modern Viennese school to the centuries-old tradition of Italian vocal lyricism. "The twelve-tone method," he stated, "must not be so tyrannical as to exclude a priori both expression and humanity. The only relevant issue is whether a work is a genuine work of art or not, irrespective of what technique may have been employed in its creation." His music, suffused with lyricism, bore the personal stamp of a visionary artist who never lost his sense of wonder at the mystery of life, yet whose almost childlike faith went hand in hand with an inquiring, incisive intellect. Among his works available on records are *Cori di Michelangelo* (Choruses of Michelangelo, 1936); *Canti di prigionia*, for chorus and instruments (Songs of Prison, 1941); *Il prigioniero* (The Prisoner, 1944–1948), opera on a libretto by the composer after Villier de l'Isle-Adam and Charles de Coster; *Piccola musica notturna* (A Little Night Music, for orchestra, 1954); and *Preghiere* (Prayers, for baritone and chamber orchestra, 1962).

Mario Davidovsky (Buenos Aires, 1934–) came to this country in his early twenties. He has been associated with the Columbia-Princeton Electronic Music Center and teaches at the City College of the City University of New York. Davidovsky has written ballet, chamber, theater, and film music, but is best known for his electronic works. Highly regarded is a series of pieces called *Synchronisms*, for electronically synthesized sounds in combination with conventional instruments. It is Davidovsky's signal achievement to have introduced an element of wit and personal charm into an idiom that can all too easily become impersonal. On records: *Electronic Studies Nos. 1, 2, 3* (1961–1965); *Synchronisms Nos. 1–7* (1963–1976); *Inflexions* for fourteen players (1965); *Junctures*, for flute, clarinet, and violin (1966); *Chacona*, for violin, cello, and piano (1972).

Peter Maxwell Davies (Manchester, England, 1934–) has moved in recent years to the forefront of the contemporary British school. He studied at the Royal College of Music in his native city and at Manchester University, also at Princeton with Roger Sessions. He was one of the founders of the chamber ensemble known as The Fires of London (originally Pierrot Players), which has presented a number of his works. Maxwell Davies favors the chamber ensemble, with emphasis on nontraditional instruments and percussion. A powerful dramatic imagination manifests itself in his music. He has made his own a novel type of theater piece for a single actor-singer that can be either fully or partly staged. The best-known example is *Eight*

Songs for a Mad King (1969), based on the court journals of George III. Equally strong is *Miss Donnithorne's Maggot,* for soprano and chamber ensemble (1974), about the eccentric old lady—she was more than a little mad—upon whom the cobwebbed Miss Havisham in Dickens's *Great Expectations* was based. On records: *Second Fantasia* on Taverner's *In nomine,* for orchestra (1964); *Antechrist,* for piccolo, bass clarinet, violin, cello, and percussionists (1967); *Eight Songs for a Mad King; Points and Dances,* from the opera *Taverner*—one of the few, along with Pfitzner's *Palestrina,* about a composer—for chamber ensemble (rev. 1970); *Vesalii icones,* a piece for dancer and chamber ensemble, inspired by the anatomical drawings in the sixteenth-century textbook of Andreas Vesalius (1970); *Dark Angels,* for soprano and guitar (1974).

NORMAN DELLO JOIO (New York City, 1913–) for several years was Dean of Fine Arts at Boston University. His music shows lyric invention that unfolds in broadly flowing melodies over a diatonic-modal harmonic language of a Neoromantic cast. Gregorian chant, Italian opera, and jazz have influenced his style. Dello Joio's list includes piano music, songs, chamber and orchestral works, operas, several ballets for Martha Graham, theater and television music, and a considerable amount of choral music, both with orchestra and a cappella. The recorded works include *Sonata No. 3* for piano (1947); *New York Profiles,* for orchestra (1949); *Two Nocturnes,* for piano (1949); and *Homage to Haydn,* for orchestra (1969).

DAVID DEL TREDICI (Cloverdale, California, 1937–) stands out for the broad lyric appeal of his music. As a result, he is one of the widely performed composers of his age-group. Del Tredici teaches at Boston University and has written several large works based on Lewis Carroll's *Alice in Wonderland* that have found favor with the public. On records: *Scherzo* for piano four hands (1960); *Fantasy Pieces for Piano* (1962); *I Hear an Army,* for soprano and string quartet (1964); *Night-Conjure Verse,* for soprano, countertenor or mezzo-soprano, string quartet, and winds (1965); and several piano works.

DAVID DIAMOND (Rochester, N.Y., 1915–) studied with Bernard Rogers at the Eastman School, with Roger Sessions in New York, and with Nadia Boulanger in Paris. He now teaches at the Juilliard School. Diamond blended his innate romanticism with Neoclassic elements, the result being a style marked by melodic grace, a crisply dissonant texture, and tightly knit forms that use the classical procedures in a highly personal way. His eight symphonies (1940–1961) and nine string quartets (1940–68) occupy a central position in a variegated list that includes concertos, much chamber music, ballet and incidental music, songs and choral works, orchestral pieces and a choral symphony, *To Music,* for tenor, bass-baritone, chorus, and orchestra (1967). On records: *Quintet in B minor* for flute, string trio, and piano (1937); *Music for Shakespeare's Romeo and Juliet,* one of his most attractive works (1947); *Nonet* (1962); and *String Quartet No. 9* (1968).

EMMA LOU DIEMER (Kansas City, Missouri, 1927–) studied with Bernard Rogers and Howard Hanson at the Eastman School; also with Gardner Read and Roger Sessions. She teaches at the University of California in Santa Barbara. Her list centers around the large instrumental forms, including two symphonies and two concertos, works for brass and percussion, as well as piano and choral pieces. On records: *Toccata* for flute chorus.

LUCIA DLUGOSZEWSKI (Detroit, 1931–) was a pupil of Edgard Varèse. As in his case, her studies included work in physics and mathematics. She also inherited his abiding interest in pure sound textures. She has developed over a hundred pitched and unpitched percussion instruments made of glass, metal, and other materials, which she herself plays. She invented a timbre piano in 1951 that, in addition to a keyboard, uses bows and a variety of plectra. Like John Cage, she has been profoundly influenced by Oriental philosophy. Paralleling his close association with the dance of Merce Cunningham, she has worked with Eric Hawkins and his dancers, and has written a number of works for them. On records: *Space Is a Diamond*, for trumpet (1970); *Angels of the Inmost Heaven*, for brass (1972).

CHARLES DODGE (Ames, Iowa, 1942–) studied at Columbia University, where his early interest in computer music probably originated. His very personal approach to this medium is manifest in *Earth's Magnetic Field*, "a realization in electronic sound on tape of an index of the sun's radiation on the magnetic field of the earth" (1970). Dodge, who teaches at Brooklyn College, has recently turned to computer-synthesized vocal music, in which the voice is used as a primary sound source, manipulated by computer program, and then resynthesized to form the actual piece. Several examples of his synthesized speech music have been recorded: *In Celebration, Speech Songs,* and *The Story of Our Lives* (1972–1975). Also *Folia,* for chamber ensemble (1965); *Changes,* an electronic piece (1967–1970); and *Extensions,* for trumpet and tape (1973).

JACOB DRUCKMAN (Philadelphia, 1928–) studied at the Juilliard School, Tanglewood, the Columbia-Princeton Electronic Music Center, and in France. He is currently professor of music at Yale University. Endowed with a highly developed sense of the dramatic, Druckman has become one of the best-known composers of his generation. He views the concert hall as a form of theater; a concert for him is a dramatic ritual. In his instrumental works he is involved, as he says, "with the actual presence of the performers theatrically as well as musically." Behind this preoccupation is the idea that "theatrical and musical elements are inseparable; the ideal performance of the music already embodies the performance of the drama." In short, he is one of several contemporary composers who are seeking new ways of combining music and drama. Given this orientation, Druckman realized that the combination of electronic music with live performance restored the human, the unpredictable elements that give a concert its appeal and justification. Accordingly, he has been in the forefront of those composers who are exploring the possibilities of electronic-plus-live music. A number of his works are available on records: *String Quartet No. 2* (1966); *Incenters*, for chamber orchestra (1968); *Animus II*, for female voice, 2 percussion players, and electronic tape (1968); *Animus III*, for clarinet and prerecorded tape (1969); *Valentine*, for double bass (1969); *Synapse*, for electronic tape (1971). In several of his orchestral works, Druckman has allowed spatial elements to shape the form, as in *Lamia*, for soprano and divided orchestra with two conductors (1974). Also on records is *Delizie contente che l'alme beate* (Delicious Contentments that Beautify the Soul, 1973), for woodwind quintet and tape, in memory of Bruno Maderna.

HENRI DUTILLEUX (Angers, France, 1916–) is, like most French composers, a product of the Paris Conservatory. To the heritage of Debussy, Ravel, and Roussel he added influences emanating from Stravinsky and Schoenberg. He is one of a number of composers, both past and present, who enjoy much greater appreciation in their native land than abroad. On records: *Sonatine for Flute and Piano* (1943); *Piano Sonata* (1948); *Loup*, a ballet (1953); *Cello Concerto* (1970).

JOHN EATON (Bryn Mawr, Pennsylvania, 1935–) studied with Roger Sessions, Milton Babbitt, and Edward Cone. He has been concerned with the development of live electronic music through the use of a live-performance synthesizer known as the Synket, which allows for the introduction of chance and performer-choice elements into what had become a prerecorded, therefore fixed, idiom. He is also interested in the assimilation of microtones into the Western tradition. On records: *Concert Music*, for solo clarinet (1961); *Blind Man's Cry* (1968) for soprano and synthesizers; *Mass* (1970). Eaton teaches at Indiana University.

GEORGE EDWARDS (Boston, 1943–) studied with Richard Hoffman, Milton Babbitt, and Earl Kim. He teaches at the New England Conservatory. His works *Monopoly*, for orchestra (1972), and *Three Hopkins Songs* (1971) show a fully developed style that espouses the center of the road. On records: *String Quartet* (1967); *Kreuz und Quer*, for quintet (1971); and *Exchange-Misère*, for chamber ensemble (1974).

CECIL S. EFFINGER (Colorado Springs, 1914–) was a pupil of Bernard Wagenaar and Nadia Boulanger. He teaches at the University of Colorado. His list includes five symphonies, five string quartets, a three-act opera based on Rostand's Romantic play *Cyrano de Bergerac*, and a number of large works for chorus and orchestra. On records: *Little Symphony* (1945).

HANNS EISLER (Leipzig, 1898–1962, Berlin) began his career as a student of Schoenberg. Unsatisfied with his position as an avant-garde composer, he found a place in the revolutionary workers' movement, for which he wrote the political songs and choruses that brought him an international reputation in anti-Fascist circles during the thirties. Eisler came to the United

States in 1938, taught at the New School in New York and the University of Southern California. In 1947 the House Un-American Activities Committee sought to have him deported. After an international protest he was permitted to leave of his own accord in 1948. He spent his last years in East Germany. On records: *Klavierstücke*, Op. 3 (1923); *Piano Sonata No. 3* (1943).

DUKE ELLINGTON (Edward Kennedy Ellington, Washington, D.C. 1899–1974, New York City) achieved his nickname because of his sartorial elegance, but he lived up to the aristocratic implications of the title both as man and musician. It was said of him that although he played the piano, his real instrument was the orchestra. He left behind a body of music that ranged from simple tunes, theater songs, piano pieces, and works for jazz groups, to instrumental compositions for jazz and/or symphony orchestra. Whatever he touched showed, as Gunther Schuller put it, his passion "for translating the raw materials of musical sounds into his own splendid visions." His was perhaps the most seminal influence on the jazz music of our time. His enormous catalogue is well represented on records.

DAVID N. EPSTEIN (New York City, 1930–) studied with Roger Sessions, Irving Fine, and Milton Babbitt. His musical imagery was shaped by a blend of atonal Expressionism, Neoclassicism, and twelve-tone thinking, a stylistic synthesis that he has shaped into large instrumental works. Epstein teaches at M.I.T. and is the author of *Studies in Musical Structure*. On records: *The Seasons*, a song cycle (1956); *String Trio* (1964); *Ventures for Symphonic Wind Ensemble* (1970); *String Quartet* (1971).

DONALD ERB (Youngstown, Ohio, 1927–) studied, among others, with Bernard Heiden and Nadia Boulanger. He has taught a large number of young musicians at various schools, among them the Cleveland Institute of Music and Indiana University, and is active in various musical capacities in Cleveland. Among his recorded works are a number of orchestral works, including *Symphony of Overtures* (1964); *Phantasma*, for chamber group (1965); *Diversion for 2 (other than sex)*, for trumpet and percussion (1966); an electronic piece, *Reconnaissance* (1967); *Harold's Trip to the Sky*, for viola, piano, and percussion (1972).

ROBERT ERICKSON (Marquette, Michigan, 1917–) studied with Ernst Krenek. After several years as a serial composer he became preoccupied with exploring the possibilities of timbre and rhythm, greater freedom of tempo, and improvisational techniques. In 1964 he began to work with tape. Erickson is also interested in the construction of special instruments to play the music he writes. On records: *Chamber Concerto* (1960); and *End of the Mime*, for a capella chorus (1962). Erickson teaches at the University of California at San Diego.

ALVIN ETLER (Battle Creek, Iowa, 1913–1973, Florence, Massachusetts) studied, among others, with Paul Hindemith. He used serial techniques without ever entirely abandoning the use of tonal centers and was strongly influenced by jazz. Etler believed art depends on the purposeful handling of materials within a form; hence he was not oriented toward indeterminacy. His recorded works include *Triptych for Orchestra* (1961); *Quintet for Brass Instruments* (1964); and *Concerto for Brass Quintet, Strings, and Percussion* (1967).

RICHARD FELCIANO (Santa Rosa, California, 1930–), who teaches at the University of California at Berkeley, studied with Darius Milhaud and Luigi Dallapiccola. His music uses electronics, some indeterminate procedures, and is strongly influenced by Eastern music, as in his use of the Javanese gamelan. His emphasis, as he says, is on sound rather than system. On records: *Gravities,* for piano four-hands (1965), *Crasis,* for seven instruments and electronics (1967); *Spectra,* for piccolo, flute, alto flute, and contrabass (1967); *"and from the abyss,"* for tuba and electrically derived sounds (1976).

MORTON FELDMAN (New York City, 1926–) favors low dynamic levels in a music marked by quietude of spirit and subtlety of sound. A pupil of Wallingford Riegger and Stefan Wolpe, his aesthetic was shaped in the circle that revolved around John Cage during the '50s. Early in his career he developed a graphic notation that indicated relative durations but allowed the player to choose the pitches within a given register; or the pitches might be specified but the durations left to the performer. The music itself achieves its tensions through extreme delicacy of nuance, exploiting contrasts of timbre and register to a remarkable degree within the firmly held dynamic range. Behind it stands an aural imagination of extraordinary refinement. Feldman's music forms a very special enclave on the contemporary scene and is well represented on records. Among the available works are *Structures,* for string quartet (1951); *King of Denmark,* for percussion (1964); *Rothko Chapel,* for chorus, viola, and percussion (1972); *For Frank O'Hara,* for chamber ensemble (1973). Feldman teaches at the State University of New York at Buffalo.

BRIAN FENNELLY (Kingston, N.Y., 1937–) studied with Mel Powell, Donald Martino, and George Perle. He teaches at New York University. Fennelly's interests embrace music for both traditional instruments and electronics. On records: *Wind Quintet* (1967); *Evanescences,* for chamber group (1969); *Prelude and Elegy for Brass Quintet* (1973).

PAUL FETLER (Philadelphia, 1920–) studied, among others, with Paul Hindemith and Boris Blacher. He teaches at the University of Minnesota. Fetler is a middle-of-the-roader, whose varied list includes symphonies, concertos, opera, music for films, theater, and the dance, chamber music, as well as choral works with and without orchestra. On records: *Pastorale Suite,* for violin, cello, and piano.

IRVING FINE (Boston, 1914–1962, Natick, Massachusetts) studied at Harvard, where he later taught. Subsequently, he moved to Brandeis University where he became chairman of the School of Creative Arts in 1950. Fine was deeply committed to the Neoclassic aesthetic and its emphasis on the eighteenth-century values of order and control. These manifested themselves in his music even after he became preoccupied with twelve-tone techniques, which he used in an altogether personal manner, retaining throughout the refined lyricism, rhythmic charm, and overall elegance that characterized his earlier style. Fine favored chamber music and choral works, but in his *Symphony* (1960–1962), he showed his ability to handle the large orchestral forms. This work is available on records, as are several attractive choral pieces; *Toccata concertante* for orchestra (1946); the suite *Music for Piano* (1947); *Partita for Wind Quintet* (1948); the song cycle *Mutability* (1952); and *Serious Song: Lament for String Orchestra* (1955).

VIVIAN FINE (Chicago, 1913–) had among her teachers Ruth Crawford Seeger and Roger Sessions. She teaches at Bennington College. As musical director of the Bethsabee de Rothschild Foundation (1955–1961), she became interested in the relationship of modern music to modern dance and produced a number of scores for Martha Graham, Doris Humphrey, and others. Fine was also actively associated in New York City with a group of young composers sponsored by Aaron Copland and was one of the founders of the American Composers' Alliance. On records: *Sinfonia and Fugato for Piano* (1963); *Paean on the Sound "I"* for tenor, women's chorus, and 12 brass instruments (1968–1969).

ROSS LEE FINNEY (Wells, Minnesota, 1906–) studied, among others, with Nadia Boulanger in Paris, with Alban Berg in Vienna, and with Roger Sessons in New York. He taught at the University of Michigan, where he established the electronic music studio. His music is rooted in tonality; yet he assimilated twelve-tone techniques and various implications of serialism. Finney's compositions include four symphonies, eight string quartets, and two piano concertos. On records: *Cello Sonata No. 2* (1950); *Chromatic Fantasy in E* (1957); *Symphony No. 3* (1964); *Concerto for Alto Saxophone and Winds* (1974).

IRWIN FISCHER (Iowa City, 1903–) studied, among others, with Nadia Boulanger. He teaches at the American Conservatory of Music. Fischer turned from a Neoclassical orientation to a very free handling of twelve-tone technique marked by an element of humor and fantasy. Characteristic is his *Overture on an Exuberant Tone Row* (1964), which has been recorded.

NICOLAS O. FLAGELLO (New York City, 1928–) studied with Vittorio Giannini and Ildebrando Pizzetti. He taught at the Manhattan School of Music. Flagello belongs to the conservative wing. He is well represented on records. Among the works available are *Burlesca for Flute and Guitar* (1961); *Capriccio for Cello and Orchestra* (1962); and *Lautrec: Suite for Orchestra* (1965).

WILLIAM FLANAGAN (Detroit, 1926–1969, New York City) studied at the Eastman School with Bernard Rogers and worked later with several others, among them Honegger, Barber, Copland, and Diamond. His Neoromantic lyricism found its outlet in vocal music, especially songs, on texts that show his discriminating literary taste. He also left behind a number of instrumental works. Flanagan wrote reviews for the *New York Herald Tribune;* at the time of his death at the age of 43 (by suicide), he was working on a book about American composers. On records: *Another August,* for soprano, piano, and orchestra (1967); also a group of songs.

CARLISLE FLOYD (Latta, South Carolina, 1926–) studied with Ernest Bacon at Converse College in his native state and at Syracuse University. He taught at Florida State University for some time and is now affiliated with the University of Houston. Floyd is best known as a composer of theatrically effective operas in a Neoromantic idiom, including *Susannah* (1955), *Wuthering Heights* (1959), and *Of Mice and Men* (1969). On records: *Pilgrimage: Three Sacred Songs* (1956); *In Celebration: Overture for Orchestra* (1969).

LUKAS FOSS (Berlin, 1922–) came to the United States in 1937, when he was fifteen, his parents having left Germany upon Hitler's accession to power. His identification with his new homeland found expression in *The Prairie,* a full-length cantata for four soloists, large chorus, and orchestra, on the poem by Carl Sandburg (1944). This Americanist strain commingled in his style with the Romantic heritage of Mahler, the Neoclassicism emanating from Hindemith, and the inescapable influence—for any musician at that time— of Stravinsky. With *Time Cycle* (1960) and *Echoi* (1961–1963) Foss took his place in the forefront of those who were experimenting with indeterminacy, group improvisation, and fresh approaches to sound. For example, in his *Concert* for cello, orchestra, and tape, the soloist at one point has a choice of three orchestral accompaniments; the two that are not used become the accompaniment for the next movement. Foss was also a leader in the trend toward collage, whereby contemporary composers use for their own purpose material borrowed from the past. This orientation is manifest in the *Baroque Variations for Orchestra* (1967), which is one of a number of works by Foss available on records. Others are *The Prairie; Behold, I Build an House,* for chorus (1950); *Psalms,* for chorus with orchestra or two pianos (1956); *Time Cycle,* four songs for soprano and orchestra or chamber ensemble; *Elytres* for flute, violins, piano, harp, and percussion (1964).

PETER RACINE FRICKER (London, 1920–), who teaches at the University of California at Santa Barbara, has written in all the standard genres except opera. Fricker was one of the first composers in England who, fascinated by the influences that were emanating from the Continent immediately after the war, assimilated those into his personal style. The strongly emotional impact of his music belies the charge of cerebralism that has sometimes been leveled against him, as do the speed and sureness with which he composes. His list of works includes five symphonies, two string quartets, and several large choral works. On records: *Wind Quintet* (1947) and *Symphony No. 1* (1948–1949).

KENNETH GABURO (Sommerville, New Jersey, 1926–) teaches at the University of California at San Diego. He founded the New Music Choral Ensemble, which enlarged the repertory of contemporary vocal music through improvisation, electronics, and the incorporation of theatrical elements. His music has been influenced by his experience as conductor of this group, as well as by his interest in electronics. On records: *Line Studies,* for flute, clarinet, trombone, viola (1956–1957); *Lingua II: Maledetto,* for seven virtuoso speakers (1967–1968); also several pieces involving electronic sound, among them *Lemon Drops* (1965), *For Harry* (1966), and *Antiphony III* (Pearl-White Moments, 1962) and *IV* (1967).

ROBERTO GERHARD (Valls, Catalonia, Spain, 1896–1970, Cambridge, England) left Spain at the beginning of the Civil War and settled in England. Recognition was slow in coming, but in the 1950s Gerhard achieved a high reputation on the Continent. He adapted the Schoenbergian canon to his own expressive needs, which reflected the Spanish temperament without the picturesque elements of those of his compatriots who were oriented toward French Postimpressionism. His music rather represents a blend of dodecaphonic with Neoclassical and Spanish elements. In his *Symphony No. 3, "Collages,"* for tape and orchestra (1960), Gerhard combined the grand form with electronic sound. On records: *Alegrias,* ballet suite (1944); *Don Quixote,* ballet suite (1957); *The Plague,* cantata (1964), *Concerto for Orchestra* (1965); *Symphony No. 4* (1967).

EDWIN GERSHEFSKY (Meriden, Connecticut, 1909–) studied composition with Joseph Schillinger and piano with Arthur Schnabel. He is head of the department of music at the University of Georgia. His varied list includes symphonic, choral, and chamber music. He has written motion picture scores and articles of various facets of the contemporary music scene. On records: *Fanfare, Fugato and Finale,* for orchestra (1937).

EMANUEL GHENT (Montreal, 1925–) studied with Ralph Shapey, worked at the Columbia-Princeton Electronic Music Center, and is associated with the computer-music studio of Bell Telephone Laboratories in Murray Hill, New Jersey. Ghent, who practices psychiatry in New York City, has been specifically interested in combining electronic and live sound. He has written electronic scores for the Mimi Garrard Dance Company and worked on computer-generated lighting for the dance. On records: *Helices,* for violin, piano, and tape (1969).

DINU GHEZZO (Tusla, Romania, 1941–) teaches at New York University. His music reveals his interest in new instrumental effects, extension of timbres through amplification, aleatory procedures, and improvisation; also microtones, as in his *Kanones* for flute, cello, and harpsichord (1972). These tendencies are manifest in *Thalla* for piano, electric piano, and sixteen instruments (1974), which has been recorded. Also available: *Ritualen* for piano (1969) and the aforementioned *Kanones.*

VITTORIO GIANNINI (Philadelphia, 1903–1966, New York City) studied at the Royal Conservatory in Milan, the Juilliard School (where he later taught), and the American Academy in Rome. His operas combine the Italian verismo tradition with late Romantic tunefulness, especially *The Scarlet Letter*, from the novel by Hawthorne (1937), and *The Taming of the Shrew*, after Shakespeare (1950). The latter work is available on records, as is also *Symphony No. 3*, for band (1959).

MIRIAM GIDEON (Greeley, Colorado, 1906–) was influenced by the aesthetic of atonal Expressionism, but adapted its vocabulary to her own expressive ends. Her output features vocal music, for which she has a marked affinity, and chamber works, but includes also the *Symphonia brevis* for orchestra (1953). She is represented on records by *The Hound of Heaven* for voice, oboe, and string quartet (1945); *The Adorable Mouse*, for narrator and orchestra (1960); *The Condemned Playground*, a song cycle for two soloists and chamber ensemble (1963); *Piano Suite No. 3* (1963); *Questions on Nature*, for voice, oboe, piano, and percussion (1964); *Rhymes from the Hill*, for voice, clarinet, cello, marimba (1968); and *Seasons of Time* for voice and 4 instruments (1969).

ALBERTO GINASTERA (Buenos Aires, 1916–), Argentina's foremost composer, is a substantial figure on the international scene. His music draws nourishment from folklore but is cast in an advanced harmonic idiom. Ginastera established himself in the opera houses of the world with *Don Rodrigo* (1964), *Bomarzo* (1966), and *Beatrice Cenci* (1971). These works have to a remarkable degree succeeded in combining the gestures of traditional grand opera with contemporary modes of thought. Notable too is his handling of the large instrumental forms. The recorded works include *Panambi* and *Estancia*, two picturesque ballet suites (1940, 1941); *String Quartet No. 2* (1958); *Cantata para América mágica* (1960); and *Piano Concertos Nos. 1* (1961) and *2* (1971).

PHILIP GLASS (Baltimore, Maryland, 1937–) studied with Vincent Persichetti, William Bergsma, and Nadia Boulanger. He has developed a system of composing "based on amplified ensembles of keyboard instruments, winds, and voice," his aim being to achieve music that would be perceived "as a pure medium of sound freed of dramatic structure." Glass is related to the school of so-called minimal composition, based on the repetition and slow change of short modal fragments. It is a style cultivated by Steve Reich, Terry Riley, and their adherents. He is best known for the opera *Einstein on the Beach* (lyrics and music by P. Glass, spoken text by Christopher Knowles, Lucinda Childs, and Samuel M. Johnson, 1977), which fully set forth his theory and practice. On records: *North Star*, for chamber ensemble, and *Two Pages*, for electric organ and piano.

ALEXANDER GOEHR (Berlin, 1932–), who is professor of music at Cambridge University, studied at the Royal Manchester College and with Olivier Messiaen in Paris. In 1967 he organized the Music Theater Ensemble, a group of singers, actors, dancers, mimes, and instrumentalists who function in the spirit of multimedia theater and have presented Goehr's theater pieces. He has used serial techniques freely, combining them with more traditional procedures. On records: *Two Choruses* (1962); *Piano Trio* (1966); *Quartet No. 2* (1967).

JOSEPH GOODMAN (New York City, 1918–) studied with, among others, Paul Hindemith, Walter Piston, and Francesco Malipiero. He teaches at Queens College. Goodman's music reflects a mystical bent that inclines him toward liturgical works. He is one of the few Americans who have added significantly to the contemporary literature for the organ. His list includes a concerto for that instrument as well as a piece for organ and tape. On records: *Quintet for Wind Instruments* (1954), and *Jadis III*, for flute and bassoon (1972).

MORTON GOULD (New York City, 1913–) made his mark by fusing the elements of popular American music with Classical form and structure. In his later works he moved away from the facile popularity of his earlier style and reached out toward deeper levels both in technique and expression. His language became increasingly contrapuntal, dissonant, and harmonically complex. Among his widely played works on records are *American Salute*, for orchestra (1940); *Latin American Symphonette* (1941); *Spirituals for Orchestra* (1941); *Derivations*, for clarinet and band (1957); and—illustrative of the later style—*Soundings*, for orchestra (1969).

GEORGE C. GREEN (Mt. Kisco, N.Y., 1930–) studied with Aaron Copland, Robert Palmer, Bernard Rogers, and Alan Hovhaness, among others. He teaches at Skidmore College. Green's instrumental music is adroitly written, especially for the winds, and exemplifies his basically Neoromantic orientation. On records: *Triptych for Trumpet Along* (1970); *Perihelion*, for concert band (1973).

ROBERT A. GROSS (Colorado Springs, 1914–) studied with Rubin Goldmark, Bernard Wagenaar, and Arnold Schoenberg. Gross's Neoromanticism was broadened by contact with dodecaphonic modes of thought. Chamber music and works for the violin predominate in a list that also includes vocal music. On records: *3–4–2*, for violin and cello (1969); *Passacaglia* for violin and organ (1974); and *Chacounne*, for soprano and violin (1976).

LOUIS GRUENBERG (Brest-Litovsk, Russia, 1884–1964, Beverly Hills, California) achieved his reputation through the imaginative use of Negro spirituals and folk material. He is best remembered for his opera *Emperor Jones*, on a libretto after Eugene O'Neill (1932). On records: *Polychromatics*, Opus 6, for piano (1924).

CAMARGO GUARNIERI (Tiete, Brazil, 1907–) writes music that is largely nationalistic and uses polyphonic textures extensively. He is best known in this country for the *Danza Brasileira*, which has been recorded.

IAIN HAMILTON (Glasgow, 1922–), who teaches at Duke University in North Carolina, belongs to a group of British composers who were first influenced by Hindemith, Bartók, and Stravinsky, and then adopted the techniques of serialism. His works include two symphonies, the operas *Agamemnon* (1967–1969) and *The Royal Hunt of the Sun* (1969); *The Cataline Conspiracy* (1974); also ballet, film, chamber, and vocal music, and solo sonatas for various instruments. Among the recorded works are *Nocturnes with Cadenzas*, for piano (1963); *Threnos—In Time of War*, for organ (1966); *Epitaph for This World and Time*, for three choruses and two organs (1970); and *Voyage*, for horn and orchestra (1970).

CALVIN HAMPTON (Kittatinny, Pennsylvania, 1938–) is organist at the Calvary Episcopal Church in New York City. He is one of a small number of composers who have sought to bring the organ into the electronic-music age, as in *God Plays Hide and Seek* for organ with Moog synthesizer (1971). On records: *Catch Up*, for 2 pianos and tape (1967); *Triple Play*, for piano and Ondes Martenot (1967).

JOHN HARBISON (Orange, New Jersey, 1938–) teaches at the Massachusetts Institute of Technology. His outlook was shaped by his training at Princeton under Earl Kim and Roger Sessions, his expertness as a jazz and string-quartet player, and his considerable activity as a conductor of Baroque and new music. On records: *Confinement*, for 12 players (1965); *Parody-Fantasia*, for piano (1968); *Bermuda Triangle*, for tenor saxophone, amplified cello, and electronic organ (1970); *Five Songs of Experience*, on poems of Blake, for four soloists, chorus, string quartet, and percussion (1971).

DONALD HARRIS (St. Paul, Minnesota, 1931–) studied with Ross Lee Finney, Nadia Boulanger, and Lukas Foss, among others. He teaches at the Hartt College of Music. Harris favors instrumental music in the Classical forms. On records: *Fantasy* for violin and piano (1957); *String Quartet* (1965); *Ludus I*, for ten instruments (1966); *Ludus II*, for flute, clarinet, violin, cello, piano (1973).

LOU HARRISON (Portland, Oregon, 1917–) is one of a group of composers from the West Coast who derived inspiration from the Far East rather than Europe. He was a pupil of Henry Cowell, organized concerts in collaboration with John Cage, studied with Arnold Schoenberg, accompanied and composed music for dancers (he was a dancer himself), spent a decade in New York City as critic and copyist, returned to California, visited several countries in Asia on a Rockefeller Fellowship, and now teaches at San José State University. Harrison has been strongly influenced by serial and aleatory procedures, by medieval and Renaissance polyphony, and—as already indicated—by the musical cultures of the Far East. His unceasing desire to expand the boundaries of music has impelled him to use nontraditional sources of sound: brake drums, coffee cans, flower pots, and the like. He has also been active as a builder and designer of instruments. On records: *Suite for Percussion* (1940); *Canticle No. 1 for Percussion* (1940); *Song of Queztalcoatl*, for percussion orchestra (1941); *Symphony on G* (1954–1968); *Concerto* for violin and percussion orchestra (1959); *Concerto in Slendro*, for violin, celesta, and percussion (1961), a work that evokes the Javanese gamelan; *Pacifika*

Rondo for chamber orchestra of Western and Asian instruments (1963); *Elegiac Symphony* (1975).

WALTER S. HARTLEY (Washington, D.C., 1927–) studied at the Eastman School with Bernard Rogers and Howard Hanson. He teaches at State University College in Fredonia, N.Y. Hartley is a professional pianist who, unusually enough, has written largely for the winds, as in his *Concerto for Saxophone and Band* (1967) and *Octet for Saxophones* (1975). Both works have been recorded. Also available: *Sonata Concertante,* for trombone and piano (1958); *Sonata* for tuba and piano (1962); *Caprice* for trumpet and piano (1967); *Concerto* for alto saxophone, tuba, and wind octet (1969); *Octet* for saxophones (1975).

ROMAN HAUBENSTOCK-RAMATI (Cracow, Poland, 1919–) began his career in Cracow, continued it in Tel Aviv and Paris, where he worked at the *musique concrète* studio of the French radio, then settled in Vienna as a reader for new music for Universal Edition. He belongs to the post-Webern generation of serialists, and like many another member of the avant-garde, has been concerned with the new methods of notation that center about musical graphics. On records: *String Quartet No. 1, "Mobile"* (1973).

BERNARD HEIDEN (Frankfurt, Germany, 1910–) was a pupil of Hindemith, from whom he took over not only a Neoclassic orientation but also an affinity for the wind instruments, as is manifest in his *Four Dances* for brass quintet (1967) and *Intrada* for woodwind quintet and alto saxophone (1970). Heiden, who teaches at Indiana University, has written two symphonies. Like his teacher, he never relinquished the concept of a tonal center. On records: *Sonata* for alto saxophone and piano (1937); *Quintet* for horn and string quartet (1952); *Quintet* for woodwinds (1965).

JOHN HEISS (New York City, 1938–) studied, with Otto Luening and Milton Babbitt among others. He teaches at the New England Conservatory and has been active as flutist and promoter of new techniques for the flute. His manner of writing for his instrument is manifest in *4 Movements for 3 Flutes* (1969). Also available on records are the *Quartet* for flute, clarinet, cello, and piano (1971) and *Inventions, Contours and Colors,* for chamber ensemble (1973).

WILLIAM HELLERMAN (Milwaukee, Wisconsin 1939–) attended the Juilliard School and Columbia University, where he studied with Chou Wen-chung, Otto Luening, and Vladimir Ussachevsky. He subsequently worked with Stefan Wolpe and came under the influence of various composers at the summer seminars in Darmstadt and at Tanglewood. Hellerman, who teaches at Columbia, is active as organizer of new-music concerts, performs on the classical guitar, and conducts chamber ensembles. On records: *Ek-Stasis II* for piano, percussion, and tape (1970); *Passages 13—The Fire,* for trumpet and electronic equipment (1971); *On the Edge of a Node,* for violin, cello, and guitar (1974).

ROBERT HELPS (Passaic, New Jersey, 1928–) studied with and was strongly influenced by Roger Sessions. He has made a reputation as a pianist, especially as a performer of contemporary music, and teaches at Princeton University and the Manhattan School of Music. He is represented on recordings by several piano pieces: *Three Etudes* (1956); *Recollections* (1959); *Portrait* (1960); and *Quartet* (1971).

HANS WERNER HENZE (Gutersloh, Westphalia, Germany, 1926–) has made a great reputation in Europe through his operas and ballets. Indeed, he is one of the most widely performed composers of his generation. Four of his operas have been produced in this country—*Boulevard Solitude* (1951), *Elegy for Young Lovers* (1959–1961), *The Young Lord* (1964), and *The Bassarids* (1965). He has assimilated successfully the heritage of Viennese dodecaphony, the rhythmic élan of Stravinsky, the lyricism of Italian opera, the symphonic tradition of German music-drama, and a scintillating orchestral coloring that his admirers like to think of as French. Altogether personal is his ability to spin out a long melodic line, as well as to suggest character and action, mood and drama through music. While these are primarily the gifts of the opera composer, they are present too in his instrumental music, much of which is cast in the large forms; six symphonies, two piano concertos, two violin concertos, and a number of sonatas for various instruments. Henze's political orientation, which is decisively to the left, is reflected in his choice of texts and his inclusion of popular elements such as rock music and popular tunes, along with electronic sounds, microtones, and tone clusters. On records: *Violin Concerto No. 1* (1948); *Piano Variations* (1948); *Piano Sonata* (1949); *Apollo und Hyazinthus,* for alto and small orchestra (1949); *Labyrinth,* a ballet (1952); *Wind Quintet* (1952); *Kammermusik I–XII* (1958–1963); *In Memoriam,* for chamber ensemble (1965); *Violin Concerto No. 2* (1971). Several other works, including the symphonies and *The Young Lord,* are no longer listed in the record catalogues but can be found in libraries and record collections.

WILLIAM HIBBARD (Newton, Massachusetts, 1939–) teaches at the University of Iowa, where he also directs the Center for New Music. He has explored the possibilities of extending serial techniques to the area of improvisation. On records: *String Quartet* (1971) and *Bass Trombone, Bass Clarinet, Harp* (1973).

LEJAREN HILLER (New York City, 1924–) is one of several contemporary composers who began as scientists. He received his Ph.D. in chemistry, worked as a research chemist, wrote articles and a textbook in his field, and obtained a number of patents. He had studied composition with Roger Sessions and Milton Babbitt at Princeton, and was thus in a unique position to coordinate computer programming with musical composition as founder and director of the Experimental Music Studio at the University of Illinois. In 1968 he transferred to the State University of New York at Buffalo, as codirector of the Center for the Creative and Performing Arts. Hiller's compositions range from abstract instrumental to multimedia works for the theater, to pieces that depend wholly or in part on computer and/or electronic techniques. Examples of the first and third categories are available on records, such as the *Piano Sonatas No. 4* (1950) and *No. 5* (1961); *String Quartets No. 5* (1962) and *No. 6* (1973); and *Machine Music,* for piano, percussion, and tape (1964).

SYDNEY HODKINSON (Winnipeg, Canada, 1934-) was trained at Princeton and the University of Michigan, as well as the Eastman School, where he now teaches. He has been active in organizing concerts of contemporary music, especially during the period when he directed the Rockefeller New Music Project at the University of Michigan, and has appeared in concerts both as a conductor and clarinetist. On records: *Dissolution of the Serial,* for clarinet and piano (1967); *Valence,* for chamber orchestra (1970); *Megalith Trilogy,* for organ (1973).

RICHARD HOFFMANN (Vienna, 1925-) was brought to New Zealand as a boy. He studied with Arnold Schoenberg in Los Angeles and became the master's secretary and amanuensis. In this capacity he filed Schoenberg's letters for the Library of Congress and coedited the collected edition of the latter's writings. He teaches at Oberlin College and has lectured widely on Schoenberg's works. Hoffmann has adapted the serial technique to his own compositional needs, which are based on the systematic organization of the various parameters—intervals, dynamics, timbres, rhythms, and meters. On records: *Trio* for strings (1963).

LEE HOIBY (Madison, Wisconsin, 1926-) studied composition with Gian Carlo Menotti and has continued in the Menotti tradition of modernized romantic opera. He is best known for *The Scarf* (after Chekhov, 1955) and *Natalia Petrovna* (after Turgenev, 1964). These works show to good advantage his capacity for lyric melody and his ability to suggest mood, character, and dramatic situation through music. On records: *Concerto for Piano* (1958); *After Eden,* for orchestra (1966).

ALAN HOVHANESS (Somerville, Massachusetts, of Armenian and Scottish parentage, 1911-) was strongly influenced by the music of the Middle and Far East. His style combines the Western tradition with elements drawn from Oriental cultures, especially Armenian and Indian. His music is enveloped in the atmosphere of rhapsodic improvisation so indigenous to those cultures, projected with all the exuberance of a totally uninhibited temperament. Hovhaness is an exceptionally productive composer; few of his colleagues can match the scope and diversity of his list. He is very well represented on records. Among the works available are *Armenian Rhapsody No. 1,* for chamber orchestra (1944); *Avak the Healer,* a cantata for soprano, trumpet, and strings (1946); *Prayer of St. Gregory,* for trumpet and strings (1946); *Sharagan and Fugue for Brass Choir* (1949); *Khaldis,* a concerto for piano, four trumpets, and percussion (1951); *Magnificat,* for chorus and orchestra (1959); *Silver Pilgrimage* (*Symphony No. 15,* 1962); *And God Created Great Whales,* for orchestra (1970); *Symphony No. 25, "Odysseus"* (1973).

KAREL HUSA (Prague, 1921–) is professor of composition at Cornell University and is also active as conductor and editor. To the middle-European tradition of Janáček and Bartók, he has assimilated elements of Stravinskyan Neoclassicism—he studied, among others, with Nadia Boulanger—as well as the serial techniques and advanced harmonies of the twelve-tone school. He also makes use of aleatory techniques. Husa is well represented on records by orchestral works such as *Symphony No. 1* (1953); *Quartets No. 2* (1959) and *3* (1963); *Mosaiques* (1961); *Serenade* for woodwind quintet and piano (1963); *Concerto for Saxophone* (1967); *Music for Prague* (1968); *Apotheosis of This Earth* (1971).

THOMAS SCOTT HUSTON (Tacoma, Washington, 1916–) studied at the Eastman School of Music with Howard Hanson, Bernard Rogers, and Burrill Phillips. He teaches at the University of Cincinnati. Huston's four symphonies are the central item in a varied list that includes some unusual instrumental combinations, as in his *Sounds at Night*, for 13 brass instruments (1972) and *Suite for Our Time*, for brass sextet (1973), both of which have been recorded. Also on records: *Penta-Tholoi*, for piano (1968); *Phenomena*, for string quartet (1970); *Idioms*, for violin, clarinet, and French horn (1970); *A Game of Circles*, for clarinet, piano, and celesta (1974); *Lifestyles*, for clarinet, cello, and piano (1975); *Shadowy Waters*, for clarinet, piano, and cello, commissioned by Sonos III Trio (1977).

ANTHONY IANNACCONE (Brooklyn, N.Y., 1943–) studied, among others, with Vittorio Giannini, David Diamond, and Samuel Adler. He teaches at Eastern Michigan University. Iannaccone has adapted the Neoromantic aesthetic to a lively personal style, and is one among a group of younger composers who are going back to composing symphonies. His list already includes two, as well as a variety of instrumental and vocal works and music for tape. On records: *Partita* for piano (1967); *Hades*, for brass quartet (1968); *Rituals*, for violin and piano (1973); *Bicinia*, for flute and alto saxophone (1974); *Sonatina* for trumpet and tuba (1975).

ANDREW IMBRIE (New York City, 1921–) teaches at the University of California at Berkeley. He studied with and was strongly influenced by Roger Sessions. Imbrie's output consists principally of symphonic and chamber works, but does include vocal music and two operas: *Christmas in Peebles Town* (1960) and *Angle of Repose* (1976), commissioned by the San Francisco Opera for the Bicentennial. In Imbrie's music, the solution of compositional problems springs from the particular context rather than from predetermined procedures. On records: *Concerto for Violin and Orchestra* (1954); *Quartets No. 2* (1953) and *No. 3* (1957); *Sonata for Cello and Piano* (1966); *Dandelion Wine*, for oboe, clarinet, string quartet, and piano (1967); *Symphony No. 3* (1970).

JEAN EICHELBERGER IVEY (Washington, D.C., 1923–) studied at the Eastman School with Wayne Barlow, Bernard Rogers, and Kent Kennan. She is one of a number of composers who strive to achieve a synthesis of the many diverse influences playing upon our time. "I aim at combining tonal and atonal elements, and I consider all the musical resources of the past and present as being at the composer's disposal." Ivey teaches at the Peabody Conservatory, where she directs the Electronic Music Studio. On records: *Cortege—for Charles Kent,* for electronic tape (1969); *Terminus,* for mezzo-soprano and tape (1970); *Three Songs of Night,* for soprano, five instruments, and tape (1971); *Aldebaran,* for viola and tape (1972); *Hera, Hung from the Sky,* for mezzo-soprano, winds, percussion, piano, and tape (1973). She is especially concerned with combining tape with live performers, which seems to her "to offer the best of both worlds, plus a dimension which neither live performer nor tape can reach alone."

ROGER JOHNSON (San Mateo, California, 1941–), who teaches at Ramapo College, has been active on several levels, as a composer of serious concert music and a writer of popular songs, a performer on the French horn, a pianist, conductor, music editor, copyist, and university teacher. He studied, among others, with Mel Powell, Chou Wen-chung, and Otto Luening. Johnson has adapted serial procedures to a style that is increasingly rooted in lyricism. On records: *Woodwind Quintet.*

BEN JOHNSTON (Macon, Georgia, 1926–), who teaches at the University of Illinois, studied at the Cincinnati Conservatory, subsequently with Darius Milhaud at Mills College and at the Columbia-Princeton Electronic Music Center with Otto Luening and Vladimir Ussachevsky. He also worked with John Cage. From all these influences emerged an idiom that includes nonstandard tunings, microtones (smaller than the standard semitones of the major-minor system), serialism, indeterminacy, and improvisation within a predetermined framework. On records: *Quartet No. 2* (1964); *Sonata for Microtonal Piano* (1965); and *Casta Bertram,* for double bass (1969).

BETSY JOLAS (Paris, 1926–) studied at Bennington College and at the Paris Conservatory with Darius Milhaud and Olivier Messiaen. She is one of a group of French composers who turned from serialism to aleatory procedures. She has also experimented with spatial effects based on the separation of instrumental groups, her closely woven polyphonic textures deriving their clarity from the skillful exploitation of the chamber-orchestra sound. Her music is becoming increasingly well known in the United States. On records: *Quatuor III* (*9 Etudes,* 1973).

CHARLES JONES (Tamworth, Ontario, 1910–) teaches at the Aspen Music School, the Juilliard School, and the Mannes College of Music. At Mills College he was closely associated with Darius Milhaud, who had a strong influence on his thinking. Jones's music is marked by a strong lyrical strain that expresses itself in broadly flowing lines. He favors the polytonal textures and compact forms native to French Neoclassicism. On records: *Sonatina for Violin and Piano* (1942); *String Quartet No. 6* (1970).

MAURICIO KAGEL (Buenos Aires, 1932–), after studying at the University of Buenos Aires, began his career in his native city. His most important works, however, were written after he moved to Cologne in 1957. It was there that he established his reputation as one of the most innovative members of the avant-garde. He has been a pathbreaker in various fields— graphic notation, the production of mixed-media theater pieces, in which visual images are combined with acting, singing, miming, and traditional instruments as well as electronic sounds; and the use of aleatory procedures, performer choice, and improvisation to achieve indeterminacy. On records: *Transition II*, for piano, percussion, and two tapes (1958–1959); *Improvisation ajoutée*, for organ (1961).

WILLIAM N. KARLINS (New York City, 1932–) studied with both Stefan Wolpe and Vittorio Giannini. He teaches at Northwestern University. His list centers about orchestral and chamber works couched in a concentrated idiom marked by dramatic tension. On records: *Variations on "Obiter dictum"* for amplified cello, piano, and percussion (1965).

WALTER KAUFMAN (Karlsbad, Czechoslovakia, 1907–), who teaches at Indiana University, was a pupil of Franz Schreker. He has been strongly influenced by the music of the Orient, especially the Indian ragas, and has combined this element with a Neoromantic tradition. He is a prolific composer whose list includes four operas, five symphonies, seven string quartets, chamber and piano pieces, and songs. On records: *Partita* for woodwind quintet.

ULYSSES KAY (Tucson, Arizona, 1917–) is one of our leading black composers. He studied with Bernard Rogers and Howard Hanson at the Eastman School, also with Hindemith at Yale and Luening at Columbia University. Kay, who teaches at Herbert Lehman College of the City University of New York, has turned out a varied list of works marked by appealing lyricism, spontaneity, and rhythmic verve. Behind these is a highly musical personality that has absorbed important aspects of contemporary musical thought but has steadfastly maintained a middle-of-the-road position. His oeuvre includes pieces for orchestra, piano, chorus, and solo voice; a symphony and two operas— *The Juggler of Our Lady* (1956) and *The Capitoline Venus* (1970). On records: *Short Overture* (1947); *Six Dances* for string orchestra (1954); *Fantasy Variations* for orchestra (1963); *Markings*, for orchestra (1966).

KENT KENNAN (Milwaukee, Wisconsin, 1913–) received his training at the Eastman School, and now teaches at the University of Texas. His expertise in orchestration engendered a textbook that is used throughout the country. Kennan is best known for *Night Soliloquy*, a rhapsodic mood-piece for flute and orchestra (1938) in a Neoromantic style. Also available on records are *Three Pieces* for orchestra (1936); *Concertino* for piano and wind orchestra (1946–1963), and *Sonata* for trumpet and piano (1956).

NELSON KEYES (Tulsa, Oklahoma, 1928–) studied, among others, with Ingolf Dahl, Halsey Stevens, and Kent Kennan. He teaches at the University of Louisville. Keyes's list includes chamber music, choral pieces both with and without accompaniment, ballets, dramatic music, and solo vocal pieces. His best-known work, *Abysses, Bridges and Chasms* (1971), is available on records.

EARL KIM (Dinuba, California, 1920–), who teaches at Harvard, was a pupil of Roger Sessions. Kim's music displays the tensions we associate with atonal Expressionism, although blended with the lyricism of his own style. His vocal works, which occupy a prominent place on his list, show his fastidious literary taste. Several are on texts by Samuel Beckett. On records: *Earthlight*, for soprano, violin, and piano (1973).

LEON KIRCHNER (Brooklyn, N.Y., 1919–) received most of his training in Los Angeles; he studied with Schoenberg, among others. His music bears the imprint of a powerful, creative imagination; it is personal, uncompromising, moving. Kirchner takes his stand with those who regard music primarily as an expression of thought and feeling. "An artist," he wrote, "must create a personal cosmos, a verdant world in continuity with tradition, and bringing new subtilization, vision, and beauty to the elements of experience." Kirchner's roots are to be found in the tradition of central European Expressionism, but at the same time he belongs to a generation for whom Stravinsky was a seminal influence. Out of this amalgam came an intensely expressive style that exemplifies the significant process of acculturation whereby even those who were not strictly twelve-tone composers carried the Schoenbergian influence into the mainstream of contemporary American musical thought. On records: *Sonata Concertante*, for violin and piano (1952); *Toccata* for strings, winds, and percussion (1955); *Quartet No. 3* for strings and electronic tape (1967).

MORRIS KNIGHT (Charleston, South Carolina, 1933–) teaches at Ball State University. Choral and chamber-orchestra works are included in a list that features chamber music for trumpets and trombones; he has written six brass quartets and four brass quintets. Knight is the author of a book, *Aural Comprehension in Music*, and is represented on records by both his instrumental and electronic works: *Refractions* for clarinet and tape; *Sweetkind and Origin of Prophesy*; *Miracles*, for string ensemble; *Luminescences*; *Cassation* for trumpet, horn, and trombone; *Five Quartets* for two trumpets and two trombones.

KARL KOHN (Vienna, 1926–) studied, among others, with Walter Piston, Irving Fine, and Randall Thompson. He teaches at Pomona College. Kohn's catalog includes a variety of works in a Neoromantic style: orchestral pieces, compositions for piano, with and without orchestra; chamber music, and choral pieces. He is represented on records by *Little Suite* for wind quintet (1963) and by *Madrigal* (1966), which displays his fluent choral writing.

ELLIS KOHS (Chicago, 1916–) studied at Harvard with Walter Piston, among others, from whom he took over the Neoclassic aesthetic that informs his works. These are notable for transparency of texture and compactness of form. Kohs teaches at the University of Southern California. He is represented on records by *Short Concert* for string quartet (1948) and *Symphony No. 1* (1950).

BARBARA KOLB (Hartford, Connecticut, 1939–) studied at the Hartt College of Music and at Tanglewood with Lukas Foss and Gunther Schuller. She has emerged in the 1970s as one of our most widely performed composers. Her recorded works include *Rebuttal*, for two clarinets (1964); *Trobar Clus*, for chamber ensemble (1970); *Solitaire*, for piano, vibraphone, and tape (1972); they bespeak a vivid sonic imagination.

KARL KORTE (Ossining, N.Y., 1928–), who teaches at the University of Texas in Austin, studied with four composers—Mennin, Persichetti, Luening, and Copland. His list includes three symphonies and two string quartets, but he has also an affinity for choral music. On records: *Four Songs* (1961); *Aspects of Love*, a choral cycle (1965); *Matrix* for woodwind quintet, percussion, and piano (1968); *I Think You Would Have Understood*, for jazz ensemble (1971); *Libera me*, for chorus (1974).

LEO KRAFT (Brooklyn, N.Y., 1922–) studied with Karol Rathaus at Queens College, where he now teaches. He also worked with Randall Thompson at Princeton and with Nadia Boulanger in Paris. Kraft began in a Neoclassic idiom tempered with Romantic elements, and has moved on to a chromatic harmonic language that freely uses serial procedures. On records: *Partita No. 3*, for wind quintet (1964); *Statements and Commentaries*, for piano (1965); *Dialogues for flute and tape* (1968); *Spring in the Harbor*, for soprano, flute, cello, and piano (1968); *Concerto No. 3* for cello, winds, and percussion (1969); *Line Drawings*, for flute and percussion (1972).

WILLIAM KRAFT (Chicago, 1923–) is principal timpanist and percussionist of the Los Angeles Philharmonic. His music has incorporated his experiences as a jazz performer and arranger. He has also been profoundly influenced by Stravinsky and Varèse. Among his recorded works are *Nonet* for brass and percussion (1958); *Concerto Grosso* (1961–1962); *Concerto for Four Percussion Soloists and Orchestra* (1964); *Encounters II for Unaccompnied Tuba* (1966); *Momentum*, for percussion (1966); *Triangles*, a concerto for percussion and ten instruments (1968); and *Encounters IV, a Duel for Trombone and Percussion* (1972).

GAIL KUBIK (South Coffeyville, Oklahoma, 1914–) writes music abounding in bright sonorities and gay rhythms, and bearing the imprint of a vividly pictorial imagination. Hence his success with film and radio music. At the same time, his Neoclassic orientation has drawn him to the large forms of absolute music; his list includes three symphonies and the *Symphonie-Concertante* (1952), a modern concerto grosso. Kubik studied with Bernard Rogers, Leo Sowerby, and Walter Piston, among others, and came under the influence of Nadia Boulanger. He teaches at Scripps College in Claremont, California. On records, besides the *Symphonie-Concertante*, are *Celebrations and Epilogue*, for piano (1938–1950); *Sonatina* for piano (1941); *Sonata* for piano

(1947); *Divertimenti 1 and 2* for thirteen and eight players (1959); *Sonatina* for clarinet and piano (1959); *Five Theatrical Sketches,* for piano, violin, and cello (1971); and *Scholastica: A Medieval Set,* for chorus a cappella (1972).

MEYER KUPFERMAN (New York City, 1926–) studied at Queens College, but was self-taught in composition; he is now on the faculty at Sarah Lawrence College. Kupferman is a prolific composer who has absorbed jazz elements into his style, as well as twelve-tone technique. His broadly unwinding melodies can be fiercely atonal, but have a distinctive physiognomy. His list takes in operas, ballets, symphonies, concertos, and chamber works, as well as film and television scores. The recorded works include *Libretto for Orchestra* (1949); *Chamber Symphony* (1950); *Chamber Concerto* for flute, piano, and quartet (1955); *Lyric Symphony* (1957); *Concerto* for cello and jazz band (1962); *Mask of Electra,* for mezzo-soprano, oboe, and electric harpischord (1968); *Superflute,* for flute and tape (1972).

ROBERT KURKA (Chicago, 1921–1957, New York City) was a natural musician, worthy heir to the spontaneous lyric tradition of his Czech forebears. Kurka's major work is the opera *The Good Soldier Schweik,* after the novel by Jaroslav Hasek (1957). Aware that he was fatally ill of leukemia, he raced against time to finish the score. He left behind a variety of compositions, among them two symphonies, five string quartets, four sonatas for violin and piano, and shorter works for orchestra. His death at thirty-six robbed American music of a major talent. On records: Suite from *The Good Soldier Schweik.*

EZRA LADERMAN (New York City, 1924–) is one of the consistently productive composers of his generation. His chamber compositions use the thematic idea as basis for a continuous process of development. These unfold in ample sonata forms couched in an atonal-chromatic idiom that can be powerfully expressive; for example, *Cadence,* for strings and flute, commisioned by New Music for Young Ensembles. In his theater works Laderman writes in a more or less tonal style marked by a simple lyricism. He is represented on records by a number of compositions, among them *Stanzas* for chamber orchestra (1960); *Songs for Eve* (1962–1963); *Quartet No. 2* (1964–1965); *Concerto for Orchestra* (1968); and *Duo for Violin and Piano* (1970).

JOHN LA MONTAINE (Oak Park, Illinois, 1920–) combines a Postromantic idiom with influences stemming from the French school; he studied at Eastman with Bernard Rogers and Howard Hanson, and with Nadia Boulanger. His amply designed *Piano Concerto* attracted much notice when it was first played in 1958. Also on records: *Birds of Paradise,* for piano and orchestra (1964); *Incantation for Jazz Band* (1971); *The Nine Lessons of Christmas,* for soloists, chorus, harp, and percussion (1976); *Conversations for Violin and Piano* (1977); and a varied list of piano pieces.

PAUL LANSKY (New York City, 1944–) studied at Queens College with George Perle; also with Milton Babbitt, and Edward Cone at Princeton, where he now teaches. Lansky has adopted serial procedures in his chamber works, and has produced several highly original examples of computer music on tape. On records: *Modal Fantasy,* for piano (1970); and the electronic work *Mild und leise* (1974).

BILLY JIM LAYTON (Corsicana, Texas, 1924-) had among his teachers Quincy Porter and Walter Piston. He teaches at the State University of New York at Stony Brook. Layton's musical imagery was shaped, on the one hand, by the Neoclassic aesthetic; on the other, by his experience as a saxophonist and arranger for jazz and dance groups during the 1940s. Out of the blend has come a vivacious instrumental style that is sustained by a firm sense of form. On records: *Five Studies for Violin and Piano* (1952); *String Quartet* (1956); *Three Studies for Piano* (1957).

HENRI LAZAROF (Sofia, Bulgaria, 1932-) covered a far-flung itinerary in his student years; he attended the Sofia Academy, the New Conservatory in Jerusalem, the Accademia di Santa Cecilia in Rome, and topped those off with two years at Brandeis University. He teaches at U.C.L.A. Lazarof's is primarily an instrumental imagination, projected in a strikingly dissonant idiom through both conventional instruments and electronic sound. His recorded works include *Cadence II,* for viola and tape (1969); *Cadence III,* for violin and two percussionists (1970); *Cadence VI,* for tuba and tape (1973); *Concertazioni,* for trumpet, six instruments, and tape (1973); *Third Chamber Concerto,* for twelve soloists (1974).

BENJAMIN LEES (Harbin, China, 1924-) attended the University of Southern California and studied also with George Antheil. He is one of the most prolific composers of his generation and one of the most widely performed. His is a fairly accessible idiom based on the free use of the twelve tones around a center, propelled by striking dissonances and energetic rhythms that unfold in large, well-shaped forms. "I thrive on diversity," he has stated. "The tools of composition are everywhere for everyone to use, and I have employed them all from a simple triad to controlled chaos." On records: *Concerto for Orchestra* (1962); *Symphony No. 3* (1968); *Sonata No. 2* for violin and piano (1973).

FRED LERDAHL (Madison, Wisconsin, 1943-) studied with Roger Sessions, Arthur Berger, Earl Kim, and Milton Babbitt. He teaches at Harvard University and is beginning to stand out among the composers of his generation for his imaginative instrumental writing. On records: *Piano Fantasy* (1964); *String Trio* (1965-1966).

JOHN LESSARD (San Francisco, 1920-) studied with Nadia Boulanger in Paris. From her he took over the Neoclassic orientation that has persisted throughout his career. Lessard, who teaches at the State University of New York at Stony Brook, has produced a varied list of vocal, chamber, and orchestral works. On records: *Partita for Wind Quintet* (1948); *Toccata for Harpsichord* (1951); *Octet for Winds* (1954); *Sinfonietta Concertante* (1961); *Wind Quintet* (1970).

MARVIN LEVY (Passaic, New Jersey, 1932–) has the distinction of being the only member of his generation to have had a full-length opera performed at the Metropolitan Opera House: *Mourning Becomes Electra,* based on the trilogy of Eugene O'Neill (1967). In 1978 he completed *The Balcony,* an opera based on the play by Genet. Levy's music, with its high dissonance tension, was well adapted to interpreting the explosive emotions projected by both plays. His impressive ability to create on a large canvas is manifest in two oratorios—the Christmas piece *For the Time Being,* on a poem by W. H. Auden, for narrator, six soloists, large chorus, and orchestra (1960), and *Masada,* on his own text, for tenor, chorus, and orchestra (1973). On records: an aria from *Mourning Becomes Elektra,* sung by Sherrill Milnes.

PETER TODD LEWIS (Charlottesville, Virginia, 1932–) numbered among his teachers Lukas Foss, Arthur Berger, and Stefan Wolpe. He teaches at the University of Iowa. Lewis has combined tape with live music. His list includes also chamber and orchestral works. On records: *Gestes,* for electronic equipment (1973).

ROBERT HALL LEWIS (Portland, Oregon, 1926–) teaches at Goucher College and Johns Hopkins University. He has abandoned the serial manner of his earlier works for a style based on the interplay of continuity-discontinuity, contrasts of timbre and rhythm, and structural flexibility. In this regard he is typical of a new group of composers who, having derived much from serialism, are seeking other methods of organizing the musical continuum. Lewis's list centers around instrumental and vocal chamber music, as well as orchestral pieces. On records: *Toccata* for solo violin and percussion (1963); *Divertimento* for chamber orchestra (1969); *Symphony No. 2* (1971).

PETER LIEBERSON (New York City, 1946–) has been influenced by his teachers, specifically Milton Babbitt and Charles Wuorinen, and also by the expressive tensions of Elliott Carter's harmony. On records: *Concerto for Four Groups of Instruments* (1973), in which he adapts the concerto grosso manner to an idiom replete with dissonance tension. Lieberson has also succeeded to a degree rare with the composers of his age-group in transferring to the piano keyboard the jagged polyphony and continual interplay of textures characteristic of his style. His *Piano Fantasy* (1975) has been recorded.

GYÖRGY LIGETI (Diciosanmartin, Transylvania, 1923–) received his musical training at the Academy of Music in Budapest, where he later taught. He settled in Vienna and became active at the electronic studio in Cologne, as well as the summer courses at Darmstadt. There he established his reputation as a leader of the European avant-garde. Ligeti achieved an unexpected popular success in this country—unexpected, that is, for a serious contemporary composer—when his *Atmosphères* was used to accompany the psychedelic flight through infinity in Stanley Kubrick's film *2001: A Space Odyssey.* *Atmosphères* well illustrates Ligeti's method of "composition with blocks of sound." He came to believe that serial composition, with its emphasis upon pitch relationships, series of intervals, and linear texture, was obscuring the identity of individual intervals and rhythmic patterns in relation to the vertical dimension of music. He therefore began to depart from the serial organization of intervals and rhythms, concentrating instead on the sonorous material itself, its color, density, volume, texture. Like Xenakis and Penderecki, he found the solution in the interweaving of a large number of separate parts in a fabric whose shape derived from subtle changes in timbre, dynamics, density, and other parameters. He named this sometimes static texture "Mikropolyphonie"—that is, a polyphony based on minute details. Here was an interesting extension of the theory of "tone-color-melody" that Schoenberg promulgated in his Opus 16, No. 3, according to which—as he told Mahler—it should be possible to create a melody by sounding a single tone on different instruments. Ligeti's subtly shifting textures carries this theory of *Klangfarbenmelodie* one step further, the result being a texture based on blocks of sound rather than on single notes. On records: *Atmosphères*, for orchestra (1961); *Aventures* (1962) and *Nouvelles Aventures*, for three singers and seven players (1962–1965); *Volumina*, for organ (1962); *Requiem*, for two vocal soloists, two choruses, and orchestra (1963–1965); *Lux aeterna*, for sixteen-part chorus (1966); and *Ten Pieces for Wind Quintet* (1969).

ROBERT LINN (San Francisco, 1925–), who teaches at the University of Southern California, studied with Halsey Stevens and Darius Milhaud; also with Roger Sessions and Ingolf Dahl. These influences were amalgamated with his activity, during his twenties, as a jazz pianist and arranger. Linn's is a varied list that centers about the large instrumental forms—symphony, overture, chamber music—but also includes film and vocal music. On records: *Concertino* for violin and wind octet; *Dithyramb*, for 8 cellos; *Vino*, for violin and piano; *Woodwind Quintet*.

WENDEL M. LOGAN (Thomson, Georgia, 1940–) studied, among others, with Richard Hervig. He teaches at Oberlin Conservatory. Logan's list includes instrumental and vocal music as well as electronic pieces. On records: *Songs of our Time* (1969).

EDWIN LONDON (Philadelphia, 1924–) numbered among his teachers Luigi Dallapiccola and Darius Milhaud. He studied the French horn with Gunther Schuller and combined his composing with a performer's career. London, who teaches at the University of Illinois, has used his intimate knowledge of the brass instruments to explore new ways of playing them. For example, in his *Brass Quintet* of 1965 he combines vibrato controls with trills and tremolo effects, which results in subtle nuances of pitch inflection. His list includes instrumental and vocal music as well as examples of multimedia theater. *Portraits of 3 Ladies* (1967) calls for narrator, mezzo-soprano, optional dancer, 14 instrumentalists, film projections, and electronic amplification. On records: *Trio* for flute, clarinet, and piano (1956).

NIKOLAI LOPATNIKOFF (Reval, Russia, 1903–1976, Pittsburgh, Pennsylvania) was trained in civil engineering as well as music. He came to the

United States in 1939 and taught at the Carnegie-Mellon Institute in Pittsburgh for almost a quarter of a century (1945–1969). He adhered throughout his career to the Neoclassic aesthetic he inherited from Hindemith, and he left behind a considerable body of instrumental music, and an opera, *Danton*, after Büchner (1930–1933). On records: *Variazioni concertanti* (1956).

OTTO LUENING (Milwaukee, Wisconsin, 1900–) studied in Munich and Zurich, and privately with Ferruccio Busoni and Philipp Jarnach. He spent the greater part of his teaching career at Columbia University, where with Milton Babbitt and Vladimir Ussachevsky he founded and directed the Columbia-Princeton Electronic Center. His almost three hundred works, in every medium, exhibit Luening's strong lyric gift and his sensitive ear for sonorities, as well as his imaginative manipulation of the tensions born of dissonance and the juxtaposing of unrelated tonalities. No less imaginative was his pioneering work in the then new electronic idiom. He was one of the first composers to use magnetic tape, both for *musique concrète* (developed from man-made and/or natural sounds) and synthetic (electronic) sound sources. He also produced the first work to combine tape-recorded sounds with live performers: *Rhapsodic Variations,* composed in 1954 with Vladimir Ussachevsky. Luening is well represented on records. Characteristic of his style are *String Quartets No. 2* (1922) and *No. 3* (1928); the electronic pieces *Legend* (1951), *Invention on 12 Notes* (1952), *Fantasy in Space* (1952), *Low Speed* (1952), and *In the Beginning* (1956); *Synthesis,* for orchestra and electronic sound (1960); *Trio,* for flute, cello, and piano (1962); *Sonata for Piano* (1966); *Solo Sonata No. 3,* for violin (1971); *Fugue and Choral Fantasy with Electronic Doubles,* for organ and tape (1973); and *Short Suite,* for woodwind trio (1974).

ERIK LUNDBORG (Helena, Montana, 1949–) stands out among the younger composers. He studied, among others, with Charles Wuorinen and Harvey Sollberger. Thus far he has displayed an affinity for vivid, virtuosic instrumental music. On records; *Passacaglia,* for sixteen instruments (1973–1974); *From Music Forever, No. 2,* for chamber group (1974).

WITOLD LUTOSŁAWSKI (Warsaw, 1913–) has emerged as one of the foremost figures in present-day Poland even though he composes slowly, with long breaks between works. He began in a traditional style, turned for a time to twelve-tone serialism, and in recent years has made more and more use of aleatory procedures in combination with traditional devices such as ostinatos, static textures, and harmonies that derive a certain degree of solidity from quasi-tonal patterns. On records: *Variations on a Theme of Paganini* (1941); *Concerto for Orchestra,* his best-known work (1950–1954); *Five Dance Preludes,* for clarinet, strings, harp, piano, and percussion (1955); *Funeral Music,* for orchestra (1958); *Venetian Games* (1960–1961), for orchestra; *Paroles tisées,* for tenor and orchestra (1965); *Concerto for Cello and Orchestra* (1970).

ELISABETH LUTYENS (London, 1906–) has been active not only as composer, but also as organizer of musical events featuring contemporary music. She has written over 100 scores for films and radio, as well as music for the theater. She belongs among the composers who achieve high esteem in their homeland without finding a comparable reception abroad. She was influenced by Schoenberg and Webern, but in recent years has worked in a free atonal idiom. On records: *Motet,* Opus 27, for chorus (1953). Lutyens is also the author of a whimsical autobiography called *A Goldfish Bowl.*

DONALD LYBBERT (Cresco, Iowa, 1923–), who teaches at Hunter College in New York City, numbered among his teachers Otto Luening and Elliott Carter. He abandoned his originally Neoclassic orientation for serial procedures, and has been strongly influenced by Messiaen's teachings. His works include two operas, *Uitstel voor Monica* (1953) and *The Scarlet Letter* (1964–1967); vocal, chamber, and orchestral music; and works combining electronic sounds with live performance. On records: *Sonata Brevis* for piano (1962); *Lines for the Fallen,* for soprano and two pianos (1967).

TEO MACERO (Glen Falls, N.Y., 1925–) studied at the Juilliard School and with Henry Brant. He has been producer, conductor, arranger, and composer at Columbia Records since 1955, and has written much film and television music. He has been influenced by Cage and Varèse, as well as Copland and Riegger. On records: *One—Three Quarters,* for two pianos and chamber ensemble (1969–1970).

DONALD MACINNIS (New York City, 1923–) studied with Milton Babbitt, Roger Sessions, Bohuslav Martinu, and Randall Thompson. He teaches at the University of Virginia. In addition to his instrumental compositions he has produced several striking works that combine music for cello, piano, and orchestra with tape. Characteristic is *Collide-A-Scope,* for twelve brass instruments and stereo tape (1968), which has been recorded. Also on records: *Variations* for brass and percussion (1964).

BRUNO MADERNA (Venice, Italy, 1920–1972, Darmstadt, Germany) was one of the founders of the Electronic Music Studio of the Milan Radio, where he established his reputation as one of the leaders of the Italian avant-garde. He was also closely associated with the summer courses at Darmstadt. His experience with electronic music and with post-Webern serialism went hand in hand with a keen sensitivity to the expressive potential of dramatic action and gesture, as well as with his essential lyricism—Maderna's birthright as an Italian. Out of the mixture came a style intensely personal and fresh. His death from cancer at the age of fifty-three robbed contemporary music of a major artist, as well as a brilliant conductor. On records: *Dedication* and *Pièce pour Ivry,* for violin (1971); *Serenata No. 2,* for chamber orchestra (1954); *Il giardino religioso,* for chamber ensemble (1972).

URSULA MAMLOK (Berlin, 1928–) came to this country in her teens. She studied with Roger Sessions, Ralph Shapey, and Stefan Wolpe. Her roots are in the middle-European atonal tradition, on which she has imposed a firm twelve-tone technique. She teaches at the Manhattan School of Music. On records: *Stray Birds,* for soprano, flute, and cello (1963).

DONALD MARTINO (Plainfield, New Jersey, 1931–) attended Syracuse University and Princeton. He is chairman of the composition department at the New England Conservatory. Martino is a serialist whose Neoromantic tendencies reveal themselves in the fluent melodic lines of his music. Characteristic is a tightly woven polyphony activated by the interplay of motives and propelled by virtuoso instrumental writing. On records: *A Set for Clarinet* (1954); *Trio* for violin, clarinet, and piano (1959); *Fantasy-Variations* for solo violin (1962); *Concerto for Wind Quintet* (1964); *B,a,b,b,i,t,t* for clarinet (1968); *Notturno,* for chamber ensemble (1973); *Paradiso Choruses* for fourteen soloists, chorus, orchestra, and 8-track tape (1973); *Seven Pious Pieces,* for chorus (1976).

SALVATORE MARTIRANO (Yonkers, New York, 1927–) studied with, among others, Luigi Dallapiccola at the Cherubini Conservatory in Florence. He teaches at the University of Illinois. Martirano has been partial to serial techniques; has combined instrumental and vocal sounds with prerecorded tape; has experimented with aleatory and computer-generated music; and in some works has with great effectiveness juxtaposed jazz and concert elements. He has also been resourceful in combining the visual and sound elements of multimedia theater. On records: *Mass* (1955); *Chansons innocentes,* for soprano and piano (1957); *O O O O that Shakespeherian Rag,* for chorus and chamber ensemble (1959); *Cocktail Music* for piano (1962).

RICHARD MAXFIELD (Seattle, Washington, 1927–1969, Los Angeles) studied with Roger Sessions at the University of California at Berkeley and at Princeton. He also worked with Copland, Dallapiccola, and Maderna. Maxfield attended John Cage's class at the New School in New York and ultimately replaced him as its instructor. Until his death (by suicide) he worked as an engineer and composer in southern California. He played an important role in assimilating aleatory procedures to electronic technique. The following electronic pieces are available on records: *Pastoral Symphony* (1960); *Amazing Grace* and *Night Music* (1960); *Piano Concert for David Tudor* (1961); *Bacchanale* (1963).

PETER MAXWELL DAVIES. See DAVIES.

WILLIAM MAYER (New York City, 1925–) numbers among his teachers Otto Luening and Roger Sessions. His is a lyrical music that follows the middle of the road, favored with an unusual flow of fancy and wit, and marked by what he calls "a free use of compositional techniques and disparate material with the aim of synthesizing so-called opposites into a coherent whole." With this goes a rhythmic verve and feeling for color. On records: *Andante for Strings* (1956); *Concert Piece,* for trumpet (1957); *Overture for an American* (1958); *Country Fair,* for orchestra (1963); *Brass Quintet* (1964); *Brief Candle,* for chamber orchestra and chorus (1965); *Six Miniatures,* for brass quintet (1968); *Octagon,* for piano and orchestra (1971).

TOSHIRO MAYUZUMI (Yokohama, Japan, 1929–) was trained in Paris as well as at the Tokyo University of Art. He is active in organizing festivals of contemporary music in Japan. His musical thinking derives from Stravinsky and Messiaen, coupled with an inner quietude of spirit that flows out of Oriental, especially Buddhist philosophy. On records: *Pieces for Prepared Piano and Strings* (1957); *Nirvana-Symphonie* (1957–1958); *Mandala-Symphonie* (1960); *Sameara*, symphonic poem (1962).

JOYCE MEKEEL (New Haven, Connecticut, 1931–) studied, among others, with Nadia Boulanger and Earl Kim. Her music reflects great technical discipline and coloristic sensitivity. She teaches at Boston University and is a sculptor and anthropologist, as well as composer. On records: *Corridors of Dream*, for mezzo-soprano and chamber ensemble (1972); *Planh*, for solo violin (1975).

JOHN MELBY (Whitehall, Wisconsin, 1941–) teaches at the University of Illinois. He studied, among others, with Milton Babbitt and George Crumb. Melby is interested in combining live with computer music, as in *91 Plus 5*, for brass quintet and computer or *Valedictory*, for soprano and tape (1973). On records: *2 Stevens Songs*, for soprano and tape (1975).

PETER MENNIN (Erie, Pennsylvania, 1923–) studied at Oberlin Conservatory, then at the Eastman School with Howard Hanson and Bernard Rogers. Since 1962 he has been president of the Juilliard School, a post that gives him scope to influence the course of music education in this country. His works have established themselves because of his assured handling of the large forms and the sense of exuberant energy that flows from his writing. Mennin's list centers about eight symphonies (1942–1973); a number of concertos, including a brilliant showpiece for piano (1958); string quartets; and orchestral pieces. It also includes songs, cantatas, an opera, and a variety of choral works. The impression of bigness in his music springs from his adroitness in shaping long, singing melodies that flow easily and confidently. Propulsive rhythms impart to his works their high spirits and relentless forward drive. Mennin is a natural contrapuntist whose Neoclassic orientation manifests itself in his use of instrumentlal color to reinforce the formal structure, never as an end in itself. His harmonic idiom, basically modal-diatonic, relies on an effective but circumspect use of dissonance. On records: *Symphonies Nos. 3* (1946), *4*, *"The Cycle"* (1949), and *5* (1961); *Canto and Toccata*, from *Five Pieces for Piano* (1950); *Quartet No. 2* (1952); *Cello Concerto* (1956).

GIAN CARLO MENOTTI (Cadegliano, Italy, 1911–) springs out of the tradition of Italian opera, was nourished by Puccini, Mascagni, and late Verdi; also by the tensions of Expressionistic theater, the suspense and horror of Grand Guignol, the powerful harmonies of Musorgsky, the *diablerie* of Mahler and Prokofiev. He writes his own librettos, and thus is sure of having the kind of story that will release the music in him. Menotti is able to transform familiar events and everyday experiences of our time into a popular musical theater all his own, impregnated with compassion for the little man who is the victim of circumstances beyond his control. In so doing he has produced several works that have become staples of the international repertory: *Amelia Goes to the Ball* (1934); *The Old Maid and the Thief* (1938); *The Medium* (1946); *The Consul* (1950); *Amahl and the Night Visitors* (1951); and *The Saint of Bleecker Street* (1954). The later operas seem to have less staying power. They include *Maria Golovin* (1958), *The Last Savage* (1963), and *Tamu-Tamu*, a fervid allegory about the Vietnam War (1972). Menotti's list also includes cantatas, songs, ballets, and instrumental works. On records: *Sebastian*, a ballet (1944); *Piano Concerto* in F (1945). Most of the operas have been recorded, but not all are currently available.

DONAL R. MICHAISKY (Pasadena, California, 1928–) studied with Ingolf Dahl and in Germany with Wolfgang Fortner. He teaches at the California State University in Fullerton. Chamber music for winds is prominent on his list, which also includes a choral symphony, *Wheels of Time*, and the *Sinfonia Concertante* for clarinet, piano, and orchestra. On records: *Divertimento* for 3 clarinets (1952); *Partita Piccola*, for flute and piano (1962).

ELLSWORTH MILBURN (Greensburg, Pennsylvania, 1938–) studied, among others, with Henri Lazarof and Darius Milhaud. He teaches at Rice University. Milburn is one of several composers who have a basically dramatic approach to instrumental music. As he puts it, "Underlying the structural aspects and the note-to-note process is a belief that music, whether or not it has a program or scenario, is inherently dramatic, in the work itself as well as in the performance." On records: *String Quartet* (1974).

EDWARD J. MILLER (Miami, Florida, 1930–) studied, among others, with Boris Blacher and Carlos Chávez. He teaches at Oberlin Conservatory. Miller's list includes orchestral as well as choral works, and an opera, *The Young God* (1968). On records: *Folly Stone*, for brass quintet (1966); *Quartet Variations* for percussion (1972).

ILHAN MIMAROGLU (Istanbul, Turkey, 1926–) left a career as a music critic in his homeland to settle in New York and devote himself to electronic music. He became active at the Columbia-Princeton Electronic Music Center, where he studied with Chou and Ussachevsky; also with Beeson and Varèse. Mimaroglu has succeeded in imparting to his electronic pieces an emotional intensity and a personal quality that are unusual in this medium. His works are well represented on records, among them *Bowery Bum* (1964); *Le Tombeau d'Edgar Poe* (1964); *Eight Preludes for Magnetic Tape* (1965–1967) *Tract* (1972); *Music for Jean Dubuffet's Coucou Bazaar* (1973).

ROBERT MOEVS (La Crosse, Wisconsin, 1920–), who teaches at Rutgers University, studied at Harvard with Walter Piston and in Paris with Nadia Boulanger. Moevs uses serial procedures and has been influenced by the theoretical writings of Pierre Boulez. His list includes vocal and instrumental works based on a technique of motivic expansion and what he calls "systematic chromaticism," in which a collection of pitches is used with greater freedom than in strict dodecaphony. On records: *Brief Mass* (1968); *Musica da Camera*, for chamber orchestra (1965); *Variazioni sopra una melodia*, for violin and cello (1961); *Piano Sonata* (1950).

JACQUES-LOUIS MONOD (Paris, 1927–) studied with Olivier Messiaen and the leading Schoenberg disciple in France, René Leibowitz. He represents the type of artist for whom twelve-tone technique was filtered through French tradition and sensibility. Monod's concern has been to reconstitute, within the context of the Schoenbergian method, those concepts of late-tonal music that were temporarily thrust aside by Schoenberg. On records: *Cantus Contra Cantum I*, for soprano and chamber orchestra (1972).

CARMAN MOORE (Lorain, Ohio, 1936–) studied with Hall Overton, Vincent Persichetti, and Luciano Berio. He has derived his materials from his Negro heritage, combining those with what he calls "the twentieth-century classical tradition of daring and fresh statement." On records: *Youth in a Merciful House*, for chamber ensemble (1966).

JEROME MOROSS (Brooklyn, N.Y., 1913–) was able to combine a Neoromantic orientation with folk and popular elements, as in his ballet *Frankie and Johnny* (1938). His list includes, besides ballets and theater pieces, orchestral works and sonatinas for various instuments; also four stage works on texts by John LaTouche, of which the best known is *The Golden Apple* (1950–1952). On records: *Sonatina for Clarinet Choir* (1966); *Sonatina for Bass and Piano* (1967); *Sonatina for Brass Choir* (1969); *Sonatina for Woodwind Quintet* (1970).

LAWRENCE MOSS (Los Angeles, 1927–), who teaches at the University of Maryland, was a pupil of Leon Kirchner and Ingolf Dahl. From Kirchner he took over the Expressionistic intensity that informs his instrumental and vocal works. His operas—*The Brute* (1960) and *The Queen and the Rebels* (1965)—show his approach to a new kind of lyric theater in which the Expressionism of the older generation is united with the techniques that attract the younger. On records: *Sonata for Violin* (1959); *Omaggio* for piano four-hands (1966); *Elegy*, for two violins and viola (1969); *Timepiece*, for violin, piano, and percussion (1970); *Auditions*, for wind quintet (1971); *Evocation and Song*, for saxophone and electronic equipment (1972).

ROBERT MUCZYNSKI (Chicago, 1929–) was a pupil of Alexander Tcherepnin, from whom he took over a fundamentally Neoromantic orientation, a penchant for the large instrumental forms, and a love for the piano. He has written a concerto for that instrument, and much chamber music with piano. Muczynski, who teaches at the University of Arizona, has also been active in writing music for documentary films. On records: *Suite* for piano (1960); *Sonata* for flute and piano (1961); *Three Preludes* for flute (1962); *Dance Movements*, Opus 17 (1963); *Sonata No. 2*, for piano (1966); *Sonata* for cello and piano (1968); *Fantasy Trio* for clarinet, cello, and piano (1969); *Sonata* for alto saxophone and piano (1970); *Piano Trio No. 2* (1975); *A Serenade for Summer* (1976).

GORDON MUMMA (Framingham, Massachusetts, 1935–) studied at the University of Michigan and was one of the founders of the Studio for Electronic Music in Ann Arbor. He was a cofounder of the ONCE Festival there and a member of the Sonic Arts Group, a New York–based ensemble that performed live, that is nonrecorded, electronic music. He worked for a decade with the Merce Cunningham Dance Company and now teaches at the University of California at Santa Cruz. Mumma was one of the first composers to integrate the decisions of composer and performer with an electronic system that employed computer logic. To this end he designed circuitry that provided for a semiautomatic control system to share in the compositional and performance aspects of a work. He uses the term "cybersonics" to denote this approach, which is typified in such works as *Digital Process* for acoustical and electronic instruments, digital control circuitry, tape, and motion-picture projectors (1967–1969), or *Beam* for violin, viola, cybersonic modification, and digital-computer control (1969). Mumma is represented on records by several electronic pieces: *Music for the Venezia Space Theatre,* for four-channel tape and electronic apparatus (1964); *Mesa,* for bandoneon with cybersonic console (1966); *Hornpipe,* for horn and cybersonic console (1967); *Cybersonic Cantilevers* (1973).

THEA MUSGRAVE (Edinburgh, Scotland, 1928–) studied at Edinburgh University and in Paris with Nadia Boulanger. Her list includes a variety of chamber and vocal works, concertos for various instruments, and songs. But she is best known in this country for *The Voice of Ariadne,* presented by the New York City Opera in 1977, a work whose delicate orchestral textures and subtle nuances continue in the path of Britten's chamber operas. *Mary, Queen of Scots* was introduced to this country by the Virginia Opera Company in 1978. Musgrave, who teaches at the University of California at Santa Barbara, is well represented on records: *Monologue* (1960) and *Excursions* (1965), for piano; *Chamber Concerto No. 2,* for five instruments (1966); *Concerto for Orchestra* (1967); *Clarinet Concerto* (1969); *Night Music,* for two horns and orchestra (1969); *Horn Concerto* (1971).

RON NELSON (Joliet, Illinois, 1929–) studied with Arthur Honegger, Howard Hanson, and Bernard Rogers. He teaches at Brown University. Nelson's grass-roots bent manifests itself in his spontaneous treatment of popular materials, as in his *Rocky Point Holiday* for band (1969), and *Savannah River Holiday* for orchestra (1973), both of which have been recorded.

BO NILSSON (Skelleftehama, Sweden, 1937–) is self-taught in music. He attracted attention when his *Frequenzen* was performed at Darmstadt in the summer of 1956. Nilsson belongs to the generation of composers who extended the serialization of pitches to other parameters of music, and has also experimented with open-form structures. On records: *Frequenzen,* for clarinet, flute, percussion, vibraphone, guitar, double bass (1956); *Szene III,* for chamber ensemble (1962).

LUIGI NONO (Venice, Italy, 1924–) came to music after earning a degree in law at the University of Padua. He studied composition with Malipiero and Bruno Maderna, and was soon known as one of the outstanding figures in the postwar avant-garde. In 1955 he married Schoenberg's daughter Nuria. Nono has pursued his career as a composer alongside an equally active political career; he is one of the leaders of the Venice section of the Italian Communist Party. He was one of a group of composers who, starting out from the heritage of Webern, extended the serialization of pitches to include durations, intensities, timbres, and types of articulation. However, in doing so he loosened the procedure and tried to free it from a doctrinaire approach. In his later electronic works Nono has included *concrète* material such as factory noises, market cries, tolling bells, and the breaking up of text into words, syllables, and phonemes in such a way that the word sounds become an integral component of the music. The texts he has set reflect such political movements as the struggle against Fascism in the Thirties and the rise of the Italian resistance during the war. In his latest works Nono has moved away from the elitism of the concert world and has addressed himself to a universal public of workers, peasants, and guerrillas. On records: *Polifonica-Monodia-Ritmica* for orchestra (1951); *Espressione,* for orchestra (1953).

PAULINE OLIVEROS (Houston, Texas, 1932–) worked at the San Francisco Tape Center for five years and during that time was also involved with group improvisation. In 1966 she became director of the Tape Music Center at Mills College, and a year later began teaching electronic music at the University of California at San Diego. She has explored mixed media and the possibilities of multichannel tape interacting with live situations and theatrical forms. She has also experimented with live electronic music, in which electronic or electronically modified sounds are generated during the performance. Her feeling for the theater spills over into her instrumental, choral, and orchestral music. On records: *Sound Patterns,* for chorus (1961); *Outline,* for flute, percussion, and string bass (1963); *I of IV,* on tape (1966).

ROBERT PALMER (Syracuse, N.Y., 1915–), who teaches at Cornell, stands among the moderates on the contemporary scene, with a Neoclassic orientation that was influenced by his teachers Aaron Copland and Roy Harris. He derived much too from the music of Bartók and his long personal association with Quincy Porter. On records: *Quintet* for clarinet, string trio, and piano (1952); *Choric Song and Toccata,* for wind ensemble (1968–1969).

ROBERT PARRIS (Philadelphia, 1924–) studied, among others, with Peter Mennin, Aaron Copland, and Arthur Honegger. He teaches at George Washington University and has been active as pianist, harpsichordist, and music critic. His list includes chamber music, orchestral works, compositions for solo voice, and choral music. On records: *Concerto* for trombone (1964); *Concerto* for percussion, violin, cello, and piano (1967); *Book of Imagi-*

nary Beings, for instrumental trio (1973). The *Concerto for Trombone* exemplifies an important trend among today's composers: their tendency to derive creative excitement from the medium itself. Parris found the sonorous possibilities of the instrument "endlessly fascinating. To this excitement of the imagination was added the exhilaration of being able to pull out all the stops, to take advantage of the technical prowess of a virtuoso trombonist." In such cases the performer for whom the work is written enters indirectly into the compositional process.

HARRY PARTCH (Oakland, California, 1901–1974, San Diego, California) single-mindedly pursued the goal of a microtonal music—a music based, that is, on intervals smaller than the standard semitone of our chromatic scale. In his early twenties, he evolved a scale of forty-three microtones to the octave and devised instruments with this tuning, ingenious adaptations of Hindu and African instruments. He also invented a special notation for his works. This activity emanated from an unconventional personality who stood completely outside the musical establishment. Before foundations and universities began to contribute to his livelihood, Partch supported himself by doing odd jobs; during part of the Depression he was a hobo. His aesthetic theories found expression in his book *Genesis of a Music*, which he completed in 1928; it was not published until more than two decades later (revised edition, 1974). Partch's music is dominated by plucked-string and percussion sounds, to which instruments such as his cloud-chamber bowls impart a special color. Several works of this highly original musician are available on records: *Barstow: 8 Hitchhiker Inscriptions from a Highway Railing at Barstow, California* (1941); *Plectra and Percussion Dances* (1949–1952); *Daphne of the Dunes* (1958); *And on the Seventh Day Petals Fell in Petaluma* (1966). Late in life, Partch taught at the University of California, San Diego.

KRZYSZTOF PENDERECKI (Debica, Poland, 1933–) studied at the Music Academy in Cracow, where he later taught; he is now on the faculty of Yale University. As far as the big public is concerned, he is Poland's foremost composer. His reputation in the West rests on his capacity for powerful emotional expression, which in his case is fostered by a strong mystical streak in his makeup; and his assured handling of the large forms, as in the opera *The Devils of Loudon*, after Aldous Huxley's novel (1969) and *The Passion according to St. Luke*, for narrator, solo voices, and orchestra (1963–1965). Penderecki's search for new sonorities and new ways of producing them has impelled him to use noises such as the sawing of wood and the clicking of typewriters. In this domain he has been much influenced by Iannis Xenakis. His choral music includes such special effects as hissing, shouting, whistling, articulating rapid consonants, and the like. Practically all his important pieces are available on records, among them: *Threnody—To the Victims of Hiroshima*, for string orchestra (1960); *Polymorphia*, for 48 string instruments (1961); *Fonogrammi*, for flute and chamber orchestra (1961); *Kanon*, for orchestra and tape (1962); *Capriccio No. 2*, for violin and orchestra (1967); *De natura sonoris*, for orchestra (1967); *Diesirae* (*Auschwitz Oratorio,* 1967); *The Devils of Loudon; Partita* for harpsichord and orchestra (1971); *De natura sonoris No. 2* (1971).

WILLIAM PENN (Long Branch, N.J., 1943–) studied, among others, with Henri Pousseur and Mauricio Kagel. His composing interests cover a wide range, from orchestral and chamber music to jazz, multimedia theater, film music, and electronics. He has also written a number of articles on the theory and practice of film music. Penn teaches at the Eastman School. On records: *Chamber Music II,* for cello and piano; *Fantasy for Harpsichord; Four Preludes for Marimba; Ultra Mensuram,* for three brass quintets.

RONALD PERERA (Boston, 1941–), who teaches at Smith College, studied composition principally with Leon Kirchner. He has produced a number of works that combine instruments and/or voice with electronic sounds; also choral works and song cycles. He is the author of *The Development and Practice of Electronic Music.* On records: *Alternate Routes,* an electronic piece (1971); *Apollo Circling,* for voice and piano (1971–1972); *Reflex,* for viola and tape (1973).

JOHN MACIVAR PERKINS (St. Louis, Missouri, 1935–) studied with Nadia Boulanger, Luigi Dallapiccola, and Arthur Berger, among others. His music, twelve-tone in orientation, is elegantly made and full of character. He teaches at Washington University. On records: *Caprice for Piano* (1963); *Music for Thirteen Players* (1964).

GEORGE PERLE (Bayonne, New Jersey, 1915–), who teaches at Queens College of the City University of New York, has attempted throughout his career to expand the Schoenbergian concept so as to include the possibilities for harmonic tension and direction inherent in the major-minor system. In a language based on the twelve-tone scale he has retained the concept of tonal centers and the traditional differentiation between the vertical and horizontal dimensions of music. In order to achieve a systematic organization of the harmonic material, he has modified the Schoenbergian canon by providing what he calls "harmonic modes" for twelve-tone music. These modes are generated by certain symmetrical tone rows, as in his *Piano Sonata* (1950) and *Rhapsody for Orchestra* (1953). A number of works for unaccompanied clarinet, bassoon, violin, and other instruments do not employ a tone row but are freely conceived in a twelve-tone idiom that combines various serial details with melodically generated tone centers, intervallic cells, symmetrical formations, and similar devices. Perle is thus in the forefront of those contemporary composers who have tried to adapt the Schoenbergian doctrine to their particular expressive needs. He is the author of two books, *Serial Composition and Atonality* (1962) and *Twelve-Tone Tonality* (1978), which are milestones in contemporary theory. On records: *Six Preludes,* for piano (1946); *String Quartet No. 5* (1960–1967); *Three Inventions for Solo Bassoon* (1962); *Three Movements for Orchestra* (1963); *Toccata* for piano (1969).

JULIA PERRY (Lexington, Kentucky, 1924–) studied with Nadia Boulanger and Luigi Dallapiccola, among others. Among the black composers of her generation she stands with those who are oriented toward the large forms of the Classical tradition rather than with those who draw specifically upon the Afro-American heritage. Nine symphonies form the centerpiece of her output, flanked by several concertos, an opera-ballet, and shorter instrumental and vocal works. On records: *Homunculus C. F.,* for ten percussionists (1960).

VINCENT PERSICHETTI (Philadelphia, 1915–) teaches at the Juilliard School. His impressive compositional technique is at its best in the large forms of instrumental music. His harmonic language is strongly tonal; the texture of his music is predominantly homophonic, being based on the vertical progression of harmonies rather than on the contrapuntal interplay of lines. Persichetti's instrumental writing is notable for its warmth and brilliance, and shows an imaginative adaptation of traditional patterns to the demands of contemporary style. He is well represented on records. The list includes *Hollow Men,* for trumpet and string orchestra (1946); *Serenade No. 6,* for trombone, viola, and cello (1950); *Pageant,* for wind ensemble (1953); *Symphonies No. 6* (1956) and *No. 8* (1967); *Serenade No. 10,* for flute and harp (1957); *Serenade No. 11,* for band (1960); *Parable IV,* for solo bassoon (1969).

GOFFREDO PETRASSI (Zagarola, Italy, 1904–) moved from the Neoclassical orientation of his earlier works, which showed the influence of such composers as Stravinsky, Hindemith, and Casella, toward dodecaphonic thinking. In a number of large choral and orchestral works he incorporated serial techniques in a highly expressive language marked by economy of means, terseness of statement, and the continuous interplay of motives in a densely woven texture. Seven concertos for orchestra form the central item in a list that includes orchestral, chamber, and choral works as well as operas and ballets. On records: *Noche oscura,* a cantata (1950); *Nonsense,* a setting of limericks by Edward Lear for chorus a cappella (1952); *Concerto No. 5 for Orchestra* (1955).

BURRILL PHILLIPS (Omaha, Nebraska, 1907–) studied with Howard Hanson and Bernard Rogers at the Eastman School. He tends to think in terms of theater and ballet even when writing in the abstract forms; his music is on the conservative side. Phillips's Neoclassic orientation makes him responsive to Stravinsky and to the aesthetic goals of eighteenth-century music, especially its light-hearted spirit. On records: *Selections from McGuffy's Reader,* suite for orchestra (1934); *Canzona III,* for poet and chamber orchestra (1964); *Sonata* for violin and harpsichord (1966).

DANIEL PINKHAM (Lynn, Massachusetts, 1923–) studied at Harvard and numbers among his teachers Piston, Copland, Honegger, and Nadia Boulanger. He is one of a fairly large group of composers who began as Neoclassicists but later turned to twelve-tone writing. Essentially a lyricist, Pinkham has a keen ear for unusual combinations of sound. On records: *Christmas Cantata* (1957); *Signs of the Zodiac,* for orchestra (1964); *Toccata for the Vault of Heaven,* for organ, English horn, and percussion (1972).

PAUL AMADEUS PISK (Vienna, 1893–) studied at the Vienna Conservatory and also with Schoenberg. He comes out of the middle-European tradition. Trained in musicology as well as composition, Pisk was able to bring to his espousal of twelve-tone thought a broad historical background. On records: *Three Ceremonial Rites,* for orchestra (1958).

RAOUL PLESKOW (Vienna, 1931–) grew up in New York City; he studied with Karol Rathaus at Queens College and with Otto Luening at Columbia. But the most important influence upon him was his close association with Stefan Wolpe, whose music and thought served as point of departure for his own development. In 1959 he went to C. W. Post College as Wolpe's assistant. Pleskow, like several members of his generation, has expanded the Schoenbergian canon in order to fit it to the aesthetic currents of the '70s. On records: *Movement for Oboe, Violin and Piano* (1966); *Movement for 9 Players* (1967); *Bagatelles,* for violin (1967); *Three Movements for Quintet* (1970); *Motet and Madrigal,* for soprano, tenor, and chamber ensemble (1973); *Pentimento,* for piano (1974).

HENRI POUSSEUR (Malmedy, Belgium, 1929–) took his point of departure from the music of Webern, worked in close contact with Boulez, Stockhausen, and Berio in the early '50s, and was cofounder of the Apelac Electronic Studio in Brussels. Rejecting traditional concepts, Pousseur derives his forms from the context of a particular work, basing it on the dialectical unity of opposites—for example, greater against lesser instrumental activity, contrasts in speed, register, timbre, type of articulation, as well as the various parameters—such as duration, dynamics, and timbre—to which post-Webern composers extended the concept of serialization. On records: *Trois Visages de Liège,* an electronic piece (1961); *Madrigal III,* for clarinet, violin, cello, piano, 2 percussionists (1962).

MEL POWELL (New York City, 1923–) came to serious music from jazz; he made his reputation, while still in his teens, as the pianist of Benny Goodman's band. He studied with Paul Hindemith at Yale, was influenced by Stravinsky, and adopted the post-Webern orientation that attracted so many young composers in the '50s. Within this frame Powell evolved a language of his own marked by a fastidious musicality, in which predominated the Classical virtues of moderation, proportion, and carefully wrought form. Powell for several years was director of the California Institute of the Arts in Los Angeles, where he now teaches. After a long period of silence he is composing again. The last of his instrumental pieces increasingly pointed in the direction of electronic music, an area in which he has made a significant contribution. Several of his electronic pieces are available on records: *Second Electronic Setting* (1962); *Two Prayer Settings,* for voice, instruments, and tape (1963); *Events* (1963).

MORGAN POWELL (Graham, Texas, 1938–) studied with Samuel Adler and Kenneth Gaburo. He teaches at the University of Illinois. Powell has introduced jazz elements into his music, as in his *Music for Jazz Ensemble* and

Bird Merchant for Jazz Band. Although his list includes vocal music, his imagery is predominantly instrumental. On records: *Music for Brass Ensemble.*

WILLIAM PRESSER (Sanginaw, Michigan, 1916–) studied, among others, with Bernard Rogers and Burrill Phillips at the Eastman School. He teaches at the University of Southern Mississippi. Presser's list includes a symphony, but much of his music centers around the brass instruments, as in his *Symphony No. 2* for band and *Concerto for Tuba and Strings.* On records: *Prelude, Fugue and Postlude* for brass trio (1962); *Serenade for Four Tubas* (1963); *Sonatina for Trombone* and *Suite for Brass Quartet* (1964); *Suite for Trumpet* (1967).

THOMAS PUTSCHÉ (Scarsdale, N.Y., 1929–) studied, among others, with Milton Babbitt, Aaron Copland, and Vittorio Giannini. He teaches at the Hartt College of Music (University of Hartford). On records: *The Cat and the Moon,* a one-act opera based on the play by W. B. Yeats, the music of which captures the fantasy of the text. Putsché has also been active as a music critic.

PHILIP RAMEY (Chicago, 1939–) studied mainly with Alexander Tcherepnin. He is a pianist himself, and piano music—with and without orchestra—looms large on a list that includes orchestral works, chamber music, and vocal pieces. Ramey is one of a number of younger composers who, after a certain involvement with atonality and serial techniques, are moving toward a lyricism based on tonality. As a writer on music he is known to a large public through his program notes for the New York Philharmonic. On records: *Piano Sonata No. 4* (1968); *Piano Fantasy* (1969–1972); *Leningrad Rag* (*Mutations on Scott Joplin,* 1972).

SHULAMITH RAN (Tel Aviv, Israel, 1947–) studied with Paul Ben Haim, Alexander Boscovitz, and in this country with Norman Dello Joio. She teaches at the University of Chicago. Ran has combined her Neoromantic orientation with elements drawn from her Israeli heritage. She is represented on records by *O the Chimneys,* a moving elegy for her compatriots who died in the extermination camps, for voice, instrumental ensemble, and tape (1968).

JAMES K. RANDALL (Cleveland, Ohio, 1929–) studied at Columbia, Harvard, and Princeton, where he now teaches. He is one of a number of twelve-tone composers who have expanded the possibilities of the system through mathematical treatment, by applying computations of the set to parameters other than pitch. On records: *Improvisation* for soprano and flute (1961); *Mudgett,* for soprano and tape (1965); *Quartersines* (1969).

ALAN RAWSTHORNE (Haslingden, Lancashire, England, 1905–1971, Cambridge, England) represents that section of the New Classicism which finds inspiration in the Baroque rather than the Classical era proper. The variation and concerto grosso procedures of the seventeenth and early eighteenth century have influenced his idiom, which is marked by consistency of texture and intensity of expression. He is unique among the English composers of his generation, who favor pieces for solo voice and chorus, in that he devoted himself almost exclusively to the large instrumental forms. On records: *Symphonic Studies* (1938); *Symphony No. 1* (1950); *Elegy for Guitar* (1971).

STEVE REICH (New York City, 1936–) studied with Berio and Milhaud, among others. He worked as a composer-performer at the San Francisco Tape Music Center and later established his own electronic studio in New York. He is one of several composers who use specially designed electronic equipment to produce, alter, or extend live-performance sonorities, whether vocal or instrumental. Reich has been influenced by Asian and other non-Western traditions, especially in regard to simplicity of material and a tendency to long durations. His music seems to come out of another time sense than our own; this is particularly true of the works on tape. He describes this lengthening of time as "a musical process happening so gradually that listening to it resembles watching the minute hand of a watch—you perceive it moving after you stay with it a little while." It is his answer—and that of the Orient—to the hustle and bustle of an overly competitive society. On records: *Come Out,* an electronic piece (1966); *Four Organs,* for four electric organs and maracas (1970); *Drumming,* for bongo drums, marimbas, glockenspiels, and voices (1971); *Six Pianos* (1973); *Music for Mallet Instruments, Voices and Organ* (1973); *Music for 18 Musicians* (1976).

PAUL REIF (Prague, 1910–1978, New York City) studied with Franz Schalk and—a rare privilege in those days—submitted his early works to Richard Strauss for discussion and guidance. He moved from the dissonant Expressionism of the 1930s to a mellower Neoromantic style. His catalogue includes much chamber music, orchestral works, and vocal compositions—songs and choral pieces—marked by fantasy and wit. He was working on an opera, *Portrait in Brownstone,* at the time of his death. On records: *Monsieur le Pelican* for wind ensemble (1960); *Philidor's Defense—A Musical Chess Game* (1965); *Four Songs on Words of Kenneth Koch,* for voice and string quartet (1972); *8 Vignettes for 4 Singers* (1975); *Duo for 3,* for soprano, clarinet, and cello (1976).

ROGER REYNOLDS (Detroit, 1934–) studied with Ross Lee Finney and Roberto Gerhard. He was a cofounder of the ONCE Group in Ann Arbor, Michigan, which presented programs that explored the possibilities of live electronics and group improvisation. Reynolds has worked with the electronic music studio in Cologne and been active in organizing concerts of contemporary music in Paris and Tokyo. He teaches at the University of California in San Diego. His music has been influenced by that of Charles Ives; also by his personal contacts with John Cage and Edgard Varèse. Several of his pieces combine instruments with film and slides, tape, and electronic equipment. Such a one is *Ping* (1968), for piano, flute, harmonium, cymbals, and tom-tom, which has been recorded. Also on records: *Fantasy for Pianist* (1963–1964); *Quick Are the Mouths of Earth* (1964–1965), *Ambages,* for solo flute (1965); *Blind Men* (1966); *Traces,* for piano, flute, cello, tape, and electronic modification (1969); *From Behind the Unreasoning Mark,* for trombone and percussion (1975).

TERRY RILEY (Colfax, California, 1935–) studied at San Francisco State College and the University of California at Berkeley. He was influenced by the musics of the Far East, by jazz and ragtime, and by John Cage's theories. Riley is one of several composers who, through the use of tape loop, feedback systems during performance, and kindred devices, has introduced into electronic music the elements of performer choice, improvisation, and chance (indeterminacy). His compositions, as he explains, "take the form of charts of repeated patterns and series, which must assume a form during rehearsal and performance." On records: *In C*, for any number of instruments (1964); *Poppy Nogood and the Phantom Band* (1968), for organ, soprano saxophone, percussion, and electronic equipment; *A Rainbow in Curved Air* (1969).

GEORGE ROCHBERG (Patterson, N.J., 1918–) studied with Hans Weisse and Rosario Scalero. He assimilated into his style a diversity of influences, from Hindemith, Bartók, and Stravinsky, to Mahler, Schoenberg, Berg, and Webern; also Varèse and Ives. Twelve-tone devices seemed to him to open up a new way of hearing, imagining, and organizing sound. At the same time he felt that serialism could lead to "a sterile and mechanical academicism" unless it were balanced by the composer's constant preoccupation with the expressive as well as technical aspects of music. It has been his goal to balance the two and to unite them in a higher synthesis in the great tradition of music as an emotion-arousing art. Rochberg has increasingly drawn inspiration from the Classic-Romantic period, when the expressive goals he now espouses were in the ascendent. Recent works use collage and the juxtaposition of varying styles, along with traditional tonality. On records: *Symphony No. 1* (1949–1955) and *No. 2* (1958); *String Quartets No. 1* (1952), *No. 2* (1959–1961), and *No. 3* (1972); *Chamber Symphony for Nine Instruments* (1953); *Serenata d'estate* (Summer Serenade, 1955), for chamber ensemble; *Duo Concertante*, for violin and cello (1955–1959); *Blake Songs*, for soprano and instrumental ensemble (1961); *Contra mortem et tempus* (Against Death and Time, 1965), for violin, flute, clarinet, and piano; *Music for the Magic Theater*, for chamber orchestra (1965); *Tableaux*, for soprano and eleven players (1968); *Songs in Praise of Krishna* (1970).

ROBERT ROLLIN (New York City, 1947–) studied with Mark Brunswick, Robert Palmer, and Karel Husa. He teaches at North Central College. Rollin's major works include music for piano and orchestra, for string quartet, for concert band, and various chamber groups. On records: *Aquarelles*, for wind ensemble; *Reflections on Ruin by the Sea*, for trumpet and piano.

JOHN RICHARD RONSHEIM (Cadiz, Ohio, 1927–) studied, among others, with Luigi Dallapiccola. He teaches at Antioch College. His compositions have been mostly vocal, with several instrumental pieces among them. On records: *Easter-Wings* (1964) and *Bitter-Sweet*, on the mystical poems of George Herbert, for mezzo-soprano and chamber ensemble (1969).

NED ROREM (Richmond, Indiana, 1923–) studied with several teachers, of whom Virgil Thomson and Aaron Copland had the greatest influence on him. The five years he spent in France oriented him to the Gallic view of life and art, most especially to the tradition of Satie and Poulenc. Rorem is the foremost American composer of the art song; his are in the direct line of descent from the great French *mélodie* of the Postromantic period. A gifted writer as well, he brings to the choice of text a literary taste that is all too rare among musicians. He has drawn his texts from a varied group of writers, ranging from Dryden, Herrick, Browning, and Walt Whitman, to Kafka, Rilke, Cocteau, Gide, Roethke, and Sylvia Plath. His instrumental works bespeak the lyricist as well, in their broadly flowing melodic lines. They bear the imprint of a fastidious artist in the subtlety of detail, limpidity of texture, and luminous color. In the large instrumental works written since the *Third Symphony* (1957), Rorem has favored multimovement forms with a vaguely programmatic atmosphere. He is well represented on records: *Symphony No. 3* (1957); *King Midas*, a cantata (1960–1961); *Poems of Love and the Rain*, for voice and piano (1962–1963); *Eleven Studies for Eleven Players* (1963); *Lions*, for orchestra (1963); *Lovers*, for harpsichord, oboe, cellos, and percussion (1964); *Water Music*, for violin, clarinet, and orchestra (1967); *Piano Concerto in Six Movements* (1969); *War Scenes*, for voice and piano (1969); *Gloria* (1970); *Ariel*, for soprano, clarinet, and piano (1971); *Day Music*, for violin and piano (1971); *Night Music*, for violin and piano (1972); *Book of Hours*, for flute and harp (1975), and a variety of songs.

HILDING ROSENBERG (Bosjökloster, Sweden, 1892–) is an important figure in contemporary Scandinavian music. To the influences emanating from Sibelius's Postromantic nationalism he has assimilated elements of Neoclassicism and the aesthetic of Schoenberg. His list includes six symphonies, eight string quartets, concertos for various instruments, chamber music, opera, vocal and piano works. On records: *Symphony No. 2, "Sinfonia grave"* (1928–1935).

WALTER ROSS (Nebraska, 1936–) studied with Alberto Ginastera and Robert Palmer. He teaches at the University of Virginia in Charlottesville. Ross favors the brass instruments; he has written concertos for brass quintet, for tuba, and for trombone. His recorded works include *Concerto for a Trombone* and *Fancy Dances*, for three bass tubas (1972).

NICHOLAS ROUSSAKIS (Athens, 1934–), who teaches at Columbia, came to the United States at the age of fifteen. He has been influenced by serial procedures, especially those of Milton Babbitt; by his studies with Pierre Boulez at Darmstadt; and by the music of Ligeti. In recent years he has aimed for a more sensuous sound based on the attempt to fuse serial procedures with tonal language. On records: *Sonata for Harpsichord* (1967); *Night Speech*, for chorus and instruments (1968).

DANE RUDHYAR (pseudonym of Daniel Chennevière, Paris, 1895–) was largely self-taught as a composer. He was influenced by Liszt, Scriabin,

Debussy, and early Stravinsky. A painter and poet as well as composer, he has written a number of books on what he calls a "humanistic approach to astro-psychology." On records: *Tetragrams 1, 4, and 5,* for piano (1924–1927); *Stars,* for piano (1925); *Three Paeans,* for piano (1927); *Granites,* for piano (1929).

FREDERICK RZEWSKI (Westfield, Massachusetts, 1938–) was influenced by John Cage and Stockhausen, as well as by the ideas of Herbert Marcuse. While living in Rome he helped found Musica Elettronica Viva (1966), a group that used live electronics in a multi-media theater based on improvisation and audience participation. Rzewski believes that in a truly collective art form the distinction between composer and performer would be abolished: "each term would be assimilated into a higher unity." His music reflects his political orientation, which is left-wing. After returning to New York Rzewski adopted the "minimal" techniques of composers such as Steve Reich. He has recently written large piano pieces in an eclectic style influenced by late Beethoven and Busoni, as in *The People United Will Never Be Defeated,* for solo piano (1977), a set of variations on *La Bandera Rosa,* one of the popular songs of the Loyalists during the Spanish Civil War. On records: *Les Moutons de Panurge,* for any number of melody instruments (1969); *Attica,* for narrator and instruments (1972); *Coming Together,* for narrator and instruments (1972); *Variations on No Place to Go But Around,* for piano (1973); *Three Songs* (1974).

PETER SACCO (New York City, 1928–) studied, among others, with Kent Kennan, Bernard Rogers, and Howard Hanson at the Eastman School. He teaches at San Francisco State College. Sacco's music evolved from moderately chromatic textures to what he calls "a highly personalized twelve-tone style, a style which could be lyric, dramatic, or dissonant." His list includes symphonies, concertos, songs, and choral works. On records: *3 Psalms,* for brass quintet and tenor voice (1966).

AULIS SALLINEN (Salmi, Finland, 1935–) is a leading representative of Finland's contemporary school. He has written in the various media, including a symbolic Expressionist opera *Ratsumeir* (The Horseman), which made a strong impression when it was first presented during the summer festival directed by Marti Talvela at Savonlinna. On records: *Kamarimusikki No. 1* (Chamber Music, 1975).

ERIC SALZMAN (New York City, 1933–) numbers among his teachers Otto Luening, Vladimir Ussachevsky, Roger Sessions, and Milton Babbitt. Equally decisive in his development was the influence of Ives, Varèse, Ruggles, Cowell, and Cage. In 1970 he organized a multimedia ensemble, Quog, which has presented his theater pieces. These combine voices, electronic media, and instrumental music with dramatic-visual imagery. His aim, as he puts it, is to cut through "various kinds of 'styles' and experiences" to achieve a music theater that functions on a number of levels: "group study, workshops, exercises, performance games, interaction and improvisation as well as creation and realization integrating movement and sound, music and language, dance and theater, image and idea." On records: *The Nude Paper Sermon,* for actor, Renaissance consort, chorus, and electronics, on texts by Stephen Wade and John Ashbery (1968–1969); *Helix,* for choral ensemble and tape (1971–1972).

GIACINTO SCELSI (La Spezia, Italy, 1905–) studied with Respighi and Casella. He was one of the first Italians to use twelve-tone elements in his music. His compositions, in many genres, are only now attracting international attention. On records: *String Quartet No. 4* (1964).

R. MURRAY SCHAFER (Sarnia, Ontario, 1933–) is a leading figure in the contemporary movement in Canada. He has responded strongly to modern poetry, painting, and film as exemplified in the works of Paul Klee, Ezra Pound, and Sergei Eisenstein. He teaches at Simon Fraser University in Vancouver, where he founded and directs the Studio for Sonic Research and Electronic Music. On records: *Requiems for a Party-Girl,* for soprano and nine instruments (1966).

GUNTHER SCHULLER (New York City, 1925–) was largely self-taught. He was influenced, on one hand, by the rhythmic freedom and instrumental innovations of experimental jazz; on the other, by the serial techniques of the twelve-tone method, which he handles in an unorthodox and altogether personal way. Schuller combined basic techniques drawn from jazz and so-called serious music in what he named "third stream," a free style in which improvisation plays an important part. He has drawn inspiration from a variety of styles and idioms, but possesses a strong enough musical personality to fuse those into a unity. He leans toward an expressively chromatic atonal idiom, which he uses with poetic imagination and a flair for vivid timbres. Of special interest is his book *Early Jazz: Its Roots and Musical Development* (1968). Schuller is represented on records by a number of instrumental works: *Sonata for Oboe and Piano* (1948–1951); *Symphony for Brass and Percussion* (1949–1950); *Lines and Contrasts,* for horn ensemble (1950–1960); *Dramatic Overture,* for orchestra (1951); *Contours,* for chamber ensemble (1955–1958); *String Quartet No. 1* (1957); *Woodwind Quintet* (1958); *Five Bagatelles,* for orchestra (1964); *Five Moods for Tuba Quartet* (1972); *Tre Invenzioni,* for chamber ensemble (1972).

WILLIAM SCHUMAN (New York City, 1910–), who studied composition privately with Roy Harris, is primarily a composer of large-scale symphonic works. His music, stemming from a temperament that is optimistic, assertive, and thoroughly at home in the world, has vigor and energy. The melodic line is long of breath and shaped into bold tunes; the harmonic language, rooted in tonality, is direct; the rhythmic impulse is powerful; the sonorities are predominantly bright. Nine symphonies form the central item in a list that includes concertos, chamber and choral works, ballet music, and a one-act opera, *The Mighty Casey* (1953). On records: *Symphony No. 3* (1939), *No. 4* (1942), *No. 5* (1943), *No. 7* (1960), *No. 8* (1960–1962); *Quartet No. 3* (1939); *Con-*

certo for Violin (1947); *Credendum,* for orchestra (1955); *Chester Overture* (1956); *New England Triptych,* three pieces for orchestra (1956); *Carols of Death,* for chorus (1958); *Variations on "America" after Charles Ives* (1962).

CHARLES SCHWARTZ (New York City, 1933–) studied with Darius Milhaud, Aaron Copland, and Charles Jones. He teaches at Hunter College. As director of Composers Showcase in New York City Schwartz has played an important part in the propagation of contemporary music. His list includes jazz-oriented pieces, such as *Riffs for Jazz Trumpeter and Ensemble,* as well as works in traditional forms, like the *Passacaglia for Orchestra.* On records: *Professor Jive,* a jazz symphony for solo trumpet and orchestra (1976).

ELLIOTT S. SCHWARTZ (New York City, 1936–) studied with Otto Luening, Jack Beeson, Paul Creston, and Henry Brant. He teaches at Bowdoin College. His acquaintance with several of the new crop of virtuosos who play contemporary music has prompted him—as it has a number of his colleagues—to write works designed for specific players and for the particular resources of their instruments. Schwartz is the author of *Electronic Music: A Listener's Guide,* and has assembled some interesting reflections in a volume entitled *Contemporary Composers on Contemporary Music.* On records: *Interruptions,* for woodwind quintet (1964); *Concert Piece for Ten Players* (1965); *Textures,* for strings, winds, and brass (1966).

PETER SCULTHORPE (Launceston, Tasmania, Australia, 1929–) is one of Australia's leading composers. He studied with Edmund Rubbra and Egon Wellesz, and teaches at the University of Sydney. He has been influenced by serialism and by the newer instrumental techniques of such composers as Penderecki; more recently by the music of the Far East. He feels strongly that, because of geographical proximity, Australian music should turn for inspiration to Asia rather than to Euope. On records: *Sun Music III,* for orchestra (1967).

HUMPHREY SEARLE (Oxford, England, 1915–) attended the Royal College of Music in London, where he now teaches. He also studied with Anton Webern in Vienna. His five symphonies are flanked by concertos, ballets, choral works, operas, and music for theater, films, and television. His music has its spiritual roots in post-Webern aesthetics. On records: *Aubade,* for horn and orchestra (1955).

MATYAS SEIBER (Budapest, Hungary, 1905–1960, Capetown, South Africa) was a pupil of Zoltán Kodály at the Academy of Musical Art in Budapest. He taught composition and jazz at the Frankfurt Conservatory, at a time when no one taught jazz in Germany. After Hitler took over, Seiber left Germany and settled in London. His fine sense of craftsmanship stemmed from the heritage of Hindemith, even as his inventive rhythmic sense owed much to Bartók. Seiber was a fluent composer who absorbed a variety of influences, but in his last years was increasingly interested in serialism. He died in an automobile accident. On records: *Concertino* for clarinet and strings; *French*

Folksongs, for tenor and guitar; *Permutazioni a cinque,* a serial work for wood-wind quintet (1958).

KAZIMIERZ SEROCKI (Torun, Poland, 1922–) was one of the founders of the Warsaw Annual Festival of Contemporary Music. He was originally oriented toward Neoclassicism and a stylized Polish Nationalism, but in the mid-1950s turned to serial and aleatory techniques. On records: *Sonatina for Trombone and Piano* (1966).

HAROLD SHAPERO (Lynn, Massachusetts, 1920–) studied with Walter Piston and Ernst Krenek at Harvard, as well as with Nadia Boulanger. He teaches at Brandeis University. For most of his creative career Shapero adhered to the Neoclassic aesthetic. Strongly influenced by Stravinsky and Copland, he refined their harmonic language to a personal idiom projected through the large forms of the Classic-Romantic period, which he handled with technical adroitness and melodic-rhythmic invention. He subsequently became interested in the Buchla synthesizer and produced several works on tape for synthesizer and piano. Shapero's early *Three Sonatas for Piano* (1944) have retained their freshness through the years. Also on records: *Quartet No. 1* (1940); *Sonata* for trumpet and piano (1940); *Partita in C,* for piano and small orchestra (1960).

RALPH SHAPEY (Philadelphia, 1921–) studied with Stefan Wolpe and at the University of Chicago where he directs the Contemporary Chamber Players. His music is instinct with energy and tension. Under the influence of Varèse and Schoenberg, he shaped his intuitions into a powerfully expressive idiom. The disciple of Varèse speaks in Shapey's definition of music as "an object in Time and Space: aggregate sounds structured into concrete sculptural forms." From the same provenance comes his conception of the composer as "an architect of sound, time, space, and flux." Shapey's forms unfold with cumulative energies which at their points of maximum tension explode into blocklike masses of sound. He has combined the disciplined use of avant-garde techniques with his belief in the validity of music as a passionate expression of man's emotional life. His output is mostly instrumental; but he was one of the first American composers to view the voice as an instrument, "using syllables," as he put it, "in organized sound-structures." On records: *Evocation,* for violin, piano, and percussion (1959); *Rituals,* for symphony orchestra (1959); *Incantations,* for soprano and ten instruments (1961); *String Quartet No. 6* (1963); *Songs of Ecstasy,* for voice, piano, percussion, and tape (1967); *Praise,* an oratorio for bass-baritone, chorus, and chamber orchestra (1971).

RODION SHCHEDRIN (Moscow, 1932–) was trained at the Moscow Conservatory. While adhering to the doctrine of "socialist realism" that prevails in his country, a doctrine inhospitable to the avant-gardism of the West, he has incorporated in his scores some of the orchestral techniques common among advanced composers in Europe and America. On records: *Carmen,* a ballet after Bizet (1967); *Anna Karenina,* a ballet (1971).

SEYMOUR SHIFRIN (Brooklyn, N.Y., 1926–) studied with William Schuman, Otto Luening, and Darius Milhaud. He teaches at Brandeis University. Shifrin's output includes pieces for solo voice, chorus, and orchestra, but is devoted mainly to chamber ensembles. He is one of a fairly large group of composers who have enriched their basically Neoclassic aesthetic with elements of serial thinking; he regards tone rows as one other of a number of viable contemporary techniques. The rapidly shifting harmonies in his music stem from the fundamentally chromatic nature of his language, combined with extremely elastic rhythms. His forms derive their dramatic tension from the powerful contrast of heterogeneous elements within a firmly drawn frame. On records: *Serenade for Five Instruments* (1954); *Three Pieces for Orchestra* (1958); *The Odes of Shang* for chorus, piano, and percussion (1962); *Satires of Circumstance*, for mezzo-soprano and chamber ensemble (1964); *String Quartet No. 4* (1967).

ELIE SIEGMEISTER (New York City, 1909–), who teaches at Hofstra University, studied with Wallingford Riegger and Nadia Boulanger. He has used our American heritage as source material for a large output that includes symphonies, concertos, orchestral pieces, and much chamber music; over a dozen theater works, including four operas; well over one hundred songs; and works for chorus, band, and piano. Jazz, blues, and folk-song elements are combined with twentieth-century devices within ample forms whose ideas range from tensely compact motives to broadly flowing lines. The vocal works are based on texts of "social significance," from *Strange Funeral in Braddock*, for solo voice and orchestra (1933), and *Abraham Lincoln Walks at Midnight*, for chorus (1937), to the opera *The Plough and the Stars*, on Sean O'Casey's play about the Easter rebellion, which made a strong impression when it was given in Europe. It has not yet been presented in this country. On records: *Western Suite* (1945); *Concerto* for clarinet and orchestra (1956); *Symphony No. 3* (1957); *Concerto* for flute and orchestra (1960); *Sonata No. 2* for piano (1964); *Fantasy and Soliloquy*, for solo cello (1964); *Sextet* for brass and percussion (1965); *Sonata No. 3* for violin (1965); *Sonatas No. 2* and 4 for violin and piano (1970, 1971); and songs.

STANLEY SILVERMAN (New York City, 1938–) studied with Kirchner, Milhaud, Cowell, and Roberto Gerhard. He was music director of the Repertory Theater of Lincoln Center from 1965 to 1973. In stage works such as *Elephant Steps* (1968) and *Dr. Selavy's Magic Theatre* (1972) he shows a fresh and imaginative approach to the problem of combining operatic tradition with contemporary modes of thought. His music combines disparate elements, from pop and rock to traditional serial procedures. On records: *Pianh*, a chamber concerto for guitar (1967).

NETTY SIMONS (New York City, 1923–) studied with Stefan Wolpe. Her use of twelve-tone and serial techniques is marked by an extreme economy of means and imaginative control of color. Her recent chamber and orchestral works adhere to aleatory principles within a framework of controlled pitch groupings and interval relationships. She has developed a graphic notation in which these principles are combined with traditional notation. On records: *Design Groups No. 1,* for one to three percussion players (1967); *Design Groups No. 2,* duo for any combination of low-pitched and high-pitched instruments (1968); *Silver Thaw,* for any combination of eight players (1969).

NIKOS SKALKOTTAS (Halkis, Greece, 1904-1949, Athens) studied with Kurt Weill, Philipp Jarnach, and Schoenberg, among others. His important works were crowded into the last fifteen years of his life—a varied output of chamber and orchestral music, concerted works, piano pieces, songs, and ballets. Writing in a dense twelve-tone idiom, he composed with extreme speed and sureness. He expanded classical twelve-tone procedures to include the use of several independent rows in the same work, and combined dodecaphonic processes with variation, sonata form, and a polyphonic texture consisting of long lyric lines. Many of his works still remain unperformed. On records: *Greek Dances,* for orchestra (1936); several piano works.

LEO SMIT (Philadelphia, 1921-) studied with Nicolas Nabokov and has combined his composing career with that of concert pianist. He teaches at the State University of New York at Buffalo. As pianist for George Ballanchine's American Ballet Caravan he came into close contact with Stravinsky, who had a decisive influence on his music. On records: *Copernicus—Narrative and Credo* for chorus and orchestra (1973); *At the Corner of the Sky* (1976) and *Songs of Wonder* (1976) for men's chorus.

HALE SMITH (Cleveland, Ohio, 1925-), one of the outstanding black composers of his generation, writes works marked by a high order of craftsmanship. His list includes orchestral, chamber, and piano pieces. On records: *In Memoriam—Beryl Rubinstein* (1953), for chamber orchestra; *Valley Wind,* for soprano (1955); *Evocation,* for piano (1965); *Expansions,* for wind ensemble (1967); *Ritual and Incantations,* for orchestra (1974).

JULIA SMITH (Denton, Texas, 1911-) attended the Juilliard School, where she subsequently taught. She has incorporated Americanist elements into a variety of orchestral, chamber, choral, and piano pieces. She has also written music for school use, and a book on Aaron Copland. On records: excerpts from *Daisy,* an opera (1973).

RUSSEL SMITH (Tuscaloosa, Alabama, 1927-) studied at Columbia University and was composer-in-residence with the Cleveland Orchestra and the New Orleans Philharmonic. His *Piano Concerto No. 2* (1957), which is available on records, fills a large form with bravura writing for the solo instrument and orchestra.

WILLIAM O. SMITH (Sacramento, California, 1926-) studied with Milhaud and Sessions. He teaches at the University of Washington. Music for clarinet stands out in his list of instrumental works that combine jazz elements with harmonic tensions whose roots go back to atonal Expressionism; a clarinetist himself, Smith has pioneered in new playing techniques for the instrument. On records: *Capriccio* for violin and piano (1952); *Suite* for violin and clarinet (1952); *Quartet* (1952); *Concerto* for solo jazz clarinet (1957); *Four Pieces* for clarinet, violin, piano (1957); *Five Pieces* for clarinet alone (1958); *Mosaic,* for clarinet and piano (1964); *Fancies,* for clarinet alone (1969); *Straws,* for flute and bassoon (1974).

HARVEY SOLLBERGER (Cedar Rapids, Iowa, 1938–) studied with Jack Beeson and Otto Luening at Columbia University, where he subsequently taught. With Charles Wuorinen he founded the Group for Contemporary Music, which began its activity at Columbia and later transferred to the Manhattan School of Music. He has been affected by post-Webern developments within the twelve-tone system, especially the extension of serial procedures to include registers, timbres, and dynamics. On the one hand he has followed the lead of Milton Babbitt in exploring the combinatorial possibilities of the basic set. On the other he has been influenced by the freer Expressionism of Stefan Wolpe and Elliott Carter, in which the shaping of the various parameters springs out of a particular context and in turn determines its progression to the next. A flutist himself, Sollberger writes exceptionally well for the instrument. Chamber music occupies a prominent place on his list. On records: *Chamber Variations,* for chamber ensemble (1964); *Divertimento* for flute, cello, and piano (1970); *Riding the Wind I,* for flute and chamber ensemble (1974).

HARRY STUART SOMERS (Toronto, Ontario, 1925–) is a leading figure on the contemporary-music scene in Canada. He is a prolific composer whose list includes operas, ballets, symphonies, concertos; orchestral, chamber, and choral works; songs and piano pieces. He achieves contrast by juxtaposing tonal and twelve-tone materials, and has also written tape music. On records: *Passacaglia and Fugue* for orchestra (1954).

JOEL SPIEGELMAN (Buffalo, New York, 1933–) studied at Brandeis University with Harold Shapero, Irving Fine, and Arthur Berger, and took over the Neoclassic aesthetic that they espoused during the '50s and '60s. He then began composing electronic music. Spiegelman teaches at Sarah Lawrence College, where he also directs the Studio for Electronic Music and Experimental Sound Media. Within the context of contemporary style he has tried to revive the *Gebrauchsmusik* (functional music) ideal of the 1920s. On records: *Kousochki,* for piano four-hands (1966).

CLAUDIO SPIES (Santiago, Chile, 1925–), who teaches at Princeton, has lived in the United States since his late teens. Among his teachers were Nadia Boulanger, Harold Shapero, Irving Fine, Hindemith, and Piston. About half his output is devoted to compositions for voice, solo and choral, accompanied by a variety of instrumental combinations ranging from piano to orchestra. The rest includes chamber, orchestral, and piano music. Spies moved from a strong Stravinskyan influence to the use of twelve-tone procedures, which he uses freely in a personal manner. His music is marked by melodic and rhythmic invention. On records: *Impromptu,* for piano (1963); *Viopiacem,* for viola and harpsichord or piano (1965).

LEWIS SPRATLAN (Miami, Florida, 1940–) studied with Gunther Schuller, Yehudi Wyner, and Mel Powell. He teaches at Amherst College. His list includes orchestral and chamber works, and he is now writing for a wide variety of media. On records: *Two Pieces for Orchestra* (1970).

ROBERT STARER (Vienna, 1924–) began his studies at the Vienna Academy and continued them, after Hitlerism sent his family out of Austria, first at the Jerusalem Conservatory, then at the Juilliard School. He teaches at Brooklyn College. Starer's large output is evenly divided between vocal and instrumental works. He favors the large forms, such as symphony and concerto. In these, as in his opera *Pantagleize* (1966–1970), based on the play by the Belgian dramatist Michel de Ghelderode, he adapts the central European heritage of Expressionism to an idiom impregnated with dramatic tension. On records: *Five Miniatures,* for brass quintet (1949); *Concerto à tre,* for clarinet, trumpet, trombone, and strings (1954); *Ariel,* for soprano, baritone, chorus, and orchestra (1959); *Concerto for Viola, Strings, and Percussion* (1959); *Dialogues,* for clarinet and piano (1961); *Variants,* for violin and piano (1963); *Mutabili, Variants for Orchestra* (1965); *Sonata No. 2,* for piano (1965); *On the Nature of Things,* for chorus (1969); *Evanescents* for piano (1976); *Piano Quartet* (1977).

ROBERT L. STERN (Paterson, N.J., 1934–) studied with Bernard Rogers, Lukas Foss, and Howard Hanson. He teaches at the University of Massachusetts and is visiting composer in electronic music at Hampshire College. His lyricism shows to fine advantage in *Terezin* (1967), a song cycle dedicated to the memory of the children of the death-camp and based on the poems they wrote (from the collection entitled *I Never Saw Another Butterfly*). This work has been recorded. Also on records: *Carom,* for orchestra and tape; *In Memoriam Abraham,* for orchestra.

HALSEY STEVENS (Scott, N.Y. 1908–) was influenced by Ernest Bloch, with whom he studied, and Bartók, of whom he wrote an outstanding biography. He teaches at the University of Southern California. Stevens's large list includes piano music, sonatas for various instruments, much chamber and orchestral music, songs, and choral pieces. He is represented on records by *Symphony No. 1* (1945; revised 1950); *Sonata* for horn and piano (1953); *Suite* for solo violin (1954); *Sonata* for trumpet and piano (1956); *Sonata* for trombone and piano (1965); *Concerto* for clarinet and string orchestra (1969); *Dittico,* for alto saxophone and piano (1972).

DAVID STOCK (Pittsburgh, 1939–) studied with Arthur Berger, Nikolai Lopatnikoff, and Alexei Haieff. He teaches at Antioch College. Stock's catalogue includes a number of carefully crafted, tightly knit instrumental works that show his Neoclassic orientation. On records: *Quintet* for clarinet and strings (1966). Here, the composer explains, "instrumental virtuosity is one of the primary determinants of the shape and textures of the piece."

ALAN STOUT (Baltimore, Maryland, 1932–) studied at Johns Hopkins University and the Peabody Institute. Among his teachers were Henry Cowell and Wallingford Riegger. Stout teaches at Northwestern University. His list includes four symphonies; ten string quartets; a Passion for soloists, chorus, and orchestra (1975); as well as a variety of instrumental and choral pieces and songs. On records: *Sonata* for cello (1966).

GERALD STRANG (Clareshold, Alberta, Canada, 1908–) studied with Schoenberg and was in close personal contact with him, first as teaching assistant, then as editorial assistant. He worked on electronic and computer music at the Bell Telephone Laboratories in New Jersey, and now teaches at the University of California at Los Angeles. His list includes both instrumental and tape music. Strang is also well known for his writings on computer music. On records: *Percussion Music* (1935); *Cello Concerto* (1951).

TISON STREET (Boston, 1943–) studied with Leon Kirchner and David Del Tredici. He favors the large forms of chamber music. On records: *String Quartet* (1972); *String Quintet* (1974).

MORTON SUBOTNIK (Los Angeles, 1933–) studied with Darius Milhaud and Leon Kirchner. He teaches at the California Institute of the Arts in his native city. Primarily interested in electronic music, he feared that the medium was losing the personal touch and succeeded in introducing into it an element of immediate popular appeal—what he thinks of as the spirit of "play." Subotnik aspires to get away from what he calls the "museum" quality of most concerts today by creating a live and lively electronic music that can involve listeners not only through its accessibility but also through audience participation. Hence his interest in fusing film, projections, kinetic light, and taped and live electronic music in a popular multimedia theater. Given this orientation, it is not surprising that he is very well represented on records: *Prelude No. 4* for piano and electronic tape (1966); several electronic pieces, among them *Silver Apples of the Moon* (1967); *Sidewinder* (1970); *Four Butterflies* (1972); *Until Spring* (1975).

ROBERT SUDERBURG (Spencer, Iowa, 1936–) studied with Paul Eitler, Quincy Porter, and George Rochberg. He teaches at the University of Washington. Suderburg writes in a style that combines elements of romanticism with more advanced techniques. On records: *Chamber Music II* (1967); *Concerto "within the mirror of time"* for piano and orchestra (1974).

CARLOS SURINACH (Barcelona, Spain, 1915–) divides his time between New York, Madrid, and wherever else his conducting engagements take him. He has worked within the national tradition of the modern Spanish school—Albéniz, Granados, and Falla. Surinach's is a colorful idiom flavored with a discreet use of those contemporary idioms that suit his style. An important element is the spirit of rapturous improvisation emanating from flamenco song and dance. His varied list includes two symphonies and several important ballets—*Ritmo Jondo*, with choreography by Doris Humphrey (1953), and three written for Martha Graham—*Embattled Garden* (1958), *Acrobats of God* (1960), and *The Owl and the Pussycat*, after a poem by Edward Lear (1978). On records: *Symphonic Variations* (1963); *Melorhythmic Dramas*, for orchestra (1966); *Spells and Rhythms*, for orchestra (1966); *Piano Concerto* (1973).

HOWARD SWANSON (Atlanta, Georgia, 1907–), one of the outstanding black composers of his generation, studied with Herbert Elwell and Nadia Boulanger. He favors the large forms of classical music, as in his three symphonies. He is best known for *Short Symphony* (1948), which is available on records, and *Night Music*, for small orchestra (1950), which is not.

WILLIAM SYDEMAN (New York City, 1928–) was influenced by Roger Sessions, with whom he studied. He combines the use of contemporary materials with the Classic-Romantic concept of music as an emotionally expressive art. His works range from *Homage to "L'Histoire du Soldat,"* for chamber group (1962), to *Projections No. 1*, for amplified violin, tape, and slides (1968). On records: *Music for Flute and Piano* (1960); *Quartet* for oboe and strings (1961); *Quintet No. 2* (1961); *Orchestral Abstractions* (1963); *Concerto* for piano four-hands and chamber orchestra (1967).

YUJI TAKAHASHI (Tokyo, 1938–) studied at the Toho School of Music and at Tanglewood. The formative influence was exerted by Iannis Xenakis, with whom he studied privately. Takahashi is a brilliant pianist, especially in the contemporary repertory, and teaches piano at the San Francisco Conservatory. He took over Xenakis's concept of stochastic music—that is, a music based on probabilities, and in recent years has turned his attention to computer music. On records: *Metatheses*, for piano (composed with the aid of a computer, 1968); *Six Stocheia*, for four violins (1969).

TORU TAKEMITSU (Tokyo, 1930–), one of the foremost representatives of the contemporary movement in Japan, was mostly self-educated in music. With Toshi Ichiyanagi and Seiji Ozawa, he founded a biennial festival for contemporary music called Orchestral Space, and for the 1970 World Exposition at Osaka he conceived and directed the Space Theater, a concert hall equipped with laser beams and 800 loudspeakers. His earlier compositions combined chromaticism of Schoenberg and Berg with the sustained melodic lines and powerful chordal masses of Messiaen. In some works, Takemitsu uses both Japanese and Western instruments, as in *November Steps* (1967). His tape compositions, which derive from the aesthetic and techniques of *musique concrète*, have an attractive bell-like lightness. On records: *Textures*, for orchestra (1964); *November Steps*, for two Japanese instruments and orchestra.

LOUISE TALMA (Arachon, France, 1906–), professor emeritus of music at Hunter College of the City University of New York, started out from the sound-world of Stravinskyan Neoclassicism; her thinking was shaped by a long personal association with Nadia Boulanger. In the '50s she embraced serial techniques. Pieces for solo voice and chorus occupy a prominent place in her output; those for piano display her profound knowledge of the instrument. The list also includes orchestral works. Talma's music shows expert craftsmanship and refinement of taste. Her three-act opera *The Alcestiad,* on a libretto by Thornton Wilder (1955–1958), has been presented in Germany but not yet in the United States. On records: *Six Etudes* for piano (1954); *Sonata No. 2* for piano (1955); *3 Dualogues* for clarinet and piano (1968).

ELIAS TANENBAUM (Brooklyn, N.Y., 1924–) studied, among others, with Bohuslav Martinu, Otto Luening, and Wallingford Riegger. He is director of electronic music at the Manhattan School of Music. Tannenbaum's list includes theater music, orchestral and chamber works, and electronic pieces. He is one of a number of composers who increasingly combine their tape music with instrumental and/or vocal performance. Several of his electronic works are available on records, among them *Movements, Contrasts, Blue Fantasy for the "Bird."*

FRANCIS THORNE (Bay Shore, N.Y., 1922–) studied at Yale University. Among his teachers were Hindemith and David Diamond. Thorne was active as a jazz pianist, and has combined elements of modern jazz with twelve-tone serialism. On records: *Sonatina* for solo flute (1962); *Rhapsodic Variations* for orchestra (1965); *Symphony No. 3* (1969); *Lyric Variations II,* for wind quintet and percussion (1971); *Fanfare, Fugue, and Funk,* for orchestra (1972); *Concerto* for piano and chamber orchestra (1973).

MICHAEL TIPPETT (London, 1905–) studied at the Royal Academy of Music in London. His style was nourished by a variety of influences—the Elizabethan madrigal; harpsichord music of the sixteenth and seventeenth centuries, especially that of Purcell; Negro spirituals; Stravinsky, Bartók, and Hindemith. Since the death of Britten he has emerged as England's most important composers and is a major figure on the contemporary scene. His four full-length operas—*Midsummer Marriage* (1955), *King Priam* (1962), *The Knot Garden* (1970), and *The Ice Break* (1977)—have been overshadowed on the international circuit by those of Britten. Their highly complex librettos, written by the composer, and somewhat intellectual posture do not make for easy popularity. On the other hand, his oratorio *A Child of Our Time* (1939–1941) has established itself firmly in the repertory. Among the important works are four symphonies (1945, 1957, 1971, 1977) and an oratorio, *Vision of St. Augustus* (1965). Both the *Piano Concerto* (1955) and *Concerto for Orchestra* (1963) display the composer's penchant for contrapuntal texture and brilliant instrumental writing. Recorded works include *A Child of Our Time, The Knot Garden, Midsummer Marriage, Concerto for Orchestra, Concerto for Double String Orchestra* (1939), three string quartets (1935, 1942, 1946), the first three symphonies, songs, and piano works.

JOAN TOWER (New Rochelle, N.Y., 1938–) studied with Ralph Shapey and Benjamin Boretz, among others. She has been strongly influenced by Stravinsky as well as Beethoven. Tower has moved from the twelve-tone virtuosity of the '60s to a more accessible, lyrical style that does not exclude tonal elements. On records: *Prelude for Five Players* (1970); *Hexachords,* for flute (1972); *Breakfast Rhythms I and II,* for clarinet and five instruments (1975).

ROY TRAVIS (New York City, 1922–) studied with Bernard Wagenaar at the Juilliard School, Otto Luening at Columbia University, and Darius Milhaud at the Paris Conservatory. He teaches at the University of California at Los Angeles and has been active in the university's electronic studio. His choice of subjects has been influenced by his studies in Greek drama and African primitive music. On records: *Symphonic Allegro* (1951); *Songs and Epilogues,* for bass and piano (1965); *The Passion of Oedipus,* an opera (1966); *Duo Concertante* for violin and piano (1967); *Collage for Orchestra* (1968); *Piano Concerto* (1970).

LESTER TRIMBLE (Bangor, Wisconsin, 1923–), who teaches at the Juilliard School, studied with Nikolai Lopatnikoff at Carnegie-Mellon University, and with Milhaud, Honegger, and Nadia Boulanger in Paris. His style, as he describes it, amalgamates American elements with the Germanic striving for formal unity through thematic-motivic development and the French love of elegance through instrumental and harmonic color. He has used twelve-tone procedures among other techniques, and is attracted "to the use of poly-rhythms, melodies, and harmonies in montagelike groupings." On records: *String Quartet No. 1* (1950); *Four Fragments from the Canterbury Tales* (1958); *Five Episodes,* for orchestra (1962); *In Praise of Diplomacy and Common Sense,* for baritone and chamber ensemble (1965); *Panels 1,* for chamber orchestra (1973).

GILBERT TRYTHALL (Knoxville, Tennessee, 1930–) studied with Robert Palmer and Wallingford Riegger, among others. He teaches at George Peabody College. His music combines tape with various types of live music—chorus, brass, and, in *Parallax,* brass, tape, and slides. He is the author of a book, *Electronic Music: Principles and Practice.* On records: *Entropy* for stereo brass, improvisation group, and tape (1971).

RICHARD TRYTHALL (Knoxville, Tennessee, 1939–) studied with Roger Sessions, among others. He lives in Italy, where he is active as a free-lance composer and pianist. His list includes orchestral music and several works that combine live instruments and tape. On records: *Coincidences,* for piano (1969); *Variations on a Theme by Franz Joseph Haydn,* an electronic piece (1976).

PAUL TUROK (New York City, 1929–) studied with Karol Rathaus at Queens College, also with Roger Sessions and Bernard Wagenaar. He is attracted to the large forms of instrumental music—symphony, concerto, string quartet. *A Joplin Overture* is his homage to the "primitive" whom Turok's generation rediscovered. He is also one of the handful of American composers who have tried to subjugate the music of Shakespeare's verse to their own music, in his opera *Richard III.* On records: *Little Suite* for piano (1955); *Passacaglia* for piano (1955); *Three Transcendental Etudes* for piano (1970); *Lyric Variations* for oboe and strings (1971).

CHINARY UNG (Cambodia, 1942–) moved to the United States in 1964. He studied with Chou Wen-Chung, Vladimir Ussachevsky, and Bulent Arel, among others. Ung combines Cambodian elements with Western techniques. On records: *Mohori,* for soprano and chamber orchestra (1974).

VLADIMIR USSACHEVSKY (Hailar, Manchuria, of Russian parents, 1911–) came to the United States when he was nineteen. He studied with Bernard Rogers and Howard Hanson at the Eastman School and at Columbia with Otto Luening, with whom he has been closely associated at the Columbia-Princeton Electronic Music Center. His instrumental and tape pieces are marked by timbral variety, rhythmic complexity, and structural tightness, based on the alteration through tape speed and multiple-recording techniques of a few sound sources that have a common timbral origin. In recent years Ussachevsky has also worked in the field of computer music. On records: *Three Scenes from The Creation,* for four choruses and electronic sounds (1961); with Otto Luening, *Concerted Piece for Tape Recorder and Orchestra* (1952). The electronic pieces on records include *Sonic Contours* (1952), *Piece for Tape Recorder* (1956), *Metamorphosis* (1957), *Linear Contrasts* (1958), *Wireless Fantasy* (1960), *Creation Prologue* (1962), *Of Wood and Brass* (1965), *Computer Piece No. 1* (1968), *Two Sketches* (1971).

JOHN W. VERALL (Britt, Iowa, 1908–) numbers among his teachers Aaron Copland, Roy Harris, and Zoltán Kodály. He is on the faculty of the University of Washington. His list centers about chamber music for various instrumental combinations, including seven string quartets. He has also written a textbook, *Fuge and Invention in Theory and Practice.* "I have always been interested," he states, "in warm, rich combinations of sound, and yet have desired to carry my music into new areas of texture and design." On records: *String Quartet No. 7; Sonata* for horn and piano.

GEORGE WALKER (Washington, D.C., 1922–) studied with Nadia Boulanger, among others. He is one of the outstanding black composers of his generation, and established his reputation through his assured handling of the large forms of instrumental music. On records: *Lyric for Strings* (1945); *Piano Sonata No. 1* (1953); *Trombone Concerto* (1957); *Piano Sonata No. 2* (1957); *Variations for Orchestra* (1971); *Piano Concerto* (1975); *Music for Brass* (1975); *Piano Sonata No. 3* (1975).

ROBERT WARD (Cleveland, Ohio, 1917–) studied at the Eastman and Juilliard Schools, also at Tanglewood. He has held various teaching and managerial positions, including the presidency of the North Carolina School of the Arts in Winston-Salem. He combines a vivid interest in American folk song and jazz with "the more basic penchant for austere contrapuntal writing, simple slow melodies with elaborate obbligato, and fast rhythmic dance tunes." His list includes four symphonies, chamber music, orchestral pieces, and vocal music, but he is best known as the composer of two successful operas: *Pantaloon (He Who Gets Slapped,* after Andreyev's play, 1956) and *The*

Crucible, after the drama of Arthur Miller (1961). On records: *The Crucible; Piano Concerto* (1968).

DAVID WARD-STEINMAN (Alexandria, Louisiana, 1936–) studied, among others, with Wallingford Riegger, Darius Milhaud, Milton Babbitt, and Nadia Boulanger. He has written over fifty works in various media—symphony, concerto, oratorio, ballet, opera, and, in *Antares,* tape, choir, and orchestra. Ward-Steinman teaches at the California State University in San Diego. On records: *Fragments from Sappho,* a song cycle for soprano and chamber ensemble (1966).

GERALD WARFIELD (Fort Worth, Texas, 1940–) did his student work with Samuel Adler and Milton Babbitt. He has taught at Princeton and the University of Illinois, but at present is devoting himself entirely to composition. He has adapted serial techniques to a fundamentally romantic point of view, and has espoused what he calls "contemporary transformation"—that is, the basing of a new work on the music of a master such as Bach or Chopin by "viewing it through a contemporary filter." He has written several textbooks: *Layer Analysis, Layer Dictation, How to Write Music Manuscript.* On records: *Variations and Metamorphosis,* for two cellos (1974).

ROBERT WASHBURN (Bouckville, N.Y., 1928–) studied, among others, with Darius Milhaud, Nadia Boulanger, and Alan Hovhaness. His list features orchestral and chamber music; he is the author of a textbook, *Comprehensive Foundations of Musicianship.* Washburn teaches at State University College in Potsdam, New York. Several works for wind ensemble have been recorded, among them *Ceremonial Music, Chorale for Band, Epigon IV,* and *Symphony for Band.*

BEN WEBER (St. Louis, Missouri, 1916–) was one of the first American composers to use twelve-tone procedures, even though his music never wholly relinquished tonal implications. His strong lyric gift expresses itself in the flowing lines of his counterpoint and the shapely outlines of his large forms. Chamber works, some with solo voice, form a large part of his output. Characteristic is the *Symphony on Four Poems of William Blake,* for baritone and chamber ensemble (1951). On records: *Three Pieces,* Opus 23 for piano (1946); *String Quartet No. 2* (1951); *Piano Concerto* (1961); *Dolmen, An Elegy* (1964); *Consort of Winds* (1974).

HENRY WEINBERG (Philadelphia, 1931–) studied with Roger Sessions, Luigi Dallapiccola, and Milton Babbitt, among others. He teaches at Queens College. Weinberg has been concerned, in much of his music, with extending Schoenbergian techniques into the domain of rhythm. The object is to enlarge, as he expresses it, "the number and kinds of interrelationships one hears in music of even the recent past." A strong lyric bent has nourished his sense of being rooted in the traditional bases of Western music. On records: *Cantus Commemorabilis I,* for chamber ensemble (1966).

HUGO WEISGALL (Ivancice, Czechoslovakia, 1912–), who teaches at Queens College, came to the United States in 1920. He attended the Peabody Conservatory and Johns Hopkins University, from which he received a doctorate in German literature. Essentially an opera composer, Weisgall writes in a contemporary idiom that ranges from atonal chromaticism to the twelve-tone style, an area he describes as "pretty much the place where Schoenberg was before his final decisive leap into serialism, and where Berg was in *Wozzeck.*" His surcharged harmonic language lends itself ideally to the tensions of the Expressionist theater. Hence his affinity for the European dramatists from whom he derived the librettos for several of his operas: Luigi Pirandello (*Six Characters in Search of an Author,* 1956); Frank Wedekind (*The Tenor,* 1949); August Strindberg (*The Stronger,* 1952); and William Butler Yeats (*Purgatory,* 1958). On records: *The Tenor; The Stronger; End of Summer,* for tenor and chamber ensemble (1973–1974); *Fancies and Inventions,* for baritone and chamber ensemble (1974).

RICHARD WERNICK (Boston, 1934–) studied at Brandeis University and Mills College, also at Tanglewood. He teaches at the University of Pennsylvania. His intensely expressive style, based on what he calls "the impulse to sing," favors the vocal medium, although his list includes instrumental pieces, too. On records: *A Prayer for Jerusalem,* for female voice and percussion ensemble (1970–1971); *Kaddish-Requiem,* for mezzo-soprano, chamber ensemble, and tape (1971); *Songs of Remembrance,* for mezzo-soprano and woodwind (1974).

PETER WESTERGAARD (Champaign, Illinois, 1931–) attended Harvard and Princeton, where he worked with Piston, Sessions, and Babbitt. He has been especially concerned with the relation of language to music and with the problems of text setting, as in his opera *Mr. and Mrs. Discobbolos,* a chamber opera after Edward Lear (1965), and several cantatas and chamber operas. His list also includes instrumental works. *Mr. and Mrs. Discobbolos* has been recorded, as well as a *Divertimento on Discobbolic Fragments* for flute and piano (1967).

CLIFTON WILLIAMS (Traskwood, Arkansas, 1923–) studied at the Eastman School with Howard Hanson and Bernard Rogers. He teaches at the University of Miami. Williams's works are for band, and two have been recorded: *Fanfare and Allegro* and *The Sinfonians.*

GEORGE BALCH WILSON (Grand Island, Nebraska, 1927–) studied with Ross Lee Finney, Roger Sessions, and Nadia Boulanger, among others. He teaches at the University of Michigan, where he directs the Electronic Music Studio and a concert series called Contemporary Directions. His list includes both instrumental and tape music. On records: *Exigencies* on 4-track tape (1968); *Cancatenations,* for 12 instruments (1969).

OLLIE WILSON (St. Louis, Missouri, 1937–) teaches at the University of California at Berkeley. He belongs among the black composers who combine

Afro-American musical influences with the mainstream of contemporary practice. On records: *Pieces* for piano and tape; *Piece for Four* (1966); *Akwan*, for piano, electric piano, amplified strings, and orchestra (1973); *Echoes*, for clarinet and tape (1975); *Sometimes*, for tenor and tape (1976).

BEATRICE WITKIN (New York City, 1916–) studied with Roger Sessions, Stefan Wolpe, and Edward Steuerman. Her list includes vocal and instrumental works, with greater emphasis in recent years on electronic music. Hers is a serial language that does not exclude tonal elements. On records: *Parameters*, for eight instruments (1964); *Prose Poem*, on a text by James T. Farrell, for narrator, mezzo-soprano, and instrumental ensemble (1964); *Triads and Things*, for brass quintet (1968); *Breath and Sounds*, for tuba and tape (1971).

CHRISTIAN WOLFF (Nice, France, 1934–) studied classics and comparative literature at Harvard and has participated in avant-garde music events in the United States and Europe. He is at present teaching at Dartmouth. His thinking was shaped through personal contact with John Cage, David Tudor, and Morton Feldman; he was also influenced by the music of Webern, Varèse, and Boulez. Wolff has consistently tried to unite the role of the composer with that of the performer, an attitude that involves giving the performer maximum choice during his performance. A composition, Wolff maintains, "must make possible the freedom and dignity of the performers. It should have in it a persistent capacity to surprise even the performers themselves and the composer." Hence his conviction that a performance "is a unique living organism passing through a stage of its life." The performers must therefore be free to react to one another and to the audience. "The listeners must be as free as the players." On records: *Duo* for violin and piano (1961); *Duet* for horn and piano (1961); *Summer*, for string quartet (1961); *Lines*, for quartet (1972); *Accompaniments for Piano* (1972).

CHARLES WUORINEN (New York City, 1938–) studied at Columbia University with Otto Luening, Jack Beeson, and Vladimir Ussachevsky, and taught there for a time. He and Harvey Sollberger organized the Group for Contemporary Music, which is now active at the Manhattan School of Music. Starting out from the sound-world of Stravinsky, Schoenberg, and Varèse, Wuorinen in the 1960s found his way to the twelve-tone system. He has been preoccupied, as have several of his contemporaries, with the attempt to integrate the various parameters of music in a manner that fulfills all the possibilities—and demands—of the particular context within which those unfold. This implies, of course, a close union of the systematic aspects of serialism with the nonsystematic or contextual approach that has grown up alongside it. Wuornin is a prolific composer. His list includes all the genres, including opera, but the bulk of it centers around chamber works that range from solo pieces to concertos. The recorded works include *Chamber Concerto*, for cello and ten players (1963); *Chamber Concerto*, for flute and ten players (1964); *Piano Concerto* (1965–1966); *Janissary Music*, for one percussionist (1966);

Making Ends Meet, for piano four-hands (1966); *String Trio* (1968); *Time's Encomium,* for synthesizer (1968–1969); *Ringing Changes,* for percussion ensemble (1970); *Speculum Speculi,* for chamber ensemble (1973).

YEHUDI WYNER (Calgary, Canada, 1929–) studied with Paul Hindemith at Yale and Walter Piston at Harvard, among others. He taught for a number of years at Yale. Wyner's output centers around chamber music and piano works; a prominent item is liturgical music for the synagoguge. His is a romantic expressivity manifesting itself in a harmonic language that is essentially chromatic, a rhythmic élan that unites the motoric power of the neo-Baroque with the excitement of jazz, and a freely flowing melodic line that takes on a quality of rhapsodic improvisation. A virtuoso pianist himself, Wyner brings to his music an appreciation of virtuosity and a feeling for what will go in a concert hall. On records: *Concert Duo* for violin and piano (1957); *Three Short Fantasies* for piano (1963–1971); *Intermedio,* a Lyric Ballet for soprano and strings (1974).

IANNIS XENAKIS (Braila, Rumania, of Greek parents, 1922–) moved with his family to Greece when he was ten. He graduated from the Athens Polytechnic School with a degree in engineering. His activities in the anti-Nazi Resistance had resulted in a severe face wound, imprisonment, and a death sentence. In 1947 he moved to Paris, where he studied with Honegger, Milhaud, and—his most important teacher—Messiaen. He also worked with the architect Le Corbusier and, for the 1958 Brussels Exhibition, helped design the Philips pavilion for which Varèse wrote his *Poème electronique.* In 1966 Xenakis founded a School of Mathematical and Automated Music in Paris, and subsequently established its counterpart at Indiana University. He bases his musical theories on the laws of mathematics and physics, and has called his music *stochastic,* a term related to Bernoulli's Law of Large Numbers or Probabilities. The title of one of his best-known works, *Pithoprakta* (1955–1956), means "action by probabilities." Xenakis's music maintains the principle of determinacy, as against John Cage and other proponents of indeterminacy. He determines the parameters of a piece, ordering their events according to mathematical calculation and choice rather than chance. The massed sonorities of his music, prominent use of glissandi, and a texture woven out of individual parts for each instrument in the orchestra—including the strings—gives his music a very special sound. It is a sound that has influenced a number of composers, especially Penderecki. On records: *Metastaseis* for orchestra (1955); *Pithoprakta,* for string orchestra; *Achoripsis,* for chamber ensemble (1957); *Herma,* for piano (1960–1961); *Eonta,* for piano and brass (1963); *Akrata,* for sixteen winds (1965).

ROLV YTTREHUS (Duluth, Minnesota, 1926–) studied, among others, with Ross Lee Finney, Nadia Boulanger, Roger Sessions, and Goffredo Petrassi. His music has been influenced by serial thinking and a preoccupation with sonority not as an end in itself but in terms of expressivity. These trends are in evidence in two of his recorded works: *Sextet* for strings and winds, and

The Terrible Event, for instrumental ensemble. Yttrehus teaches and directs the electronic music studio at the University of Wisconsin in Oshkosh.

BERND ALOIS ZIMMERMAN (Bliesheim, Germany, 1918–1970, Cologne) studied at the Universities of Bonn, Cologne, and Berlin while earning his living as a laborer and dance-band musician. Zimmerman was influenced by Webern and Stravinsky. His best-known work, the opera *Die Soldaten* (The Soldiers, 1958–1960, subsequently revised) exemplifies an eclectic style that ranges from electronic sounds and serialism to graphic notation and collage. The work uses mixed-media techniques, including a spherical distribution of sound sources, films and loudspeakers, orchestral instruments and singing voices, along with noise, *Sprechstimme,* electronic and concrete sounds. Also, the action does not unfold as a sequence in real time but shuffles events freely or presents them simultaneously. On records: *Concerto* for violin and orchestra (1950).

PAUL ZONN (Boston, 1938–) studied with Richard Hervig. He teaches at the University of Illinois. His list centers about instrumental music; typical is the *Concerto* for viola and thirteen players. On records: *Chroma* (1967), for oboe and piano; *Lieberata,* for chamber ensemble (1967); *Divertimento No. 1,* for tuba, double bass, and two percussion (1968).

RAMON ZUPKO (Pittsburgh, 1932–) was a student of Vincent Persichetti's. He now teaches at Western Michigan University. Typical of his approach to sound is *Trichromes,* for winds, percussion, and tape. On records: *Fixations,* for violin, cello, piano, and tape (1974); *Fluxus I,* for tape (1977).

Appendices

Appendix I Basic Concepts

a. *Melody* (Background Material for Chapter 3)

Melody during the Classic-Romantic era tended toward symmetrical structure. Melodies consisted of phrases that were generally four measures long, with a cadence at the end of each. For example:

The incomplete cadence, like the comma in punctuation, indicates that more is to come. The complete cadence, like the period in punctuation, gives a sense of finality. In the above example, the first and third phrases end in incomplete cadences. The final cadence is the point where the melody line reaches its destination and comes to rest.

b. Harmony (Background Material for Chapter 4)

Intervals. By an interval we mean the distance—that is the difference in pitch—between two tones; also the relationship between them. If two tones are sounded in succession they outline a melodic interval; if simultaneously, they establish a harmonic interval. The combination of the two tones creates a sonorous entity with a quality of its own quite distinct from either of its constituents.

Intervals are named according to the distance between the tones.

A minor interval is a half-tone smaller than a major interval. A diminished interval is a half-tone smaller than a perfect or minor interval. An augmented interval is a half-tone larger than a perfect or major interval.

Chords. Harmony pertains to the movement and relationship of chords. A chord may be defined as a combination of tones that occur simultaneously and are conceived as an entity. (In broken chords—arpeggios—the tones of the chord are heard in succession.) The melody unfolds above the harmony, and together they constitute a single entity.

The *triad* is a three-tone chord formed by combining every other degree of the scale; that is, steps 1–3–5 (*do-mi-sol*); 2–4–6 (*re-fa-la*); 3–5–7 (*mi-sol-ti*); 4–6–8 (*fa-la-do*), and so on. In other words, the triad consists of two intervals of a third superimposed upon each other. Following are triads based on the scale of C major.

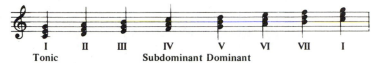

The tonic or I chord is the chord of rest. The other triads, representing a greater or lesser degree of activity, seek to be resolved to the tonic. The dominant or V chord represents a greater degree of activity than the subdominant or IV chord. The tonic, dominant, and subdominant triads suffice to harmonize many a famous tune, as in the following example:

Way down upon the   Swanee River   Far, far, a-way,
I——————————— IV——————— I——— V———
There's where my heart is turning ever, There's where the Old Folks stay.
I——————————————— IV—————————I——————————————— V———— I——
All the world is   sad and dreary,   Everywhere I   roam,
V——————————— I————————————— IV——————— I ——(V)———
Oh brothers, how my heart grows weary, Far from the Old Folks at home.
I ——————————————— IV ————————————— I ————————— V————————I——

When the process of chord building is carried one step further, we obtain a seventh chord (steps 1–3–5–7 of the scale, or 2–4–6–8, 3–5–7–9, and so on). Continuing the process of superimposing thirds, we obtain ninth chords (steps 1–3–5–7–9, 2–4–6–8–3, 3–5–7–9–4, and so on).

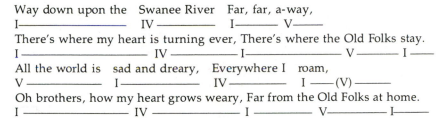

The dominant-seventh chord resolving to the tonic is the standard final cadence of the Classic-Romantic period. It is especially prominent in works dating from 1775–1825, the era of Haydn, Mozart, Beethoven, and Schubert.

c. Tonality (Background Material for Chapter 5)

If we look at the piano keyboard we observe that from one tone to its octave—for example, from C to the C above it—there are twelve keys, seven white and five black. These are a half tone or semitone apart. From C to C-sharp is a half tone; from C-sharp to D the same. From C to D is a whole tone. The seven white and five black keys thus represent the twelve semitones into which the octave is divided in our system of music.

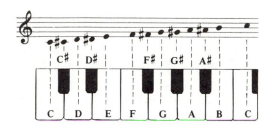

A scale is an arrangement of a series of tones in consecutive order, as-cending or descending. (The word is derived from the Latin *scala*, "ladder.") The twelve semitones of the octave pictured above comprise the chromatic scale. *Chromatic* implies movement by semitones.

A key is a group of related tones with a common center or tonic. This "loyalty to the tonic" is inculcated in us by most of the music we hear. It is the unifying force in the *do-re-mi-fa-sol-la-ti-do* scale. You can test for your-self how strong is the pull to the tonic by singing the first seven tones of this pattern, stopping on *ti*. You will experience an almost physical compulsion to resolve the *ti* up to *do*. This sense of relatedness to a central tone is what we mean by *tonality*. When we listen to a composition in the key of A we hear a piece based in large part upon the family of tones that revolve around and gravitate to the common center A.

A scale presents the tones of the key in consecutive order. It is, really, a statement of movement. The music of the eighteenth and nineteenth cen-turies was based on two contrasting scales, the *major* and the *minor*. These consisted of seven tones—eight, if you prefer, as the *do* is duplicated at the end of the series. The major scale is the familiar *do-re-mi-fa-sol-la-ti-do* pat-tern. Its seven tones were chosen out of the possible twelve in order to form a centralized family or key out of which musical compositions could be fash-ioned. The relationship of the major scale to the chromatic scale is manifest in the piano keyboard. The chromatic scale, we saw, included the seven white and five black keys. The major scale is sounded by the seven white keys from C to C. In other words, the major scale represents the "seven-out-of-twelve" way of listening that prevailed in the period from Bach and Han-del to Tchaikovsky and Brahms.

The Major-Minor System. If you look at the diagram of the keyboard given above, you will notice that the seven white keys from C to C are not equally distant from one another. Where the white keys have a black between, they are a whole tone (two half tones) apart. This is the rule, with two important exceptions: there is no black key between the third and fourth steps, E–F, and between the seventh and eighth steps, B–C. These tones, therefore, are a semitone apart. When we sing the *do-re-mi-fa-sol-la-ti-do* sequence we are measuring off a pattern of eight tones that are a whole tone apart except steps 3–4 (*mi-fa*) and 7–8 (*ti-do*). Sing this scale and try to distinguish between the whole- and half-tone distances.

The major scale implies certain relationships based on tension and resolution. We have already indicated the most important of these—the thrust of the seventh step to the eighth (*ti* seeking to be resolved to *do*). There are others. If we sing *do-re* we are left with a sense of incompleteness which is resolved when *re* moves down to *do*. *Fa* gravitates to *mi*; *la* descends to *sol*. Most important of all, the major scale defines the two poles of Classical harmony—the *do* or tonic, the point of ultimate rest; and the *sol* or dominant, representing the active harmony. Tonic going to dominant and returning to tonic became the basic progression of Classical harmony, as well as the basic principle of Classical form.

The major scale, we saw, is a "ladder" of whole and half tones. A ladder may be placed on high ground or low, but the distance between its steps remains the same. So too the major scale may be measured off from one starting point or another without affecting the sequence of whole and half steps within the pattern.

Any one of the twelve tones of our octave may serve as starting point for the scale. Whichever it is, that tone at once assumes the function of the tonic or key center. The other tones are chosen according to the pattern of the ladder. They immediately assume the functions of activity and rest implicit in the major scale. Most important, they all take on the impulse of gravitating more or less directly to the tonic.

With each different tonic we get another group of seven out of the possible twelve. In other words, every major scale has a different number of sharps or flats. The scale of C major is the only group that has no sharps or flats. If we build the major scale from G we must include an F-sharp in order to conform to the pattern of whole and half steps. (Try building the pattern whole step, whole step, half step, whole step, whole step, whole step, half step, from G. You will find that there is no F in this group.) If we build the major scale pattern from D, we get a group of seven that includes two sharps. If F is our starting point the scale includes B-flat. (See page 608 for table of major and minor scales.)

Whether the major scale begins on C, D, E, or any other tone, it follows the same model in the arrangement of the whole and half steps. This model is known as a *mode*. All the major scales exemplify the major mode of arranging whole and half steps. There is also a minor mode, which complements and serves as a foil to the major. This differs from the major primarily in that its third degree is flatted; that is, the scale of C minor has E-flat instead of E. In the harmonic minor the sixth step is also flatted: C–D–E♭–F–G–A♭–B–C. (The minor scale exists in two other versions, the melodic minor and natural minor.) The minor is pronouncedly different from the major in mood and coloring. *Minor*, the Latin word for "smaller," refers to the fact that the distinguishing interval C–E♭ is smaller than the corresponding interval C–E in the major ("larger") scale.

Like the major, the pattern of the minor mode may be duplicated from each of the twelve tones of the octave. In each case there will be another group of seven out of twelve—that is, the scale will have another number of sharps and flats. It becomes clear that every tone in the octave may serve as

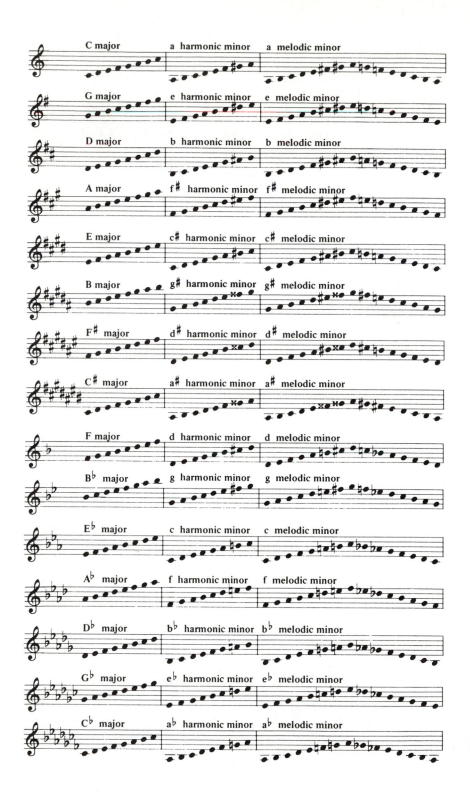

starting point or keynote for a major and minor scale. This gives us twelve major keys and twelve minor keys.

Just as we are able to build a scale from any one of twelve tones, we are able to sing or play the same melody beginning on C, C-sharp, D, and so on. In each case the tune will be in another key. The pitch and the keynote will be different, as will the number of sharps or flats. But the melody line will remain unchanged because the pattern of whole and half steps is retained in the new key as in the old. This is why the same song can be published in various keys for soprano, alto, tenor, or bass. When we shift a piece of music from one key to another we *transpose* it. Transposition should be carefully distinguished from *modulation,* the act of going from one key to another. Modulation is a highly emotional factor in music, for it opens up the circle of the key and shifts the listener into a new key area. Modulation consequently is a prime factor for variety in music. Transposition, on the other hand, is simply the shifting of the melody and its harmonies to a higher or lower key.

d. *Rhythm and Meter* (Background Material for Chapter 6)

Rhythm denotes the controlled movement of music in time. *Meter* denotes the organization of time within which that movement takes place. In other words, meter connotes the fixed time units—the *measures*—within which musical events unfold. Within these units the rhythm flows freely, now more, now less eventfully. Meter involves the arrangement of beats into measures, while rhythm pertains to the arrangement of time values within the measure. Every waltz has the same meter: ONE-two-three ONE-two-three. Within that meter, each waltz follows its own rhythm. In the jazz band, the drum, double bass, and the pianist's left hand establish the pattern of the meter. The melody instruments and the pianist's right hand articulate the rhythm that flows above that pattern.

In Classic-Romantic music meter depends upon the organization of time in equal measures marked by the regular recurrence of accent. There are two basic metrical patterns—duple and triple meter. Duple meter, generally encountered as two-four time (2/4), consists of a succession of beats in which a strong alternates with a weak: ONE-two ONE-two; or in marching, LEFT-right LEFT-right. That is to say, there are two beats in the measure, the accent on the first. The pattern is familiar from many nursery rhymes and marching songs.

Twín - kle	twín - kle	lít - tle	stár———,
ONE - two	ONE - two	ONE - two	ONE - two
Hów I	wón - der	whát you	áre———
ONE - two	ONE - two	ONE - two	ONE - two

The other basic metrical pattern is that of an accented beat followed by two unaccented: three beats to the measure, or triple meter. This is the pattern of three-four time (3/4) traditionally associated with the waltz and minuet. A celebrated example of triple meter is *The Star-Spangled Banner*.

Oh	sáy can you	sée_____by the
three	ONE - two - three	ONE - two - three

	dáwn's ear - ly	líght _____
	ONE - two - three	ONE - two

Duple and triple are the primary meters; all others are compound. By combining two measures of duple we obtain a measure of four beats, or quadruple meter. The primary accent falls on the first beat of the measure, with a subsidiary accent on the third: ONE-two-Three-four. Quadruple meter, generally encountered as four-four time (4/4), is found in some of our most widely sung melodies:

Wáy _____down u - pon the	Swá nee River_____
ONE two Three four	ONE two Three four

Fár, _____ fár a -	wáy _____
ONE - two Three - four	ONE two - Three - four

Two measures of triple time may be combined to make sextuple meter: six-four or six-eight time. This is often marked by a gently flowing effect.

Drínk to me ōn - - ly	wí - ith thine ēy - es and
ONE - two - three - Four - five - six	ONE - two - three - Four - five - six

Í _____will plē - edge with	míne _____
ONE - two - three - Four - five - six	ONE - two - three - Four - five - six

Other compound meters are based on five, seven, nine, eleven, or twelve beats to the measure. However, the four patterns just discussed are the ones most frequent in the music of the nineteenth century.

e. Tempo

Meter tells us how many beats there are in the measure, but it does not tell us whether these beats occur slowly or rapidly. The *tempo*, by which we mean the rate of speed, the pace of the music, provides the clue to this vital matter. Consequently the rhythmic organization of music involves three things: meter, which organizes musical time into measures; rhythm, which organizes time values within the measure; and tempo, which determines the speed of the measures, their duration in actual time.

Because of the close connection between tempo and mood, tempo markings have come to indicate not only the pace of the music but its character as well. The tempo terms are generally given in Italian, a survival from the time when the opera of that nation dominated the European scene. Most frequently encountered are the following.

Very slow: *Largo* (literally, "broad")
              Grave (literally, "heavy")

Slow: *Lento*
              Adagio (literally, "at ease")

Moderate: *Andante* (literally, "going")—at a walking pace
              Andantino—somewhat faster than *andante,* "sauntering"
              Moderato

Fairly fast: *Allegretto* (literally, "a little lively")—not as fast as *allegro*

Fast: *Allegro* (literally, "cheerful," "happy," "lively")

Very fast: *Vivo*—lively
              Vivace—vivacious
              Allegro molto—very fast
              Presto—quick
              Prestissimo—as quick as possible

As important as the tempo terms are those indicating a change of pace. The principal ones are *accelerando* (getting faster) and *ritardando* (holding back, getting slower); *a tempo* (in time) indicates a return to the original tempo.

f. Dynamics

Dynamics denotes the degree of loudness or softness at which the music is played. Modern instruments place a wide gamut of dynamic effects at the composer's disposal. The principal dynamic indications are:

Very soft: *pianissimo (pp)*
Soft: *piano (p)*
Moderately soft: *mezzo piano (mp)*

Moderately loud: *mezzo forte (mf)*
Loud: *forte (f)*
Very loud: *fortissimo (ff)*

As the modern orchestra increased in size and precision, composers extended the range of dynamic shadings in both directions, so that we find *ppp* and *fff*. In late nineteenth-century scores, four and even five *p*'s or *f*'s were used.

Of special importance are the changes in dynamics. The commonest are:

Growing louder: *crescendo* (◁━━━)
Growing softer: *decrescendo* or *diminuendo* (━━━▷)
Sudden stress: *sforzando* (*sf*), literally, "forced"—accent on a single note or chord

8. *Devices of Counterpoint* (Background Material for Chapter 7)

When several independent lines are combined, composers try to give unity and shape to the texture. A basic procedure for achieving this end is *imitation,* in which a *subject* or motive is presented in one voice and then duplicated in another. While the imitating voice restates the theme, the first voice goes on to a *countersubject.* This duplication of an idea—at different times and pitches—by all the voice parts is of the essence in contrapuntal thinking.

How long is the statement that is to be imitated? This varies considerably. It may be the entire length of a voice part that runs from the beginning to end of a piece. Or the imitation may occur intermittently. When the whole length of a voice part is imitated, we have a strict type of composition known as a *canon.* The name comes from the Greek word for "law" or "order." Each phrase heard in the leading voice is repeated almost immediately in an imitating voice throughout the length of the work. The most popular form of canon is the *round,* in which each voice enters in succession with the same melody. Composers do not often cast an entire piece or movement in the shape of a canon. What they do is to use canonic imitation as an effect in all sorts of pieces.

Contrapuntal writing is marked by a number of devices that have flourished for centuries. *Inversion* is a species of imitation in which the melody is turned upside down; that is, it follows the same intervals but in the opposite direction. Where the melody originally moved up by a third, the inversion moves down a third. Where it descended by a fourth, it now ascends a fourth. Thus, D–E–F inverted becomes D–C–B. *Augmentation* consists of imitating a theme in longer time values. A quarter note may become a half, a half note a whole, and so on. In consequence, the theme in its new version sounds slower. *Diminution* consists of imitating a theme in shorter time values. A whole note may become a half, a half note a quarter, which makes the theme in its new version sound faster. *Retrograde,* also known as *cancrizans* or *crab motion,* means to imitate the melody backwards. If the original sequence of notes reads B–D–G–F, the imitation reads F–G–D–B. Retrograde-and-inversion imitates the theme by turning it upside down and backwards. These devices of sixteenth-century counterpoint have been revived in contemporary music, especially by Arnold Schoenberg and his school.

The Fugue. From the art and science of counterpoint issued one of the most exciting types of Baroque music, the *fugue.* The name is derived from *fuga,* the Latin for "flight," implying a flight of fancy (possibly the flight of the theme from one voice to the other). In a fugue, several independent voices—generally three or four—take turns in presenting a striking theme or subject. A fugue may be written for a group of instruments; for a solo instrument such as organ, harpsichord, or even violin; for several solo voices or for full chorus. Whether the fugue is vocal or instrumental, the several lines are called *voices*, which indicates the origin of the type. In vocal and orchestral fugues each line is articulated by another performer or group of performers. In fugues for keyboard instruments the ten fingers—on the organ, the feet as well—manage the complex interweaving of the voices.

The subject is stated at the outset in one of the voices (soprano, alto, tenor, or bass) without accompaniment. It is then imitated in another voice—this is the answer—while the first continues with a countertheme or countersubject. It will then appear in a third voice and be answered in the fourth, if there are four, while the first two weave a free contrapuntal texture against these. When the theme has appeared in each voice once, the first section of the fugue—the *exposition*—is at an end. The exposition may be repeated, in which case the voices will enter in a different order. From there on the fugue alternates between exposition sections that feature the entrance of the subject, and less weighty interludes known as *episodes*. The latter serve as areas of relaxation.

Each recurrence of the theme reveals new facets of its nature. It may be presented in longer or shorter note values, turned upside down, presented backwards, or upside down and backwards. It may be combined with new subjects or with some other version of itself. It may be presented softly or vigorously. The composer manipulates the subject as pure musical material in the same way that the sculptor molds his clay. Especially effective is the *stretto* (from the Italian for "close") in which the theme is imitated in close succession, with the subject entering in one voice before it has been completed in another. The effect is one of voices crowding upon each other, creating a heightening of tension that brings the fugue to its climax. There follows the final statement of the subject, generally in triumphal mood. The mission has been accomplished, the tension released.

Another important form of contrapuntal music is the *concerto grosso*, a composition based on the opposition between two dissimilar masses of sound. (The verb *concertare* means "to fight side by side," "to vie with one another as brothers in arms.") A small group of instruments known as the *concertino* is pitted against the large group, the concerto grosso or tutti. The contrast is one of color and dynamics. The concerto grosso was extensively cultivated during the Baroque era, and has been revived in the twentieth century.

h. Instruments of the Orchestra (Background Material for Chapter 8)

The same tone will sound different when produced by a trumpet or a violin. The difference lies in the characteristic color, or *timbre*, of each instrument. (The word retains its French pronunciation, *tam'br*.) Timbre focuses our musical impressions. By the way in which the composer chooses his timbres, blending and contrasting them, he creates the particular sound-world that a given piece inhabits.

The orchestra is organized in four sections or choirs—string, woodwind, brass, and percussion. Known as "the heart of the orchestra," the string section played a most important part—both for lyric and dramatic effects—in the scores of the Classic-Romantic era. The string section includes four instruments—violin, viola, cello, and double bass—which correspond roughly to soprano, alto, tenor, and bass. In these instruments the strings are set vibrating by the action of the bow. The player *stops* the string by pressing down a finger of his left hand at a particular point, thereby changing the length of that portion of the string which is free to vibrate, and with it the rate of vibration and the pitch.

The string instruments are preeminent in playing *legato* (smooth and connected), though they are capable too of the opposite quality of tone, *staccato* (short and detached). A special effect, *pizzicato* ("plucked"), is executed by the performer's plucking the string with his finger instead of playing with the bow, thereby producing a guitarlike tone. *Vibrato* refers to the throbbing tone which the violinist achieves by moving his finger slightly away from and back to the required spot, thus enriching the resonance. In *glissando* the player moves his hand rapidly along the string, sounding all the pitches of the scale. *Tremolo*, the rapid repetition of a tone through a quick up-and-down movement of the bow, is associated in the popular mind with suspense and excitement. No less important is the *trill*, a rapid alternation between a tone and its neighbor, giving a birdlike effect. *Double-stopping* involves playing on two strings simultaneously. It is possible too to sound three or four notes together. Thereby the violin, essentially a melody instrument, becomes capable of harmony. The *mute* is a three-pronged clamp which is slipped onto the bridge of the instrument to muffle the tone. *Harmonics* are flutelike crystalline tones in the very high register, produced by lightly touching the string at certain points instead of stopping it in the usual way.

The woodwind section of the orchestra consists of four principal instruments—flute, oboe, clarinet, and bassoon. Each of these is supplemented by at least one instrument of the same family: the flute by the piccolo, the oboe by the English horn, the clarinet by the bass clarinet, and the bassoon by the contrabassoon. Saxophones too are included in this group. The woodwinds are not as homogeneous a group as the strings. They are not necessarily made of wood; and they represent several methods of setting in vibration the column of air within the tube. The clarinet and saxophone are single-reed instruments; the oboe and bassoon are double-reed instruments; while in the flute the player blows directly across a mouth hole cut in the side of the pipe (the *embouchure*). The woodwinds do, however, have two features in common: first, the holes in the side of the pipe; and second, their timbres, which are such that composers think of them and write for them as a group. Because they are more vivid and distinctive in color than the more neutral strings, they must be used somewhat more sparingly.

The brass section is the "heavy artillery" of the orchestra. Its four members—trumpet, horn, trombone, and tuba—are indispensable for melody, for sustaining harmony, for rhythmic accent, for the weight of their massed tone, and for the flamelike sonority they contribute to climaxes. These instruments have a cup-shaped mouthpiece. The column of air within the tube is set vibrating by the tightly stretched lips of the player, which act as a kind of double reed. To go from one pitch to another requires not only mechanical means, such as a slide or valves, but also variation in the pressure of the lips and breath, which demands great muscular control. Fatigue of the lip muscles will cause even an expert player to go off pitch.

The percussion section, sometimes referred to as "the battery," comprises a variety of instruments that are made to sound by striking or shaking. Certain ones consist of an elastic material such as metal or wood. In others, such as the drums, vibration is set up by striking a stretched skin. The percussion instruments fall into two categories, those of definite and those of indefinite pitch. In the former class are the kettledrums or timpani, which are used in sets of two or three. Also of definite pitch are the glockenspiel, celesta, xylophone, marimba, and chimes. Among the percussion instruments of indefinite pitch are the bass drum, the side drum (also known as snare drum); tambourine and castanets; the triangle, cymbals, and gong. We have mentioned in the text, in connection with particular works, such exotic percussion instruments as the guiro, claves, and bongo drums.

The harp, a plucked-string instrument, is a charter member of the orchestra. Modern orchestral scores frequently call for a piano. The orchestra as a whole is constituted with a view to securing the best balance of tone. Approximately two-thirds of the ensemble are string players, one-third are wind players. The following distribution is typical of our larger orchestras.

Strings, about 65:	18 first violins 16 second violins 12 violas 10 violoncellos 10 double basses
Woodwinds, about 15:	3 flutes, 1 piccolo 3 oboes, 1 English horn 3 clarinets, 1 bass clarinet 3 bassoons, 1 double bassoon
Brass, 11:	4 horns 3 trumpets 3 trombones 1 tuba
Percussion, 5:	2 kettledrum players 3 men for bass and side drum, glockenspiel, celesta, xylophone, triangle, cymbals, tambourine, etc.

The conductor has before him the score of the work. This consists of from a few to as many as twenty-five or more lines, each representing an instrumental part. All the staves together comprise a single composite line. What is going on at any moment in the orchestra is indicated at any given point straight down the page. (See music examples on pages 44 and 45.) The term *tutti* ("all") refers to the orchestra as a whole. The term *concertante*, on the other hand, refers to an orchestral style in which single instruments or groups are pitted against each other in a soloistic manner.

The following table illustrates the comparative range of the various instruments.

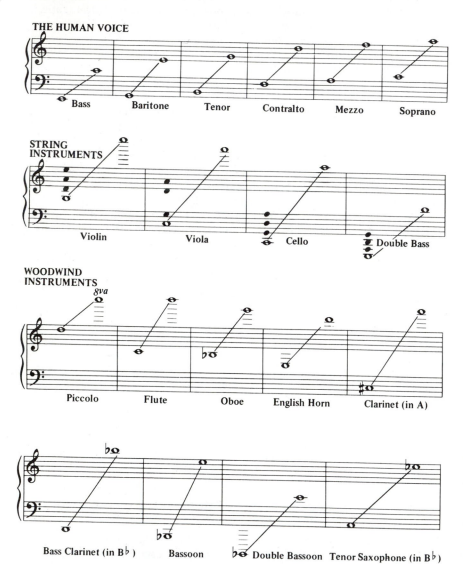

BRASS INSTRUMENTS

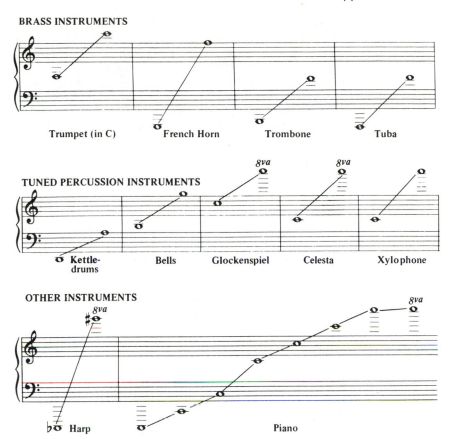

Trumpet (in C)   French Horn   Trombone   Tuba

TUNED PERCUSSION INSTRUMENTS

Kettle-drums   Bells   Glockenspiel   Celesta   Xylophone

OTHER INSTRUMENTS

Harp   Piano

i. The Large Musical Forms (Background Material for Chapter 9)

The Sonata-Symphony. The grand form in music, the sonata-symphony, is based on the exposition, development, and restatement of themes. The theme becomes the first in a chain of musical situations, all of which grow out of the basic idea as naturally as does the plant from the seed. Hence the term *germ theme*, which indicates the capacity of the initial idea to flower, to expand, and to develop in such a way as to create an effect of organic unity. The most tightly knit kind of expansion in our music is known as *thematic development*. To develop a theme means to unfold its latent energies, to search out its capacities for growth and bring them to fruition.

In the process of development, certain procedures have proved to be particularly effective. The simplest is repetition, which may occur either at the same pitch or at another. A basic technique is the breaking up of the theme into its constituent fragments, the *motives*. A motive is the smallest segment of a theme that forms a melodic-rhythmic unit. The motives are the germ cells of musical growth. Through fragmentation of themes, through repeating and varying the motives and combining them in ever fresh patterns, the composer imparts to the musical organism the quality of dynamic evolution and growth. Development may also proceed by imitation—that is, the theme is presented in one voice and forthwith imitated in another. Or the theme may be combined with other melody lines or fragments in an intricate texture. Through these and kindred devices the theme takes on fresh forms and displays unsuspected facets of its personality.

The name sonata comes from the Italian *suonare,* "to sound," indicating a piece to be sounded on instruments, as distinct from *cantata,* a piece to be sung. A sonata is an instrumental work consisting of a cycle of contrasting movements, generally three or four in number. The name sonata is used when the music is intended for one or two instruments. If more than two are involved the work is called, as the case may be, a trio, quartet, quintet, sextet, septet, octet, or nonet. A sonata for solo instrument and orchestra is called a concerto; for full orchestra, a symphony. The sonata cycle, clearly, accounts for a large part of the instrumental music we hear.

The First Movement. The most highly organized and characteristic member of the several movements that make up the cycle is the opening *allegro.* This is in *sonata form.* The terms *first-movement form* and *sonata-allegro form* are also used to describe this movement. *First-movement form* is somewhat misleading, as this type of structure is also used for the last movement. *Sonata-allegro form* correctly suggests that this type of structure is at its most characteristic in a lively or allegro movement, but fails to take into account that slow movements, especially in the eighteenth-century symphony, were also cast in this form.

Sonata form is summed up in the following somewhat simplified outline:

Exposition	*Development*	*Recapitulation* (or *Restatement*)
(Slow introduction)	Frequent modulation (away from home key)	First theme or thematic group in home key
First theme or theme group in home key	Fragmentation and manipulation of themes	Bridge
Bridge—modulates	Building up of tension against return to home key	Second theme or thematic group transposed to home key (or close to it)
Second theme or thematic group in contrasting key	Retransition to home key	Coda. Cadence in home key
Codetta. Cadence in contrasting key		

Even as the dramatist creates opposing personalities as the chief characters of his work, so the composer achieves a vivid contrast between the musical ideas that form the basis of the movement. The opposition between two themes may be underlined in a number of ways: through a contrast in dynamics—loud against soft; in register—low against high; timbre—strings against winds, one instrumental combination against another; rhythm and tempo—an animated pattern against one that is sustained; tone quality—legato against staccato; type of melody—an active melody line with wide range and leaps against one that is quieter; type of harmony—consonance against dissonance, diatonic harmony against chromatic; type of accompaniment—quietly moving chords against extended arpeggios. One contrast is required, being the basis of the form: the contrast of key. And the opposition may be further intensified by putting one theme in the major and the other in minor.

The conventional description of sonata form, by its emphasis upon the two or three themes that serve as building blocks for an instrumental movement, seems to imply that everything between these themes is in the nature of transitional material. On the contrary: the sonata movement is an organic unity in which the growth, the development, the destiny of the idea is no less important than the idea itself (just as in a human action whose consequences are no less important than the deed proper). From the symphonic point of view the theme includes not only the germinal idea *but also its expansion and development;* not only the few notes given in the musical examples in the text but also the *"etc."*—that is, the passage or section into which the initial idea flowers. It is only when we take this larger view of the theme that we come to understand the symphonic movement for what it is: a continuous expansion and growth of musical ideas from first note to last, from which not a measure may be omitted without disturbing the equilibrium and the organic oneness of the whole.

The Other Movements. The second movement of the symphonic cycle is generally the slow movement. This may be a simple A-B-A form, in which the middle section contrasts with the outer two. Or it may be a theme and variations. Or, as we already have indicated, it could be—and in the eighteenth-century symphony frequently was—a sonata form. The third movement in the Classical cycle was the minuet and trio, an A-B-A form in which the minuet was repeated after the middle part (the trio). The minuet was displaced, in the nineteenth-century symphony, by the scherzo, which differs from the minuet in its headlong pace, vigorous rhythm, and more varied character.

The final movement in the Classical cycle was often a rondo. This is a movement consisting of symmetrical sections and based on the recurrence of a central idea—the rondo theme—in alternation with one or more subsidiary themes; as in the pattern A-B-A-B-A, in which there is only one other theme; or A-B-A-C-A, where there are two; or some variation, as in the pattern A-B-A-C-A-B-A. The rondo furnished a happy ending for the Classical symphony. The final movement might also be a rondo-sonata, a type that joined the lightness of the rondo with the developmental procedures of sonata form; or a theme and variations; or a sonata form. Nineteenth-century composers favored a large sonata form that would balance the first movement and bring the symphony to a rousing conclusion.

Following is an outline of the cycle of movements in the sonata-symphony of the Classic-Romantic era:

MOVE-MENT	FORM	CHARACTER	TEMPO	
			Mozart: Symphony No. 40	*Beethoven: Symphony No. 5*
First	Sonata form	Epic-dramatic	*Allegro molto*	*Allegro con brio*
Second	A-B-A Sonata form Theme and variations	Slow lyrical movement. May range, however, from the whimsical to the tragic	*Andante*	*Andante con moto*
Third	A-B-A	Dance movement: Minuet (18th century) Scherzo (19th century) Both in 3/4 time	*Allegretto*	*Allegro*
Fourth	Rondo Sonata form Rondo-sonata Theme and variations	Lively finale (18th century Triumphal ending: the Romantic "apotheosis" (19th century)	*Allegro molto*	*Allegro*

(For a more detailed discussion of melody, harmony, tonality, rhythm and meter, tempo, dynamics, devices of counterpoint, instruments of the orchestra, form, and the sonata-symphony, see the appropriate chapters in Machlis, *The Enjoyment of Music*, Fourth Edition.)

j. The "Chord of Nature": The Harmonic Series

Musical tones are produced by vibrations. The pitch of a tone—by which we mean its location in the musical scale in relation to high or low—is determined by the rate of vibration. This in turn depends on the length of the vibrating body. The shorter a string or column of air, the more rapidly it vibrates and the higher the pitch. The longer a string or column of air, the fewer the vibrations per second and the lower the pitch. The width, thickness, density, and tension of the vibrating body also affect the outcome.

When a string or a column of air vibrates, it does so not only as a whole but also in segments—halves, thirds, fourths, fifths, sixths, sevenths, and so on. These segments produce the *overtones*, which are also known as *partials* or *harmonics*. What we hear as the single tone is really the combination of the fundamental tone and its overtones, just as what we see as white light is the combination of all the colors of the spectrum. Although we may not be conscious of the partials, they play a decisive part in our listening; for the presence or absence of overtones in the sound wave determines the timbre, the color of the tone. Following is the table of the Chord of Nature: the fundamental and its overtones or harmonics. Those marked with an asterisk are not in tune with our tempered scale.

The fundamental tone and its overtones comprise the harmonic series, the "Chord of Nature" that resounds when any string or column of air is set vibrating. Half the string gives the second member of the series, the octave above fundamental. This interval is represented by the ratio 1:2; that is to say, the two tones of this interval are produced when one string is half as long as the other and is vibrating twice as fast. The one-third segment of the string produces the third member of the harmonic series, the fifth above the octave. This interval is represented by the ratio 2:3. We hear it when one string is two-thirds as long as the other and is vibrating one and a half times (3/2) as fast. The one-fourth segment of the string produces the fourth member of the series, the fourth above. This interval is represented by the ratio 3:4, for its two tones are produced when one string is three-fourths as long as the other and vibrates one and a third times (4/3) as fast. One fifth of the string produces the fifth member of the harmonic series, the major third, an interval represented by the ratio 4:5. Its two tones are produced when one string is four-fifths as long as the other and vibrates one and a fourth (5/4) times as fast. One sixth of the string produces the sixth member of the series, the minor third, represented by the ratio 5:6; and so on. As the segments grow shorter, the intervals they produce grow correspondingly smaller. From the seventh to the eleventh partials we find whole tones; this interval is represented by the ratio 7:8. Between the eleventh harmonic and its octave, 22, the semitone appears. This interval is represented by the ratio 11:12. After partial 22 we enter the realm of microtones—third tones, quarter tones, sixth and eighth tones, and so on.

The triad is given by the first six tones of the series, specifically by tones 4–5–6. The chord of the dominant seventh is represented by tones

4–5–6–7; the dominant ninth chord by tones 4–5–6–7–9; an eleventh chord by tones 4–5–6–7–9–11; and a thirteenth chord by tones 4–5–6–7–9–11–13.

The evolution of man's harmonic sense seems to have followed the harmonic series. Music began as monophonic—that is, single-line melody. In other words, the early musicians were aware only of the fundamental. The Greeks appear to have developed a style of singing in which men and women, or men and boys, sang the same melody an octave and/or a fifth apart. In other words, the ancients discovered the perfect consonances—octave, fifth, fourth—formed by the first four tones of the harmonic series. This covers the period of ancient and primitive music, up to the period of organum about a thousand years ago. Toward the end of the Middle Ages the major third and the minor third were accepted, first as dissonances, ultimately as imperfect consonances. This made possible the introduction of the triad (tones 4–5–6 of the series), and prepared the way for the supplanting of the medieval modes by triadic harmony—a development that carried music well into the Renaissance. The dominant seventh chord (tones 4–5–6–7 of the series) was a governing force in harmony throughout the Baroque and Classical eras. With the addition of the ninth overtone, which introduces the chord of the dominant ninth (tones 4–5–6–7–9 of the series), we are in the period of Wagner, Liszt, and César Franck. Thus, by the end of the nineteenth century Western harmony had pretty thoroughly explored the possibilities of the first nine tones of the Chord of Nature.

Debussy's experiments, which ushered in the twentieth century, centered about the whole-tone scale: tones 7, 8, 9, 10, 11, 13 of the series. At the same time composers moved forward to the eleventh and thirteenth chords formed by those harmonics. The next step was taken with the turning from triadic to quartal harmony: from chords based on the third to those based on the fourth. A leader in this development was Scriabin, whose "mystic chord" consisted of tones 8, 11, 14, 10, 13, and 9 of the harmonic series. (For this chord and other examples of quartal harmony, see page 22.) In other words, twentieth-century harmony moved with astonishing rapidity to explore the higher overtones of the harmonic series. This development was given enormous impetus by Schoenberg, who based his harmonic language on the chromatic—better, the twelve-tone—scale found in the harmonic series between tones 11 and 22. Indeed, theorists used to explain the difference between Stravinsky and Schoenberg by saying that Schoenberg's harmony explored higher overtones than did Stravinsky's. (This, of course, was in the days before Stravinsky turned to twelve-tone music.)

If the historical analogy holds, then the next century will be spent in exploring still higher reaches of the Chord of Nature—that is to say, the realm of microtones now being opened up by the development of electronic music.

The harmonic series shows why the octave is the basic interval in all music. The octave is the first overtone, and is so close to the fundamental that when both tones are struck together they practically sound like one.

k. The Twelve-Tone Method

As originally formulated by Schoenberg, the twelve-tone method "consists primarily of the constant and exclusive use of a set of twelve different tones." No tone is repeated within the set, and all twelve tones must be used. Here is a typical set, that of Schoenberg's *Suite*, Opus 25:

In addition to the original form, the set may also be used in its mirror forms—that is, retrograde (the notes in reverse order, from back to front), inversion (the intervals in the opposite direction—those that went down now go up the same distance), and retrograde inversion (the inversion backwards). Here are these forms of the set given above.

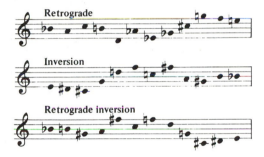

In addition, each of these four forms may be transposed to begin on any of the twelve notes, yielding a total of forty-eight possible forms of the set, all of which preserve the interval succession of the original. A note within a set may be played in any octave: thus, a C may be middle C, the C an octave above, or any other C. The above set might thus be used in the following form:

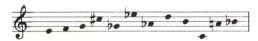

There is no requirement that all the available forms of a set be used in a particular piece, and Schoenberg normally confined himself to relatively few, especially in shorter pieces. He discovered early that certain forms of certain sets had musically useful relationships (and others have since discovered more about such sets and their properties). For example, in the basic set of the *Suite*, Opus 25, there is a conspicuous tritone (diminished fifth or augmented fourth) between the third and fourth notes (G–C♮); at a certain transposition of the set, the corresponding tritone is formed of the same notes, though in reverse order. And a certain inversion of the basic set also gives these same notes in the same reverse order (the example shows only the first four notes of the set, for simplicity's sake):

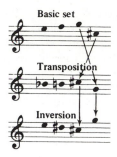

Many similar and more extensive relationships among the forms of certain sets have been discovered and musically exploited by Schoenberg and his successors. For a fuller discussion, the interested reader is referred to George Perle, *Serial Composition and Atonality* (see Bibliography).

The sets of other twelve-tone works discussed in this book are given below. The original version is labelled O, the retrograde R, the inversion I, and the retrograde inversion RI.

a. Schoenberg, *Variations*, Opus 31

b. Webern, *Symphony*, Opus 21

This row has special characteristics. The second six notes are the (transposed) retrograde of the first six. Thus, if the whole row is transposed up a tritone, it is exactly equivalent to the retrograde form shown above.

c. Schoenberg, *A Survivor from Warsaw*

Appendix II Texts and Translations of Vocal Works

Mahler, *Das Lied von der Erde*

I. Das Trinklied vom Jammer der Erde

I. The Drinking Song of the Earth's Lament

Schon winkt der Wein im gold'nen Po-
kale,
Doch trinkt noch nicht, erst sing' ich
euch ein Lied!
Das Lied vom Kummer
Soll auflachend in die Seele euch
klingen.
Wenn der Kummer naht,
Liegen wüst die Gärten der Seele,
Welkt hin und stirbt die Freude, der
Gesang.
Dunkel ist das Leben, ist der Tod.

Herr dieses Hauses!
Dein Keller birgt die Fülle des goldenen
Weins!

The wine gleams in the golden goblet,

But do not drink yet—first I'll sing you a
song!
Let the song of sorrow
Resound with laughter in your souls.

When sorrow approaches,
The gardens of the soul lie waste,
Joy and song wither away and die.

Dark is life, dark is death.

Master of this house!
Your cellar hides a wealth of golden
wine.

Hier, diese Laute nenn' ich mein!
Die Laute schlagen und die Gläser
  leeren,
Das sind die Dinge, die zusammen pas-
  sen.
Ein voller Becher Weins zur rechten Zeit
Ist mehr wert, als alle Reiche dieser
  Erde!
Dunkel ist das Leben, ist der Tod.

Das Firmament blaut ewig und die Erde

Wird lange fest steh'n und aufblühn im
  Lenz.
Du aber, Mensch, wie lang lebst denn
  du?
Nicht hundert Jahre darfst du dich
  ergötzen
An all dem morschen Tande dieser Erde!

Seht dort hinab! Im Mondschein auf den
  Gräbern
Hockt eine wild-gespenstische Gestalt—
Ein Aff' ist's! Hört ihr, wie sein Heulen
Hinausgellt in den süssen Duft des Le-
  bens!

Jetzt nehmt den Wein! Jetzt ist es Zeit,
  Genossen!
Leert eure gold'nen Becher zu Grund!
Dunkel ist das Leben, ist der Tod!

But I can call this lute my own!
The lutes resound and the wine glasses
  are emptied.
These are the things that go well
  together.
A full cup of wine at the right time
Is worth more than all the treasures of
  this earth.
Dark is life, dark is death.

The firmament is forever blue, and the
  earth
Will stand firm and blossom in the
  spring.
But you, o mortal, how long is your
  span?
You have no hundred years to delight

In all the fleeting pleasures of this earth!

Look over there! In the moonlight on the
  graves
A ghostly apparition crouches.
It is an ape! Listen, how his howling
Cuts across the sweet scent of life!

Now drink the wine. Now it is time, my
  friends!
Drain your golden cups to the botton.
Dark is life, dark is death!

II. *Der Einsame im Herbst*

Herbstnebel wallen bläulich überm See;
Vom Reif bezogen stehen alle Gräser;
Man meint, ein Künstler habe Staub von
  Jade
Über die feinen Blüten ausgestreut.

Der süsse Duft der Blumen ist verflogen;
Ein kalter Wind beugt ihre Stengel nie-
  der.
Bald werden die verwelkten, gold'nen
  Blätter
Der Lotosblüten auf dem Wasser zieh'n.

Mein Herz ist müde. Meine kleine
  Lampe

II. *The Lonely One in Autumn*

Bluish autumn mists drift over the sea;
The grass is covered with frost.
One would think an artist had scattered

Dust of jade over the delicate leaves.

The sweet scent of flowers has vanished;
A cold winds bends the stems.

Soon the faded golden leaves of the lotus
  blossoms
Will float on the water.

My heart is weary. My little lamp

Erlosch mit Knistern, es gemahnt mich
  an den Schlaf.
Ich komm' zu dir, traute Ruhestätte!
Ja, gib mir Ruh', ich hab' Erquickung
  not!

Ich weine viel in meinen Einsamkeiten.
Der Herbst in meinem Herzen währt zu
  lange.
Sonne der Liebe, willst du nie mehr
  scheinen,
Um meine bittern Tränen mild aufzu-
  trocknen?

Goes out sputtering, I long for sleep.

I come to you, trusty house of rest!
Yes, give me rest, for I have need of re-
  freshment!

I weep often in my loneliness.
The autumn in my heart lasts too long.

O bright sun of love, will you shine no
  more
And gently dry my bitter tears?

III. *Von der Jugend*

Mitten in dem kleinen Teiche
Steht ein Pavillon aus grünem
Und aus weissem Porzellan.

Wie der Rücken eines Tigers
Wölbt die Brücke sich aus Jade
Zu dem Pavillon hinüber.

In dem Häuschen sitzen Freunde,
Schön gekleidet, trinken, plaudern,
Manche schreiben Verse nieder.

Ihre seidnen Ärmel gleiten
Rückwärts, ihre seidnen Mützen
Hocken lustig tief im Nacken.

Auf des kleinen Teiches stiller
Wasserfläche zeigt sich alles
Wunderlich im Spiegelbilde.

Alles auf dem Kopfe stehend
In dem Pavillon aus grünem
Und aus weissem Porzellan;

Wie ein Halbmond steht die Brücke,
Umgekehrt der Bogen. Freunde,
Schön gekleidet, trinken, plaudern.

III. *Of Youth*

In the middle of the little pond
There stands a pavilion
Of green and white porcelain.

Like a tiger's back
A bridge of jade
Arches to the pavilion beyond.

In the little house friends sit,
Well-dressed, drinking, chatting;
Some are writing little verses.

Their silken sleeves slip
Backward, their silken caps
Perch merrily on the back of their heads

In the quiet surface of the little pond
Everything is reflected
Wonderfully, as in a mirror.

Everything standing on its head
In the pavilion
Of green and white porcelain;

Like a half-moon stands the bridge,
With its arch upside down. Friends,
Well dressed, drink and chat. . . .

IV. *Von der Schönheit*

Junge Mädchen pflücken Blumen,
Pflücken Lotosblumen an dem Ufer-
  rande.

IV. *Of Beauty*

Young maidens pick flowers,
Pick lotus flowers on the river bank.

Zwischen Büschen und Blättern sitzen
    sie,
Sammeln Blüten in den Schoss und
    rufen
Sich einander Neckereien zu.

Gold'ne Sonne webt um die Gestalten,
Spiegelt sie im blanken Wasser wider.

Sonne spiegelt ihre schlanken Glieder,

Ihre süssen Augen wide,
Und der Zephir hebt mit Schmeichel-
    kosen
Das Gewebe ihrer Ärmel auf,
Führt den Zauber
Ihrer Wohlgerüche durch die Luft.

O sieh, was tummeln sich für schöne
    Knaben
Dort an dem Uferrand auf mut'gen Ros-
    sen,
Weithin glänzend wie die Sonnen-
    strahlen;
Schon zwischen dem Geäst der grünen
    Weiden
Trabt das jungfrische Volk einher!

Das Ross des einen wiehert fröhlich auf

Und scheut und saust dahin,
Über Blumen, Gräser wanken hin die
    Hufe,
Sie zerstampfen jäh im Sturm die hinge-
    sunk'nen Blüten.
Hei! Wie flattern im Taumel seine
    Mähnen,
Dampfen heiss die Nüstern!

Gold'ne Sonne webt um die Gestalten,

Spiegelt sie im blanken Wasser wider.
Und die schönste von den Jungfrau'n
    sendet
Lange Blicke ihm der Sehnsucht nach.
Ihre stolze Haltung ist nur Verstellung.
In dem Funkeln ihrer grossen Augen,
In dem Dunkel ihres heissen Blicks
Schwingt klagend noch die Erregung
    ihres Herzens nach.

They sit among the bushes and leaves,

Gathering blossoms in their lap and
    calling
Each other all kinds of teasing names.

The golden sunlight envelops them,
Throwing their reflection in the glisten-
    ing water.
The sunshine mirrors their slender
    limbs
And their sweet eyes,
And the gentle breeze with a
    caress
Lifts the fabric of their sleeves,
Wafting the magic
Of their fragrance through the air.

O see, where a group of handsome lads

Rides noisily along the bank on bold
    steeds,
Glistening far-off like the rays of the
    sun;
Already through the branches of the
    green willows
The youthful company advances, trot-
    ting gaily!
The horse of one of the youths neighs
    delightedly,
Shies and dashes forward,
His hoofs poised over flowers and grass,

Trampling like a storm the hidden blos-
    soms.
Hei! His mane waves in a frenzy,

His nostrils steaming.

Golden sunlight envelops the young fig-
    ures,
Mirrors them in the shining water.
And the loveliest of the maidens

Sends him a parting glance of longing.
Her proud bearing is only a pretense.
In the sparkle of her wide eyes,
In the darkness of her hot glance
There reveals itself sadly the excitement
    of her heart.

V. Der Trunkene im Frühling

Wenn nur ein Traum das Leben ist,
Warum denn Müh und Plag'!?
Ich trinke, bis ich nicht mehr kann,
Den ganzen, lieben Tag!
Und wenn ich nicht mehr trinken kann,
Weil Kehl' und Seele voll,
So tauml' ich bis zu meiner Tür
Und schlafe wundervoll!

Was hör ich beim Erwachen? Horch!

Ein Vogel singt im Baum.
Ich frag' ihn ob schon Frühling sei,
Mir ist als wie im Traum.
Der Vogel zwitschert: Ja!
Der Lenz ist da, sei kommen über
    Nacht!
Aus tiefstem Schauen lauscht' ich auf,
Der Vogel singt und lacht!

Ich fülle mir den Becher neu
Und leer' ihn bis zum Grund
Und singe, bis der Mond erglänzt
Am schwarzen Firmament!
Und wenn ich nicht mehr singen kann,
So schlaf' ich wieder ein,
Was geht mich denn der Frühling an!?
Lasst mich betrunken sein!

VI. Der Abschied

Die Sonne scheidet hinter dem Gebirge.
In alle Täler steigt der Abend nieder
Mit seinen Schatten, die voll Kühlung
    sind.
O sieh! Wie eine Silberbarke schwebt
Der Mond am blauen Himmelssee
    herauf.
Ich spüre eines feinen Windes Weh'n
Hinter den dunklen Fichten!

Der Bach singt voller Wohllaut durch
    das Dunkel.
Die Blumen blassen im Dämmerschein.
Die Erde atmet voll von Ruh' und Schaf,

Alle Sehnsucht will nun träumen.
Die müden Menschen geh'n heimwärts,
Um im Schlaf vergess'nes Glück

V. The Drunken One in Spring

Since life is but a dream,
Why then toil and trouble?
I drink till I can hold no more,
So pleasantly the livelong day!
And when I can drink no more
Because gullet and soul are full,
I stagger home to my door
And sleep marvelously well.

What is this sound when I awake? Listen!

A bird is singing in the tree.
I ask him if spring has come,
I seem to be in a dream.
The bird chirps: Yes!
Spring is here, spring came overnight!

I look up and gaze intently,
The bird sings and laughs!

I fill my cup anew
And empty it to the bottom,
And sing until the moon lights up
The darkening firmament.
And when I can no longer sing,
I fall asleep again.
What matters spring to me?
Let me get drunk again!

VI. The Farewell

The sun sets behind the hills.
Evening descends upon all the valleys
With its shadows, bringing coolness.

O see how the moon, like a silver boat,
Floats up on the blue sea of heaven.

I feel a soft wind stirring
Behind the dark pine trees.

The brook sings sweetly in the dark.

The flowers grow pale in the twilight.
The earth breathes gently, full of rest
    and sleep.
All longing flows into a dream.
Weary men go homewards,
So that in sleep they may recapture

Und Jugend neu zu lernen!
Die Vögel hocken still in ihren Zweigen.
Die Welt schläft ein!

Es wehet kühl im Schatten meiner Fich-
ten.
Ich stehe hier und harre meines Freun-
des;
Ich harre sein zum letzten Lebewohl.
Ich sehne mich, o Freund, an deiner
Seite
Die Schönheit dieses Abends zu genies-
sen.
Wo bleibst du! Du lässt mich lang allein!

Ich wandle auf und nieder mit meiner
Laute
Auf Wegen, die vom weichen Grase
schwellen.
O Schönheit! O ewigen Liebens—
Lebens—trunk'ne Welt!

Er stieg vom Pferd und reichte ihm den
Trunk
Des Abschieds dar.
Er fragte ihn, wohin er führe
Und auch warum es müsste sein.
Er sprach, seine Stimme war umflort:
Du, mein Freund,
Mir war auf dieser Welt das Glück nicht
hold!
Wohin ich geh'? Ich geh', ich wand're in
die Berge.
Ich suche Ruhe für mein einsam Herz.

Ich wandle nach der Heimat, meiner
Stätte.
Ich werde niemals in die Ferne schwei-
fen.
Still ist mein Herz und harret seiner
Stunde!
Die liebe Erde allüberall
Blüht auf im Lenz und grünt aufs neu!

Allüberall und ewig blauen licht die Fer-
nen!
Ewig . . . ewig . . .

—*Adapted from the Chinese by H. Bethge*

Forgotten joy and youth!
The birds crouch in the branches.
The world goes to sleep.

It is cool in the shadows of my pine
trees.
I stand here and await my friend;

I await his last farewell.
I long, o my friend, to enjoy

The beauty of this evening by your side.

Where do you tarry? You leave me too
long alone.

I wander up and down with my lute

Along paths billowing with soft grass.

O beauty! O world drunk with eternal
love and life!

He alighted from his horse and offered
him
The cup of farewell.
He asked him where he was journeying
And why it must be so.
He spoke, his voice was veiled: O my
friend,
My lot was hard in this world.

Where do I go? I go wandering in the
mountains.
I seek rest for my lonely heart.

I journey to my homeland, my abode.

I will nevermore roam afar.

My heart is still and awaits its hour!

The lovely earth everywhere
Blossoms in the spring and becomes
green again.
The distant sky shines blue everywhere,
ever . . .
Ever . . . ever . . .

—*English translation by Joseph Machlis*

Strauss, Final Scene from *Salome*

Salome

Ah! Du wolltest mich nicht deinen
   Mund küssen lassen, Jochanaan!
Wohl, ich werde ihn jetzt küssen.
Ich will mit meinen Zähnen hineinbeis-
   sen, wie man in eine reife Frucht beis-
   sen mag.
Ja, ich will ihn jetzt küssen deinen
   Mund, Jochanaan.
Ich hab' es gesagt.
Hab 'ich's nicht gesagt?
Ja, ich hab' es gesagt. Ah! Ah!
Ich will ihn jetzt küssen.
Aber warum siehst du mich nicht an,
   Jochanaan?
Deine Augen, die so schrecklich waren
   so voller Wut and Verachtung, sind
   jetzt geschlossen.
Warum sind sie geschlossen?
Öffne doch die Augen, so hebe deine
   Lider, Jochanaan!
Warum siehst du mich nicht an?
Hast du Angst vor mir, Jochanaan, dass
   du mich nicht ansehen willst?
Und deine Zunge, sie spricht kein Wort,
   Jochanaan, diese Scharlachnatter, die
   ihren Geifer gegen mich spie.
Es ist seltsam, nicht?
Wie kommt es, dass diese rote Natter
   sich nicht mehr rührt?
Du sprachst böse Worte gegen mich,
   gegen mich, Salome, die Tochter der
   Herodias, Prinzessin von Judäa.
Nun wohl! Ich lebe noch, aber du bist
   tot, und dein Kopf, dein Kopf gehört
   mir!
Ich kann mit ihm tun, was ich will.
Ich kann ihn den Hunden vorwerfen
   und den Vögeln der Luft.
Was die Hunde übrig lassen, sollen die
   Vögel der Luft verzehren.
Ah! Ah! Jochanaan, Jochanaan, du warst
   schön.
Dein Leib war eine Elfenbeinsäule auf
   silbernen Füssen.
Er war ein Garten voller Tauben in der
   Silberlilien Glanz.

Ah! Thous wouldst not suffer me to kiss
   thy mouth, Jokanaan!
Well, it shall now be kissed.
And with my teeth I'll bite it as one bites
   in a ripe fruit.

Yes I will kiss it now, kiss thy mouth,
   Jokanaan.
I said that I would.
Did I not say it?
Yes, yes, so I have said. Ah! Ah!
I will now kiss thy mouth.
But wherefore dost thou not look at me,
   Jokanaan?
Thine eyes that were so terrible, so full
   of rage and contempt, they are now
   closed.
Wherefore then are they closed?
Open thou thine eyelids, Jokanaan!

Why dost thou not look at me?
Art thou afraid of me, Jokanaan, that
   thou wilt not look at me?
And thy red tongue doth speak no word,
   Jokanaan, that scarlet viper spitting its
   poison.
It is strange, aye?
How is it that this small scarlet viper
   doth stir no more?
Thou didst use evil language against
   me, against me, Salome, the daughter
   of Herodias, Princess of Judaea.
Well then! I'm living still, but thou art
   dead, and thy head belongs to me!

I'm free to do with it what I will.
I may give it to the dogs to feed on, and
   the birds in the air.
What is left by the dogs may be de-
   voured by the birds of the air.
Ah! Ah! Jokanaan, Jokanaan, thou wert
   fair!
Thy body was a column of ivory set on a
   silver socket.
It was a garden full of doves and lillies of
   silver.

Nichts in der Welt war so weiss wie dein Leib.
Nichts in der Welt war so schwarz wie dein Haar.
In der ganzen Welt war nichts so rot wie dein Mund.
Deine Stimme war ein Weirauchgefäss und wenn ich dich ansah, hörte ich geheimnisvolle Musik . . .

Ah! Warum hast du mich nicht angesehn, Jochanaan?
Du legtest über deine Augen die Binde eines, der seinen Gott schauen wollte.
Wohl! Du hast deinen Gott gesehn, Jochanaan, aber mich, mich hast du nie gesehn.
Hättest du mich gesehn, du hättest mich geliebt!
Ich dürste nach deiner Schönheit.
Ich hungre nach deinem Leib.
Nicht Wein noch Äpfel können mein Verlangen stillen . . .
Was soll ich jetzt tun, Jochanaan?
Nicht die Fluten, noch die grossen Wasser können dieses brünstige Begehren löschen . . .
Oh! Warum sahst du mich nicht an?

Hättest du mich angesehn, du hättest mich liebt.
Ich weiss es wohl, du hättest mich geliebt.
Und das Geheimnis der Liebe ist grösser als das Geheimnis des Todes . . .

Herod

Sie ist ein Ungeheuer, deine Tochter.
Ich sage dir, sie ist ein Ungeheuer!

Herodias

Meine Tochter hat recht getan.
Ich möchte jetzt hierbleiben.

Herod (rising)

Da spricht meines Bruders Weib.
Komm, ich will nicht an diesem Orte bleiben.

No thing on earth was so white as thy skin.
No thing on earth was so black as thy hair.
And in all the world was no thing so red as thy mouth.
But thy voice was a censer of sweet scents, and when I looked on thee I could hear a music of strange sounds . . .

Ah! Wherefore didst thou not look at me, Jokanaan?
Thou didst put upon thine eyes the covering of him who would see his God.
Well! Thou mayst have seen thy God, Jokanaan, but me, me thou didst never see.
If thou hadst looked at me, thou wouldst have loved me.
I thirst for all thy beauty.
I'm hungry for thy body.
Neither wine nor apples can appease all my desire . . .
What shall I do now, Jokanaan?
Neither floods nor the great waters can ever quench my passion . . .
Oh! Wherefore didst thou not look at me?

If thou hadst looked at me, thou wouldst have loved me.
I know it well, thou wouldst have loved me,
And the mystery of love is greater than the mystery of death . . .

Herod

She is a hideous monster, thy daughter.
I tell she is thee, monstrous!

Herodias

My daughter did well.
And I will now stay here.

Herod (rising)

There speaks my brother's wife.
Come, I will no longer stay in this place.

Komm, sag ich dir!
Sicher, es wird Schreckliches geschehn.
Wir wollen uns im Palast verbergen,
Herodias, ich fange an zu erzit-
tern . . .
Mannassah, Issachar, Ozias, löscht die
Fackeln aus.
Verbergt den Mond, verbergt die
Sterne!
Es wird Schreckliches geschehn.

Come, I tell thee!
Surely, something terrible will happen.
Let us hide ourselves in the palace,
Herodias, I am beginning to
tremble . . .
Manasseh, Isachar, Ozias, put out the
torches.
Hide the moon, hide the stars!

Something terrible will happen.

Salome

Ah! Ich habe deinen Mund geküsst, Jo-
chanaan.
Ah! Ich habe ihn geküsst, deinen Mund,
es war ein bitterer Geschmack auf
deinen Lippen.
Hat es nach Blut geschmeckt?
Nein! Doch es schmeckte vielleicht nach
Liebe . . .
Sie sagen, dass die Liebe bitter
schmecke . . .
Allein was tut's?
Was tut's?
Ich habe deinen Mund geküsst, Jocha-
naan.
Ich habe ihn geküsst deinen Mund.

Ah! I have kissed thy mouth, Jokanaan.

Ah! I have kissed thy mouth, there was a
bitter taste on thy lips.

Was it the taste of blood?
Nay! But perchance this is the taste of
love . . .
They say that love hath a bitter taste . . .

But what of that?
What of that?
I have kissed thy mouth, Jokanaan.

I have kissed thy mouth.

Herod

Man töte dieses Weib!

Kill that woman!

Schoenberg, *Pierrot lunaire*

Part I

1. Mondestrunken

Den Wein, den man mit Augen trinkt,
Giesst Nachts der Mond in Wogen nieder,

1. Moondrunk

The wine that only eyes can drink
Pours nighttimes from the moon in
waves,

Und eine Springflut uberschwemmt
Den stillen Horizont.

Gelüste schauerlich und suss,
Durchschwimmen ohne Zahl die Fluten!

Den Wein, den man mit Augen trinkt,
Giesst Nachts der Mond in Wogen nieder.

Der Dichter, den die Andacht treibt,
Berauscht sich an dem heilgen Tranke,
Den Himmel wendet er verzückt

Das Haupt und taumelnd saugt
und schlürit er
Den Wein, den man mit Augen trinkt.

And its springtime tide floods over
The horizon's quiet bowl.

Aching lusts, shocking and sweet,
Float beyond measure in the gushing
philter!

The wine that only eyes can drink,
Pours nighttimes from the moon in
waves.

The poet, under piety's cover,
Gets fuddled on the holy brew;
Towards Heaven, rapt, tilts back his
head
And giddily reeling laps and swills

The wine that only eyes can drink.

2. Columbine

Des Mondlichts bleiche Bluten,
Die weissen Wunderrosen,
Bluhn in den Julinachten—
O brach ich eine nur!

Mein banges Leid zu lindern,
Such ich am dunklen Strome
Des Mondlichts bleiche Bluten,
Die weissen Wunderrosen.

Gestillt war all mein Sehnen,
Dürft ich so märchenheimlich,
So selig leis—enblattern
Auf deine braunen Haare
Des Mondlichts bleiche Blüten!

2. Columbine

The moonlight's pallid blossoms,
The white and wondrous roses,
Bloom in midsummer midnights—
O! could I pluck but one!

To still my luckless grieving
I seek in Lethe's murky stream
The moonlight's pallid blossoms,
The white and wondrous roses.

All my yearning would be sated
Could I, in fairytale secret,
In gentle bliss . . . rip petal from petal
And scatter in your auburn hair
The moonlight's pallid blossoms.

3. Der Dandy

Mit einem phantastischen Lichtstrahl
Erleuchtet der Mond die krystallnen
Flacons
Auf dem schwarzen, hochheiligen
Waschtisch
Des schweigenden Dandys von
Bergamo.

In tonender, bronzener Schale
Lacht hell die Fontaine, metallischen
Klangs.
Mit einem phantastischen Lichtstrahl
Erleuchtet der Mond die krystallnen Fla-
cons.

Pierrot mit dem wächsernen Antlitz

3. The Dandy

With a fantastical ray of light
The moon strikes sparks from the crystal
flacons
On that ebony high altar, the washstand

Of the laconic dandy from Bergamo.

In the resonant bronze basin
Water spurts noisily with metallic
laughter.
With a fantastical ray of light
The moon strikes sparks from the crystal
flacons.

He of the waxworks face, Pierrot,

Steht sinnend und denkt: wie er heute
  sich schminkt?
Fort schiebt er das Rot und des Orients
  Grün
Und bemalt sein Gesicht in erhabenem
  Stil
Mit einem phantastischen Mondstrahl.

Racks his brain and thinks: How shall I
  make me up today?
Vetoes rouge and Orient green

And paints his phizz in loftier style—

With a fantastical ray of light.

4. *Eine blasse Wäscherin*

4. *A Pale Washerwoman*

Eine blasse Wäscherin
Wäscht zur Nachtzeit bleiche Tücher;
Nackte, silberweisse Arme
Streckt sie nieder in die Flut.

A washerwoman pale as a sheet
Washes nights her bleachpale linen,
Dips naked arms white as silver
Glistening down into the stream.

Durch die Lichtung schleichen Winde,
Leis bewegen sie den Strom.
Eine blasse Wäscherin
Wäscht zur Nachtzeit bleichte Tücher.

Through the clearing sidle breezes
Gently ruffling up the river.
A washerwoman pale as a sheet
Washes nights her bleachpale linen.

Und die sanfte Magd des Himmels,
Von den Zweigen zart umschmeichelt,
Breitet auf die dunklen Wiesen
Ihre lichtgewobnen Linnen—

Heaven's lovely livid scullion,
By the branches gently tickled,
Lays out upon the darkling meadows
Her bedlinen woven of threads of
  light—

Eine blasse Wäscherin.

A washerwoman pale as a sheet.

5. *Valse de Chopin*

5. *Valse de Chopin*

Wie ein blasser Tropfen Bluts
Färbt die Lippen einer Kranken,
Also ruht auf diesen Tönen
Ein vernichtungssüchtger Reiz.

Like a spitwatered drop of blood
Rouging the lips of the phthisic sick.
So upon these morbid tones
There lies a soul-destroying spell.

Wilder Lust Accorde stören
Der Verzweiflung eisgen Traum—
Wie ein blasser Tropfen Bluts
Färbt die Lippen einer Kranken.

Crimson chords of fierce desire
Splatter despair's white-icy dream—
Like a spitwatered drop of blood
Rouging the lips of the phthisic sick.

Heiss und jauchzend, suss und
  schmachtend,
Melancholisch düstrer Walzer,
Kommst mir nimmer aus den Sinnen!
Haftest mir an den Gedanken,
Wie ein blasser Tropfen Bluts!

Hot exultant, sweetly longing,

Melancholy nightwood waltz
Nagging sleepless at my brain,
Cleaving to my every thought,
Like a spitwatered drop of blood!

6. *Madonna*

6. *Madonna*

Steig, o Mutter aller Schmerzen,
Auf den Altar meiner Verse!
Blut aus deinen magren Brüsten
Hat des Schwertes Wut vergossen.

Mount, Madonna of all sorrows,
Upon the altar of my verses!
Blood from out thy milkless breasts
Spilled at the saber's angry slash.

Deine ewig frischen Wunden

Thy wounds, fresh always, weeping
  blood,

Gleichen Augen, rot und offen.
Steig, o Mutter aller Schmerzen,
Auf den Altar meiner Verse!

In den abgezehrten Händen
Hätst du deines Sohnes Leiche.
Ihn zu zeigen aller Menschheit—
Doch der Blick der Menschen meidet
Dich, o Mutter aller Schmerzen!

7. Der kranke Mond

Du nächtig todeskranker Mond

Dort auf des Himmels schwarzem Pfühl,
Dein Blick, so fiebernd übergross,
Bannt mich wie fremde Melodie.

An unstillbarem Liebesleid
Stirbst du, an Sehnsucht, tief erstickt,

Du nächtig todeskranker Mond

Dort auf des Himmels schwarzem Pfühl.

Den Liebsten, der im Sinnenrausch
Gedankenlos zur Liebsten schleicht,
Belustigt deiner Strahlen Spiel—
Dein bleiches, qualgebornes Blut,
Du nächtig todeskranker Mond.

Are sleepless eyes, red and staring.
Mount, Madonna of all sorrows,
Upon the altar of my verses!

In thy fleshless wasted hands
Thou holdst the corpse that was thy Son
As tidings to a careless world
But still they turn their eyes away
From thee, Madonna of all sorrows.

7. The Sick Moon

You darkgloomed lifesick deathbed
    moon
Splayed white on night-sky's pillow,
Your huge and feverswollen face
Holds me fast, like alien tones.

From stanchless quenchless ache of love
You'll die of yearning, choked and
    smothered,
You darkgloomed lifesick deathbed
    moon
Splayed white on night-sky's pillow.

The lovedrunk lover on his way
Thoughtless to his lover's bed
Applauds as charming silver rays
The hueless pain-born blood you spill,
You darkgloomed lifesick deathbed
    moon.

Part II

8. Night (Passacaglia)

Finstre, schwarze Riesenfalter
Töteten der Sonne Glanz.
Ein geschlossnes Zauberbuch,
Ruht der Horizont—verschwiegen.

Aus dem Qualm verlorner Tiefen
Steigt ein Duft, Erinnrung mordend!
Finstre, schwarze Riesenfalter
Töteten der Sonne Glanz.

Und vom Himmel erdenwärts
Senken sich mit schweren Schwingen
Unsichtbar die Ungetüme
Auf die Menschenherzen nieder . . .
Finstre, schwarze Riesenfalter.

8. Night (Passacaglia)

Sinister giant black butterflies
Eclipse the glazing disk of sun.
Like a sealed-up book of wizard's spells
Sleeps the horizon—secret silent.

From dank forgotten depths of Lethe
A scent floats up, to murder memory.
Sinister giant black butterflies
Eclipse the blazing disk of sun.

And from heaven downward dropping
To the earth in leaden circles,
Invisible, the monstrous swarm
Descends upon the hearts of men,
Sinister giant black butterflies.

9. Gebet an Pierrot

Pierrot! Mein Lachen
Hab ich verlernt!
Das Bild des Glanzes
Zerfloss-Zerfloss!

Schwarz weht die Flagge
Mir nun vom Mast.
Pierrot! Mein Lachen
Häb ich verlernt!

O gieb mir wieder,
Rossarzt der Seele,
Schneemann der Lyrik,
Durchlaucht vom Monde,
Pierrot—mein Lachen!

9. Prayer to Pierrot

Pierrot! My laughter's
All forgot!
The radiant image
Dissolved—dissolved!

Black blows the flag
That flies at my mast.
Pierrot! My laughter's
All forgot!

O give me back—
Soul's Veterinarian,
Snowman of Verse,
Your Way-Up-Highness the Moon,
Pierrot—my laughter!

10. Raub

Rote, fürstliche Rubine,
Blutge Tropfen alten Ruhmes,
Schlummern in den Totenschreinen,
Drunten in den Grabgewölben.

Nachts, mit seinen Zechkumpanen,
Steigt Pierrot hinab—zu rauben
Rote, fürstliche Rubine,
Blutge Tropfen alten Ruhmes.

Doch da—sträuben sich die Haare,
Bleiche Furcht bannt sie am Platze:
Durch die Finsternis—wie Augen!—
Stieren aus den Totenschreinen
Rote, fürstliche Rubine.

10. Theft

Red and princely rubies,
Bloody drops of fabled fame,
Slumber with dead men's bones
Beneath the vaults of sepulchers.

At night, with fellow tipplers,
Pierrot breaks in—to steal
Red and princely rubies,
Bloody drops of fabled fame.

But there!—their hair's on end—
Livid fear turns them to stone:
Through the dark like gleaming eyes
Goggle from the chests of bones
Red and princely rubies

11. Rote Messe

Zu grausem Abendmahle,
Beim Blendeglanz des Goldes,
Beim Flackerschein der Kerzen,
Naht dem Altar—Pierrot!

Die Hand, die gottgeweihte,
Zerreisst die Priesterkleider
Zu grausem Abendmahle,
Beim Blendeglanz des Goldes.

Mit segnender Geberde
Zeigt er den bangen Seelen
Die triefend rote Hostie:
Sein Herz—in blutgen Fingern—

Zu grausem Abendmahle!

11. Red Mass

At the gruesome Eucharist,
In the trumpery golden glare,
In the shuddering candlelight,
To the altar comes—Pierrot!

His hand, by Grace annointed,
Rips open his priestly vestment
At the gruesome Eucharist,
In the trumpery golden glare.

With hand upraised in blessing
He holds aloft to trembling souls
The holy crimson-oozing Host:
His ripped-out-heart—in bloody
     fingers—
At the gruesome Eucharist.

12. Galgenlied

Die dürre Dirne
Mit langem Halse
Wird seine letzte
Geliebte sein.

In seinem Hirne
Steckt wie ein Nagel
Die dürre Dirne
Mit langem Halse.

Schlank wie die Pinie,
Am Hals ein Zöpfchen—
Wollüstig wird sie
Den Schelm umhalsen,
Die dürre Dirne!

12. Gallows Ditty

The wood-dry whore
With rope-long neck
Will be the last lover
To hold him tight.

She sticks in his brain
Like a hammered-in nail,
The wood-dry whore
With rope-long neck.

Pinetree-scrawny
With hank of hair,
The lecher, she'll grab
The wretch's neck,
The wood-dry whore!

13. Enthauptung

Der Mond, ein blankes Türkenschwert
Auf einem schwarzen Seidenkissen,
Gespenstisch gross—dräut er hinab
Durch schmerzensdunkle Nacht.

Pierrot irrt ohne Rast umher
Und starrt empor in Todesängsten
Zum Mond, dem blanken Türken-
schwert
Auf einem schwarzen Seidenkissen.

Es schlottern unter ihm die Knie,
Ohnmächtig bricht er jäh zusammen.
Er wähnt: es sause strafend schon
Auf seinen Sünderhals hernieder
Der Mond, das blanke Türkenschwert.

13. Beheading

The moon, a naked scimitar
Upon a black silk cushion,
Ghostly huge hangs threatening down
Through night as dark as woe.

Pierrot, who paces about in panic,
Stares up and feels the clutch of death
At sight of moon, a naked scimitar

Upon a black silk cushion.

Knees atremble, quaking, shaking,
He falls into a faint of fright,
Convinced it's slashing down already
On his guilty sinful neck,
The moon, the naked scimitar.

14. Die Kreuze

Heilge Kreuze sind die Verse,
Dran die Dichter stumm verbluten,
Blindgeschlagen von der Geier
Flatterndem Gespensterschwarme!

In den Leibern schwelgten Schwerter,
Prunkend in des Blutes Scharlach!
Heilge Kreuze sind die Verse,
Dran die Dichter stumm verbluten.

Tot das Haupt—erstarrt die Locken—
Fern, verweht der Lärm des Pöbels.
Langsam sinkt die Sonne nieder,
Eine rote Königskrone.—
Heilge Kreuze sind die Verse!

14. The Crosses

Poems are poets' holy crosses
Where they, silent, bleed to death,
Eyes struck blind by beating wings
Of a spectral vulture swarm.

Their ragged flesh the prey of daggers
Reveling in their scarlet blood!
Poems are poets' holy crosses
Where they, silent, bleed to death.

Bowed and wounded sinks the head,
Afar the silly mob still prattles.
Slowly solemn sinks the sun,
Gold and red of royal crown.
Poems are poets' holy crosses.

Part III

15. *Heimweh*

Lieblich klagend—ein krystallnes Seufzen
Aus Italiens alter Pantomime,
Klingts herüber: wie Pierrot so hölzern,

So modern sentimental geworden.

Und es tönt durch seines Herzens Wüste,
Tönt gedämpft durch alle Sinne wieder,
Lieblich klagend—ein krystallnes Seufzen
Aus Italiens alter Pantomime.

Da vergisst Pierrot die Trauermienen!
Durch den bleichen Feuerschein des Mondes,
Durch des Lichtmeers Fluten—schweift die Sehnsucht
Kühn hinauf, empor zum Heimathimmel
Leiblich klagend—ein krystallnes Seufzen!

15. *Homesickness*

Gently keening, a crystalline sighing

Voice out of Italy's old pantomime
Complains how Pierrot's grown so wooden,
So trite and mawkish, inanely à la mode.

When its voice is heard in the wilderness
Of his heart and all his senses,
Gently keening, a crystalline sighing
Voice out of Italy's old pantomime.

Pierrot drops his churlish sulking,
And through wan flame of moonlight,

Through tides of light, his homesick yearning
Soars abroad to happier skies,

Gently keening, a crystalline sighing.

16. *Gemeinheit!*

In den blanken Kopf Cassanders,
Dessen Schrein die Luft durchzetert,

Bohrt Pierrot mit Heuchlermienen,
Zärtlich—einen Schädelbohrer!

Darauf stopft er mit dem Daumen
Seinen echten türkischen Taback
In den blanken Kopf Cassanders,
Dessen Schrein die Luft durchzetert!

Dann dreht er ein Rohr von Weichsel
Hinten in die glatte Glatze
Und behäbig schmaucht und pafft er
Seinen echten türkischen Taback
Aus dem blanken Kopf Cassanders!

16. *Vulgar Horseplay!*

Into Pantaloon's bonebald head—
who screams and shrieks and rends the air—
Pierrot, that ace of hypocrites,
Drills—tenderly!—with a surgeon's borer.

Then uses his thumb to pack and tamp
His choicest blend of Turkish tobacco
Into Pantaloon's bonebald head—
who screams and shrieks and rends the air.

Then screws a stem of cherry wood
Into the back of the polished pate,
Lights up and nonchalantly puffs away
At his choicest blend of Turkish tobacco
Through Pantaloon's bonebald head!

17. *Parodie*

Stricknadeln, blank und blinkend,
In ihrem grauen Haar,
Sitzt die Duenna murmelnd,
Im roten Röckchen da.

17. *Parody*

With knitting needles steely bright
Stuck in her mousegray hair,
The duenna sits there all atwitter
In her best red party frock.

Sie wartet in der Laube,
Sie liebt Pierrot mit Schmerzen,
Stricknadeln, blank and blinkend,
In ihrem grauen Haar.

Da plötzlich—horch!—ein Wispern!
Ein Windhauch kichert leise:
Der Mond, der böse Spötter,
Äfft nach mit seinen Strahlen—
Stricknadeln, blink and blank.

She's waiting 'neath the bower,
Ablaze for Pierrot with passion,
With knitting needles steely bright
Stuck in her mousegray hair.

Suddenly—hark!—a whisper,
The titter of a puff of wind:
The moon, coldhearted cynic,
Is aping with quicksilver beams
Those knitting needles steely bright.

18. *Der Mondfleck*

Einen weissen Fleck des hellen Mondes

Auf dem Rücken seines schwarzen
    Rockes,
So spaziert Pierrot im lauen Abend,

Aufzusuchen Glück und Abenteuer.

Plötzlich stört ihn was an seinem
    Anzug,
Er beschaut sich rings und findet
    richtig—
Einen weissen Fleck des hellen Mondes

Auf dem Rücken seines schwarzen
    Rockes.

Warte! denkt er: das ist so ein Gipsfleck!

Wischt und wischt, doch—bringt ihn
    nicht herunter!
Und so geht er, giftgeschwollen, weiter,

Reibt und reibt bis an den frühen
    Morgen—
Einen weissen Fleck des hellen Mondes.

18. *The Moonfleck*

With a fleck of white—bright patch of
    moonlight—
On the back of his black jacket,

Pierrot strolls about in the mild evening
    air
On his night-time hunt for fun and good
    pickings.

Suddenly something strikes him as
    wrong,
He checks his clothes over and sure
    enough finds
A fleck of white—bright patch of moon-
    light—
On the back of his black jacket.

Damn! he thinks, There's a spot of white
    plaster!
Rubs and rubs, but can't get rid of it,

So goes on his way, his pleasure
    poisoned,
Rubbing and rubbing till dawn comes
    up—
At a fleck of white, a bright patch of
    moonlight!

19. *Serenade*

Mit groteskem Riesenbogen
Kratzt Pierrot auf seiner Bratsche,
Wie der Storch auf einem Beine,
Knipst er trüb ein Pizzicato.

Plötzlich naht Cassander—wütend
Ob des nächtgen Virtuosen—
Mit groteskem Riesenbogen
Kratzt Pierrot auf seiner Bratsche.

19. *Serenade*

With grotesquely giant-sized bow
Pierrot draws cat-squeals from his viola.
Like a stork, on one leg balanced,
He plucks a doleful pizzicato.

Out pops furious Pantaloon
Raging at the night-time virtuoso—
With grotesquely giant-sized bow.
Pierrot draws cat-squeals from his viola.

Von sich wirft er jetzt die Bratsche:	So the player drops his fiddle;
Mit der delikaten Linken	Delicately, with his skilled left hand,
Fasst den Kahlkopf er am Kragen—	Grabs old baldy by the collar—
Träumend spielt er auf der Glatze	And dreamily plays upon his pate
Mit groteskem Riesenbogen.	With grotesquely giant-sized bow.

20. *Heimfahrt (Barcarole)* — 20. *Homeward Journey (Barcarole)*

Der Mondstrahl ist das Ruder,	With moonbeam as his rudder,
Seerose dient als Boot;	His boat a water lily,
Drauf fährt Pierrot den Süden	Pierrot sails softly southward
Mit gutem Reisewind.	Driven onward by the wind.
Der Strom summt tiefe Skalen	The river hums its watery scales
Und wiegt den leichten Kahn.	And gently rocks his skiff,
Der Mondstrahl ist das Ruder,	With moonbeam as his rudder,
Seerose dient als Boot.	His boat a water lily.
Nach Bergamo, zur Heimat,	To Bergamo, his native land,
Kehrt nun Pierrot zurück;	Pierrot is homeward bound.
Schwach dämmert schon im Osten	Pale dawns already in the east
Der grüne Horizont.	The green of morning's rim
—Der Mondstrahl ist das Ruder.	—With moonbeam as his rudder.

21. *O alter Duft* — 21. *O Scent of Fabled Yesteryear*

O alter Duft aus Märchenzeit,	O scent of fabled yesteryear,
Berauschest wieder meine Sinne;	Befuddling my senses with bygone joys!
Ein närrisch Heer von Schelmerein	A silly swarm of idle fancies
Durchschwirrt die leichte Luft.	Murmurs through the gentle air.
Ein glückhaft Wünschen macht mich froh	A happy ending so long yearned for
Nach Freuden, die ich lang verachtet:	Recalls old pleasures long disdained:
O alter Duft aus Märchenzeit,	O scent of fabled yesteryear,
Berauschest wieder mich!	Befuddling me again!
All meinen Unmut gab ich preis;	My bitter mood has turned to peace;
Aus meinem sonnumrahmten Fenster	My sundrenched window opens wide
Beschau ich frei die liebe Welt	On daytime thoughts of world I love,
Und träum hinaus in selge Weiten . . .	To daydreams of a world beyond . . .
O alter Duft—aus Märchenzeit!	O scent of fabled yesteryear!

—*Albert Giraud*

—*English translation by
Robert Erich Wolf*

Poulenc, *Banalités*

Chanson d'Orkenise — The Song of Orkenise

Par les portes d'Orkenise	Through the gates of Orkenise
Veut entrer un charretier	A wagoner wants to enter;

Par les portes d'Orkenise	Through the gates of Orkenise
Veut sortir un vanupieds.	A vagabond wants to leave.
Et les gardes de la ville	And the guards of the town
Courant sus au vanupieds:	Falling on the vagabond:
"Qu'emportes-tu de la ville?"	"What are you carrying out?"
"J'y laisse mon coeur entier."	"I left my heart there."
Et les gardes de la ville	And the guards of the town
Courant sus au charretier:	Falling on the wagoner:
"Qu'apportes-tu dans la ville?"	"What are you bringing into town?"
"Mon coeur pour me marier."	"My heart in order to marry."
Que des coeurs dans Orkenise!	Nothing but hearts in Orkenise!
Les gardes riaient, riaient.	The guards laughed and laughed.
Vanupieds la route est grise	Vagabond, the road is grey
L'amour grise, ô charretier.	Love is befuddling, o wagoner.
Les beaux gardes de la ville	The handsome town guards
Tricotaient superbement;	Knitted superbly;*
Puis les portes de la ville	Then the gates of the town
Se fermèrent lentement.	Closed slowly.

Hôtel	*Hotel*
Ma chambre a la forme d'une cage	My room has the shape of a cage
Le soleil passe son bras par la fenêtre	The sun stretches his arm through the window
Mais moi, qui veut fumer	But I, who wish to smoke
Pour faire des mirages	In order to day dream
J'allume au feu du jour ma cigarette	I light my cigarette at the fire of the day.
Je ne veux pas travailler	I don't want to work
Je veux fumer.	I want to smoke.

Fagnes de Wallonie	*The Heaths of Walloon*
Tant de tristesses plénières	So many deep sorrows
Prirent mon coeur aux fagnes désolées	Bear my heart to the desolate heaths
Quand las j'ai reposé dans les sapinières	Where, weary, I put to rest among the fir trees,
Le poids des kilomètres pendant que	The weight of kilometers
râlait	
Le vent d'ouest	While the west wind sounds its death rattle
J'avais quitté le joli bois	I left the lovely woods
Les écureuils y sont restés	The squirrels remained there
Ma pipe essayait de faire des nuages	My pipe tried to make clouds
Au ciel	In the sky
Qui restait pur obstinément	Which, obstinately, remained pure.
Je n'ai confié aucun secret	I have not confided any secret
Sinon une chanson énigmatique	Except for an enigmatic song
Aux tourbières humides	To the damp peat moss.

*In slang, this means they have splendid moustaches.

Les bruyères fleurant le miel
Attiraient les abeilles
Et mes pieds endoloris
Foulaient les myrtilles et les airelles.

Tendrement mariée
Nord Nord La vie s'y tord
En arbres forts Et tors
La vie y mord La mort
A belle dents
Quand bruit le vent.

The heather, smelling of honey
Attracted the bees
And my aching feet
Trampled the huckleberries.

Tenderly married,
North, north, life twists there
In trees strong and twisted
Life bites death
to pieces there
When the wind roars.

Voyage a Paris

Ah! la charmante chose
Quitter un pays morose
Pour Paris
Paris joli
Qu'un jour dut créer
l'Amour

Trip to Paris

Ah, what a charming thing
To leave the dull country
For Paris
Darling Paris
That one day
Love must have created . . .

Sanglots

Notre amour est règlé par les calmes
    étoiles
Or nous savons qu'en nous beaucoup
    d'hommes respirent
Qui vinrent de très loin
et sont un sous nos fronts
C'est la chanson des rêveurs
Qui s'étaient arraché le coeur
Et le portaient dans la main droite
Souviens t'en cher orgueil des tous ces
    souvenirs
Des marins qui chantaient comme des
    conquérants
Des gouffres de Thulé des tendres cieux
    d'Ophir
Des malades maudits de ceux qui fuient
    leur ombre
Et du retour joyeux des heureux ém-
    igrants
De ce coeur il coulait du sang
Et le rêveur allait pensant
A sa blessure délicate
Tu ne briseras pas la chaîne de ces
    causes
Et douloureuse et nous disait
Qui sont les effets d'autres causes
Mon pauvre coeur mon coeur brisé
Pareil au coeur de tous les hommes

Sighs

Our love is ruled by the calm stars

For we know that in us breathe many
    men
Who came from very far
And are one underneath.
It is the song of dreamers
Who tore out their heart
And carried it in the right hand
(Remember, dear pride, all those memo-
    ries
Of sailors who sang like conquerors

Of the abyss of Thule, of the tender skies
    of Ophir
Of the cursed sick who fled from their
    own shadows
And of the joyful return of happy emi-
    grants)
This heart ran with blood
and the dreamer continued to think
Of his wound, delicate
(You will not break the chain of these
    causes)
and painful said to us
(which are the results of other causes)
My poor heart, my wounded heart
Like the heart of all men

Voici, voici nos mains que la vie fit es-
claves
Est mort d'amour ou c'est tout comme
Est mort d'amour et le voici
Ainsi vont toutes choses
Arrachez donc le vôtre aussi
Et rien ne sera libre jusqu'à la fin des
temps
Laissons touts aux morts
Et cachons nos sanglots.

—*Guillaume Apollinaire*

(Here, here are our hands which life has
enslaved)
Has died of love, or it seems so.
Has died of love and here it is.
Such is the way of everything
Tear yours out too
And nothing will be free until the end of
time.
Leave everything to the dead
And hide our sighs.

—*English translation by Claire Brook*

Webern, *Four Songs*, Opus 13

1. Wiese im Park

Wie wird mir zeitlos. Rückwärts hinge-
bannt
weil' ich und stehe fest im Wiesenplan,
wie in dem grünen Spiegel hier der
Schwan.
Und dieses war mein Land.
Die vielen Glockenblumen! Horch und
schau!
Wie lange steht er schon auf diesem
Stein,
der Admiral. Es muss ein Sonntag sein
und alles läutet blau.
Nicht weiter will ich. Eitler Fuss, mach
Halt!
Vor diesem Wunder ende deinen Lauf.
Ein toter Tag schlägt seine Augen auf.
Und alles bleibt so alt.

—*Karl Kraus*

1. Lawn in the Park

All time has vanished. With a backward
view,
pausing, I stand with green on ev'ry
side
and see the mirror'd swans that calmly
glide.
This was my country too.
O what a host of bluebells! Look and
hear!
And see how long and still a butterfly
sits on this stone. Now surely Sunday's
nigh,
bluebells ring far and near.
I'll go no farther; it's in vain, so hold!
Before you wonder upon wonder lies.
A day that's dead opens its blue eyes.
And ev'ry thing is old.

2. Die Einsame

An dunkelblauem Himmel steht der
Mond.
Ich habe meine Lampe ausgelöscht,—
schwer von Gedanken ist mein einsam
Herz.
Ich weine, weine; meine armen Tränen

rinnen so heiss und bitter von den
Wangen,

2. Lonely Girl

In dark blue fields of heaven walks the
moon.
A lamp stands by my side: I put it out.
Heavy and pensive is my lonely heart.

I weep, weep; my poor tears are running,
running all down my cheek so warm and
bitter,

weil du so fern bist meiner grossen
    Sehnsucht,
weil du es nie begreifen wirst, wie weh
    mir ist, wenn ich nicht bei dir bin.

because you're so far from my great
    longing,
because you'll never understand how
    great my pain when I'm not with you.

*—Adapted from the Chinese
by Hans Bethge*

3. In der Fremde

In fremden Lande lag ich. Weissen
    Glanz
malte der Mond vor meine Lagerstätte.

Ich hob das Haupt,—ich meinte erst, es
    sei
der Reif der Frühe, was ich schimmern
    sah,
dann aber fühlte ich: der Mond, der
    Mond,
und neigte das Gesicht zur Erde hin,

und meine Heimat winkte mir von fern.

*—Adapted from the Chinese by Hans
    Bethge*

3. In a Strange Land

In a strange land I was sleeping.
    Shimm'ring light
spread by the moon around my couch
    and pillow.
I raised my head, and thought at first it
    was
the edge of morning that was shining
    so;
but suddenly I felt the moon, the moon,

and dropped my head upon my pillow
    then,
until I saw my country far away.

4. Ein Winterabend

Wenn der Schnee ans Fenster fällt,
    lang die Abendglocke läutet,
    vielen ist der Tisch bereitet
und das Haus ist wohl bestellt.
Mancher auf der Wanderschaft
    kommt ans Tor auf dunklen Pfaden.
    Golden blüht der Baum der Gnaden
aus der Erde kühlem Saft.
Wanderer tritt still herein;
    Schmerz versteinerte die Schwelle.
    Da erglänzt in reiner Helle
auf dem Tische Brot und Wein.

4. A Winter Evening

When the snow has fall'n by night,
    long the ev'ning bell is ringing,
    trav'llers to their home is bringing,
to their food and rest and light.
Many in their wandering,
    wearily in darkness going,
    see the tree of gold that's growing
here by mercy's cooling spring.
Wanderer, rest shall be thine;
    leave the world of pain, derision.
    See this pure and shining vision;
on the table bread and wine.

—Georg Trakl

Vaughan Williams, *Seranade to Music*

How sweet the moonlight sleeps upon this bank!
Here will we sit and let the sounds of music
Creep in our ears. Soft stillness and the night
Become the touches of sweet harmony.

Look how the floor of heaven
Is thick inlaid with patines of bright gold.
There's not the smallest orb that thou behold'st
But in his motion like an angel sings,
Still quiring to the young-ey'd cherubins;
Such harmony is in immortal souls;
But whilst this muddy vesture of decay
Doth grossly close it in, we cannot hear it.

Come, ho, and wake Diana with a hymn!
With sweetest touches pierce your mistress' ear
And draw her home with music.
I am never merry when I hear sweet music.
The reason is, your spirits are attentive.
The man that hath no music in himself,
Nor is not mov'd with concord of sweet sounds,
Is fit for treasons, stratagems, and spoils;
The motions of his spirit are dull as night,
And his affections dark as Erebus.
Let no such man be trusted.

Music! hark! It is your music of the house.
Methinks it sounds much sweeter than by day.
Silence bestows that virtue on it.
How many things by season season'd are
To their right praise and true perfection!
Peace, ho! The moon sleeps with Endymion,
And would not be awak'd.

—William Shakespeare

Britten, *War Requiem*

I. Requiem aeternam

Chorus

Requiem aeternam dona eis Domine,
et lux perpetua luceat eis.

Rest eternal grant unto them, O Lord:
and let light eternal shine upon them.

Boys' Choir

Te decet hymnus, Deus in Sion;
et tibi reddetur votum in Jerusalem;

Thou, O God, art praised in Sion;
and unto Thee shall the vow be performed in Jerusalem;

exaudi orationem meam, ad te omnis
caro veniet.

Thou who hearest the prayer, unto Thee
shall all flesh come.

Tenor Solo

What passing-bells for these who die as cattle?
Only the monstrous anger of the guns.

Only the stuttering rifles' rapid rattle
   Can patter out their hasty orisons.
No mockeries for them from prayers or bells,
   Nor any voice of mourning save the choirs,—
The shrill, demented choirs of wailing shells;
   And bugles calling for them from sad shires.

What candles may be held to speed them all?
   Not in the hands of boys, but in their eyes
   Shall shine the holy glimmers of goodbyes.
The pallor of girls' brows shall be their pall;
   Their flowers the tenderness of silent minds,
   And each slow dusk a drawing-down of blinds.

Chorus

Kyrie eleison, Christe eleison, Kyrie eleison.   Lord have mercy upon us. Christ have
      mercy upon us. Lord have mercy
      upon us.

II. Dies irae

Chorus

Dies irae, dies illa,   Day of wrath and doom impending,
Solvet saeclum in favilla,   Heaven and earth in ashes ending!
Teste David cum Sibylla.   David's words with Sibyl's blending!

Quantus tremor est futurus,   Oh, what fear man's bosom rendeth
Quando Judex est venturus,   when from heaven the judge descend-
                eth,
Cuncta stricte discussurus!   on whose sentence all dependeth!

Tuba mirum spargens sonum   Wondrous sound the trumpet flingeth,
Per sepulchra regionum   through earth's sepulchres it ringeth,
Coget omnes ante thronum.   all before the throne it bringeth.

Mors stupebit et natura,   Death is struck and nature quaking,
Cum resurget creatura,   all creation is awaking,
Judicanti responsura.   to its judge an answer making.

Baritone Solo

Bugles sang, saddening the evening air,
And bugles answered, sorrowful to hear.

Voices of boys were by the river-side.
Sleep mothered them; and left the twilight sad.
The shadow of the morrow weighed on men.

Voices of old despondency resigned,
Bowed by the shadow of the morrow, slept.

Soprano Solo and Chorus

Liber scriptus proferetur,	Lo! the book exactly worded,
In quo totum continetur,	wherein all hath been recorded;
Unde mundus judicetur.	thence shall judgement be awarded.
Judex ergo cum sedebit,	When the judge his seat attaineth,
Quidquid latet, apparebit:	and each hidden deed arraigneth,
Nil inultum remanebit.	nothing unavenged remaineth.
Quid sum miser tunc dicturus?	What shall I, frail man, be pleading?
Quem patronum rogaturus,	Who for me be interceding,
Cum vix justus sit securus?	when the just are mercy needing?
Rex tremendae majestatis,	King of majesty tremendous,
Qui salvandos salvas gratis,	who dost free salvation send us.
Salva me, fons pietatis.	Fount of pity, then befriend us!

Tenor and Baritone Solos

Out there, we've walked quite friendly up to Death;
  Sat down and eaten with him, cool and bland,—
  Pardoned his spilling mess-tins in our hand.
We've sniffed the green thick odour of his breath,—
Our eyes wept, but our courage didn't writhe.
  He's spat at us with bullets and he's coughed
  Shrapnel. We chorussed when he sang aloft;
We whistled while he shaved us with his scythe.

Oh, Death was never enemy of ours!
  We laughed at him, we leagued with him, old chum.
No soldier's paid to kick against his powers.
  We laughed, knowing that better men would come,
And greater wars; when each proud fighter brags
He wars on Death—for Life; not men—for flags.

Chorus

Recordare Jesu pie,	Think, kind Jesus—my salvation
Quod sum causa tuae viae:	caused Thy wondrous incarnation;
Ne me perdas illa die.	leave me not to reprobation.
Quaerens me, sedisti lassus:	Faint and weary Thou has sought me;
Redemisti crucem passus:	on the cross of suffering bought me;
Tantus labor non sit cassus.	shall such grace be vainly brought me?
Ingemisco, tamquam reus:	Guilty, now I pour my moaning,
Culpa rubet vultus meus:	all my shame with anguish owning;
Supplicanti parce Deus.	spare, O God, Thy suppliant groaning!
Qui Mariam absolvisti,	Through the sinful Mary shriven,
Et latronem exaudisti,	through the dying thief forgiven,
Mihi quoque spem dedisti.	Thou to me a hope hast given.

Inter oves locum praesta,	With Thy sheep a place provide me,
Et ab haedis me sequestra,	from the goats afar divide me,
Statuens in parte dextra.	to Thy right hand do Thou guide me.
Confutatis maledictis,	When the wicked are confounded,
Flammis acribus addictis,	doomed to flames of woe unbounded,
Voca me cum benedictis.	call me, with Thy saints surrounded.
Oro supplex et acclinis,	Low I kneel with heart-submission;
Cor contritum quasi cinis:	see, like ashes, my contrition!
Gere curam mei finis.	Help me in my last condition!

Baritone Solo

Be slowly lifted up, thou long black arm,
Great gun towering toward Heaven, about to curse;

Reach at that arrogance which needs thy harm,
And beat it down before its sins grow worse;

But when thy spell be cast complete and whole,
May God curse thee, and cut thee from our soul!

Chorus and Soprano Solo

Dies irae, dies illa,	Day of wrath and doom impending,
Solvet saeclum in favilla,	Heaven and earth in ashes ending!
Teste David cum Sibylla.	David's words with Sibyl's blending!
Quantus tremor est futurus,	Oh, what fear man's bosom rendeth
Quando Judex est venturus,	when from heaven the judge descend-eth,
Cuncta stricte discussurus!	on whose sentence all dependeth!
Lacrimosa dies illa,	Ah! that day of tears and mourning!
Qua resurget ex favilla,	From the dust of earth returning,
Judicandus homo reus,	man for judgement must prepare him:
Huic ergo parce Deus.	Spare, O God, in mercy spare him!

Tenor Solo

Move him into the sun—
Gently its touch awoke him once,
At home, whispering of fields unsown.
Always it woke him, even in France,
Until this morning and this snow.
If anything might rouse him now
The kind old sun will know.

Think how it wakes the seeds,—
Woke, once, the clays of a cold star.
Are limbs, so dear-achieved, are sides,
Full-nerved—still warm—too hard to stir?
Was it for this the clay grew tall?

—O what made fatuous sunbeams toil
To break earth's sleep at all?

Chorus

Pie Jesu Domine, dona eis requiem. Amen.   Lord, all-pitying, Jesu blest, grant them
rest. Amen.

III. Offertorium

Boys' Choir

Domine Jesu Christe, Rex gloriae,   O Lord Jesus Christ, King of Glory,
libera animas omnium fidelum   deliver the souls of all the faithful
defunctorum de poenis inferni,   departed from the pains of hell
et de profondo lacu: and from the depths of the pit:
libera eas de ore leonis,   deliver them from the lion's mouth,
ne absorbeat eas tartarus,   that hell devour them not,
ne cadant in obscurum.   that they fall not into darkness.

Chorus

Sed signifer sanctus Michael   But let the standard-bearer Saint
                                     Michael
repraesentet eas in lucem sanctam: bring them into the holy light:
quam olim Abrahae promisisti,   which, of old, Thou didst promise
et semini ejus.   unto Abraham and his seed.

Baritone and Tenor Solos

So Abram rose, and clave the wood, and went,
And took the fire with him, and a knife.
And as they sojourned both of them together,
Isaac the first-born spake and said, My Father,
Behold the preparations, fire and iron,
But where the lamb for this burnt-offering?
Then Abram bound the youth with belts and straps,
And builded parapets and trenches there,
And stretched forth the knife to slay his son.
When lo! an angel called him out of heaven,
Saying, Lay not thy hand upon the lad,
Neither do anything to him. Behold,
A ram, caught in a thicket by its horns;
Offer the Ram of Pride instead of him.
But the old man would not so, but slew his son,—
And half the seed of Europe, one by one.

Boys' Choir

Hostias et preces tibi Domine laudis of-   We offer unto Thee, O Lord, sacrifices of
ferimus: prayer and praise:

tu suscipe pro animabus illis, quarum hodie memoriam facimus:	do Thou receive them for the souls of those whose memory we this day recall:
fac eas, Domine, de morte transire ad vitam.	make them, O Lord, to pass from death unto life.

IV. Sanctus

Soprano Solo and Chorus

Sanctus, sanctus, sanctus Dominus Deus Sabaoth.	Holy, Holy, Holy, Lord God of Sabaoth.
Pleni sunt coeli et terra tua, Hosanna in excelsis.	Heaven and earth are full of Thy glory: Glory be to Thee, O Lord most high.
Benedictus qui venit in nomine Domini. Hosanna in excelsis.	Blessed is he that cometh in the name of the Lord. Glory be to Thee, O Lord most high.

Baritone Solo

After the blast of lightning from the East,
   The flourish of loud clouds, the Chariot Throne;
After the drums of Time have rolled and ceased,
   And by the bronze west long retreat is blown,

Shall life renew these bodies? Of a truth
   All death will He annul, all tears assuage?—
Fill the void veins of Life again with youth,
   And wash, with an immortal water, Age?

When I do ask white Age he saith not so:
"My head hangs weighed with snow."
   And when I hearken to the Earth, she saith:
   "My fiery heart shrinks, aching. It is death.
Mine ancient scars shall not be glorified,
Nor my titanic tears, the sea, be dried."

V. Agnus Dei

Tenor Solo

One ever hangs where shelled roads part.
   In this war He too lost a limb,
But His disciples hide apart;
   And now the Soldiers bear with Him.

Chorus

Agnus Dei, qui tollis peccata mundi, dona eis requiem.	O Lamb of God, Who takest away the sins of the world, grant them rest.

Tenor Solo

Near Golgotha strolls many a priest,
And in their faces there is pride
That they were flesh-marked by the Beast
By whom the gentle Christ's denied.

Chorus

Agnus Dei, qui tollis peccata mundi, dona
  eis requiem.

O Lamb of God, Who takest away the
  sins of the world, grant them rest.

The scribes on all the people shove
And bawl allegiance to the state,
But they who love the greater love
Lay down their life; they do not hate.

Chorus

Agnus Dei, qui tollis peccata mundi, dona
  eis requiem sempiternam.

O Lamb of God. Who takest away the
  sins of the world, grant them eternal
  rest.

Dona nobis pacem.

Grant us peace.

VI. Libera me

Chorus and Soprano Solo

Libera me, Domine, de morte aeterna, in
  die illa tremenda:
Quando coeli movendi sunt et terra: Dum
  veneris judicare saeculum per ignem.

Deliver me, O Lord, from death eternal, in that fearful day:
When the heavens and the earth
  shall be shaken: When Thou shalt
  come to judge the world by fire.

Dies illa, dies irae, calamitatis et miseriae,

O that day, that day of wrath, of calam-
  ity and misery,

dies magna et amara valde.

a great day and exceeding bitter.

Tenor Solo

It seemed that out of battle I escaped
Down some profound dull tunnel, long since scooped
Through granites which titanic wars had groined.
Yet also there encumbered sleepers groaned,
Too fast in thought or death to be bestirred.
Then, as I probed them, one sprang up, and stared
With piteous recognition in fixed eyes,
Lifting distressful hands as if to bless.

And no guns thumped, or down the flues made moan.
"Strange friend," I said, "here is no cause to mourn."

Baritone Solo

"None," said the other, "save the undone years,
The hopelessness. Whatever hope is yours,
Was my life also; I went hunting wild
After the wildest beauty in the world.

For by my glee might many men have laughed,
And of my weeping something had been left,
Which must die now. I mean the truth untold,
The pity of war, the pity war distilled.
Now men will go content with what we spoiled.
Or, discontent, boil bloody, and be spilled.
They will be swift with swiftness of the tigress,
None will break ranks, though nations trek from progress.
Miss we the march of this retreating world
Into vain citadels that are not walled.
Then, when much blood had clogged their chariot-wheels
I would go up and wash them from sweet wells,
Even from wells we sunk too deep for war,
Even the sweetest wells that ever were.

I am the enemy you killed, my friend.
I knew you in this dark; for so you frowned
Yesterday through me as you jabbed and killed.
I parried; but my hands were loath and cold."

Tenor and Baritone Solos

"Let us sleep now . . ."

Boys' Choir, Chorus and Soprano Solo

In paradisum deducant te Angeli:
in tuo adventu suscipiant te Martyres,

et perducant te in civitatem sanctam Jeru-
salem.
Chorus Angelorum te suscipiat,
et cum Lazaro quondam paupere aeternam
  habeas requiem.

Requiem aeternam dona eis, Domine;
et lux perpetua luceat eis.
Requiescant in pace. Amen.

Into Paradise may the Angels lead thee:
at thy coming may the Martyrs receive
  thee,
and bring thee into the holy city Jerusalem.
May the Choir of Angels receive thee,
  and with Lazarus, once poor, mayest
  thou have eternal rest.

Rest eternal grant unto them, O Lord:
and let light eternal shine upon them.
May they rest in peace. Amen.

—English poetry by Wilfred Owen

Babbitt, *Philomel*

I.

Sounds of the Thracian Woods (*Tape*)	*Philomel*
(Eeeeeeeeeeeeeee)	
	Eeeeeeeeeeeeeeeeeeeeee! Feeeeeeeeeeeeeeeeeeeee! Feeeeeeeeeeeeeeeeeeeel! I feel— Feel a million trees And the heat of trees
Not true trees—	
	Feel a million tears
Not true tears— Not true trees—	
	Is it Tereus I feel?
Not Tereus; not a True Tereus—	
	Feel a million filaments; Fear the tearing, the feeling Trees, that are full of felony—
	Trees tear, And I bear Families of tears—
	I feel a million Philomels—
Trees filled with mellowing Feminine fame—	
	I feel trees in my hair And on the ground, vines, Honeymelons fouling My knees and feet Soundlessly in my Flight through the forest; I founder in quiet.
	Here I find only Famine of melody, Miles of felted silence Unwinding behind me, Lost, lost in the wooded night.
Pillowing melody, Honey unheard—	
	My hooded voice, lost.
	Lost, as my first Unhoneyed tongue; Forced, as my last Unfeathered defense;

Fast-tangled in lust
Of these woods so dense.
Emptied, unfeeling and unfilled
By trees here where no birds have
    trilled—

Feeling killed
Philomel stilled
Her honey unfulfilled.

Feeling killed
Philomel stilled
Her honey unfulfilled

What is that sound?
A voice found;
Broken, the bound
Of silence, beyond
Violence of human sound,
As if a new self
Could be founded on sound.

Oh, men are sick:
The gods are strong.
Oh, see! Quick! Quick!
The trees are astounded!
What is this humming?
I am becoming
My own song. . . .

Oh, men are sick:
The gods are strong.
Oh, see! Quick! Quick!
The trees are astounded!
What is this humming?
I am becoming
My own song. . . .

II. *Echo Song*

Echoes as Answers
(Tape)

Philomel

O Thrush in the woods I fly among,
Do you, too, talk with the forest's
    tongue?

Stung, stung, stung;
With the sting of becoming
I sing

O Hawk in the high and widening sky,
What need I finally do to fly
And see with your unclouded eye?

Die, die, die;
Let the day of despairing
Be done

O Owl, the wild mirror of the night.
What is the force of the forests light?

Slight, slight, slight,
With the slipping-away of
The sun

        O sable Raven, help me back!
        What color does my torn robe lack?

Black, black, black;
As your blameless and long-
Dried blood

        O bright Gull, aid me in my dream!
        Above the foaming breaker's cream!

Scream, scream, scream,
For the scraps of your being;
Be shrill

        The world's despair should not be
           heard!
        Too much terror has occurred:
        The Gods who made this hubbub erred!

Bird, bird, bird!
You are bare of desire:
Be born!

        Oh green leaves! through your rustling
           lace
        Ahead, I hear my own myth race.

Thrace, Thrace, Thrace!
Pain is unchained,
There is change!
There is change!
In the woods of Thrace!

III. *Philomel*

Living, growing, changing, being in the hum always
Of pain! The pain of slow change blows in our faces
Like unfelt winds that the spinning world makes in its turning:
Life and feeling whirl on, below the threshold of burning.

           I burn in change.
           Far, far I flew
           To this wailing place.
           And now I range
(with tape)   Thrashing, through
           The woods of Thrace.

If pain brush against the rushing wings of frightened change,
Then feeling distills to a burning drop, and transformation
Becomes intolerable. I have been raped and had my tongue
Torn out: but more pain reigns in these woods I range among.

           I ache in change,
           Though once I grew
           At a slower pace.
           And now I range

(*with tape*)   Thrashing, through
                    The woods of Thrace.

Crammed into one fell moment, my ghastly transformation
Died like a fading scream: the ravisher and the chased
Turned into one at last: the voice Tereus shattered
Becomes the tiny voice of night that the God has scattered.

                    I die in change.
                    Pain tore in two
                    Love's secret face.
                    And now I range
(*with tape*)   Thrashing, through
                    The woods of Thrace.

Love's most hidden tongue throbbed in the barbarous daylight;
Then all became pain in one great scream of silence, fading,
Finally, as all the voices of feeling died in the west
And pain alone remained with remembering in my breast.

                    I screamed in change.
                    Now all I can do
                    Is bewail that chase.
                    For now I range
(*with tape*)   Thrashing, through
                    The woods of Thrace.

Pain in the breast and the mind, fused into music! Change
Bruising hurt silence even further! Now, in this glade,
Suffering is redeemed in song. Feeling takes wing:
High, high above, beyond the forests of horror I sing!

                    I sing in change
                    And am changed anew!
                    (O strange, slow race
                    That I ran with grace!)
                    I sing in change.
                    Now my song will range
                    Till the morning dew
                    Dampens its face;
                    Now my song will range
                    As once it flew
                    Thrashing, through
                    The woods of Thrace.

                                      —*John Hollander*

Crumb, *Ancient Voices of Children*

1.

El niño busca su voz.
(La tenía el rey de los grillos.)

1.

The little boy was looking for his voice.
(The king of the crickets had it.)

En una gota de agua
buscaba su voz el niño.

No la quiero para hablar;
me haré con ella un anillo
que llevará mi silencio
en su dedo pequeñito.

2.

Me he perdido muchas veces por el mar
con el oído lleno de flores recién cor-
   tadas,
con la lengua llena de amor y de agonía.
Muchas veces me he perdido por el mar,
como me pierdo en el corazón de
   algunos niños.

3.

¿De dónde vienes, amor, mi niño?

De la cresta del duro frío.
¿Qué necesitas, amor, mi niño?
La tibia tela de tu vestido.
¡Que se agiten las ramas al sol
y salten las fuentes alrededor!
En el patio ladra el perro,
en los árboles canta el viento.
Los bueyes mugen al boyero
y la luna me riza los cabellos.
¿Qué pides, niño, desde tan lejos?

Los blancos montes que hay en tu
   pecho.
¡Que se agiten las ramas al sol
y salten las fuentes alrededor!
Te diré, niño mío, que sí,
tronchada y rota soy para ti.
¡Cómo me duele esta cintura
donde tendrás primera cuna!
¿Cuando, mi niño, vas a venir?
Cuando tu carne huela a jazmín.

¡Que se agiten las ramas al sol
y salten las fuentes alrededor!

4.

Todas las tardes en Granada,
todas las tardes se muere un niño.

In a drop of water
the little boy was looking for his voice.

I do not want it for speaking with;
I will make a ring of it
so that he may wear my silence
on his little finger.

2.

I have lost myself in the sea many times
with my ear full of freshly cut flowers,
with my tongue full of love and agony.
I have lost myself in the sea many times
as I lose myself in the heart of certain
   children.

3.

From where do you come, my love, my
   child?
From the ridge of hard frost.
What do you need, my love, my child?
The warm cloth of your dress.
Let the branches ruffle in the sun
and the fountains leap all around!
In the courtyard a dog barks,
in the trees the wind sings.
The oxen low to the ox-herd
and the moon curls my hair.
What do you ask for, my child, from so
   far away?
The white mountains of your breast.

Let the branches ruffle in the sun
and the fountains leap all around!
I'll tell you, my child, yes,
I am torn and broken for you.
How painful is this waist
where you will have your first cradle!
When, my child, will you come?
When your flesh smells of jasmine-
   flowers.
Let the branches ruffle in the sun
and the fountains leap all around!

4.

Each afternoon in Granada,
a child dies each afternoon.

5.

Se ha llenado de luces
mi corazón de seda,
de campanas perdidas,
de lirios y de abejas.
Y yo me iré muy lejos,
más allá de esas sierras,
más allá de los mares,
cerca de las estrellas,
para pedirle a Cristo
Señor que me devuelva
mi alma antigua de niño.
—*Federico García Lorca*

5.

My heart of silk
is filled with lights,
with lost bells,
with lilies, and with bees,
and I will go very far,
farther than those hills,
farther than the seas,
close to the stars,
to ask Christ the Lord
to give me back
my ancient soul of a child.
—*Translations by W. S. Merwin (1),
Stephen Spender and
J. L. Gili (2), J. L.
Gili (3 and 5), and Edwin Honig (4)*

Appendix III A Reading List of Books and Articles on Twentieth-Century Music

Books prefaced by an asterisk (*) are paperback editions.

General

Anderson, E. Ruth. *Contemporary American Composers: a Biographical Dictionary*. Boston: G. K. Hall, 1976.

Apel, Willi. *The Harvard Dictionary of Music*. 2nd rev. ed. Cambridge: Harvard, 1969.

*————, and R. T. Daniel. *The Harvard Brief Dictionary of Music*. Cambridge: Harvard, 1960.

Austin, William. *Music in the Twentieth Century*. New York: Norton, 1966.

Baker's Biographical Dictionary of Musicians. 5th ed. Ed. Nicolas Slonimsky. New York: Schirmer, 1958, with 1971 supplement.

*Boretz, Benjamin, and Edward T. Cone, eds. *Perspectives on American Composers*. New York: Norton, 1971.

*Brindle, Reginald Smith. *The New Music: the Avant-Garde Since 1945*. New York: Oxford, 1975.

Chase, Gilbert. *America's Music.* 2nd rev. ed. New York: McGraw-Hill, 1966.

———, ed. *The American Composer Speaks.* Baton Rouge: Louisiana State University Press, 1966.

*Copland, Aaron. *The New Music, 1900–1960.* New York: Norton, 1968.

*Cowell, Henry. *American Composers on American Music.* New York: Ungar, 1962.

Grove's Dictionary of Music and Musicians. 6th ed. Ed. Stanley Sadie. New York: St. Martin's, 1979.

Hamilton, David. "A Synoptic View of the New Music," *High Fidelity,* 18 (Sept. 1968), pp. 44–61.

Hartog, Howard, ed. *European Music in the Twentieth Century.* Westport, Conn.: Greenwood, 1976.

Hays, William, ed. *Twentieth-Century Views of Music History.* New York: Charles Scribner's Sons, 1972.

Hines, Robert S., ed. *The Composer's Point of View.* Norman: University of Oklahoma, 1963.

———, ed. *The Orchestral Composer's Point of View.* Norman: University of Oklahoma, 1970.

*Hitchcock, H. Wiley. *Music in the United States: A Historical Introduction.* 2nd rev. ed. Englewood Cliffs, N.J.: Prentice-Hall, 1974.

Krebs, Stanley D. *Soviet Composers and the Development of Soviet Music.* New York: Allen & Unwin, 1970.

*Lang, Paul Henry, and Nathan Broder, eds. *Contemporary Music in Europe: A Comprehensive Survey.* New York: Norton, 1967.

MacMillan, Keith, and John Beckwith, eds. *Contemporary Canadian Composers.* New York: Oxford, 1975.

*Mellers, Wilfred. *Music in a New-Found Land.* 2nd ed. New York: Hillstone, 1975.

*———. *Romanticism and the Twentieth Century.* New York: Schocken, 1969.

Meyer, Leonard B. *Music, the Arts, and Ideas.* Chicago: University of Chicago Press, 1967.

*Mitchell, Donald. *The Language of Modern Music.* New York: St. Martin's, 1970.

Murdoch, James. *Australia's Contemporary Composers.* Melbourne: Sun Books, 1975.

Myers, Rollo W. *Modern French Music from Fauré to Boulez.* New York: Praeger, 1971.

The New Oxford History of Music. Vol. 10: *The Modern Age, 1890–1960.* Ed. Martin Cooper. London, New York: Oxford, 1974.

Nyman, Michael. *Experimental Music.* New York: Schirmer Books, 1974.

Problems of Modern Music. Ed. Paul Henry Lang. New York: Norton, 1962.

Rosenfeld, Paul. *Musical Impressions.* Ed. Herbert A. Leibowitz. New York: Hill & Wang, 1969.

Routh, Francis. *Contemporary British Music.* London: Macdonald, 1972.

*Salzman, Eric. *Twentieth-Century Music: An Introduction.* 2nd ed. Englewood Cliffs, N.J.: Prentice-Hall, 1974.

Samson, Jim. *Music in Transition: A Study of Tonal Expansion and Atonality, 1900–1920*. New York: Norton, 1977.

Scholes, Percy A. *Concise Oxford Dictionary of Music*. 2nd ed. Ed. J. O. Ward. New York: Oxford, 1964.

Schwartz, Elliot. *Electronic Music: A Listener's Guide*. New York: Praeger, 1973.

———, and Barney Childs, eds. *Contemporary Composers on Contemporary Music*. New York: Holt, Rinehart, & Winston, 1967.

*Schwarz, Boris. *Music and Musical Life in Soviet Russia 1917–1970*. New York: Norton, 1973.

Searle, Humphrey, and Robert Layton. *Britain, Scandanavia and the Netherlands*. New York: Holt, Rinehart, & Winston, 1972.

Slonimsky, Nicolas. *Music Since 1900*. 4th ed. New York: Charles Scribner's Sons, 1971.

Sternfeld, F. W., ed. *Music in the Modern Age*. Praeger History of Music, Vol. V. New York: Praeger, 1973.

Stuckenschmidt, H. H. *Germany and Central Europe*. New York: Holt, Rinehart & Winston, 1970.

———. *Twentieth Century Music*. New York: McGraw-Hill, 1969.

Thompson, Kenneth. *A Dictionary of Twentieth-Century Composers (1911–1971)*. London: Faber & Faber, 1973.

Thompson, Oscar. *The International Cyclopedia of Music and Musicians*. 10th rev. ed. Ed. Bruce Bohle. New York: Dodd, Mead, 1975.

Vinton, John, ed. *Dictionary of Contemporary Music*. New York: Dutton, 1974.

Westrup, J. A., and F. Ll. Harrison. *The New College Encyclopedia of Music*. Rev. ed. Ed. Conrad Wilson. New York: Norton, 1977.

Yates, Peter. *Twentieth Century Music*. New York: Pantheon, 1967.

Music Theory

*Boretz, Benjamin, and Edward T. Cone, eds. *Perspectives on Contemporary Music Theory*. New York: Norton, 1972.

*———. *Perspectives on Notation and Performance*. New York: Norton, 1976.

Brindle, Reginald Smith. *Serial Composition*. New York: Oxford, 1966.

Cowell, Henry. *New Musical Resources*. New York: Something Else Press, 1969 (reprint of 1930 ed.).

Forte, Allen. *Contemporary Tone Structures*. New York: Teachers College, Columbia University, 1955.

———. *The Structure of Atonal Music*. New Haven: Yale University Press, 1973.

Hindemith, Paul. *Craft of Musical Composition*. New York: Associated Music Publishers, 1941–45.

Messiaen, Olivier. *The Technique of My Musical Language*. Paris: A. Leduc, 1956.

Partch, Harry. *Genesis of a Music*. 2nd rev. ed. New York: Da Capo, 1974.
Perle, George. *Serial Composition and Atonality*. 4th rev. ed. Berkeley, Los Angeles, & London: University of California, 1977.
———. *Twelve-Tone Tonality*. Berkeley, Los Angeles, & London: University of California, 1977.
Persichetti, Vincent. *Twentieth-Century Harmony*. New York: Norton, 1961.
Piston, Walter. *Harmony*. 4th rev. ed., rev. and expanded by Mark DeVoto. New York: Norton, 1978.
Rufer, Joseph. *Composition With Twelve Notes*. London: Rockliff, 1954.
Wittlich, Gary E., ed. *Aspects of Twentieth-Century Music*. Englewood Cliffs, N.J.: Prentice-Hall, 1975.

By and About Twentieth-Century Composers

BARTÓK

Bartók, Béla. *Essays*. Ed. Benjamin Suchoff. New York: St. Martin's, 1976.
———. *Letters*. Ed. János Demény. New York: St. Martin's, 1971.
Lesznai, Lajos. *Bartók*. London: Dent, 1973.
*Stevens, Halsey. *The Life and Music of Béla Bartók*. Rev. ed. New York: Oxford, 1967.

BERG

Adorno, Theodor W. *Alban Berg: A Biography of the Music*. New York: Grossman, 1975.
Carner, Mosco. *Alban Berg: The Man and the Work*. New York: Holmes and Meier, 1977.
Reich, Willi. *Alban Berg*. New York: Harcourt, Brace & World, 1965.

BERNSTEIN

*Bernstein, Leonard. *The Joy of Music*. New York: New American Library, 1967.
———. *The Unanswered Question: Six Talks at Harvard*. Cambridge: Harvard, 1976.

BOULEZ

Boulez, Pierre. *Boulez on Music Today*. Cambridge: Harvard, 1971.
———. *Notes of an Apprenticeship*. New York: Knopf, 1968.
Peyser, Joan. *Pierre Boulez*. New York: Macmillan, 1976.

BRITTEN

Gishford, Anthony, ed. *Tribute to Benjamin Britten on his Fiftieth Birthday*. London: Faber & Faber, 1963.
White, Eric Walter. *Benjamin Britten: His Life and Operas*. Berkeley: University of California, 1970.

CAGE

*Cage, John. *M: Writings '67–'72*. Middletown, Conn.: Wesleyan, 1973.
*———. *Silence*. Middletown, Conn.: Wesleyan, 1961.

*——. *A Year From Monday: New Lectures and Writings*. Middletown, Conn.: Wesleyan, 1969.

——, and Alison Knowles, eds. *Notations*. West Glover: Something Else Press, 1969.

Kostelanetz, Richard, ed. *John Cage*. New York: Praeger, 1970.

CARTER

Carter, Elliott. *The Writings of Elliott Carter: An American Composer Looks at Modern Music*. Ed. Else and Kurt Stone. Bloomington: Indiana University Press, 1977.

Edwards, Allan. *Flawed Words and Stubborn Sounds: A Conversation with Elliott Carter*. New York: Norton, 1971.

COPLAND

Berger, Arthur. *Aaron Copland*. New York: Oxford, 1953.

*Copland, Aaron. *Copland on Music*. New York: Norton, 1963.

*——. *Music and Imagination*. New York: Mentor, 1959.

*——. *What to Listen For in Music*. New York: Mentor, 1964.

DEBUSSY

*Debussy, Claude. "Monsieur Croche," in *Three Classics in the Esthetics of Music*. New York: Dover, 1962.

*Lockspeiser, Edward. *Debussy*. 4th ed. New York: McGraw-Hill, 1972.

——. *Debussy: His Life and Mind*. 2 vols. New York: Macmillan, 1962–65.

*Vallas, Leon. *Claude Debussy: His Life and Works*. New York: Dover, 1973.

GERSHWIN

Jablonski, Edward, and Lawrence Stewart. *The Gershwin Years*. New York: Doubleday, 1973.

Kimball, Robert E., and Alfred Simon. *The Gershwins*. New York: Atheneum, 1973.

Schwartz, Charles. *George Gershwin: His Life and Music*. Indianapolis: Bobbs Merrill, 1973.

HINDEMITH

Hindemith, Paul. *A Composer's World*. Garden City, N.Y.: Doubleday, 1961.

Skelton, Geoffrey. *Paul Hindemith: The Man Behind the Music*. London: Victor Gollancz, 1975.

IVES

Cowell, Henry, and Sidney Cowell. *Charles Ives and His Music*. New York: Oxford, 1955.

Hitchcock, H. Wiley. *Ives*. New York: Oxford, 1977.

——, and Vivian Perlis, eds. *An Ives Celebration*. Urbana: University of Illinois Press, 1977.

Ives, Charles. *Charles E. Ives Memos*. Ed. John Kirkpatrick. New York: Norton, 1972.

*——. *Essays Before a Sonata and Other Writings*. Ed. Howard Boatwright. New York: Norton, 1962.

*Perlis, Vivian. *Charles Ives Remembered: An Oral History*. New York: Norton, 1976.

Rossiter, Frank. *Charles Ives and His America*. New York: Liveright, 1975.

JANÁČEK

Evans, Michael. *Janáček's Tragic Operas*. London: Faber, 1978.

MAHLER

Cardus, Neville. *Gustav Mahler: His Mind and His Music*. New York: St. Martin's, 1965.

Kennedy, Michael. *Mahler*. Totowa, N.J.: Rowman and Littlefield, 1976.

La Grange, Henri-Louis de. *Mahler*. New York: Doubleday, 1973.

*Mahler, Alma Schindler. *Gustav Mahler: Memories and Letters*. Ed. Donald Mitchell. Rev. and enlarged. Seattle: University of Washington Press, 1971.

Mitchell, Donald. *Gustav Mahler: The Wunderhorn Years*. Berkeley: University of California Press, 1975.

Newlin, Dika. *Bruckner, Mahler, Schoenberg*. Rev. ed. New York: Norton, 1978.

Redlich, H. F. *Bruckner and Mahler*. New York: Octagon, 1955.

MESSIAEN

Johnson, Robert Sherlaw. *Messiaen*. Berkeley: University of California Press, 1975.

Samuel, Claude. *Conversations With Olivier Messiaen*. London: Stainer & Bell, 1976.

MILHAUD

Milhaud, Darius. *Notes without Music*. New York: Da Capo, 1970 (reprint of 1953 ed.).

POULENC

Bernac, Pierre. *Francis Poulenc*. New York: Norton, 1978.

Hell, Henri. *Poulenc*. London: J. Calder, 1959.

PROKOFIEV

Nestyev, Israel V. *Prokofiev*. Tr. Florence Jonas. Stanford, California: Stanford University Press, 1960.

PUCCINI

Ashbrook, William. *The Operas of Puccini*. New York: Oxford, 1968.

Carner, Mosco. *Puccini: A Critical Biography*. 2nd ed. New York: Holmes & Meier, 1977.

RACHMANINOV

Bertensson, S., and J. Leyda. *Sergei Rachmaninoff: A Lifetime in Music*. New York: New York University Press, 1956.

RAVEL

Myers, Rollo W. *Ravel*. London: G. Duckworth, 1960.

Nichols, Roger. *Ravel*. London: Dent, 1977.

Orenstein, Arbie. *Ravel: Man and Musician.* New York: Columbia University Press, 1975.

SATIE

Myers, Rollo. *Erik Satie.* New York: Dover, 1968.
Templier, Pierre-Daniel, ed. *Erik Satie.* Tr. Elena L. and David S. French. Cambridge, Mass.: MIT Press, 1969.

SCHOENBERG

*Boretz, Benjamin, and Edward T. Cone, eds. *Perspectives on Schoenberg and Stravinsky.* Rev. ed. New York: Norton, 1972.
*Leibowitz, René. *Schoenberg and His School.* New York: Da Capo, 1975.
MacDonald, Malcolm. *Schoenberg.* London: Dent, 1976.
Newlin, Dika. *Bruckner, Mahler, Schoenberg.* Rev. ed. New York: Norton, 1978.
Reich, Willi. *Schoenberg: A Critical Biography.* New York: Praeger, 1971.
Rosen, Charles. *Arnold Schoenberg.* New York: Viking, 1975.
Schoenberg, Arnold. *Letters.* Ed. E. Stein and E. Kaiser. New York: St. Martin's, 1958.
————. *Style and Idea.* Ed. Leonard Stein. New York: St. Martin's, 1975.
Stuckenschmidt, H. H. *Arnold Schoenberg.* London: J. Calder, 1959.

SESSIONS

*Sessions, Roger. *The Musical Experience of Composer, Performer, Listener.* Princeton: Princeton University Press, 1971.
*————. *Questions About Music.* New York: Norton, 1971.

SHOSTAKOVICH

*Kay, Norman. *Shostakovich.* London, New York: Oxford, 1971.

SIBELIUS

Layton, Robert. *Sibelius and His World.* New York: Viking, 1970.
Tawaststjerna, Erik. *Sibelius.* Berkeley: University of California Press, 1975.

STOCKHAUSEN

Cott, Jonathan. *Stockhausen: Conversations with the Composer.* New York: Simon & Schuster, 1973.
Harvey, Jonathan. *The Music of Stockhausen.* Berkeley: University of California Press, 1975.
Maconie, Robin. *The Works of Karlheinz Stockhausen.* London, New York: Oxford, 1976.

STRAUSS

Del Mar, Norman. *Richard Strauss.* Vol. 1: New York: Free Press of Glencoe, 1962; Vols. 2–3: Philadelphia: Chilton, 1969, 1973.
Mann, William S. *Richard Strauss: A Critical Study of the Operas.* New York: Oxford, 1966.
Marek, George. *Richard Strauss: The Life of a Non-Hero.* New York: Simon & Schuster, 1967.

STRAVINSKY

*Boretz, Benjamin, and Edward T. Cone, eds. *Perspectives on Schoenberg and Stravinsky*. Rev. ed. New York: Norton, 1972.

*Craft, Robert. *Stravinsky: Chronicle of a Friendship 1948–1971*. New York: Vintage, 1973.

*Lang, Paul Henry, ed. *Stravinsky: A New Appraisal of His Work*. New York: Norton, 1963.

*Stravinsky, Igor. *An Autobiography*. New York: Norton, 1962.

*———. *Poetics of Music*. Cambridge, Mass.: Harvard, 1970.

———, and Robert Craft. *Conversations with Igor Stravinsky*. New York: Doubleday, 1959.

———. *Dialogues and a Diary*. New York: Doubleday, 1963.

———. *Expositions and Developments*. New York: Doubleday, 1962.

———. *Memories and Commentaries*. New York: Doubleday, 1960.

———. *Retrospectives and Conclusions*. New York: Knopf, 1969.

———. *Themes and Episodes*. New York: Knopf, 1966.

*Vlad, Roman. *Stravinsky*. 2nd ed. London: Oxford, 1967.

White, Eric Walter. *Stravinsky, the Composer and His Works*. Berkeley: University of California Press, 1966.

THOMSON

*Thomson, Virgil. *American Music Since 1910*. New York: Holt, Rinehart, & Winston, 1971.

———. *The Art of Judging Music*. New York: Greenwood, 1969.

*———. *The State of Music*. New York: Vintage, 1962.

———. *Virgil Thomson*. New York: Knopf, 1966.

TIPPETT

Kemp, Ian, ed. *Michael Tippett: A Symposium on His 60th Birthday*. London: Faber & Faber, 1965.

Tippett, Michael. *Moving into Aquarius*. London: Routledge & Paul, 1959.

VARÈSE

Ouellette, Fernand. *Edgard Varèse*. New York: Orion, 1968.

Varèse, Louise. *Varèse: A Looking-Glass Diary*. New York: Norton, 1972.

VAUGHAN WILLIAMS

Kennedy, Michael. *The Works of Ralph Vaughan Williams*. London, New York: Oxford, 1964.

Vaughan Williams, Ralph. *The Making of Music*. Westport, Conn.: Greenwood, 1976.

Vaughan Williams, Ursula. *R.V.W.: A Biography of Ralph Vaughan Williams*. London, New York: Oxford, 1964.

WEBERN

Kolneder, Walter. *Anton Webern: An Introduction to His Works*. Berkeley: University of California Press, 1968.

Webern, Anton. *The Path to the New Music*. Bryn Mawr, Pa.: Theodore Presser, 1963.

Appendix IV A Synoptic Table

of Modern Composers, World Events, and Prominent Figures in Literature and the Arts since 1900

Emmanuel Chabrier
    1841–1894
Gabriel Fauré
    1845–1924
Sir Charles Hubert
    Parry 1848–1918
Henri Duparc
    1848–1933
Vincent d'Indy
    1851–1931
Sir Charles Villiers
    Stanford 1852–1924
Arthur Foote
    1853–1937
Alfredo Catalani
    1854–1893
Engelbert Humper-
    dinck 1854–1921

1900. Boxer Rebellion in China. Count Zeppelin tests dirigible balloon. Dr. Walter Reed organizes campaign against yellow fever. Philadelphia Symphony founded.

1901. President McKinley assassinated. Queen Victoria dies, succeeded by Edward VII. Marconi sends first signal across Atlantic. De Vries's mutation theory.

1902. Boer War ends in British victory. Cuba becomes a republic. First International Arbitration Court at The Hague.

Pierre Auguste Renoir
    1841–1919
W. H. Hudson
    1841–1922

Stéphane Mallarmé
    1842–1898
George Brandes
    1842–1927
Henry James 1843–1916
Paul Verlaine
    1844–1896
Gerard Manley Hop-
    kins 1844–1899
Friedrich Nietzsche
    1844–1900
Henri Rousseau
    1844–1910

669

Leoš Janáček 1854–1928
George W. Chadwick
1854–1931
Ernest Chausson
1855–1899
Anatole Liadov
1855–1914

Sir Edward Elgar
1857–1934
Edgar Stillman Kelley
1857–1944
Ruggiero Leoncavallo
1858–1919
Giacomo Puccini
1858–1924

Hugo Wolf 1860–1903
Gustav Mahler
1860–1911
Isaac Albéniz
1860–1919
Gustave Charpentier
1860–1956
Anton Arensky
1861–1906
Edward MacDowell
1861–1908
Charles Martin Loeffler
1861–1935

Claude Debussy
1862–1918
Frederick Delius
1862–1934
Horatio Parker
1863–1919
Pietro Mascagni
1863–1945
Richard Strauss
1864–1949
Alexander Grechan-
inov 1864–1956

Paul Dukas 1865–1935
Alexander Glazunov
1865–1936
Jean Sibelius
1865–1957

145,000 miners strike in Pennsylvania.

1903. Wright Brothers' first successful flight. Ford organizes
motor company. Panama de-
clares its independence of Colombia, encourages U.S. to
build canal. Massacre of Jews
in Kishinev, Russia. First
transcontinental automobile
trip.

1904. Russo-Japanese War. London Symphony founded. New
York subway opened.

1905. Fort Arthur surrendered to
Japan. Opening of Duma, first
Russian parliament. Norway
separates from Sweden. Freud
establishes psychoanalysis.
Einstein's theories, 1905–1910.

1906. San Francisco earthquake
and fire. Harry K. Thaw shoots
famous architect Stanford
White.

1907. Financial panic in U.S. Second Hague Conference. Triple
Entente. First round-the-world
cruise of U.S. fleet. William
James's *Pragmatism*.

1908. Model T Ford produced.
Fire destroys Chelsea, Mass.

1909. Peary reaches North Pole.
First flight across English
Channel.

1910. Discovery of protons and
electrons. Edward VII dies,
succeeded by George V. J. B.
McNamara and brother tried
for dynamite explosion at Los
Angeles *Times*; defended by
Clarence Darrow. Pathé
Newsreel appears in Paris.

Anatole France
1844–1924
Robert Bridges
1844–1930
Max Liebermann
1847–1935
Paul Gauguin
1848–1903
Augustus Saint-
Gaudens 1848–1907
Joris-Karl Huysmans
1848–1907
August Strindberg
1849–1912
Guy de Maupassant
1850–1893
Robert Louis Steven-
son 1850–1894
George Moore
1852–1933
Vincent van Gogh
1853–1890
Arthur Rimbaud
1854–1891
Oscar Wilde 1856–1900
Louis H. Sullivan
1856–1924
John Singer Sargent
1856–1925
Sigmund Freud
1856–1939
George Bernard Shaw
1856–1950
Joseph Conrad
1857–1924
Hermann Sudermann
1857–1928
Selma Lagerlöf
1858–1940
Georges Seurat
1859–1891
Childe Hassam
1859–1935
A. E. Housman
1859–1936
Henri Bergson
1859–1941
Knut Hamsun
1859–1952

Ferruccio Busoni
1866–1924
Erik Satie 1866–1925
Francesco Cilèa
1866–1950
Enrique Granados
1867–1916
Mrs. H. H. A. Beach
1867–1944
Umberto Giordano
1867–1948
Henry F. Gilbert
1868–1928
Albert Roussel
1869–1937
Hans Pfitzner
1869–1949

Henry Hadley
1871–1937
Frederick Shepherd
Converse 1871–1940
Alexander Scriabin
1872–1915
Alexander von Zem-
linsky 1872–1942
Arthur Farwell
1872–1952
Ralph Vaughan Wil-
liams 1872–1958
Edward Burlingame
Hill 1872–1960

Max Reger 1873–1916
Sergei Rachmaninov
1873–1943
Daniel Gregory Mason
1873–1953
Josef Suk 1874–1935
Arnold Schoenberg
1874–1951
Charles Ives 1874–1954

Samuel Coleridge-
Taylor 1875–1912
Maurice Ravel
1875–1937
Italo Montemezzi
1875–1952

1911. Mexican Revolution.
Amundsen reaches South
Pole. *Mona Lisa* stolen from
Louvre. Supreme Court anti-
trust decisions against Standard Oil and American To-
bacco Co.

1912. Capt. Robert F. Scott
reaches South Pole; dies on return journey. China becomes a
republic. Balkan Wars: Mon-
tenegro, Bulgaria, Serbia, and
Greece defeat Turkey. Wilson
elected. *Titanic* sunk.

1913. Peace Palace dedicated at
The Hague. Federal income tax
in U.S.

1914. Archduke Francis Fer-
dinand of Austria assassinated
at Sarajevo. Outbreak of World
War I. German army invades
Belgium. U.S. intercedes in
Mexico; Marines land at Vera
Cruz. First ship through
Panama Canal.

1915. German submarines blockade England. *Lusitania* sunk.
Nurse Edith Cavell shot. First
transcontinental telephone,
New York to San Francisco.

1916. Battle of Verdun. German
submarine *Deutschland* visits
New York. Rasputin killed.
Easter Rebellion in Dublin;
Tom Mooney sentenced for
bomb explosion at Pre-
paredness Day parade in San
Francisco.

1917. Balfour Declaration on Palestine. Germany begins unrestricted submarine warfare.
United States enters war. Mata
Hari shot. Russian Revolution.

Anton Chekhov
1860–1904
Sir James Barrie
1860–1937
Rabindranath Tagore
1861–1941
Aristide Maillol
1861–1945
O. Henry 1862–1910
Arthur Schnitzler
1862–1931
Edith Wharton
1862–1937
Gerhart Hauptmann
1862–1946
Maurice Maeterlinck
1862–1949
Konstantin Stanis-
lavski 1863–1938
Edvard Munch
1863–1944
George Santayana
1863–1952
Henri de Toulouse-
Lautrec 1864–1910
Frank Wedekind
1864–1918
Gabriele D'Annunzio
1864–1938
George Grey Barnard
1864–1938
Louis Eilshemius
1864–1941
Irving Babbitt
1865–1933
Rudyard Kipling
1865–1936
William Butler Yeats
1865–1939
Bernard Berenson
1865–1959
Lincoln Steffens
1866–1936
Romain Rolland
1866–1943
Wassily Kandinsky
1866–1944
Benedetto Croce
1866–1952

Reinhold Glière
1875–1956
Julián Carrillo
1875–1965
Manuel de Falla
1876–1936
Ernest H. Schelling
1876–1939
Ermanno Wolf-Ferrari
1876–1948
John Alden Carpenter
1876–1951
Carl Ruggles 1876–1971

David Stanley Smith
1877–1946
Ernö (Ernst von) Doh-
nányi 1877–1960
Franz Schreker
1878–1934
Ottorino Respighi
1879–1937
John Ireland 1879–1962

Arthur Shepherd
1880–1958
Ernest Bloch 1880–1959
Béla Bartók 1881–1945
Nikolai Miaskovsky
1881–1950
Georges Enesco
1881–1955
Ildebrando Pizzetti
1881–1968
Karol Szymanowski
1882–1937

Joaquín Turina
1882–1949
Arthur Schnabel
1882–1951
Lazare Saminsky
1882–1959
Igor Stravinsky
1882–1971
Gian Francesco Mali-
piero 1882–1973
Zoltán Kodály
1882–1967
John Powell 1882–1963

Bolsheviks seize power. Prohibition Amendment.

1918. Wilson's Fourteen Points.
Russia makes separate peace.
Paris bombarded. Battles of
Somme, Aisne, Argonne. Ger-
many surrenders. Kaiser ab-
dicates.

1919. Treaty of Versailles. Third
International formed. Anti-
British demonstrations in
India. First nonstop flight New
York to San Francisco.

1920. League of Nations con-
venes at Geneva. Women's
suffrage. Sacco and Vanzetti
accused of murder in payroll
holdup. First transcontinental
air-mail route.

1921. Peace treaty signed with
Germany. Limitation of Ar-
maments Conference meets in
Washington.

1922. Mussolini marches on
Rome. Violence in coal strike
at Herrin, Ill. Discovery of in-
sulin. John Dewey's *Human
Nature and Conduct.*

1923. French and Belgian troops
occupy Ruhr. Adolf Hitler attempts Beer Putsch in Munich.
Pancho Villa killed in ambush.

1924. Lenin dies at 54. Dawes
Reparations Plan. Mrs. Nellie
Tayloe Ross first woman gov-
ernor (Wyoming). Leopold-
Loeb case.

1925. Locarno Conference.
Rhineland demilitarized. John
T. Scopes, defended by
Clarence Darrow, found guilty

Arnold Bennett
1867–1931
John Galsworthy
1867–1933
Luigi Pirandello
1867–1936
Käthe Kollwitz
1867–1945
Edmond Rostand
1868–1918
Stefan George
1868–1933
Edgar Lee Masters
1868–1950
Edwin Arlington Rob-
inson 1869–1935
André Gide 1869–1951
Norman Douglas
1869–1952
Henri Matisse
1869–1954
Frank Lloyd Wright
1869–1959
Stephen Crane
1870–1900
Ernst Barlach
1870–1938
John M. Synge
1871–1909
Leonid Andreyev
1871–1919
Marcel Proust
1871–1922
Theodore Dreiser
1871–1945
Paul Valéry 1871–1945
Georges Rouault
1871–1958
Aubrey Beardsley
1872–1898
Serge Diaghilev
1872–1929
Piet Mondrian
1872–1944
John Marin 1872–1953
Bertrand Russell
1872–1970
Pío Baroja 1872–
Jakob Wassermann
1873–1934

Riccardo Zandonai
1883–1944

Anton Webern
1883–1945

Alfredo Casella
1883–1947

Lord Berners (Gerald
Tyrwhitt) 1883–1950

Sir Arnold Bax
1883–1953

Edgard Varèse
1883–1965

Charles Tomlinson
Griffes 1884–1920

Bernard van Dieren
1884–1936

Emerson Whithorne
1884–1958

Louis Gruenberg
1884–1964

Alban Berg 1885–1935

Wallingford Riegger
1885–1961

Deems Taylor
1885–1966

Humberto Allende
1885–1959

John J. Becker
1886–1961

Marion Bauer
1887–1955

Nadia Boulanger 1887–

Heitor Villa-Lobos
1887–1959

Ernst Toch 1887–1964

Bohuslav Martinu
1890–1959

Jacques Ibert
1890–1962

Sergei Prokofiev
1891–1953

Frederick Jacobi
1891–1953

Frank Martin
1891–1974

Sir Arthur Bliss 1891–

Richard Donovan
1891–1970

of teaching evolution in Day-
ton, Tenn.

1926. General strike in Britain.
Germany admitted to League
of Nations.

1927. Lindbergh flies across Atlantic. Sacco-Vanzetti executed
despite worldwide protest.
Trotsky expelled from Communist Party.

1928. First all-talking film. *Graf
Zeppelin* crosses Atlantic. First
radio broadcast of New York
Philharmonic Orchestra.

1929. Teapot Dome scandal.
Stock market crash. Papal State
reconstituted as State of Vati-
can City.

1930. London Naval Reduction
Treaty. Penicillin discovered.
Judge Crater vanishes.

1931. Japan invades Manchuria.
Spain becomes a republic. Empire State Building completed.

1932. Japan establishes puppet
state in Manchukuo. Franklin
D. Roosevelt elected. James J.
Walker, under investigation,
resigns as Mayor of New York.

1933. Hitler becomes German
Chancellor. Germany quits
League of Nations. Roosevelt
proclaims bank holiday, signs
National Recovery Act, recog-
nizes Soviet Union. Prohibition repealed. TVA es-
tablished.

1934. Chancellor Dollfuss of Austria assassinated by Nazis.
Hindenburg dies; Hitler becomes Fuehrer.

Max Reinhardt
1873–1943

Willa Cather 1873–1947

Colette 1873–1953

Max Beerbohm
1873–1956

Amy Lowell 1874–1925

Hugo von Hof-
mannsthal 1874–1929

Henri Barbusse
1874–1935

G. K. Chesterton
1874–1936

Gertrude Stein
1874–1946

W. Somerset
Maugham 1874–1965

Rainer Maria Rilke
1875–1926

Thomas Mann
1875–1955

Albert Schweitzer
1875–1965

Jack London 1876–1916

Sherwood Anderson
1876–1941

José Maria Sert
1876–1945

Constantin Brancusi
1876–1957

Maurice Vlaminck
1876–1958

Marsden Hartley
1877–1943

Mikhail Artzybashev
1878–1927

Isadora Duncan
1878–1927

Ferenc Molnar
1878–1952

Carl Sandburg
1878–1967

John Masefield
1878–1967

Upton Sinclair
1878–1968

Vachel Lindsay
1879–1931

Paul Klee 1879–1940

E. M. Forster
1879–1970

Arthur Honegger
1892–1955
Darius Milhaud
1892–1974

Eugene Goossens
1893–1962
Arthur Benjamin
1893–1960
Paul Pisk 1893–
Federico Mompou
1893–
Douglas Moore
1893–1969
Bernard Rogers
1893–1968

Willem Pijper
1894–1947
Walter Piston
1894–1976
Bernard Wagenaar
1894–1971

Karol Rathaus
1895–1954
Paul Hindemith
1895–1963
Carl Orff 1895–
Mario Castelnuovo-
Tedesco 1895–1968
William Grant Still
1895–
Leo Sowerby
1895–1968

Virgil Thomson 1896–
Roger Sessions 1896–
Howard Hanson 1896–
Ernesto Lecuona
1896–1963

Alexander Tansman
1897–
Henry Cowell
1897–1965
Quincy Porter
1897–1966
Francisco Mignone
1897–

1935. Hitler reintroduces universal military training. Nuremberg Laws deprive German Jews of citizenship and ban intermarriage. Italy invades Ethiopia. John L. Lewis founds CIO. Social Security Act signed. Will Rogers dies in plane crash.

1936. Civil War in Spain. Italy annexes Ethiopia. First socialist government in France, under Léon Blum. German-Japanese anti-Comintern Pact, later joined by Italy. George V of England dies, succeeded by Edward VIII, who renounces throne for Mrs. Wallis Simpson. Sulfa drugs introduced in U.S. First sitdown strike.

1937. Loyalist government moves to Barcelona. Japan seizes Peiping. Hitler repudiates Treaty of Versailles. Italy withdraws from League of Nations. Marshall Tukhachevsky and other Soviet generals executed for treason.

1938. Insurgent planes bomb Barcelona. Hitler annexes Austria. Betrayal at Munich: Britain and France agree to dismemberment of Czechoslovakia.

1939. Spanish Civil War ends in victory for Franco. Hitler enters Prague. Germany and Italy form Axis. German-Russian Pact. Russia invades Finland. Nazi invasion of Poland precipitates World War II.

1940. Nazis overrun Netherlands, Belgium, Luxembourg. Churchill becomes Prime Minister. Evacuation of Dunkirk.

Wallace Stevens
1879–1955
Raoul Dufy 1879–1953
Guillaume Apollinaire
1880–1918
Ernst Kirchner
1880–1938
André Derain
1880–1954
Scholem Asch
1880–1957
Henry L. Mencken
1880–1959
Sir Jacob Epstein
1880–1959
Emil Ludwig
1881–1948
Pablo Picasso
1881–1973
Sean O'Casey
1881–1964
Fernand Léger
1881–1955
Max Weber 1881–1961
James Joyce 1882–1941
Virginia Woolf
1882–1945
Sigrid Undset
1882–1949
Georges Braque
1882–1963
Jacques Maritain
1882–1973
Franz Kafka 1883–1924
Kahlil Gibran
1883–1931
José Ortega y Gasset
1883–1955
William Carlos Williams 1883–1959
José Clemente Orozco
1883–1949
Walter Gropius
1883–1969
Max Eastman
1883–1969
Amadeo Modigliani
1884–1920
Maurice Utrillo
1884–1955

George Gershwin
1898–1937
Vittorio Rieti 1898–
Marcel Mihalovici
1898–
Roy Harris 1898–
Ernst Bacon 1898–
E. K. ("Duke") Elling-
ton 1899–1974

Silvestre Revueltas
1899–1940
Francis Poulenc
1899–1963
Georges Auric 1899–
Alexander Tcherepnin
1899–1977
Randall Thompson
1899–
Carlos Chávez 1899–
Domingo Santa Cruz
1899–

Amadeo Roldán
1900–1939
Kurt Weill 1900–1950
Ernst Krenek 1900–
George Antheil
1900–1959
Henry Barraud 1900–
Aaron Copland 1900–
Otto Luening 1900–
Henri Sauguet 1901–
Edmund Rubbra 1901–
Werner Egk 1901–
Marcel Poot 1901–
Harry Partch 1901–1974

Sir William Walton
1902–
Stefan Wolpe
1902–1972
Theodore Chanler
1902–1961
Mark Brunswick
1902–1971
John Vincent 1902–
Aram Khatchaturian
1903–1978
Boris Blacher
1903–1975

Germans enter Paris; France
capitulates. Japan invades
French Indo-China. R.A.F.
halts invasion threat. Roosevelt elected to third term.

1941. Hitler attacks Russia. Japan
attacks Pearl Harbor. U.S.
enters the war. Nazis enter
Athens. FDR and Churchill
agree on war aims, announce
Atlantic Charter.

1942. British stop Rommel at El
Alamein. U.S. forces land in
North Africa; army under Pat-
ton lands in Sicily. Six million
Jews die in Nazi extermination
camps. First nuclear chain reaction achieved by Enrico
Fermi, among a group of scientists.

1943. Germans defeated at Sta-
lingrad and in North Africa.
Mussolini deposed. Italy surrenders. Teheran Conference:
Roosevelt, Churchill, and Stalin decide on invasion of
France. Race riots in Detroit.

1944. Hitler wounded in bomb
plot. Gen. MacArthur returns
to Philippines. Invasion of
France. Battle of the Bulge.
Roosevelt elected to fourth
term.

1945. Yalta Agreement. Roosevelt dies at 63, succeeded by
Truman. United Nations Conference opens at San Francisco.
U.S. troops cross Rhine, invade Iwo Jima and Okinawa.
Hitler, Goebbels commit suicide. Germany surrenders.
Atom bomb dropped on Hiroshima. Japan surrenders.

1946. Philippines become independent. First meeting of

Lion Feuchtwanger
1884–1958
D. H. Lawrence
1885–1930
Sinclair Lewis
1885–1951
Sascha Guitry
1885–1957
André Maurois
1885–1967
François Mauriac
1885–1970
Ezra Pound 1885–1972
William Rose Benét
1886–1950
Diego Rivera
1886–1957
Oskar Kokoschka
1886–
Thornton Wilder
1887–1975
Robinson Jeffers
1887–1962
William Zorach
1887–1966
Alexander Archipenko
1887–1964
Marc Chagall 1887–
Le Corbusier
1887–1965
Arnold Zweig 1887–
Georgia O'Keeffe
1887–
Eugene O'Neill
1888–1953
Maxwell Anderson
1888–1959
Giorgio di Chirico
1888–
T. S. Eliot 1888–1965
John Crowe Ransom
1888–1974
Thomas Hart Benton
1889–1975
Arnold J. Toynbee
1889–1975
Karel Čapek 1890–1938
Franz Werfel 1890–1945
Christopher Morley
1890–1957
Mark Tobey 1890–1976

Vittorio Giannini
1903–1966
Nikolai Lopatnikov
1903–1976

Manuel Rosenthal
1904–
Dmitri Kabalevsky
1904–
Luigi Dallapiccola
1904–1975
Goffredo Petrassi
1904–

Constant Lambert
1905–1951
Erich Itor Kahn
1905–1956
André Jolivet
1905–1974
Michael Tippett 1905–
Alan Rawsthorne
1905–1971
Marc Blitzstein
1905–1964

Alejandro Caturla
1906–1940
Dmitri Shostakovich
1906–1975
Paul Creston 1906–
Ross Lee Finney 1906–
Louise Talma 1906–
Normand Lockwood
1906–
Robert Sanders 1906–
Miriam Gideon 1906–

Henk Badings 1907–
Burrill Phillips 1907–

Olivier Messiaen 1908–
Elliott Carter 1908–
Daniel Ayala 1908–

Elie Siegmeister 1909–
Howard Swanson
1909–
Paul Nordoff 1909–

U.N. General Assembly. Victor Emmanuel III abdicates. Nuremberg trials.

1947. Truman Doctrine. Marshall Plan. India wins independence. Moscow forms Cominform. Communists take power in Hungary and Romania.

1948. Gandhi assassinated. Communists take over Czechoslovakia. Israel proclaimed a nation, attacked by Arabs. Soviet blockade of Berlin; airlift begun. Tojo and other Japanese leaders hanged as war criminals. Organization of 21 American states.

1949. Truman's Point Four Program to aid backward areas. Communists defeat Chiang Kai-shek in China. USSR explodes atomic bomb. North Atlantic Defense Pact. Trial and conviction of U.S. Communist leaders.

1950. North Koreans invade South Korea. U.S. plans hydrogen bomb.

1951. Schuman Plan pools coal and steel markets of six European nations. Truce talks in Korea.

1952. George VI dies; succeeded by Elizabeth II. Eisenhower elected President.

1953. Stalin dies. Armistice in Korea. Mount Everest scaled. Beria executed in USSR.

1954. First atomic-powered submarine, *Nautilus*, launched. War in Indo-China. Supreme

Henry Miller 1891–
Jean Cocteau
1891–1963
Grant Wood 1892–1944
Jean Giraudoux
1892–1944
Edna St. Vincent Millay 1892–1950
Rebecca West 1892–
Sir Osbert Sitwell
1892–1969
Elmer Rice 1892–1967
Pearl S. Buck
1892–1973
Ernst Toller 1893–1939
George Grosz
1893–1959
John P. Marquand
1893–1960
Herbert Read 1893–
S. N. Behrman
1893–1973
Joan Miró 1893–
Carlos Mérida 1893–
Dorothy Parker
1893–1967
E. E. Cummings
1894–1962
Katherine Anne Porter
1894–
James Thurber
1894–1961
Aldous Huxley
1894–1963
Ben Hecht 1894–1964
David Siqueiros
1894–1974
László Moholy-Nagy
1895–1946
Paul Eluard 1895–1952
Lin Yutang 1895–
Edmund Wilson
1895–1972
Abraham Rattner
1895–
F. Scott Fitzgerald
1896–1940
Robert Sherwood
1896–1955

Rolf Liebermann 1910–
Samuel Barber 1910–
Charles Jones 1910–
Paul Bowles 1910–
William Schuman
1910–
Josef Alexander 1910–
Blas Galindo 1910–

Gian Carlo Menotti
1911–
Alan Hovhaness 1911–
Vladimir Ussachevsky
1911–

Igor Markevitch 1912–
Jean Françaix 1912–
Arthur Berger 1912–
John Cage 1912–
Hugo Weisgall 1912–
Peggy Glanville-Hicks
1912–
Wayne Barlow 1912–
Tom Scott 1912–
Salvador Contreras
1912–
Pablo Moncayo 1912–

Benjamin Britten
1913–1976
Tikhon Khrennikov
1913–
Norman Dello Joio
1913–
Morton Gould 1913–
Jan Meyerowitz 1913–
Gardner Read 1913–
Henry Brant 1913–
Roger Goeb 1914–
Alexei Haieff 1914–
Gail Kubik 1914–
Charles Mills 1914–

David Diamond 1915–
Irving Fine 1915–1962
Robert Palmer 1915–
Vincent Persichetti
1915–
George Perle 1915–
Carlos Surinach 1915–

Court rules segregation in
public schools illegal. Communist Party outlawed in U.S.

1955. Churchill, at 80, succeeded
by Anthony Eden. Peron
ousted in Argentina. Salk
serum for infantile paralysis.
Warsaw pact signed.

1956. Egypt seizes Suez Canal.
Russia launches Sputnik, first
man-made satellite.

1957. Eisenhower Doctrine for
aid to Middle East. First underground atomic explosion.

1958. Egypt and Syria form
United Arab Republic under
Nasser. Alaska becomes 49th
state. Fifth Republic in France
under De Gaulle.

1959. Castro victorious over Ba-
tista. Soviet launches first
man-made planet. Hawaii becomes 50th state.

1960. South African natives revolt against *apartheid.* Syng-
man Rhee forced out by popular discontent in South Korea.
American U-2 plane shot
down in Russia. Kennedy
elected President.

1962. Cuban missile crisis.
Algeria declared independent
of France. Opening of Lincoln
Center for the Performing Arts
in New York.

1963. President Kennedy assassinated. Lyndon Johnson be-
comes 36th President.

1965. First walk in space. White
minority in Rhodesia pro-
claims itself independent of

John Dos Passos
1896–1970
William Faulkner
1897–1962
Louis Aragon 1897–
Liam O'Flaherty 1897–
Kenneth Burke 1897–
Sergei Eisenstein
1898–1948
Bertolt Brecht
1898–1956
Ludwig Bemelmans
1898–1962
Erich Maria Remarque
1898–1970
Alexander Calder
1898–1976
René Clair 1898–
Ernest Hemingway
1898–1961
Hart Crane 1899–1932
Federico García Lorca
1899–1936
Stephen Vincent Benét
1899–1943
Noel Coward
1899–1973
Elizabeth Bowen
1899–1973
Rufino Tamayo 1899–
Eugène Berman
1899–1972
Allen Tate 1899–
Thomas Wolfe
1900–1938
Antoine de Saint-
Exupéry 1900–1944
Ignazio Silone 1900–
John van Druten
1901–1957
Vittorio de Sica
1901–1974
André Malraux
1901–1976
John Steinbeck
1902–1968
Langston Hughes
1902–1967
Kenneth Fearing 1902–

Ben Weber 1916–
Milton Babbitt 1916–
Alberto Ginastera
1916–

Ulysses Kay 1917–
Robert Ward 1917–
Lou Harrison 1917–

Gottfried von Einem
1918–
Leonard Bernstein
1918–
George Rochberg
1918–
Frank Wigglesworth
1918–

Leon Kirchner 1919–
Bruno Maderna
1920–1972
Harold Shapero 1920–
John Lessard 1920–

Robert Kurka
1921–1957
Jack Beeson 1921–
Andrew Imbrie 1921–

Lukas Foss 1922–
Iannis Xenaxis 1922–
Peter Mennin 1923–
Mel Powell 1923–
Ned Rorem 1923–
Leo Kraft 1923–
Gyorgy Ligetti 1923–

Raffaello de Banfield
1924–
Billy Jim Layton 1924–
Luigi Nono 1924–
Pierre Boulez 1925–
Gunther Schuller 1925–
Luciano Berio 1925–

Hans Werner Henze
1926–
Morton Feldman 1926–
Carlisle Floyd 1926–
Lee Holby 1926–

Britain. Alabama Civil Rights
March.

1966. France withdraws from
NATO alliance.

1967. Israeli-Arab "6-Day War."
First successful heart trans-
plant in South Africa.

1968. Richard M. Nixon elected
President. Soviet occupation
of Czechoslovakia. Martin
Luther King and Robert F.
Kennedy assassinated.

1969. Apollo II: first manned
landing on the moon. De
Gaulle resigns as French president.

1970. U.S. intervention in Cambodia. Nobel Prize in Literature to Aleksandr Solzhenit-
syn.

1971. Publication of the "Pen-
tagon Papers." Peoples Republic of China admitted to
the U.N.

1972. Richard Nixon re-elected.
Attempted assassination of
Governor George Wallace.

1973. Vietnam War ends. The
"Watergate Affair" begins.
Energy crisis. Vice President
Agnew resigns.

1974. President Nixon resigns.

1975. Francisco Franco dies. Civil
War in Angola.

1976. Viking spacecraft lands on
Mars. U.S. celebrates its Bicentennial. Mao Tse-tung dies.
Jimmy Carter elected president.

George Orwell
1903–1950
Kay Boyle 1903–
Ogden Nash 1903–1971
Erskine Caldwell 1903–
Mark Rothko
1903–1970
Salvador Dali 1904–
Graham Greene 1904–
George Balanchine
1904–
Christopher Isher-
wood 1904–
James T. Farrell 1904–
Isamu Noguchi 1904–
Willem de Kooning
1904–
Lillian Hellman 1905–
Jean-Paul Sartre 1905–
Arthur Koestler 1905–
John O'Hara 1905–1970
Mikhail Sholokhov
1905–
Roberto Rossellini
1906–1977
Clifford Odets
1906–1963
W. H. Auden
1907–1973
Christopher Fry 1907–
Alberto Moravia 1907–
William Saroyan 1908–
Stephen Spender 1909–
Eudora Welty 1909–
Jean Anouilh 1910–
Nicholas Montserrat
1910–
Terence Rattigan 1911–
Lawrence Durrell
1912–
Jackson Pollock
1912–1956
Albert Camus
1913–1960
Irwin Shaw 1913–
William Inge
1913–1973
Dylan Thomas
1914–1953
Tennessee Williams
1914–

William Flanagan
1926–
Seymour Schrifrin
1926–

Salvatore Martirano
1927–
Russel Smith 1927–

Jacob Druckman 1928–
Karlheinz Stockhausen
1928–

George Crumb 1929–
Yehudi Wyner 1929–
David Baker 1931–
Marvin David Levy
1932–

Easley Blackwood
1933–
Kryzsztof Penderecki
1933–
Mario Davidovsky
1934–
Peter Maxwell Davies
1934–

Aribert Riemann 1936–
Charles Wuorinen
1938–
Frederic Rzewski 1938–

1977. Egypt's President Anwar el-Sadat makes historic visit to Israel for peace talks with Prime Minister Menachem Begin. United States signs treaty giving Panama control of Panama Canal and Canal Zone as of 1999.

1978. Pope John Paul I elected. First baby born of extrauterine conception. Death of Pope John Paul I. Pope John Paul II elected.

Thomas Merton 1915–
Arthur Miller 1915–
Robert Motherwell
1915–
Robert Lowell
1917–1977
Carson McCullers
1917–1967
Jerome Robbins 1918–
J. D. Salinger 1919–
Howard Nemerov
1920–
James Jones 1921–1977
Norman Mailer 1923–
Paddy Chayefsky
1923–
Truman Capote 1924–
James Baldwin 1924–
Kenneth Koch 1925–
Robert Rauschenberg
1925–
Allen Ginsberg 1926–
John Ashbery 1927–
John Hollander 1928–
John Barth 1930–
Jean-Luc Godard 1930–
Jasper Johns 1930–
Harold Pinter 1930–
Andy Warhol 1931–
Yevgeny Yevtushenko
1933–
Tom Stoppard 1937–

Index